THE
unofficial GUIDE®
ᴛᴏLondon

5TH EDITION

THE *unofficial* GUIDE®

TO London

5TH EDITION

LESLEY LOGAN

WILEY

This is for Sylvana Grodin with thanks for the memories.

Published by:
John Wiley & Sons, Inc.
111 River Street
Hoboken, NJ 07030-5774

Produced by Menasha Ridge Press

Cover design by Michael J. Freeland

Interior design by Vertigo Design

For information on our other products and services or to obtain technical support, please contact our Customer Care Department within the United States at 800-762-2974, outside the United States at 317-572-3993, or by fax at 317-572-4002.

John Wiley & Sons, Inc. also publishes its books in a variety of electronic formats. Some content that appears in print may not be available in electronic formats.

ISBN 978-0-470-13829-8

Manufactured in the United States of America

5 4 3 2 1

CONTENTS

LIST *of* MAPS

ABOUT
the AUTHOR

LESLEY LOGAN is a freelance writer who has worked in publishing for more than two decades as an author, ghostwriter, copywriter, and editor. She is the author of *Frommer's London Day by Day* and has cowritten a number of nonfiction books. Originally from New York, she and her husband, Tom, and daughter, Nora, have lived abroad, first in Hong Kong and then in London, since 1994. Lesley holds both U.K. and U.S. passports, a distinction that, among other extraordinary liberties, is a big plus at airport immigration lines.

ACKNOWLEDGMENTS

FOR THIS LATEST EDITION I am indebted to Jacqueline Kispal for all her hard work, braving pubs, clubs, restaurants, and tourist spots, and writing about it so well; to Laurie Palomaki (and her tireless traveling toddler twins, Zoe and Lily) for rewriting and updating the children's chapter with such thorough intelligence and enthusiasm; and to Sally Harclerode for her shopping savoir faire and astonishing general knowledge of London. Thanks also to K. Khan for his help. A special thanks to Amanda Barclay for all she has taught me about writing, London, and the art of facing a challenge.

To Bob Sehlinger and Molly Merkle of Menasha Ridge Press, thanks for a wonderful assignment. Much appreciation to the brilliant and eagle-eyed Ritchey Halphen and Lady Vowell Smith for wrestling a monster manuscript into shape, and also to Tanya M. Hines-Wright for expertly proofreading the galleys.

A heartfelt thanks to the legions of anonymous curators, cab drivers, Transport for London people (especially Jax's buddy Alfie), London Tourist Board employees, shopkeepers, waiters, concierges, hotel managers, bellhops, B&B owners, and people on the street, who generously gave me tips, information, and guided tours, and unfailingly pointed me in the right direction.

I have appreciated the letters and evaluations I received from so many readers, the kind and the critical. Your generosity in taking the time to write makes me grateful to be able to continue updating this book, to make right some wrongs, and to learn from your own London experiences.

Lastly, thanks to Tom and Nora Logan, who are my home, no matter where we each may live.

—Lesley Logan

INTRODUCTION

◼ LONDON CALLING

LET'S JUST GET IT OUT OF THE WAY, SHALL WE? There seems to be no discussing London without some reference to Samuel Johnson's quote about his beloved city: "When a man is tired of London, he is tired of Life, for there is in London all that Life can afford." It might even be said that when one is tired of quoting Dr. Johnson's well-worn line, one must surely be tired of promoting London. Call it a bit of erudite whistling in the dark by tourist boards and local politicians, travel writers, and London business boosters, but you will rarely come upon such a city, where the words of an 18th-century writer and lexicographer should be employed with such gusto by modern public-relations maestros, repeated with as much pride as if they had written the boast themselves. Certainly it is exactly this easy—even surreal—conversation between past and present that reveals something profound about London's appeal to both visitors and residents. The city has the enviable ability to show off its attic of past charms without ever moldering into boring irrelevance. London is Miss Havisham's frozen wedding day, but with a wicked DJ and free alcopops; it is forever young in its senescence, traditionally cutting edge, classically vulgar, and raffishly refined.

Check out the historical free-for-all of this city where against the gorgeous Georgian facade of the Royal Academy is pitted a series of seriously modern sculptures; where horse-drawn carriages and soldiers on horseback in full regalia merit barely a passing glance from Londoners whizzing around in their energy-efficient Smart cars; where the Liberty department store on the 18th-century John Nash–designed Regent Street is housed in a Tudor building straight out of a fairy tale and filled with 21st-century gadgets, potions, and products. This wonderful palimpsest of centuries—the layering of today's global village on top of post–World War II London over Edwardian elegance, draped upon Victorian glory, laid over 18th-century exuberance, under which the medieval and even the Roman city can be appreciated—is, especially to the North American eye, a miracle of conservation and civic pride. But if London were only the sum of its past, it would be an inert monument, not the contemporary scene of a constantly evolving culture of theater, arts, music, and fashion for which it's justifiably celebrated.

In 1978, Bette Midler said of the time difference between the two cities, "When it's three o'clock in New York, it's still 1938 in London." Thirty years ago, this was a spot-on quip, referring to the gloom of postwar austerity that still clung to London's coal-dirty buildings and the utter lack of good food or central heating. Although to many of us, raised to believe that all shops should open on Sunday and not close till well past six on weekdays, and who would like to be able to hop on an Underground train after midnight, London still has a way to go to rival the 24-7 charms of, say, the island of Manhattan. Yet despite the minor irritations and the major expenses of this vast city, about 30 million visitors a year come to enjoy the city known as the Big Smoke, the Great Wen, and the most expensive city in Europe, the numbers swelling its resident population of almost 8 million. And that's not even counting the transient young people who, like Dick Whittington and his cat, come to London to seek fame and fortune, people from all over Great Britain, the European Union, the commonwealths and ex-colonies of England, looking for a stroke of luck, a second chance, or their own history. They work in the service industries, on the streets, up on scaffolds, or in the shadows, essential ingredients in the madcap stew that is London.

Of course, all visitors to this capital quickly discover that London is no quaint theme park. It takes a bit of dedication and determination to unlock London's enchantments, and visitors may struggle to reconcile the soft-lit picture of the fabled metropolis carried in their minds against the often dirty, indifferent, and confusing modern reality of the place. But the payoff for a little footwork and a lot of curiosity is huge.

London can be many cities to many people. Contrast Dr. Johnson's hymns of worship ("The happiness of London is not to be conceived but by those who have been in it. . . .") with Percy Bysshe Shelley's assessment of early-19th-century London: "Hell is a city much like London—a populous and smoky city." We who live here tend to agree with both of these writers, at least a few times a day. People may have a wide range of feelings about London, but indifference is usually not one of them. It's rare for an English speaker (or reader, or film viewer) to come here without a mental trunk full of preconceptions. Those of a certain age had an intimate acquaintance with the bells of St. Clements, London Bridge, and the Drury Lane home of the muffin man even before we knew the alphabet. When we could read, we inhaled deeply the pungent London of Charles Dickens, who captured the 19th-century city in all its degradation and beauty, and who left his unforgettable impressions on the pages of his novels and in the psyches of his readers. Whether it's the London of Arthur Conan Doyle or Will Self, Virginia Woolf or Zadie Smith, Henry James or Martin Amis, this city has appeared so frequently as a character in literature (not to mention painting and film) that it is a place we carry in our collective consciousness like a time-traveling dream.

Waking up to London is another story. To arrive here for the first time is to suddenly confront fantasy with fact. The most outstanding fact about London is its sprawling geography—there is nothing so neat as a "downtown" of London. It is a metropolis whose former hamlets and villages became connected by urban sprawl over the centuries, allowing one to identify the still-distinct boroughs, many of which have held on to their pleasingly human-sized scale placed among liberal plots of green breathing spaces. London takes a lifetime to explore fully, and a tourist with only a week to cover the major sights will be hard-pressed to make even a dent. But you can make a start. The best approach is to decide where your interests lie; you will soon discover that there are few interests known to humanity that London cannot entertain.

London has the best museums in the world, the world-famous as well as some lesser-known ones. Its miles of parks offer some of the loveliest natural scenery to be found in any metropolis. Part of London's charm—although debatably so, as its climate is hardly celebrated—lies in the sudden deluges from leaden skies that will just as quickly be sliced open with swords of sunlight, and in those frequently single days that feature four seasons of weather.

Just as mercurially appealing are the people of London, who speak in a rich concoction of accents, in more than 200 languages, and represent a teeming multitude of personalities, classes, attitudes, nationalities, and political views. No matter what moves you—theater, architecture, sports, antiques, markets, designer duds, contemporary art and old masters, heart-stopping cathedrals, louche cafes, palaces, poetry readings, gambling, lunatic nightclubs, pubs, horticulture, witchcraft, fencing, boating—there truly is, as the good doctor pointed out almost three centuries ago, "in London all that Life can afford."

ABOUT *this* GUIDE

WHY "UNOFFICIAL"?

MOST LONDON TRAVEL GUIDES follow the usual tracks of the typical tourist, automatically sending everyone to the well-known sights without offering any information about how to do this painlessly; recommending restaurants and hotels indiscriminately; and failing to recognize the limits of human endurance in sightseeing. This guide attempts to be different: we understand that in a huge city like London, it is essential to discriminate, make plans, and be flexible when hours-long lines appear out of nowhere or the clouds burst and you've forgotten your umbrella.

We'll tell you what we think of certain tourist traps, give you the real story on famous restaurants and hotels, show you options for going off the beaten track, and advise you how to spend a little less money on some things so you can spend more on others. We'll complain about rip-offs, and we'll fill you in on bargains. We also hope to give you the kind of information that will make you love London all the more—some of the endearing eccentricities that make you realize you're definitely not in Kansas anymore.

We've tried in this book to anticipate the special needs of older people, families with young children, families with teenagers, solo travelers, and people with physical challenges.

We cover the hotels, restaurants, and attractions in seemingly insane detail because we want you to be able to make the most informed decisions possible about where to go and what to do. For those of you who don't want to have to figure it all out yourself, we've listed a number of good commercial and customized tours on pages 100–109 in Part Six, Sightseeing, Tours, and Attractions.

Please do remember that prices and admission hours—and, worst of all, exchange rates—change. We've listed the most up-to-date information we can get, but it never hurts to double-check before you head out the hotel door. Remember, this is one of the busiest tourist towns in the world, so in the case of a hot exhibit, a trendy restaurant, or a theatrical phenomenon, be sure to make your reservations early and reconfirm.

About *Unofficial Guides*

Readers care about authors' opinions. The authors, after all, are supposed to know what they are talking about. This, coupled with the fact that the traveler wants quick answers, dictates that travel authors be explicit, prescriptive, and, above all, direct. The authors of the *Unofficial Guide* try to be just that. We spell out alternatives and recommend specific courses of action. We simplify complicated destinations and attractions to allow the traveler to feel in control in the most unfamiliar environments. Our objective is not to give the most information or all the information, but the most accessible, useful information. Of course, in a city like London, many hotels, restaurants, and attractions are so closely woven into the fabric of the city that to omit them from this guide because we can't recommend them would be a disservice to our readers. We've included all the famous haunts, giving our opinions and experiences of them, in the hopes that you will approach (or avoid) these institutions armed with the necessary intelligence.

An *Unofficial Guide* is a critical reference work; we focus on a travel destination that appears to be especially complex. Our authors and researchers are completely independent from the attractions, restaurants, and hotels we describe. The *Unofficial Guide to London* is designed for individuals and families traveling for fun as well as for business, and it will be especially helpful to those hopping "across the pond" for the first time. The guide is directed at value-conscious, consumer-oriented adults who seek a cost-effective but not overly Spartan travel style.

SPECIAL FEATURES

- Vital information about traveling abroad
- Friendly introductions to London's "villages"
- Listings keyed to your interests, so you can pick and choose
- Advice to sightseers on how to avoid the worst crowds, as well as advice to business travelers on how to avoid traffic and excessive costs
- Recommendations for lesser-known sights that are off the well-beaten tourist path but no less worthwhile
- Maps that make it easy to find places you want to go—or avoid
- A hotel section that helps you narrow down your choices quickly, according to your needs and preferences
- A table of contents and detailed index to help you find things fast

WHAT YOU WON'T GET

- Long, useless lists in which everything looks the same
- Information that gets you to your destination at the worst possible time
- Information without advice on how to use it

HOW THIS GUIDE WAS RESEARCHED AND WRITTEN

IN PREPARING THIS WORK, we took nothing for granted. Each hotel, restaurant, shop, and attraction was visited by trained observers who conducted detailed evaluations and rated each according to formal criteria. Team members conducted interviews with tourists of all ages to determine what they enjoyed most and least during their visits to London.

Though our observers are independent and impartial, they are otherwise "ordinary" travelers. Like you, they visited London as tourists or business travelers, noting their satisfaction or dissatisfaction.

The primary difference between the average tourist and the trained evaluator is the latter's skills in organization, preparation, and observation. A trained evaluator is responsible for more than just observing and cataloging. Observer teams use detailed checklists to analyze hotel rooms, restaurants, nightclubs, and attractions. Finally, evaluator ratings and observations are integrated with tourist reactions and the opinions of patrons for a comprehensive quality profile of each feature and service.

In compiling this guide, we recognize that a tourist's age, background, and interests will strongly influence his or her taste in London's wide array of attractions and will account for a preference for one sight or museum over another. Our sole objective is to provide the reader with sufficient description, critical evaluation, and pertinent data to make knowledgeable decisions according to individual tastes.

LETTERS, COMMENTS, AND QUESTIONS FROM READERS

WE EXPECT TO LEARN FROM OUR MISTAKES, as well as from the input of our readers, and to improve with each new book and edition. Many of those who use the *Unofficial Guides* write to us asking questions, making comments, or sharing their own discoveries and lessons learned in London. We appreciate all such input, both positive and critical, and encourage our readers to continue writing. Readers' comments and observations will frequently be incorporated into revised editions of the *Unofficial Guide* and will contribute immeasurably to its improvement.

How to Write the Author

Lesley Logan
The Unofficial Guide to London
P.O. Box 43673
Birmingham, AL 35243
unofficialguides@menasharidge.com

When you write, be sure to put your return address on your letter as well as on the envelope—sometimes envelopes and letters get separated. And remember that our work takes us out of the office for long periods of time, so forgive us if our response is delayed.

HOW INFORMATION
is ORGANIZED

TO GIVE YOU FAST ACCESS to information about the best of London, we've organized material in several formats.

HOTELS

THERE ARE SO MANY DRAMATICALLY different hotels in London that range from the small and quirky to the big and boring, even within the same price range and class. To further complicate matters, room types often vary wildly within each of these establishments. Even the world-class, well-known, expensive hotels will offer rooms of totally different size and with totally different amenities, and a midpriced boutique hotel will often have under one charming roof and at a similar price both closet-sized attic rooms with tiny beds and no views and magnificent salons with French windows opening onto balconies. The converted town houses, the updated terminus grand hotels, the homey B&Bs have only so much to work with: grade-listed historical buildings cannot freely make structural changes, so gutting interiors in order to make the rooms homogeneous is usually out of the question. We have tried to focus on hotels that offer a more consistent type—or at least clearly delineated selection—of lodgings, and we have attempted to summarize this somewhat unwieldy and problematic subject in ratings and rankings that allow you to quickly crystallize your choice. We concentrate on the specific variables that differentiate one hotel from another: location, size, room quality, services, amenities, and cost.

ENTERTAINMENT AND NIGHTLIFE

VISITORS WILL HAVE VERY PERSONAL ideas of what constitutes a good night out on the town, depending on their age, background, bank account, and bedtime. Some night owls will want to hit as many different clubs as possible during their stay in London, but they will probably prefer to party with like-minded people, or at least want to blend in a bit. Because nightspots so often have a very specific clientele and ambience, we believe that detailed descriptions are warranted, so that you don't end up in a lager-soaked mosh pit when you're dressed for cool jazz and cold mojitos. The best nightspots in London are profiled in Part Nine, Entertainment and Nightlife. Be warned, though, that the popularity and character of clubs can change quite literally overnight; they also go out of business without warning. We have made a point of selecting places that seem to have withstood the tests of time and fluctuations of fashion—although, obviously, one person's mead is another person's poison when it comes to late-night entertainment. Just because Princes William and Harry party at a certain club doesn't mean you'd want to be caught dead there. Of course, the preferred haunts of, say, fashionistas, glitterati, football legends, celebutantes, screen and stage luvvies, or billionaire babies can change as fast as their entourages, so try to do some on-the-spot research when you get here before pitching up someplace where you may be disappointed—or horrified.

RESTAURANTS

WE PROVIDE PLENTY OF DETAILS when it comes to restaurants, and we wish we could promise you they will be just as fresh as the daily catch by the time you have this book in your hands. But as with everything in the universe, the only constant is change. All we can do is try to focus on those things less likely to do a sudden about-face: location, reputation, clientele, service standards, and caliber of chefs. Given the high cost of eating in London, and the fact that you will probably eat at a dozen or more restaurants during your stay, you may benefit from discussing your choices with a concierge or soliciting the opinions of other visitors or acquaintances before you make your reservation. Try to vary your restaurant experiences according to cuisine, price, and location—our dining profiles in Part Eight can get you started in that direction, and we hope the standards we observed at all these many tables have not slipped in the slightest by the time you put your napkin in your lap.

LONDON'S NEIGHBORHOODS

ONCE YOU'VE DECIDED where you're going, getting there becomes the issue. To help you do that, we refer consistently to five groups of London neighborhoods, described briefly below to give you a vague idea of what they're about. All profiles of hotels, restaurants, attractions, and nightspots include these neighborhood references. The post codes that appear at the end of London addresses are for the purpose of delivering mail and are known to the citizens as shorthand for a certain area: residents know that SW1, for example, is part of the royal borough of Westminster and includes the neighborhoods of Victoria, Pimlico, and parts of Knightsbridge and Belgravia. Chelsea and Kensington are in the SW3 and SW7 codes. Neighborhoods to the north are known by their N prefix followed by a number. They represent compass directions (N, S, W, E) that radiate generally from central London (C), with the lowest numbers being in the center of London, roughly to the east of Hyde Park and west of The City. With a few exceptions, the higher the number, the farther the area is from central London.

West End (includes Bloomsbury, Holborn, Mayfair, Piccadilly, Regent's Park, Soho, Waterloo, and the West End)

You will certainly spend time in this fun-filled, attraction-rich collection of neighborhoods. Most of the theaters are here, as are **St. Martin-in-the-Fields, Trafalgar Square,** rowdy **Leicester Square, Chinatown, Somerset House,** the **National Gallery,** and pubs, pubs, pubs. **Covent Garden** has shops and street entertainment, as well as the **London Transport Museum.** You might want to stay at a hotel around the West End or Soho, but it can get loud at night, with drunks roaring up and down side streets and tourists as far as the eye can see. Of course, that may be precisely the appeal. Other attractions include the **Royal Academy,** the **National Portrait Gallery,** the **Horse Guards Parade,** and the **British Museum,** along with portions of **Regent's, Green,** and **St. James's** parks.

The **West End** embraces the shopping of New and Old Bond Street, Oxford Street, Baker Street, Leicester Square, Carnaby Street, Neal's Yard, Covent Garden, and more. This area was the heart of London life in the centuries following the Great Fire of 1666 and remains the pulsating center of the entertainment industry (in **Soho**), the legal profession (in **Lincoln's Inn**), and higher education (in the ivory towers of the **University of London Colleges,** the **London School of Economics,** and **King's College**). Blue plaques commemorating London addresses of various historical giants abound in this area, from Handel and Karl Marx in Soho, to Virginia Woolf and her pals around the British Museum, to worthy lords and ladies off Piccadilly.

Posh old **Mayfair,** long a haven of gentility, is home to the most expensive shops in the world, including the bespoke-clothing establishments of St. James and Jermyn streets and the international designers of Bond Street. There are hotels here of every imaginable type, except for modestly priced ones—sheiks, celebs, and captains of industry stay at the **Atheneum,** the **Ritz, Brown's, Claridge's,** or the **Savoy. Hatchard's,** the oldest bookstore in London, is on Piccadilly, as are **Fortnum & Mason** and the **Burlington** and **Piccadilly arcades,** dignified ancestors of the modern strip mall. Nearby is **Shepherd's Market,** which in the 1600s was the site of a riotous saturnalia known as the May Fair and a place for the entertainers of the day—jugglers, fire eaters, boxers, prostitutes—to parade their talents. Today, Shepherds' Market is a mere shadow of its former self, but charming nonetheless.

In fact, it is quite possible to have a rollicking great time in London without once stepping out of this area. Wandering all the side streets and visiting the major sights in the area can eat up a month's holiday. Overheating your credit cards and dodging all the traffic around here can wear down your nervous system, so be sure to take a break and hop a bus to other areas that are less frenetic but equally interesting.

The City (includes Barbican, Brixton, Clerkenwell, the East End, South Bank, Tower Hill, and Whitechapel)

This is the oldest part of London, where you'll find the unsinkable St. Paul's Cathedral, the occasional whispers of a medieval past, and some remnants of the town that the occupying ancient Romans called Londinium. The square mile of **The City** has long been and continues to be where most of London's financial business is conducted. The area pretty much dies at night and on weekends, but during the day you'll find plenty of good restaurants here, along with lots of historic pubs. The **Bank of England Museum** and Richard Rogers's **Lloyd's of London** building are here, along with some amusing architectural visions, such as the grasshopper on the top of the **Stock Exchange** and **30 St. Mary Axe,** a glass high-rise nicknamed "The Gherkin" for its picklelike shape. The old markets, rigorously updated—**Smithfield's, Spitalfields,** and **Leadenhall**—are fun to check out. This area also offers Victorian architecture, art galleries, churches, and the faintest echo of Cockney English life.

The **East End** is, like so much of this crushingly expensive city, experiencing great gentrification, as the prices of real estate in central London push people ever farther afield. New luxury apartments, artsy nightspots, and the **Prince of Wales's Institute of Architecture** now share the streets where Jack the Ripper stalked his prey and Sweeney Todd made mincemeat of his customers. Here, too, you can get a boat to Greenwich, see some of the old Roman wall around

central london

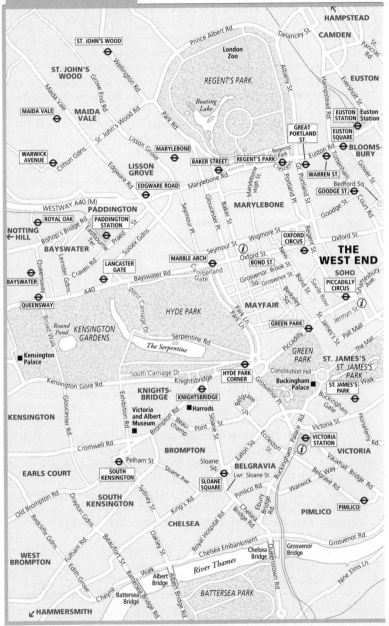

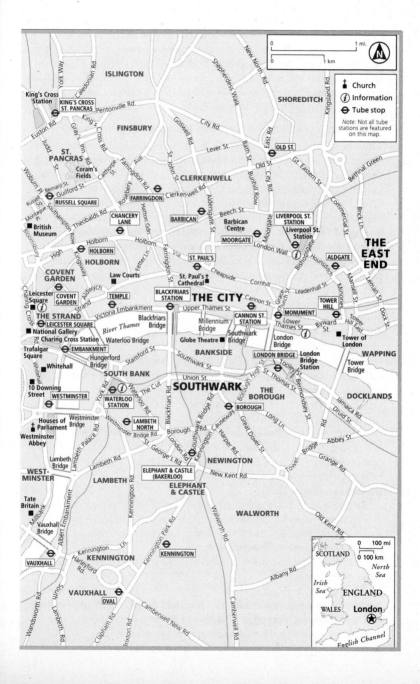

ISLINGTON

King's Cross Station
KING'S CROSS ST. PANCRAS
Pentonville Rd.

SHOREDITCH

Church
Information
Tube stop
Note: Not all tube stations are featured on this map.

FINSBURY

ST. PANCRAS

Coram's Fields

CLERKENWELL

OLD ST.

RUSSELL SQUARE

FARRINGDON

Clerkenwell Rd.

British Museum

CHANCERY LANE

BARBICAN

LIVERPOOL ST. STATION

THE EAST END

Barbican Centre

Liverpool St. Station

HOLBORN

MOORGATE

Holborn

London Wall

ALDGATE

COVENT GARDEN

Law Courts

ST. PAUL'S

Cheapside

Cornhill

Leicester Square

COVENT GARDEN

TEMPLE

St. Paul's Cathedral

BLACKFRIARS STATION

THE CITY

Cannon St.

TOWER HILL

THE STRAND

LEICESTER SQUARE

Upper Thames St.

CANNON ST. STATION

MONUMENT

National Gallery

Charing Cross Station

River Thames

Blackfriars Bridge

Millennium Bridge

Southwark Bridge

Lower Thames St.

Byward St.

Tower of London

WAPPING

Trafalgar Square

EMBANKMENT

Waterloo Bridge

Globe Theatre

London Bridge

LONDON BRIDGE

London Bridge Station

Tower Bridge

Whitehall

Hungerford Bridge

Stamford St.

BANKSIDE

DOCKLANDS

SOUTH BANK

Southwark St.

10 Downing Street

WESTMINSTER

Union St.

SOUTHWARK

THE BOROUGH

Jamaica Rd.

Druid St.

Houses of Parliament

WATERLOO STATION

LAMBETH NORTH

BOROUGH

Westminster Bridge

Westminster Abbey

Westminster Bridge Rd.

Borough Rd.

Long Ln.

Abbey St.

Lambeth Bridge

WEST-MINSTER

Lambeth Rd.

St. George's Rd.

London Rd.

Harper Rd.

Great Dover St.

Grange Rd.

LAMBETH

ELEPHANT & CASTLE (BAKERLOO)

NEWINGTON

New Kent Rd.

Tate Britain

Millbank

ELEPHANT & CASTLE

Old Kent Rd.

Vauxhall Bridge

WALWORTH

Walworth Rd.

VAUXHALL

KENNINGTON

KENNINGTON

SCOTLAND

North Sea

Irish Sea

VAUXHALL

OVAL

Camberwell New Rd.

WALES

ENGLAND

London

English Channel

London, or visit the drunk-with-history **Tower of London** and the Victorian marvel that is **Tower Bridge.** Walk across the **Millennium Bridge,** which spans both the Thames and the centuries between the old power station that houses the art of the **Tate Modern** and Christopher Wren's 17th-century **Cathedral of St. Paul.** The City is a wonderful mélange of old and new (and, in the case of the re-creation of Shakespeare's **Globe Theatre,** the newly old), where modern needs push up against, but never entirely overcome, the proud footprints of the past.

Westminster and Victoria (includes Belgravia and Pimlico)

This area runs from the semiseedy to the sublime. It encompasses the august halls of government and power in London in **Whitehall,** where statues everywhere memorialize the great and powerful of England: Oliver Cromwell, Lord Nelson, the two King Charleses, Winston Churchill, and others, all left out in the rain with pigeons desecrating them. There are plenty of hotels to go along with the attractions of the **Houses of Parliament,** the **Queen's Gallery,** the **Churchill Museum and Cabinet War Rooms, Westminster Abbey,** and **Tate Britain.** Because of the heavy concentration of World War II bombing in this area, there are patches of real ugliness here and there where rebuilding paid no attention to architectural coherence. Much of Westminster simply closes down on the weekend—not the attractions but the eateries, which cater mainly to the business crowd. **Pimlico,** to the south of Westminster, has lots of cheap hotels but may not be the greatest place to stay in terms of transportation and street interest.

Here lies the august triangle of **Buckingham Palace,** which the queen calls her London home; **Number 10 Downing Street,** the official residence of the Prime Minister; and the **Banqueting Hall** where Charles I was beheaded—the three points neatly take the measure of power throughout England's history. There are magnificent vistas here—the fairy-tale view from Buckingham Palace across **St. James's Park** toward Westminster Abbey will have you reaching for your camera, and who can ever have enough photos of **Big Ben** and the wildly neo-Gothic Houses of Parliament, now looked over by the graceful spectacle of the **London Eye** Ferris wheel?

Belgravia is an enclave of ambassadors and billionaires, with enormous mansions, some of which are made up of as many as five massive houses strung together, as in the humble home of the Sultan of Brunei. On the **Westminster Embankment** you can watch the Thames flow past or jump on a sightseeing boat that will take you to the Tower of London or Greenwich.

The area also encompasses the great renaissance of the **South Bank**—the **London Aquarium,** the **Marriott Hotel,** the **Royal Festival Hall** and **National Theatre,** the **Hayward Gallery,** the London Eye—as well as the ancient palace of **Lambeth,** where the archbishop of Canterbury lives. From the South Bank you get the very best views of the halls of Westminster and Big Ben, and year-round you can stroll along the promenade and enjoy the parade of life that is always marching by.

Knightsbridge, South Kensington, and Chelsea (includes Earls Court)

This group of neighborhoods is the stronghold of the wealthy—British aristocrats, Russian oligarchs, expatriates on expense accounts, brilliant (or lucky) entrepreneurs, and petroleum-enriched sheiks coexist in the splendor of Georgian town houses built around generous garden squares, or in deceptively simple mews houses that once stabled horses. **Knightsbridge** is mainly about shopping: augmenting **Harrods** and **Harvey Nichols** are the world-class designer shops on **Sloane Street, Fulham Road,** and **Beauchamp Place.** The auction house **Bonhams** is in **Knightsbridge Village,** as is an assortment of secondhand designer-clothes shops, and on busy **Brompton Road** you'll find the full complement of high-street chains: **H&M, Gap, Benetton, Jigsaw, Monsoon, Burberry,** and more.

Besides its overkill of commerce, Knightsbridge is also famous for having the most consonants in a row in any English word, surely a fact to be savored. The area is a convenient place to stay, with buses and tube lines going from there to everywhere in London. The **Victoria and Albert, Natural History,** and **Science museums** are only a stone's throw from **Hyde Park,** through which you can horseback-ride, skate, or bicycle.

South Kensington was once known as Albertopolis and Museumland because of the Great Exhibition of 1851 that Prince Albert organized. The marvelous collections of treasures and curiosities of the exhibition formed the basis for these great museums, which are as beautiful on the outside as they are fascinating within. **Royal Albert Hall,** the **Royal Art College, Imperial College,** and numerous learned societies, institutes, and foreign embassies give the area yet more gravitas. Today South Kensington is known by a different nickname: "Little France," thanks to the **Lycée Français** and the **Institut Français** in the middle of town. There are lots of great patisseries, some good restaurants, and plenty of hotels.

To the south, **Chelsea** boasts the famous **King's Road,** the once-swinging high street for 1960s hipsters and 1970s punks that gave way to yawn-inspiring 1980s yuppies and 21st-century just-plain-rich folk. The absurdly unsuitable SUVs that are popular in this area are wittily referred to as "Chelsea tractors." The days of these overweight vehicles driven by underweight women may be numbered as the mayor of London proposes to charge SUVs more than double the cost of a normal, less polluting automobile for the privilege of entering the area (in February 2007, Kensington and Chelsea opened the western part of the capital to enlarge the eight-quid-a-day congestion-charging area). It's a good idea, but probably not very effective: being grotesquely overcharged for everything raises very few eyebrows and not many hackles here, especially among the Richie Riches.

In the neighborhoods off the King's Road are a multitude of blue plaques identifying the many writers and artists who once called Chelsea home: Oscar Wilde, George Eliot, Whistler . . . the list goes on and on. Chelsea is a very smart area—and the property prices reflect this, as do the price tags in the swanky shops.

Marylebone to Notting Hill Gate (includes Kensington, Bayswater, Holland Park, and Regent's Park)

At the northern border of Hyde Park, **Bayswater** and **Marylebone** are home to fabulous Middle Eastern restaurants, lots of fun shopping areas, and some cheap and cheerful daily street markets. Here you'll find the **Wallace Collection, Whiteley's Shopping Mall, Queensway**'s strange combo skating rink and bowling alley, the burgeoning bustle of chi-chi shops on the once-funky **Westbourne Grove, Madame Tussauds,** and two horseback-riding stables that offer trots around Hyde Park. **Paddington Station** is the terminus for the Heathrow Express, as well as for trains that serve the West Country and South Wales.

Marylebone is a charming little village north of bustling Oxford Street, with a number of good restaurants and excellent shops. **Regent's Park** houses the **London Zoo,** the **London Central Mosque,** and **Regent's Park Open Air Theatre;** it also affords some of the most beautiful 18th-century vistas in London. Designed in concert with King George IV, who was regent at the time, this area is the crowning achievement of architect John Nash, even though it was a financial failure that remained uncompleted in his lifetime.

In 1689, King William and Queen Mary moved their royal residence to the then far-flung country village of **Kensington** for the king's health, and their court followed suit, building grand manors far more impressive than the homely **Kensington Palace** of the era—some of which are still private homes to this day. As rich attracts rich, in the following centuries the neighborhoods to the west and north, **Notting Hill** and **Holland Park** developed into the highly exclusive areas that they are today, give or take a few wobbles in their fortunes during the intervening centuries. **Kensington High Street** is a big, bustling shopping street, with a huge range of stores selling clothing, accessories, housewares, and electronics; it also boasts a number of popular restaurants, as well as the wildly popular grocery store–eatery **Whole Foods Market.**

Notting Hill, after its genteel heyday in Victorian times, became run-down enough to attract new immigrants. In the early 1960s, it was a Jamaican enclave that yearly celebrated its Caribbean roots with the vibrant Notting Hill Carnival. Before long, the spacious flats with communal gardens started attracting young aristo hippies living on family funds. Notting Hill is a very popular place, as it had been long before the Richard Curtis movie with Julia Roberts and Hugh Grant came along. This is the site of the famous **Portobello Market,** which is worth a look on Saturday—as long as you're not prone to agoraphobia or manic spending sprees.

PART ONE

An OVERVIEW *of* LONDON

LONDON IS ONE OF THE WORLD'S BEST CITIES and has been for centuries, give or take an outburst or two of social and economic depredations, class oppression, maniacal monarchies, puritan repressions, and worse. This capital city has been through invasion, warfare, famine, plague, and rebellion, but age has yet to wither London or custom to stale her infinite variety. Nor is it completely pretentious to parrot a line from Shakespeare to praise this city—it used to be his town, too.

As coolly modern and urbane as London is now, there is something profoundly mysterious and majestic about this 21st-century city when you tune out the neon and push away the traffic to grasp the deeper dimensions of its fascinating and long life. A bit of the history of this town on the Thames is just as useful for the discerning visitor as a street map. So here we go.

The LONG LIFE *of an* ANCIENT CITY

INITIALLY, LONDON'S HISTORY IS ONE OF INVASION and conquest, perhaps because the city is situated on the banks of a wide river cutting through a large island; its later history, owing to England's system of monarchy, is one of bloody factionalism and revolving persecutions. During the empire's formative years, British blood was shed on foreign soil as England's sovereignty was propped up by the exploitation of far-off continents and by the labor of underpaid, often underage workers in London.

But through it all, the story of London has been intertwined with the history of commerce: this port city has beckoned to artisans, sailors, farmers, prostitutes, and wheelers and dealers of all shades of corruption for two millennia. London shows no signs of losing its mojo in the third millennium.

WHEN ROME RULED LONDINIUM

JULIUS CAESAR'S FAMOUS REMARK about how Britons made terrible slaves was based both in fact and in no small measure of sour grapes: in 55 BC and 56 BC, he tried to subdue England twice and failed. In AD 43, the Romans again sent an army to conquer the island. This time they built a bridge over the Thames at the narrowest crossing, near the present London Bridge. Soon, this small Roman outpost, called Londinium, grew into a thriving port of commerce, as luxury goods from all over the Roman Empire arrived and were exchanged for corn, iron, and—Julius Caesar notwithstanding—slaves.

The Roman historian Tacitus wrote that Londinium was "famed for commerce and crowded with merchants," a description that would remain accurate for the next 2,000 years (and will doubtless continue to be). Roadways, the most ubiquitous and long-lasting feature of Roman rule, soon headed in every direction from this trading post and were well traveled by Romans and Britons in search of adventure and wealth. After a period of Pax Romana (a "peace" imposed martially by Rome on its dominions), foreign rule became increasingly unbearable to the local tribes. Queen Boudicca (also spelled Boadicea) of the Iceni tribe was at the head of a violent revolt, leading hordes of warriors to invade Londinium, where they massacred everyone in sight and burned the Roman fortress to the ground. The revolution was short-lived, however, and the rebels were mercilessly repaid with extreme interest. Londinium was rebuilt with an encircling wall, encompassing the present-day City and Barbican area. A piece of the wall is preserved near the Museum of London, and a heart-stirring statue of the ferocious Boudicca stands near Westminster Bridge.

By AD 410, the sun had dipped below the horizon on the once-unbeatable Roman Empire. Troops withdrew gradually, leaving behind the sprouts of Rome's newly adopted Christian faith. London then dwindled into a ghost town. When new invaders from the north arrived, they superstitiously stayed away from the Roman ruins, which were soon buried under the silt of the river and would lie undiscovered until the end of World War II.

THE SAXONS' LUNDENWIC

IN THE FIFTH CENTURY, immigration of Saxon tribes from the north of Europe to the southeast of England led to an inevitable move toward the well-situated former Londinium, abandoned on the Thames. By the late 400s, London slowly shook off its Roman ashes and began to reestablish itself as a trading post, now known as Lundenwic. After starting his reign as the leader of a pagan society, King Ethelbert converted to Christianity and built the first church of St. Paul on roughly the same site where today's edifice stands. The Saxon kings spent most of the next five centuries fighting Viking invaders and fortifying their kingdom and its capital at Winchester, in the West Country. London has King Alfred to thank for rebuilding it after Danish invaders left it in ruins, as well as for lighting a few other candles in those dark ages.

The tenth century saw a new prosperity as neighborhoods and parishes sprang up on the banks of the Thames. In the 11th century, the Danes finally won the day, and England was forced to kneel to its king, Canute. He put London on the map as the capital of the kingdom, and by 1042, when Edward the Confessor took the scepter, London was poised on the brink of a great architectural leap forward. Westminster Abbey and the Palace at Westminster gave the raucous commercial port a dignity that was soon complemented by the White Tower, the tallest building at the Tower of London.

WILLIAM THE CONQUEROR

IN 1066, AT THE BATTLE OF HASTINGS, a Norman army led by William vanquished the Saxon troops and with that victory signaled a new dawn for London. William decided to hold his coronation at Westminster Abbey, where virtually every British monarch since has been crowned. The king recognized that London was perfectly placed to be a rich capital, and he built his White Tower next to the river, not just for the strategic value but also to show the inhabitants of this headstrong city who was in charge. However, William was also a smart politician who granted freedoms to the Saxon-dominated church and local governors, ensuring a pleasant and profitable back-scratching all around.

London grew rich under the watchful eye of the kings who followed, who knew that the key to their power lay in the wealth and goodwill of London's merchants and churchmen. In 1180, William Fitzstephen, in the preface to his *Life of Thomas à Becket,* sang high praises of London: "It is blessed by a wholesome climate. . . . in the strength of its fortifications, in the nature of its site, the repute of its citizens, the honour of its matrons; happy in its sports, prolific in noble men . . . I can think of no other city with customs more admirable. . . . The only plagues of London are the immoderate drinking of fools and the frequency of fires."

A VIBRANT MEDIEVAL PORT

LONDON IN THE MIDDLE AGES was a crazy salad of streets, alleys, markets, outdoor brothels, bear-baiting pits, pubs, and theaters. The vibrancy of the streets was matched in energy by the jostling for power among the court, the burgesses, and the church. In 1215, the Magna Carta, a revolutionary document of the time that attempted to limit the excesses and power of the king and establish personal rights and political freedom for the nobility, was signed by King John, who was forced to do so by rebellious barons and the newly created lord mayor of London. Soon Parliament and the House of Commons were created, and England became a place of liberty and justice for at least a few more than before. Though the Magna Carta was designed to free the aristocracy from the despotism of a monarch, it also contained the fateful word *freemen,* and so signaled at least theoretical rights for the common people.

The port was thriving. Houses and warehouses lined the riverbanks, and the power of the guilds and merchants grew apace. But London's position as one of the world's great ports—crowded with thousands of people living in appalling sanitary conditions—led to the first outbreak of bubonic plague. The Black Death of 1348 traveled across the English Channel from the European continent, which was already reeling from the dread disease. Nearly half of London's population succumbed to the plague, infected by rats that multiplied in the filthy streets and fetid sewers. The debacle, with its attendant economic disaster, led to an egregiously ill-advised poll tax imposed in 1381 by a financially strapped court—a shilling a person, regardless of income or situation. The Peasants' Revolt, led by Jack Straw and Wat Tyler, put every future monarch on notice that Londoners had a breaking point that should be studiously avoided. After a riotous spree of looting, burning, and murder, the rebels were overcome, and a young King Richard II restored order, but the point was well taken: the poll tax was quietly dropped.

A new intellectual age dawned around this time. In the 1390s, Geoffrey Chaucer wrote *The Canterbury Tales,* and in 1476 William Caxton set up his printing press at Westminster. His apprentice, the aptly named Wynkyn de Worde, took over when Caxton died in 1491 and relocated the press to Fleet Street in 1500, turning the making of books into a real business, publishing volumes on a wide variety of subjects and even setting up a bookstore in St. Paul's. At the same time, London's monasteries became centers for teaching and learning, and literacy began creeping into the merchant and upper classes, setting the scene for the Renaissance culture of the Tudor era.

TUDOR LONDON

THE WAR OF THE ROSES BETWEEN the fractious factions of the House of Plantagenet—the York and Lancaster branches—provided William Shakespeare with a superabundance of material for his tragedies. As he wrote in *Richard III,* "England hath long been mad, and scarred herself; / The brother blindly shed the brother's blood, The father rashly slaughtered his own son, / The son, compelled, been butcher to the sire: / All this divided York and Lancaster. . . ."

The bloody dynastic feud for the throne had relatively little effect on the daily lives of Londoners scrambling for a living. But when Richard III allegedly smothered his two young nephews, the rightful heirs to the throne, in the Tower of London, the citizenry strenuously disapproved, and few regretted the end of Richard's reign. Enter the Tudor dynasty, whose heirs were at least as ruthless when it came to insulting and disposing of relatives as any of the previous Plantagenets had been.

Henry VIII married his elder brother Arthur's widow, Catherine of Aragon, to keep the peace with Spain. After 20 years of marriage and one daughter, Mary, Henry fell in love with Anne Boleyn and was spurred by his emotions to make the momentous decision that he must marry again in order to have a male heir. He petitioned the Catholic Church in Rome for an annulment, but for all his diplomatic wiles, he was refused absolutely. Not one to take no for an answer, and a man who willingly threw out both baby and bathtub with the bathwater, Henry broke with the Vatican and created the Church of England, installing himself as de facto Pope. This shocking maneuver kicked off a complicated crisis of faith and politics, one in which old supporters were forced to choose between their Catholicism and their king. All too many were burned or beheaded as heretics.

When his queen failed to produce the desired male heir (although her one child, Elizabeth, was to become one of the most powerful monarchs of England), Henry trumped up charges of adultery and incest against Anne Boleyn, and she was executed at the Tower of London, where her unquiet ghost apparently makes the rounds nightly. The king then embarked on a serial marital spree that left in its wake a total of six wives—as the nursery rhyme goes, "two beheaded, two divorced, one died, and one survived."

One of the most long-reaching secular expressions of this religious overhaul was in the dissolution of the monasteries, as Henry rather gleefully took for the crown all the Catholic Church's property in England—cathedrals, churches, priories, convents, and monasteries. Huge numbers of beautiful Gothic and medieval buildings were put to fire and other depredations, and the king redistributed the land among the new loyal-to-Henry aristocracy, creating new streets, houses, and courtyards where there had once been wealthy Catholic establishments. Resistant nuns and clergy were hung, drawn, and quartered; the army of crippled, diseased, and homeless who had been supported by the charity of the churches was thrown upon its own resources, and the streets of London resounded with the cries of their misery.

After Henry VIII died, syphilitic and obese, the sickly child-king Edward VI took the throne; his six-year reign, cut short by his death from consumption, amounted to little more than a vicious power struggle among his courtiers. After "Bloody" Mary, Henry's first daughter, ascended the throne, she imprisoned her half-sister, Elizabeth, in the Tower of London to prevent any uprisings against her iron-fisted reign. Under the staunchly (some would say fanatically) Catholic Mary, it was the Protestants' turn to have their property seized and be hung or burned alive. The daily spectacle of burning heretics at the marketplace of Smithfields finally disgusted even Londoners accustomed to gruesome public punishments.

In another turn of the dynasty, Elizabeth returned England to its still-unsteady Protestant base, forestalling any Catholic overthrow by having her cousin, Mary, Queen of Scots, executed at Fotheringay Castle in Northamptonshire in 1587. (Mary's son, King James I, ordered her body exhumed in 1612 and reinterred at Westminster Abbey, producing the grim irony of two rival queens resting for eternity within a few feet of one another.)

THE ELIZABETHAN FLOWERING OF LONDON

WHAT WERE THE GOOD CITIZENS of London doing while all the royal-kin-killing kerfuffle and musical thrones were being played out? Well, while the aristocrats built over-the-top estates from the remains of the monasteries and Hyde Park became a happy hunting ground for King Henry VIII, the ordinary Londoner went about the usual daily rounds of earning and eating, fornicating and frolicking, marrying and burying. In 1586, William Shakespeare arrived in London, joining Ben Jonson, Christopher Marlowe, John Donne, and others of the day's glitterati in an extraordinary flowering of English letters.

The city now had a population of 200,000 people, up from 50,000 in the 1300s, and more arrived every day. The great era of exploration was under way as the English plied the oceans in search of riches, returning with sugar, spice, coffee, and tobacco. Sir Thomas Gresham started the Royal Exchange from its humble beginnings as a coffeehouse and made London the world's most important financial center, a position it maintained into the early 20th century. Even more important was the establishment of the printing press.

Although Queen Elizabeth could be as dangerous a friend (and relative) as she was a foe, she was devoted to the welfare of her kingdom and understood that her greatest power lay in the love her subjects had for her—she had an instinctive gift for almost-modern public relations. Perhaps the greatest gift she gave the nation was her much-vaunted virginity: by not marrying a foreign prince, she kept England solidly English for 45 prosperous years (and, not coincidentally, kept for herself the power that she otherwise would have had to cede to any husband). By the end of her long reign, the memories of those ugly battles of succession had faded, but more cataclysms lay ahead for the monarchy and for London.

ROUNDHEADS AND RESTORATION

THE GUNPOWDER PLOT OF 1605, in which a group of Catholic conspirators, including the celebrated Guy Fawkes, was thwarted in a plan to blow up King James I (Mary, Queen of Scots's son), his ministers, and Parliament at the Palace of Westminster, rather appropriately opened London's apocalyptic 17th century. King James died in 1625, leaving on the throne a backward and vain son, Charles I.

Although at this time London was the wealthiest city in the world, Charles I simply could not leave well enough alone. He insisted on the divine right of kings, a philosophy that was anathema to the Parliament and businessmen of London, and a civil war was waged over the principle.

The monarchist Cavaliers were defeated by the Puritan Roundheads, and Charles I was beheaded outside his beloved Banqueting Hall, which had been designed by Inigo Jones. It's the only part of the massive Palace of Westminster that remains intact, and the ceiling painting by Rubens gives you a hint of the megalomania that led to Charles I's downfall: the Stuart dynasty is depicted as sitting at the right hand of God, and glorified beyond all recognition is the short, awkward king who managed to lose his throne and his head. Although the majority of London had been on the side of the antiroyalist Commonwealth, 18 years of dour Puritanism under Oliver Cromwell's rule, during which all fun was canceled, left the city gasping for a breath of fresh air. The diarist John Evelyn wrote at Cromwell's death that "it was the joyfullest funeral I ever saw, for there were none that cried but dogs."

In 1661, London warmly welcomed the exiled Charles II back from France, "shouting with inexpressible joy" and watching undismayed when Charles ordered the three-year-old corpses of Cromwell and two cronies exhumed for the dubious purpose of hanging and beheading them publicly for the murder of his father. (Perhaps the citizens thought it fitting punishment for the closing of theaters, brothels, and gambling houses.)

1660S: PLAGUE AND FIRE

CHARLES II BARELY HAD TIME TO ADJUST his crown when disaster struck. In early 1665, the first cases of a new outbreak of bubonic plague were seen in London. Samuel Pepys, the great diarist, first heard of the contagion in April, writing, "Great fear of the sickness here in the city, it being said that two or three houses are already shut up. God preserve us." The hot summer saw the outbreak burst into an epidemic, with affected houses painted with red crosses and shut up with a guard outside—people trapped inside died either of the plague or starvation. By September, red crosses bloomed everywhere, and the rattle of the death cart was heard in the streets with its mournful accompaniment, "Bring out your dead!"—a wretched parody of the cries of the apple- and mussel-mongers that had been silenced by the calamity. On September 7, 1665, John Evelyn wrote, "I went all along the city and suburbs from Kent Street to St. James's, a dismal passage and dangerous, to see so many coffins exposed in the streets thin of people, the shops shut up and all mournful silence, as not knowing whose turn might be next."

It was not humanity's finest hour. The stricken were incarcerated in their homes or, if they had escaped London, prevented from traveling on roads, as the sight of one suppurating sore could touch off a riot. Fleeing Londoners, whether infected or not, were often pelted with rocks and dung at the outskirts of villages. Con artists and quacks peddled phony cures, and the rich and powerful jumped ship like the rats that were carrying the plague. The horror of the disease was unspeakable, dispatching an estimated 100,000 by the time this epidemic began to abate, around Christmas 1665, when the cold started to kill off the fleas. In February, the king returned to London to survey—in safety, he thought—the melancholy scene of a decimated London still smelling of rotted flesh. But the rough hand of fate hadn't finished with London yet.

On September 2, 1666, a baker's oven in Pudding Lane was left unbanked. Its sparks, teased out of the chimney by a stiff wind, fired like tinder the dry wood of summer-baked houses, igniting the entire city in a matter of hours. Pepys was called at three in the morning by a servant to look at the fire, and, being used to little local fires in the cramped wooden alleys and byways of London, he "thought it to be on the back side of Mark Lane at the furthest. . . . I thought it far enough off, and so went back to bed."

The lord mayor also brushed off the fire, saying, "a woman might piss it out," and no measures were taken to control the conflagration until it was too late. Amazingly, only a handful of people lost their lives, one of them a servant in the house of the baker where the fire had started. John Evelyn described a ghastly picture of the event two days after it started: "The burning still rages, and it was now gotten as far as the Inner Temple; all Fleet Street, the Old Bailey, Ludgate Hill, Warwick Lane, Newgate, Paul's Chain, Watling Street, now flaming, and most of it reduced to ashes; the stones of St. Paul's flew like grenados, the melting lead running down the streets in a stream, and the very pavements glowing with fiery redness, so as no horse nor man was able to tread on them, and the demolition had stopped all the passages, so that no help could be applied."

King Charles finally stepped in and did what the lord mayor should have done sooner: he had his navy blow up the houses in the way of the fire, creating a break in its path. After four grim days, the driving wind died down and the fire finally ended. In its wake lay an unrecognizable London, which had suffered untold losses in its architecture, parish records, art treasures, and books. In all, 436 acres of London had been consumed: 13,200 houses, 87 parish houses and many of their churches, 44 merchants' halls, the Royal Exchange, the magnificent medieval Guildhall, and St. Paul's Cathedral. It was, if nothing else, an opportunity to rebuild the city along straight and reasonable lines, obliterating the medieval maze of tiny streets that had contributed to the tragedy.

But this was not to be. Although both John Evelyn and the young Christopher Wren submitted designs for a new London with wide thoroughfares and sensible squares and circuses, the urgent need for housing and the legal problems of land ownership assured that the rebuilding followed the original "plan" of medieval London rather too faithfully. The only real improvements were lanes widened to a mandatory 14 feet and buildings made of stone. This was Wren's great opportunity, as he rebuilt 51 of the ruined churches, including St. Paul's Cathedral. Despite the loss of many of those edifices during World War II, Wren's name will forever be associated with the glory of his age, as London rose like a phoenix from the ashes of the fire into the magnificence of the 18th century. But before the glory of that age came the bloodless Glorious Revolution, which changed forever the roles of monarch and Parliament.

THE CROWDED THRONE: KING JAMES AND WILLIAM AND MARY

THE THREE-YEAR REIGN OF JAMES II followed the death of his brother Charles II in 1685, and once again the old Catholic–Protestant enmities reared their ugly heads. James II (also styled James VII of Scotland) was raised Catholic, and once he ascended the throne, his sympathies were evidenced in his appointments of Catholics to key positions in the armed forces. His antipathy to Parliament—certainly influenced by his father Charles I's own disdain of that governing body that left James fatherless—was indicated by the camp of soldiers he placed at the outskirts of London. When Parliament protested, James took a page out of his beheaded father's book and decided that he did not require Parliament's approval to rule.

Bad move. James kept his head but lost his throne in a coup that saw not one bullet fly. The Stuarts may be thanked for the rise of Parliament and the reduction of monarchical powers that over the centuries diminished the roles of English regents to little more than extremely overpaid ribbon cutters and fodder for gossip.

James's Protestant daughter Mary had been wife to one William of Orange, a Dutch prince, for years when the call came for her to ascend the throne of England. Her husband had been a head of state in the Protestant Netherlands who had watched with ill ease as James's second marriage produced a Catholic male heir to the throne. The idea of a religious alliance between France and England would have put the squeeze on the Netherlands and its busy trade. William of Orange led an invasion of a smaller army against James's English forces, whose soldiers switched sides with alacrity. James II, like his brother Charles II before him, cut and ran to France, and William of Orange was welcomed warmly into London.

There was dissent between Whigs and Tories regarding which spouse should be regent and which consort, but ultimately the crown was offered to be shared equally between the two, thus giving us England's first royal power couple. Good old John Evelyn was kind enough to weigh in with his opinion on the two: "She seems to be of a good nature, and that she takes nothing to heart; whilst the Prince her husband has a thoughtful countenance, is wonderfully serious and silent, and seems to treat all persons alike gravely, and to be very intent on affairs: Holland, Ireland, and France are calling for his care." The common people never took to William with the same affection as they did to Mary—and the feelings were reciprocated all around—but with Parliament having passed a Bill of Rights limiting the actual powers of the throne, London could now rest easy that its interests were being looked after by politicians at least theoretically devoted to the city and its business.

Despite their moving to the pleasant countryside of Kensington from the palace of Whitehall in the first year of their reign to avoid central London's dread contagions and mephitic stink, Mary II died of smallpox in 1694. William III died in 1702 after being thrown from a horse. Mary's sister Anne succeeded the couple quietly; her relatively dull 12-year reign is remembered primarily for the naming of a lacy wildflower and a style of furniture. The last of the Stuart line and the last monarch to veto an act of Parliament, Anne was on the throne when England and Scotland were unified as Great Britain. *1066 and All That,* a hilarious history of England published in 1930, summed up the queen thus: "Finally the Orange . . . was succeeded by the memorable dead queen, Anne. . . . The Whigs being the first to realize that the Queen had been dead all the time, chose George I as King."

GEORGIAN LONDON

TO MOST LONDON CONNOISSEURS, the 1700s remain the very apex of the city's greatness: in architecture, literature, theater, painting, sculpture, philosophy and sciences, and the building of stately homes and parks, no other epoch can rival 18th-century London for its verve and creativity. The artists, thinkers, and artisans of the day have come to define their disciplines: William Hogarth, Sir Joshua Reynolds, and Thomas Gainsborough (painting); Jonathan Swift, Henry Fielding, and Oliver Goldsmith (literature); David Garrick (theater); Alexander Pope (poetry); Mary Wollstonecraft Shelley (feminism and philosophy); John Nash and Robert Adams (architecture); Capt. James Cook (exploration); Adam Smith and Jeremy Bentham (economics); and composer George Frederic Handel, a naturalized British subject.

Of course, one can hardly mention London and the 18th century in the same breath without a bow to the looming figure of the formidable writer, lexicographer, and London lover Dr. Samuel Johnson, immortalized by his quotable words as much as by his biographer and friend, James Boswell. Countless other less acclaimed but no less important figures—sadly, it is mostly men who make the list—made major breakthroughs in technology, medicine, and science in this robust century.

There was something in the air, it would seem, and not just the stench of the tanneries, slaughterhouses, and privies. In the 100-year span of this period, London grew from 650,000 souls to close to a million. The small villages north and west of the city were embraced by London's expansion. Near the hamlet of Knightsbridge, a country house was bought and grandly rebuilt by the duke of Buckingham, then later purchased by King George III as a private royal residence.

From Germany in 1714 came the Hanoverian succession, from whom the present royal family is descended. Georges I through IV presided over the acquisition of land from Canada to Australia and the ignominious loss of the wealthy American colonies to the war of independence. They saw the rise of a new technology that revolutionized the cotton and wool trades of England. They watched as the Bastille was stormed, igniting the French Revolution, and managed to keep their crowns steady while the aristocracy across the channel were losing their heads. They continued to speak German while ruling an English-speaking kingdom. Because of this undiplomatic oddity, the position of prime minister came to be necessary. The absolute rule of royalty began to be challenged: thanks to the madness of King George III (later identified as porphyria), the dissolute lifestyle and limited intellect of prince regent George IV, and, later, the age and gender of young Queen Victoria, the policymaking powers of the monarch were quietly whittled away by an increasingly powerful Parliament and a succession of prime ministers who rejected the role of royal flunkie.

Despite the philosophical advances of the period, the daily life of London as it expanded was attended by an increase in crime, corruption, drinking, and poverty. Dr. Johnson—whose remark that "when a man is tired of London, he is tired of life" was not without its irony—wrote a poem about London that exposed this dark underbelly:

> Here malice, rapine, accident, conspire,
> And now a rabble rages, now a fire;
> Their ambush here relentless ruffians lay,
> And here the fell attorney prowls for prey;
> Here falling houses thunder on your head,
> And here a female atheist talks you dead. . . .
> Prepare for death if here at night you roam,
> And sign your will before you sup from home. . .

An increasing polarization—owing to the incipient Industrial Revolution—shaped London society into strict camps of owners and workers, rich and poor. The middle and upper classes' brutal insensitivity to the less fortunate was about as pervasive and shocking as the casual violence of Dark Age societies. The entertainments of the bourgeoisie included outings to insane asylums for a laugh—Bethlehem Hospital, aka Bedlam, was a favorite venue—and attendance at public executions, where they were fleeced by locals who charged outrageous prices for a window seat overlooking Newgate Prison's scaffold. There was (as always, but particularly pronounced in those days) one law for the rich and one for the poor; criminals who weren't executed for the slightest offense were forced to endure a grueling and often fatal passage to the new penal colony in Australia, or they were offloaded to the colonies of the Americas. Many of London's powerless, often guilty of nothing more than being in the wrong place at the wrong time (typically, dead drunk in a tavern), were press-ganged into the Navy, as dire a fate as any jail or colony. It was only by the most vigorous repression of dissent that the revolution in France did not spread to London, which was hardly unaccustomed to anarchy in the streets, especially after the Gordon Riots of 1780, in which Newgate was stormed by an anti-Catholic mob and 300 were left dead.

London was not, however, lacking in notable reformers and pro-gressive thinkers (most memorably Jonathan Swift, whose "Modest Proposal" to solve the problem of the Irish poor involved feeding their babies to the rich), whose pamphlets, essays, and the newfangled fad of the novel helped midwife a tradition of savage English satire and social commentary that found many outstanding exponents in the Victorian century.

VICTORIAN LONDON

QUEEN VICTORIA'S REIGN KICKED OFF IN 1837, after the unla-mented last gasp of Georgian rule by the grotesque George IV, whose years as prince regent during his father's illnesses inspired a kind of Sodom-on-the-Thames license among the upper classes, and who rivaled the Sun King in his noble excess and addiction to pleasure. George may have been the patron of John Nash, who developed Regent's Park and filled the city with white-stucco-covered houses, but other than that, he didn't do much for London, although the extrava-gance and vice of his court certainly filled the coffers of moneylenders, gambling dens, and whorehouses.

At his death, a very different kind of social order was born, or at the very least a reactionary new brand of hypocrisy was embraced. Only 18 years old when she became queen, Victoria gave her name to an age of moral rectitude and social mobility, reform and wretched-ness, empire and exploitation.

Another name is so completely identified with 19th-century Lon-don that it has become an adjective describing certain awful aspects of it: Charles Dickens. He is never far from the hearts and minds of the London dweller (his face appears—appropriately, for one who wrote so much about money's awful power—on the £10 note). It is Dickens's London that we tend to think of when we envision the 19th century: poor Bob Cratchit freezing in Scrooge's office; Pip and the convict Magwitch fleeing on the Thames under the cover of pea-soup fog; Oliver Twist asking for more gruel in the orphanage; the endless court case of *Jarndyce v. Jarndyce*.

Dickens was an insomniac who walked the streets of London for hours every night, alertly absorbing the sounds and secrets of the city. His is the resounding voice of 19th-century London, just as Pepys's and John Evelyn's were of the 17th. Through his compassionate reporting and fiction, Dickens awakened middle-class readers and the politicians who represented them to the misery of the poor. He helped steer England toward a more humane course, as reformers worked to abolish the slave trade, put limits on child labor, allow married women property and personal rights, extend suffrage, and open the first state schools.

The Industrial Revolution didn't so much flower as detonate in the 19th century, crushing centuries of social, familial, and economic tra-ditions in its coal-powered mechanical maw. The gulf between rich and poor widened, landscape and atmosphere degraded, and farming villages destabilized, as impoverished people from the country trickled into a city already bursting at the seams with immigrants from the far reaches of the empire.

With this desperate pool of cheap labor at hand, London grew at an amazing rate. New houses were built in every direction, bringing formerly quiet outlying villages into London's urban scene. The first Underground train tunnels were excavated, sewers were built, transatlantic cable was laid, and the first police force was established. Overground train tracks originating in London crisscrossed the country, omnibuses were pulled through the streets by huge workhorses, streets were gaslit, and circuses bloomed among busy thoroughfares all over the city. Museums, monuments, learned societies, and public libraries flourished. The Great Exhibition of 1851, organized by Victoria's husband, Prince Albert, showed the world that London was a city of cosmopolitan suavity and culture, firmly looking to the future.

That Karl Marx wrote *Das Kapital* while living in this two-faced city has a persuasive epic logic. The terrible contrast between the shiny new city, with its shops and theaters, hotels and town houses, and the unmitigated squalor of the East End slums in many ways defined the Victorian Age.

Yet it was a time in which enormous changes took place, a time in which terrible injustices were institutionalized, uncovered, and, in some cases, at last redressed. It was also a time of unforgettable literature and indelible heroes. Any age that could produce Florence Nightingale, Oscar Wilde, and Lewis Carroll can't be all bad, after all.

WORLD WAR I

QUEEN VICTORIA MADE A PERFECT EXIT in January 1901, keeping her era tidily defined by century. Her eldest son, Albert Edward (whom she always called "poor Bertie"), after years of dallying at dining, bridge, and adultery, finally emerged from his mother's long shadow to be crowned King Edward VII. His was a short reign—only a decade, a mere fraction of his mother's 64 years on the throne—but it was distinctive enough to earn the title of the Edwardian Age, England's last era to be named for a monarch. It was a clear cusp between the centuries, a time of accelerated progress during which motorcars became common, corsets came off, women demonstrated for the vote, and a number of Victorian verities began to be challenged.

A well-known sensualist of the time, King Edward helped unleash a more permissive era in which free love, divorce, and bohemian living arrangements could be practiced without complete social ostracism. The famously free-thinking Bloomsbury Group formed around this time, comprising certain artists and writers living in the then–shabby-genteel neighborhood near the British Museum. The Bloomsburyites redefined not only their artistic disciplines but also their relationships. A famous quote of Virginia Woolf's—"In or about December 1910, human character changed"—underscores the leap made in thought and behavior by this new generation, one whose youth was stolen or poisoned by the conflagration then gathering in Europe.

In 1914, London and the British Empire enjoyed the zenith of their world power. The British pound sterling, as safe as gold, was the currency of commerce all over the globe. There was peace and prosperity. Social activists were busy working to secure the vote for women, get children out of the factories and into classrooms, and force legislation making government responsible for its neediest citizens.

But the shadow of German zeppelins loomed above London. Despite the efforts of pacifists like George Bernard Shaw, England plunged into the ghastly battles fought across the channel, battles that very nearly wiped out an entire generation of young Englishmen. By the time World War I ended in 1918, the whole social order had changed again. It was a completely different London, filled with shell-shocked veterans, emancipated women, and tumbrel-talking aristocrats.

THE LONG WEEKEND: 1918–1939

IT COULD BE SAID THAT THE PERIOD BETWEEN the two World Wars was a last glimmer of glamour for London. There is truth in that observation, despite the ugly rumblings of black-shirted British fascists led by Nazi sympathizer Sir Oswald Mosley, despite the economic depression that left millions unemployed, and despite the terrible losses of life, limb, and hope during WWI. It may be that we view this interlude with an acute awareness of how much was soon to be buried under the Blitz, making any frivolity of that time seem more poignant than silly.

People embraced the work of humorist P. G. Wodehouse, who helped his readers shake off the blues of the war and the depression. To this day, the country loves Wodehouse's vision of London between the wars: gin-soaked parties with bright young things, dim Right Honorables, creaking lords and terrifying aunts, the Drones Club, and of course the unflappable Jeeves and his young master, Bertie Wooster. They inhabit a hilarious and strangely innocent fictional world that reveals what made London laugh between cataclysms. Noël Coward, Cecil Beaton, Siegfried Sassoon, Virginia Woolf, Robert Graves, George Orwell, Nancy Mitford, W. H. Auden, and T. S. Eliot captured other shades of feeling and insights of that brief respite between the horrors, which Graves summed up aptly in the title of his book *The Long Weekend*.

London gave Hollywood a run for its money during this time, making movies with such luminaries as Laurence Olivier, Peggy Ashcroft, Charles Laughton, and Alfred Hitchcock. Agatha Christie and Dorothy Sayers fed the increasing demand for murder mysteries. The West End was alive with plays, from melodramas to social realism. But nothing cooked up in the imagination could even come close to the real-life drama of 1936: the abdication of King Edward VIII for the woman he loved, the American divorcée Mrs. Wallis Simpson. Although the event was billed as a grave constitutional crisis, the British monarchy clearly was becoming increasingly irrelevant to its subjects, save as newsreel filler. The citizens were mainly concerned with their own lives as they joined trade unions, built suburban communities, and tried to figure out the map of the Underground. In 1931, this tangled web was brought to heel by a man named Harry Beck and simplified into the sleek Art Deco design we know and love, and the population of eight million began using the tube not only to commute to work but also to escape the befogged, coal-smutted city to ever-more-distant reaches of residential London.

Meanwhile, across the English Channel, Europe was increasingly threatened by Adolf Hitler, who had been dismissed by most intelligent Londoners as a twisted clown but admired by a shameful number of hate-filled fascists and dim-witted minor (and some major) aristocrats. But England's initial inaction, for whatever reasons, soon reaped a whirlwind, as his Luftwaffe rained destruction on London and Europe's fleeing Jews came to town with stories of concentration camps and genocide too horrible to countenance.

THE BLITZ: "THEIR FINEST HOUR"

WORLD WAR I, THE "WAR TO END ALL WARS," couldn't live up to that promise for long: only two decades after the armistice was signed, London was once again anxiously watching the skies over Whitehall. This time the threat came not from lumbering zeppelins but from significantly-more-deadly Messerschmitts, Stukas, and unpiloted "doodlebugs" filled with deadly ordnance. The attacks started in earnest on the sunny day of September 7, 1940, when hundreds of fighter planes and bombers buzzed up the Thames and destroyed docks, gasworks, and power stations. The Luftwaffe went on to bomb London nightly for 76 consecutive nights, dropping more than 27,000 high explosives and thousands more incendiaries. The Blitz was on.

The night of December 29, 1940, was the worst, with the city almost burned to the ground and St. Paul's Cathedral under serious threat. Children were hurriedly sent to the countryside or to America, but the royal family made a point of staying in town, even after nine bombs fell on Buckingham Palace. People sought shelter in the tube stations in staggeringly large numbers, sleeping on the ground or in bunk beds placed on the tracks and platforms. Above ground, civilians coped with bombed-out streets, nightly fires, disrupted railways, power and water failures, the destruction of their homes, and, most terribly, the deaths of their friends, neighbors, and families. Novelist Nancy Mitford described the scene vividly in a letter to a friend:

> I find my nerves are standing up to the thing better now—I don't tremble quite all the time as I did. . . . NOBODY can have the slightest idea of what it is like until they've experienced it. As for the screaming bombs, they simply make your flesh creep but the whole

thing is so fearful that they are actually only a slight added horror.
The great fires everywhere, the awful din which never stops, and
wave after wave after wave of aeroplanes, ambulances tearing up
the street and the horrible unnatural blaze of lights from search-
lights, etc.—all has to be experienced to be understood. Then in the
morning the damage—people ring one another up to tell one how
their houses are completely non-existent. . . . People are beyond
praise, everyone is red eyed and exhausted but you never hear a
word of complaint or down-heartedness. It is most reassuring.

—From *Nancy Mitford*, by Selena Hastings
(Hamish Hamilton, 1985)

The bombardment put to the test the famous English stiff upper lip,
and London's rise to the challenge earned the admiration of the rest of
the country and the world. To this day, veterans of the Blitz are notably
tough-minded about their experience; ask an old woman about living
through the war, and you won't get much more from her than the
simple declaration, "We just got on with it—what else could we do?"
Winston Churchill was more eloquent as the voice of the people during
those dark days, author of such unforgettable war cries as "We shall
defend our island, whatever the cost may be, we shall fight on the
beaches, we shall fight on the landing grounds, we shall fight in the
fields and in the streets, we shall fight in the hills; we shall never surrender," and "Let us therefore brace ourselves to our duties, and so bear
ourselves that, if the British Empire and its Commonwealth last for a
thousand years, men will still say, 'This was their finest hour.' "

And so it was. Despite the thousands killed, the millions wounded
and displaced, the destruction of hundreds of thousands of dwelling
places and buildings, and the near-total destruction of the city and the
East End, London pulled up its socks and carried on. "Mustn't grum-
ble" was the motto of the day, as people were keen to the even-worse
suffering of others around them and on the Continent. When the bomb
sirens wailed, Londoners took refuge in corrugated steel caves called
Anderson shelters (to be replaced later by the heavier Morrison shelters)
buried three feet underground. The homeless were sheltered by hotels—
when the East End was first bombed, a huge crowd marched to the
Savoy and demanded to be admitted, which they were—as well as by the
not-completely-invulnerable tube stations. Brigades of men and women
pulled all-night duties to put out fires in likely targets such as Westminster Abbey and St. Paul's Cathedral, saving some of the precious treasures of London's past. When the war finally ended, it could be well said
of the blitzed Londoners that, again in the words of Churchill, "their
will was resolute and remorseless, and as it proved, unconquerable."

SUNSET OF THE EMPIRE

IN 1948, ENGLAND LOST THE JEWEL of her colonial crown when
India became independent, and over the next decade she continued to

lose colonies around the world, as well as much of the shipping and manufacturing business that had made her rich. The 1950s were spent cleaning up the wreckage of the Blitz and maneuvering around strict food rationing. There was a grayness in the city: the gaps of bombing sites yawned among the old Victorian buildings that were still black with coal grime and sagging under the weight of the years. Many people abandoned the city for the suburbs, whose spread was contained by the public lands of the Green Belt on the outer perimeters of London. The welfare improvements of the Labour government helped people rebuild their lives and gave them a sense of security unknown up to that time. In 1946, Heathrow Airport was opened, followed by Gatwick Airport three years later; the city was quickly rebuilt with modern glass-and-steel towers. People began to buy motorcars, and domestic-labor-saving devices were new, plentiful, and affordable.

The most influential advance of the time was certainly the "telly," on which people watched the coronation of Elizabeth II on June 2, 1953, from the comfort of their armchairs. Prime Minister Harold Macmillan said in 1959, "Most of our people never had it so good."

The Festival of Britain celebrated the centennial of Prince Albert's Great Exhibition, and it was on that site the South Bank Centre came to be. The fog lifted, thanks to antipollution measures, and the future looked as bright as the sky on a clear day. A new age was indeed coming, and it was a doozy. After the war, a quarter of the map of the world was colored pink to denote English colonial possessions; by the mid-1960s, England had lost almost all of her empire.

THE SWINGING '60s AND PUNK '70s

WHATEVER ENGLAND MAY HAVE LOST in world supremacy, London compensated for by becoming ground zero of the 1960s "youthquake." The iconic figures of the Beatles and James Bond joined the thinner ones of Twiggy and Julie Christie in making all things British very hip. England was swinging like a pendulum, and London, as always, was the epicenter of the groove.

Movies such as *A Hard Day's Night, Blow-Up, To Sir with Love,* and *A Man for All Seasons* were worldwide hits. The comedy of Spike Milligan gave way to that of Monty Python. Michael Caine, Vanessa and Lynn Redgrave, Oliver Reed, and Terence Stamp were among the many English stars who could pull off a Hollywood blockbuster as adeptly as a Pinter or Shakespeare play in the West End. Peter Sellers's Inspector Clouseau made him a superstar—a word and concept born in the bright light of the 1960s.

Fashion designers of Carnaby Street and the King's Road started the miniskirt and bell-bottom trends, and fashion photographers such as David Bailey became as famous as their subjects. The Beatles, the Rolling Stones, The Kinks, Cream, Small Faces, Fairport Convention, Pink Floyd, The Yardbirds, Led Zeppelin, The Who . . . London's bands in the 1960s were a veritable *Debrett's Peerage* of rock and roll.

Twenty-something rock stars and their birds got their clothes at Granny Takes a Trip and Biba, drove around in Bentleys, and bought stately old piles in the country from hard-up toffs. *Hair* was performed in the West End, scandalizing audiences with its on-stage nudity. The Rolling Stones put on a free concert in Hyde Park, which was also the scene of political demonstrations and love-ins. Sex, drugs, and rock and roll became a way of life for many of the new generation.

No one did sex, drugs, and rock and roll better than the glam rockers and punks of the 1970s, who went to extremes. Green mohawk hairdos, safety pins piercing cheeks, very high platform shoes, and in-your-face attitudes were commonplace sights along the King's Road, where designer Vivienne Westwood and impresario Malcolm McLaren (who later managed the Sex Pistols) ran a punk-rock clothing shop— still open, with the crazy backward-moving clock outside. If you'd told Westwood that she would one day receive an Order of the British Empire from the queen and have her own exhibition at the V&A, this peroxided punk goddess with the artfully ripped shirts would have told you to sod off, or words to that effect.

Feminism had many local, brilliant exponents, with Angela Carter writing in south London and Aussie expat Germaine Greer writing *The Female Eunuch* in her flat on the King's Road. The literature of the day was pretty dark; Martin Amis's *Dead Babies* was a savage and chilling portrait of young people in 1970s London that opened the door to many imitators. The film *A Clockwork Orange,* adapted by Stanley Kubrick in 1972 from the novel by Anthony Burgess, was a surreal prediction of a London gone viciously mad in the not-too-distant future. Squatters took over entire buildings that had been earmarked for renovation; the 17.5% value-added tax was introduced; and a Women's Year Rally coincided with the election of Margaret Thatcher as leader of the Conservative Party. By the time Sex Pistol Sid Vicious had stabbed his girlfriend to death and then overdosed in New York City, people were exhausted and disillusioned with the so-called Me Decade of the 1970s. It seemed time to get on to more-upbeat pastimes—like that old-time London passion, making money.

THE THATCHER YEARS

WHEN MARGARET THATCHER WAS ELECTED prime minister in 1979, she announced the somewhat astonishing goal of returning to Victorian values. She axed 40,000 civil-service jobs and wrested control of Transport for London from the Greater London Council (GLC), selling it to private investors. The gap between rich and poor widened, as a very Victorian economic and social Darwinism—the survival of the fittest and fattest cats—took shape. After fighting constantly with the Labour-based GLC over social services and privatization, Thatcher abolished the council altogether in 1986, and the building on the Thames that housed it stood empty until the Marriott Hotel moved in.

People in The City (the financial district of London) were suddenly making big money, property prices skyrocketed, and the materialistic yuppie came to define the era in both England and the United States.

London in the 1980s also saw race riots in Brixton, the first cases of AIDS, strikes by tube- and steelworkers, and a ban on smoking on the Underground after a fire at King's Cross killed 31 people. Homelessness rose disturbingly as Thatcher ripped holes in the socialist safety net, and the real-estate boom took its toll on government housing.

But all that money had a salubrious affect on the surface of London, as many of the old white-stucco fronts of private homes and the marble of grand old buildings got a good scrub, erasing years of coal smoke from their faces. Look at any photo of London in the mid–20th century and compare it to contemporary views: even allowing for sepia-toned discolorment, the change is startling. Throwing off the old habits of war blackouts, London became luminous, shining arc lights on its many monuments and museums. Even Harrods started lighting up, outlined in white bulbs that locals called tawdry but secretly admired. Another bright (and tawdry) spot in the 1980s was, of course, the "fairy tale" marriage of Lady Diana Spencer and Prince Charles at St. Paul's Cathedral in 1981, watched by millions on TV and providing a much-needed popularity punch to the boring old House of Windsor. In 1989, Thatcher closed out her decade by resigning (to put it nicely—she was pushed out with extreme prejudice), and John Major took over as prime minister.

COOL BRITANNIA: THE 1990S

THIS DECADE STARTED WITH THE HISTORICAL joining of the French and English sides of the new "chunnel" beneath the English Channel, linking Paris and London with a three-hour train ride whose duration gets shorter every decade (it's currently down to two and a half hours). The xenophobic fear that hordes of foreigners would breach London by rail never quite materialized, although the train surely had a part to play in the huge upsurge of tourism in the 1990s.

In 1992, Queen Elizabeth II suffered her famous *annus horribilis* (you've got to love a monarch who uses Latin the way other people use slang). It was indeed a pretty bad year for her: a fire at Windsor Castle caused extensive damage, and the marital troubles of Charles and Diana and Andrew and Fergie went horrendously public. Worst of all, the queen herself, one of the richest women in the world, learned that she would have to pay taxes for the first time in her life. Not one to leave books unbalanced—this is a woman who lived through the Blitz and food rationing—she decided to pay for the repair of Windsor Castle by opening Buckingham Palace to the public for two months a year. Both residences now rake in so much money that there was enough left over to upgrade the Queen's Gallery, where we can now see even more royal treasures.

The 1990s saw a number of cultural developments, such as the rise of the "Britpack" of young artists whose work made traditionalists wonder if they were losing touch: Damien Hirst's animal carcasses floating in formaldehyde, Chris Ofili's elephant-dung Virgin Mary, and Tracy Emin's unmade bed won prizes and patrons. Brits started being funny again, with *French and Saunders,* Absolutely Fabulous, Eddie Izzard, *The Fast Show,* and *Blackadder* whizzing around the globe on DVD to amuse Anglophones everywhere. By the time the Britpop explosion signaled the start of "Cool Britannia," everyone in the world knew that London was again the place to be. The Spice Girls, Oasis, All Saints, and Robbie Williams put British music back at the top of the charts. London Fashion Week became one of the hottest tickets in Europe, rivaling even Milan and Paris as the event at which to showcase new collections.

In May 1997, Tony Blair of the Labour Party was voted in as prime minister, signaling an end to the Conservative Party's 18-year run and beginning a historic three-term reign. Blair ran on a platform of finding the "third way" between the policies of Tory and Labour, and he succeeded mainly in annoying both parties. In August, the world was stunned by the death of Diana, Princess of Wales, in a Paris car crash inspired a week of completely un-British mourning. It was a spasm of national grief that had Buckingham Palace going head-to-head with Tony Blair, who convinced the queen that she must show her subjects that she cared about the "People's Princess." It was a weird moment in media culture: the queen was scolded daily by the newspapers, which later had no objection to the stiff upper lip with which the queen mourned her mother's and sister's deaths. But Diana had been a media creation, and the queen quickly discovered that the media was in charge of this circus; she was soon seen wading through the flowers piled in front of Buckingham Palace, affecting interest in the notes left by an unprecedentedly emotional populace. People stood in line for days to sign the condolence book at St. James's Palace, while a sea of flowers numbering in the millions was left at the gates of Kensington Palace. It was a London no one had ever seen before and will likely never see again—only a few years later, people who had participated in the orgy of public mourning admitted to being slightly bewildered and red-faced over it all.

A NEW WORLD: AFTER SEPTEMBER 11

THE TERRORIST ATTACKS ON THE PENTAGON in Washington, D.C., and the World Trade Center in New York City threw the world into a state of panic, and the hardest-hit business was the travel trade, from airlines to souvenir shops. London, as significant a symbol of Western capitalism and culture as New York, went into high alert. Having coped with years of terrorism wrought by the Irish Republican Army, the city went quietly into action, permanently closing the street in front of the U.S. Embassy, arresting suspected Al Qaeda members, and stepping up security in Parliament and other high-profile institutions.

The number of visitors to London dropped dramatically in the months following the attack, and the buoyant financial outlook of the 1990s gave way to a nervous slide in the stock market, real estate, and consumer goods. Tourism took an even greater hit when England and Tony Blair became partners with the United States in the coalition forces in Iraq. The dearth of tourists, ironically, corresponded to the completion of new hotels and restaurants responding to the boom trend of the '90s; by the time people began getting on planes again, the exchange rate of dollar to pound was topping out at $1.95, transforming even midrange hotel prices of £150 to a terrifying $292 a night.

The year 2002 was the queen's Golden (50th) Jubilee, which turned out to be a total lovefest for Lizzie. She certainly needed the cheering up, as she had recently lost her sister, Princess Margaret, and her mother, the Queen Mum Elizabeth, who died at age 101.

In April 2005, Prince Charles finally wed his mistress of 30 years, Camilla Parker Bowles, who became the Duchess of Cornwall to mixed reactions. The following month, Tony Blair was reelected prime minister for a historically unprecedented third time for a Labour Party member. Then, on July 7, 2005, in what have come to be called the 7/7 attacks, four British-born Muslim terrorists detonated four bombs on the Underground and on a bus, killing an estimated 55 innocent people but producing the finest example of grace under fire seen since the Blitz. While American soldiers at a nearby military base were ordered to stay out of London for five days, Londoners were back on the tube the next day and continued to display implacable calm in the face of the horror.

As of this writing, the city is still unwieldy and difficult for the average citizen. Public transportation suffers from high fares and low expectations. Tube strikes often bring the city to a standstill (though thankfully not with the regularity of Métro strikes in Paris), automobile traffic is still bad, roadwork causes constant traffic jams, and the streets after midnight are rife with the shouts of drunken louts and the assault of the occasional mugger. Pubs are now allowed to stay open past 11 p.m., a baffling "solution" to the public drunkenness associated with the drink-all-you-can-before-closing syndrome. To the delight of many, smoking has finally been banned in restaurants and other public places. Now if they could do something about the air pollution, public-transport problems, airport delays, street crime, and high prices, we might start breathing more easily.

The bottom line is that London is and always has been a big city with big problems, along with its myriad delights. But no matter what the century, London will *always* remain a fascinating, fast-paced, infuriating, and fun-filled destination of choice.

QUEUES, *the* WEATHER, *and a* STIFF UPPER LIP

A FOREIGN TRIBE

ENGLISH-SPEAKING TRANSATLANTICS enjoy the great advantage of sharing a language with Londoners. That is not to say that you won't encounter communication problems, but at least you'll know the words, if not always the meaning behind them. The great misunderstandings are not in language but in nuance. This is a society based on the oblique and the tacit, with an intrinsic orderliness that springs from the old class system. You'll never understand it in the course of a visit, so just be polite and go along with the program. Nobody's going to change a hair for you.

George Bernard Shaw said that it is impossible for one Englishman to open his mouth without inviting the disdain of another. These days, some people would very much like to believe this is no longer true; whether it is still reality is open to argument. What is referred to as "received BBC pronunciation" has wrought some changes in the various accents of England. Professor Henry Higgins, in Shaw's *Pygmalion,* had the entertaining ability to identify the very street on which a Londoner grew up by his accent. You don't have to be a linguist to ascertain who was raised in South London, East London, or in a boarding school, but these accents are no longer strictly defined by class. (In fact, a recent article claimed that casting agents are having a harder time finding actors who can speak with the upper-class accent; today's posh hide their origins behind what's called Estuary English—a cross between the BBC accent and the working-class pronunciation of the Home Counties.) It is certain, however, that whether you are American, Australian, South African, or Kiwi, you'll be treated with curious amusement and the occasional flicker of contempt.

GET IN LINE: THE ENGLISH ART OF QUEUING

ALL THE RUMORS ARE TRUE: the British line up for pretty much everything—not for them the mad dash and bowling over of obstacles in the race for your objective. It's just common sense: find your place at the back of a line and hold it against certain chaos and injustice. Even soccer hooligans queue for tickets and beer. To jump the queue is the height of bad manners, and to do so is to invite certain tut-tutting, raised eyebrows, muttered comments, or, in the case of soccer games, a punch in the face. In fact, breaking in line is such a breach of etiquette that it is about the only time the British will break another taboo: the one that prohibits raising one's voice—or speaking to a stranger—in public (markets, pubs, and soccer stadiums notwithstanding). Nowadays, the order of the bus queue has been breached, and you no longer see neat single-file lines along the pavement, but please do not give a little old lady the elbow and jump ahead of her. You'll regret it.

In some travel situations—buses included, usually long-distant coaches—you will find a line formed, in which case you should take your place at the back. Don't even think of playing the befuddled foreigner and pushing in at the front.

WEATHER REPORTS

THE BRITISH PASSION for talking about the weather amounts nearly to an obsession. They will even go so far as to discuss it vigorously with complete strangers: as Dr. Johnson observed back in the day, "When two Englishmen meet, their first talk is of the weather." And frankly, it's rich material for discussion—London can easily go through four seasons in one day. The casting of aspersions on the abilities of the forecasters is a tried-and-true ice-breaker that will pave the way for inquiries about the extreme and interesting weather (tornadoes, blizzards, hurricanes, monsoons, sandstorms, and so on) of former colonial continents. As everyone must know by now, the famous London fogs of the past were a result of the coal burned in the city, and a bona fide "pea souper" hasn't been sighted since the early 1960s, after the Clean Air Act of 1956 put a stop to industrial pollution.

unofficial **TIP**
Always stand to the right when riding on escalators. The locals, even if they have no intention of passing you, hate it when tourists stand two abreast and clog up the path.

The idea that it rains constantly in London is also a myth, although there isn't one Londoner who doesn't own at least one umbrella (called a brolly; some 7,000 are lost on London buses and trains a year), nor will you find many visitors who haven't been forced to buy a rain poncho or an umbrella on short notice. The once reliably cool summers have, like so much of the world, fallen prey to ferocious heat spells, made more hellish by the lack of air-conditioning on public transport and in some restaurants and hotels. However, such sweltering is short-lived compared with the blistering heat of southern Europe.

THE GREAT BRITISH RESERVE

THIS IS ALIVE AND WELL, stiffening the upper lip and continuing to define "Englishness." Anthropologist Kate Fox maintains that this detachment is a function of social uneasiness rather than coldness or arrogance. It is also manifest in a reluctance to toot one's own horn: if anything, the English are competitive in their self-deprecation, which is almost always based on humor. You will see it displayed in the advertising, in which wit and wordplay take precedence over volume, sloganeering, and repetition (although this may come to be a relic of the past, as ads with vulgar wording and scantily clad models grow apace on the sides of buses and on billboards). It is apparent in the weather forecasts—"Today will be rather damp, with a possibility of patchy fog and maybe a spot of drizzle in between clear intervals"— and on the tube at rush hour, where instead of mouthing off at an annoying commuter who refuses to move down in the carriage, passengers will mutter excuse-me's, issue exasperated coughs, and initiate great flappings of newspapers.

Such quietude can be almost soothing and welcome to an American accustomed to the chattering hordes of compatriots asking personal questions, bragging about themselves, and offering the usual too much information, but it can take a bit of getting used to at first and might leave the visitor feeling a little out in the cold. The traditional silence on buses and trains has been broken by people shouting into their mobile phones, but the prevailing mood on public transport can still be strangely meditative—Fox calls it denial: denial that there are other people around you, mixed with a strange denial that you are there as well.

However, such reserve is not to be taken for granted, as there are exceptions to this cloak of invisibility in which the British perceive others as being clad, and which also covers them when in public. Road rage is a big problem in traffic-choked London, but luckily gun laws are stringent enough that it results in shouting matches and fisticuffs rather than more-serious consequences. And there is nothing quite as ominous to the uninitiated as the roar of 10,000 grown men at a soccer game singing with one voice, "You're shite and you know you are!" Not for them the cozy familiarity of the seventh-inning stretches and the lilting tones of "Take Me Out to the Ballgame."

A similar contradiction to the stereotype is found during the prime minister's question period in the House of Commons. Barely veiled or even naked insults are hurled by members of Parliament at one another, while howls of derision and guffaws of braying laughter render the institution more like a classroom whose teacher has stepped out than a hallowed hall of government. There is something rather invigorating about this cacophony, and it gives you an idea of the healthy self-regard in which the English hold themselves, despite their protestations of humility. The great paradox is that they yield to no one, even if some of them get weak at the knees before the queen.

TO DO OR NOT TO DO: THAT IS THE CULTURE

AN ARTICLE IN *THE SPECTATOR* MAGAZINE a few years ago gave the worst possible advice to put in a tourist guide to London. The writers came up with, among other "tips," "Introduce yourself and shake hands all around in your train compartment" and "Try out the famous echo in the British Library Reading Room." As funny as we find this concept, we will resist temptation and will give you some do's and don'ts guaranteed to be 100% valid. (Exceptions to all of the following, based on class, manners, eccentricity, and specific circumstances, will apply.)

- **Don't** call older people by their first names unless expressly invited to do so—in fact, it is considered normal not to use any names at all when addressing people.

- **Don't** expect people to introduce you to others. One can spend an entire evening with a group of people who introduce neither themselves nor their friends to you. This is not bad manners; rather, it has something to do with the don't-be-pushy rule that prevails at most gatherings. Introductions can only be undertaken by the correct factotum, and nobody will know who that might be, so they keep quiet (as may the correct factotum, not wanting to look self-important).

- **Don't** try to intervene in soccer arguments—it's a very serious subject, one that no outsider can comprehend properly. Remember at games that the hooligans mean business.

- **Don't** take it personally when people act as if you're invisible, correct your pronunciation, look at you with disdain when you ask for directions to "Lye-cester Square," act slightly exasperated by your inability to read a byzantine map of London, or try to run you down in the street. You'll run across a lot of this—get used to it.

- **Don't** brag about how much sunlight you get at home; this will not endear you to anyone.

- **Don't** tell anyone that their accent is "cute." It is you who has the accent, and it is not considered remotely cute by the British.

- **Don't** gloat about the American Revolution, the bracing but (to Londoners) rather last-minute entrance of Yankee troops into World War II, or the sunset on the British Empire. Again, not cute.

- **Do** watch out for queues and take your place in them.

- **Do** be polite. Courtesy is appreciated much more than friendliness, and it's more likely to be reciprocated.

- **Do** remember that this is a country of rules, rules, rules—and that people aren't just making them up as they go along, though it sometimes seems that way.

- **Do** be patient in restaurants and stores; use your vacation as an opportunity to slow down and practice your good manners.

- **Do** learn to enjoy being called "luv" and "darling" and "sweetheart" by certain strangers.

- **Do** prepare for your visit by reading as much as you can about London, and when here, try to listen more than you speak. This is a very interesting place, and the people are fascinatingly foreign, in speech, attitudes, and humor.

Divided by a Common Language: A British-English Glossary

Thanks to the broadcasting of American television shows and films (in London, people go see films at the cinema, as opposed to viewing movies or flicks at the theater), the British are more hip to our lingo than we are to theirs. Even if you've read the English versions of the Harry Potter books, watched plenty of Britcoms on cable and Britflicks at the cinema, or been a *Masterpiece Theatre* junkie for decades, you may need a bit of a leg up. We've assembled a short glossary of words you may not have caught watching *Pride and Prejudice, Little Britain,* or *King Lear.* With the globalization of culture, it is almost quaint to assume that we English speakers might misunderstand each other, but just in case, here goes. . . .

AMERICAN ENGLISH	BRITISH ENGLISH
AT THE AIRPORT	
cart	trolley
bill	bank note
wallet	billfold/purse
ON THE ROAD	
baby carriage/stroller	pram/buggy
baggage room	left-luggage office
detour	diversion
divided highway	dual carriageway
highway exit	motorway junction
hood (car)	bonnet
minivan	people carrier
sedan car	saloon car
overpass	flyover
one-way ticket	single journey
round-trip ticket	return ticket
truck	lorry
trunk	boot
underpass (pedestrian, under streets)	subway
AT THE HOTEL	
baby crib	cot
closet	cupboard/wardrobe
coffee/tea with or without milk	black or white
cot	extra bed or camp bed
first floor	ground floor
long-distance call	trunk call
outlet/socket	power point
second floor	first floor
vacuum	Hoover

IN A RESTAURANT OR FOOD STORE

buffet	sideboard
check	bill
cookie	biscuit
cracker	savoury biscuit
dessert	pudding
French fries	chips
ground beef	mince
molasses	black treacle
potato chips	crisps
smoked herring	kipper
zucchini	courgette

AT THE THEATER

aisle	gangway
balcony	gallery/upper circle
intermission	interval
mezzanine/loge	dress circle
movie theater	cinema

IN THE MARKETS AND ON THE HIGH STREET

diaper	nappy
eraser	rubber
hardware store	ironmonger
liquor store	off-license
panties	knickers
panty hose	tights
raincoat	macintosh (or mac)/cagoule
restroom	public convenience/loo/w.c./lavatory
sneakers	trainers or plimsolls
shorts (underwear)	pants
sweater	jumper
undershirt	vest
vest	waistcoat

IN SICKNESS AND IN HEALTH

acetaminophen (Tylenol)	paracetamol
adhesive bandages	plasters
emergency room	casualty department
rubbing alcohol	surgical spirit

PART TWO

PLANNING YOUR VISIT

■■ AIRLINE DEALS

THE TWO LARGEST TRANSATLANTIC CARRIERS in and out of London are **British Airways** (☎ 800-AIRWAYS; **www.britishairways.com**) and **Virgin Atlantic Airways** (☎ 800-862-8621; **www.virgin-atlantic.com**); they're certainly the ones to check with first to get a baseline on a fare. They often engage in price wars, which means the other airlines will lower their prices, too, or at least try to match the lowest rate. Other airlines will tempt you with low prices on flights that may have you cooling your heels in Reykjavík or some other far-flung airport hub for hours, so if time is not an issue and money is, go for it.

Obviously, if you are collecting frequent-flyer miles with a particular carrier, that airline is the one to use because you will accumulate a tidy sum of miles with a round-trip to London. Some of the United States–based transatlantic airlines are **American** (☎ 800-433-7300; **www.aa.com**); **Delta** (☎ 800-241-4141; **www.delta.com**); and **United** (☎ 800-241-6522; **www.united.com**). All fly into either Heathrow or Gatwick.

unofficial **TIP**
Flight consolidators are a good way to shop for the best deal, but be sure that the one you use books foreign travel.

Consolidators buy up blocks of unsold seats from airlines and resell them to you. Some consolidators deal primarily with domestic tickets, and while they may be able to get you a ticket to London, it might be the same price as the published fare from an airline, and more restrictions may apply. The Internet has made shopping for fares incredibly easy, but there is a here-today-gone-tomorrow quality to many travel sites, not to mention the gobbling-up of small sites by larger ones, such as Travelocity's merger with the U.K.'s LastMinute.com. Some of the so-called discount Web sites are actually owned by or partnered with various airlines and offer very few discounts, if any, and some are merely agencies to sell tickets.

Before you start searching the Internet, first call a couple of the big airlines to get a baseline on prices. Sometimes it helps to talk to a person; sometimes a particular airline will offer Web-only discounts, which they will be happy to steer you toward.

Check the back of the travel section of your Sunday newspaper for ads of consolidators, and make a few calls to them. You can often save money by taking a nondirect flight and changing planes in a major hub city in Europe or Scandinavia, but this option requires the patience of Job and the resilience of a backpacker, turning a seven- to ten-hour flight into a (possibly overnight) marathon.

unofficial **TIP**
Beware of airfare prices that look too good to be true: they are probably the lowest seasonal fare minus all those extra fees and taxes that can really add up.

Here are a few tried-and-true Web sites (arranged alphabetically):

www.bestfares.com Big database; lots of vacation options (cars, hotel rooms, packages).

www.cheapflights.com Easy-to-use site with discount prices from airlines, agents, and discount specialists in the United Kingdom and the United States.

www.cheaptickets.com Finds cheapest Web fares available; offers an affiliate program with travel rewards.

www.expedia.com Well-established Web site; always check its prices against the airlines' Web sites before booking.

www.goodfare.com International travel discounts, including consolidator fares.

www.opodo.com Worldwide travel company; offers flights, hotels, and car rental. Prices may be in pounds, which will add to the cost when booking with a non-U.K. credit card.

www.priceline.com Site where you "bid" for a price but rarely get it. (Best deals here are for the hotel rooms and some packages.)

www.orbitz.com Good place to browse (thousands of fares); doesn't always have the best prices.

www.travelocity.com Full-service everything; hotels, flights, rental cars, and tourist-attraction ticket packages are decent, with a wide variety of hotels to choose from.

Winter is London's off-season, when airlines and some hotels offer impressive packages. For information about finding and negotiating hotel deals, see page 67 in Part Three, Accommodations.

QUICK CHECK

TRAVEL INSURANCE Your own insurance company may offer travel insurance, so check there first before buying any additional coverage. You can purchase insurance for canceled travel, lost luggage, and medical emergencies through **Travel Guard International** (☎ 800-826-1300; **www.travelguard.com**) or **Travel International, Inc.** (☎ 800-243-3174; **www.travelinsured.com**).

While we're on the subject of emergencies, here's a Web site for worriers: **travel.state.gov**, a U.S. State Department site that will apprise you of any health, political, or terrorist risks current in a given part of the world; it also provides special reports on safety and security. Being operated by the government, this site tends to err on the side of extreme caution, but an ounce of prevention is worth a pound of cure.

LUGGAGE Every airline has different rules—all veering toward the draconian these days, even in business and first class—so call ahead to find out the number of bags that can be checked, maximum baggage weight, and size and weight of carry-ons. (Virgin Atlantic, for instance, is very strict about carry-on luggage and will make you check even a backpack if it is too heavy.) Weight allowances go up with the class you are flying—if you're in the economy section, you may have to pay extra for overweight. On some airlines, they won't even let you pay; you just flat can't fly with the extra weight.

The carry-on rules are also tightening: one bag only is the standard, and it must be of a reasonable size and weight. The Web site of the airline you choose will have a link to its latest luggage policy.

With the more stringent security enforced for carry-on luggage, you must stow the following items in your checked luggage: scissors, nail files and clippers, penknives, razors or razor blades, or any other sharp object that could conceivably be used as a weapon. Bottles of liquid (other than duty-free perfume) are no longer allowed on board; plus, laptops and other electronic equipment may cause delays if you don't take them out of your carry-on and put them in the plastic box provided, as you will usually be asked to do. You can speed things up by removing your keys, change, any heavy metal belt, shoes, electronics, and cosmetics before you hit the x-ray machine. It's getting crazy, especially as you will find that there is no global template to these security precautions, so when in Rome . . .

unofficial **TIP**
If you lose your medicine, it helps if you know its generic name so you can get a new prescription.

VALUABLES Cameras, jewelry, money, and anything particularly fragile or precious, including medication, should go on the plane with you. If your bags have been lost and they sit in the baggage hall for any length of time, some malefactor may seize the opportunity to steal whatever looks attractive in your bag—and unless you have reams of receipts and ticket stubs, you won't get a thing back from the airline.

MEDICATIONS You may want to bring an extra supply of any medicine you are taking, as well as a spare pair of eyeglasses. Prescriptions from a foreign doctor will usually be honored in England, so ask your doctor for a backup before you go. Wear a MedicAlert tag if you have a serious health condition.

PERSONAL ELECTRONICS Your laptop has a built-in electrical transformer, and all you'll need to do is buy a plug adapter at any electronics shop at home or at the airport. In London you can pick one up at newsstands, grocery shops, department stores, or any electronics retailer. The common U.K. electrical plug is the large three-prong type, which is different from the two-round-prong type used in the rest of Europe. **RadioShack** and **Brookstone** carry adapter packages that cover pretty much any type of plug.

To use hair dryers, electric toothbrushes, and other personal electronics, you will need to run them through an electrical transformer, which will enable you to use 110-volt U.S. appliances in the British 220-volt system without blowing them up or burning them out. These transformers are now small enough to travel with. Check the small print on your appliances to see if the voltage will work here: if it says "Input AC 100–240V," you're OK. If the number on the label doesn't go higher than AC 110V, you'll need to buy a transformer or leave the appliance at home.

unofficial **TIP**
Many hotels rent cell phones, and you can pick up a pay-as-you-go U.K. phone for about £90 plus the cost of minutes. Seasoned travelers will have a tri-band cell phone that will work around the world; to avoid appalling roaming charges, you can buy a pay-as-you-go SIM (subscriber-identity module, or "smart card")— that is, if your phone uses the Global System for Mobile Communications (GSM) option.

CAR RENTAL It's not a bad idea to reserve a rental car before you go to London; you can often get a better price from your country of origin. Check with your hotel to see if there is a rental place nearby, so you don't have to cross the entire city to pick up and drop off the car. You must be over 25 years of age, have a driver's license (no need for an international license) that's valid for two years, and a credit card.

BRITRAIL If you plan to travel around rural England by train, you can purchase a BritRail Pass before you leave and save a bundle. Call **Rail Europe** at ☎ 888-382-RAIL in the United States or ☎ 800-361-RAIL in Canada, or visit **www.raileurope.com.** You can also order Travelcards for London public transport at the Rail Europe Web site, but there's no financial incentive, only convenience, as you can easily get Travelcards or stored-value Oyster cards (see pages 152 and 153) when you get to London at any tube station or London Tourist Office.

MONEY ATMs with Cirrus, MAC, and credit-card-account systems can be found all over London. You'll avoid many extra bank fees (and maybe get the value-added tax (VAT) knocked off at some little shops) by paying cash: credit-card companies charge foreign-currency conversion fees, which can really add up. Also, remember that you can't get a cash advance from an ATM without your card's PIN number—not something we all necessarily have memorized or even know about—so

unofficial **TIP**
Note: Traveler's checks in non-British currency are useless in England.

get it from your credit-card company before you leave home. They'll probably insist on mailing the number to you, so leave yourself enough advance time. If you don't have a credit or ATM card, go to the bank and buy good old-fashioned traveler's checks in British pound sterling notes only.

The WEATHER

LONDON MEASURES ITS MILD WEATHER in degrees Celsius, or centigrade, rather than Fahrenheit; zero Celsius is freezing, and anything over 30 Celsius is tropical. Get the weather report online at **uk.weather.com; weather.cnn.com;** or the Web sites of such London newspapers as the *Times* (**www.timesonline.co.uk**), the *Guardian* (**www.guardian.co.uk**), and the *Telegraph* (**www.telegraph.co.uk**).

To convert temperatures (approximately) from Celsius to Fahrenheit, double the Celsius value and add 30. Here are some more-exact numbers:

–3°C	=	26.7°F	15°C	=	59°F
–1°C	=	30.2°F	20°C	=	68°F
0°C	=	32°F (freezing)	25°C	=	77°F
1°C	=	33.8°F	30°C	=	86°F
5°C	=	41°F	37°C	=	98.6°F (normal
10°C	=	50°F			body temperature)

WHAT *to* BRING

PACKING FOR YOUR TRIP TO LONDON depends on the weather, which we've mapped out seasonally, but there are a few things that you might appreciate having handy at all times of the year:

• This book.
• A small map of central London and a pocket-sized street atlas that has exhaustive maps of every neighborhood in London, a tool even the natives can't do without; *London A–Z* and *Nicholson's London Street Atlas* are equally good.
• One hundred pounds, which you can buy from your bank at home, to pay for transportation from the airport in case the ATM at the airport is on the fritz (alternatively, you can ask the taxi driver to stop at a money machine). If you are taking the tube or the bus, you will only need about £10 per person.
• A good backpack or shoulder bag.
• A small collapsible umbrella.

MONTH	TEMPERATURE (°F/°C)	RAINFALL (INCHES)
January	40°/4°	2.1"
February	40°/4°	1.6"
March	44°/7°	1.5"
April	49°/9°	1.5"
May	55°/13°	1.8"
June	61°/16°	1.8"
July	64°/18°	2.2"
August	64°/18°	2.3"
September	59°/15°	1.9"
October	52°/11°	2.2"
November	46°/8°	2.5"
December	42°/6°	1.9"

AVERAGE DAYTIME TEMPERATURES AND RAINFALL IN LONDON

- A rain poncho.
- A currency converter.
- A portable electrical transformer, if you can find one small enough and you want to bring your own hair dryer, electric toothbrush, or the like (check amps to make sure this transformer can handle your appliances—hair dryers are notorious for blowing out the smaller, more portable transformers); the electrical input from the wall outlet is 220 volts, which must be transformed and stepped down to 110 volts for American electronics or else those appliances will burn out. (See pages 45 and 52 for more information.)
- A camera and extra film—like everything else, film is expensive here.
- An extra memory card for a digital camera, and either extra batteries or a recharger with an electrical transformer that can be plugged into 220 volts.
- Sugar substitute (if you have a favorite brand).
- Books on London that relate to your interests.
- Comfortable walking shoes.

CLOTHING

LONDON IS A CITY OF MANY economic classes and sartorial styles. There are lots of rich young things for whom dressing for dinner means a pair of £250 jeans, some fab shoes, and an outrageously expensive jacket, while women of the WWII generation wear skirts and sensible shoes on the street and into restaurants, still taking their fashion cues from their contemporary, the queen. If you happen to come across a

unofficial **TIP**
Theaters no longer require dressing up, thank goodness. We advise dressing in layers, as it can get pretty warm in the middle of a sold-out play.

wedding, you'll see how seriously Londoners take their formal clothing—morning suits and eye-catching hats are de rigueur at most British nuptials, even at civil ceremonies. Harrods, which has a ridiculously high opinion of itself, actually has a dress code, as does the Ritz: no jeans or sneakers at the hotel's restaurant and bar; at Harrods, it's completely and mysteriously at the store's discretion. Generally speaking, urban Westerners all dress pretty much the same way (and in the very same designers), and except for very fancy and/or uptight places, there is no need to change the way you dress in London.

Bring one or two good comfortable outfits for stepping out to restaurants; smart casual is always safe. There's not a lot of snobbery about clothing here. As a nation of grand old eccentrics, Britons are mostly unflappable when it comes to other people's personal styles. If you do end up at a restaurant with a tie-and-jacket code, the maître d' will likely be happy to lend you one.

WHEN *to* GO

THE BEST TIME TO GO TO LONDON is whenever it's possible for you. If you want more than anything to see this remarkable city but can't afford the high-season airfare, then by all means go in the winter, when fares drop by as much as 75%—if you book sufficiently in advance and look around for the good deals. Other considerations might include the special events you're eager to see—perhaps Wimbledon or the Chelsea Flower Show—or the attractions in which you're most interested. Some of your choices (stately homes, for example) are usually closed between October 31 and April 1. Although the winter is dark and dreary, it's free of the swarms of tourists that you find in the summer. Let's take it season by season.

SUMMER Though unpredictable, summer in London is often quite gorgeous. Writer Henry James was probably thinking of England, his adopted home, when he declared the two most beautiful words in the English language to be "summer afternoon." One thing that these summer afternoons can't promise, though, is consistent heat—three consecutive days of 75°F and sun is considered a heat wave. However, the global-warming trend is upsetting London's traditionally brisk summer, and the past few years have seen record-breaking high temperatures that upset both residents and visitors, as air-conditioning is relatively rare in shops, restaurants, and many hotels. Even worse, it's nonexistent in buses and trains, where the heat can get dangerously high—you'd be arrested for transporting animals in conditions similar to those on the tube during an August heat wave.

Do check to make sure that your hotel has air-conditioning if you're coming in July or August; more and more hotels are taking the recent heat waves seriously and have added climate controls to their rooms. Nighttime temperatures, even on a hot day, do drop, and often a fan will suffice to cool a hotel room.

On the plus side, summer in London means that the parks are at their most riotously floral and that all the stately homes and palaces are open. Buskers (street performers) are everywhere on the streets; there are carnivals, street fairs, and more outdoor dining than makes sense in a country with such variable weather. Private garden squares are open to the public on one Sunday in June; check **www.timeout.com/london** for details.

FALL Many Londoners prefer the autumn to the summer in London for many reasons, one of which is that the crowds simmer down. Autumnal London has a soulful atmosphere, with the leaves turning brown and winds twisting them off the branches and twirling them along the streets. Because of London's mild climate, many flowers in the parks last all the way into November; to see their radiance blending with the hues of the changing leaves is wonderful. The sunny days are mood lifting and the brisk air invigorating. The main thing to remember is that most of the stately homes and palaces close October 30, so come before then if these sights are at the top of your list. (Buckingham Palace closes at the end of September or in the first week of October.) November can get as cold as 40°F, but not usually much below that. Bring gloves and a hat for the windy days. The days get shorter and shorter, too.

> *unofficial* **TIP**
> Plan to dress in layers during the summer in London, as the weather can change dramatically in one day. Bring socks, at least one sweater, trousers ("pants" here are underpants, also known as knickers), a light jacket, and a rain poncho. The most crucial piece of clothing is a pair of comfy walking shoes.

WINTER There is a beautiful old English folk song heard at Christmas called "In the Bleak Midwinter" ("ground as hard as iron, water like a stone"), which plays in many Londoners' minds as they wake up to a flat darkness that returns around 4:30 p.m. The ancient trees in the parks have shed their leaves, standing like skeletons against a leaden sky. The bleakness has its own poetic appeal, as it rarely includes freezing temperatures and the museums are warm and inviting in the winter. Airline deals can be fantastic, hotels are cheaper, crowds are lighter (save for busloads of uniformed schoolchildren flooding the museums), and your choice of plays at the half-price-ticket booths expands considerably. All in all, it's an economical time to make a cultural holiday.

No one does Christmas quite like the English. They aren't constrained by the observation of Thanksgiving a month earlier, so they start their decorating and selling in October. (Last year, Harrods and

Selfridges opened their Christmas shops in August!) November is when the Oxford Street and Regent Street Christmas lighting ceremonies take place, and Santa, better known as Father Christmas, arrives with great fanfare at Harrods. There are scores of wonderful candlelit Christmas concerts at churches and cathedrals—check *Time Out London* or *What's On* for where and when. What you won't find much of is snow, which may be a relief for some of you. But there is plenty of rain, and it's the cold, biting kind. The best news is that after the winter solstice on December 21, the days begin to get longer.

SPRING This season starts early in London. Carpets of crocus cover Hyde Park as early as February, with daffodils not far behind. It's a fine time to visit; the stately homes reopen at the end of March or beginning of April, and the parks and gardens come into bloom. Early May is a time when Londoners fall in love all over again with their city, despite the pummeling from the pollen and the flying fluff from the flowering trees (the allergy prone should pack plenty of meds). Lovely as it is, though, May can also be downright nippy.

London revels in its outdoor life, with events such as the London Marathon, boat races on the Thames, and the Chelsea Flower Show. The weather can be fantastic, with not as much rain as in winter, but no matter how cloudless the morning, only an optimist ventures into parks for long walks without an umbrella.

GATHERING INFORMATION

FOR ASSISTANCE IN PLANNING your vacation; contact the **British Tourist Authority** (☎ 800-462-2748; in London: ☎ 0208-846-9000; **www.visitbritain.com**). Available resources include brochures, maps, and a free London Planner booklet. Make a point of calling, writing, or going in for these goodies at the following U.S. and international locations:

CHICAGO No phone calls; write or walk in at 625 North Michigan Avenue, Suite 1510, Chicago, IL 60611.

NEW YORK 555 Fifth Avenue, Seventh Floor, New York, NY 10176; ☎ 800-462-2748 or 212-986-2200. A bookstore next door to the office offers many London-related items of interest.

AUSTRALIA University Centre, Eighth Floor, 210 Clarence Street, Sydney NSW 2000; ☎ 011-61-02-267-4555; fax 011-61-02-267-4442.

CANADA 111 Avenue Road, Suite 450, Toronto, Ontario M5R 3J8; ☎ 800-847-4885.

NEW ZEALAND Dilworth Building, Suite 305, Queen and Customs streets, Auckland 1; ☎ 011-64-09-303-1446; fax 011-64-09-377-6965.

WEB SITES

There are so many Web sites about London, it's hard to keep up with them all. They are always being improved (or removed), but the following sites should provide enough links to keep you glued to your computer for weeks:

www.visitlondon.com This is the Web site of London's official visitors bureau, with up-to-the-minute information on events, hotels, restaurants, sightseeing, exhibits, and more.

www.royal.gov.uk Official Web site of the British monarchy, with information on royal palaces, castles, and museums.

www.allinlondon.co.uk Comprehensive site that lives up to its name.

www.riverthames.co.uk Good source for all things riverine: the pubs, the events, the walks, the history.

www.photograph-london.com Thousands of professional images of London's sights, events, and people. You can even buy them.

www.timeout.com/london The online presence of *Time Out London* magazine, this is city's best source for event listings.

www.londonnet.co.uk Magazine-style guide to events, plus articles and info on hotels, restaurants, and entertainment.

www.guardian.co.uk The *Guardian* and *Observer* newspapers online.

www.thisislondon.co.uk Event listings and local news from the *Evening Standard.*

SPECIAL CONSIDERATIONS

PASSPORT, VISAS, AND CUSTOMS

IF YOU'RE AMERICAN, CANADIAN, OR from New Zealand, all you need to enter England is a valid passport. Make sure your passport is up to date; you may not be allowed in if you have less than two months' validity remaining on it. Americans can find passport information, including forms to download, at the **U.S. Department of State Bureau of Consular Affairs** Web site, **travel.state.gov.** Alternatively, you can call the **National Passport Information Center** at ☎ 877-487-2778.

You don't need a visa for a vacation of up to 90 days. Make two copies of the information page of your passport, and give one to someone at home to keep. Put the other in your luggage to expedite replacement in case your passport gets lost or stolen.

WHAT YOU MAY AND MAY NOT BRING INTO THE UNITED KINGDOM

YOU CAN BRING IN, DUTY FREE:

- 200 cigarettes, 100 cigarillos, 50 cigars, or 250 grams of tobacco
- 2 liters of table wine and 1 liter of alcohol over 22% by volume (most spirits) and either 2 liters of alcohol under 22% by volume (fortified or sparkling wine or liqueurs) or 2 more liters of table wine

- 60 milliliters of perfume or 250 milliliters of eau de toilette
- Other goods up to a value of £145 (about $290)

You may not bring in controlled drugs (any medication you take should be in its original bottle with your name on it), firearms and/or ammunition, plants and vegetables, fresh meats, or any kind of animal. British Customs is currently somewhat relaxed about cigarettes—two or three cartons won't set off any alarms.

ELECTRICITY

THE ELECTRICITY SUPPLY IN THE UNITED KINGDOM is 220 volts AC, which, as mentioned earlier, will blow out any American 110-volt appliance you bring, specifically hair dryers, electric toothbrush chargers, and electric razors. Electric lamps are the only items that don't require a transformer. Check that your laptop computer has a built-in transformer; it's a standard feature, as it tends to be with digital camera and iPod chargers—look at the small print on the actual plug: if it says "Input AC 100–220V," it's good to go once you fit a plug adapter to suit the large three-prong wall sockets in England. These plug adapters are easily found at travel and airport shops at home and at ironmongers (hardware stores), chemists (drugstores), supermarkets, news agents (newsstands), and corner shops in the United Kingdom. Don't plug in anything until you've checked the voltage on the transformer!

unofficial **TIP**
Some electrical transformers require your participation: they *must* be be set to "input AC 220 volt, output AC 110 volt." You'll know by the pop, flash, and smoke if you got it wrong.

POUNDS, PENCE, AND TRAVELER'S CHECKS

THE BRITISH ARE GOING SLOWLY into this European Union business, taking a wait-and-see attitude toward the euro. At this writing, they still use pounds (£), one of which converts to $2.10. This can make visiting London extremely painful to the pocketbook—in fact, let's just say that no matter what currency you bring to this stunningly expensive city, it will shrink with a shock once it's converted to pounds and you start spending it. Check any major newspaper's business section for current exchange rates, or go to **www.xe.com.** The pound is divided into 100 pence, abbreviated *p* (a single unit is called a penny). Gone are the days of the shilling, the tuppence, and the farthing; what we lose in quaintness we make up for in manageability.

There are no longer any £1 notes, but there are red 50s, purple 20s, brown 10s, and green 5s. Coins are divided into £2, £1, 50p, 20p, 10p, 5p, 2p, and 1p. Coins cannot be changed into foreign cash, so spend them while you're in London. Better still, donate them on your way home to the brilliant UNICEF Change Collection scheme that most airlines sponsor. (See Part Four, Arriving and Getting Oriented, for details on ATMs, changing money, and using credit cards.)

VALUE-ADDED TAX (VAT)

THIS IS ONE OF THE GREAT FRUSTRATIONS of shopping in London: a 17.5% tax slapped on everything from hotel rooms to lipstick; the only exceptions are food, children's clothes, and books, yet these are still very expensive. There are ways to get the VAT refunded, and we'll tell you about them in Part Ten, Shopping. Almost everything for sale has the tax added into the sticker price, except for merchandise sold in some small shops, as well as various services.

unofficial **TIP**
Go to your bank before you leave home and buy about £100 worth of British pound sterling notes so you will have plenty of cash on hand to pay for transportation from the airport and maybe even that first meal.

EMBASSIES AND HIGH COMMISSIONS

United States

The **U.S. Embassy** is housed in Mayfair at 24 Grosvenor Square, London W1A 2LQ; ☎ 0207-499-9000; **www.usembassy.org.uk** (tube: Bond Street). Go here if you've lost your passport or have some other emergency. Hours are 8:30 a.m. to 5:30 p.m. Passports are handled Monday through Friday, 8:30 to 11 a.m., and Monday, Wednesday, and Friday, 2 to 4 p.m. The Passport Office is on 55 Upper Brook Street, around the corner from the main entrance (tube: Marble Arch or Bond Street).

Canada

The **High Commission** is at MacDonald House, 38 Grosvenor Street, W1K 4AA; ☎ 0207-258-6600; **www.canada.org.uk** (tube: Bond Street). It is open Monday through Friday, 8 to 11 a.m.

Australia

The **High Commission** is at Australia House, Strand, WC2B 4LA; ☎ 0207-379-4334; **www.australia.org.uk** (tube: Charing Cross) and is open Monday through Friday, 10 a.m. to 4 p.m.

New Zealand

The **High Commission** is at New Zealand House, 80 Haymarket at Pall Mall, SW1Y 4TQ; ☎ 0207-930-8422; **www.nzembassy.com** (tube: Charing Cross). It's open Monday through Friday, 9 a.m. to 5 p.m.

Ireland

The **Irish Embassy** is at 17 Grosvenor Place, SW1X 7HR; ☎ 0207-235-2171; **www.ireland.embassyhomepage.com** (tube: Hyde Park Corner). Hours are Monday through Friday, 10 a.m. to 4 p.m. Visa and passport services are located in Montpelier House, 106 Brompton Road, SW3 1JJ; ☎ 0207-225-7700.

TRAVELING WITH CHILDREN

REMEMBER THAT CHILDREN GET JET LAG, too, so plan your first day so you all can recover from it. Our rating system for attractions attempts to gauge suitability for children and adults of various ages, but bear in mind that all children have different interests and differing levels of tolerance for museums and attractions. See Part Seven, Children's London, for more information.

DISABLED ACCESS IN LONDON

LONDON MAY BE MORE WHEELCHAIR- and disabled-access-ready than many cities in Europe, but with the strict rules governing historic buildings, accessibility features can be impossible to implement in many of its attractions. In America you can count on wheelchair access and disabled restrooms in public buildings; in London you need to call ahead or use any of the following excellent references:

ARTSLINE is the best resource available. The organization's Web site has links and information on just about anything you would want to know about living with a disability, specifically as it pertains to visiting London's cultural attractions. With the power of the Internet, they have expanded their information impressively. They are at 54 Chalton Street, NW1 1HS; ☎ 0207-388-2227; **www.artsline.org.uk.**

ACCESS IN LONDON is published with the assistance of Artsline and the Pauline Hephaistos Survey Projects (PHSP). It's researched by disabled people and is updated regularly. Look for it at various bookstores in London, or contact Access Project, 39 Bradley Gardens, W13 8HE; ☎ 0208-858-2375; **www.accessinlondon.org.** Online bookstores also carry it.

ACCESS TO THE UNDERGROUND, a brochure published by Transport for London, is available at Underground stations or by writing the Transport for London Unit for Disabled Visitors, 172 Buckingham Palace Road, SW1 9TN.

INFORMATION FOR WHEELCHAIR USERS VISITING LONDON is a pamphlet that you can find at any tourist office in London.

CAN BE DONE is a tour operator that specializes in London holidays and tours for people with disabilities; call ☎ 0208-907-2400 or visit **www.canbedone.co.uk.**

EASING JET LAG

JET LAG IS A VERY REAL PROBLEM, as any long-distance traveler can tell you. The number of time zones you pass through is directly proportional to how much jet lag you'll suffer, meaning that visitors from Los Angeles, for example, will feel more out of sorts than New Yorkers. The common wisdom is that you will have roughly one day of symptoms for each hour of time difference. Though some people don't experience jet lag at all, most of us do to varying degrees. The symptoms include fatigue, muscle aches and headaches, changes in appetite, sleep disturbances, irritability, forgetfulness, confusion, and dizziness. The best remedy is to try to reset your internal clock as soon as possible. On the plane, drink lots and lots of water, but no alcohol, and eat sparingly. Sleeping on the plane is not always an option, but do try.

When you arrive, change your watch immediately and try to forget what time it is "for you." You might use your first day to take an open-top-bus tour, not just for the great introductory overview of the city but also for the generous helping of sunlight you (might) get. Exercise also helps; a walk in the park stretches muscles that are achy from hours of immobilization on a plane.

unofficial **TIP**
The best way to reset your clock is to get as much sunlight as possible when you arrive—not always easy in London.

For those who can afford it, massage can be of great benefit in treating jet-lag symptoms. It is not only a natural remedy but also very pleasant. **Body Tissue Service** (☎ 0207-000-1900; **www.bodytissue .com**) offers a reputable and convenient in-room massage-therapy service (plus beauty treatments, should you be so inclined), available from 8 a.m. to midnight seven days a week.

HEALTH

YOU MAY WANT TO TAKE OUT MEDICAL INSURANCE before you leave—you won't be covered by Britain's National Health Service unless you're a citizen of a nation in the European Union. You may be eligible for free emergency care, but anything else, including follow-up or specialist services, will come out of your pocket. Check your existing policies to see if they cover medical services abroad. If they don't, **Health Insurance Finders** (☎ 800-259-0307; **www.healthinsurancefinders.com**) offers temporary coverage at a good price.

PHARMACIES Oddly, just one chemist (drugstore) in London is open 24-7: **Zafash Pharmacy** in Earls Court (233–235 Old Brompton Road, SW5; ☎ 0207-373-2798; tube: Earls Court). More centrally located, **Bliss Chemist** (5 Marble Arch, W1; ☎ 0207-723-6116; tube: Marble Arch) is open from 9 a.m. until midnight every day. In South Kensington, **Dajani Chemist** (92 Old Brompton Road, SW7; ☎ 0207-589-8263; tube: South Kensington) keeps its doors open from 9 a.m. until 10 p.m. every weeknight, closing at 9 p.m. on Saturday and 8 p.m. on Sunday. Some **Boots** stores stay open until 8 or 9 at night depending on the area.

unofficial **TIP**
The only real threat to your health here—London has good water and food—is from the street traffic. Keep a beady eye out for bikers and motorcyclists—they drive like maniacs here, and they seem to come out of nowhere.

DENTISTS To get help with tooth problems, call the **Dental Emergency Care Service** 24 hours a day at ☎ 0207-937-3951. They will give you the name of the nearest dental clinic.

DOCTORS The better hotels will have their own doctors on call. If your hotel doesn't, get in touch with **Doctors Direct** (☎ 0207-751-9701; **www.doctorsdirect.co.uk**). **Medical Express,** a private clinic

(117a Harley Street, W1; ☎ 0207-486-0516; tube: Baker Street), is open 9 a.m. to 6 p.m. Monday through Friday.

In England the emergency room is called the *casualty department*. Call ☎ 999 or 112 for an ambulance. You'll be taken to the nearest hospital, or, if your symptoms aren't life threatening, you'll be advised where to go for further help. The biggest difference in medical care between England and the States is that if you get in an accident here, emergency services are provided free. As one journalist noted in the aftermath of the 7/7 bombing, the victims were treated equally and professionally and did not have insult added to injury by being presented with huge bills at the end of their hospital stays. However great the National Health Service is, though, let's hope you stay healthy enough on holiday never to require its care.

SELF-HELP

If you're looking for 12-step meetings, you'll find plenty of them in London. Call for times and places.

Alcoholics Anonymous ☎ 0207-833-0022; www.alcoholics-anonymous.org.uk

Narcotics Anonymous ☎ 0207-730-0009; www.ukna.org

Overeaters Anonymous ☎ 0142-698-4674; www.oagb.org.uk

A **CALENDAR** *of* **FESTIVALS** *and* **EVENTS**

LONDON PLAYS HOST TO A HUGE NUMBER of traditional and modern events each month, so many that we had to try to narrow them down to the most interesting and important. When you arrive in London, pick up a *Time Out* magazine for the full selection, dates, and times, or if you're the kind of person who likes to plan ahead, go to **www.time out.com/london**, **www.visitbritain.com**, or the London Tourist Board's Web site at **www.visitlondon.com**. For a list of exhibitions, festivals and events on the South Bank, visit **www.southbanklondon.com**.

January

NEW YEAR'S DAY LONDON PARADE January 1. A big, brash spectacle with giant balloons, marching bands, clowns, vintage cars, and more, much in the style of the big Fifth Avenue parades in New York City. Starting at Parliament Square at noon, the parade follows Whitehall, Trafalgar Square, Lower Regent, and Piccadilly, ending up at Green Park at 3 p.m. Lots of spillover fun can be had in Hyde Park later that day. ☎ 0208-566-8586; **www.london parade.co.uk**. (Tube: for start of parade, Westminster; for middle, Charing Cross; for end, Green Park.)

CHARLES I COMMEMORATION Last Sunday of January. The English Civil War Society, dressed in authentic 17th-century uniforms complete with arms, follows the route King Charles I took on January 30, 1649, before he lost his head. The corps marches from St. James's Park at 11:30 a.m., down the mall, through the Horse Guards, to lay a wreath at the site of his execution in front of the Banqueting House. (Tube: St. James's Park.)

February

kids **CHINESE NEW YEAR CELEBRATIONS** The date of this holiday changes annually but is always in either late January or early February. The celebration usually takes place on the first Sunday after the first day of the Chinese New Year. London's Chinatown, in Soho, around Garrard Street, comes alive with bright decorations, red streamers, and the Lion Dance. Great food is everywhere. Visit **www.chinatownchinese.com** and click on "London Chinatown." (Tube: Piccadilly Circus.)

GREAT SPITALFIELDS PANCAKE RACE Shrove Tuesday (changes yearly; check calendar—it can also fall in early March). Starts at noon, usually at Dray Walk, Old Truman Brewery, Tower Hamlets, E1, near Brick Lane (starting place is subject to yearly change, so call the number that follows or check at **www.visitlondon.com** or **www.timeout.com/london**). Here's some fun: teams of people running around the East End flipping pancakes as they go, in the name of charity. If you want to join in, call ☎ 0207-375-0441 a few days ahead. (Tube: Liverpool Street or Aldgate East; depends on starting place.)

March

kids **ST. PATRICK'S DAY CELEBRATIONS** Weekend nearest March 17. With two-day celebrations in Trafalgar Square, Covent Garden, and South Bank, this holiday has grown considerably in London over the past five years. Music, Irish-produce stalls, entertainment, and a walloping big parade. See **www.timeout.com/london** or **www.bbc.co.uk** for details. (Tubes: Piccadilly Circus, Covent Garden, and Charing Cross.)

HEAD OF THE RIVER BOAT RACE End of March (usually the Saturday before the Oxford and Cambridge Boat Race). Starting at Mortlake and ending at Putney, this is a smaller affair than the mighty Oxford–Cambridge race but no less interesting to observe from the banks of the Thames. The Surrey Bank above Chiswick Bridge is a good viewing station, or you can park yourself in any of the riverside pubs along the way. Call ☎ 0193-222-0401 or go to **www.riverthames.co.uk** for date and starting time. (BritRail: Mortlake for start; tube: Hammersmith for midpoint, Putney Bridge for finish.)

OXFORD AND CAMBRIDGE BOAT RACE This takes place on a Saturday in late March or early April and is considered the big magilla of boat races, held since 1829. Teams of eight battle the current, rowing 6.8 kilometers upriver from Putney to Mortlake. Be prepared for crowds on the bridges, on banks, and in riverside pubs. Call ☎ 0207-379-3234 or go to **www.theboatrace.org** for information. (BritRail: Mortlake for finish; tube: Putney Bridge for start, Hammersmith for midpoint.)

April

GUN SALUTE TO MARK THE QUEEN'S BIRTHDAY April 21. Features a 41-gun royal salute to Queen Elizabeth II, fired at noon by the King's Troop Royal House Artillery in Hyde Park (opposite the Dorchester Hotel), then a 62-gun fiesta at the Tower of London at 1 p.m. Take your pick or enjoy both. Bring earplugs. If the date falls on a Sunday, the event will take place on the Monday that follows. (Tube: Marble Arch for Hyde Park, Tower Hill for Tower of London.)

kids **LONDON HARNESS HORSE PARADE** Easter Monday, Battersea Park. This competition of magnificent "working" horses drawing carriages and carts makes the parade a treat unlike any other. Battersea Park is a beautiful place in which to enjoy it. For information, call ☎ 0173-323-4451 or visit **www.eastofengland.org.uk** (where you'll find information on all kinds of seasonal events for country folk and animal fanciers) or **www.batterseapark.org**. (Tube: Sloane Square, then bus to Battersea.)

LONDON MARATHON Occurs on a Sunday in mid-April, starting at Greenwich Park and ending at Buckingham Palace. On average, 35,000 competitors participate, so if you want in you'd better apply early. Entries close in October. Call ☎ 0207-620-4117 or check **www.londonmarathon.co.uk**. (BritRail: Blackheath or Greenwich for start; tube: Green Park for finish.)

May

CHELSEA FLOWER SHOW Runs for five or so days in late May at the Chelsea Royal Hospital. This is the ne plus ultra of London's spring affairs, so you'd better get tickets in advance and prepare to be jostled. Go early in the morning to see the amazing flora and garden accoutrements, a great passion of even the city-dwelling English. The last day is a madhouse, as people buy up goods at bargain prices. For tickets, call ☎ 0845-260-5000 or see **www.rhs.org.uk**. (Tube: Sloane Square.)

kids **COVENT GARDEN PUPPET FESTIVAL AND MAY FAIR** Second Sunday at St. Paul's Church (not to be confused with St. Paul's Cathedral) Garden and Covent Garden. A procession, a service at St. Paul's, and then hours of Punch-and-Judy shows amount to family fun. Call Alternative Arts at ☎ 0207-375-0441. (Tube: Covent Garden.)

ROYAL WINDSOR HORSE SHOW Mid-May, Home Park, Windsor Castle. A wonderful day out for everyone, equestrian or not. Besides the jumping and showing competitions, there are amazing Pony Club games, booths galore, and a few carnival rides, all conducted under the impressive, hulking shadow of Windsor Castle. For information, call ☎ 0175-386-0633 or visit **www.royal-windsor-horse-show.co.uk.** (BritRail: Windsor.)

June

BEATING RETREAT HOUSEHOLD DIVISION June 1 or 2, Whitehall Horse Guards Parade. Part of the big celebration of the queen's coronation anniversary, this is a spectacle of sound and sight, with troops in full regalia in the Horse Guards Parade. To get your tickets, call ☎ 0207-414-2479 or see **www.trooping-the-colour.co.uk.** (Tube: Green Park.)

TROOPING THE COLOUR June 1 and 2, Horse Guards Parade, Whitehall. Yes, the lucky queen gets two birthdays: April 21, when she was actually born, and June 2, the anniversary of her coronation, which is considered her "official" birthday. There's a procession to Buckingham Palace, where the air force flies overhead and a gun salute is fired. Watch from the Mall or try to get a ticket for a good view. Tickets are awarded by ballot; call ☎ 0207-414-2479 or see **www.trooping-the-colour.co.uk** for details. Check in Hyde Park during the preceding Saturdays—you may catch a full-dress rehearsal. (Tube: Westminster.)

 KENWOOD LAKESIDE CONCERTS These are held at the beautiful Kenwood House grounds every Saturday night until September in Hampstead Heath, and they feature headliners in jazz, classical, pop, and rock. A 50-year-old tradition, these open-air events also feature laser shows, fireworks displays, and the Heath at sundown— enchanting. For information, call ☎ 0207-973-3427 or see **www.picnic concerts.com.** (Tube: Archway, Golders Green, or Highgate, then bus #210.)

 ROYAL ACADEMY SUMMER EXHIBITION From early June to mid-August, the Royal Academy in Piccadilly. For more than 200 years, the Royal Academy of Art has been showing the work of contemporary artists in its summer exhibitions, many of which have caused scandals in their day. You can browse or buy. Call ☎ 0207-300-8000 or see **www.royalacademy.org.uk.** (Tube: Green Park or Piccadilly Circus.)

ROYAL ASCOT Mid-June, Ascot Racecourse, Berkshire. Made famous to Americans by the scene in the movie *My Fair Lady,* Ascot brings out all of social London. It's almost more entertaining to dish the outfits and hats than it is to watch the races. For information, go to **www .ascot.co.uk;** for tickets, call ☎ 0870-727-1234. (BritRail: Ascot.)

WIMBLEDON LAWN TENNIS CHAMPIONSHIPS Late June to early July, Wimbledon, Southwest London. This is where all true tennis fans want to be, and everyone else loves the strawberries and cream. Demand for tickets always exceeds supply, so plan way in advance—at least three months. (Queuing on the day you want to go is possible, but there's no guarantee you'll get in.) Tickets for Centre and Number One courts are awarded by ballot. Tours of the courts and club can be booked outside of championship time. Call ☎ 0208-971-2473 or see **www.wimbledon .org** for information. (Tube: Wimbledon.)

TASTE OF LONDON FESTIVAL IN REGENT'S PARK Late June. Sponsored by the Channel 4 television network, this is a guaranteed great day out for food lovers. Under white tents set up on the immaculate green lawns of Regent's Park, you can sample savory dishes from more than 40 of London's top restaurants. There are activities for all tastes: see celebrity chefs at work, participate in a beer master class, drink deep of the wine experience, or just enjoy the crowds and live music. Visit **www.tasteoflondon.co.uk** to book your tickets.

July

BBC HENRY WOOD PROMENADE CONCERTS (THE PROMS) Mid-July through September, Royal Albert Hall, Kensington Gore. Known affectionately as "the Proms," this eight-week series of various orchestral concerts, from classical to contemporary, can be seen for a small fee (standing) or for significantly more (sitting); it can also be enjoyed on a blanket in Kensington Gardens, where the music is piped in. The last night is the big extravaganza, with fireworks. For tickets and information, see **www.bbc.co.uk/proms,** or call the Royal Albert at ☎ 0207-589-8212. Tickets go on sale in mid-June. (Tube: South Kensington or Gloucester Road.)

August

OPENING OF BUCKINGHAM PALACE Early August through October. While the queen is away, the tourists will play. Lines of camera-laden hoi polloi wait to take the grand tour through Elizabeth II's pied-à-terre while she summers in Scotland. Order tickets in advance by calling ☎ 0207-766-7300, or buy them at the ticket booth in Green Park. Visit **www.the-royal-collection.com** for online booking and information. (Tube: Green Park or St. James.)

NOTTING HILL CARNIVAL End of August, Ladbroke Grove and Portobello Road. It's Europe's biggest street party, with a mad parade of floats and freaks, all dressed to the teeth in Caribbean-queen costumes (male and female varieties); steel bands provide the beat, West Indian food the aromas of the islands. The route of the parade is constantly being re-evaluated—residents go nuts over the inconvenience of the three-day event. Prepare to stand shoulder to shoulder in the midst of wild partying and (hopefully) sunny street fun. The best information is available at **www.bbc.co.uk/ london/carnival.** (Tube: Notting Hill.)

September

GREAT RIVER RACE Mid-September, starting on the Thames at Richmond. You've never seen such a collection of boats. Some 200 traditional crafts—including such diverse specimens as whalers,

Viking longboats, Chinese dragon boats, and canoes—race from Ham House in Richmond at 10:30 a.m., finishing at Island Gardens, across from Greenwich Pier, about three hours later. Call ☎ 0208-398-9057 or see **www.greatriverrace.co.uk.** (Tube: Richmond for start; Docklands Light Railway: Island Gardens for finish.)

 OPEN HOUSE LONDON Mid-September. Finally, a chance to look (free!) inside more than 500 amazing houses and buildings that are usually off-limits to the likes of us commoners. Additionally, Open House offers four London architectural tours throughout the year. Call ☎ 0207-383-2131 for information, or visit **www.londonopenhouse.org.**

LONDON FASHION WEEKEND Late September at the Natural History Museum in South Kensington. The ultimate venue for fashionistas to pick up designer clothing at greatly reduced prices. Sign up for catwalk shows, or visit an Elizabeth Arden Masterclass for tips on new makeup trends. Tickets for Saturday and Sunday are sold on timed entry, either for the morning or afternoon. To book tickets, call the hotline at ☎ 0870-890-0097, or visit **www.londonfashionweekend.co.uk.**

October

PEARLIES COSTERMONGER HARVEST FESTIVAL First Sunday in October, St. Martin-in-the Fields, Trafalgar Square. An old Cockney tradition celebrating the apple (coster) harvest that starts with a service at the church and introduces the newly crowned Pearly King or Queen decked out in a costume festooned with white buttons. Musical merrymakers are everywhere. Service starts at 3 p.m.; call ☎ 0207-930-0089 for details. (Tube: Charing Cross.)

kids **TRAFALGAR DAY PARADE** Third Sunday in October, Trafalgar Square. Large, traditional military-style parade commemorating Lord Nelson's sea victory at the Battle of Trafalgar in 1805. Marching bands, Sea Cadets. Call ☎ 0207-928-8978. (Tube: Charing Cross.)

November

BONFIRE NIGHT AND GUY FAWKES DAY FIREWORKS DISPLAYS November 5, all over London. Guy Fawkes was the Catholic conspirator who led the narrowly averted Gunpowder Plot to blow up King James I and Parliament. To make up for all that unexploded gunpowder, the day is celebrated with huge fireworks, public and private. For the best displays, consult *Time Out London,* call the London Tourist Board at ☎ 0207-971-0026, or check the LTB Web site at **www.visitlondon.com.**

kids **LORD MAYOR'S SHOW** Mid-November. This event goes back 700 years—old even by England's standards. The lord mayor rides through the city in a let-them-eat-cake-type gilded carriage (which can be seen at the Museum of London during the rest of the year), followed by a retinue of floats, bands, and military marchers. For a map of the procession, starting times, and more, visit **www .lordmayorsshow.org.** (Tube: Mansion House.)

REMEMBRANCE DAY November 11. At the 11th hour on the 11th day of the 11th month, all of England falls silent in remembrance of those who died in the two World Wars. Red poppies are bought and worn by a majority of Londoners to show respect for the soldiers who gave their lives for England. On the nearest Sunday to the 11th, a service is held for the war dead at the Cenotaph in Whitehall. Buy a poppy and wear it. For information about various Remembrance Day observations, check *Time Out London.* (Tube: Whitehall.)

December

CHRISTMAS LIGHTS AND TREE Late November and December, central London. Various Christmas lighting ceremonies take place on Regent, Oxford, Bond, and Jermyn streets, among others. The switch is flipped by some flavor-of-the-month celeb who gets a dollop of publicity in return. The real fun is the tree-lighting ceremony in Trafalgar Square, which is followed by caroling around the tree each evening, between 4 and 10 p.m. Consult the London Tourist Board at **www.visit london.com,** or try **www.timeout.com/london.**

OLYMPIA INTERNATIONAL SHOW JUMPING CHAMPIONS Mid-December, Grand Hall, Olympia. This is a fun-filled exhibition, rivaling even the Wembley Show for sheer excitement. Lots of trade booths provide plenty of Christmas-shopping opportunities for horse lovers. Call the box office for tickets at ☎ 0870-143-2020, or see **www.olympiahorse show.com.** (Tube: Olympia.)

PART THREE

ACCOMMODATIONS

SELECTING ACCOMMODATIONS

YOUR "HOME AWAY FROM HOME" is crucial to the pleasure of your vacation or business trip. Traveling is stressful, touring around London is certainly tiring, and nothing takes the edge off exhaustion and jet lag like sinking into a warm, comfortable hotel room—that doesn't cost an arm and a leg—after a long day.

London hotels, like everything else here, are just too expensive for you not to make an effort to strike deals or take advantage of specials in order to whittle down the often-breathtaking expense of even ordinary hotels. Although the prices given in the following profiles represent rack rates for the range of double rooms, don't let that scare you off: talk to the manager, and/or check out the Internet for promotions.

unofficial **TIP**
No hotel wants to have empty rooms, and most staff are willing to offer you upgrades and discounts without too much pushing. Call the reservations manager and ask for a better rate than the one quoted.

Although it may seem somewhat cheeky for a guidebook to send you to the Internet (we're supposed to save you that effort, theoretically), one way of getting your vacation in order is to check into the travel-shopping Web sites that offer discount rooms or packages—you will often see as much as 50% off rooms at some of the nicer hotels, which need to push their product during slow times. We like **www .travelocity.com, www.expedia.com,** and **www.hotelsoflondon.com,** but be wary of the many opportunistic sites that act primarily as advertising outlets for hotels: you won't get any deals, and you may not even get a shot at a reservation, as any time period you select will come up as "No rooms available for that day." Travelocity or Expedia may not net you any deep discounts, but they do include a wide range of hotels, with photos and maps showing their locations, and they give you the total cost for your entire stay. They also offer extras such as discounted car rentals, museum passes, and tour-bus tickets. It's very convenient to have all your confirmation numbers and directions in hand before arriving in a foreign city.

WHAT *to* EXPECT

Here are some important facts to remember—and resign yourself to—regarding London hotels:

1. Expect small rooms. *Single* usually means a very small room with one window and a single bed.

2. Certain amenities are not a given. Air-conditioning is not always available; neither are minibars, safes, pay TV, health facilities, or even private bathrooms (hostels and bed-and-breakfasts usually offer you the choice of private or shared baths).

3. If the price is really low, say, £35 a night, chances are the hotel is going to be pretty funky and the bathroom will be down the hall (and possibly shared).

4. When you're looking for a discount, first check for Web discounts to get a bottom line on available prices, and then call the hotel and deal with the reservations manager directly.

5. Take advantage of the weekend rates at many of the five-stars, and spend the weekdays at a moderately priced hotel.

6. Don't expect the same level of service you'd get in a moderate-to-expensive hotel in the United States in a comparable London hotel. It's pretty much only the five-star hotels here that offer the customer-is-always-right-what-can-I-do-for-you-right-away-sir-yes-ma'am kind of service. However, some small, inexpensive hotels managed by their owners will make a point of providing friendly service with genuine concern for your well-being.

7. Always check to see if breakfast is included in your price. Also, it's very important to know if service and the 17.5% value-added tax (VAT) are included in the price. These two add-ons can add considerably to your bill. In our listed prices, we've added VAT where necessary. If you're talking directly to the hotel, ask if VAT and/or service charges are part of the quoted price.

THE BEST OF BRITAIN

WE'VE TRIED TO LIST A GOOD RANGE OF HOTELS in every price range, and with such a huge choice of establishments, we've necessarily picked ones that we like. Many of the hotels profiled have traditional English atmosphere and charm, but it must be admitted that budget is budget in every language. Also, the hotel world is constantly in a state of flux, with new owners chucking the chintz and Ye Olde England type of decor, but the period details often remain. We appreciate the attractions of elegant minimalism, but there is nothing more appealing than the kind of hotel that builds on the natural beauty of, for instance, a Georgian terrace house, where architectural details and leafy gardens are a constant reminder of a more gracious era. Many hotels in the city have pleasing sitting rooms with gas fires, antiques, and deep sofas, and serve authentic cream teas and massive English breakfasts—meals that simply must be experienced to get the full flavor of a certain ideal of London.

Of course, some of the standard chain hotels might well have features that make the most sense for you, such as wheelchair access, fitness clubs, frequent-flyer-mile tie-ins, good incentive packages, and the price and location you prefer. We have our own preference for certain neighborhoods, but that may not be yours.

NEIGHBORHOODS FOR HOTELS

A NUMBER OF POPULAR NEIGHBORHOODS seem to work well for leisure visitors to London. Here are our favorites:

SOUTH KENSINGTON This neighborhood has a lot going for it: an easy walk to **Hyde Park** and **Kensington Gardens,** three museums, **Harrods, Albert Hall,** and the shops of **Knightsbridge** and **Chelsea;** three tube lines and many buses; French bakeries and restaurants for every budget; plus a small-town feeling in the big city. Filled with white-stucco-front Georgian houses and garden squares, South Kensington is a pleasant area to stroll around. Anchoring the area are the **Victoria and Albert Museum,** the **Brompton Oratory** church, and the **Natural History Museum,** with their ornate Victorian facades and interior splendors. The **Lycée Français Charles de Gaulle** and the **French Embassy** in the center of South Kensington lend a charming Parisian vibe to the area—here you'll find French bookshops, chic mothers and bilingual children, and some of the best pastries in London. If you're an avid museumgoer, all three museums (the above mentioned plus the **Science Museum,** which is just up Exhibition Road) are free, so staying nearby is a grand idea, allowing you to pop in and out of the exhibits to your heart's content.

EARLS COURT Farther west, in Earls Court, you can definitely get a better deal, and you're only a few bus or tube stops from **Holland Park, Hyde Park,** the Thames, and central London. There are lovely neighborhood squares, the atmospheric **Brompton Cemetery,** and a huge range of restaurants, pubs, and shops, including the only all-night pharmacy for miles around. Earls Court has a less precious, more real-world vibe than the more expensive South Ken, and it's more appropriate for young people, backpackers, and people allergic to pretentious redevelopment (although Earls Court is bound to join in that trend one of these days). It's also got a lot of gay-friendly hotels and pubs, and the cemetery has a reputation as a hangout for gay guys. The **Earls Court Arena** plays host to concerts and other events; check online or locally to see what's on.

KENSINGTON Above Earls Court, across the busy six-lane Cromwell Road (we have avoided listing many otherwise decent hotels on Cromwell, as the noise from the street can be deafening), is Kensington, an upscale area that nevertheless has a number of inexpensive hotels, small mum-and-pop shops, and lots of restaurants. It's bounded by **Kensington Gardens** to the north and **Holland Park** to the northwest, with Gloucester Road running through the middle of it, leading to **Kensington High Street** and **Kensington Palace.** It features residential streets of beautiful white-stucco Georgian homes, a few garden squares, and some very charming rose-covered cottages tucked away in elegant little neighborhoods and mews. Hotels here range from very expensive to budget, making for a nice mix of people on the street (though only the very rich or very old can afford to live here). Kensington High Street has every shop you could possibly want, including Marks and Spencer, Topshop, Whole Foods Market, and a big variety of cafes and eateries. There's a multiplex cinema at the western end, with Holland Park across the street. Buses and Underground trains (Circle and District lines) can take you from here to just about anywhere in London with ease and dispatch.

> *unofficial* **TIP**
> It's still more affordable and attractive to stay in South Kensington than in, say, Mayfair, but you would be wise to agitate for package deals, upgrades, or discounts in the many hotels within this borough.

MAYFAIR AND PICCADILLY Here you'll find **Hyde Park, Green Park, St. James's Park, Bond Street** shopping, art galleries everywhere, the **Royal Academy,** an easy walk to the West End, and good transportation. No matter where you're staying, do take a stroll through the neighborhood, where you'll be enchanted by streets of mews houses, mansions, and cottages. You'll catch the scent of very old money, as well as the newer perfume of oil fortunes (the **Saudi Embassy** is gorgeous, and we're told that the huge building across the street houses a single billionaire family). Indeed, this is one of London's most exclusive areas, and has been for 300 years. **Berkeley Square, Curzon Street, Charles Street,** and the surrounding area have maintained a large number of quaint buildings, many of which missed being bombed in the Blitz by inches, as you can see from the sore thumbs of modernity sticking out here and there. The shopping of nearby Bond Street, Old and New, should not be approached unless you're fully armed with a platinum credit card, but anyone can window-shop or browse.

> *unofficial* **TIP**
> Be sure to visit **Shepherd's Market,** a quiet area of Mayfair that was once the shopping and gossiping center for the multitude of servants who maintained the grand houses around it.

SOHO AND THE WEST END This is where you'll strike the mother lode of entertainment: street musicians, nightclubs, theaters, cinemas, strip clubs, lap dancing, and every kind of shop imaginable (or unimaginable . . . you may want to cover your children's eyes as you pass some sex shops). **Covent Garden,** the **Royal Opera House, Leicester Square, Soho Square, Piccadilly Circus, Regent Street, Trafalgar Square, Chinatown,** the **National Gallery,** and **Somerset House** are some of the bigger attractions here; the smaller seductions include street markets, **Carnaby Street,** the bookshops of **Charing Cross,** and **St. Martin-in-the-Fields Church.** There's a superabundance of inexpensive and not-too-grotty hotels as well as some budget busters, along with the best people-watching and nightlife opportunities in London. This is where everyone comes out to play. The downsides include a lot of noise and traffic fumes, and it can get a bit dicey at night. When the bars close, the drunks and louts roar into the streets, sometimes heaving up their dinner onto the pavement as they go (mind where you walk); and the after-midnight street dramas can hold their own against any of the stage action you may have seen earlier.

> *unofficial* **TIP**
> Obviously, there is a downside to this neighborhood, and it's a stubborn stumbling block to most mere mortals: the majority of the hotels are crushingly expensive. But you can always stop in at **Claridge's, Brown's,** or **The Ritz** for a drink or afternoon tea. Plus, you may find that even the snootiest grand hotel will have weekend package deals or be amenable to striking a deal—it never hurts to ask.

BLOOMSBURY This is a much quieter option, and yet still within walking distance of the nightlife of Soho and the West End. Its biggest attraction is the unparalleled **British Museum,** and if you look around at the blue plaques celebrating its literary inhabitants, you'll get a feel for how bohemian and intellectual it used to be. It still has interesting shops and a variety of restaurants; best of all, there are so many affordable hotels here that the competition among them all has kept the quality just a bit higher than in some of the other budget-lodging areas. Bookstores that have been around forever still ply their trade, and there is an umbrella ("brolly") shop here that has been in business since before World War I.

> *unofficial* **TIP**
> Bloomsbury is one neighborhood that has not fully succumbed to developers' greed.

Cheap (But Not Always Cheerful) Hotel Neighborhoods

BAYSWATER, PIMLICO, KING'S CROSS, AND VICTORIA This is not to say that these neighborhoods don't have some very attractive hotels at reasonable prices; it's just that they have a discouraging number of fleabags, so beware of low-priced hotels in these areas—you won't be able to know just how sleazy a place is by looking on the Internet.

CALL FOR DEALS

AS WE STATE ABOVE, ALMOST EVERY HOTEL in London—except for the already cut-rate ones—will have some kind of saver scheme, be it a weekend reduction, a package that includes breakfast and a free night, price reductions during the seasonal (January and August) sales held in London's big shops, a summer season, a low season, a Christmas season, a corporate rate, a half-price scheme, a desperate-for-business rate, a no-reason discount, and so on. Hoteliers want you to come to London, and they want you to stay in their hotel. There is also the possibility of a last-minute room, in which a hotel with an empty room will agree to a huge reduction just to fill it. This requires flexibility, but it can spell big savings.

Rule number one in making any of these deals is to talk to the reception manager—she or he is the only person who can agree to make deals. Chat him or her up and see what can be arranged; service is managers' business, and they do aim to please. But remember that some hotels don't need to make deals; check out the listings and see how many rooms a hotel has. Chances are that the more rooms there are, the more of them will be vacant. Often the rooms that remain empty are the junior, executive, or superior suites. To get one of those for the price of a standard double is a worthy coup, and you will be very happy in such a room, especially one in a grand hotel.

BED-AND-BREAKFASTS

B&BS ARE BIG IN BRITAIN, AND IN LONDON there are some drop-dead gorgeous homes that are open to you through agencies. The price (with a few exceptions) is per person, per night; includes breakfast; and offers you so much more than any hotel will, and at half the price. Be aware that the majority of these don't have air-conditioning in the rooms (though fans are always available). Also note that some B&Bs require a two-night minimum stay. Most small establishments ask for a credit-card deposit and a small booking fee, and then you'll pay your host the full cost of your stay in cash or by credit card when you arrive.

The author of our Shopping chapter (Part Ten) runs a women-only bed-and-breakfast in Knightsbridge, called **Lennox B and B.** The rates are wonderfully reasonable, the breakfasts are sumptuous, and if there is any concierge in London who knows more about what's going on in this city than she does, well, we'll eat every page of this guidebook. Contact Sara Louise at **lennoxbandb@aol.com,** and she'll give you all the details about how to book.

Some Excellent Companies

THE BULLDOG CLUB (☎ 0870-803-4414; fax 0870-622-0021; **stay@bull dogclub.com; www.bulldogclub.com**) Only the crème de la crème of houses are included in this exclusive group, with grand homes in May-fair, Belgravia, Chelsea, and other beautiful neighborhoods. About 30 properties are available. The criteria demand that each guest have a room separate from the host family's quarters; that the home is within a five-minute walk to public transportation; that guests are given such amenities as bathrobes and tea- and coffeemakers; and that the home holds to a high decorative standard. You'll probably find high-quality bedding, chocolates on your pillow, organic food for breakfast, and fine china for your tea. All Bulldog rooms are non-smoking, and you will have your own keys to the house; you may also get Internet access, your own entrance, a work area, and possibly a balcony or little garden spot. Prices start at around £65 for single occupancy and £90 for double; breakfast, obviously, is included. You pay a small fee of £25 to join the "club" for a three-year membership. The Bulldog Club also runs properties in Scotland and various rural areas, should you wish to take a side trip.

LONDON HOMESTEAD SERVICES (☎ 0207-286-5115; **www.lhslondon.com**) This service represents about 200 homes in the London area, many of which you can see on the Web site. There are three categories: Budget and Standard rooms range from £16 to £30 per person per night but tend to be outside central London; Premier prices generally fall between £30 and £50 for rooms within the central-London area. Before you commit to renting a room, ask the agency for details on bathroom facilities, transportation in the neighborhood, the number of steps to your room, elevator availability, and room size.

UPTOWN RESERVATIONS (☎ 0207-351-3445; fax 0207-351-9383; **www.uptownres.co.uk**) This is an extremely upscale B&B agency, with fine houses of high standards in central neighborhoods as well as London's leafy areas. Uptown offers out-of-town properties, self-serviced flats, and long-term apartments. Singles start at £75 a night, double or twin rooms go for £95 and up, and rooms for four begin at £135. The agency takes all major credit cards and offers more than 80 properties in the best neighborhoods.

SERVICED AND SELF-SERVICED APARTMENTS

A SERVICED APARTMENT CAN BE A GOOD ALTERNATIVE to a hotel room, with commensurate prices and much more room—to be able to close a door on your traveling companion(s) once in a while can be a delightful luxury. The best of these offer the same services a hotel does; some even provide breakfast. You may get a 24-hour concierge, satellite TV, laundry, and daily maid service; you may even get a washer and dryer, secretarial services, guest membership to a health club, a fully equipped kitchen, and more.

unofficial **TIP** When you factor in the costs of eating all your meals in restaurants, a hotel costs considerably more than its nightly rate; get an apartment and you can spend your restaurant budget on the less perishable pleasures of shopping sprees.

CENTRAL LONDON APARTMENTS (☎ 0845-644-2714; fax 0845-644-2715; **www.central-london-apartments.com**) This firm specializes in short-term rental of hotel rooms, suites, and serviced apartments in every good neighborhood in London. The prices are guaranteed to be at least 30% less than standard hotel prices; though the costs are high for a one- or two-bedroom suite, you can get a studio flat for as little as £50 a night, although the average price is more likely to be in the £80 to £125 range. The properties are generally nicely appointed lodgings in desirable areas. Make sure the prices quoted include VAT, and negotiate a lower rate for stays of more than a week.

HOME FROM HOME (☎ 0207-233-8111; fax 0207-233-9101; **www .homefromhome.co.uk**) With more than 200 properties in London, Home from Home can be dialed from America toll free (☎ 800-748-9783) for a brochure, but its Web site suffices to show you what attractive houses and decent prices they offer, from £85 to £220 and up per night. A minimum stay of seven days is required, although you may be able to negotiate a shorter stay.

LONDON FIRST CHOICE APARTMENTS (☎ 0208-990-9033; fax 0208-754-1200; **www.lfca.co.uk**) LFCA has a large assortment of hotels and serviced and nonserviced apartments. The prices may look a bit high, but if you get a place with a kitchen, you can save a bundle by staying away from restaurants. The prices quoted are competitive with the B&B agencies (see the Web site for more information). Prices vary according to season, neighborhood, and type of accommodation, from £100 a night for a studio in Earls Court to £3,400 per week for a three-bedroom apartment in Mayfair.

LONDON'S LUXURY HOTELS

EVERYONE KNOWS ABOUT THE STAR SYSTEM used to rate restaurants and hotels—one is at the bottom of the scale, and five is at the top. In the *Unofficial Guides,* we also use a rating system of stars, and we too grade hotels from the lowly one to the pinnacle of five. However, please be alert to the fact that our stars have little, if anything, to do with the universal hotel-star system. We apologize in advance for any confusion that might result when you see that we've given just two stars overall to a hotel advertised in other publications as four-star, or when what is clearly a one-star hotel gets a rating of four stars from us. Our star rating is based strictly in the *relative context of the hotels covered in this book,* and is arrived at by looking at value, quality, and cost.

Having said that, we do know that *five-star* is as informative an adjective as one such as *country:* in the same way we know that the latter will be rustic, so we will instantly know that the former will be expensive and grand, no doubt providing impeccable service and costly amenities. We've taken the most famous five-star hotels of London, such as **The Ritz** and **Claridge's,** and separated them from the other profiles for the simple reason that they are classic London establishments and no book on this city would be complete without them. But if you can afford the £250- to £600-plus a night that these hotels charge, you probably don't need the kind of detail our other profiles provide: you know you'll get the best bedding, furnishings, toiletries, and services money can buy. If you aren't the kind of person who's accustomed to (or financially capable of) splurging on accommodations, you may find one of the following hotels worth spending a weekend in, as many of them often offer package deals to fill rooms when their corporate clients leave town. But be careful—this kind of luxury can spoil you completely, and you may never look at a good three-star hotel in quite the same way again.

unofficial **TIP**
Buyer beware: if you decide to splurge on a luxury hotel for a special occasion, question the reservations clerk closely regarding what is offered, and make a point of requesting a good view, a spacious room, and a convenient yet quiet location on your floor—never settle for so-so when spending this kind of money!

You can, however, call any of the following hotels and ask about discounts. A number of possibilities exist: low-season rates, applicable in January and February; summer discounts; promotions for the citywide retail-shop sales during August and January; weekend break rates; upgrading to a bigger room; paying for your room in advance in dollars; executive discounts; and frequent-flyer tie-ins. Talk to the reservations manager to see if you can work something out—many of the high-end hotels have toll-free numbers in the United States. There are also some Internet-only prices that you might check and then use as a challenge to the manager to sweeten the deal.

Some of these otherwise astronomically priced hotels have single rooms at not-too-shocking rates—while the room may be small, you'll have the best comfort and service you can imagine. Reservations managers may upgrade you to a junior suite if there's one available. Remember that an empty hotel room is a perishable commodity, as hotels are well aware. All the prices we quoted are for *two people sharing a standard double room,* and we've calculated and included the 17.5% VAT (unless otherwise noted), which adds up to a sizable dollop on top of a sizable basic rack rate—many of the most expensive hotels just don't have the nerve to include it in quoted prices and only mention this exclusion in small print below the rates (they may also slip in a 3%-to-5% service charge, which we haven't included in the price).

THE BERKELEY (Wilton Place, SW1; ☎ 0207-235-6000; fax 0207-235-4330; **www.theberkeleyhotellondon.com;** tube: Knightsbridge or Hyde Park Corner) Right off Knightsbridge, west of Hyde Park Corner, this hotel has what are widely considered the best spa and gym in London, and Marcus Wareing's restaurant Pétrus won a second Michelin star in 2007; less formal but equally impressive is the Boxwood Café. For cocktails, try the enchanting Blue Bar. The Berkeley is owned by the Maybourne group, which also owns Claridge's and The Connaught. There are 214 serenely spacious rooms, starting at £269, with upgrades to deluxe king-size rooms and suites available at a not-unreasonable extra cost.

BLAKES (33 Roland Gardens, SW7; ☎ 0207-370-6701; fax 0207-373-0442; **www.blakeshotel.com;** tube: South Kensington) This utterly gorgeous and very intimate hotel in South Kensington caters to rock stars, models, actors, and aristos. Although Blakes is slightly less expensive than the others in this class, you can still fracture your credit card between the tariff and the extras, such as the eponymous restaurant. The rooms are exuberantly and individually decorated in styles ranging from expensive bordello to country squire to raj's field tent. Good value for a five-star hotel, even though some of the rooms are small. The restaurant serves a delightfully untraditional afternoon tea, with sandwiches presented in little glass boxes and the best tiny-but-tall homemade scones. There are 47 rooms, starting at £320.

CLARIDGE'S (Brook Street, W1; ☎ 0207-629-8860; fax 0207-499-2210; **www.claridges.co.uk;** tube: Bond Street) Bold decor evokes Jazz Age glamour and royal luxury. A fantastic (and fantastically expensive) afternoon tea is served in impressive surroundings. On Saturdays there's a good chance of seeing a society wedding, featuring women in charming *chapeaux* and men in morning coats. The restaurant, Gordon Ramsay at Claridge's, is one of London's best. The Art Deco period details are deliciously evocative of the kind of sophisticated mansions imagined in 1930s screwball-comedy flicks; Jean Harlow or Mary Astor would look right at home here, and Jay Gatsby would have tried to buy it. There are 203 rooms, starting at £500.

THE CONNAUGHT (16 Carlos Place, W1; ☎ 0207-499-7070; fax 0207-495-3262; **www.theconnaughthotellondon.com;** tube: Bond Street) The Connaught has been in business since 1897; Charles de Gaulle made it his wartime headquarters, and Cecil Beaton and David Niven called it home. It attracts so many regulars that it's almost a club, so reserve well in advance of your visit. There are 92 rooms, starting at £360 plus service charge.

THE DORCHESTER (53 Park Lane, W1; ☎ 0207-629-8888; fax 0207-409-0114; **www.dorchesterhotel.com;** tube: Marble Arch) One of London's grandest establishments, this hotel is right across from Hyde Park and within walking distance to some of the toniest shops in London. Restaurants and the health club are of the highest standards, as are the rooms and the decor. There are 244 rooms and suites, starting at £350.

THE LANDMARK (222 Marylebone Road, NW1; ☎ 0207-631-8000; fax 0207-631-8080; **www.landmarklondon.co.uk;** tube: Marylebone) The Landmark gives good value for the money because it's out of the Mayfair-Piccadilly high-rent district, located instead in the charming and convenient Marylebone Village. There's an impressive atrium for dining, a fitness center and pool, and good-sized rooms. All 298 rooms are doubles and start at £300.

THE LANESBOROUGH (Hyde Park Corner, SW1; ☎ 0207-259-5599; fax 0207-259-5606; **www.lanesborough.com;** tube: Hyde Park Corner) Looking at the elaborately Georgian interior, you'd never guess that gurneys used to roll around these floors instead of room-service carts. This former hospital is now a formal hotel, full of charm and mahogany-paneled splendor, which blends interestingly well with the Asian decoration of the fine restaurant. Each room has a butler call button—need we say more? There are 95 rooms, starting at £450 for a standard double.

THE METROPOLITAN (Old Park Lane, W1; ☎ 0207-447-1000; fax 0207-447-1100; **www.metropolitan.co.uk;** tube: Hyde Park Corner) This hotel is home not only to the esteemed and expensive sushi restaurant Nobu but also the renowned Metropolitan Club, a private hot-spot that was at the top of the social ladder when it opened in 1997 and is still formidable. Guests of the hotel get complimentary membership, a big plus for young social types. There's also a state-of-the-art gym. There are 155 rooms, from £380.

ONE ALDWYCH (1 Aldwych, WC2; ☎ 0207-300-1000; fax 0207-300-1001; **www.onealdwych.co.uk;** tube: Covent Garden or Charing Cross) Where to start? This elegant and modern hotel has so many amenities that we can only list the highlights: a 56-foot pool in a magnificent spa; a multimedia screening room with wide-body seats; 350 important works of art scattered throughout the rooms; three bars; a good restaurant; and a clientele that will have you itching to grab your camera. Doubles start at £400, with lower rates on weekends and in summer.

 THE RITZ (150 Piccadilly, W1; ☎ 0207-300-2308; toll free from the United States, 877-748-9536; fax 0207-493-2687; **www.theritz london.com;** tube: Green Park) What else can you say about the place that has given its name to the dictionary as a definition of luxury and extravagance? Before you think The Ritz is just plain out of the question, call and see what kind of deals they're offering: you might happen upon a weekend deal or discounted summer rate. The decor is Versailles-on-Piccadilly, and the accommodations are sumptuousness itself. Individually decorated rooms, 131 in all, start at £390 and go up, up, up.

 SANDERSON (50 Berners Street, W1; ☎ 0207-300-1400; fax 0207-300-1401; **www.sandersonlondon.com;** tube: Oxford Circus or Tottenham Court) Sanderson, part of the Ian Schrager–owned Morgans Hotel Group, is favored by rich, high-profile media personalities, whose personal needs may be inferred by the excessive luxury offered here: 450-thread-count cotton, three phones with two private lines in each room, private fitness areas in some rooms, a yoga studio, and a two-story holistic bathhouse. There's even the very rare feature of a children's play area—most luxury hotels hope that kids will stay home. The decor is quirky, dreamy, Dalí-esque, with eclectic furnishings in an array of colors and periods. There are 150 rooms, priced from £400 upward.

THE SAVOY (1 Savoy Hill, Strand, WC2; ☎ 0207-950-5492; toll free from the United States, 800-637-2869; fax 0207-950-5482; **www.fairmont.com/savoy;** tube: Charing Cross) The

Savoy has undergone what's known as a sympathetic renovation recently: like Claridge's, it maintains the decor of its salad days, and its service is impeccable. It's right in the thick of things, perfect for theatergoers. Rooms, 161 in all, start at £370. The only rooms with river views are the suites, which start at £650.

HOTEL RATINGS

OVERALL RATINGS We've distinguished the properties that follow according to relative quality, tastefulness, state of repair, cleanliness, and size of standard rooms, grouping them into classifications denoted by stars. Overall star ratings in this guide apply to London properties only and do not correspond to ratings awarded by the British Tourist Authority, automobile clubs, or other travel critics. Overall ratings are presented to show the difference we perceive between one property and another. They are assigned without regard to location or to whether a property has restaurants, recreational facilities, entertainment, or other extras.

★★★★★	Superior	Tasteful and luxurious by any standard
★★★★	Extremely nice	Above average in appointments and design; very comfortable
★★★	Nice	Average but quite comfortable
★★	Adequate	Plain but meets all essential needs
★	Budget	Spartan; not aesthetically pleasing, but clean

QUALITY RATINGS In addition to overall ratings (which delineate broad categories), we also employ quality ratings. They apply to room quality only and describe the property's standard accommodations. In addition to standard accommodations, many hotels offer luxury rooms and special suites that are not rated in this guide. Our rating scale is ★ to ★★★★★, with ★★★★★ as the highest possible rating and ★ as the lowest.

VALUE RATINGS We also provide a value rating to give you some sense of the quality of a room in relation to its cost. As before, the ratings are based on the quality of room for the money and do not take into account location, services, or amenities. Our scale is as follows:

★★★★★	An exceptional bargain
★★★★	A good deal
★★★	Fairly priced—you get exactly what you pay for
★★	Somewhat overpriced
★	Significantly overpriced

A ★★½ room at £100 may have the same value rating as a ★★★★★ room at £180, but that does not mean that the rooms will be of comparable quality. Regardless of whether it's a good deal or not, a ★★½ room is still a ★★½ room.

For each hotel we also provide the London neighborhood in which the property is located.

HOW THE HOTELS COMPARE

ON THE FOLLOWING PAGES is a table that lists the hotels we've researched and profiled, organized by overall rating. To find a particular hotel listed in this table, look through the alphabetical section of profiles later in the chapter.

If you use subsequent editions of this guide, you will notice that many of the ratings and rankings change. In addition to the inclusion of new properties, these changes also reflect guest-room renovations or improved maintenance and housekeeping. A failure to properly maintain guest rooms or a lapse in housekeeping standards may negatively affect the ratings or even result in our deleting the hotel from this book altogether.

Finally, before you begin to shop for a hotel, take a hard look at this letter we received from a couple in Hot Springs, Arkansas:

> We canceled our room reservations to follow the advice in your book [and reserved a hotel room highly ranked by the Unofficial Guide]. We wanted inexpensive, but clean and cheerful. We got inexpensive, but [also] dirty, grim, and depressing. I really felt disappointed in your advice and the room. It was the pits. That was the one real piece of information I needed from your book! The room spoiled the holiday for me aside from our touring.

Needless to say, this letter was as unsettling to us as the bad room was to our reader. Our integrity as travel journalists, after all, is based on the quality of the information we provide our readers. Even with the best of intentions and the most conscientious research, however, we can't inspect every room in every hotel. What we do, in statistical terms, is take a sample: we check out several rooms selected at random in each hotel and base our ratings and rankings on those rooms. The inspections are conducted anonymously and without the knowledge of the management. Although unusual, it is certainly possible that the rooms we randomly inspect are not representative of the majority of rooms at a particular hotel. This is particularly true in the smaller London hotels that offer such a variety of room sizes and styles.

Another possibility is that the rooms we inspect in a given hotel are representative, but that by bad luck a reader is assigned a room that is inferior. When we rechecked the hotel our reader disliked, we discovered our rating was correctly representative, but that he and his wife had unfortunately been assigned to one of a small number of threadbare rooms scheduled for renovation.

How the Hotels Compare

HOTEL	OVERALL QUALITY	ROOM QUALITY	VALUE
Dukes Hotel	★★★★★	★★★★★	★★★
Goring Hotel	★★★★★	★★★★	★★★
Thistle Victoria	★★★★★	★★★★	★★★★
Brown's Hotel	★★★★	★★★★★	★★
Charlotte Street Hotel	★★★★	★★★★	★★★
The Colonnade	★★★★	★★★★	★★★★
Covent Garden Hotel	★★★★	★★★★½	★★★
The Draycott Hotel	★★★★	★★★★★	★★★
The Gore	★★★★	★★★★½	★★★
Great Eastern Hotel	★★★★	★★★★	★★½
Hazlitt's	★★★★	★★★★	★★½
Haymarket Hotel	★★★★	★★★★	★★★
Hotel Russell	★★★★	★★★★	★★★★
London Marriott Hotel County Hall	★★★★	★★★★	★★★
Miller's Residence	★★★★	★★★	★★★½
Radisson Edwardian Hampshire	★★★★	★★★★	★★½
The Rookery	★★★★	★★★½	★★½
The Soho Hotel	★★★★	★★★★	★★★
The Sumner Hotel	★★★★	★★★★	★★★★
Threadneedles	★★★★	★★★★½	★★★
The Zetter Restaurant & Rooms	★★★★	★★★★	★★★★
The Abbey Court Hotel	★★★½	★★★★	★★★★½
The Cadogan Hotel	★★★½	★★★½	★★
Collingham Suites and Apartments	★★★½	★★★★	★★★½

The key to avoiding disappointment is to snoop around in advance and to protest vigorously if your room is not up to the standards of the photos at the Web site or in a promotional brochure. Demand a different room for the same price.

HOTEL PROFILES

ALL PRICES INCLUDE THE 17.5% value-added tax (VAT) and refer to the range of prices for a double room for two people: we assume that

HOTEL	OVERALL QUALITY	ROOM QUALITY	VALUE
Durrants	★★★½	★★★½	★★★½
Grange White Hall Hotel	★★★½	★★★½	★★★
Lincoln House Hotel	★★★½	★★★½	★★★★½
The Mayflower	★★★½	★★★½	★★★★
The Portobello Hotel	★★★½	★★★★	★★★
Number Sixteen	★★★½	★★★★	★★½
The Pelham Hotel	★★★½	★★★★	★★½
St. Giles Hotel London	★★★½	★★★½	★★★½
Columbia Hotel	★★★½	★★★	★★★★★
Saint Gregory Hotel	★★★½	★★★	★★★½
Ambassadors Bloomsbury	★★★	★★	★★★
The Gainsborough	★★★	★★★	★★★★
The Gallery Hotel	★★★	★★★½	★★★½
The Hoxton	★★★	★★★	★★★
Park Inn Hyde Park	★★★	★★★	★★★
The Rembrandt Hotel	★★★	★★★	★★★★½
The Sloane Square Hotel	★★★	★★★★	★★★½
Barkston Gardens Hotel	★★½	★★½	★★★★
Best Western Paddington Court Hotel	★★½	★★½	★★★
Strand Palace Hotel	★★½	★★½	★★★
Ruskin Hotel	★★	★★½	★★★★★
Fielding Hotel	★½	★★	★★½

unless you're on business, you'll be with a traveling companion. Some double rooms have only one rather smallish double bed; others have two single beds or a king- or queen-size bed. In England, "king-size" is what Americans call a queen, and "super-king" is the U.K. equivalent of a U.S. king-size bed.

Obviously, single rooms will be less expensive, but as noted in the reviews, these are often tiny and depressing, no matter how great the hotel is in general. We've suggested in some cases that you upgrade to a double room even if you're traveling alone—the additional space is often worth the additional cost. At some B&Bs, the total quoted

west end accommodations

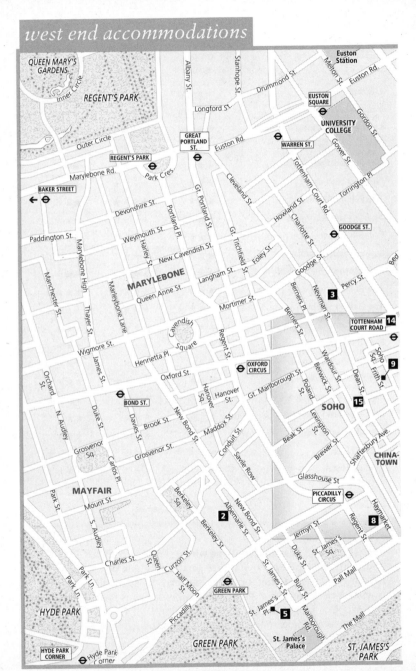

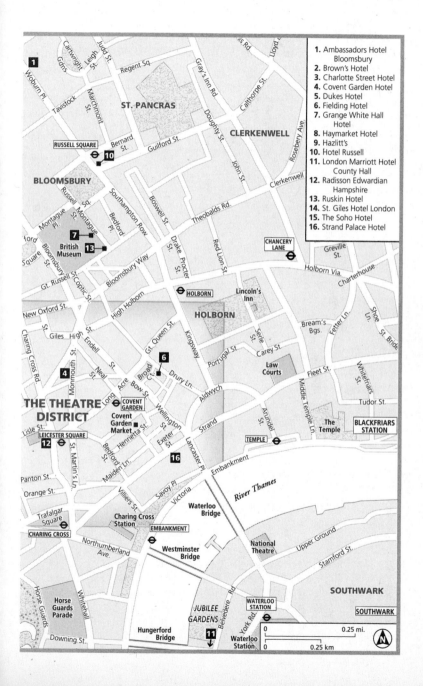

1. Ambassadors Hotel Bloomsbury
2. Brown's Hotel
3. Charlotte Street Hotel
4. Covent Garden Hotel
5. Dukes Hotel
6. Fielding Hotel
7. Grange White Hall Hotel
8. Haymarket Hotel
9. Hazlitt's
10. Hotel Russell
11. London Marriott Hotel County Hall
12. Radisson Edwardian Hampshire
13. Ruskin Hotel
14. St. Giles Hotel London
15. The Soho Hotel
16. Strand Palace Hotel

westminster and victoria
accommodations, dining, and nightlife

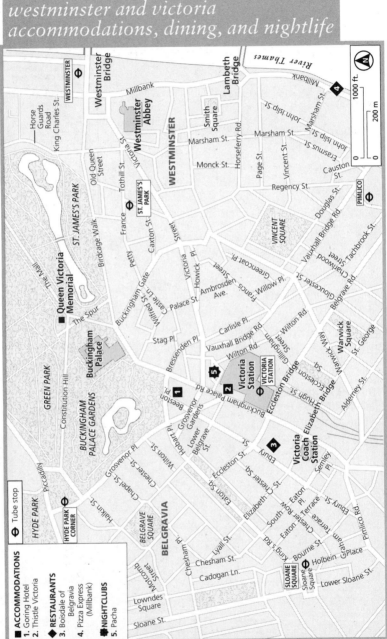

the city accommodations

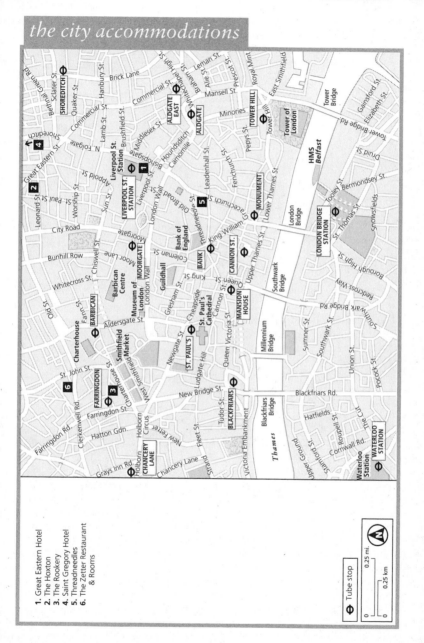

1. Great Eastern Hotel
2. The Hoxton
3. The Rookery
4. Saint Gregory Hotel
5. Threadneedles
6. The Zetter Restaurant & Rooms

Ф Tube stop

0   0.25 mi.

0   0.25 km

knightsbridge to south kensington

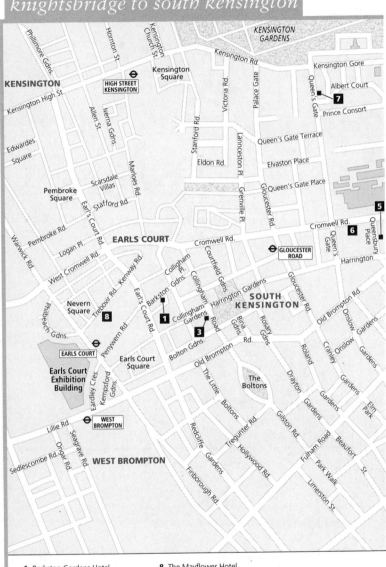

1. Barkston Gardens Hotel
2. The Cadogan Hotel
3. Collingham Suites and Apartments
4. The Draycott Hotel
5. The Gainsborough
6. The Gallery Hotel
7. The Gore
8. The Mayflower Hotel
9. Number Sixteen
10. The Pelham Hotel
11. The Rembrandt Hotel
12. The Sloane Square Hotel

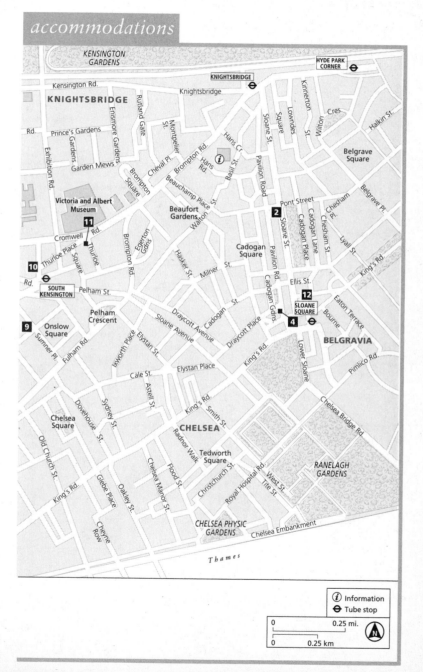

accommodations

KENSINGTON
GARDENS

HYDE PARK
CORNER

KNIGHTSBRIDGE

Kensington Rd.
Knightsbridge

KNIGHTSBRIDGE

Kinnerton St.
Lowndes Square
Wilton Cres.
Halkin St.

Prince's Gardens
Rd.
Exhibition Rd.
Ensmore Gardens
Gardens
Garden Mews
Rutland Gate
Montpelier St.
Cheval Pl.
Brompton Rd.
Brompton Square
Hans Cr.
Hans Rd.
Basil St.
Sloane St.
Sloane Square
Belgrave Square
Belgrave Pl.

ⓘ

Victoria and Albert
Museum

11

Beauchamp Place
Beaufort Gardens
Walton St.
Pont Street
2
Chesham Pl.
Chesham St.
Cadogan Lane
Cadogan Place
Lyall St.
King's Rd.

Cromwell   Rd.
10
Thurloe Place
Thurloe Square
Thurloe
Brompton Rd.
Egerton Gdns.
Hasker St.
Milner   St.
Cadogan Square
Pavilion Rd.
Sloane St.

Rd.
**SOUTH
KENSINGTON**
Pelham St.
Ellis St.
12
**SLOANE
SQUARE**
4
Eaton Terrace
Bourne

Pelham Crescent
Draycott Avenue
Sloane Avenue
Cadogan   St.
Draycott Place
Cadogan Gdns.
BELGRAVIA

9
Onslow Square
Summer Pl.
Fulham Rd.
Ixworth Place
Elystan St.
Elystan Place
King's Rd.
Lower Sloane
Pimlico Rd.

Cale St.
Astell St.
Sydney St.
King's Rd.
Smith St.
Chelsea Bridge Rd.

Chelsea Square
Dovehouse St.
CHELSEA
Radnor Walk
Tedworth Square
Christchurch St.
Royal Hospital Rd.
West St.
Tite St.
**RANELAGH
GARDENS**

Old Church St.
King's Rd.
Glebe Place
Oakley St.
Chelsea Manor St.
Flood St.
Cheyne Row
**CHELSEA PHYSIC
GARDENS**
Chelsea Embankment

Thames

ⓘ Information
⊖ Tube stop

0   0.25 mi.

0   0.25 km

N

marylebone to notting hill gate

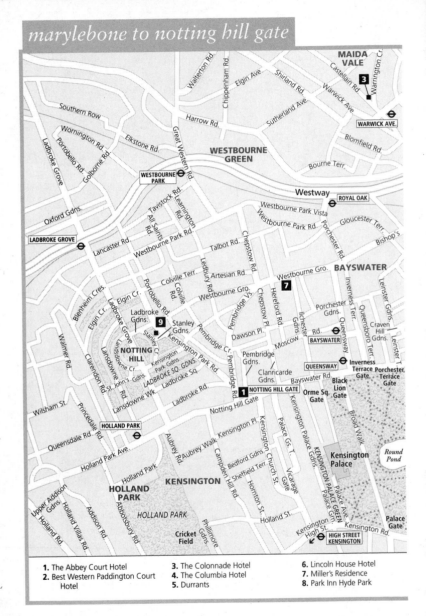

1. The Abbey Court Hotel
2. Best Western Paddington Court Hotel
3. The Colonnade Hotel
4. The Columbia Hotel
5. Durrants
6. Lincoln House Hotel
7. Miller's Residence
8. Park Inn Hyde Park

accommodations

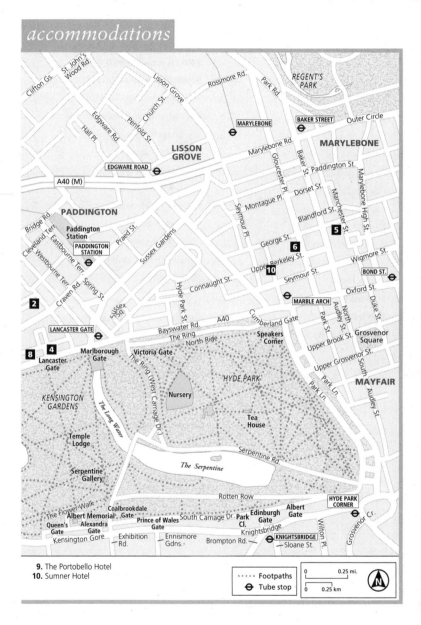

9. The Portobello Hotel
10. Sumner Hotel

····· Footpaths
⊖ Tube stop

0   0.25 mi.
0   0.25 km

ACCOMMODATIONS BY NEIGHBORHOOD

WEST END

Ambassadors Bloomsbury

Brown's Hotel

Charlotte Street Hotel

Covent Garden Hotel

Dukes Hotel

Fielding Hotel

Grange White Hall Hotel

Haymarket Hotel

Hazlitt's

Hotel Russell

London Marriott Hotel County Hall

Radisson Edwardian Hampshire

Ruskin Hotel

St. Giles Hotel London

The Soho Hotel

Strand Palace Hotel

THE CITY

Great Eastern Hotel

The Hoxton

The Rookery

Saint Gregory Hotel

Threadneedles

The Zetter Restaurant & Rooms

WESTMINSTER AND VICTORIA

Goring Hotel

Thistle Victoria

KNIGHTSBRIDGE TO SOUTH KENSINGTON

Barkston Gardens Hotel

The Cadogan Hotel

Collingham Suites and Apartments

The Draycott Hotel

The Gainsborough

The Gallery Hotel

The Gore

The Mayflower Hotel

Number Sixteen

The Pelham Hotel

The Rembrandt Hotel

The Sloane Square Hotel

MARYLEBONE TO NOTTING HILL GATE

The Abbey Court Hotel

Best Western Paddington Court Hotel

The Colonnade

Columbia Hotel

Durrants

Lincoln House Hotel

Miller's Residence

Park Inn Hyde Park

The Portobello Hotel

The Sumner Hotel

price per night is for two people sharing a room, including breakfast for two. Other establishments may charge you for one room and two breakfasts, so be clear what the *final* cost will be, and always check the fine print.

We've added VAT to all rates, so if you see a lower price on a Web site, you will probably see written in tiny type somewhere on the page, "Rates are subject to 17.5% VAT," "Rates are exclusive of VAT," or some variation thereof. We haven't factored in the 3%-to-5% charge some hotels add for service, because it differs from hotel to hotel; many hotels do not endorse this stealth surcharge and leave you to decide on tipping for service. What you want to see above or below the prices is "Rates include VAT, service charge, and breakfast." (We admire a hotel that adds it all up and publishes the total on their rate cards or advertising.) Prices for deluxe, executive, triple-occupancy, and family rooms, as well as suites and rooms with special features (such as a four-poster bed, fireplace, or balcony), will be significantly higher.

Many hotel groups will not publish a rack rate on their Web sites—you have to choose a date and room in order to get a price, which allows them to change their prices according to demand. The best advice is to call for a firm final cost per night, with all the extras added in.

The Abbey Court Hotel ★★★½

QUALITY ★★★★   VALUE ★★★★½   PRICE RANGE £120–£175

20 Pembridge Gardens, Notting Hill Gate, W2; ☎ 0207-221-7518; fax 0207-792-0858; www.abbeycourthotel.co.uk

BUILT IN 1830, THE ABBEY COURT is housed in a lovely old Victorian mansion in a white-stucco-front neighborhood close to Portobello Road. It's a real beauty, and well priced, too. It's popular with antiques dealers, not only because they can walk to Kensington Church Street and all the antiques warrens along Portobello, but also because it has plenty of really fine old furniture, art, and decorations to admire. It's comfortable and homey as well as elegant and serene—almost like visiting the home of a rich aunt with very good taste. Downstairs is a small conservatory where breakfast is served (Continental breakfast is included), and an honor bar is set out all day. Newspapers are ordered for you free, and there are plenty of English magazines in each room. Reductions are available for stays of more than a week; and you will find special deals or upgrades on the Web site. Please note that there is no elevator.

SETTING AND FACILITIES
Nearest tube station Notting Hill Gate. Quietness Rating A in back, B+ in front (quiet street). **Dining** Small breakfast room. **Amenities** Newspapers, bathrobes, cookies, and bottled water; in-room Internet, computers for your use; use of nearby health club (for a fee); honor bar. **Services** Multilingual staff; 24-hour room service, bellhop, laundry; receptionist does work of concierge and can organize tickets, beauty treatments, restaurant reservations, and whatever else you desire.

ACCOMMODATIONS
Rooms 22. **All rooms** Telephone, Internet modem, satellite TV, hair dryer, iron, bathrobe. **Some rooms** Antique four-poster or brass beds, sitting areas. **Bed and bath** Italian-marble bathrooms with jetted tubs, showers, heated towel racks. Mattresses and sheets are of high quality. **Favorites** The four-poster rooms are the biggest and the nicest. **Comfort and decor** The decor is traditional, with lovely antiques and prints all around, fantastic mirrors, and nice wallpaper. It's a

pleasure to see how well appointed the Abbey Court is, and for us that spells comfort. There's no elevator for the 5 floors, which may spell discomfort for many, but the stairway is beautiful.

PAYMENT, RESERVATIONS, AND RESTRICTIONS
Deposit Credit card; 48-hour cancellation policy. **Credit cards** All major. **Check-in/out** 3 p.m./11 a.m. **Pets** Not allowed. **Elevator** No. **Children** Yes. **Disabled access** No elevator.

Ambassadors Bloomsbury ★★★

QUALITY ★★	VALUE ★★★	PRICE RANGE £80–£165

12 Upper Woburn Place, Bloomsbury, WC1; ☎ 0207-387-1456; fax 0207-388-9930; www.ambassadors.co.uk

CLEAN, SLIGHTLY SWANKY, AND EFFICIENT, this hotel is big on accommodating business types, but it also lays plenty of style over its solid substance. The rooms feel a little small for a long visit, even in the deluxe rooms—no big shock in London hotels. But despite this small quibble, the Ambassadors can confidently check all the important boxes: good bed, good bath, and good breakfast. The hotel was reopened in 2007, and so is on the cutting edge of modern amenities, as well as pristinely clean and fresh looking. On another positive note, very good discounts are available if you book online—up to 44% savings on a double room. The Ambassadors' location near the newly opened St. Pancras Eurostar terminal means that discounts (if not reservations) will become harder to come by.

SETTING AND FACILITIES
Nearest tube station Euston. **Quietness rating** B. **Dining** Breakfast, lunch, and dinner. **Amenities** Restaurant, bar/lounge, free wireless access, conference rooms, safe-deposit box at front desk. **Services** Concierge, 24-hour room service, bellhop, multilingual staff, babysitting.

ACCOMMODATIONS
Rooms 105. **All rooms** Internet access, cable TV, air-conditioning, telephone, voice mail, tea and coffee, wake-up calls, hair dryer. **Some rooms** Work area, more space. **Bed and bath** High standard for a hotel in this price range. **Favorites** Deluxe rooms are more appealing. **Comfort and decor** Modern but not minimalist; very colorful and decorated in a cheerfully stylish manner.

kids Barkston Gardens Hotel ★★½

QUALITY ★★½	VALUE ★★★★	PRICE RANGE £55–£135

34–44 Barkston Gardens, Earls Court, SW5; ☎ 0207-373-7851; fax 0207-370-6570; www.barkstongardens.com

IN AN AREA KNOWN for its backpacker hostels and low-cost B&Bs, this is one of the best places to stay. Yes, some of the rooms are small and the decor is uninspired, but Barkston Gardens is clean, relatively well run, and convenient to transportation and shops—overall, a good value for the money. Rooms for £55 to £65 a night (these are the rates with Internet discount;

rack rates are higher) are few and far between in a city like London, or at least they're hard to find if you have higher standards than a backpacking student. The nine family rooms are a good deal at £95. The redbrick Victorian town house has a charming exterior. The lobby has white marble floors and not a whole lot else, but what it lacks in sumptuousness it makes up for in convenience: the hotel is a 15-minute walk to the museums and Hyde Park; Earls Court High Street, around the corner, has all the shops and pubs you could want (the tube station is yards from the hotel, and Earls Court Arena is a block away). There are two eating venues in the hotel: Brewster's Bar, which serves sandwiches and spirits, and Le Rendez-vous, where you can eat breakfast and dinner. Some of the rates include Continental breakfast; otherwise, it costs a reasonable £6.25 for Continental or £8.50 for full English breakfast. There is no air-conditioning, so bear that in mind if you're booking for summer; heat waves have become less of a rarity these days, even if they last only a week.

SETTING AND FACILITIES

Nearest tube station Earls Court. **Quietness rating** A/B. **Dining** Yes, at Brewster's Bar or Le Rendezvous. **Amenities** Newspapers, Internet access in public area, breakfast and dinner. **Services** Concierge, limited room service.

ACCOMMODATIONS

Rooms 93. **All rooms** Telephone, TV, hair dryer, tea and coffee, trouser press. No air-conditioning. **Some rooms** View of gardens. **Bed and bath** Basic and functional. **Favorites** Family and first-floor rooms. **Comfort and decor** Plain-Jane, though there are some period details in place that give it a more distinguished appearance than similarly priced hotels. For 2 people, make sure you have a queen-size bed or twins—the doubles aren't big enough.

PAYMENT, RESERVATIONS, AND RESTRICTIONS

Deposit Credit card; 24-hour cancellation policy. **Credit cards** All major. **Check-in/out** 2 p.m./11:30 a.m. **Pets** Not allowed. **Elevator** Yes. **Children** Yes. **Disabled access** Limited.

Best Western Paddington Court Hotel ★★½

QUALITY ★★½	VALUE ★★★	PRICE RANGE £95–£120

27 Devonshire Terrace, Paddington, W2; ☎ 0207-745-1200; fax 0207-745-1201; www.paddingtoncourt.com

THE PADDINGTON COURT is part of the Best Western chain (the world's largest), so you can expect the usual: so-so service, acceptable rooms, and reasonable rates. It's a five-minute walk from Paddington Station and next to Hyde Park and Kensington Gardens; the surrounding aesthetic is serene and busy in equal measure. This is essentially a hotel by numbers: the rooms are simple, the beds are fine, the bathrooms are clean—in other words, everything you'd expect from a large chain, with none of the characteristic little nuances that decorate some of the smaller, more expressive hotels in London. Still, it'll do for the price. The more expensive suites, however, have a bit more going for them; you get a kitchenette with all conveniences, plus wooden flooring. There is a nice lounge area, and the morning breakfast is hearty. The bar, open from 6 p.m., could provide that perfect nightcap. At the moment, the hotel offers a deal whereby if you stay five nights, you get the sixth free.

SETTING AND FACILITIES

Nearest tube station Paddington. **Quietness rating** A/B. **Dining** Breakfast and dinner. **Amenities** Restaurant for breakfast, snacks, and evening meal; hospitality tray; cable TV; radio; telephone; modem connection; digital alarm clock; en suite bathroom with bath and/or shower. **Services** Concierge, 24-hour room service.

ACCOMMODATIONS

Rooms 195. **All rooms** Cable TV, radio, telephone, Internet, en suite bathroom. **Some rooms** Studio accommodation with kitchen. **Bed and bath** Adequate. **Favorites** The suites are a lot more enticing than the standard doubles and go for as little as £30 extra in some cases. **Comfort and decor** Decor is standard hotel issue, but nothing is terribly objectionable. Workmanlike might be the best way to describe it, and you'll have no real complaints about the comfort.

PAYMENT, RESERVATIONS, AND RESTRICTIONS

Deposit No deposit, but payment in full upon arrival. **Credit cards** All major. **Check-in/out** 2 p.m./noon. **Pets** No. **Elevator** Yes. **Children** Yes. **Disabled access** Yes.

Brown's Hotel ★★★★

QUALITY ★★★★★	VALUE ★★	PRICE RANGE £360–£725

30–34 Albemarle Street, Mayfair, W1; ☎ 0207-493-6020; fax 0207-493-9381; www.brownshotel.com

THIS FIVE-STAR HOTEL has gained something of a reputation among Americans as *the* English hotel to stay in, and it is indeed a venerable old London institution. Recently purchased by the Rocco Forte hotel group, it was closed for two months in summer 2005 for a major (and admittedly necessary) refurbishment. The period details remain—a carved fireplace, ornate molding, leaded windows in the dining room, and in the Donovan Bar a gorgeous stained-glass window depicting the dragon-slaying St. George. The lounge, the bar, and the lobby have been spruced up, but no major changes in the essential Britishness of the establishment have been made, thank goodness. The rooms are more elegant, with nicer furnishings and better bathrooms than before; there's now a spa offering beauty treatments and a small gym.

Brown's history is distinguished: Alexander Graham Bell made the first telephone call in Britain from here; Rudyard Kipling wrote books, poems, and articles in what is now the Kipling Suite; and Theodore Roosevelt got married while staying here. Lord Byron's valet, James Brown, started the hotel in 1837. He and his wife had learned a thing or two from living in the "mad, bad, and dangerous to know" lordship's household, and the hotel was a success from the start. After the Browns sold it in 1859, the next owner made it the first hotel in London to have an elevator, telephone, and electricity. It grew from a single town house to 11 (the next-door St. George's Hotel was the first purchase), which is why you'll find the configurations of the rooms so completely unpredictable. Brown's is all about service: for 117 rooms, there are 160 staff. The prices are astronomical, but you may be able to wheedle a deal out of the manager.

SETTING AND FACILITIES
Nearest tube station Green Park. **Quietness rating** A. **Dining** The Grill serves breakfast, lunch, and dinner. Try the Drawing Room for tea and the Donovan Bar for cocktails or coffee. **Amenities** Spa and fitness room, afternoon tea, business center. **Services** Concierge, 24-hour room service and valet, laundry, business support.

ACCOMMODATIONS
Rooms 117. **All rooms** Multiline telephone with voice mail, Internet access, minibar, sitting area, writing desk, satellite TV, air-conditioning. **Some rooms** Sitting area with sofa, working fireplace, four-poster bed, French doors. **Bed and bath** Expect heated towel racks, bespoke toiletries, bathrobe, and slippers; queen- or king-size beds with top-of-the-line mattresses and bedclothes. **Favorites** Mayfair and Royal suites. First-floor rooms are the best, with high ceilings and big windows. Avoid the rooms at the top—they are low-ceilinged; some of the junior suites are small for the price. **Comfort and decor** You will find the comfort factor high, although some of the rooms are not as large as one would expect, and some are downright cramped. The decor is English deluxe: leather chairs, deep sofas, and thick rugs, with some fine pieces of furniture, carvings, and art here and there.

PAYMENT, RESERVATIONS, AND RESTRICTIONS
Deposit Credit card; 24-hour cancellation policy. **Credit cards** All major. **Check-in/out** 2 p.m./noon. **Pets** Not allowed. **Elevator** Yes. **Children** Yes. **Disabled access** Limited.

The Cadogan Hotel ★★★½

QUALITY ★★★½	VALUE ★★	PRICE RANGE £340–£465

75 Sloane Street, Knightsbridge, SW1; ☎ 0207-235-7141; fax 0207-245-0994; www.cadogan.com

THIS LONDON INSTITUTION was taken over by the Stein Group, which operates luxury hotels all over the world, and they made a lot of changes to the clubby old country-house decor in the public areas, which was unfortunate. They refurbished the place in a kind of generic deluxe-hotel style that seems at odds with the Victorian bone structure of the old building. Sure, it's nice enough, and if you aren't into faux-historical decor, you'll probably breathe easier, but it is bewildering that one would take a place as historical as this and make it look like a million other hotels: it's like a bad face-lift on a beloved old granny.

The building was constructed in 1887 along with the scores of redbrick private homes in the exclusive development of Cadogan Gardens. It was here, in 1895, that Oscar Wilde was arrested for sodomy amid great publicity and outrage. Actress Lillie Langtry, mistress of the Prince of Wales (later King Edward VII), lived in a house next door that she sold to the hotel, and she kept a bedroom suite here until 1897. These two artists represent a particular time and place in Victorian London that the Cadogan was part of; all Wilde devotees will want to come have a look at this first station of his crucifixion.

Be sure to ask about the rooms on the first floor: they're likely to have bowfront windows, French doors, and an eye-level view of the leafy trees in Cadogan Square (hotel guests are given access to these gardens as well as to the tennis court within). Langtry's Restaurant, in what once was drawing room of the "Jersey Lily," offers an excellent menu of old English dishes made with local produce. The prices are reasonable, as you will see if you walk around and check out the menus of the many restaurants and cafes in the area.

SETTING AND FACILITIES

Nearest tube station Knightsbridge or Sloane Square. **Quietness rating** A in the interior, C on Sloane Street, and B on Pont Street. **Dining** Breakfast, lunch, and dinner in Langtry's; tea in the lounge or bar. **Amenities** Health-club affiliation, access to gardens and tennis. **Services** Concierge, 24-hour room service, bellhop, laundry, touring suggestions and packages.

ACCOMMODATIONS

Rooms 65. **All rooms** Telephone, voice mail, Internet access, satellite TV, air-conditioning, hair dryer, iron, writing desk. **Some rooms** Sitting room, 1 bedroom, 2 bathrooms, or view of gardens. **Bed and bath** High standard of both. **Favorites** The Lillie Langtry room; any of the luxury doubles on first floor. **Comfort and decor** All comfort is catered to, and decor is restful and expensive looking, but we miss the period wallpaper in the hallways. Plus, all rooms are individually decorated and very comfortable.

PAYMENT, RESERVATIONS, AND RESTRICTIONS

Deposit Credit card; 24-hour cancellation policy. **Credit cards** All major. **Check-in/out** Noon/noon. **Pets** Small dogs allowed and given a "designer pet bed." **Elevator** Yes. **Children** Yes. **Disabled access** Yes, but wheelchair access is limited.

Charlotte Street Hotel   ★★★★

QUALITY ★★★★	VALUE ★★★	PRICE RANGE £246–£336

15–17 Charlotte Street, Fitzrovia, W1; ☎ 0207-806-2000; fax 0207-806-2002; www.charlottestreethotel.com

THIS SMALL, LUXURIOUS HOTEL is located in a district known as Fitzrovia. London's epicenter of media activity, the area includes production houses, TV stations, and advertising agencies. It's a busy neighborhood, with plenty of restaurants and bars up and down Charlotte Street. The hotel has been decorated and furnished in a fresh, modern English style, with light wood paneling, wooden floors, soft furnishings, and leather chairs. The large lobby area leads into the Oscar Bar & Restaurant, which serves modern European cuisine; the bar is popular with local media lushes and big shots.

Bedrooms are individually decorated; the traditional British touches, such as floral curtains and floral wallpaper, somehow manage to avoid looking chintzy. The designer, Kit Kemp, who with her husband, Tim, runs Firmdale Hotels, is renowned for her trademark mannequin dummies that stand sentry-style in every room (a quirky, superfluous detail, yet good for draping your jacket on). If it's within your budget, try staying in a loft suite; these rooms have stairs leading to the bedroom area on a mezzanine level and seem to be more like a doll's house than a hotel room. Although more useful for those attending a corporate event or for a local film director, another cool feature is the state-of-the-art screening room, which hosts the Sunday Film Club.

SETTING AND FACILITIES
Nearest tube station Tottenham Court Road or Goodge Street. **Quietness rating** A/C. All windows are double glazed, but street noise in front can be bothersome if you like to sleep with the window open. **Dining** Oscar Restaurant & Bar for breakfast, lunch, dinner, and exotic cocktails. **Amenities** Restaurant, lounge areas, 24-hour gym, 2 meeting rooms, 1 screening room (67-seat minicinema). **Services** Concierge, 24-hour room service, same-day laundry service, bellhop.

ACCOMMODATIONS
Rooms 52. **All rooms** Air-conditioning, en suite bathrooms, 2-line telephone with voice mail, Internet access, satellite TV, VCR/DVD and CD player, mini-TV in bathroom, minibar, safe, movies and music to rent, hair dryer, writing desk; fax machine, mobile phone, laptops available on request. **Some rooms** Walk-in shower and bidet. The more deluxe rooms have bigger beds (super-king-size, which is the U.S. king-size), some four-poster beds. **Bed and bath** Bathrooms are decorated in solid granite and oak, with a shower and tub, plus a mini-TV. Regular rooms have big beds that can be split into twins. **Favorites** Room 108, one of the loft suites, is popular, as are the penthouse suites, which offer good views. **Comfort and decor** The rooms all have a sophisticated yet homey feel and are very comfortable.

PAYMENT, RESERVATIONS, AND RESTRICTIONS
Deposit Credit card; 24-hour cancellation policy. **Credit cards** All major, except DC. **Check-in/out** 1 p.m./11 a.m. **Pets** Not allowed. **Elevator** Yes. **Children** Yes. **Disabled access** Good (includes 2 modified rooms).

kids Collingham Suites and Apartments ★★★½

QUALITY ★★★★	VALUE ★★★½	PRICE RANGE £155–£215

26–27 Collingham Gardens, South Kensington, SW5; ☎ 0207-244-8677; fax 0207-244-7331; www.collinghamapartments.com

HERE'S A CHANCE TO STAY at a serviced apartment in the leafy area west of South Kensington. At first glance the prices seem a tad high, but the savings in dining out make it a good, economical option: instead of dropping

£10 per person for breakfast, buy some eggs or a box of cereal and prepare breakfast in the kitchen. The area is good: you're about a 10-minute walk to Hyde Park and the museums of South Kensington; at Earls Court Underground station, you can catch the Piccadilly, Circle, and District lines to get anywhere quickly. The neighborhood has rows of redbrick early-Victorian-style (from 1830) town houses, many of which have beautiful stained-glass windows in the doors and white columns supporting ornate entryways above which are balconies.

Collingham Apartments comprises two adjoining houses. Of the 25 rooms, there are 10 one-bedrooms and studios, 10 two-bedrooms, 3 three-bedrooms, and 2 penthouses. Bought and upgraded in 1998, when London was on an economic upswing, the new owners spared no expense on the details, and they pretty much covered all the conveniences. The apartments are nicely located across the street from the verdant greenery of Collingham Square, to which, sad to say, you don't have access, but the front rooms afford pleasant views.

The best thing about this establishment is the variety of rooms. It's perfect for a family with small children: you can close a door on them when they go to sleep. The two-bedrooms start at £355, and one unit with two bedrooms and two bathrooms costs £425, which sounds steep, but you could share the expense with one or two (very close) friends. The first-floor rooms have cute little balconies and French doors, and the penthouses are stunning, with a terrace overlooking the gardens behind each house. The elevator is a crucial and excellent feature, tiny as it is. You'll be glad of it when you're struggling home from the nearby Sainsbury's or Waitrose supermarkets with bags of food to cook. Be very careful with your booking—you can get a full refund only if you cancel more than 28 days before arrival date.

SETTING AND FACILITIES

Nearest tube station Earls Court or Gloucester Road. **Quietness rating** A in rear, B in front. **Dining** Self-service in kitchen or order takeout. **Amenities** Bathrobes, hair dryer, stove, refrigerator, kitchen utensils, toiletries. **Services** Concierge, 24-hour reception and security porter, babysitting, bellhop, laundry facilities on-site plus dry cleaning sent out, food delivery from local restaurants.

ACCOMMODATIONS

Rooms 25. **All rooms** Telephone with voice mail, high-speed Internet modem, satellite TV, modern full kitchen, air-conditioning, DVD player and DVD library, CD player, hair dryer, safe, bathrobes. **Some rooms** Balcony and terrace, 3 bedrooms. **Bed and bath** Well-appointed bathrooms with jetted tubs, showers, and heated towel racks; big, comfortable beds with good cotton sheets. **Favorites** Penthouses and front first-floor apartments. **Comfort and decor** Furnished to a high standard, with all considerations of comfort looked after. The decor is neutral but pleasing.

PAYMENT, RESERVATIONS, AND RESTRICTIONS

Deposit Credit card; 28-day full-refund cancellation policy, 7-day partial refund. **Credit cards** All major. **Check-in/out** 2 p.m./noon. **Pets** Not allowed. **Elevator** Yes. **Children** Yes. **Disabled access** 6 steps into buildings.

kids The Colonnade ★★★★

| QUALITY ★★★★ | VALUE ★★★★ | PRICE RANGE £135–£235 |

2 Warrington Crescent, Little Venice (Maida Vale), W9; ☎ 0207-286-1052; fax 0207-286-1057; www.theetoncollection.com

IF YOUR MAIN CONCERN is comfort and quiet, this elegant hotel in Maida Vale may be for you. It's one of three boutique hotels that the Eton Collection recently opened in London, and it shares the same dedication to pleasing surroundings and luxurious extras that those hotels are all about. The location may appear too far northwest of central London for your touring plans, but it is an excellent introduction to the quiet joys of walking along Grand Union Canal and looking into the colorful houseboats moored there. It's this once-busy canal that gave the area the nickname of Little Venice. You can walk to the waterbus dock and take a pretty canal trip to Regent's Park and the London Zoo, both of which will thrill the youngsters. Children under age 16 stay free, and the patio with tables outside is a safe place for them to burn off some energy without endangering the antiques. A few adjoining rooms or suites will do nicely for a family room.

The hotel is made up of two imposing Victorian mansions built in 1865. There are suites named for John F. Kennedy and Sigmund Freud, who each stayed here briefly in 1962 and 1938, respectively (the bed built for President Kennedy's state visit is still here). It's a great hotel for those who prefer relatively fresh air and the Victorian vibe that the hotel has re-created so convincingly. The centerpiece is the museum-quality late-19th-century Wedgwood fireplace, from which the decor has wisely taken its cue. Thanks to The Colonnade's location on the outskirts, the prices here are reasonable for the luxury within, but you should still check into any promotions or Web site deals to whittle down the cost further—budget it's definitely not. If you're making your first trip to London, you may want to stay someplace a little more central—and to be honest there are some unattractive areas nearby—but if you've already experienced trying to sleep with the noise of London's traffic outside your window, definitely check out this little jewel.

SETTING AND FACILITIES
Nearest tube station Maida Vale. **Quietness rating** A. **Dining** The E Bar serves authentic Spanish tapas for lunch and dinner and all-day snacks; nice breakfast room. **Amenities** Newspapers, bathrobes, breakfast included with some rates, bar. **Services** Concierge, 24-hour room service, bellhop, laundry, in-room spa treatments.

ACCOMMODATIONS
Rooms 43. **All rooms** Telephone, satellite TV, hair dryer, bathrobe, wireless broadband, air-conditioning, minibar. **Some rooms** Bowfront windows or French doors. **Bed and bath** Comfortable beds dressed in Frette linens, down pillows, and duvets; interesting and pleasing furnishings. Bathrooms are either showers-only or full baths with showers in tubs; designer toiletries and heated towel rack. **Favorites** First-floor rooms. **Comfort and decor** Luxuriously comfortable in the traditional Victorian style; rich, dark fabrics for curtains and bed covers, comfortable chairs, and fine antique pieces and other period details.

PAYMENT, RESERVATIONS, AND RESTRICTIONS
Deposit Credit card; 24-hour cancellation policy. **Credit cards** All major. **Check-in/out** 2 p.m./11 a.m. **Pets** Not allowed. **Elevator** Yes. **Children** Yes (those under age 16 stay free). **Disabled access** Steps to entrance and steps from elevator on 3rd floor to 4th floor.

kids Columbia Hotel ★★★½

QUALITY ★★★	VALUE ★★★★★	PRICE RANGE £79–£146

95–99 Lancaster Gate, Bayswater, W2; ☎ **0207-402-0021;** **fax 0207-706-4691; www.columbiahotel.co.uk**

THIS IS ONE OF THE BETTER DEALS in the area—and amazingly, the Columbia hasn't raised its prices one pound since the last edition of this book. There may be cheaper rooms to be had, but not with the amenities and friendliness of this hotel—breakfast is included, and they run special discounts even in summer that take about £15 off the rack rate. Created from five huge Victorian mansions, the hotel fronts busy Bayswater Road in an area that was the height of gentility for merchants and professionals in its heyday; the abundance of space and the nearness of Hyde Park were custom-made for their typically large families and armies of servants. Those days are gone, as the roar of the traffic below reminds you constantly, but the riotous thoroughfare does afford easy access to public transportation (and we don't need to tell you how great Hyde Park is for a family with young kids).

The rooms are done in standard hotel style, but they're clean and some are fairly roomy, with period details such as bay windows and fireplaces. Because of the layout of the original buildings, there is great disparity among the sizes and shapes of the rooms. Unfortunately, the first floor, with its elegant high ceilings and huge windows, is taken up by conference rooms, but there are many park-view rooms on the remaining floors. The only problem with having the beautiful park view is the attendant traffic noise, which includes hundreds of buses a day. This is a well-priced hotel that nicely accommodates families, pets, and even automobiles (parking on a first-come, first-serve basis). Rooms with three beds go for £112, but we suggest spending the extra money a night for what is still a good deal to get a larger and possibly more interesting room (a four-bed is £129; a four-bed plus rollaway is £146). Queensway, a few minutes' walk away, has lots of great restaurants (not to mention a skating rink and bowling alley). The staff is friendly and helpful.

SETTING AND FACILITIES
Nearest tube station Lancaster Gate. **Quietness rating** C– in front, A in back. **Dining** Breakfast included. **Amenities** Newspapers, lounge, maps, family rooms, crib rental, bar. **Services** 24-hour reception desk, laundry, overnight luggage storage.

ACCOMMODATIONS .
Rooms 100. **All rooms** Shower and toilet, telephone, BBC TV, hair dryer. **Some rooms** View over park, connecting rooms, 4 beds in 1 room. **Bed and bath**

Clean and satisfactory; mostly showers. **Favorites** Big rooms. **Comfort and decor** Very plain and simple.

PAYMENT, RESERVATIONS, AND RESTRICTIONS
Deposit Credit card; 24-hour cancellation policy. **Credit cards** All major except DC. **Check-in/out** 2 p.m./11:30 a.m. **Pets** Allowed. **Elevator** Yes, 2. **Children** Yes. **Disabled access** 1 disabled room and a room for deaf or hearing-impaired guests.

 **Covent Garden Hotel** ★★★★

QUALITY ★★★★½   VALUE ★★★   PRICE RANGE £264–£376

10 Monmouth Street, Covent Garden, WC2; ☎ 0207-806-1000; fax 0207-806-1100; www.firmdale.com

HERE'S ANOTHER FINE PROPERTY owned by Firmdale Hotels, which also owns the Charlotte Street, Haymarket, Number Sixteen, Pelham, and Soho hotels (see respective reviews). The Covent Garden is more spacious than the other five and offers more square footage, both in the size of the beds and the size of the rooms and hallways. It's such a great collection of hotels, we just wish they didn't charge so much—a fact that lowers their value rating—but it's true that you get what you pay for. Look for summer and weekend promotion packages, which shave a bit off the overhead. Amenities offered include wireless access, laptop rental, cell phones, and in-room entertainment centers (DVD, VCR, CD). A fitness area has treatment rooms for massage and beauty services. Brasserie Max has become a favorite London hangout for the young and famous, and why not: fine food, attractive surroundings, exotic cocktails, and a good-looking staff and clientele are a fantastic combo, especially if you're seated by a window for optimal people-watching. The Covent Garden has two screening rooms, letting you enjoy first-run films in comfort and style. But the outstanding thing about this hotel is the decor. It's just a place where all the taste and talents of the designer come together effortlessly and pleasingly. The location is superb: Monmouth Street, on which the hotel is situated, is a relatively quiet street in Seven Dials but lies within skipping distance of Soho, Covent Garden, Bloomsbury, and the theaters of the West End.

SETTING AND FACILITIES
Nearest tube station Covent Garden. **Quietness rating** B normally, C– on weekend nights (all rooms are double-glazed and air-conditioned). **Dining** Brasserie Max is a modern dining room with good food. **Amenities** 2 drawing rooms, 1 very large, with working fireplaces; restaurant; honor bar with snacks; personal safe; cell phone for rent; workout room; 2 screening rooms. **Services** Concierge, 24-hour room service, valet, bellhop, laundry.

ACCOMMODATIONS
Rooms 50. **All rooms** U.S.-size queen/king bed (even in singles), air-conditioning, telephone with extra line and voice mail, wireless access or high-speed modem,

satellite TV, DVD/VCR and movies to watch, CD player and music discs to borrow, writing desk, bathtub, umbrella. **Some rooms** Ornamental fireplace, four-poster bed, sofa and sitting area, roof terrace. **Bed and bath** Bathrooms are splendid, all gray marble and perfection. The beds are huge, outfitted in all-cotton sheets and covered with the most beautiful duvets and pillows. **Favorites** Number 304 is a deluxe double with a blue theme, a gorgeous four-poster bed, and an ornamental fireplace with 2 big chairs in front of it. The terrace suite is preferred by the many movie stars who stay here; it has its own little terrace, a library, a sofa, and a sweetly appointed queen-size bed. **Comfort and decor** Comfort is of a very high standard, to a degree you probably don't have at home. The decor is sublime—Tim and Kit Kemp are geniuses at interior decoration, neatly blending traditional antiques with their own brand of quirky taste.

PAYMENT, RESERVATIONS, AND RESTRICTIONS

Deposit Credit card; 24-hour cancellation policy. **Credit cards** All major. **Check-in/out** 1 p.m./11 a.m. **Pets** Not allowed. **Elevator** Yes, 2. **Children** Yes. **Disabled access** Yes; big elevators and wide hallways.

 The Draycott Hotel   ★★★★

QUALITY ★★★★★	VALUE ★★★	PRICE RANGE £250–£346

26 Cadogan Gardens, Knightsbridge/Chelsea, SW3; ☎ 0207-730-6466; fax 0207-730-0236; www.draycotthotel.com

BUILT IN THE 1890S, The Draycott is a wonderfully grand Victorian mansion that isn't pretentious or stiff—it feels like a really beautiful home. The prevailing decor is of the Edwardian period, and compared with the usual Victorian-era style, it is simple elegance itself. The prevailing theme of the hotel was conceived back when it was the Cliveden Townhouse, owned and run by the Cliveden Hotel outside of London. The rooms are named after theatrical legends—Laurence Olivier, Edmund Kean, Edith Evans, George and Ira Gershwin, the Redgraves, Noël Coward, James Barrie, and so on. Each room is decorated with corresponding memorabilia, whose sepia tones nicely complement the wood paneling and leaded windows. The lovely drawing room has a welcoming, comfortable atmosphere and opens onto a nice-sized garden where you can relax with a book in good weather. A self-service tea is set out each day at 4 p.m., and a complimentary bottle of Champagne is uncorked at 6 p.m. The Draycott is a short walk from Sloane Square and Knightsbridge, but you'd swear you're in the country when you're in a room with a bay window overlooking the garden. The only downside is that you may never want to leave.

SETTING AND FACILITIES

Nearest tube station Knightsbridge or Sloane Square. **Quietness rating** A. **Dining** Dinner on request, but there is no public dining room. Breakfast room is gorgeous and bright. **Amenities** Private dining room, drawing room, smoking room, afternoon tea, Champagne at 6 p.m., honor bar, breakfast room, garden, public computer and wireless Internet access. **Services** Concierge, complimentary chauffeur service into the city each weekday, 24-hour room service, laundry, babysitting.

ACCOMMODATIONS
Rooms 35. **All rooms** Telephone, voice mail, fax and modem line, wireless connection, air-conditioning, satellite TV, DVD/VCR, stereo CD. **Some rooms** Garden view, fireplace. **Bed and bath** Excellent quality; bathrooms are superior, as would be expected, and have some Edwardian period details, including some very big tubs. **Favorites** Any of the deluxe junior suites overlooking gardens; the deluxe doubles are very nice. **Comfort and decor** Highest standard of comfort; the decor is delightful—sumptuous but not overbearing.

PAYMENT, RESERVATIONS, AND RESTRICTIONS
Deposit Credit card; cancellation policy of 24 hours. **Credit cards** All major. **Check-in/out** 2 p.m./11 a.m. **Pets** Dogs allowed on ground-floor rooms. **Elevator** Yes, 2. **Children** Yes. **Disabled access** No, too many stairs.

Dukes Hotel ★★★★★

QUALITY ★★★★★	VALUE ★★★	PRICE RANGE £300–£410

35 St. James's Place, St. James's, SW1; ☎ 0207-491-4840; toll free from U.S., 800-381-4702; fax 0207-493-1264; www.dukeshotel.co.uk

BEHIND A CHARMING COURTYARD in one of the most appealing areas of central London is the deluxe Dukes Hotel. The neighborhood has been one of grandeur, populated by courtiers and aristocrats jousting to be near the power of St. James's Palace in the 18th century, and it continued its association with royalty when Buckingham House became another royal residence.

You know you're in for a treat when you approach the hotel by night: authentic gas lamps light your way in. Inside, you'll find a sumptuous hotel that promises the highest standards in service and accommodation; Dukes has won numerous awards, even boasting a Zagat Best Martini citation. It's terribly expensive, of course, catering to the kind of clientele who like amenities such as 100-year-old Cognac and an elliptical cross-trainer in the gym. It's an intimate, clubby kind of place, which is why we've included it in the main review section rather than with its high-priced brethren earlier in the chapter. Although Dukes hardly needed it, it's been renovated and re-equipped over the past few years, dropping the smaller single rooms in favor of a double-size for a single guest; installing wireless Internet access throughout the hotel; updating the fitness room; and refining the climate control and noise filters that one takes for granted in a luxury hotel. The location is fantastic: besides all the bespoke shops and handy restaurants around the corner on Piccadilly, you also are within minutes of St. James's and Green parks, which is rather like having two magnificent backyard gardens. You couldn't ask for a more central yet quiet spot in which to enjoy London.

SETTING AND FACILITIES
Nearest tube station Green Park. **Quietness rating** A. **Dining** Private dining room can be booked. **Amenities** Bar with exceptional Cognacs and wines; health

club with massage and personal trainer available. **Services** Concierge, butler, valet, secretarial services, 24-hour room service.

ACCOMMODATIONS
Rooms 89. **All rooms** Telephone, satellite TV, air-conditioning, private bar, writing desks. **Some rooms** Oversize (7-foot-square) "Emperor" beds; sitting rooms; views of Big Ben, Westminster Abbey, parks, and Parliament; exceptional amount of space (the penthouse is 700 square feet). **Bed and bath** Magnificent marble bathrooms with bathrobes and beds that you'd be proud to call your own. **Favorites** The penthouses are more like flats, huge and unimaginably luxurious, but even the standard doubles, averaging 190 square feet, are very big by any hotel standard, much less hotels in London. You can't go wrong in any of the rooms here. **Comfort and decor** Highest standards of comfort and pleasing decor—not overdone, just serene and elegant.

PAYMENT, RESERVATIONS, AND RESTRICTIONS
Deposit Credit card. **Credit cards** All major. **Check-in/out** 2 p.m./noon. **Pets** Not allowed. **Elevator** Yes. **Children** No children under age 5. **Disabled access** Limited.

Durrants   ★★★½

QUALITY ★★★½	VALUE ★★★½	PRICE RANGE £195–£340

George Street, Marylebone, W1; ☎ 0207-935-8131; fax 0207-487-3510; www.durrantshotel.co.uk

A HOTEL THAT HAS BEEN RUN by the same family since 1921, Durrants has a lot going for it, not the least of which its proximity to the Wallace Collection, Oxford Street, Marylebone High Street, and Regent's Park. The building dates from 1790, and the decor is resolutely Regency, with authentic prints gracing the walls and plenty of dark-wood paneling that evokes the past nicely without overdoing it or being too faux. The rooms are a wee bit bigger than those in comparably priced hotels, and they're also a lot nicer than most, furnished with some genuine antique pieces as well as standard-issue wallpaper and fabrics. If your room is too small, ask for an upgrade or a change. The atmosphere in the public part of the hotel is that of a leather-chaired gentlemen's club, with oil paintings and gas fires. There's a tiny bar called the Pump Room, from which women were once banned, apparently giving the proprietor license to hang paintings of nudes on the walls. Breakfast (an expensive one) is served by waiters in a very charming breakfast room, and the restaurant on the other side of the lobby is of good quality. The hotel faces the back of the Wallace Collection, which you can explore for free as many times as you want.

SETTING AND FACILITIES
Nearest tube station Baker Street or Bond Street. **Quietness rating** A. **Dining** The restaurant has intimate booths and decent British food besides. **Amenities** Air-conditioning in public area, on request when booking; Pump Room, lounges with fireplaces, bar downstairs. **Services** Concierge, 24-hour room service, bellhop, laundry, airport transfer, babysitting.

ACCOMMODATIONS

Rooms 92. **All rooms** Telephone, Internet access, satellite TV, hair dryer, iron, writing desks. **Some rooms** Air-conditioning, separate sitting rooms, minibars. **Bed and bath** All remodeled and upgraded in the past 2 years; beds are comfortable, and bathrooms are attractive and relatively spacious. **Favorites** Suite number 305 is a 2-room pleasure: the sitting room has lots of conversation areas and is beautifully decorated with old portraits. **Comfort and decor** Except for the lack of air-conditioning in some rooms (this amenity is spreading slowly), it's a fine hotel. There's an effortlessness that is very appealing, and the comfort is part of this.

PAYMENT, RESERVATIONS, AND RESTRICTIONS

Deposit Credit card; must cancel by noon on the day before arrival hour. **Credit cards** All major except DC. **Check-in/out** 2 p.m./noon. **Pets** Not allowed. **Elevator** Yes, 2. **Children** Yes; babysitting and cribs can be arranged. **Disabled access** Ground-floor accessible rooms, but discuss when booking; call ahead.

Fielding Hotel ★½

QUALITY ★★	VALUE ★★½	PRICE RANGE £105–£125

4 Broad Court at Bow Street, Covent Garden, WC2; ☎ 0207-836-8305; fax 0207-497-0064; www.the-fielding-hotel.co.uk

THE FIELDING IS LIKE a college dormitory, completely utilitarian and inoffensive, though it does manage a small amount of charm. Certainly the exterior is attractive, with its ivy-covered leaded windows, and you are free from traffic noise and fumes. It sits prettily on a pedestrian court with 19th-century lamps in the shadow of the Royal Opera House. The setting is unique and pleasant; you may hear glorious voices practicing arias day or night. It's all inexpensive pine furnishings and hard beds inside, but you don't have to share bathrooms, even at the cheapest rate, and everything is as clean and simple as you could ask for at the price (warning: no elevator). The proprietors and staff are friendly and helpful. They used to offer a good cheap breakfast but decided to withdraw that option, as there are so very many cafes in every direction. This change has worked out fine for them—there's a lot less stress, as the hotel tends to be booked solid. The superior double rooms in front are a bit nicer than the rest and are worth the extra dough. The Fielding is around the corner from Covent Garden and is within a healthy walking distance of The City, the British Museum, the Thames, and Piccadilly. It's a fabulous location at a very low price. No air-conditioning, but you'll find fans in each room. There is no lift for the three floors.

SETTING AND FACILITIES

Nearest tube station Covent Garden. **Quietness rating** A/B. **Dining** No. **Amenities** Lounge, honor bar. **Services** Helpful reception desk.

ACCOMMODATIONS

Rooms 24. **All rooms** Telephone, 5-channel TV, toilet. **Some rooms** Sitting area, writing desk. **Bed and bath** Hard beds, clean bathrooms with showers only. **Favorites** Superior doubles in the front of the building have the most space and light. **Comfort and decor** Somewhere between utilitarian and spartan.

Deposit One night's rate; 72-hour cancellation policy. **Credit cards** All major.
Check-in/out Noon/11 a.m. **Pets** Not allowed. **Elevator** No. **Children** No
children under age 13. **Disabled access** No (3 floors).

The Gainsborough ★★★

QUALITY ★★★	VALUE ★★★★	PRICE RANGE £144–£188

7–11 Queensberry Place, South Kensington, SW7; ☎ 0207-838-1700;
toll free from U.S., 800-270-9206; fax 0207-970-1805; www.eeh.co.uk

IF YOU LOOK ON THE WEB SITE, you will *always* find some kind of promotional discounts available that will lop off a third or more of the rack rates,
both here and at The Gainsborough's sister hotel across the street, The
Gallery. The Gainsborough is clearly the younger, less sophisticated sister of
the two, in that there are no large sitting rooms, conference rooms, or fanci-
fully dressed lounges, but it is still serviceable and well decorated. The smallish
rooms are comfortable and tasteful; the staff is helpful and friendly. Walk
out of the hotel and you'll see the magnificent Alfred Waterhouse–designed
Natural History Museum—one of three museums practically on your doorstep
(the Victoria and Albert and the Science museums are the other two). The bus
that goes past can present a noise problem for those in the front rooms.

SETTING AND FACILITIES
Nearest tube station South Kensington. **Quietness rating** B in back, C– in front
and on lower floors (the number 74 bus goes past the hotel). **Dining** Breakfast;
24-hour room service. **Amenities** Breakfast room and bar, wired and wireless
broadband, fax in lobby, discount at fitness club nearby. **Services** Concierge,
room service, laundry, breakfast, bellhop.

ACCOMMODATIONS
Rooms 49. **All rooms** Telephone, wireless Internet, satellite TV, tea and coffee,
safe, hair dryer, iron. **Some rooms** French windows, balcony, bigger TVs, air-
conditioning. **Bed and bath** Beds are firm and comfortable. Singles all have
showers only; doubles have shower-tub combinations; suites have spa baths.
Nicely decorated bathrooms. **Favorites** Number 112 has a balcony and French
windows and seems a little bigger than the others. **Comfort and decor** Rooms
are small, but everything is clean and nicely presented. The decor, individual in
each room, is subdued but homey.

PAYMENT, RESERVATIONS, AND RESTRICTIONS
Deposit Credit card; 24-hour cancellation policy. **Credit cards** All major. **Check-
in/out** 1 p.m./noon. **Pets** Not allowed. **Elevator** Yes. **Children** Yes. **Disabled
access** Call ahead to discuss.

The Gallery Hotel ★★★

QUALITY ★★★½	VALUE ★★★½	PRICE RANGE £144–£225

8–10 Queensberry Place, South Kensington, SW7; ☎ 0207-838-1700;
toll free from U.S., 800-270-9206; fax 0207-970-1805; www.eeh.co.uk

THIS IS THE PREVIOUSLY MENTIONED sister of The Gainsborough, and you must forgive us for repeating ourselves by telling you that this is another good hotel in the heart of South Kensington, with the imposing Natural History Museum at the end of the street, the tube a two-minute walk away, and Kensington Gardens and Hyde Park a five-minute walk away. The rooms are not big, except for the fabulous suite (at £325), which has a private garden terrace. An attractive breakfast room (breakfast is included in some rates) serves a well-stocked buffet. Upstairs you'll find a pleasant sitting room with a bar and a chessboard. Recently refurbished, the decor is attractive. Check the Web site for deals that can as much as halve the rack rates, or ask for an upgrade to a suite. The more expensive doubles and singles have air-conditioning. The bus that goes past can present a noise problem for those in the front rooms.

SETTING AND FACILITIES
Nearest tube station South Kensington. **Quietness rating** A in back, C– in front and on lower floors (the number 74 bus goes past the hotel). **Dining** Breakfast room; 24-hour room service. **Amenities** Telephone with modem, wireless Internet (charges apply), minibar, satellite TV, iron, tea and coffee, safe, writing desk, fitness club nearby, music in bar on occasion, fax in lobby. **Services** Concierge, 24-hour room service.

ACCOMMODATIONS
Rooms 36. **All rooms** Telephone, wireless Internet access, satellite TV, hair dryer, safe. **Some rooms** Air-conditioning, fax, couches, spa bathtubs. **Bed and bath** Excellent on both counts. Baths in doubles and suites, shower stalls in singles. **Favorites** Number 502 is a penthouse suite with a huge bed, a private garden terrace, a dining table, 2 couches, 3 phone lines, broadband and wireless Internet access. **Comfort and decor** Care has been taken to ensure all comforts, and the decor is individual and restful—a bit plain but clean and pleasing to the eye.

PAYMENT, RESERVATIONS, AND RESTRICTIONS
Deposit Credit card; 24-hour cancellation policy. **Credit cards** All major. **Check-in/out** 1 p.m./noon. **Pets** Not allowed. **Elevator** Yes. **Children** Yes. **Disabled access** No.

The Gore ★★★★

QUALITY ★★★★½	VALUE ★★★	PRICE RANGE £275–£350

189 Queen's Gate, South Kensington/Kensington, SW7;
☎ **0207-584-6601; fax 0207-589-8127; www.gorehotel.com**

THERE'S A NEW WIND BLOWING at The Gore, and it's not just the air-conditioning that's been installed in all the rooms. It's been bought by first-time hotel owners who are dedicated to keeping all its best parts and adding some new touches and improvements of their own, such as the all-day snacks and the espresso machine in the drawing room, plus a number of themed packages that tie in with what's happening in London. The origi-nators of The Gore were two antiques dealers who started their hotel careers at the wonderful Hazlitt's in Soho (see page 109). Their philosophy was to create hotels they would like to live in, decorated with authenticity and flair, and they hung 4,500 prints and paintings and artfully displayed a serious collection of antiques. The new owners know better than to mess around with the unique visual feast, and they've dedicated themselves to upgrading the service and amenities.

The most amazing room in the hotel is the Tudor Room, which could be part of a National Trust property, and its 16th-century bed could easily find a home in a museum. Even the single rooms are extraordinary, with beds and furnishings from the 19th century. The bathrooms are good, with attention paid to details. The restaurant, Bistro One Ninety Queen's Gate, is fairly priced and very pretty, serving breakfast, lunch, and dinner, and the bar off the reception is a candlelit lounge that feels like a traditional men's club, with wood paneling and leather couches. The Gore's location is good for lovers of Hyde Park and is also walking distance from South Kensington, the Albert Hall, and Kensington High Street.

SETTING AND FACILITIES

Nearest tube station Gloucester Road. **Quietness rating** A in back and top floors, B in lower front floors. **Dining** Bistro One Ninety Queen's Gate for all meals. **Amenities** Use of 2 nearby fitness centers. **Services** Concierge, 24-hour room service, wireless Internet access, bellhop, laundry.

ACCOMMODATIONS

Rooms 48. **All rooms** Telephone with voice mail, high-speed broadband access, satellite TV, air-conditioning, minibar, antiques and art, genuine Victorian beds, fans, writing desks. **Some rooms** Stained-glass windows, French doors and balcony, sitting area, fireplace. **Bed and bath** The beds have been upgraded recently to accommodate people used to modern king-size hotel beds. Try the twin-bedded rooms if a double might be too small for you and your partner. The bathrooms are amazing: many of them have the old-fashioned wooden loo chair above an antique Thomas Crapper porcelain toilet—a genuine "throne." Showerheads are big; tubs are deep. **Favorites** The Tudor Room is astonishing: a Victorian re-creation of an Elizabethan gallery, complete with huge stone fireplace (with gas flames) and stained-glass images of Elizabeth I herself. Carved lintels of heads and gargoyles are not for the faint of heart. The Miss Ada Room (number 207) has a lovely Victorian theme, with dark mahogany and a very good double bed with a bust of Queen Victoria at the foot of it. In the Venus Room, also known as the Judy Garland Room, you can sleep in an antique rococo bed once owned by the singer-actress. **Comfort and decor** There is a sense of easy comfort throughout the hotel, and the decor is endlessly fascinating, although a minimalist would run screaming from The Gore's portals.

PAYMENT, RESERVATIONS, AND RESTRICTIONS

Deposit Credit card; 48-hour cancellation policy. **Credit cards** All major. **Check-in/out** 1 p.m./11:30 a.m. **Pets** Not allowed; exceptions made for guide dogs and perhaps well-behaved lapdogs. **Elevator** Yes. **Children** Yes. **Disabled access** No.

Goring Hotel ★★★★★

| QUALITY ★★★★ | VALUE ★★★ | PRICE RANGE £311–£334 |

Beeston Place, Victoria, SW1; ☎ 0207-396-9000; fax 0207-834-4393; www.goringhotel.co.uk

EXUDING PURE ELEGANCE AND COMFORT, the Goring is a gracious and lovely hotel a few steps from Victoria Station and within easy reach of the wonders of Westminster Abbey and Buckingham Palace. It has the great benefit of being on a tiny street where any traffic tends to be specifically for the hotel; in the back is a lawn that's a real oasis of peace, even though you can only look at it. The hotel is justifiably proud of having remained in the same family since 1911, and it does indeed call to mind a fine country club of the early 1900s. It doesn't have any Victorian frippery, just a cool Edwardian elegance and comfort, from the bright yellow and marble of the beautiful lobby to the lounge tables that look as if they've seen quite a few bridge games in their day. There's a finely carved fireplace and a wall of windows through which you can view the garden, and drinks and light food are served in the drawing room all day. The dining room is of very high quality, serving English food that has won the applause of some of London's toughest food critics. The Goring plays to a lot of repeat customers—generations of them—and it's easy to see why. Special rates are available on weekends, which is the only time we who are without a luxury-hotel budget can afford to stay.

SETTING AND FACILITIES

Nearest tube station Victoria. **Quietness rating** A (double-glazed windows). **Dining** Beautiful dining room, plus garden bar and drawing room for teas and light meals. **Amenities** A very attractive and capacious drawing room and bar, a splendid expanse of lawn out back to admire, wireless Internet access, complimentary membership at nearby health club. **Services** Concierge, 24-hour room service, bellhop, laundry.

ACCOMMODATIONS

Rooms 75. **All rooms** Individual temperature controls (including air-conditioning), telephone, high-speed modem, satellite TV, hair dryer, writing desk. **Some rooms** Balcony overlooking garden, fax. **Bed and bath** Beautiful wood-and-marble bathrooms and good-sized beds in all the rooms. **Favorites** A few rooms have balconies that overlook the garden. These are fantastic and quite a rarity in London (or in any big city, for that matter). **Comfort and decor** The decor is extremely well done, suggesting a quite pleasing elegance and cheerfulness. All the common areas and the individual rooms are bright and warmly welcoming.

PAYMENT, RESERVATIONS, AND RESTRICTIONS

Deposit Credit card. **Credit cards** All major. **Check-in/out** Noon. **Pets** Dogs and birds not allowed (since 1911, when, judging from the posted restriction, apparently many people traveled with birds in hand). **Elevator** Yes. **Children** Yes. **Disabled access** Yes.

Grange White Hall Hotel   ★★★½

QUALITY ★★★½	VALUE ★★★	PRICE RANGE £150–£235

2–5 Montague Street, Bloomsbury, WC1; ☎ 0207-233-7888; fax 0207-630-9897; www.grangehotels.com

THIS PLEASANT, WELL-APPOINTED HOTEL is literally in the shadow of the British Museum (which just doesn't look quite as magnificent from the back—the red bricks are less impressive than the front's stone sheath). The large, exquisite garden has a glassed-in, air-conditioned conservatory that can be used for afternoon teas or private functions. The rooms are as small as most London hotel rooms, but if you require space, ask for the lower-ground (basement) rooms—some have more space for the same price as an upstairs room. The ambience is pleasing, and although the furniture is reproduction, the decor still has a certain flair and cleanliness. There are some really lovely touches, such as the elaborate molding in every room that has been painstakingly painted, the glass-and-brass elevator, and the sumptuous curtains. The Grange White Hall offers a number of brilliant money-saving schemes—one of which is to book through the hotel's Web site, though you can also call and negotiate a deal. Weekend stays cost less than weekday ones, and discounts are available depending upon the length of your stay.

SETTING AND FACILITIES

Nearest tube station Russell Square. **Quietness rating** A on garden in back, B+ in front (double glazing helps). **Dining** Breakfast, lunch, and dinner in the gorgeous English Garden Restaurant; the Museum Wine Bar is attached to the hotel but has a separate entrance. **Amenities** Buffet breakfast, conservatory and garden, smoking and nonsmoking rooms, daily newspaper. **Services** Concierge, 24-hour room service, bellhop, laundry, fitness center a 2-minute walk away, business facilities.

ACCOMMODATIONS

Rooms 60. **All rooms** Telephone, high-speed modem, satellite TV, in-house movies, minibar, iron, tea and coffee, hair dryer, writing desk, computer modem. **Some rooms** Four-poster bed, balcony, garden view, French doors, sofa bed. **Bed and bath** Bathrooms are in perfect condition; most beds are OK, the four-posters wonderful. **Favorites** Numbers 109 and 106 each have a balcony that looks out onto the garden; all the rooms on the 1st floor have high ceilings and French doors. **Comfort and decor** Decor is handsome. Care has clearly been taken to make this hotel visually gratifying, although it lacks a certain authenticity (not a lot of real antiques). It is comfortable enough, even though rooms are of the usual smallish variety.

PAYMENT, RESERVATIONS, AND RESTRICTIONS

Deposit Credit card; 24-hour cancellation policy. **Credit cards** All major. **Check-in/out** 2 p.m./11 a.m. **Pets** Not allowed. **Elevator** Yes. **Children** Yes. **Disabled access** Limited.

Great Eastern Hotel   ★★★★

QUALITY ★★★★   VALUE ★★½   PRICE RANGE £385–£565

Liverpool Street, by The City and East End, EC2; ☎ 0207-618-5000; fax 0207-618-5000; london.greateastern.hyatt.com

IN 2006 THE HYATT HOTEL GROUP bought the Great Eastern, and not only have the prices come down a bit, but more discounted deals are on offer. It's one of the best full-service hotels in the Square Mile, as the financial center of the city is known. It's a great boon to business travelers as well as those who want to stay farther east than is common for the sightseeing visitor. Liverpool Street, a major transportation hub of London, is adjacent to the hotel, and while the neighborhood is not quite as appealing as many others in London, there is the ever-increasing trendiness of Hoxton Square and Spitalfields, once the center of French Huguenot weavers.

The Great Eastern was one of the grand old Victorian terminus hotels, built in 1884 and expanded in 1901. A massive renovation, taking three years and millions of pounds, brought this old warhorse into the 21st century with modern aplomb. The rooms are spare and minimalist, all sharp angles and fluffy pillows, attractive and functional, with Eames chairs at the desks and bright colors accenting earth tones. Great care was taken to preserve some of the fine Victorian-period elements, the best being the stained-glass dome in the restaurant Aurora, and much of the oak paneling and moldings. The hotel has everything a traveler could want, including a special jet-lag treatment and massage any time of day or night. Attracting as they do a large number of well-traveled corporate types and big-name performers at the nearby Barbican Centre, the management knows just what kind of sharp service is essential to their success, and they deliver: efficient room service, 24-hour business center, high-speed Internet access in every room, a top-shelf fitness room, and fine dining. All appetites are catered to: there's Miyabi for Japanese, the Fishmarket for guess-what, George for Olde England pub-style food, Aurora for fancy European dining under the glorious stained-glass dome, and Terminus for unfussy brasserie food with artful desserts and a large menu. Weekend and special promotions are available, with rooms going for as little as £117.50 a night.

SETTING AND FACILITIES

Nearest tube station Liverpool Street or Bishopgate. **Quietness rating** B/C. **Dining** 5 restaurants, all pretty pricey but of good quality. **Amenities** Bars and lounges, newspapers, business center, health club with treatment facilities. **Services** Concierge, room service, same-day laundry, body treatments, mobile-phone rental, shoe shine, shops, valet parking.

ACCOMMODATIONS

Rooms 267, including 21 suites. **All rooms** Ergonomically designed workstation with 2-line telephone, voice mail, high-speed modem and wireless access, fax, satellite TV with on-demand movies, hair dryer, minibar, safe, CD player, DVD player and DVD library. **Some rooms** Fireplaces, high ceilings, big windows;

other rooms have more of a modern loft effect. **Bed and bath** Splendid, with Frette sheets and the latest bathroom fittings. **Favorites** We prefer the rooms on the lower floors of the east block because they've retained the most Victorian features; rooms on the higher floors are more modern. **Comfort and decor** As you'd expect from furniture magnate Terence Conran, the decor is modern, solid, and comfy, with clean lines and relaxing colors.

PAYMENT, RESERVATIONS, AND RESTRICTIONS
Deposit Credit card. **Credit cards** All major. **Check-in/out** 2 p.m./noon. **Pets** Not allowed. **Elevator** Yes. **Children** Yes. **Disabled access** Yes.

Haymarket Hotel ★★★★

QUALITY ★★★★	VALUE ★★★	PRICE RANGE £287–£365

1 Suffolk Place, West End, SW1; ☎ 0207-470-4000; fax 0207-470-4004; www.firmdale.com

THIS LATEST ADDITION TO the Firmdale Hotels collection has everything that the others provide in abundance—great service, mood-lifting colors and witty decor, serious antiques, and the kind of stylish comfort you wish you could replicate at home. The Haymarket manages to one-up the others, with a location that puts you splat in the middle of all that London is best known for and a swimming pool that would be the envy of a posh health club. You can fall out of your well-appointed room and roll right over to Trafalgar Square, the National Gallery, Piccadilly, the Royal Academy, St. James's and Green parks, Bond Street, Soho, and the West End theaters (the hotel is next door to the Haymarket Royal Theatre).

The hotel's decor elicits oohs and ahhs and a few giggles (chandeliers in the shape of umbrellas in the restaurant Brumus, enormous bouquets of naked lightbulbs in the gallery, massively oversize articulated desk lamps in the pool lounge). One appreciates the increasing mastery of designer Kit Kemp in the Haymarket—she takes calculated design risks that pay off charmingly, mixing fabrics, patterns, and colors in ways that must in theory break rules but that in practice break right through into the realm of fabulous. Original details of this Regency building (past uses include gentlemen's club, shooting gallery, and an American Express office) don't clash with or mock modern aesthetics, as they do in many minimalist or achingly contemporary hotels—the decor is as exuberantly creative as the era in which the building was designed.

The guest rooms, whether the smallish standard doubles or the deluxe suites, offer the kind of comfort and attention to detail that lure guests who need long-term lodgings in London—the Firmdale group gets more than its fair share of film people shooting movies in the city. Plasma TVs, free wireless access, heated racks for thick, fluffy towels, Miller Harris toiletries, double sinks, bidets, sheets of the best Egyptian cotton, and eiderdown pillows are standard in all rooms. Probably the most impressive room in the Haymarket is for the disabled: everything has been adapted for the comfort and ease of wheelchair users, with lowered sinks, an easy-access open shower, handrails, and ramps.

As with all great hotels, the biggest drawback of the Haymarket is the cost—one always gets sticker shock on receiving the final bill. Also, the area is famous for its noisy activity: theatergoers, traffic, late-night crowds stumbling out of clubs toward the after-midnight buses around Trafalgar Square, and the daytime crush of office workers—no amount of double glazing will entirely dull those sound waves.

SETTING AND FACILITIES

Nearest tube station Piccadilly Circus. **Quietness rating** C/D. **Dining** Brumus Restaurant serves breakfast, lunch, and dinner. **Amenities** Restaurant, bar, 2 lounges, swimming pool, gym, beauty-treatment room. **Services** Full concierge services, 24-hour room service.

ACCOMMODATIONS

Rooms 50. **All rooms** Flat-screen TV (also in bathroom), free DVD library, minibar, telephone, wireless access, desk, individual decor. **Some rooms** Fireplace, sofa, and balcony. **Bed and bath** High-count cotton sheets and down pillows, granite-walled bathrooms with big baths and nice toiletries. **Favorites** Junior suites in the rear of building. **Comfort and decor** Decor is absolutely something to write home about, and comfort is up to global diva standards.

PAYMENT, RESERVATIONS, AND RESTRICTIONS

Deposit No deposit, but payment in full upon arrival. **Credit cards** All major. **Check-in/out** 2 p.m./11 a.m. **Pets** Guide dogs only. **Elevator** Yes. **Children** Yes. **Disabled access** Yes; a room on the ground floor is specially designed to accommodate wheelchair users.

 **Hazlitt's** ★★★★

| QUALITY ★★★★ | VALUE ★★½ | PRICE RANGE £240–£311 |

6 Frith Street, Soho Square, W1; ☎ 0207-434-1771; fax 0207-439-1524; www.hazlittshotel.com

HAZLITT'S, WHICH HAPPENS TO BE author Bill Bryson's favorite home away from home, perfectly evokes another time, with handsome antiques and decor in the Georgian style, in the heart of Soho, where sleepy London tends to stay wide awake. It is a simple hotel, with no elevator and only a tiny sitting room for communal lounging. Staying here is more like staying at a particularly well-appointed rooming house from days gone by. The house was built in 1718, and the floors sag and droop as you would, too, if you'd been trod on for close to 300 years. The rooms are luxuriously comfortable, with beautiful antique bedsteads and cotton sheets. Busts sculpted by one of the owner's relatives grace many of the bathrooms and rooms, and antique prints adorn the walls. The period verisimilitude is strict: the house of a writer like William Hazlitt would not have been overdone with gimcrackery or knickknackery.

Hazlitt's attracts writers like honey draws flies, partly because of the respect they get here and perhaps because they're the only people who know who Hazlitt was. In the sitting room is a bookcase containing signed copies of books written by guests, and it's an impressive collection: Seamus Heaney, Ted Hughes, Vikram Seth, Jostein Gardner, Susan Sontag, Dava Sobel, and scores of others. Of course, the brilliant Bill Bryson's books are here; he sent the phones ringing off the hook when he mentioned his favorite hotel in his hilarious book on England, *Notes from a Small Island*. Hazlitt's attracts a loyalty—or eccentricity—hardly ever met with: one of the regulars paid for double glazing to be put on the windows of his favorite room. This is not to say that you will indubitably love Hazlitt's; it's for a particular type of person, one who likes the noise and action of the present-day West End as much as the atmosphere of long-ago Soho. Look for promotional deals at the Web site.

SETTING AND FACILITIES
Nearest tube station Tottenham Court. **Quietness rating** D/F in front on weekend nights, A/B in back at all times. **Dining** No. **Amenities** Writing desks and modems, cotton sheets, Continental breakfast at extra charge. **Services** Receptionist, bellhop, laundry, 24-hour room service.

ACCOMMODATIONS
Rooms 23. **All rooms** Telephone, high-speed modem, satellite TV, bathtub, antiques, writing desk. **Some rooms** Ornamental fireplace, four-poster, high ceilings. **Bed and bath** Superb on both scores: Victorian tubs, deep and delicious, have huge showerheads; beds are comfortable, high off the ground, big, and cotton sheeted. **Favorites** The suite on the ground floor, the double-glazed-windowed Jonathan Swift room, and a small room in the back are best. Really, there are no rooms here that aren't charming and inviting; the higher ceilings are on the 1st and 2nd floors. **Comfort and decor** Top-notch comfort (unless you require an elevator), and the decor is nourishing to the eye and soul.

PAYMENT, RESERVATIONS, AND RESTRICTIONS
Deposit Credit card; 48-hour cancellation policy. **Credit cards** All major. **Check-in/out** 2 p.m./noon. **Pets** Not allowed. **Elevator** No. **Children** Yes. **Disabled access** No.

Hotel Russell   ★★★★

QUALITY ★★★★	VALUE ★★★★	PRICE RANGE £152–£210

Russell Square, Bloomsbury, WC1; ☎ 0207-837-6470;
fax 0207-837-2857; www.principal-hotels.com/hotelrussell/index.aspx

THIS GRAND OLD TERRA-COTTA–FACED edifice, built in 1898, underwent a years-long renovation that cost upward of £20 million, which was money well spent on this landmark building in Bloomsbury. We're happy to report that not much has changed—and why would it, since there are so many antique details that would be a shame to lose, such as the sweeping marble staircase. There are contemporary rooms, as well as ones decorated in a more classic style; air-conditioning in every room; and all the communications conveniences you could want. The hotel attracts a business crowd on account of its conference facilities, and it's accustomed to demanding customers. The restaurants are just OK but quite convenient, and the location is nice and close to the West End, The City, and the British Museum. The building is magnificent—one of the great Victorian hotel palaces.

SETTING AND FACILITIES
Nearest tube station Russell Square. **Quietness rating** C in front (double glazing), B in back. **Dining** Fitzroy Doll's bar and restaurant serves European and British food; Virginia Woolf's Brasserie serves burgers, pastas, and so on. Tempus and Benjamin's bars have a club atmosphere, with fireplaces, red leather couches, and drinks. **Amenities** Full business support, executive floor with lounge and Continental breakfast gratis (most rates don't include breakfast, which can run you £20, so take advantage of the many cafes in the area). **Services** Concierge, 24-hour room service, bellhop, laundry, conference ready.

ACCOMMODATIONS
Rooms 373. **All rooms** Telephone, modem, satellite TV, air-conditioning, hair dryer, iron, tea and coffee. **Some rooms** Minibar, writing desk, wide-screen plasma TV, bathrobes, balcony. **Bed and bath** Excellent; some bathrooms are quite big. **Favorites** A suite with a sitting room and French doors in both rooms looking out onto Russell Square. **Comfort and decor** It's got all the luxury trappings of a Meridien hotel without Meridien prices: old-fashioned huge hallways, high ceilings, and big rooms. The common areas are appealing, with a grand staircase in the beautiful Victorian lobby.

PAYMENT, RESERVATIONS, AND RESTRICTIONS
Deposit Credit card; must cancel before 2 p.m. on day of arrival. **Credit cards** All major. **Check-in/out** 2 p.m./noon. **Pets** Not allowed. **Elevator** Yes, 3. **Children** Yes. **Disabled access** As a Grade II historic building, the hotel can't be altered to accommodate wheelchair ramps, but management can help a lot.

The Hoxton ★★★

QUALITY ★★★	VALUE ★★★	PRICE RANGE £59–£169

81 Great Eastern Street, Hoxton, EC2; ☎ 0207-550-1000; fax 0207-550-1090; www.hoxtonhotels.com

WHEN YOU TAKE INTO ACCOUNT the cool and vibrant location, this hotel is remarkably inexpensive, especially considering the really quite nice decor and general cleanliness of the place. Being a new project, it has some small flaws, such as erratic room service, but this kind of little wrinkle can be ironed out in time. Sleek and trendy with moody lighting and a clean, earth-toned decor, the Hoxton has real star potential. The lobby has a beautiful stone fireplace and exposed brick walls. A breakfast of yogurt, fruit, and fresh orange juice is included, and although the Wi-Fi access is free, if you don't have your own laptop, they charge £7.50 a day for Web access via the television. To get the best price, you need to book in advance; the Web site has offers that will knock your jaw off your face: they ran an introductory £1-a-night deal that was a master stroke of PR—bring in the punters, impress them, and they will return.

SETTING AND FACILITIES

Nearest tube station Old Street. **Quietness rating** C/D. **Dining** The Hoxton Grill. **Amenities** Lounge, restaurant, Wi-Fi, use of nearby gym (hotel guests pay £5 for a day pass). **Services** Full concierge services, 24-hour room service.

ACCOMMODATIONS

Rooms 205. **All rooms** Flat-screen TV, Frette sheets, duck-down duvets and pillows, Wi-Fi access, free water and milk in minibar. **Some rooms** Bigger ones have tubs in the bathrooms instead of showers. **Bed and bath** Clean and to a good standard. **Favorites** The rooms are all similar except in size; go for a suite if you can afford it. **Comfort and decor** Tasteful, contemporary, snug.

PAYMENT, RESERVATIONS, AND RESTRICTIONS

Deposit No deposit, but payment in full upon arrival. **Credit cards** All major. **Check-in/out** 2 p.m./noon; £5 an hour for late checkout. **Pets** No. **Elevator** Yes. **Children** Yes. **Disabled access** Yes.

Lincoln House Hotel ★★★½

| QUALITY ★★★½ | VALUE ★★★★½ | PRICE RANGE £89–£115 |

33 Gloucester Place, Marble Arch, W1; ☎ 0207-486-7630; fax 0207-486-0166; www.lincoln-house-hotel.co.uk

WE'VE BEEN MEANING to put this lovely little B&B in this guide for ages, having heard so many good things about it from people who should know. Its reputation for friendliness and cleanliness is way up there, while the prices are way down. The neighborhood is north of Oxford Street and south of Regent's Park; transportation to everywhere is a short walk away, as are the conveniences of picturesque Marylebone. The proprietor, Joseph Sheriff, is a smart, well-traveled guy who takes great pride in knowing just what guests want, and he provides much more than you would find at a comparably priced hotel, such as air-conditioning (in most of the rooms), free wireless access, and a public-use computer in the lobby. The Lincoln House is on a busy road, with buses going to and fro, but the rooms in the back are quieter, looking over the mews. You can be in Hyde Park in five or ten minutes, or you might prefer shopping at Selfridges department store, which is even closer. The rooms are, naturally, on the small side: big Americans may want to spring for the family room at £115—Sheriff offers special discounts for guests from the States. There is an additional cost of £3.50 for a Continental or English breakfast, which is served in the pleasant breakfast room or brought to your room. The price is more than fair, as the menu is extensive (even Middle Eastern and vegan breakfasts are available)—and just go look at what the cafes in the surrounding area charge. This is a lovely old town house from the late 18th century, and many of the most charming period details have been lovingly restored. The Web site is extremely comprehensive, including a list of bed and room sizes (they're in meters, which may not be useful, but you'll get the idea).

SETTING AND FACILITIES

Nearest tube station Marble Arch. **Quietness rating** C in front rooms, B+ in rear. **Dining** Breakfast room. **Amenities** Breakfast (full English, vegetarian, or Continental); laptop rental, wireless Internet access, and computer in lobby. **Services** Touring and ticket advice; breakfast brought to room free of charge; friendly, helpful staff.

ACCOMMODATIONS

Rooms 23. **All rooms** Telephone, satellite TV, hair dryer, trouser press, tea and coffee. **Some rooms** Minifridge, period details, high ceilings. **Bed and bath** Showers only. **Favorites** 1st-floor rooms with nice windows or quieter rooms overlooking the mews. **Comfort and decor** Simple, clean, and pleasing, with some lovely Georgian architectural features. More than half the rooms have air-conditioning; rooms without have water-based air coolers (electric fans available on request).

PAYMENT, RESERVATIONS, AND RESTRICTIONS

Deposit Credit card; 72-hour cancellation policy. credit Cards All major. **Check-in/out** 2 p.m./11:30 a.m. **Pets** Not allowed. **Elevator** No. **Children** Yes. **Disabled access** No.

London Marriott Hotel County Hall ★★★★

QUALITY ★★★★	VALUE ★★★	PRICE RANGE £292–£362

County Hall, South Bank, SE1; ☎ 0207-928-5200; toll free from U.S., 888-236-2427; fax 0207-928-5300; www.marriott.com

THIS HOTEL HAS THE LARGEST ROOMS of any Marriott in London, and it has all the amenities you'd expect from the chain, but with one major difference: it's located in the old County Hall building right on the Thames, which has spectacular, postcard-perfect views of Parliament, Big Ben, the London Eye, and the tower of Westminster Abbey. You can stroll down the Thames Path, browsing the secondhand-book stalls or popping in for a concert at the Royal Festival Hall, a play at the National Theatre, or a late-night film at the cinema. In summer, all the world's a stage on the South Bank, even if there's not a whole lotta shakin' going on in the neighborhood to the south of the Marriott. Across the bridge is Westminster, which tends to roll up the sidewalks at night and on weekends. The hotel has a 25-meter pool and an excellent gym; beauty and health treatments are available. There are some delightful eating and lounging areas, which you should visit even if you don't stay here—the view is magnificent, especially at night. There are wood-paneled walls everywhere and all kinds of interesting architectural features in this certified-historic building. And the beds are huge. Ask for deals and promotions, as the rack rate is steep.

SETTING AND FACILITIES

Nearest tube station Westminster or Waterloo. **Quietness rating** A/B. **Dining** County Hall Restaurant serves English cuisine and offers an oyster-and-seafood bar, plus great views of the Thames. Library Lounge has tea and snacks. Try

Leader's Cocktail Bar for a nightcap. **Amenities** Restaurant, lounge, bar, views of Parliament and Big Ben, health club with big pool, disabled rooms, valet parking. **Services** Concierge, 24-hour room service, valet parking, bellhop, laundry.

ACCOMMODATIONS

Rooms 186. **All rooms** Telephones, voice mail, high-speed modem, satellite TV, air-conditioning, minibar, hair dryer, tea and coffee, iron, safe. **Some rooms** Separate sitting room, river views. **Bed and bath** Excellent bathrooms; beds are queen- or king-size. **Favorites** Any of the rooms with a view of Parliament; inside rooms on courtyard are quiet. **Comfort and decor** Comfort is high; decor is high-standard hotel type, with some unfortunate choices in fabrics.

PAYMENT, RESERVATIONS, AND RESTRICTIONS

Deposit Credit card; must cancel by 4 p.m. on day of arrival. **Credit cards** All major. **Check-in/out** 2 p.m./noon. **Pets** Not allowed. **Elevator** Yes. **Children** Yes. **Disabled access** 6 disabled rooms of a very high standard.

The Mayflower Hotel ★★★½

QUALITY ★★★½	VALUE ★★★★	PRICE RANGE £92–£165

26–28 Trebovir Road, Earls Court, SW5; ☎ 0207-370-0991; fax 0207-370-0994; www.mayflowerhotel.co.uk

THE MAYFLOWER GROUP RUNS TWO OTHER HOTELS and a complex of serviced apartments. The Mayflower Hotel in Earls Court offers real value for the money, with standard double rooms starting at £92. The individually designed rooms, the amenities and services, and the general look and feel are not often found in a hotel of this price bracket. The rooms are on the small side, but nicely presented and rather chicly modern. The staff is helpful and actually looks happy—not necessarily a prerequisite for working in London's service business. Continental breakfast is included in the rate, but a fry-up can be ordered for a little extra. Rates can come down to under £75 with the right planning (for instance, booking in advance or through the Internet). The Earls Court Underground station is down the road, with links to Heathrow and all over London; the hotel is also conveniently within walking distance to many restaurants and a 24-hour supermarket.

SETTING AND FACILITIES

Nearest tube station Earls Court. **Quietness rating** A/B. **Dining** Breakfast. **Amenities** Lounge and juice bar, breakfast room, newspapers, conference rooms, Wi-Fi, parking, multilingual staff, safe-deposit box at front desk. **Services** Concierge, 24-hour front desk, airport transportation (surcharge), dry-cleaning service, secretarial services.

ACCOMMODATIONS:

Rooms 66. **All rooms** Cable TV, telephone, air-conditioning and ceiling fan, CD player, electronic room safe, free Wi-Fi access, tea and coffee, hair dryer, trouser press. **Some rooms** High ceilings, period details, additional space. **Bed and bath** High standards. **Favorites** The luxury doubles are very nice at £165; for the same price you could get a triple, which will ensure a good-sized room. **Comfort and decor** Good-quality furnishings, newly renovated bathrooms, and attractive design and decor.

PAYMENT, RESERVATIONS, AND RESTRICTIONS
Deposit No deposit, but payment in full upon arrival. **Credit cards** All major. **Check-in/out** 2 p.m./11 a.m. **Pets** No. **Elevator** Yes. **Children** Yes. **Disabled access** Yes, except for steps to front door, which can be negotiated with the help of staff.

 **Miller's Residence**   ★★★★

QUALITY ★★★	VALUE ★★★½	PRICE RANGE £176–£217

111a Westbourne Grove, Notting Hill Gate, W2 (entrance on southeast side of Hereford Road); ☎ 0207-243-1024; fax 0207-243-1064; www.millersuk.com

SINCE MILLER'S RESIDENCE OPENED IN 1997, it has been quietly drawing strength from the numbers of people who love it and keep going back, as well as the numerous newspaper and magazine people who keep writing about it. The owners have created an eccentric and beautiful "rooming house" in Notting Hill Gate, filled to bursting in the common areas with sublime antiques. The drawing room is wonderful, with a stunningly carved fireplace and still more antiques.

The eight rooms (two are suites, at £270 a night) are named after English Romantic poets and have lines from their masterworks inscribed on the back of each door. The Coleridge Room, for example, features an old model of the HMS *Bounty*, and "Rime of the Ancient Mariner" is quoted on its door. This is the kind of quirky and interesting inn that appeals to a certain kind of sensibility—if you're looking for a predictable hotel experience, this is not really the place to get it, and if you have small children it probably wouldn't be very relaxing, what with all the valuables on display here. But if you love antiques and you like being in the very hip Westbourne Grove area, you'll find Miller's a delightful break from the usual hostelries. The house is on a busy stretch of Westbourne Grove full of restaurants and interesting shops. Breakfast is included in the price of a room; guests who book long stays get discounts. Reserve well in advance.

SETTING AND FACILITIES
Nearest tube station Bayswater. **Quietness rating** C/D. **Dining** Breakfast only. **Amenities** 24-hour computer access, wireless access, exuberant drawing room (illuminated by candles at night) with fireplace and another equally gorgeous lounge. **Services** Reception acts as concierge; limited room service (from local restaurants); laundry.

ACCOMMODATIONS
Rooms 6; 2 apartment suites. **All rooms** Telephone, voice mail, satellite TV, wireless access, wonderful antiques. **Some rooms** four-poster, even more

wonderful antiques. **Bed and bath** Good-quality beds, and the bathrooms are of a high standard. **Favorites** All rooms are different and very cool. Try the red Coleridge Room or the lighter Tennyson Room. **Comfort and decor** Comfort is fine, except for the lack of an elevator and the possibility of a hot day or two without air-conditioning. The decor has to be seen to be believed. The owners have spent their time amassing stunning antiques that they have spread wildly and well all over this wonderful rooming house.

PAYMENT, RESERVATIONS, AND RESTRICTIONS
Deposit Credit card; cancellation policy seven days prior to arrival. **Credit cards** All major. **Check-in/out** 2 p.m./noon. **Pets** Not allowed. **Elevator** No. **Children** Yes. **Disabled access** No.

Number Sixteen ★★★½

QUALITY ★★★★	VALUE ★★½	PRICE RANGE £176–£293

16 Sumner Place, South Kensington, SW7; ☎ 0207-589-5232;
toll free from U.S., 800-592-5387; fax 0207-584-8615;
www.numbersixteenhotel.co.uk

THIS TOWN-HOUSE HOTEL, an old favorite among visitors who love South Kensington, has undergone a renovation that may have some of the former customers feeling a bit uncomfortable: gone is the chintz of yesteryear, as well as the old descriptive names of the rooms. It's now a modern, but not minimalist, boutique hotel whose prices have also caught up to the present. Quirky ethnic decorations—huge birdcages, driftwood lamps, and the like—work well in the formerly staid conservatory. The bathrooms have been seriously upgraded, with gray granite and power showers, and the bedrooms are all individually decorated. What couldn't be upgraded was the size of the rooms, which are pretty small except for the superior deluxes. The lower ground floor has a few rooms with their own entrance to the garden, which is a nice plus. There is no breakfast room, but food will be brought to your room, the conservatory, or one of the public sitting areas 24 hours a day. Big beds are draped in cotton sheets, appealing to the 80%-American clientele. Good service. Ask about promotional deals.

SETTING AND FACILITIES
Nearest tube station South Kensington. **Quietness rating** B. **Dining** 24-hour room service. **Amenities** Air-conditioning, voice mail, high-speed modem, satellite TV, DVD player (rental card for nearby video store provided), mobile-phone rental, minibar, safe, access to health club nearby (for fee). **Services** Concierge, laundry.

ACCOMMODATIONS
Rooms 42. **All rooms** Air-conditioning, telephone with voice mail, modem, minibar, DVD player, satellite TV, safe, hair dryer. **Some rooms** Balcony, French doors, access to garden. **Bed and bath** Of a very high standard; big beds, great bathrooms. **Favorites** Number 3 is on lower ground (in basement) but has space and a huge bed; 306 is red and elegant, if small. Ask for rooms on the garden, as

they're quieter. **Comfort and decor** Decor is eccentrically elegant, with faux-stone-painted walls and interesting artwork and knickknacks; comfort is top-notch.

PAYMENT, RESERVATIONS, AND RESTRICTIONS
Deposit Credit card; 48-hour cancellation policy. **Credit cards** All major. **Check-in/out** 3 p.m./noon. **Pets** Not allowed. **Elevator** Yes. **Children** Yes. **Disabled access** 4 ground-floor rooms, 3 steps to front door.

Park Inn Hyde Park ★★★

QUALITY ★★★	VALUE ★★★	PRICE RANGE £80–£110

66 Lancaster Gate, Bayswater, W2; ☎ 0207-262-5090; fax 0207-723-1244; www.parkinn.com

TAKING OVER FROM THE FORMER Gresham Hotel, Park Inn Hyde Park inherits the beautiful bone structure of the period architecture and has had quite the face-lift performed on it. It's true that the Gresham was guilty of looking a little dated; the revamp puts bold primary colors on simple modern furniture, and somehow, in an atmosphere of antique gentility provided by the glorious windows and period details, it works perfectly. The rooms here are not huge, but they are comfortable, with good beds and excellent air-conditioning; street noise is kept down by double-glazed windows. However, the size and quality of rooms are prone to differ quite substantially, so be assertive when booking and ask for the larger options. Look for good discount rates at the hotel's own Web site—the tariff can be as low as £60 per night, which, if you can get it, is a great price to pay for a room at a hotel of this quality. Breakfast is more than adequate, with hot and cold options. Note that it is worth asking for another room if you aren't satisfied with the one you have—the staff are accommodating and professional, and they'll do their best to please you.

SETTING AND FACILITIES
Nearest tube station Paddington. **Quietness rating** B/C. **Dining** Dishes Restaurant & Serpentine Bar. **Amenities** Restaurant, bar, 24-hour fitness center, meeting facilities, business center. **Services** Concierge, 24-hour room service, full secretarial facilities.

ACCOMMODATIONS
Rooms 188. **All rooms** Air-conditioning, Wi-Fi Internet access, cable and satellite TV, tea and coffee, telephone, hair dryer, in-room safe, air-conditioning, wake-up calls, trouser press, iron and ironing board (on request), nonsmoking rooms. **Some rooms** Suites are more spacious. **Bed and bath** Clean and to a good standard. **Favorites** Suites. **Comfort and decor** Good-quality amenities and comforts; decorated in a clean and colorful modern style.

PAYMENT, RESERVATIONS, AND RESTRICTIONS
Deposit No deposit, but payment in full upon arrival. **Credit cards** All major. **Check-in/out** 2 p.m./11 a.m. **Pets** No. **Elevator** Yes. **Children** Yes. **Disabled access** Yes.

The Pelham Hotel ★★★½

QUALITY ★★★★	VALUE ★★½	PRICE RANGE £265–£376

15 Cromwell Place, South Kensington, SW7; ☎ 0207-589-8288; toll free from U.S., 800-553-6674; fax 0207-584-8444; www.firmdale.com

AS WITH ALL THE FIRMDALE ESTABLISHMENTS, the Pelham Hotel is visually arresting, with each room unique and exquisitely decorated. However, the size of many of the rooms leaves something to be desired, as with many period-building conversions, but the decor lulls you into complacency. The atmosphere is that of a luxurious town house, with all the amenities you could desire. There are two sitting rooms with fireplaces; mahogany paneling; and deep, comfy chairs and sofas. The views in the front are of South Kensington, and there's not much to look at out of the rear windows except for the Lycée Français playground (expect noise on school days). The location is excellent, with the museums of South Kensington just steps away, three tube lines across the street, buses that stop in front of the hotel (a big bother to noise-phobes), and the shops of Knightsbridge a five-minute walk away. The staff is friendly, helpful, and knowledgeable; ask about special deals. Breakfast is included with some rooms.

SETTING AND FACILITIES

Nearest tube station South Kensington. **Quietness rating** B in rear, C in front (the front has *double* double glazing, a real necessity). **Dining** Kemps Restaurant has an excellent menu that changes every few weeks; the room is comfortable and relaxed. **Amenities** Sitting rooms with fireplaces, Champagne and hors d'oeuvres on Wednesdays, honor bar and coffee and tea in back sitting room. **Services** 24-hour room service, concierge, laundry—anything you can think of.

ACCOMMODATIONS

Rooms 52. **All rooms** 2 telephones, voice mail, high-speed modem, satellite TV, mobile phone rental, minibar, sitting area. **Some rooms** DVD/VCR player, sofa, balcony, four-poster bed. **Bed and bath** Twins, doubles, and kings (which can be turned into twins) are all very comfortable; bathrooms have big tubs, good showers, and granite and mahogany decor. **Favorites** Front-facing luxury double, with French doors leading to balcony; any of the deluxe doubles; the suite with the walk-in wardrobe, 2 sinks in bathroom, and shower cubicle as well as tub. **Comfort and decor** The comfort factor is what we'd all like to achieve in our own homes, and the decor is like stepping into the pages of *Architectural Digest*.

PAYMENT, RESERVATIONS, AND RESTRICTIONS

Deposit Credit card; 48-hour cancellation policy. **Credit cards** All major, except DC. **Check-in/out** 1 p.m./noon. **Pets** Not allowed. **Elevator** Yes. **Children** Yes. **Disabled access** Limited; steps into hotel must be negotiated with assistance.

The Portobello Hotel ★★★½

QUALITY ★★★★	VALUE ★★★	PRICE RANGE £190–£242

22 Stanley Gardens, Notting Hill Gate, W11; ☎ 0207-727-2777; fax 0207-792-9641; www.portobellohotel.com

THE PORTOBELLO IS A TRENDY PLACE, with corporate accounts held by a number of modeling, music, and film agencies—it's A-list all the way. It's in an old Victorian terrace house; the rooms are completely different from one another, and admirably so. The hotel has a lot of charm, blending whimsical, Asian-accented, and traditional decor nicely. Continental breakfast is included in the price of a room and can be delivered to your room. The ambience is pleasant, especially if you get one of the larger rooms, but the singles are cell-like, despite the gracious decor, and there is no space to do anything other than sleep. The most imposing room, number 16, features a big round bed and a balcony overlooking the garden; there's a deep antique copper bathtub right in the room, a saucy invitation to romance. Number 13 has a huge, high four-poster bed that requires a footstool to mount. The hotel is within walking distance of Portobello Road, which makes it good for committed Portobello and Kensington Church Street shoppers.

SETTING AND FACILITIES

Nearest tube station Notting Hill Gate. **Quietness rating** A. **Dining** Very small breakfast room. **Amenities** Tiny basement restaurant with a few tables for breakfast and lunch; drawing room with fireplace and view of garden; health-club facilities are a 4-minute walk away; computer in most rooms. **Services** Concierge, room service, Continental breakfast sent to room, laundry, all business services.

ACCOMMODATIONS

Rooms 23. **All rooms** Telephone, high-speed modem, satellite TV. **Some rooms** Balcony, couches, minibar, air-conditioning, four-poster. **Bed and bath** Beds are comfy; baths range from a huge claw-foot tub to tiny shower stalls, but all are clean and user-friendly. **Favorites** Number 16, with the balcony overlooking the garden and the big round bed, is everyone's favorite. We also like the garden-view, Asian-style number 46. Number 38, a single, is very small but has a good feeling to it. The 1st-floor rooms with the large French windows are spacious and fine. **Comfort and decor** The decoration here is extraordinary, including a range of furnishings, from traditional English antiques to exotic Asian and Middle Eastern treasures. Comfort is as high a priority as style.

PAYMENT, RESERVATIONS, AND RESTRICTIONS

Deposit Credit card; 48-hour cancellation policy. **Credit cards** All major. **Check-in/out** After noon/noon. **Pets** Not allowed for long stays, but the hotel could hardly turn away the best friends of the rich and famous. **Elevator** New elevator fitted, but only to 3rd floor. **Children** Yes. Disabled Access No.

Radisson Edwardian Hampshire   ★★★★

QUALITY ★★★★	VALUE ★★½	PRICE RANGE £282–£320

31–36 Leicester Square, Leicester Square, WC2; ☎ 0207-839-9399; toll free from U.S., 800-333-3333; fax 0207-930-8122; www.radissonedwardian.com

HOUSED IN A MAGNIFICENT BUILDING right on Leicester Square behind the tkts theater-ticket booth, the Edwardian Hampshire is a four-star hotel run by the Radisson group. It has all the amenities you'd expect from a five-star inn—though, as with so many of London's hotels, not quite as much space in some of the standard rooms as you would want. The rooms are well appointed, and there's a kind of Asian theme to the decor. The walnut-paneled lobby offers a quiet sitting place protected from, yet in view of, the madding crowds of Leicester Square. Dine and drink at the smart Hampshire Bar and Restaurant, which serves modern British and Mediterranean cuisine amid classic yet contemporary decor.

The four-poster bedrooms are beautiful, and all the junior suites are of a reasonable size, but at unreasonable prices (they start at £400!). Some of the rooms have views over Trafalgar Square in the back and Leicester Square in front. Leicester Square isn't for everyone; it's noisy and people packed, and the sleaze factor can be high on weekends after the pubs close. Ask about Radisson-related deals, but forget the theater packages: you have tkts, the official London half-price-ticket booth, outside your door. With so many variables in price at the Radisson hotels, we hesitate to even list the costs. Call or visit the Web site to see what a wide array of prices they have.

SETTING AND FACILITIES

Nearest tube station Leicester Square. **Quietness rating Rooms** on the Leicester Square side have triple glazing on the windows, ensuring quiet, but beware the occasional Carnival Fair in the square—you may want to hole up in the back. **Dining** Hampshire Bar and Restaurant. **Amenities** Small fitness room, bathrobes, telephones in bathrooms, full air-conditioning. **Services** Concierge, 24-hour room service, bellhop, laundry, business support, online check-in.

ACCOMMODATIONS

Rooms 124. **All rooms** Telephone, high-speed modem and wireless access, minibar, satellite TV, in-house movies, air-conditioning, hair dryer, bathrobe, tea and coffee, iron, writing desk. **Some rooms** four-poster, views, floor-to-ceiling windows. **Bed and bath** High quality. **Favorites** The four-poster suite with a view over Trafalgar Square. Junior suites are also great. **Comfort and decor** Five-star-hotel–style comforts and interesting decor that mixes 18th-century reproductions with Asian artwork.

PAYMENT, RESERVATIONS, AND RESTRICTIONS

Deposit Credit card; 24-hour cancellation policy. **Credit cards** All major. **Check-in/out** 2 p.m./11 a.m. **Pets** Not allowed. **Elevator** Yes. **Children** Yes. **Disabled access** Yes.

kids The Rembrandt Hotel ★★★

QUALITY ★★★	VALUE ★★★★½	PRICE RANGE £175–£209

11 Thurloe Place, South Kensington, SW7; ☎ 0207-589-8100; fax 0207-225-3476; www.sarova.com/rembrandt

A MASSIVE OVERHAUL OF THE REMBRANDT eviscerated its traditional English look, leaving it with a sleek lobby that looks like pretty much any other hotel's. Granted, the result is clean and fresh looking, but something has been lost. In any event, the main reasons to stay at the Rembrandt are location, location, location. It's across the street from the Victoria and Albert and a hop, skip, and jump from the Science Museum, the Natural History Museum, and Harrods. It is also a four-minute walk from the South Kensington tube station, where one can access the Piccadilly (which goes to Heathrow), Circle, and District lines. Three useful buses are within shouting distance, and taxis are a breeze to hail. The hotel has a big lobby with fireplace, bar service, and plenty of couches to go around. Reservations clerks usually recommend the double executive room to Americans, since they're accustomed to lots of space. Breakfast may be included in your rate and is always very hearty, served in the lobby or the Palette Restaurant. The Aquilla, the attached health club, has a small and very warm pool that welcomes children most times of the day. Kids will also like the nearness of the museums, especially on weekends when there are children's adventure activities on offer. The Rembrandt attracts a lot of business conferences and is at the top of many package tours' hotel lists. Ask about room upgrades.

SETTING AND FACILITIES

Nearest tube station South Kensington. **Quietness rating** A in rear and on top floors; D/F for front lower floors (double glazing is not 100% effective). **Dining** The Palette Restaurant serves traditional breakfast, lunch, and dinner. **Amenities** Lobby with bar and fireplace, big dining room and small conservatory, tour-bus pickup, health club with small pool (there's a daily charge for use unless it's included in your rate), conference rooms, professional business services. Breakfast included in some rates. **Services** Concierge, 24-hour room service, bellhop, laundry, fax and Internet in lobby, babysitting.

ACCOMMODATIONS

Rooms 195; 2 nonsmoking floors. **All rooms** Telephone, air-conditioning, satellite TV, modem, in-house movies, minibar on request, tea and coffee, hair dryer, writing desk. **Some rooms** Bidet, sitting area. **Bed and bath** Beds are decent. The refurbishment freshened up the bathrooms considerably; they are clean and good-sized by London standards. **Favorites** Executive-double front rooms on 1st floor facing Victoria and Albert Museum. The only drawbacks to these rooms are the roar of traffic and the bus fumes. **Comfort and decor** Unremarkable but solid on every score.

PAYMENT, RESERVATIONS, AND RESTRICTIONS

Deposit Credit card; 48-hour cancellation policy. **Credit cards** All major. **Check-in/out** 2 p.m./noon; express checkout available. **Pets** Not allowed. **Elevator** Yes, 2. **Children** Yes. **Disabled access** Yes; 3 steps in front can be accessed by a ramp that must be requested.

 **The Rookery** ★★★★

QUALITY ★★★½	VALUE ★★½	PRICE RANGE £240–£323

12 Peter's Lane, Cowcross Street, Clerkenwell, EC1; ☎ 0207-336-0931; fax 0207-336-0931; www.rookeryhotel.com

THE ROOKERY IS A CHARMING HOTEL owned by the talented team of Peter McKay and Douglas Blain, who also bring you the period authenticity of Hazlitt's (see page 109). Part of The Rookery's authenticity, unfortunately for guests, is the absence of an elevator for the four floors. If the hotel had a lift, our value and quality ratings would be higher—we can't wrap our heads around spending this kind of money if stairs were at all a problem. Located a short distance from The City, in Clerkenwell, the hotel is perfect for the businessperson. This is not an area where tourists stay, but it's definitely a viable choice, especially if you have an interest in the "real" historic London. St. Paul's Cathedral and the Old Bailey are visible from some of The Rookery's windows.

However, it is not only the neighborhood that lends appeal; the building itself is a conglomeration of restored 18th-century town houses that make for an intimate, delightful accommodation. All the modern conveniences are here, but they pale next to the glories of the past, carefully culled from auction houses, flea markets, and antiques shops. Like that of Hazlitt's, The Rookery's exterior gives no hint of the wonders that lie within: the old brick buildings are nondescript, located down a little lane and through an alley that cows used to cross on their fatal journey to the Smithfield Meat Market. Look for lanterns and a discreet sign—no waving banners here. Rooms are of a decent size, and the bathrooms are unique. Weekend breaks are more affordable, as are some other deals; check the Web site or call.

SETTING AND FACILITIES
Nearest tube station Farringdon. **Quietness rating** A. **Dining** No. **Amenities** Conservatory, meeting rooms, personal safes in each room; you can take your breakfast in the lounge or in your room. **Services** Concierge, 18-hour room service, bellhop, laundry.

ACCOMMODATIONS
Rooms 33. **All rooms** Telephone, Wi-Fi and high-speed modem, satellite TV, air-conditioning, hair dryer, writing desk, personal safe. **Some rooms** Views, four-poster. **Bed and bath** Great attention to both practical and aesthetic excellence, with the best modern mattresses fitted into unique and antique bedsteads. Every room is different, outfitted with rich woods and important antiques. The bathrooms have original Victorian fixtures; some boast free-standing claw-foot tubs and showerheads the size of dinner plates. **Favorites** The Rook's Nest has a view of St. Paul's and the Old Bailey, and if you squint your eyes to remove the modern eyesores, you can really get the measure of Old London town. **Comfort and decor** Of the highest quality on both scores, except for the lack of an elevator.

PAYMENT, RESERVATIONS, AND RESTRICTIONS
Deposit Credit card; 48-hour cancellation policy. **Credit cards** All major. **Check-in/out** 1:30 p.m./11:30 a.m. **Pets** Not allowed. **Elevator** No. **Children** Yes. **Disabled access** No.

Ruskin Hotel ★★

| QUALITY ★★½ | VALUE ★★★★★ | PRICE RANGE £72–£90 |

23–24 Montague Street, Bloomsbury, WC1; ☎ **0207-636-7388; fax 0207-323-1662; www.ruskinhotellondon.com**

THE RUSKIN HAS BEEN RUN by the same Spanish family since the mid-1980s, and it very much has the feel of an inexpensive hotel in Barcelona. It also has the loyalty of many return customers. Unlike many budget bed-and-breakfasts in London, the Ruskin has an elevator to all floors, accepts all major credit cards, and is clean and friendly. The rates for rooms with no toilet are fair enough to merit walking down the hall. The sitting room has a beautiful painting from 1801 by John Ward, a painter for the Duke of Bedford, whose estate still owns all the land around here. The house is quite old, having started out as a private residence before it served as a warren of offices where Sir Arthur Conan Doyle was reputed to have worked on his Sherlock Holmes stories. For a no-frills B&B–budget hotel with breakfast included, the Ruskin is a good bet. The single rooms have no en suite toilets; you will need to get a double for that, and indeed at £72, you should (singles start at £52).

SETTING AND FACILITIES
Nearest tube station Russell Square. **Quietness rating** A in back, B in front (double-glazed windows help). **Dining** Breakfast room. **Amenities** Breakfast included; generous portions served by waiters in a nice breakfast room. **Services** *Se habla español;* they can manage a few other languages as well.

ACCOMMODATIONS
Rooms 33; 6 with shower and toilet. **All rooms** Telephone, hair dryer, tea and coffee. **Some rooms** Garden view, bathroom. **Bed and bath** Both communal and private bathrooms are in good shape; the beds are comfortable, though the doubles might be a squeeze for large Americans. **Favorites** Number 102 is a pleasant family room. **Comfort and decor** The exuberance of the many plants and flowers on the outside may betray the utilitarian decor within: strip lights over beds, Naugahyde, fake wood, and plastic furniture. Sensitive souls might shrivel at the decor, frankly, but if you can close your eyes to it, you might find time to admire certain features, like friezes and the sitting room's mural.

PAYMENT, RESERVATIONS, AND RESTRICTIONS
Deposit 1 night nonrefundable, unless they can re-let the room. **Credit cards** All major. **Check-in/out** 1 p.m./11:30 a.m. **Pets** Not allowed. **Elevator** Yes. **Children** Yes. **Disabled access** Yes.

St. Giles Hotel London   ★★★½

QUALITY ★★★½	VALUE ★★★½	PRICE RANGE £110–£170

1 Bedford Avenue, Bloomsbury, WC1; ☎ **0207-300-3000; fax 0207-300-3001; www.stgiles.com**

THIS LARGE INDEPENDENT HOTEL keeps its reputation with a spotless lobby, good services, and attractive accommodations. The rooms, like so many in this city, are a little small, but they are nicely presented and of a relatively high quality, as are the bathrooms. The location, on the very busy intersection of Oxford Street and Tottenham Court Road, can be considered a plus or a minus, depending on your feelings toward shopping, traffic, and general urban congestion: the sidewalks pullulate with people during the day, and buses from all over London and beyond converge in this area (the Tottenham Court Road bus station is steps away) day and night. Some people will love to jump right into the mass of pedestrians and walk the short distances to the British Museum, the flagship Topshop at Oxford Circus, Soho, Chinatown, and Regent's Park. If walking is not your thing and you need to work off some of those afternoon-tea extravaganzas, St. Giles has a huge, superior gym—courtesy of the YMCA, and for which you pay a hotel-guest discounted day rate—with a swimming pool, neither of which is a common option at hotels in this price range. Check Web site for deals and promotions. There is also a St. Giles Hotel at Heathrow (Hounslow Road, Middlesex, TW1; ☎ 0208-817-7000).

SETTING AND FACILITIES
Nearest tube station Tottenham Court Road. **Quietness rating** C/D (depends on floor). **Dining** Breakfast, lunch, and dinner. **Amenities** Swimming pool, health club, gym, Lazy Dog Bar; Chikara (Asian), Kobe Jones (Japanese), and Il Grasso (Italian) restaurants. **Services** Concierge, 24-hour room service, business support.

ACCOMMODATIONS
Rooms 655. **All rooms** Tea and coffee, cable TV, pay movies, nonsmoking rooms, in-room safe, hair dryer, telephone. **Some rooms** Some are bigger and quieter than others, with better views. **Bed and bath** Up to a high global business standard for the price range. **Favorites** Rooms on higher floors. **Comfort and decor** Good on the former count, lackluster on the latter.

PAYMENT, RESERVATIONS, AND RESTRICTIONS
Deposit No deposit, but credit card details will be taken. **Credit cards** All major. **Check-in/out** 11 a.m./2 p.m. **Pets** No. **Elevator** Yes. **Children** The pool makes this a great place to bring the kids. **Disabled access** Very good.

Saint Gregory Hotel ★★★½

| QUALITY ★★★ | VALUE ★★★½ | PRICE RANGE £129–£145 |

100 Shoreditch High Street, Shoreditch, E1; ☎ 0207-613-9800; fax 0207-613-9811; www.saintgregoryhotel.com

DESCRIBED AS A "LUXURY BUSINESS HOTEL," the Saint Gregory is spacious, clean, and contemporary. Located in Shoreditch, a fashionable part of the East End, the hotel is within walking distance not only to the financial center of the Square Mile but also to a mammoth number of cool little bars and pubs all around Old Street and Hoxton. On the flip side, the location is quite busy, which may make it necessary for you to request a room on the higher floors or in the back of the hotel for some peace and quiet. The rooms are larger than the general standard in London, and the bathrooms are clean and elegant. The city vistas from many of the rooms may not be as scenic as the rooftop restaurant's magnificent panorama of the 30 St. Mary Axe building (aka "The Gherkin") through to the BT Tower, but at least you can enjoy the views during dinner or drinks. They offer buffet breakfast and good facilities for the disabled. Check the Internet for discounted rates (as low as £112 through the cheap-hotel-room booking sites).

SETTING AND FACILITIES

Nearest tube station Old Street. **Quietness rating** C/D. **Dining** Breakfast, lunch, and dinner. **Amenities** Restaurant, bar and lounge, wheelchair access, laundry facilities, gym, business and conference facilities, car park (charge). **Services** Concierge, 24-hour room service, luggage storage, foreign currency exchange, business support.

ACCOMMODATIONS

Rooms 200. **All rooms** Telephone, cable TV, trouser press, tea and coffee, radio, nonsmoking rooms, minibar, in-room safe, hair dryer, air-conditioning, broadband Internet. **Some rooms** Views, good space. **Bed and bath** Clean and to a high standard. **Favorites** Suites. **Comfort and decor** Very hip decoration, and the comforts are all you'd expect from a capital-city hotel.

PAYMENT, RESERVATIONS, AND RESTRICTIONS

Deposit No deposit, but payment in full upon arrival. **Credit cards** All major. **Check-in/out** 2 p.m./noon. **Pets** No. **Elevator** Yes. **Children** Yes. **Disabled access** Very good.

The Sloane Square Hotel ★★★

QUALITY ★★★★	VALUE ★★★½	PRICE RANGE £160–£320

Sloane Square, Chelsea, SW1; ☎ 0207-896-9988; fax 0207-751-4211; www.sloanesquarehotel.co.uk

FIRST OF ALL, THIS HOTEL is in a great location, despite the noise from busy Sloane Square in front. It's in the heart of Chelsea, with the shopping districts of Knightsbridge and King's Road at your doorstep, plus great transportation links to all over London. The Sloane Square exudes classiness and style, with a recent £7 million refurbishment of the whole hotel ensuring clean and elegant surroundings. The rooms are beautifully presented but exceedingly small: a double standard room barely leaves enough space around the bed to open a suitcase in, but the beds are comfortable and well sized, there is a desk, and the decor is soothing. Rooms fronting the square are double glazed, which helps muffle the noise of 24-hour cars and buses. Drawer and closet space are minimal; you may find yourself living out of your suitcase, if you can find a place on the floor for it. The attached Chelsea Brasserie serves up wholesome, well-put-together menus. All in all, this is a solid enough choice for the price, but do vigorously insist on a bigger room than the standard double, which, when all is said and done, ends up costing about £190, serious money in today's dollars. Visitors receive reduced rates on next-weekend stays—better than average value for the money in a very attractive location.

SETTING AND FACILITIES

Nearest tube station Sloane Square. **Quietness rating** C. **Dining** Breakfast, lunch, snacks, cocktails, and dinner at the on-site Chelsea Brasserie restaurant, headed by the excellent David Karlsson Möller of Racine fame; outdoor tables. **Amenities** Restaurant Internet access, fitness room. **Services** Concierge, 24-hour room service, dry cleaning.

ACCOMMODATIONS
Rooms 100. **All rooms** All the traditional 4-star touches, such as complimentary toiletries, flat-screen TV, safe, minibar. **Some rooms** Expect more space for more money, and if you're claustrophobic, pay it. **Rooms** fronting the square are noisy. **Bed and bath** Excellent baths, comfy beds with good linens. **Favorites** The corner rooms have window seats looking out on the square. These rooms are also larger than most and pretty quiet. **Comfort and decor** Very comfortable beds and a good shower—tubs are a rarity in the single rooms, so go double if required. Decor is nice and new and exquisitely presented; lovely wallpaper.

PAYMENT, RESERVATIONS, AND RESTRICTIONS
Deposit No deposit, but payment in full upon arrival. **Credit cards** All major. **Check-in/out** 2 p.m./11 a.m. **Pets** No. **Elevator** Yes. **Children** Yes. **Disabled access** Good.

The Soho Hotel ★★★★

| QUALITY ★★★★ | VALUE ★★★ | PRICE RANGE £265–£370 |

4 Richmond Mews (off Dean Street), Soho, W1; ☎ 0207-559-3000; fax 0207-559-3003; www.firmdale.com

THE FIRMDALE GROUP CALLS THIS gorgeous hotel "Soho's first full service luxury hotel"; the *Tatler* named it the "Most Glamourous Hotel in the World"; and *Condé Nast Traveler* declared that "the interiors are a triumph." High praise, and all of it deserved. The Soho Hotel is in the thick of party-time Soho, between Dean and Wardour streets, putting it within hopping distance of the theaters of Shaftesbury Avenue, Chinatown, and New Oxford Street. As is usual in the hotels owned by Tim and Kit Kemp, the rooms have been individually and lovingly decorated by the talented Mrs. Kemp, and no expense has been spared in piling on the amenities. Only the best linens, mattresses, towels, toiletries, and electronics will do, and judging from the high occupancy rate enjoyed at this establishment, a lot of people agree. The decor is cool and modern without being at all stark—judicious use of color, lighting, and fabric blends beautifully with the unusual furniture, art, and antiques for which the Kemps are famous. A ten-foot-high Fernando Botero cat stands guard at the entrance, with oversize urns and wide-board floors creating the sense of a stage set—appropriate given the theatrical neighborhood. The restaurant is coolly beautiful, the Crimson bar is sexy, and the screening-room seats are upholstered in red leather and crazy cow-skin. All the rooms have double-glazed windows, but if you're looking for a quiet neighborhood, you'd best keep looking.

SETTING AND FACILITIES
Nearest tube station Piccadilly Circus or Covent Garden. **Quietness rating** C/D. **Dining** Breakfast, lunch, and dinner. **Amenities** Restaurant, bar and

lounge, Wi-Fi access, 2 drawing rooms, gym, spa-treatment rooms. **Services** Concierge, 24-hour room service, beauty treatments.

ACCOMMODATIONS

Rooms 91. **All rooms** Flat-screen TV (also in bathroom), DVD and CD player, minibar, 2 telephone lines, wireless access, desk, individual decor, Miller Harris toiletries. **Some rooms** Wraparound terraces with views. **Bed and bath** Highest standards in both. **Favorites** Suite with the terrace. **Comfort and decor** World-class in both departments.

PAYMENT, RESERVATIONS, AND RESTRICTIONS

Deposit No deposit, but payment in full upon arrival. **Credit cards** All major. **Check-in/out** 2 p.m./11 a.m. **Pets** Guide dogs only. **Elevator** Yes. **Children** Yes. **Disabled access** Very good.

Strand Palace Hotel ★★½

QUALITY ★★½	VALUE ★★★	PRICE RANGE £129–£149

372 Strand, Covent Garden, WC2; ☎ 0207-836-8080; fax 0207-836-2077; www.strandpalacehotel.co.uk

THE STRAND PALACE is smack in the middle of the Strand: directly in front of the delights of Covent Garden; a stone's throw from the National and National Portrait galleries, Trafalgar Square, St. Martin-in-the-Fields, and Somerset House; and strolling distance to all the theaters of the West End (including two theaters you could do cartwheels to without getting out of breath). Besides all the culture, there's a heavy concentration of shops, banks, restaurants, historic pubs, and transportation links right outside your door.

OK, so the location is great—what about the hotel? Well, charming it isn't. It's a darn big hotel (783 rooms on nine floors) with functional rooms and concierge services. Despite the great location and reasonable rates, there are some justified complaints: it's certainly short on atmosphere; there's no air-conditioning in some of the standard rooms; tiny single rooms should be avoided, even if you're alone; none of the five bars and restaurants are that great; and check-in can be as difficult as in the precomputer age. The biggest complaints about this hotel can be traced to its size—the service is uneven, with too few workers for too many guests; the occasional cold food from room service; and the nightmare of tour buses checking in and out at all hours. It's a plain-Jane option, but if you love the neighborhood or have business here, check for deals and upgrades that might get you into, say, one of the superior rooms that does have air-conditioning, Internet access, bearable decor, and so on.

The recent renovation has helped a lot; while the rooms are still very basic at the standard level, the pricier rooms have a few more things going for them. Club rooms offer a bit more than standard rooms, and you get access to a private lounge with wide-screen television and high-speed Internet access. Superior Club rooms go much further with the amenities: in-room Internet access, more space, and a free newspaper and pay-per-view movie each day. There are many interconnecting rooms for families.

SETTING AND FACILITIES

Nearest tube station Charing Cross. **Quietness rating** C to D; rooms on the Strand are the worst. **Dining** 372 The Strand (traditional English carvery buffet); Johnston's Café & Bar; Biancone: Italian cafe and bar; Diva: coffee, snacks, and drinks; The Mask Bar: cocktail bar; Hops! Bar: pub with music and a sports screen. **Amenities** Breakfast included in most rates, minibars in some rooms. **Services** Concierge; 24-hour room service, bellhop, laundry.

ACCOMMODATIONS

Rooms 785. **All rooms** Telephone, TV, hair dryer, tea and coffee. **Some rooms** Air-conditioning, Internet access, a free newspaper and pay-per-view movie each day. **Bed and bath** Typical hotel standard—nothing special, though clean and functional. **Favorites** Superior Club rooms. **Comfort and decor** Uninspired decor, reasonable comfort.

PAYMENT, RESERVATIONS, AND RESTRICTIONS

Deposit Credit card; cancellation policy by 2 p.m. local time on day of booked arrival. **Credit cards** All major. **Check-in/out** 1 p.m./11:30 a.m. **Pets** Not allowed. **Elevator** Yes. **Children** Yes. **Disabled access** Yes.

The Sumner Hotel ★★★★

| QUALITY ★★★★ | VALUE ★★★★ | PRICE RANGE £147–£175 |

54 Upper Berkeley Street, Marble Arch, W1; ☎ 0207-723-2244; fax 0870-705-8767; www.thesumner.com

THE SUMNER OPENED RECENTLY, advertising itself as the rebirth and relocation of the popular old South Kensington Hotel, Number Five Sumner, which has closed after a decades-long run. The "new" Sumner is across the park in an 1820s Georgian terrace that has been renovated and fitted to the highest standards while also preserving many lovely old details, such as oak paneling and carved coves. It's a bit more upscale than the former incarnation, upholding and possibly surpassing the high standards of Number Five, which kept a loyal clientele coming back year after year. The staff is friendly and accommodating, and the rooms are elegant and tastefully decorated. The location is practical, close to nearly everything that both tourists and business visitors could wish for: Hyde Park, Oxford Street, Soho, and Mayfair. Similarly to its level of service, the standard of comfort and attention here distinguishes the Sumner from its many other small-hotel competitors.

SETTING AND FACILITIES

Nearest tube station Marble Arch. **Quietness rating** A/B. **Dining** Complimentary buffet breakfast. **Amenities** Breakfast room, lounge, sitting room. **Services** 24-hour concierge.

ACCOMMODATIONS

Rooms 20. **All rooms** Air-conditioning, wide-screen LCD TVs, free broadband Internet, minibar, telephone, hair dryer, ironing board. **Some rooms** All are individually decorated; some rooms are more attractive than others, especially those on the first floor. **Bed and bath** High standards, with comfortable beds and good showers. **Favorites** Rooms on the 1st floor. **Comfort and decor** The decor is stately in the lounge and reception; the rooms are slightly less so but still very pretty.

PAYMENT, RESERVATIONS, AND RESTRICTIONS
Deposit No deposit, but payment in full upon arrival. **Credit cards** All major. **Check-in/out** After 2 p.m./11 a.m. **Pets** No. **Elevator** Yes. **Children** Yes. **Disabled access** Yes.

Thistle Victoria   ★★★★★

QUALITY ★★★★	VALUE ★★★★	PRICE RANGE £162–£210

101 Buckingham Palace Road, Victoria, SW1; ☎ 0207-834-9494; fax 0207-630-1978; www.thistlehotels.com

FIRST OF ALL, DON'T BE SCARED off by the rack rates above; there's almost always a deal to be had. Thistle has frequent-flyer tie-ins, special rates and packages, and all manner of deals. You may also know that Thistle hotels run from sublime to prison cell block, depending on the property they buy. Well, here they got lucky: this is one of those grand, massive Victorian terminus hotels that make your eyes pop when you enter it, and by the time you reach the middle of the vast dome with the huge chandelier swinging from it, you've unconsciously straightened your posture. The hotel was built to accommodate the visitors coming to see the Great Exhibition of 1851, and it was built to impress. There are stained-glass windows, wrought-iron staircases, columns, marble floors and walls, carved busts on stands or in alcoves outside and in, potted plants, and huge windows. The rooms are in good shape, the common areas are impressive, and the Galleria, which extends the already huge lobby to a second floor up, is one of the grandest hotel sitting areas in London.

The Thistle Victoria provides all the services one can expect from a hotel group with global standards: wireless and wired high-speed Internet, fax on request, satellite TV, nonsmoking floors, free newspapers, business support, and so on. It's near Victoria, Westminster Abbey, and Buckingham Palace—a central location that's noisy during the day. There are two sections: the "new" wing, built in the 1870s, has generally standard-sized rooms, whereas the old wing was built at a time when a guest required a couple of rooms plus one for the maid or valet, so this wing suffers from a rather knocked-together disparity of room size. The hotel has been renovating its rooms, with a view to a full face-lift within two years. So expect fresh new furniture and beds upon arrival this year.

SETTING AND FACILITIES
Nearest tube station Victoria. **Quietness rating** A in back, C in front, D in lower floors with huge windows, but that doesn't stop people from requesting these rooms again and again. **Dining** Very stately dining room, big enough to seat the occupants of the whole hotel; Harvard Bar; Galleria and lounge for tea and meals. **Amenities** The above refreshment areas, modems, many different pillows available, newspaper. **Services** Concierge, 24-hour room service, bellhop, laundry.

ACCOMMODATIONS

Rooms 357. **All rooms** Telephone, wireless or high-speed modem, satellite TV, hair dryer, iron, tea and coffee, in-house movies, writing desk. **Some rooms** Minibar, four-poster and half-tester (half a four-poster, with a canopy) beds, separate sitting room, huge windows, and high ceilings. **Bed and bath** All-cotton sheets on the beds; you can request special hypoallergenic, foam, or 100%-down pillows. The bathrooms are good. **Favorites** The big rooms at the front in the old wing with the big windows—noisy but gorgeous. **Comfort and decor** High quality; all rooms are individually decorated in nice colors and attractive furniture.

PAYMENT, RESERVATIONS, AND RESTRICTIONS

Deposit Credit card. **Credit cards** All major. **Check-in/out** 2 p.m./noon. **Pets** Dogs allowed conditionally. **Elevator** Yes. **Children** Yes. **Disabled access** No; many steps.

Threadneedles ★★★★

QUALITY ★★★★½	VALUE ★★★	PRICE RANGE £346–£420

5 Threadneedle Street, The City, EC2; ☎ 0207-657-8080; fax 0207-657-8100; www.theetoncollection.com

THE CITY'S FINANCIAL SQUARE MILE has long needed more hotels, or at least more charming hotels. This grand boutique hotel, the first luxury hotel in The City, fills the bill admirably, if expensively (with nonbusiness rates on weekends and some seasonal discounts for us noncorporate visitors). *Condé Nast Traveler* magazine called Threadneedles the hottest hotel of 2003, and the praise went straight to the head of the Eton Collection, which immediately opened two other hotels in London, both equally boutiquey but less business oriented. A grandiose former bank built in 1856, Threadneedles has undergone a so-called sympathetic renovation that borders on codependence, so many magnificent period details have they kept: the colonnades at the base of the stained-glass atrium, the wood paneling, and the strong scent of money. It's hardly cheap, as you can see by the prices, but the weekend rates (just under £200 a night) make it a nice outing, despite the quiet streets and closed businesses that are standard for The City on weekends. The hotel is a three-minute walk from the Bank tube station and within hailing distance of St. Paul's and other old churches, the Monument, the Barbican, and the Museum of London.

Although Threadneedles has some weekday restrictions on children, they are welcome on weekends, and a couple of interconnecting rooms will suit a family nicely. A recently built health spa–gym was added to the other amenities, such as the restaurant and top-of-the-line business and conference facilities. This is a top-grade hotel, with all the friendly service and efficient care for your comfort that you should expect from a boutique property in the global financial center of England.

SETTING AND FACILITIES

Nearest tube station Bank. **Quietness rating** B, even in front thanks to double-glazed windows, C with windows open. **Dining** Bonds Restaurant & Bar for breakfast, lunch, and dinner. **Amenities** Newspapers, bathrobes, safe, bottled water, breakfast included in some rates, fitness center, well-stocked minibar. **Services** Concierge, 24-hour room service, bellhop, laundry, complimentary shoe shine, all business-center facilities.

ACCOMMODATIONS

Rooms 69. **All rooms** Telephone with voice mail, high-speed modem and wireless Internet access, air-conditioning, satellite TV, CD player and music library, bathrobe and slippers, big desk. **Some rooms** Views of St. Paul's and The City. **Bed and bath** Frette bed linens, duck-down pillows and duvets. Limestone bathrooms with chrome and glass features, jetted tubs, upscale toiletries. **Favorites** Penthouse with great view of St. Paul's. **Comfort and decor** Very high standards of excellence, with every comfort provided. But if you're looking for Jollie Olde England, keep moving: the decor is all about careful downlighting, soothing hues, and no clutter; it's minimalist in its simplicity and elegance, but somehow warmer than you'd expect.

PAYMENT, RESERVATIONS, AND RESTRICTIONS

Deposit Credit card; 24-hour cancellation policy. **Credit cards** All major. **Check-in/out** 2 p.m./11 a.m. **Pets** Not allowed. **Elevator** Yes. **Children** Weekday restrictions depending on age. **Disabled access** 4 disabled-friendly rooms.

The Zetter Restaurant & Rooms ★★★★

QUALITY ★★★★	VALUE ★★★★	PRICE RANGE £182–£240

St. John's Square, 86–88 Clerkenwell Road, Clerkenwell, EC1;
☎ **0207-324-4444; fax 0207-324-4445; www.thezetter.com**

THIS WIDELY LAUDED HOTEL-RESTAURANT has sealed Clerkenwell's recent reputation as a very happening place. The pink-neon Z outside announces the hotel's intention to amuse you with retro chic, and the Scandinavian purity of the decor tells you they won't waste your time on Olde English frippery. And the prices let you know they aren't going to mug you: the founders' most important goal was "sensible prices."

Grouped around the five-story atrium, the rooms are modern and sharp-edged, with vintage fabric providing a splash of color and pattern for a calm focal point. The standard rooms are small, though not depressing. The beds are deluxe, as are the sheets and toiletries. Occupying the ground floor, The Zetter's restaurant and bar are bathed in light from the atrium by day, and at night soft-pink lighting makes everything—and everyone—look gorgeous. (You can also switch the bedrooms' lights to pink, the advantage of which increases with one's age.) Rooms offer interactive television with broadband Internet access, movies on demand, and other such modern conveniences. The penthouses go way out on a limb, with wraparound floor-to-ceiling windows and terraces and lots of space. The funny lounge with retro 1960s chairs will make you feel as if you've stepped into an episode of *The Jetsons*. The whole establishment, in fact, will make you smile—unless you're just a grump (or you just got your final bill).

SETTING AND FACILITIES

Nearest tube station Farringdon. **Quietness rating** B/D, quiet in rear rooms, noisy in front if windows are open, but double glazing helps a lot. **Dining** Zetter Restaurant, breakfast, lunch, afternoon tea, and dinner; mostly Italian menu. **Amenities** Newspapers, bathrobes, interactive TV with broadband access, movies on demand, 4,000 CD tracks to choose from, association with nearby health club, vending machines in halls stocked with high-quality goods, wheelchair-access room on each floor. **Services** Concierge, room service, bellhop, laundry, business facilities, Clerkenwell tour packages, weekend packages.

ACCOMMODATIONS

Rooms 59. **All rooms** Telephone with voice mail, satellite and Internet-ready interactive TV, movies on demand, hair dryer, bathrobe, hot-water bottle. **Some rooms** Terrace, minibar, jetted tub. **Bed and bath** Sleek and modern, with bath products from Barefoot Botanicals; high-quality beds, good linens, down pillows and duvets. **Favorites** The penthouses. **Comfort and decor** Surprisingly comfortable for such a rigorously modern place; decor is amusingly eccentric.

PAYMENT, RESERVATIONS, AND RESTRICTIONS

Deposit Credit card; 24-hour cancellation policy. **Credit cards** All major. **Check-in/out** 2 p.m./noon. **Pets** Not allowed. **Elevator** Yes. **Children** Yes. **Disabled access** Full disabled access, with one room on each floor set aside for wheelchair users.

PART FOUR

ARRIVING *and* GETTING ORIENTED

■ ENTERING *the* COUNTRY

VISITORS AND THEIR FAMILIES WITHOUT EUROPEAN UNION (EU), Irish, or British passports must fill out arrival cards. You will be (or should have been) issued your card by the cabin crew on the plane; fill it out and stick it in your passport. Immigration takes these cards seriously, so be sure to give the complete address of the place where you'll be staying. If for some reason you didn't get landing cards on board, pick them up at the counters at the immigration queue or from airport personnel. Don't wait until you reach the immigration desk to fill them out; do so before your turn. The walk from plane to immigration may be very long, so try to keep your carry-on luggage light and easy to handle.

IMMIGRATION

KEEP YOUR EYES ON THE SIGNS AND MAKE SURE you are heading for the right immigration line. If you've been traveling in first or business class, you can usually head straight for the Fast Track line and show your Fast Track Pass or boarding ticket. Fast Tracks often close at night—check with the flight attendant so that a closed Fast Track doesn't slow you down. There are two other lines: one for EU-passport holders and one for all other nationalities. Have your passport and landing card ready for display. You may be asked pointed questions about what you're doing in London and where you're staying; immigration is a serious business in this country with National Health Service and other quality-of-life attractions, not to mention the threat of terrorism. (For now, it's not as difficult for Americans to enter England as it is for the English to enter America—there is a growing resentment here about the overzealousness of the immigration officials in the States who have hassled, detained, and returned British citizens with little rhyme or reason; consequently, there may be a backlash against

Americans here to dramatize the immigration inequity.) Nationals from the United States, Canada, Australia, New Zealand, South Africa, Japan, or Switzerland can get in without a visa as long as they are on vacation. (If you are here on a job, you must have a work visa; students need a student visa. These documents must be obtained before you leave home.) Other nationalities should check with the British consulate in their home country before making plane reservations, or go to **www .britainusa.com** for visa information.

CUSTOMS

NEXT, YOU GO TO THE BAGGAGE HALL to collect your bags. Grab a free trolley, and after you have retrieved your luggage, follow signs for customs. The Goods to Declare exit is red, the Nothing to Declare exit is green, and the European Union exit (for anyone arriving from the continent) is blue.

Guidelines for what you can bring into England are divided into two categories: one for goods bought within the EU and the other for items purchased outside the EU. The likelihood that you will bring large jewels or luxury goods to London is remote, but you may want to save some money by bringing in your own instruments of vice, bought for bargain-basement prices at the duty-free shop before leaving or on the plane during your flight. Duty-free allowances are as follows:

- 200 cigarettes, 100 cigarillos, 50 cigars, or 250 grams of tobacco
- 2 liters of table wine and 1 liter of alcohol over 22% by volume (most spirits) and either 2 liters of alcohol under 22% by volume (fortified or sparkling wine or liqueurs) or 2 more liters of table wine
- 60 milliliters of perfume or 250 milliliters of eau de toilette
- Other goods up to a value of £145 (about $290)

While these are the published customs figures, it's unlikely that you'll be stopped and questioned if you happen to be carrying two or three cartons of cigarettes and a few bottles of vodka—customs personnel here are reasonable people with grown-up attitudes, and they can tell a big drinker or chain smoker from a bootlegger or smuggler. You may not bring in controlled drugs (any medication you have should be in its original bottle with your name on it), firearms and/or ammunition, obscene material, threats to public health and the environment, plants and vegetables, fresh meats, or any kind of animal.

unofficial **TIP**
If you have any questions about import and export issues, contact the **Excise and Inland Customs Advice Centre** (☎ 0845-010-9000; **hmce.gov.uk**).

Should you need to declare goods, duties are payable in pounds sterling or by MasterCard or VISA. You have rights, which Her Majesty's customs officers are supposed to make perfectly clear to you, such as receiving help in repacking bags if you are asked to unpack them, appealing on the spot to a senior officer against a proposed search, and claiming compensation if any property is damaged in a search. If you want to appeal a written tax or duty decision, let the officer know at the time and you'll receive a leaflet that explains how to do so. Direct any complaints to the Adjudicator's Office (Haymarket House, 28 Haymarket, London, SW1 4SP; ☎ 0207-930-2292; fax 0207-930-2298). If you decide to appeal later, you must notify customs within 45 days.

If you have nothing to declare, march through the appropriate exit. If you are stopped—occasionally random checks are carried out— *never* make jokes about the contents of your bags. You could be arrested, detained, and possibly deported. This is a nation that has dealt with terrorism for decades, and the officials are very serious. *Never* leave your bags unattended: a left piece of luggage can result in the closure of the tube, the evacuation of an airport terminal or car park, and the destruction of the left luggage.

If you haven't brought English pounds to pay for transportation from the airport, ATMs, known here as "cash points," can be found in all airports and train stations. Most machines operate on the Cirrus or MacPlus system, deducting money from your checking account at home. If you only have a credit card, be sure you have a four-digit PIN to use at the cash points—these machines seldom have letters on their keypads, so memorize your PIN numerically.

GETTING *into* LONDON

CAR RENTALS

MOST MAJOR CAR-RENTAL COMPANIES, including **Avis, Hertz,** and **Europcar,** have counters at the airports. It's best to reserve before you leave home, as you will probably get a better price. You must be over age 25 and have a valid license, good for at least two years, from your home country. Only metered spots and restricted parking are available in central London, so you'll need to use a parking lot ("car park"), which is expensive unless your hotel has an agreement with one nearby. For reservations, visit **www.hertz.com, www.avis.com,** or **www.europcar.com.**

From Gatwick Airport (☎ 0870-000-2468)

It's a long drive into London from Gatwick, and chances are traffic will be bad. A taxi to central London from Gatwick costs more than £100 and takes about an hour depending on traffic. Your best transportation option by far is the **Gatwick Express** (☎ 0845-850-1530; **www.gatwick-express.co.uk**), which leaves every 15 minutes (between 5 a.m. and 1:35 a.m.) and takes you right to Victoria Station in half an hour, where you can catch a taxi, tube, or bus to your final destination. (The trains stop running around midnight, after which there is a London-bound bus, or coach, outside the arrival hall.) Follow the signs and take the escalator down to the platform; the Gatwick Express is clearly marked. You can pay on the train, where they take cash and most credit cards, or you can book a ticket ahead through the Web site (be sure to keep track of your confirmation code). The fare is £15 one-way ("single journey"), £27 round-trip ("return"), half price for children between the ages of 5 and 15, and free for children under age 5. Check the Web site for special offers, such as the four-for-two discount. Don't bother with first-class tickets—they're a rip-off.

South Eastern Trains (☎ 0845-000-2211; **www.setrains.co.uk**) run every 15 minutes between Gatwick and Victoria, and although the trip takes slightly longer than the Gatwick Express, it costs less, at about £8 one-way, £15 round-trip during peak times; off-peak costs £8.30 round-trip (no one-way tickets sold).

If you're staying in the east or north, **Thameslink** (☎ 0845-748-4950; **www.nationalrail.co.uk**) is a good choice. Stops throughout the city include Blackfriars, City Thameslink, London Bridge, Farringdon, and King's Cross. Tickets are approximately £10 single journey, £20 return.

unofficial **TIP**
In general, the state of rail travel in London is woeful. Prices vary depending on a number of factors, including times, discounts, season, and the many incremental increases that the train companies regularly institute, even as their quality of service declines.

Hotelink (☎ 0129-353-2244; **www.hotelink.co.uk**), at £24 per person, is cheaper than a taxi, and you'll be met at the plane and taken to your hotel, which is comforting after a long flight (£98 gets you a private car for up to three passengers). You must book through the Web site or ask your hotel to book for you. Shuttles run about once an hour.

From Heathrow Airport (☎ 0870-000-0123; www.heathrow.co.uk)

BY TAXI Heathrow has a number of options for getting into London. The most expensive is the black-cab taxi, which can run from £50 for a no-traffic west-London drop-off to £80 or more for a bad-traffic central- or north-London destination. The best thing about the black cabs is that they are allowed to drive in the bus lanes, which saves time in rush hour. They're roomy enough for four people plus luggage, and they drop you at your doorstep.

Car services known as "minicabs" are another option. They are normal-sized cars, but the name differentiates them from the black cabs. They don't run on a meter and are slightly cheaper than the black taxis, but unless affiliated with a reputable outfit like **Addison Lee** (book in advance by phone at ☎ 0207-387-8888 or online at **www.addisonlee.com**), minicab drivers generally aren't as London-savvy as their black-cab counterparts; plus, they aren't allowed to use the bus lanes. Take advantage of the safe and spacious black cabs, whose drivers have " the Knowledge" (a long and stringent study of London's 20,000-plus roads) to get you anywhere you want to go. Driving time varies with

unofficial **TIP**
Tipping black-cab drivers is not expected, but a few extra pounds are much appreciated, especially if the driver helps you with your bags.

traffic, but it will generally take between 45 minutes and an hour to reach most central-London locations.

BY BUS **National Express** buses (☎ 0870-580-8080; **www.national express.com**) run from Heathrow to Victoria Station from 6 a.m. to 9:30 p.m., and leave from all terminals at Heathrow about every half hour. A single one-way standard fare starts at £4 and can rise to £10 and £15 round-trip depending on the time of day; fares are half price for children, and trips take about 50 minutes to central London.

BY UNDERGROUND (AKA TUBE) (**www.tfl.gov.uk**) The **Piccadilly Line** originates at Heathrow and is a fast and inexpensive way to get into the city, with convenient stops in central London and beyond to the northern suburbs. This is a great option if you aren't carrying a lot of baggage and it's not rush hour. Note that for some routes you have to get out and change trains at Acton Town, a pain that can add a sizable chunk of time to your trip. Buy the correct ticket—you'll be going to Zone One or Zone Two—and hold on to it; you'll need it when you leave the tube station. Tickets cost £4 one-way (less if you get a stored-value Oyster Card) and can be purchased right outside the tube entrance.

Look for signs to the Underground, and make sure you have the right ticket; if not, you can be fined £20 on the other end. Take the tube into London to a stop near your destination, and if you are lugging bags, hail a cab on the street to get to your hotel for a fraction of what a taxi would cost straight from the airport. Barring delays or train changes, it takes about an hour to get from Heathrow to Piccadilly Circus.

*un*official **TIP**
The tube is the least expensive option and the best bet for large groups of travelers.

BY HEATHROW EXPRESS TRAIN (☎ 0845-600-1515; **www.heathrowexpress.co.uk**) Run and owned by British Airways, this train is the fastest way into London—at 100 miles an hour, it takes only 15 minutes, and it leaves every 15 minutes, from 5:10 a.m. to 11:10 p.m. The standard fare is £28 round-trip, £14.50 one-way. (The first-class price of £46 round-trip apparently makes Heathrow Express the most expensive public transport in the world per mile and minute traveled.) Paddington's Underground station connects with four tube trains, as well as overland trains that go west. There are plenty of cabs at Paddington Station, and they've recently instituted a taxi-share system that can save you time and money.

From Stansted Airport (☎ 0845-850-0150; www.stansted.co.uk)

This is a relatively new airport, and it functions quite smoothly. As it's 35 miles outside of London, a taxi is prohibitively expensive (the trip takes over an hour and costs more than £120). Luckily, the **Stansted Express** train is very fast: you'll arrive at Liverpool Street Station in 45 minutes. Just follow the airport signs down one floor to the train platform, and catch the train to Liverpool Street, which is a major rail hub and tube station. Trip time is 45 minutes, and the trains run from 5 a.m. to 11:30 p.m. The fare is around £15 one-way and £26 round-trip. Trains run every 30 minutes. The **Airbus A6 or A9** (☎ 0870-580-8080) takes more than an hour and a half and costs £10 one way, £15 round-trip; its only benefit over the train is that it runs 24 hours a day.

From Luton Airport (☎ 0158-240-5100; www.london-luton.co.uk)

Luton deals mostly with British charter flights and cut-rate budget airlines. Getting into London from Luton (about 30 miles north of the city) by **Blueback** taxi (☎ 0870-771-1711; **www.blueback.com**) can take more than 90 minutes in traffic and costs around £90—they charge by the mile, and there are a number of hidden fees. **National Express** (see previous page) runs a 24-hour bus service from Victoria to Luton every 45 minutes for about £9 one-way and approximately £12 return; children ride for half price. **Greenline Bus** #757 travels between Victoria Station in London and Luton at a similar cost (call ☎ 0870-608-7261 or see **www.greenline.co.uk** for times). Travel time is approximately an hour and 45 minutes.

From London City Airport
(☎ 0207-646-0000; **www.londoncityairport.com**)

This is the closest airport to central London (nine miles east of Docklands), but it services only British and European short hops. The airport is well run, and the transportation is convenient: a black-taxi ride to London runs about £30, and shuttle buses leave every 20 minutes or so for Canary Wharf (£4) and Liverpool Street (£8).

By Eurostar (☎ 0123-361-7575; **www.eurostar.com**)

This high-speed train is a fast, though not necessarily cheap, way to get from the heart of Paris or Brussels to London's St. Pancras Station. If you want to pop over for a one-night stand on the spur of the moment, a number of fares can go as high as £298 for a fully refundable, fully negotiable ticket (check the Web site for special rates). In 2007, Eurostar relocated from south of the River Thames to a new facility at the St. Pancras railway station in north London, next to King's Cross; all onward connections can be made with ease from either St. Pancras or King's Cross. The great advantage of the Eurostar over the plane or ferry is that it is absolutely the most convenient way to get to and from the Continent—only two and a half hours from London to the Gare du Nord in Paris. (Don't forget to take your passport and fill out an arrival card for the British immigration checkpoint at the Gare du Nord.)

unofficial **TIP**
You can sometimes get last-minute-type deals at the Eurostar Web site for first-class seats that will be cheaper than the standard coach fare, and you'll love the first-class service and ambience (though in our opinion these amenities aren't worth paying full price for).

GETTING ORIENTED
in LONDON

POST CODES

LONDON IS DIVIDED INTO POST CODES, which instantly identify an area to those in the know. You'll see these codes on maps, street signs, and addresses. They are not arbitrary—they represent compass directions: *W1* is "West" and *WC* is "West Central," just as *E1* is "East" and *EC* is "East Central." Post codes can encompass more than one "village" and vice versa; SW1 includes Victoria, Pimlico, and Westminster, and Chelsea extends into districts SW3, SW7, and SW10. You'll quickly figure it out, and you'll have your own favorite post code before you know it.

unofficial **TIP**
The closer an area is to central London, the lower its post-code number—those ending in *1* are the closest.

GRASPING LONDON'S GEOGRAPHY
A River Runs Through It

The most important feature of London's geography is the rolling **River Thames.** It snakes through the city, bending around boroughs and post codes, and though it may not be the great and busy highway through London that it once was, it is still the major water artery and has been described as London's "liquid history." We predict that with public transportation as crowded as it has become, more and more river taxis will start plying the river, which would be a real boon to Canary Wharf commuters. (Most of the river's old tributaries have been filled in or covered over—and thank goodness for that: the Fleet and Tyburn rivers, for example, were fetid fluvial horrors clogged with sewage and often carrying cholera.)

Starting in the east, the Thames slows down at the hairpin turn around the Isle of Dogs, with **Greenwich** on the south side of the river. A foot tunnel there was built in Victorian times, its snail's-pace construction and profound plainness earning it the double-entendre nickname of "The Great Bore." **Canary Wharf** is on the Isle of Dogs, and at the next bend of the river is the **East End.**

The river straightens out for the section that includes the **Tower of London, Tower Bridge,** and **The City.** To the south of this portion of the river is **Southwark,** which gives way to the **South Bank** to the west, with the **Globe Theatre**'s thatched roof and the mighty **London Eye** Ferris wheel in view.

On the northern side of the river is **Somerset House,** once approachable by boat until the **Victoria Embankment** was built to stay the destruction of the Thames's frequent floods (a thing of the past since the 20th-century construction of the Thames Barrier at the eastern mouth of the river). Along the embankment you'll see the **Temple,**

Cleopatra's Needle, Big Ben, the **Houses of Parliament,** and, at Lambeth Bridge, on the opposite bank, the medieval **Lambeth Palace.** Radiating north from this important stretch of the river are **Covent Garden** and **Soho,** then **Bloomsbury** and, slightly to the northwest, **Regent's Park.**

Come back down to the river, and follow it past the grand Houses of Parliament at Westminster. The earliest incarnation of **Westminster Abbey** was on a little island near the very spot where the church now stands. The river passes the **Tate Britain** museum at Pimlico on its way to **Chelsea,** where Sir Thomas More once kept a grand riverside manor house, which Henry VIII liked so much that More—who must have regretted ever inviting his boss to visit—was forced to give it over to the king.

The Thames continues to flow west through **Fulham, Hammersmith,** and **Chiswick,** toward **Richmond** and **Hampton Palace.** North of Chelsea you'll find **South Kensington, Hyde Park, Bayswater,** and **Marylebone,** beyond which lies Regent's Park. Farther north is **St. John's Wood,** and then **Hampstead Heath.**

Hyde Park

This 350-acre green space, adjoined to the west by the 250-acre **Kensington Gardens,** is another landmark that helps visitors get a handle on London's geography. The park is surrounded by central London; to the north is Bayswater, to the east lie **Marble Arch** and **Mayfair,** to the southeast are **Belgravia** and **Knightsbridge,** to the southwest is **South Kensington,** and to the west are **Kensington** and **Holland Park.** To get from one place to the other via the parks' green and pleasant pastures and pathways is a joy, if you care to make the effort.

Get Streetwise

London is a huge city, but it is divided into enough discrete areas that you can differentiate among its parts rather easily, using the river and

unofficial **TIP**
Use a street map, not a tube map, to determine distances.

Hyde Park as baselines. Study a map of the whole city, seeing how the neighborhoods intersect. Though highly stylized, a tube map can help you get a grip on this vast metropolis. (Especially useful is the map of the yellow Circle Line, which orbits central London.) The tube map was streamlined from an unreadable mess of meandering lines into what you see now. It works and it's readable, but it's not geographically exact, and map distance versus walking distance between tube stops can be misleading.

The essential navigational aid is *London A–Z* (Z being pronounced "zed" by the British). Other serviceable street atlases are available, such as those by Collins and by Nicholson, but *A–Z* is the most commonly used. And it's not for tourists only. In fact, Londoners probably rely even more on it than tourists do, because they know how devilishly devious the streets here are. Not only will you find streets of the same name in different post codes, but many major arteries also change names as they charge ahead through various areas. Thus, the A4 from Heathrow becomes the Great West Road, then Talgarth Road, then Cromwell, Thurloe Place, Brompton Road, Knightsbridge, and Piccadilly, all without making a single turn. Complicating things further, an abundance of streets share the same first name but have different suffixes: Street, Place, Road, Mews, Gardens, Crescent, Circle, Square, High Street. . . .

unofficial **TIP**
Knowing the full address and post code of a destination is crucial.

The story of the *A–Z* atlas is typically English. In 1935, Mrs. Phyllis Pearsall, one of those redoubtable Englishwomen à la Florence Nightingale, got so frustrated at being unable to find her way around London that she single-handedly walked and mapped its 23,000 streets in a year's time. We salute her.

Some of the major thoroughfares in London are of rather ancient vintage—old commercial routes for horse-drawn carts, and the streets, mews, alleys, dead ends, cul-de-sacs, terraces, and crescents that were often cowpaths, driveways, back passageways to a high street, or well-traveled footpaths between homes and pubs. This city was never brought to heel by planners in the way that New York and parts of Paris were (though the Blitz certainly took care of many exotic East End warrens), which is what makes it so much fun to explore. For seeing the best of London by foot, there is nothing better than just getting lost. Indeed, it is highly unlikely that you won't do so unintentionally at least once when you're here. But as long as you carry a copy of *A–Z* and persist in one direction or another, you are bound to eventually hit some recognizable landmark . . . or a taxi.

A fantastic shop in Covent Garden called **Stanford's** (12–14 Long Acre; ☎ 0207-836-1321; **www.stanfords.co.uk;** tube: Covent Garden) carries every map known to London. Here you can find walking maps, cycling maps, subterranean maps, backstreet maps for avoiding the large thoroughfares, and maps of the old city.

unofficial **TIP**
It's best to get the big picture with a foldout map that is relatively simple, with a bird's-eye view of London's post codes, and keep a pocket street atlas on hand for narrowing down your route.

THINGS *the* LOCALS *already* KNOW

GETTING THE LOWDOWN ON WHAT'S UP

FOR THE LATEST INFORMATION ON CURRENT PLAYS, movies, art exhibits, clubs, fairs, museum tours, lectures, walking tours, or whatever, pick up a copy of *Time Out London* magazine. This weekly is more thorough than its competitor, *What's On,* although the latter is a little simpler to read. As a cheaper alternative to the magazines, most of the daily newspapers publish weekend entertainment sections on Thursdays and Fridays.

If you want to buy a copy before you arrive, e-mail **net@timeout .co.uk,** call the distribution department at ☎ 0207-813-6060, or simply check out the Web site—a virtual magazine with some extras you won't find in the hard copy—at **www.timeout.com/london.** If you live in a big city, look for *Time Out London* at newsstands that carry foreign newspapers and magazines.

TIPPING

MANY RESTAURANTS LEVY A DEFAULT SERVICE CHARGE of between 12.5% and 15%, so examine your menu and your bill to see if it has already been applied. If it has and you still get a credit-card receipt with an empty gratuity line, just run a slash through it unless you choose to tip extra. If you pay with cash, you can leave some change from the bill if you feel like it. If service is not included, it will be mentioned in some obvious manner on the bill.

unofficial **TIP**
A tip of 12–15% is appropriate in restaurants; if you were ever a waiter or if the service was great, 20% is good.

Taxi drivers appreciate a tip and in many cases really earn it by helping with bags, taking a smart route, and providing information. Anything from 50p to £1 is usual in short-haul trips; after £10, a tip of 10% to 15% is fine. You won't be abused for giving a lousy tip or even no tip at all, and you may be warmly thanked for a good one. In the good hotels, you can tip the staff as you feel they deserve—£1 or £2 a bag for bellhops, a fiver for the maid, whatever you think the concierge deserves for whatever service he or she provides. Check to see if service is included on your bill, in which case feel free to tip only those staff who have been especially helpful.

LONDON'S MEDIA

Newspapers

London has a huge selection of newspapers, from the solemn to the sordid. Make a point of reading at least a couple of them while you're here.

The *Times* Like so much of the world's media, this is a Rupert Murdoch production. It aspires to be a great newspaper, but it falls short of the mark. The recent change to tabloid size has diminished it in more than size, but tube riders like the convenience. The *Times* does have a big Sunday edition with something for everyone.

Daily Express Conservative middlebrow newspaper.

Daily Mail Usually manages to have a star, a royal, or a socialite on the cover. Fairly good money section. Relatively free of hard news.

Daily Telegraph Right-wing broadsheet with large Saturday and Sunday editions.

Evening Standard Tabloid-sized afternoon newspaper; a little light on news, but it features good local stories and entertainment listings, plus the Metro Life entertainment supplement on Thursdays and the *Evening Standard Magazine* on Fridays.

Financial Times Printed on pink paper; a must for the businessperson.

The *Guardian* A well-written liberal newspaper, also recently reduced to tabloid size.

The *Independent* A decent broadsheet with some good writing and a very good Sunday edition.

International Herald Tribune This is the fluff-free paper of choice for American expatriates—it features the best of the *New York Times* and runs no advertising. Great editorial section with weekly contributions from America's favorite columnists, and *Doonesbury*, too.

The *Observer* A Sunday-only paper with all the sections you'd expect; a fine read.

The *Sun* Sleazy tabloid. This is the home of the (in)famous Page Three Girl, the gratuitous photo of a topless woman placed on the third page. The content is similarly absurd. Read it and laugh.

Other tabloids that you may not want to be caught dead reading include the *Daily Star*, full of the important news of women's breasts, murder, and sex scandals; and the *Sport*, which doesn't even bother to pretend it's anything but a titillation rag.

A number of free papers handed out on the street are "lite" versions of the dailies—full of ads and yesterday's (or this morning's) news.

Magazines

The Big Issue A must-read, this magazine carries some of the most interesting articles on London you'll find, and it helps provide the homeless with income (feel free to give the vendor a tip when buying it). It's often guest-edited by some literary or media worthy.

The *Economist* Very serious and informative conservative mag on money and politics.

Harpers and Queen Glossy magazine devoted to the rich, famous, and beautiful; a bit like the *Tatler* in its social coverage, but with more beauty articles.

Hello! Weekly rag that makes *People* look like the *New Yorker*. Lots of Hollywood celebs, minor royalty, gossip, puzzling media creations, and a weekly television and radio guide. *OK!* is its closest competitor, and it's easy to get them mixed up—the same photos often appear in both weeklies.

Private Eye Political satire that is the scourge of the establishment—*any* establishment. Might be obscure for nonresidents, but it's still worth a try.

Punch Now owned by Mohammed Al-Fayed, this august humor magazine is sold throughout Harrods. It's lost its punch, however—don't bother unless you happen across editions from the 19th century.

The *Spectator* Entertaining, intelligent, and politically to the right, which in England has no connection to religious fundamentalism and is often intellectually rigorous.

Tatler House (or castle) organ of aristocrats, social climbers, and wannabes. Features such edifying articles as guides to rich bachelors and bachelorettes. Endless pages of photos of dull social gatherings of marquises, dukes, and barons. Good information on how to spend all your money in one day.

Time Out London The most comprehensive weekly guide to what's going on in the city (see page 141).

The *Times Literary Supplement* Like the *New York Times Book Review,* this is a ripping-good intellectual read, with articles and book reviews written by some of the brightest people in the world of letters. After you've read a few pieces, you'll wonder how you've lived without it.

Television

The state-owned **British Broadcasting Corporation (BBC)** charges all television owners a subscription fee to the tune of £135.50 a year (that's for a color TV; amusingly, if you've held on to your antique black-and-white set, you pay just £45). This means that BBC programming is commercial free, save advertising for the network's own shows and products. It's a lovely change of pace from American television, but the sad truth is that the "Beeb" has lost its edge, and the best stuff on the telly here originated in America on F/X, HBO, or Showtime.

BBC 1 is the weakest of the British TV networks, with lots of cheaply produced cooking shows, talk shows, and animal programs. **BBC 2,** once very stuffy, now produces some decent dramas and indecent reality shows, imports the occasional good movie, and has some good current-affairs shows.

unofficial **TIP**
For sociological interest, watch the BBC—you'll find a few wonderful shows, such as Britcoms, adaptations of Dickens or less recognized English authors, and quirky gardening and house-decorating programs that wouldn't last half a minute on American TV.

The independent network **ITV,** on channel 3, currently produces the most expensive dramas seen on British TV. It's funded by commercials, which appear (mercifully) only every 15 minutes. **Channel 4** is also a commercial station, and definitely the hippest. Conscientiously irreverent and edgy, this is where you'll find last year's season of favorite American TV fare, the good ones, usually. **Five,** another indy network (found, appropriately enough, on channel 5), carries a standard mix of talk shows, sports, movies, and programming from the States.

Cable, found in all the good hotels, provides **Sky One,** which carries CNN, MTV, and plenty of movies and television programs from the United States.

Radio

Most radio programming is provided by the BBC, which operates five national networks, and is in many ways quintessentially British. (Until the 1950s, BBC radio presenters were required to wear dinner jackets when reading the news.) This Britishness is best heard on BBC Radio 3 and 4. For instance, Radio 4's shipping forecast, a maritime weather report broadcast four times daily, is eccentric and incomprehensible to the layperson, articulating perfectly the voice of an old island culture.

The local listings in newspapers and magazines will tell you what is on when.

•	**Radio 1**	Pop music at 98.8 FM
•	**Radio 2**	Light entertainment at 89.2 FM
•	**Radio 3**	Classical music and related topics at 91.3 FM
•	**Radio 4**	The best thing in British media. Like National Public Radio in America but offering much more—short stories, serials, dramatizations, interviews, quizzes, comedies, and plays.
•	**Capital FM**	Top-ten pop music at 95.8 FM and oldies on Capital Gold at 1548 AM
•	**Classic FM**	More classical music on 100.9 FM. (An English friend once told me that no Brit will ever complain about classical music played at ear-deafening decibels.)
•	**Jazz FM**	Great jazz and blues at 102.2 FM
•	**Newstalk**	All news all the time, plus often-interesting phone-in commentary, at 97.3 FM

Telephones

Criminally, British Telecom (BT) pinheads decided to remove and sell off the majority of the red phone boxes that used to be such a pleasing and distinctive hallmark of London. (OK, maybe they were used as a loo once too often in some areas, but still.) You will still see them in many of the tourist areas, but mostly you'll find soulless and ugly glass boxes plastered with tons of sex-trade advertising.

unofficial **TIP**
Important: When calling England from overseas, drop the 0 preceding the phone number, but from within the country, use the 0.

The public phone booths here take either coins or BT phone cards. Coins are your best bet, and you can make a very quick call for 20p. Some public phones in restaurants have a system in which you wait for the call to be answered before putting the money in—otherwise, you lose it. Read the directions before using a pay phone.

English telephone jacks will not fit an American modem cord, so if you have your laptop and want to get online using a dial-up Internet connection, ask the hotel for an adapter or buy one at a department store (Harrods, John Lewis, Peter Jones, Dixons, and small-electronics shops carry them).

International calls are made by dialing 00, then the country code, area code, and local number. To call through a long-distance service, dial its access lines and follow the directions, using your credit-card number:

AT&T Direct ☎ 0800-890-011; Australia, 0800-890-061
Canada Direct ☎ 0800-890-016

SOME IMPORTANT NUMBERS

00   International dialing code; that is, if you're placing a call from England to another country, dial 00 + 1 for the United States and Canada, 61 for Australia, 64 for New Zealand, etc.

100   General operator

112 or **999**   Emergency for police, fire, or ambulance

153   International directory assistance

155   International operator

118118   U.K. directory assistance

PUBLIC TOILETS

LONDON HAS EARNED THE ADMIRATION of its tourists and the appreciation of its dwellers for its plentiful and clean public conveniences, also called WCs (water closets), lavs, toilets, or loos. Because there's usually a small charge for their use, people tend to be more respectful as they've invested some money. Fifty pence gets you 15 minutes in a free-standing cubicle, which is washed and sterilized automatically after each use. There always seems to be toilet paper in these loos, as well as in the free lavatories found in the parks and some tube stations and squares.

unofficial **TIP**
Although we can't tell you it's OK to walk into a pub, hotel, or a restaurant and use the toilet if you aren't a customer, many people here aren't too uptight about that.

MAIL

GET YOUR STAMPS FOR POSTCARDS and letters from a newsagent or a **Mail Boxes Etc.** shop (visit **www.mbe.co.uk** for locations). Public post offices can get extremely crowded, as lots of people pay their bills there. If you want to buy special-edition stamps, you will have to queue up at the post office. An overseas postcard stamp costs 54p and an overseas letter 78p to £1.24, depending on weight. Remember to put an air-mail sticker on your letter, and be sure to include the name of the destination country in the address. (I once had a letter addressed to New York City returned because I didn't write "USA" on the envelope.)

Royal Mail post offices are open Monday through Friday, 9 a.m. to 5 p.m., and Saturday, 9 a.m. to 12:30 p.m. Cuts in services have rendered the wonderful old twice-daily postal delivery a thing of the past, and in order to save money, post offices are increasingly forced to share the premises of a tourist bureau, a stationery store, or a press agent—there's even one in the lobby of the Science Museum! (For more information, visit **www.royalmail.com**.)

STORE HOURS

MANY RETAIL SHOPS HERE OPERATE on a rather old-fashioned schedule of 10 a.m. to 6 p.m. Monday through Saturday. But in deference

to an encroaching 9-to-5 ethos and a global consumer culture, a number of stores, especially the
clothing chains, are now open on Sundays. Some
supermarkets and convenience stores stay open
around the clock (though some close on Saturdays
at 10 p.m. in order to restock and then reopen at
8 a.m. on Sundays). Even the great holdouts—
Harrods, John Lewis, and Peter Jones—are now
open later on Wednesdays and Thursdays. ("Later"
means only until 7 or 8 p.m., however.)

unofficial **TIP**
Call and check before
you take off for any shop,
especially on a Saturday,
when strange hours such
as noon to 5 p.m. may be
in effect.

CRIME

LONDON'S CRIME RATE SEEMS TO BE RISING with its rents and
costs. While the homicide rate remains relatively low, owing in part
to England's strict gun laws, muggings are on the rise, as the haves
seem to have so much more and the have-nots less.
Compounding the problem is a national increase
in alcoholism and drug abuse.

On the streets of London, there is definitely a
disturbing trend toward the commission of
crimes more violent than the usual purse snatch-
ings. Reports of youth gangs going on mugging
or bodily-harm sprees are not uncommon. Shouting matches on the street have likewise become

unofficial **TIP**
Women, take note:
statistics for rape are high.
Try not to travel alone
at night, and avoid the
top decks of night buses.

familiar sights, and they frequently degenerate into fisticuffs. (Even
wealthy neighborhoods are not immune to burglaries, car thefts, and
highway robbery.)

As in all cities, there's a lot of stress, and bad behavior often follows on its heels. Do keep a sharp eye out, and try to avoid areas with
a high concentration of pubs (such as Leicester Square and Soho) late
at night. If you must take a night bus, sit downstairs; the rowdies tend
to congregate on the upper deck.

Here are some safety tips, most of which are just common sense:

• Keep your purse close at all times; sling it across your chest if possible,
  and don't leave it sitting unattended in a public place—hanging a bag
  on the back of a chair at a sidewalk cafe is a temptation to thieves.

• Don't put your wallet in a backpack unless it's in an inner zipped pocket.

• Put your wallet in a front pocket.

• Use a money belt when carrying large sums.

• Don't hang around counting your money after using an ATM.

• Don't wear flashy jewelry or an expensive wristwatch.

• Watch your belongings on the tube and on buses.

• Avoid buses after midnight; use a taxi or minicab instead. Women
  may be happier using the woman-owned **Lady Mini Cabs** (☎ 0207-
  272-3300). For a black taxi, try **Dial a Cab** (☎ 0207-426-3420) or

> **Radio Taxis** (☎ 0207-272-0272). The car service **Addison Lee** is also highly recommended (☎ 0207-387-8888).

- Never accept an unsolicited ride from a minicab driver.
- Leave your passport in a safe at the hotel, and carry a photocopy of the information page.
- Ignore any implausible story you might hear on the street; this town is full of exceedingly talented con artists.
- Stay out of the parks after dark.
- Late at night, travel in groups, if possible.
- If you buy something at a very expensive store, take it back to your hotel or ask for a plain bag to carry it in.
- The emergency phone number is ☎ 999; *don't* use it except in a true emergency. To report a crime, call ☎ 112 or directory assistance at ☎ 118118 for the number of the nearest police station.

THE HOMELESS AND BEGGARS

THE BEST WAY TO HELP THE HOMELESS is to buy *The Big Issue,* a magazine that is sold on the street by licensed vendors. The magazine is almost always fascinating, featuring guest editors and words and images by the homeless, and part of the money goes to the vendors, who work hard in all weather for very little money (tips are gratefully accepted).

In London, as in other European cities, you will often see women in headscarves carrying sleeping babies and begging. You may feel moved to give a pound or two, but more often than not, such scenes are staged: many panhandlers will "borrow" a child to more effectively generate pathos, and the babies are reportedly sedated to keep them quiet.

RELIGION

OPPOSITE ARE THE PHONE NUMBERS for various religious bodies and places of worship. If you're not picky, feel free to drop into any of the wonderful churches all over London for a bit of beauty and peace.

GAY LONDON

WHEN OSCAR WILDE WAS ARRESTED ON CHARGES of sodomy at the Cadogan Hotel in the last days of the 19th century, that afternoon's boat to France was so crowded with single gentlemen that it almost sank. The law banning homosexuality was often enforced more for political reasons than anything else, but it made being gay in England fraught with real danger. And it was all the more peculiar because of the tacit acceptance of same-sex dalliances in the all-male school system of the upper classes (such experimentation was understood to be a passing phase).

Anglican
   St. Paul's Cathedral, ☎ 0207-236-4128,
   or Westminster Abbey, ☎ 0207-222-5897
Baptist
   Bethesda Baptist Church, ☎ 0207-221-7039
Buddhist
   The Buddhist Society, ☎ 0207-834-5858
Catholic
   Brompton Oratory, ☎ 0207-808-0900, or
   Westminster Cathedral, ☎ 0207-798-9055
Christian Science
   Third Church of Christ, Scientist, ☎ 0207-499-1271
Greek Orthodox
   Greek Orthodox Archdiocese, ☎ 0207-723-4787
Hindu
   Shri Swaminarayan Mandir Temple, ☎ 0208-961-5031
Islamic
   London Central Mosque, ☎ 0207-724-3363
Jewish
   Liberal Jewish Synagogue, ☎ 0207-286-5181, or
   United Synagogue, ☎ 0208-343-8989
Methodist
   Westminster Central Hall, ☎ 0207-222-8010
Quaker
   Friends House, ☎ 0207-387-3601

In 1967, the outdated law was finally changed, and today London boasts the most happening gay scene in Europe. There are gay hotels, bookshops, health clubs, religious groups, bars, nightclubs, cafes, travel agencies, publications, and even a taxi company. The liveliest areas are in Soho (Old Compton Street in particular) and Earls Court. Clapham Common, Hampstead Heath, and the Brompton Cemetery are popular green spaces for hanging out and meeting people—and maybe doing a little cruising.

Here are a few gay-friendly organizations and businesses:

The **London Lesbian and Gay Switchboard** can be reached 24 hours a day, 365 days a year at ☎ 0207-837-7324 or **www.llgs.org.uk.** The staff can offer information and counsel on any issues related to being gay in London.

Gay's the Word is the oldest gay-and-lesbian bookshop in the United Kingdom (66 Marchmont Street, Bloomsbury; ☎ 0207-278-7654; tube: Russell Square). In 2007, under threat from rising rents, the owners launched a Save the Store campaign that has forestalled the wolf at the door for now; if you want to help, visit the shop's Web site (**freespace.virgin.net/gays.theword**), or just go and spend a lot of money there.

Philbeach Hotel is a fun, reasonably priced, and exclusively gay hotel. A party for crossdressers erupts once a week. (30–31 Philbeach Gardens, Earls Court, SW5; ☎ 0207-373-1244; **www.philbeachhotel.co.uk;** tube: Earls Court.)

Check out *Time Out London* and the following Web sites to find gay-friendly and exclusively gay hotels, hostels, bars, restaurants, and so on: **www.gaytravel.co.uk** and **www.pinkuk.com** list hotel deals, information on special club nights and raves, and details about current cultural activities. Find out when the summer Gay Pride Day is held—it's one of the best parades in London and getting better every year.

LOST/STOLEN CREDIT CARDS

REPORT MISSING CREDIT CARDS to both the police and the 24-hour lost-or-stolen-card bureaus below:

American Express	☎ 0127-369-6933
Diners Club	☎ 0800-460-800
MasterCard/Eurocard	☎ 0800-964-767
Switch	☎ 0113-277-8899
VISA	☎ 0800-895-082

PART FIVE

GETTING AROUND

▌ PUBLIC TRANSPORTATION

THE MOST IMPORTANT THING TO TAKE OUT with you in London is a good map and/or the pocket-sized *London A–Z* guide (see page 140)—the former for the big picture and the latter for the details. You won't regret the extra weight in your bag. A camera is another must, because you never know when you'll run into a horse-drawn carriage or a battery of the queen's guards outfitted in the kind of full regalia that really wouldn't work in battle: gold shields, plumed hats, silver swords, and all manner of medals, loaded with significance and tradition. Strange details on buildings or gates will beg to be recorded, as will juxtapositions of interest—a horse-drawn Harrods carriage with a double-decker bus behind it, or a pigeon relaxing on the head of the lion in Trafalgar Square. Bring extra film or a second (or third) digital-camera card. Also, be sure to carry a few 50p coins for the free-standing public toilets, which may be ugly but are clean and a rare convenience in a major metropolis.

As with all large, modern cities, London's biggest problems are transportation and traffic. The congestion fee initiated in February 2003 was an attempt to limit cars in a certain central area by charging nonresidents £5 a day to drive inside its perimeter. The idea was to get more people to leave their cars at home and use public transportation, and the money generated was to be used to improve Underground and bus service. In February 2007 the congestion area was expanded to encompass most of western London as well, and the charge has risen to £8 a day. (Mayor Ken Livingstone is also seeking to charge SUV drivers £25 a day *and* rescind the 90% resident discount.) Businesses are up in arms, delivery people are irate, and traffic has improved only slightly—in the opinion of cabbies, the final authorities on such matters, it's still abysmal. In fact, because of the steep discount for residents of the charging area, the danger is

unofficial **TIP**
Avoid public transport during rush hours, and resign yourself to taking a cab late at night if your destination is not served by a night bus (a regular-route bus with an *N* prefix).

that all the people who wouldn't have gone near the previous congestion zone are now less loath to, adding a potential 60,000 cars (paying just £4) a week to the most heavily traveled neighborhoods.

The increase in people using public transportation as a result of the congestion charge has made commuting in London just that much more hellish. There are constant delays and interruptions of service on the tube, and on the weekends, when repairs are made, whole lines shut down. Buses, when not stuck in traffic, have an infuriating habit of arriving at long last in packs. But all that said, as a visitor you will be more tolerant than regular commuters, and you'll be able to travel during off-peak times. Eight times out of ten, the tube will get you wherever you're going quickly and efficiently, and the double-decker buses are a fun way to see London.

For help with any questions you might have about getting around London, call **Transport for London** at ☎ 0207-222-1234, or visit its excellent Web site at **www.tfl.gov.uk.** You can get information on any facet of travel, including the most direct tube or bus route to where you are going, how everything (or *if* everything) is running, advice on the best discount fares, and an apologia on why the tube has to stop at midnight (unlike modern subways, London's only has two tracks and cannot simply divert trains onto other tracks for servicing).

TRAVEL ZONES

TRANSPORT FOR LONDON HAS DIVIDED the city into six travel zones. **Zone 1** is in the middle of central London, and the rest radiate outward in circles that end at **Zone 6** in the suburbs and at Heathrow in the west. Most of what you'll be doing in London will most likely fall within Zones 1 and 2. Bus and tube fares rise with zone numbers. For years, transportation experts have discussed the possibility of simplifying fares by instituting one flat fee, but the size of London and the cost of fuel for buses makes such a master stroke impractical.

OYSTER CARDS

THE CHEAPEST WAY TO TRAVEL AROUND LONDON, these cards are so named because they come in a blue plastic wallet that opens up just like a crustacean (but with more ease) and are meant to protect your money as an oyster protects a pearl. A single cash-fare tube ticket for Zone 1 travel costs £4, but with an Oyster card, the same journey costs £1.50. Using Oyster also cuts your bus fare in half: single fares cost £2 when you pay on board or buy a ticket from the too-often-unreliable ticket machines in central London, but with an Oyster they're only £1. The daily price cap for using only buses and trams is £3, so you can make as many journeys as you like within a 24-hour period from 4:30 a.m. on and never pay more than £3.

Oyster cards are available at any tube or train station for a refundable deposit of £3. Once you have the card, you can store cash on it that is deducted every time you touch in and out on the yellow card reader at tube stations. A green light should appear on the reader when your card has been validated; failing to touch in correctly at the beginning and end of your journey will result in your being charged the maximum cash fare. When using the bus, you have to touch in at the start of your journey but not at the end. Every time you touch the card to the reader, you will see how much money is left on your card. When it starts getting low, you can top up the card with cash or credit at any tube-station ticket window or the easy-to-use touch-screen Oyster ticket machines inside the station; some newsagents and corner shops will replenish your card as well. Another incentive for using Oyster: the daily price cap when using tubes and buses is 50p less than the cost of a one-day Travelcard (see below).

To get your £3 deposit back at the end of your visit, return the card to a ticket kiosk at any station, and a check will be mailed to your home address. You can also keep the card for the next time you travel—Oyster cards stay active for two years, and if you don't use it within that time frame, you can take it to a station and have it reactivated. You might even give a card with some cash left on it to someone who can use it. Good deed and all that.

unofficial **TIP**
We cannot stress enough the ease and value of the Oyster card, especially as bus drivers can be implacably unhelpful if you can't get the machine at the bus stop to give you a ticket. Best of all, this one card takes care of all transportation in the Transport for London system.

TRAVELCARDS

THE BEST ONE-OFF, ONE-DAY DEAL for traveling on public transportation is the Travelcard, which gives you unlimited travel on the tube, buses, and most overland rail services in Greater London, including the Docklands Light Railway (DLR). A one-day, off-peak Travelcard for Zones 1 and 2 (bought after 9:30 a.m.) costs £5.10; a one-day peak Travelcard for these two zones costs £6.60. A seven-day Travelcard costs £23.20 for Zones 1 and 2, and a three-day Travelcard for the same two zones costs £16.40.

Since January 2007, many good and not-so-good changes have been made to fares and tickets. (The powers that be have to justify the hefty salaries of expensive consultants and transport czars and show they're always cooking up complicated new ideas.) It is no longer possible, for example, to buy a Family Travelcard, but children age 10 and younger can now travel free on the London Underground, buses, trams, and DLR. A one-day, off-peak Travelcard valid in Zones 1 through 6 costs £2 for riders ages 11 to 15; 16-to-18-year-olds pay the same rate as adults. An adult with a valid Travelcard can purchase one-day cards for up to four children between the ages of 5 and 15 for £1 each. For parties of ten or more adults and/or under-18s, go for group tickets, which cost £3.50 for each adult and £1 for each child under 18, but note that your group has to travel together all the time. Group tickets are valid on the tube, DLR, and National Rail only (no buses). Alas, there are no senior or student discounts for visitors— you have to be a London resident to qualify. Available at tube stations and at some newsagents, Travelcards can be used on buses within the same travel zones.

BUSES

 IN OUR OFTEN-CHALLENGED OPINION, there is no better view in the world than that of London from the top first-row seat of a double-decker bus. Many of the old buildings seem

kids to have been designed expressly for this vantage point; the statues and gargoyles that decorate some of the city's fine architecture are at eye level when you're riding up top. (See page 167 for some of the best double-deckers from which to view London.) With 17,000 bus stops all over London, you should be able to find one that's pretty close to your chosen destination.

The European Union forbids double-decker buses and for decades has threatened to remove them from London streets to comply with idiotic Continental regulations. Let's hope the government keeps its head in this case and tells Brussels exactly what bus it can get on.

Types of Buses

ROUTEMASTERS These wonderful buses allowed riders to hop on at the rear, where conductors would take their fares. Sadly, Routemasters have been all but phased out in London due to safety concerns about passengers jumping on and off while the buses were still moving. More convincing were the arguments that they were inaccessible to the disabled and polluted more than newer buses. Still, their loss is a shame, especially as these buses provided jobs to not just one but two people—the driver and the ticket taker, whose presence made the buses safer at night. All that remains of the beloved Routemaster (which was in fact preferred by just about every single Londoner) are the two **Heritage Routes:** Route 9, from Knightsbridge to Aldwych, and Route 15, from Aldwych up to Marble Arch. All other London buses have low floors and are wheelchair accessible.

DOUBLE-DECKER FRONT-ENTRY BUSES These have replaced the old Routemasters. You get on in front, pay the driver, and take your seat. If there is no ticket machine at the bus stop, you can pay with cash; correct change is good to have but not required. An Oyster card or Travelcard (see pages 152 and 153) makes paying much less of a hassle, not to mention more economical.

SINGLE-DECKER BUSES These nondescript, EU-approved buses are used for shorter journeys through London. They cost the same to ride as other buses but are less roomy (except for the double-length "bendy" buses). You must pay your fare with an Oyster card, a Travelcard, a day pass, or a single ticket from the machine at your bus stop. You *won't* be allowed to pay with cash, even, unbelievably, if the ticket machine is broken. On rare occasions, bus drivers have been known to wait for passengers while they run and buy a ticket at the machine . . . but don't count on it.

unofficial **TIP**
We advise against sitting alone on the top deck of a night bus late in the evening—many drunks and sinister types ride at this time, and these days there's no ticket-taking conductor to protect you.

NIGHT BUSES These follow the same routes as the daytime buses but run less often. They have an N before the route number and run from around 11 p.m. to 6 a.m. These buses are the only all-night public transport available, as the tube stops running around midnight. Most night buses have a stop at Trafalgar Square.

Here's how the buses go 'round and 'round:

GET ON THE BUS Most bus-stop shelters have a big map of London displaying the bus routes in different colors, as well as a list of the stops for each bus number on the route. Be sure that you're standing at the correct bus stop—Oxford Street and Hyde Park Corner, for example, have many buses and many stops. If you don't see your bus listed on the red-and-white sign, it won't stop where you are. A sign with a red symbol on a white background indicates a compulsory stop, while a sign with a white symbol on a red background indicates a request stop. In theory, a bus must always make a compulsory stop, but don't believe it. When you see your bus, wave your hand to flag it down, or it may just sail sedately by (if it's full, it will *definitely* sail by, so don't take it personally). When preparing to get out, press the red button on the yellow pole in advance of your stop. Ask for help if you're not sure where your stop is.

PAYING YOUR WAY In addition to being a lot more scenic than the tube, traveling by bus is cheaper when you have an Oyster card (see page 152). All Oyster-card bus fares cost £1, at all times, regardless of which zones you travel in, whereas tube fares depend upon which zones you travel in and whether you travel at peak or off-peak times. A one-day bus pass costs £3.50; a single cash-fare bus trip costs £2. You can buy a book of six **Bus Saver** tickets that cover all of London for £6; you'll find them at Travel Information Centres, Underground stations, and newsagents. When using Bus Saver tickets, board at the front of the bus and give the receipt part to the driver. These tickets are not valid on trams. (You can also use tube Travelcards on buses.)

Children age 10 and under ride free on the tube, buses, and trams, but if your child looks borderline, you may be hassled by a persnickety ticket inspector. The best option for children ages 11 to 15 who are traveling with an adult is a day Travelcard, which costs just £1 (see page 153).

THE TUBE

THE METROPOLITAN LINE—the first Underground train line—opened at 6 a.m. on Saturday, January 10, 1863, carrying 40,000 very excited Londoners on its inaugural day of service. The tube now carries millions of passengers a day; at rush hour, it feels as if there are millions in your train car alone. And no one is excited about it anymore. Nonetheless, it's the best possible way to get around London at peak times, despite breakdowns and delays.

The tube's most outstanding failing is that it doesn't run 24 hours a day: the last trains leave central London around midnight and begin again around 5:30 a.m. You pay according to transport zones, as outlined previously. A single cash-fare trip that includes travel in Zone 1 (that is, in Zone 1 only or some combination of Zones 1 through 6) costs £4; a single trip that excludes travel in Zone 1 (that is, in Zones 2 through 6 only) is £3. Your best bet is the Oyster card or Travelcard, both described earlier in this chapter. *Beware:* If you are traveling with an invalid ticket—for example, you try to leave a Zone 3 station with a Zone 1 ticket—you are liable to be fined £20 on the spot. To verify which stations fall within which zones, look on one of the big maps posted near the vending machines and ticket windows.

unofficial **TIP**
If you lose your ticket, you may be subject to a penalty fare of £20, so hold on to it.

TICKETS, PLEASE Buy a ticket for your trip at the ticket window, or use one of two machines. The larger machine lists in alphabetical order all the possible stations to which you might wish to go. Pick your station and the type of ticket you want (adult single journey, child single, adult return, and so on), and the machine will tell you how much money to insert; it takes credit cards and bills. The other, smaller machine is simpler but assumes that you know how much your ticket costs and which zones you'll be traveling in. You will most likely be buying the £4 ticket for Zone 1. You can choose one-way (single) or round-trip (return); however, each single cash fare costs £4, so if you have to make a return journey, it makes more sense to buy a day Travelcard for £5.10 (off-peak), even if you'll only use it twice.

Put the ticket in the front of the turnstile, magnetic stripe down; it will come out at the top of the turnstile. Keep your ticket within easy reach, because you will need to put it into another turnstile as you exit your destination.

READING THE MAP The tube map is an amazing feat of workmanship. Before it was streamlined in an Art Deco–ish style in 1931 by transport hero Harry Beck, it looked like an explosion in a string factory, with lines snaking all over central London, impossible to follow. The Beck tube map is not an accurate geographical representation of London, and you'll save much time and grief if you look at *London A–Z* first (see page 140).

unofficial **TIP**
Check the front of your train for its destination!

Locate your destination and identify the color and/or pattern for each Underground line. Look for the key to the lines at the bottom right of the map. There are 12 tube lines in all; to change lines, you must find the stations where the various lines converge, which are indicated by white circles outlined in black. The conductor may announce on board which lines you can catch at the next station, and newer tube trains have scrolling LED signs, but you're better off using your map and your head. If you get on a train and are totally confused, look at the map above the windows—it's a straight line of the stops on that particular train and is much easier to read than the big map. Failing that, you can ask someone on the tube. Because London is confusing even to residents, most people are friendly and tolerant toward the lost.

> *unofficial* **TIP**
> As in any big city, rush hour in London is a nightmare, so wait until the crowds thin to ride if you can. Also, never leave a bag unattended on the tube, at a tube station, or on a bus. This is not so much an invitation to thieves (although it is certainly that) as it is an alarm to commuters and Underground staff, who will treat it as a possible explosive device.

WHICH WAY? Be aware of the direction in which you're traveling. Most platforms have a sign indicating a compass direction, or at the least the final destination to which the train travels. Find where you are on your map, figure out which direction you want to go in, and go to the correct platform.

As you will see on the map, a few tube lines split off into different directions. The District Line, for example, requires close attention: instead of ending up in the northwest at Ealing Broadway, you will be heading south to Richmond. Look at the map to see where your line terminates, and make sure you get on the train with that name; the final stop is posted on the front of the train.

> *unofficial* **TIP**
> Keep a strap from your backpack or handbag wound around your wrist so you don't leave it on the tube—jet lag can make fools of us all.

TUBE ETIQUETTE

A CARDINAL RULE IS TO ALWAYS STAND in single file to the right on the escalators, giving free passage to people who want to skip up or down the steps. This means no standing and chatting next to your friend. Failure to observe this rule may be met with an impatient reprimand or a quivering ball of resentment at your back.

 ## TAXIS

THE MAJESTIC BLACK TAXICABS of London are not always black—many are now besmirched by advertising coating their exteriors—but as symbols of London, they are as distinctive as Tower Bridge or Big Ben. The cabs are designed to specifications that echo their history: the high-ceilinged passenger compartment was once meant to accommodate a gentleman's top hat, and the empty space in front next to the driver was used to store a bale of hay in the days when the cabs were horse-drawn carriages, or cabriolets.

Compared with New York City's yellow taxis or any of the small whizzing conveyances in the rest of Europe, London black cabs are the epitome of comfort and convenience. Enjoy them while you can: they are very expensive to make, and the manufacturers would prefer to put minivan-style taxis on the streets.

The taxis in London cruise the streets or line up in queues. If a cab is available, the light atop the car will be on, and you may wave it down. You can usually get a taxi on the opposite side of the road to stop for you, so don't despair if none are going your way. They are famous for being able to make U-turns on a dime—or on a 5p piece, as it were (in fact, the cars are built with this specific flexibility in mind).

unofficial **TIP**
If there are zigzagging lines running alongside the curb, the taxi cannot legally stop. Move to where those lines end to get picked up.

SEEKERS OF THE KNOWLEDGE As much a part of the London scene as their automobiles, taxi drivers are a well-respected part of the workforce. They have remarkable powers of navigation, of which they are justifiably proud. They train for three to five years, memorizing every street and landmark in London. You'll sometimes see people on mopeds with maps clipped to the handlebars, looking around and making notes. These are student cab drivers. They have to learn, by heart, some 60,000 routes across and around London. During their exams, they have to recite these "runs" to their examiner, citing traffic lights, one-way systems, roundabouts, and landmarks. During this recital, the examiner will do everything he can to distract the student, often playing a difficult customer, hurling insults, singing, or arguing. Those who pass this stringent test are said to have "the Knowledge."

HOW TO TAKE A TAXI Etiquette dictates that you not enter the cab until you have told the driver, from the curb through the passenger-side window, where you want to go. Do not ask if he knows the way;

unofficial **TIP**
Don't smoke, eat, or drink in a taxi. Many cabbies own their cars—which cost upward of £27,000—and are fiercely protective of their well-being.

he's trained to know, and what's more, he will not admit it if he doesn't (we say "he" because few women drive cabs at this time)—to be fair, though, plenty of cabbies will graciously turn to their oversize A–Z to check the route. After getting out of the cab, you are likewise expected to pay through the window, standing on the curb. This works to both your and the cabbie's advantage: you can get out and reach easily into your pocket or purse, and the driver doesn't have to turn around and reach through the partition.

In his hilarious best-selling book about England, *Notes from a Small Island*, Bill Bryson observes that London taxi drivers, despite being absolutely the most excellent in the world, do have a few idiosyncrasies. For one, they are incapable of driving for any distance in a straight line:

"No matter where you are or what the driving conditions, every 200 feet a little bell goes off in their heads and they abruptly lunge down a side street." Our own experience with London cabbies is that they are absolute geniuses at getting from point A to point B with the least amount of traffic and in the shortest amount of time. They know London better than anyone, and the more we get to know London, the more impressed we are with their ability to follow serpentine routes that lead you away from traffic and straight to the heart of where you're going.

WORTH (ALMOST) EVERY POUND We learn more about London and its roads when we take a cab, so much so that we can justify the expense, which can be considerable. The surcharge on night rides has been dropped, while the rates have crept upward. A short trip costs about £5; a trip from central London to, say, Hampstead, will be about £25-plus. Barring a breakdown, the tube is usually a quicker bet, but it's always a pleasure to jump in a taxi and watch London go by from the dark comfort of the cab's very civilized interior. Sometimes you can also get a great conversation out of the deal.

Some drivers, on hearing an American voice, will want to tell you about their experiences in the United States or give you a heads-up regarding what to expect in England. Cabbies are a talkative and opinionated lot, so much so that the satirical magazine *Private Eye* has run very funny op-ed pieces by "Lord Justice Cabdriver."

You can call a black taxi (see the list below) if you're staying in a place where they don't cruise regularly or if it's late at night. Some companies charge extra for booking over the phone or using a credit card—ask when you call.

Computer Cabs	☎ 0207-286-0286
Dial a Cab	☎ 0207-253-5000
Radio Taxis	☎ 0207-272-0272

MINICABS

MINICABS ARE MUCH LESS RELIABLE THAN THE BLACK CABS, but they're cheaper and can come in very handy in many instances, such as when you find yourself far from a tube stop in an outlying area or when you need to get back to your hotel very late at night and there's not a black cab in sight.

unofficial **TIP**
You can't hail a minicab on the street—in fact, you *shouldn't* get into one that stops and offers you a ride. It's not at all kosher; there are a lot of scams and dicey drivers out there.

There are a few reputable minicab companies, including some that employ only women drivers. You must call to book a car; that way, you have some recourse should anything go wrong. Minicab drivers are not required to have "the Knowledge"—which may be made abundantly clear by how lost they can get—but because they charge a flat fee, at least there's no economic downside.

Make sure you agree on a price when booking the cab, and confirm it with the driver when you get in. Tipping is normally between 10% and 15%. The cars are often two-door compacts—nowhere near as roomy as the black cabs—so if you have four large or five regular-size people, get a black cab, or ask if the minicab company has a people carrier (minivan). **Addison Lee** (☎ 0207-387-8888) regularly uses them, which is one reason this company is so popular. Here are a few other good ones:

A&A Chauffeurs Ltd.	☎ 0208-958-3344
College Cars	☎ 0208-955-6666
Greater London Hire Ltd.	☎ 0208-444-2468
Lady Mini Cabs	☎ 0207-254-3501

MOTORCYCLE TAXIS

THIS NEW TRAVEL TWIST IS ALSO ENJOYING SUCCESS in Paris, another clogged European city. The motorbike will get you through the worst traffic in a very short time, and the helmets are equipped with microphones so you can tell the driver to slow down. Not for the faint of heart. Call **Addison Lee Taxybike** ("Safe, Sedate, and You Won't Be Late") at ☎ 0207-255-2469, or visit **www.addisonlee.com.**

RAIL SERVICES AND
DOCKLANDS LIGHT RAILWAY

YOU CAN USE TRAVELCARDS (see page 153) on some of the local commuter lines in London. The **North London Line** is a good way to cross Greater London, cutting a swath from west (Richmond) to east (Woolwich) and stopping at various train and some tube stations along the way. And because it's aboveground, it's a nice change of pace from the mole tunneling of the tube. Call ☎ 0845-748-4950 for all train inquiries.

If you're using **National Rail** to get out of London, ask about the discounts it offers. There are a number of discount cards that you may not think apply to you, as they are good for a year, but the savings can be enormous. Ask at any major rail station or travel agency. You can apply for the discount at the same time you buy your tickets.

Docklands Light Railway (☎ 0207-363-9700) is clean, quiet, and aboveground. It services the East End, Canary Wharf, North Greenwich, the *Cutty Sark,* and Lewisham. It is also becoming a tourist option, and special tickets combine rail travel with riverboat trips. Touring trains leave from Tower Gateway and Bank every hour on the hour starting at 10 a.m., and you will hear interesting commentary from a guide as you ride.

GETTING *around* on **YOUR OWN**

RENTING A CAR AND DRIVING IN LONDON

IT'S NOT A GOOD IDEA TO RENT A CAR in London—this is a confusing, frustrating, and dangerous place to drive, even for those who are already used to driving on the left. Although you need only present a valid driver's license from any country or state to rent a car, traffic laws and driving customs are quite different from those of other countries. The driver's license here is the most difficult in the world to earn, with only Switzerland's test being harder. If you are driving out to the country and must rent a car, it might be best to take the tube to Heathrow or Gatwick and rent a car from there to avoid central London's notorious traffic and the pernicious congestion charge, which you will be responsible for.

If you do find yourself driving in England, here's a tip: the best way to remember which side of the road you're supposed to be on is simply to keep yourself and your steering wheel (which is on the right side of the car) in the middle of the road rather than hugging the side, and you'll always be in the right place. (The same principle holds in countries where one drives on the left—the driver is always in the middle of the road.) As for traffic round-abouts, "right has might, left is bereft"; that is, you should yield to the person on the right.

unofficial **TIP**
Don't let the way cars are parked throw you—you can park facing any old direction in England.

In London, the parking regulations are strict—look at lampposts to find signs outlining them. You can't park on a double yellow line ever; your car will be clamped or towed. If you're clamped, you'll find a sticker on your car telling you where to pay for the clamp's removal and the additional fine; if you're towed, call ☎ 0207-747-7474 to find out where your car was taken. The penalty is stiff: more than £200, all told.

Most neighborhoods have residential parking permits, meaning you cannot park in these areas except at night, on bank holidays, and all day on Sunday, a day when you can park pretty much

unofficial **TIP**
Expect to pay about £50 to fill an economy car with gas, or petrol, as they call it here.

anywhere, including on some red routes (red-lined avenues) and all single yellow lines. Read the signs carefully—there are meters and Pay and Display spaces for visitors to use.

Pay and Display works like this: park your car, find the ticket machine, pay the correct amount for the desired time, get your ticket, and display it on your windshield or dashboard. You'll find a number of **National Car Parks** around central London (look for the yellow NCP signs); call ☎ 0870-606-7050 or visit **www.ncp.co.uk** for locations.

The central numbers for the big rental companies (cars cost about £65-plus per day) are as follows:

Alamo	☎ 0870-400-4508	www.alamo.com
Avis	☎ 0207-917-6700	www.avis.co.uk
Budget	☎ 0800-181-181	www.gobudget.com
Enterprise	☎ 0125-235-3620	www.enterprise.com
Europcar	☎ 0870-607-5000	www.europcar.co.uk
Hertz	☎ 0870-844-8844	www.hertz.co.uk

WALKING

PLEASE DO. You'll be surprised at how far you can go by foot—a lot faster at times than on the bus, and certainly more pleasantly than on the tube. You'll get to see small architectural curios, drop into inviting shops and restaurants, and find alleys and mews that you wouldn't see by cab. Keep your A–Z handy, and go ahead and get lost. You'll thank yourself for it. Do keep an eye out for maniac drivers, and be aware that your instincts when crossing the streets are all wrong. Take it slowly, and *don't* try to outrun a walking light—the drivers will scare the devil out of you.

The zebra crossings, however, belong to the pedestrian. When you see a flashing yellow light at a crosspath marked with white stripes, you have the right of way—cars *must* stop for you. There may be one or two drivers who haven't quite gotten the hang of this system, so don't stride out without sensible caution.

unofficial **TIP**
Avoid the subways late at night; some become little villages of sleeping homeless people.

Around big intersections such as Piccadilly Circus, Marble Arch, and Hyde Park Corner are "subways," or walkways beneath the street. They are well indicated with signposts, so you will be able to know which way to go. Some are actually quite interesting—Hyde Park Corner has painted tiles giving you the goods on the Duke of Wellington (whose house is right there) and the parks of London. Others use exit numbers and seem to go on forever.

LOST AND FOUND

IF YOU'VE LEFT SOMETHING IN ONE of the public conveyances covered previously, which is easily done when you're tired and jet-lagged, take heart: you just might get it back. For insurance claims, you must inform the police of your loss. Do not call the emergency number; instead, find the nearest police station by calling ☎ 118118.

Transport for London maintains a Web site (**www.tfl.gov.uk/contact/871.aspx**) that will help you to find your property—more than 130,000 items are lost on buses, trains, and taxis a year. You can also call one of the following phone numbers:

Buses	☎ 0207-486-2496
Black taxis	☎ 0207-918-2000
Train stations (railroad)	☎ 0870-000-5151
Tube trains	☎ 0207-486-2496

PART SIX

SIGHTSEEING, TOURS, *and* ATTRACTIONS

An EMBARRASSMENT *of* RICHES

LONDON MAY NOT BE NUMBER ONE on everyone's travel wish list (it ain't Paris or Tahiti), but it certainly deserves a place in the top five. There are the obvious must-see attractions: the **Tower of London,** the **British Museum,** the **Victoria and Albert Museum, Westminster Abbey.** And then there are the other bits that make London so wonderful: the parks, the themed walking tours, the obscure collections, and the markets. Along the South Bank, there's the **London Eye,** the **Hayward Gallery,** the **National Theatre,** the **Tate Modern.** Across the river are the **Houses of Parliament, Big Ben,** and **St. James's Park,** and of course you can't miss a visit to **Buckingham Palace.**

One of the greatest things about London is that most museums are free to enter, with only a suggested donation. However, the attractions that do charge can be pricey, so a **London Pass** might be a worthy investment. The pass gives you free priority entry at 56 pay tourist attractions in London, including Buckingham Palace, the Tower of London, the London Zoo, Shakespeare's Globe Theatre, the London Aquarium, and even a free circular cruise with Catamaran Cruisers. It's available in one-, two-, three-, and six-day adult and child versions; for a few extra pounds, you can buy passes that include free travel on London public transportation (the one-day London Pass Plus Travel, for example, costs £41 for adults and £24 for children). To purchase a pass, call ☎ 0870-242-9988 or visit **www.londonpass.com.** Only you can decide on your must-sees, but we can help you to narrow—or expand—your list.

KNOW THY LIMITS

WE ALL HAVE A THRESHOLD at which sightseeing crosses the line from pleasure to torture: your feet hurt, the lines are too long, the weather is appalling, you're hungry, and jet lag has hit you hard. This threshold varies from person to person, but for the disabled, the elderly, and the very young, the passage over it can be risky as well as uncomfortable. A number of attractions in London are wheelchair inaccessible, have stairs too steep for older travelers to climb, or put their exhibits too high for a small child to see. You do not want to place yourself (or your companions, if they fall into any of the above categories) in the position of finding out too late that the attraction just won't work. Although in our listings we try to judge whether a place is disabled- or child-friendly, it's always a good idea to call first and find out for sure. Improvements are being made all the time in the interest of easier access at most attractions, museums, churches, and stately homes, so check ahead.

If you plan to visit a museum with your children, you might want to find out if any kids' activities are scheduled for the day you want to go. The **Victoria and Albert** and **British museums** are just two of the "grown-up" museums that offer plenty for children to see and do, with special activities available on weekends and school holidays. (See Part Seven, Children's London, for more specifics about touring the city with children.)

TOURIST-INFORMATION CENTERS

THE FOLLOWING WEB SITES have tons of up-to-the-minute information about attractions and sights.

www.visitbritain.com Great Britain's official tourist Web site features lots of useful information and trip-planning advice.

www.londontown.com Comprehensive site that offers specials on hotels, sells theater tickets, and provides news on the latest exhibitions.

www.visitlondon.com London's official Web site features loads of information and lets you book hotels, buy discount passes, and more.

www.thisislondon.co.uk The *Evening Standard*'s Web site is a good source for current entertainment and restaurant information.

www.timeout.com The weekly magazine features cultural event listings, as well as information on entertainment, restaurants, and nightlife.

The biggest and most comprehensive walk-in tourist office is the **Britain and London Visitor Centre** (1 Regent Street, Mayfair, SW1; tube: Piccadilly Circus; open 9 a.m. to 6:30 p.m. weekdays, 10 a.m. to 4 p.m. weekends). You can pick up an armful of pamphlets, brochures, maps, and flyers, and reserve tickets, tours, and hotel rooms. It's also a one-stop shop for souvenirs and London-related books.

TOURING

JUMP ON THE BUS

THE BEST THING TO DO ON THE FIRST DAY in any city is to take advantage of a hop-on-hop-off bus tour. This gives you the lay of the land, and if the day is bright, the open top of a double-decker bus provides the sunlight that helps you get over jet lag. Just riding up high is a thrill to most kids, and all the hopping on and off will keep them from getting restless. The buses stop at most of the major attractions and intersections, such as the Tower of London, Madame Tussauds, Green Park, Hyde Park and Hyde Park Corner, Harrods, the South Kensington museums, and so on.

You can pick up a bus at almost any of the significant attractions; check with your hotel to find the closest stop to you. Tickets can be bought on the bus or from bus employees who stand at some of the stops. You must get on the bus as early as possible to avoid the crushing traffic jams (congestion charging has eased them only slightly) that can make your tour a carbon monoxide–infused bummer. If you see traffic building up while you're touring, you can always hop off and continue your itinerary the next day or later in the afternoon, as the tour tickets are good for 24 hours—a plus that lets you can break up the tour nicely. You can also buy your tickets online and get a small discount.

Both of the following companies cover basically the same routes and offer the same services. Each sells fast-track tickets to the more overcrowded attractions, such as Buckingham Palace (when it's open in the fall), Madame Tussauds, and the Tower of London.

unofficial **TIP**
The bus companies' fast-track attraction tickets are well worth getting.

The **Big Bus Company** (☎ 0207-233-9533; **www.bigbus.co.uk**) conducts a Red Tour that starts at Green Park, includes live commentary, and lasts approximately two hours, along with a three-hour Blue Tour that commences at Marble Arch and includes digitally recorded commentary in eight languages. In the summer, the buses run every 15 minutes or so; in winter, they go about every half hour, stopping at all the major (and minor) attractions. Tickets are £22 for adults and £12 for children ages 5 to 15 (there's a £2 discount for adults when you buy online). Big Bus also offers a number of walking tours (included in ticket price), with themes such as Royal London, the Beatles' London, James Bond, ghosts, and famous movie locations. There are also river cruises and some out-of-town excursions.

The **Original London Sightseeing Tour** (☎ 0208-877-2120; **www.the originaltour.com**) offers tours in seven languages, fast-entry tickets, and four different touring options (including a river tour) as part of the ticket price. Tickets, good for 24 hours, cost £19 for adults, £12 for children, and £72 for a family of five. Original London's big advantage is its wonderful Kids Club (**www.theoriginaltour.com/kids_club**), which provides lots of fun for children in the form of activity packs, games, quizzes, and kid-focused commentary (on the red route only). Buses depart daily every 15 to 20 minutes.

ON YOUR OWN

YOU DON'T HAVE TO SPEND ALL THAT MUCH to get a decent double-decker bus ride if you use **Transport for London.** The well-known **#11** bus takes you past many of the same sights the tourist buses pass, for a mere fraction of the cost. Pick it up on King's Road at World's End or the Chelsea Town Hall stops—you'll get a good look at that famous mod street as well as ride through Victoria; past Westminster Abbey, Whitehall, and Trafalgar Square; and up the Strand to St. Paul's Cathedral before finishing in the East End at Liverpool Street. All this for only £2, less if you have the **Oyster card** (see Part 5, Getting Around).

The **#15** is also wonderful. You can pick it up at Paddington and ride to Marble Arch, up Oxford Street, down Regent Street to Piccadilly Circus, down Haymarket Street to Trafalgar Square, up the Strand (which turns into Fleet Street), by St. Paul's Cathedral and the Tower of London, and end up at Petticoat Lane (Middlesex Street), which has a market on Sunday mornings and some stalls during the week.

The **#14** goes from Tottenham Court Road (by the British Museum) over the Thames and west to Putney Heath, passing Piccadilly, Knightsbridge, the museums of South Kensington, and the shops of Fulham.

> *unofficial* **TIP**
> Get a bus map at any tourist center or hotel lobby, and check out these routes and any others that look interesting to you. If, as you're traveling, you feel you're going too far afield, just get off and jump on a bus going in the opposite direction to return to central London.

The **#24** bus will take you north from Victoria Station all the way to Hampstead Heath and Highgate, from which you can get an amazing view of London.

To take in some of South London, hop on the **#2** bus from Marylebone Station, Marble Arch, or Hyde Park Corner, and ride across the Thames through Brixton and up Tulse Hill to Crystal Palace Park, where you can get out and look at the prehistoric creatures imagined and modeled by the Victorians.

PRIVATE TOURS

YOU CAN HIRE A BLACK CAB to take you around London, creating your own tour and seeing only those sights that interest you most. Or you can leave it up to the professionals at **Black Taxi Tours of London** (☎ 0207-935-9363; **www.blacktaxitours.co.uk**) and select from an array of themed tours: Tales of the Thames River, Secret London, London's

> *unofficial* **TIP**
> The great thing about Black Taxi Tours is that you can avoid traffic jams and get into the squares, mews, and backstreets where no tour bus can take you.

Villages, and special Christmas tours, for instance. A two-hour tour costs about £90; taxis hold up to five people.

SEEING THE HIGHLIGHTS

THE DOUBLE-DECKER-BUS TOURS ARE DESIGNED to show you the sights of London in a general way. You can see where everything is in relation to everything else, perhaps find out how long the lines are for certain attractions, figure out what can be done in a day or a week, and determine which areas seem most intriguing. Taking a general tour first thing will help you plan efficiently for the days ahead. You'll learn, for example, that you won't be able to do the Tower of London on the same day you take a walk in Hampstead Heath, which is so far away that it's off any standard London tour itinerary. Or you will note that a trip to the National Gallery can be combined with a visit to any or all of the following: the adjacent National Portrait Gallery, St. Martin-in-the-Fields, Trafalgar Square, Leicester Square, Covent Garden, and Somerset House, topped off by a half-price ticket for an evening show at the theater.

SIGHTSEEING COMPANIES

A LOT OF TOUR COMPANIES IN LONDON do very similar out-of-town and in-the-city tours for roughly the same prices. You can find their brochures in any hotel lobby. A word of caution: these outfits have many courtesy hotel-pickup points in London, which sounds very convenient—who doesn't want to fall out of their hotel room into a waiting coach at 8 a.m.?—but yours may just be the first of 15 stops, and if you get stuck in the normal London traffic, you can be on the bus for an hour before you actually get started on the tour.

The major tour companies offer half-day, morning, night, full-day, or two-day tours of London, plus days-out tours to such places as Windsor and Leeds castles, Eton, Hampton Court, Stonehenge, Bath, Stratford-upon-Avon, Oxford, Cambridge, Salisbury, Brighton, Dover, Canterbury, York, Chester, Warwick Castle, the Lake District, Scotland, and even Paris and Amsterdam. They arrange bus, train, or boat transport depending on the destination. The price of the tour almost always includes entrance fees for the attractions and the cost of meals, and, in the case of overnight trips, the cost of accommodations.

Have a look at the Web sites of the following tour companies:

*un*official **TIP**
You'll probably find it most convenient to meet your tour bus at its final departure point—find this out when you reserve your tour, and then take the tube or a taxi to get there. The downside to this evasive action is that you may not get the seat you want (the best seats are clearly the top-floor front row).

Astral Travels (☎ 0870-225-5303; **www.astral travels.co.uk**) escorts small groups on minicoach day tours, as well as extended 3- to 14-day all-over tours. The range of interests covered on Astral's specialized one-day tours is most impressive. Their numerous and distinctive London tours feature a classic-car option in which you see London from the back of a beautifully restored automobile from the 1920s or '30s. Excellent value for the money.

Evan Evans Tours (☎ 0207-950-1777; fax 0207-950-1771; **www.evanevans tours.co.uk**) offers full-day, morning, and afternoon coach tours with such themes as Discovering London and London Past and Present.

Golden Tours (☎ 0208-811-2858; toll free from the U.S., 800-548-7083; **www.goldentours.co.uk**) has an immersive full-day Total London Experience, including stops at Westminster Abbey and the Tower of London, a walking tour of Covent Garden, and a "flight" on the London Eye.

For tours along the river, contact **City Cruises** (☎ 0207-740-0400; **www.city cruises.com**).

For boat rides along the canals of Little Venice and Camden Lock, call **London Waterbus Company** (☎ 0207-482-2550 or 0207-482-2660; **www.london waterbus.com**).

GET OUT *of* TOWN

ALTHOUGH GETTING EVEN A TASTE OF LONDON'S richness can take all of an extended visit, it's a nice break to get out of the Big Smoke and into the famous English countryside, which is heaving

unofficial **TIP**
Astral Travels is an
especially good option if
you're not fond of big
buses with lots of people.

with delightful medieval towns and inspiring cathedrals. The above tour companies conduct such trips conveniently and hassle free.

You may want to rent a car to do your sightseeing, but sometimes it's just easier to let others do the driving. Taking a train will work for going to Bath, Oxford, Salisbury, Cambridge, or Stratford-upon-Avon, where you can get a hotel room and walk around town, but for trips to Stonehenge or places such as the town of Laycock or Warwick Castle, you're better off going with a tour group. Visit any of the companies' Web sites on the previous pages to decide where and when you want to go. Ask how many people have already booked; perhaps you can find a day when there will be only a handful of guests.

SOME GOOD SIDE TRIPS

NOTE: ALL THE TRAVEL TIMES GIVEN below are for British Rail train service—which is notoriously unreliable.

BATH is about one and a half hours from Paddington Station (170 miles). A gorgeous Georgian town with Roman relics, it is famous for its historic buildings and Sally Lunn cakes. Jane Austen lived there during its heyday as a fashionable spa town.

kids **BRIGHTON** is one hour from Victoria Station (53 miles). The city makes for jolly seaside fun, with kid-friendly rides and games on the pier; little shopping streets and alleys; and the Royal Pavilion, Brighton, an Oriental-fantasy retreat of George IV.

CAMBRIDGE is one hour from King's Cross Station (85 miles). This quiet university town has beautiful river views and significant buildings, such as the early-Tudor King's College Chapel.

CANTERBURY is 80 minutes from Victoria Station (50 miles). The old pilgrimages used to come to the cathedral, in which Saint Augustine converted King Ethelbert in AD 597 and Thomas à Becket was murdered in 1170.

HATFIELD HOUSE is 20 minutes from King's Cross Station (20 miles). This is where Queen Elizabeth I spent her childhood.

OXFORD is one hour from Paddington Station (56 miles). This university city of "dreaming spires" is a good jumping-off place for the Cotswolds.

ST. ALBANS is 30 minutes from King's Cross Station (25 miles). It's an old Roman stronghold with ruins and rose gardens.

SALISBURY is one and a half hours from Waterloo Station (84 miles), with a magnificent cathedral, military museum, and beautiful flower-filled neighborhoods around the cathedral. Stonehenge is a short drive away.

STRATFORD-UPON-AVON is less than two hours (91 miles) from Paddington Station. This is Shakespeare's hometown—he was born, married, and buried here—and the place is devoted to him, but it has other attractions as well. See a play by the Bard during your visit; there are matinees on most days as well as evening performances, and the town is just charming, with canal boats, markets, and exquisite old architecture.

WINDSOR is 30 minutes from Waterloo Station (20 miles). See the storybook castle by the Thames, and venture into the fine old town with good pubs. The playing fields of Eton are nearby, and lovely little shops and restaurants are all around.

■ ROMANTIC LONDON

ONE REALLY DOESN'T ASSOCIATE LONDON with *amour* in the way one does Paris or Venice, but that's not to say there aren't some romantic places to explore with your beloved. Judging by the snogging (kissing) that goes on in **Hyde Park,** we'd have to say that taking a blanket, a jug of wine, and your special someone to the park for a lie-around in the sun is one of London's favorite pastimes for couples, and it's free. If you need exercise, get in a paddleboat and tool around the Serpentine. Take a night cruise along the **Thames,** or sit on a bench at sunset on the river at the end of Oakley Street, watch the birds circling overhead, and wait for the lights to illuminate the spectacular **Albert Bridge.** The ongoing rejuvenation of the South Bank makes it a midsummer night's dream in warm weather, as you stroll along and watch the boats pass by the twinkling lights of the city. Our favorite evening out is a concert at the **Royal Festival Hall** or a play at the **National Theatre,** then a walk along the river and over any of the bridges for a view of the **London Eye** and a long stare into the fast-flowing Thames.

As for romantic restaurants, **Momo** (25 Heddon Street, off Regent Street, Mayfair, W1; ☎ 0207-434-4040; tube: Oxford Circus) is a Middle Eastern restaurant done exquisitely in *Arabian Nights* fantasy style. The quite expensive **Pont de la Tour** (Butler's Wharf, 36D Shad Thames, SE1; ☎ 0207-403-8403; tube: London Bridge or Tower Hill) has good food and wonderful views of Tower Bridge, which can be pretty romantic unless you truly only have eyes for each other. **Sarastro** (126 Drury Lane, Theatreland, WC2; ☎ 0207-836-0101; tube: Covent Garden; **www.sarastro-restaurant.com**) is a restaurant designed like a theater. You can even book your own opera box.

For something unique, go to **Fig 108**, an art studio where you can paint a masterpiece for your loved one, or even paint each other. Cost is £40 per person including canvas and paint. You must book in advance (Studio 004, Westbourne Studios, 242 Acklam Road, Westbourne Park,

W10; ☎ 0870-410-3254; tube: Westbourne Park; **www.fig108.com**). Or you can dirty-dance at London's authentic Latin live-music venue, **Salsa** (96 Charing Cross Road, Charing Cross, WC2; ☎ 0207-379-3277; tube: Tottenham Court Road or Leicester Square; **www.barsalsa.info**).

The most romantic hotels are the **Portobello Hotel** (ask for the room with the round bed), the **Covent Garden Hotel** (wonderful amenities, which mean you never have to leave the premises), and **The Gore** (request the Venus, the Tudor, or the Miss Ada suite). And, of course, you can't go wrong at **The Ritz** for romance—check out the weekend break prices and request a honeymoon-type room or, better still, a suite. (See Part Three, Accommodations, for more information.)

Agent Provocateur (6 Broadwick Street, Soho, W1; ☎ 0207-439-0229; **www.agentprovocateur.com;** tube: Piccadilly) sells *very* sexy underwear that's erotic and sophisticated at the same time. Soho also has lots of playful (as well as some frankly creepy) sex shops around—you may get inspired. Then there is the popular **Myla,** an exotic and erotic shop that carries seductive clothing and sexy what-nots (4 Burlington Gardens, Mayfair, W1; ☎ 0207-491-8548; **www.myla.com;** tube: Green Park or Piccadilly). Check both shops' Web sites for other store addresses.

Oh, **SUCH** *a* **PERFECT DAY**

 WHAT CONSTITUTES A PERFECT DAY IN LONDON will naturally depend on who's in your party and what your keenest interests are. One person's poison is another one's mead, as they say. But if I were to try to conjure up a day that would hit as many of my personal favorite high notes as possible, it would go something like this:

I would want to start with a good cappuccino in a great people-watching area. Whatever neighborhood you are staying in, we can pretty much guarantee that there will be a little sidewalk cafe or a nice French or Italian joint that serves coffee. If I were in my favorite neighborhood, which is South Kensington, I would head straight for **Orsini** (8a Thurloe Place, SW7; ☎ 0207-581-5553; tube: South Kensington). Across the street from the Victoria and Albert Museum and just east of the Rembrandt Hotel, it's a friendly family-run cafe that feels like a little slice of Italy in London. I love having a cappuccino and toasted baguette at a pavement table, even with the roar of traffic. If you require a heartier breakfast, go up the street to **Patisserie Valerie**—the croissants are unlike those anywhere else, and they serve a large selection of hot breakfasts (215 Brompton Road, SW3; ☎ 0207-823-9971; tube: Knightsbridge). Another option is to go around the corner to Brompton Cross, where **La Brasserie** serves perfect Continental breakfasts as well as eggs in an authentically Parisian atmosphere, complete with sidewalk tables and brusque waiters (272 Brompton Road, SW3; ☎ 0207-584-1668; tube: South Kensington). For a fabulous selection of bread, try **Aubaine,** right next door.

After breakfast, go look at the **Brompton Oratory** (1 Thurloe Place; ☎ 0207-808-0900; **www.bromptonoratory.com;** tube: South Kensington), an imposing Catholic church. It's an inspiring edifice, with small chapels lining the enormous hall and a rotunda to rival that of St. Paul's. Go through the churchyard and out to Ennismore Gardens, which you'll take up to **Hyde Park,** a couple of blocks away. Amble around the park, and go to the riding ring to see if any of the Queen's Guards are exercising their horses or rehearsing any ceremonies. Go feed a duck or two at the **Serpentine,** and check out the problem-plagued yet charming **Diana, Princess of Wales Memorial Fountain** (it's as high-maintenance as the princess herself was).

Exit the park at Exhibition Road (take a quick look at the **Albert Memorial** on your right: you might want to stop for a photo op), and head for the **Victoria and Albert Museum** down the street (opens at 10 a.m.). The British Galleries are very interesting and charming; they're among the finest examples of modern curating in London. The outside courtyard has been redone in a pleasing, if overly modern style. If the weather is fine, have a rest and a cup of coffee there.

Then walk through South Kensington (or take a taxi or the number 49 bus from outside the South Ken tube station) up Sydney Street to the **Chelsea Old Town Hall.** Across from the hall is the **Bourbon Hanby Arcade** for antiques browsing or buying; next to it is **Daisy & Tom,** a wonderful place to buy British books for your little friends. Then, if the weather's warm, enjoy lunch outside at one of the restaurants at the **Chelsea Marketplace,** or have a less expensive ploughman's lunch at the pub next to the neo-Gothic **St. Luke's Church** (where Dickens got married). Within the marketplace you'll also find a good health-food store called **Here,** along with three eateries, a pet shop, a jewelry store, and the marvelous **Chelsea Gardener** center. You'll be sorry you can't take home some of the plants and flowering trees sold there.

Stroll down King's Road toward Sloane Square, check out the **Duke of York Square** with all its overly expensive shops and its many resting places, do a little window-shopping, and catch the #11 bus wherever possible. Take the 11 past all the great sights: **Westminster Abbey, Big Ben, Whitehall, Trafalgar Square,** and up Fleet Street to **St. Paul's Cathedral.** If you have the energy, climb to the top of St. Paul's and enjoy the view. If not, just take a seat in the church and admire the craftsmanship that went into this magnificent building, or perhaps rest in the courtyard of the church and watch the tourists. Catch a bus toward Trafalgar Square and go to **Leicester Square** to buy half-price theater tickets at the **tkts** kiosk there for that evening. There's no saying what plays will be available, but it's always a joy to see anything in these atmospheric old theaters—unless you are extremely tall, in which case seating can be

unofficial **TIP**
Although you might not find tickets for your desired play on sale at the tkts half-price kiosk, there's always something great to see, and the price is right. You may even get to watch American film or TV stars strut their stuff in a West End production.

uncomfortable, so try to get a box seat. Check to see what stars are performing: it's always a thrill to watch a big-name star performing on stage, no matter what the play is.

Then, depending on the time, your next move would be a toss-up between having tea at **Brown's Hotel** or the more economical **Fortnum & Mason** (give tea at **The Ritz** a pass—it's too expensive and not as delicious as it should be). If you're still full from lunch, skip tea altogether and go try the brass-rubbing in the crypt at **St. Martin-in-the-Fields.** It's a real treat. You pick out one of the many medieval brass plates with engraved images, get a piece of paper and a selection of colored wax, and then tease out the design by rubbing the wax stick over the plate—no artistic talent required. Take your time with the rubbing, enjoying the atmosphere and the pastime. Buy some gifts in the church's wonderful shops (one at the brass-rubbing area and one in the other part of the crypt). Then walk over to **Covent Garden** and watch the buskers (street entertainers) do their thing, or wander through the shops.

Dinner at last. For the atmosphere (and the Yorkshire pudding), try **Rules,** the oldest surviving restaurant in London (35 Maiden Lane, WC2; ☎ 0207-836-5314; **www.rules.co.uk;** tube: Charing Cross). Yes, it's a tourist trap, but it's also redolent of a long-gone era, with the photos and cartoons on the wall charting its history since it opened in 1798. And where else can you get grouse, woodcock, and partridge?

You will most likely love the play, especially because you will have paid half price for some perfectly decent seats, and the theater itself may be an architectural gem. You will love how they sell ice cream right in the theater at the intermission (or, as the Brits call it, "the interval"), and you will be proud of yourself for having already ordered your refreshments before the play started and finding them waiting for you at the bar at intermission. When the play lets out at 10:30 or 11 p.m., walk over to **Ronnie Scott's** (47 Frith Street, W1; ☎ 0207-439-0747; **www.ronniescotts.co.uk;** tube: Tottenham Court Road) and listen to jazz until you're ready to call it a day and go back to your hotel.

WALKING *in and around* LONDON

WALKING IS BY FAR THE BEST WAY TO EXPERIENCE LONDON. Grab a map and your camera, select a starting point, and just start exploring. You never know what you may find once you move off of London's bustling main thoroughfares: a cobbled alleyway with a quaint cafe, a medieval church, or even a dreamy view across the river. Following are a number of suggested walks covering a diverse range of areas. Many cross the paths of some great London attractions and can create an entire day's worth of wandering if you decide to stop off and visit some of the sights along the way.

You might also want to try out **London Walks** (☎ 0207-624-3978; **www.walks.com**), which offers 120 weekly themed walks dedicated to Jack the Ripper, ghosts of London, lost palaces, the Beatles, rock and roll, literary London (Charles Dickens, Oscar Wilde, and others), the swinging 1960s, "The Real World of Harry Potter: Wizards, Were-wolves & Vampires," and so many more. Pick up a leaflet at any hotel or check for daily events in *Time Out London*. Another option is to enjoy the encyclopedic knowledge of Diane Burstein of **Secret London Walks** (☎ 0208-881-2933; **www.secretlondonwalks.co.uk**). You can choose from a variety of themed walks, or you might prefer to arrange a private tour dedicated to your own personal interests.

WALKING ON YOUR OWN

IF YOU PREFER TO WALK at your own pace, try the strolls we've out-lined here.

City of London: Through the Centuries

TIME TO ALLOW 3–4 hours depending on indoor visits.

DISTANCE Approximately 1½ miles.

TUBE St. Paul's or Barbican.

SIGHTS Museum of London; St. Botolph, Aldersgate; Postman's Park; Priory Church of St. Bartholomew the Great; National Postal Museum; Christ Church, Greyfriars; St. Paul's Cathedral; Guildhall (including Guildhall Clock Museum and Guildhall Art Gallery); Guild Church of St. Lawrence Jewry.

THIS WALK PROVIDES JUST A GLIMPSE of the vast array of archi-tecture that has evolved in London over the centuries, from the ancient Roman wall that once enclosed the fourth-century city of Londinium to the skyscrapers of the modern financial district. Begin your wanderings at the **Museum of London,** looking out from the museum's terrace, where you are surrounded by concrete and glass. This is 20th-century London, with heavy traffic and office buildings. However, if you know where to look, you will glimpse bits of old— the London of medieval peasants, Renaissance grandeur, and Victorian sentimentality. A stop at the museum is great for getting your bearings on London's diverse historical eras.

After enjoying an engaging hour or two of well-curated history, head across the traffic circle to Aldersgate. Locate Little Britain Street on the right; **St. Botolph Church** is on the corner. The church's classical Georgian interior is in glorious contrast with its bland and unassum-ing exterior. Turn right as you exit the church and enter **Postman's Park.** This hidden churchyard was dedicated by the Victorians in 1900 as a memorial to "heroes of everyday life" who died in acts of selfless bravery (it forms an important plot twist in the 2004 movie *Closer,* with Jude Law and Natalie Portman, a great film for London-location viewing). In the center of the intimate park, you will find the protected wall of memorials. One epitaph reads, "Saved a lunatic woman from suicide at Woolwich Arsenal, but was himself run over by the train." Exiting the park on the opposite side, turn right onto King Edward Street, then follow Little Britain around to the left to where it deposits you in Smithfield Square.

In medieval times, the marketplace of **Smithfield Green** was thriving with merchants, peddlers, peasants, and livestock. Jousts, tournaments, horse fairs, and hangings have all been held here. To your left is **St. Bartholomew's Hospital.** Founded in 1123 as a priory and hospice, it is London's oldest hospital. Out front is a memorial to Sir William Wallace, known as Braveheart, the Scot who defied a king and was torn in quarters by four horses for the crime of treason. If you venture inside the hospital's main entrance, you will find the small hospital church of **St. Bartholomew the Less** and an 18th-century courtyard. Back out on the square and to your right you will see a half-timbered Tudor gatehouse. Through here is a gem of medieval London, the **Priory Church of St. Bartholomew the Great,** also dating back to 1123. Don't miss the opportunity to take a look at this breathtaking example of original 12th-century Norman architecture.

Making your way back to Little Britain, turn right onto King Edward Street, using the dome of St. Paul's Cathedral before you as a guide. Past Postman's Park and the National Postal Museum, at the end of Little Britain, are the remains of Christopher Wren's **Christ Church, Greyfriars.** Originally built in 1691, it was destroyed during air raids in World War II. Today, the tower and walls enclose a lovely trellised garden marking the original location of the church columns and center aisle. Cross Newgate Street and turn left. Beyond the tube-station entrance is the churchyard of **St. Paul's Cathedral.** Vastly different from the medieval St. Bart's, Christopher Wren's Renaissance masterpiece is the second-largest cathedral in the world. Stop here to see the glorious interior or perhaps climb the dome for unparalleled city views.

Wandering back through the churchyard, turn right and head east on Cheapside. Cross over and make a left on Wood Street and then follow Milk Street as it bears to the right. This area was another of London's medieval marketplaces, although the only remnants of its useful origins are the street names—Bread Street, Milk Street, Honey Lane—to remind you of its past. Just ahead is the entrance to the **Guildhall,** the headquarters for the Corporation of London. Behind the bleak 20th-century facade lies the impressive Great Hall, open 10 a.m. to 4:30 p.m., Monday through Friday. Next door, the Guildhall Library houses a clock museum (open 9:30 a.m. to 4:30 p.m., Monday through Friday), some glorious stained-glass windows, and an art collection. Also, if you can catch it open, be sure to stop in and see the spectacular interior of the **Guild Church of St. Lawrence Jewry** located on the main road. The name is derived from its location on the site of London's early Jewish ghetto. Finally, follow King Street south to Victoria Street. Turn right and end your walk at Mansion House tube station.

Old Hampstead Village

TIME TO ALLOW 2 hours.

DISTANCE Approximately 1½–2 miles.

TUBE Hampstead.

SIGHTS Hampstead Heath, Hampstead High Street, Church Row, St. John's-at-Hampstead, St. Mary's Church, Fenton House, Admiral's House, Well Walk and Flask Walk, Burgh House, Downshire Hill, Keats House.

ALSO NEARBY Freud Museum, Kenwood House.

THE HISTORY OF HAMPSTEAD HAS ALWAYS BEEN tied closely to its hill, its heath, and its healthy environment—in the early 1700s, Hampstead became a booming spa town. The area's iron-rich water was said to cure all manner of ailments, and you could purchase flasks of the vile-tasting stuff for three pence a bottle or bathe in it at one of the local bathhouses. Today, narrow streets lined with lovingly restored 18th-century homes help the village retain much of its charming Georgian atmosphere.

Arriving in Hampstead via the Underground, you will come up London's deepest elevator shaft near the top of Hampstead Hill in the village center. **Heath and Hampstead High streets** stretch before you, lined with shops, cafes, and restaurants—definitely a great area in which to stop for tea at the end of your walk. Exiting the tube station, cross over and turn left on Heath Street, then right on **Church Row,** one of the best-preserved streets in London. Notice the grand wrought-iron work, the remains of early-18th-century oil-lamp stands, and the intricately detailed windows over many of the homes' main entrances. These distinctively individual fanlights, illuminated from behind by candles, helped you find your home after dark in the days of strong gin and no street lighting. Famous residents here included writers George du Maurier and H. G. Wells. At the end of the line of trees sits **St. John's-at-Hampstead,** consecrated in 1747. Take some time to wander the graveyard and church, and then head up Holly Walk.

At the top of the hill on the right, **St. Mary's Church,** one of London's oldest Roman Catholic churches, is nestled among a row of homes. Its hiding-in-plain-sight location was important to nervous Catholics who were forced to be furtive before religious tolerance was officially granted in 1829. Make a right, follow Mount Vernon down to where it meets up with Hampstead Grove, and turn left. Another worthwhile stop is **Fenton House** on the right. This wonderfully preserved 17th-century home today houses an exquisite collection of Asian, European, and English china, needlework, and furniture, but its finest attraction is its unique collection of early musical instruments, including Handel's harpsichord. Beyond Fenton House, turn left onto Admiral's Walk, where you'll find the 18th-century **Admiral's House.** Look carefully and you will see the nautical alterations made by Lt. Fountain North in 1775. North adapted the roof to resemble the deck of a ship, complete with flagstaff and cannon, which was fired to celebrate naval victories. P. L. Travers and Walt Disney fans should find this all vaguely familiar; the character and home of Admiral Boom in *Mary Poppins* were based on this eccentric individual.

At the end of Hampstead Grove, where it runs into the main thoroughfare of Heath Street, is a small reservoir on the left. **Whitstone Pond,** built in 1856, allowed Londoners who had successfully navigated the steep, muddy roads to the hilltop to clean their carriages by walking their horses down the ramps and through the pond. Crossing Heath Street, begin your journey down the hill and alongside Hampstead Heath, turning right at Squire's Mount and passing some lovely cottages that date to 1704. Continue on Cannon Lane, turning left on Well Road, so named for the spring that gave the town its reputation for health. Famous residents here included D. H. Lawrence, J. B. Priestley, and John Constable. Turning left on New End Square brings you past **Burgh House,** the 1703 home of Hampstead Spa's physician, William Gibbons. Today the building is a local museum, meeting place, and exhibition space. To your left is **Well Walk** and to your right **Flask Walk.** Just up Flask Walk on your right is an old bathhouse that was still used by some locals until the late 1960s. Cross Well Walk and enjoy a downhill stroll on Willow Road. At the bottom, turn right on **Downshire Hill.** This is another picturesque street lined with 19th-century homes and gardens; its centerpiece is **St. John's Church Downshire Hill,** opened in 1823. If it's open, take a quick peek inside.

Turning left on Keats Grove brings you to our last stop, the **Keats House.** Poet John Keats lived in Hampstead from 1818 to 1820, and it is here that he produced many of his most famous works. The home is carefully restored and decorated as Keats would have known it, and the intimate museum is a wonderful tribute to his short, tragic life. Upon leaving Keats House, turn left and head back up Keats Grove, then left again on Downshire Hill. Make a right on Rosslyn Hill and enjoy some window-shopping or stop in one of the many cafes on your way back toward the Hampstead tube station, just a five-minute walk up the road.

 ROYAL LONDON:
FROM PALACE TO PARLIAMENT

TIME TO ALLOW 3–4 hours.

DISTANCE Approximately 2½ miles.

TUBE Victoria.

SIGHTS Royal Mews, Queen's Gallery, Buckingham Palace, St. James's Park, Churchill Museum and Cabinet War Rooms, Horse Guards Parade, Admiralty Arch, Trafalgar Square, National Gallery, National Portrait Gallery, St. Martin-in-the-Fields Church, Royal Horse Guards, Banqueting House, 10 Downing Street, Cenotaph, Westminster Bridge, Houses of Parliament, St. Margaret's Church, Westminster Abbey.

THIS WALK TAKES YOU PAST MANY OF LONDON'S most popular sights. The city's history, royalty, and fabulous architecture are thoroughly represented as you march through Westminster, home to London's monarchy and Parliament. The walk allows you plenty of opportunities to stop along the way, so the length of the walk depends entirely on your stamina.

Begin your walk at the Victoria tube station. Turn right on Buckingham Palace Road, following signs for the palace. Just beyond Lower Grosvenor Place is the entrance for the **Royal Mews** on the left. Housed in the palace stables is an impressive display of royal carriages; the oldest, made in 1762 for George III, is still used for coronations. Just past the Royal Mews is the **Queen's Gallery,** displaying Elizabeth II's jaw-dropping collection of privately owned artwork (although this claim is open to dispute—many people feel that these priceless works of art more properly belong to the nation, and should not be considered the private property of the Windsor family). Continuing along the road from the gallery, you soon arrive in the forecourt of **Buckingham Palace,** the official London residence of the sovereign since George III bought the place from Lord Buckingham in 1762.

The palace serves as both home and office for Her Majesty, and its elaborately decorated rooms are in continuous use for state affairs, official receptions, ceremonial occasions, and Parliamentary meetings. See the attractions listing for opening times; it is currently open to the public only from late July through late September. North of the palace is Green Park, but we are heading east to **St. James's Park,** to the right of The Mall.

Enter the park by Birdcage Walk and wander east along the pond's edge. The oldest of London's parks, St. James's started life as part of the private grounds of St. James's Palace but was opened to the public during the reign of the Stuart monarchs. Cross over the bridge, stopping to take in the stunning views of the palace to the west and the Horse Guards Parade to the east. As you continue to walk along the path beside the lake, the London Eye Ferris wheel, Westminster Abbey, and St. Stephen's Clock Tower come into view through the trees; wildlife skitter past or glide by on the water; and, if you're lucky, the sun shines a few rays through the clouds above. Charles II,

Samuel Pepys, and John Milton all enjoyed (very approximately) similar views, except for that of the London Eye, of course, which has a modern elegance they might have loved. The most famous residents of the park are the pelicans, who have delighted visitors here since the 17th century. Every afternoon they parade across the lawn on Duck Island to receive their daily fish dinner, and they thoroughly enjoy the sanctuary provided here, along with the 20 or more other species of ducks and geese that call St. James's home.

As you reach the other side of the park, cross Horse Guards Road. Just in front of you, King Charles Street ends at a stairway, and to the right of this is the entrance to the **Churchill Museum and Cabinet War Rooms,** a fascinating museum about World War II in London. Winston Churchill and his cabinet planned and plotted battle ops here while the bombs rained down on London during the desperate days of WWII. From the War Rooms, turn right on Horse Guards Road, passing the **Horse Guards Parade,** where the **Changing of the Guard** occurs daily at 11:30 a.m. (Sunday at 10 a.m.). Never take the daily Changing of the Guard as a given: it is frequently canceled (check the Web site **www.changing-the-guard.com**). Turn right on The Mall and walk under **Admiralty Arch** into **Trafalgar Square.** In the center stands Nelson's Column, the memorial to Britain's best-loved national hero, Admiral Lord Horatio Nelson, who defeated Napoléon at the Battle of Trafalgar in 1806. Today the square is the scene of frequent political demonstrations along with London's annual Christmas-tree lighting, concerts, and New Year's countdowns. (Feeding the famed pigeons here was outlawed a decade ago, to the relief of the cleaning crew and the disappointment of the ornithologically courageous.) Behind Trafalgar is the **National Gallery,** where you could spend hours enjoying one of the world's greatest art collections. To the right is the 18th-century church of **St. Martin-in-the-Fields,** definitely worth a stop to admire the elegant interior and perhaps catch a free lunchtime concert. Downstairs, the church's Café in the Crypt serves soups and sandwiches.

Leaving Trafalgar Square, walk down Whitehall (the street directly opposite the front of the National Gallery). You will pass the front of the **Horse Guards Building,** with its guards at attention, and almost directly opposite that is the **Banqueting House,** the only intact vestige of the great palace at Whitehall, which burned to the ground in 1698. Prior to this loss, the palace was the site of numerous historical events, such as the marriage of Henry VIII to Anne Boleyn and, most famously, the beheading of Charles I during the English Civil War. Others who lived in the vanished palace include Cardinal Thomas Wolsey, Oliver Cromwell, Charles II, and William III and Mary II (who abandoned it for the more salubrious country air at Kensington Palace). It's a quick-hit kind of place but still worth a stop—the Rubens ceiling celebrating the Stuart kings has a lot to do with why Charles I was executed: he truly believed in the divine right of kings, as the ceiling so absurdly demonstrates. In fact, Parliament probably could have lived with the doctrine, but when it threatened their power and, worse, when Charles I began demanding outrageous sums of government money for personal use, Parliament kicked back—hard.

Farther along Whitehall on the right is **10 Downing Street,** home of Britain's prime minister, although you are not likely to see much because the street is guarded and gated and crawling with police. The **Cenotaph,** in the middle of Whitehall, is Britain's memorial to those who died in World War I. It is the focal point of the country's Remembrance Day ceremonies, during which two minutes of silence are observed throughout the entire country on the 11th minute of the 11th hour of the 11th day of the 11th month each year.

Not far ahead, you will begin to see the buildings of Westminster coming into view. Once you've arrived in Parliament Square, you have a number of choices before you: You can wander out onto **Westminster Bridge** for the best views of **Westminster Abbey,** the **Houses of Parliament,** and **St. Stephen's Tower** and get a look at the statue of the warrior Queen Boudicca on her horse-drawn chariot, at the foot of the bridge. You can admire the madcap neo-Gothicism of the Houses of Parliament (their great architect, Augustus Pugin, ended up in the Bedlam insane asylum after either going mad or suffering from mercury poisoning) or explore the 16th-century **St. Margaret's Church** (where Sir Walter Raleigh was laid to rest). And take the opportunity at walk's end to enjoy inspiring hymns sung by the Westminster boys' choir during the daily choral evensong at Westminster Abbey, possibly the most visited tourist sight and certainly one of the most beautiful churches in London.

For MUSEUM LOVERS

IF YOU LOVE GOING TO MUSEUMS, you already have a lot in common with typical Londoners. The city is crammed with wonderful museums, many of which are free of charge.

A remarkable Web site called **24 Hour Museum** (**www.24hour museum.org.uk**) details current and upcoming exhibitions at 2,000 museums in London and across the country; it also offers virtual tours of the permanent collections of the museums featured plus links and news feeds. It's a great way to see some of the smaller, harder-to-visit museums without leaving your desk. Billed as "The National Virtual Museum," the site aims to represent Britain's entire cultural history—no small undertaking.

Saving Money on Museum Admissions

There are ways to save on the admission fees of museums, attractions, and galleries. However, let us point out that the British, Victoria and Albert, Science, Natural History, both Tates, and many other smaller museums are free of charge, except for special exhibitions. So if you

London Attractions by Neighborhood

LOCATION/ ATTRACTION NAME	DESCRIPTION	AUTHOR'S RATING
WEST END		
The British Museum	One of the most famous museums in the world	★★★★★
Charles Dickens Museum	Historic home and museum	★
London Transport Museum	Interactive museum of trams, buses, and trains	★★★★
National Gallery	Art gallery	★★★★★
National Portrait Gallery	Famous faces of England	★★★★
Royal Academy of Arts	Museum and exhibition venue	★★★½
Sir John Soane's Museum	Historic home and museum	★★★★
Somerset House	Historic home and art galleries	★★★★
THE CITY, EAST END, AND SOUTH LONDON		
Bank of England Museum	Museum of money and banking	★★
British Airways London Eye	Observation wheel	★★★★★
Clink Prison Museum	Re-creation of a medieval prison	★
Dalí Universe	Surrealist master's works	★★★★
Design Museum	Changing exhibits of exemplars of design	★★
Dr. Johnson's House	Historic home and museum	★★
Guildhall	Corporate headquarters for the City of London	★★
HMS *Belfast*	Royal Navy battleship from WWII	★★
Imperial War Museum	British military experience	★★
London Aquarium	Wonderland of fish	★★★★
London Dungeon	Horror attraction	★★★
The Monument	Memorial of the Great Fire of 1666	★★★
Museum of London	Museum of the city's history	★★★★★
Old Bailey	London's central criminal courts	★★
Old Operating Theatre, Museum, and Herb Garret	Museum of old medical equipment	★★★½
Saatchi Gallery	Best of young British modern art	★★★

LOCATION/ ATTRACTION NAME	DESCRIPTION	AUTHOR'S RATING
THE CITY, EAST END, AND SOUTH LONDON (CONTINUED)		
St. Paul's Cathedral	London's most prominent cathedral	★★★
Shakespeare's Globe Theatre	Reconstructed Shakespearean theater	★★★★
Southwark Cathedral	Small medieval church	★★½
Tate Modern	Museum of international modern art	★★★★★
Tower Bridge Exhibition	Offers terrific views	★★
Tower of London	Ancient fortress	★★★★★
V&A Museum of Childhood	Large museum of toys	★★★
Windsor Castle	Queen's country house in Hertfordshire	★★★★
WESTMINSTER AND VICTORIA		
Big Ben Clock Tower	Monument	Not rated
Buckingham Palace	Stately home of the Queen	★★★
Changing of the Guard	Grand old tradition	★★
Churchill Museum and Cabinet War Rooms	Secret WWII headquarters	★★★
Houses of Parliament	Britain's working chambers of government	★★★
Queen's Gallery, Buckingham Palace	Art gallery	★★★
Royal Mews, Buckingham Palace	Where royal carriages and queen's horses are kept	★★½
Tate Britain	Museum of English painters	★★★★
Westminster Abbey	Historically important church	★★★★
KNIGHTSBRIDGE TO SOUTH KENSINGTON		
Apsley House (The Wellington Museum)	Historic home and museum	★★★
Carlyle's House	Historic home and museum	★★★
Natural History Museum	Old and modern exhibits	★★★
Science Museum	Huge, excellent museum	★★★★
Victoria and Albert Museum	Museum of decorative arts	★★★★★
The Wellington Arch	Small specialty museum of architecture	★★

London Attractions by Neighborhood (cont'd.)

LOCATION/ ATTRACTION NAME	DESCRIPTION	AUTHOR'S RATING
MARYLEBONE TO NOTTING HILL GATE		
Albert Memorial	Outdoor monument	★★
Kensington Palace State Rooms	Stately home of Kensington Gardens	★★★★
Leighton House Museum and Art Gallery	Historic home	★★
Linley Sambourne House	Historic home	★★★
Madame Tussauds Waxworks and the Stardome	World-famous wax museum	★★★
Sherlock Holmes Museum	Real home of fictional detective	★★★
The Wallace Collection	Private collection of 19th-century Anglo-French art	★★★
NORTH LONDON		
British Library at St. Pancras	Multidisciplinary cultural collection	★★★★
Burgh House and Hampstead Museum	Museum with exhibition and concert space	★★

really want to do London on the cheap, you could skip the high ticket prices of the Tower of London, the London Eye, Madame Tussauds, and other points of interest, and you will still have so much to do you may not fit it all in.

If you want it all, as well as additional deal sweeteners, try the **London Pass,** which affords fast-track, reduced, or free entry to more than 50 fee-charging attractions; free travel on tubes, trains, and buses; discounts at a number of restaurants; free phone rental; discounts on film developing; free walking tours; and a plethora of other incentives to buy. They had to pull out all the stops to make the London Pass attractive since so many museums dropped their entrance fees in late 2001.

It's sort of like a gym membership—it makes no sense unless you plan to use it vigorously. The costs start at £36 for a one-day adult pass and £22 for a child, and increase incrementally to £79 for a six-day adult pass and £55 for a child. If you want to include travel on London public transport, the prices start at £41 for a one-day adult

LOCATION/ ATTRACTION NAME	DESCRIPTION	AUTHOR'S RATING
NORTH LONDON (CONTINUED)		
Freud Museum	Historic home and museum	★★
Kenwood House (The Iveagh Bequest)	Georgian villa and art gallery	★★★
London Zoo	Modernized old zoo	★★★★
GREENWICH AND DOCKLANDS		
National Maritime Museum and Queen's House	Largest maritime museum in the world	★★★★
Royal Observatory, Greenwich	Location of the prime meridian	★★★
WEST LONDON		
Chiswick House	Stately home and gardens	★★★
Hampton Court Palace	Royal palace and gardens	★★★★★
Hogarth's House	Artist's historic home	★★

pass (£24 for children) and go up to £117 for a six-day adult pass (£75 for children).

Only you can make the call on whether the pass is worth it. The more days you stay, the higher the savings, but you may want to get out of London for a day or two or simply rest in the hotel or at a park some days. However, if you're one of those very organized and energetic types determined to lick the last drop of honey from London's bounteous cup, the pass will definitely save you plenty. If you are planning to go to, say, the Tower of London, at £15 for adults and £9.50 for children, and then want to take a river cruise to Hampton Court or see the Tower Bridge Exhibition, the pass may be worth it, especially with some of the extra enticements, such as fast-track entry and £4.50 worth of free brass-rubbing at St. Martin-in-the-Fields. Passes can be purchased (for a £1 discount) online at **www.londonpass.com** or at the **Britain and London Visitor Centre** (1 Regent Street, south of Piccadilly Circus). Just remember that getting to and from attractions in London can take a big bite out of your day.

west end attractions

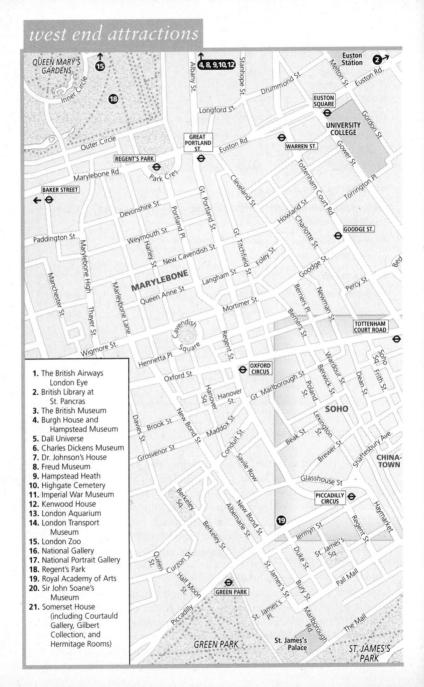

1. The British Airways London Eye
2. British Library at St. Pancras
3. The British Museum
4. Burgh House and Hampstead Museum
5. Dalí Universe
6. Charles Dickens Museum
7. Dr. Johnson's House
8. Freud Museum
9. Hampstead Heath
10. Highgate Cemetery
11. Imperial War Museum
12. Kenwood House
13. London Aquarium
14. London Transport Museum
15. London Zoo
16. National Gallery
17. National Portrait Gallery
18. Regent's Park
19. Royal Academy of Arts
20. Sir John Soane's Museum
21. Somerset House (including Courtauld Gallery, Gilbert Collection, and Hermitage Rooms)

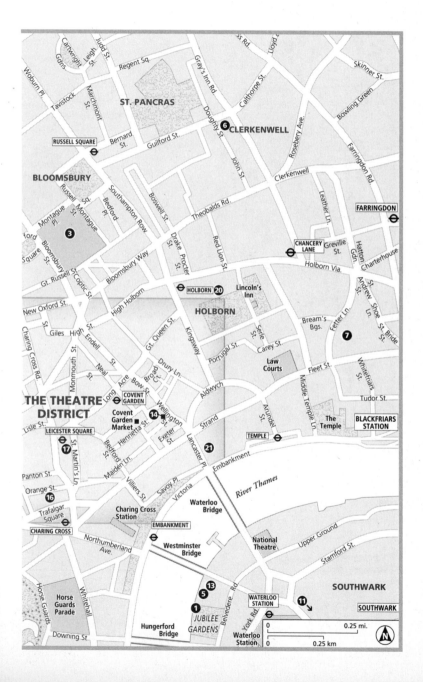

westminster and victoria attractions

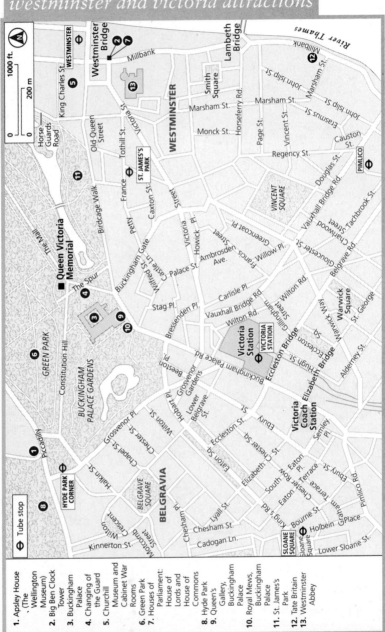

1. Apsley House (The Wellington Museum)
2. Big Ben Clock Tower
3. Buckingham Palace
4. Changing of the Guard
5. Churchill Museum and Cabinet War Rooms
6. Green Park
7. Houses of Parliament: House of Lords and House of Commons
8. Hyde Park
9. Queen's Gallery, Buckingham Palace
10. Royal Mews, Buckingham Palace
11. St. James's Park
12. Tate Britain
13. Westminster Abbey

the city attractions

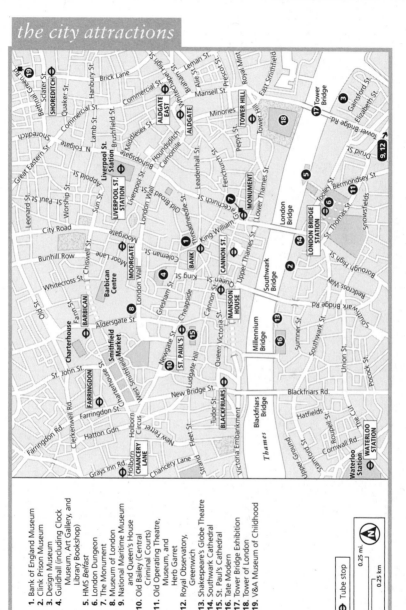

1. Bank of England Museum
2. Clink Prison Museum
3. Design Museum
4. Guildhall (including Clock
   Museum, Art Gallery, and
   Library Bookshop)
5. HMS *Belfast*
6. London Dungeon
7. The Monument
8. Museum of London
9. National Maritime Museum
   and Queen's House
10. Old Bailey (Central
    Criminal Courts)
11. Old Operating Theatre,
    Museum, and
    Herb Garret
12. Royal Observatory,
    Greenwich
13. Shakespeare's Globe Theatre
14. Southwark Cathedral
15. St. Paul's Cathedral
16. Tate Modern
17. Tower Bridge Exhibition
18. Tower of London
19. V&A Museum of Childhood

⊖ Tube stop

0   0.25 mi.
0   0.25 km

knightsbridge to south kensington

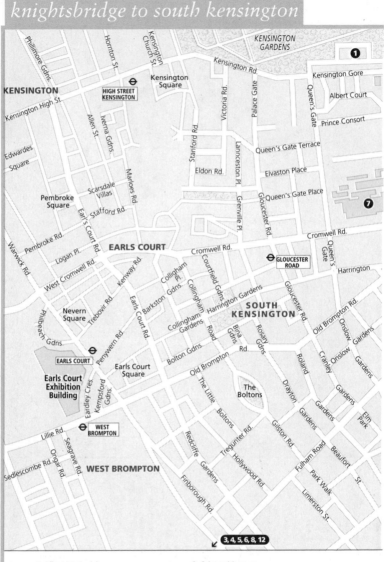

KENSINGTON GARDENS

Kensington Gore

Kensington Rd.

Kensington Road

Queen's Gate

Albert Court

Prince Consort

Phillimore Gdns.

Hornton St.

Kensington Church St.

Kensington Square

KENSINGTON

HIGH STREET KENSINGTON

Kensington Square

Kensington High St.

Allen St.

Iverna Gdns.

Victoria Rd.

Palace Gate

Queen's Gate Terrace

Stanford Rd.

Lanceston Pl.

Edwardes Square

Scarsdale Villas

Marloes Rd.

Eldon Rd.

Elvaston Place

Pembroke Square

Grenville Pl.

Gloucester Rd.

Queen's Gate Place

7

Stafford Rd.

Earl's Court Rd.

Pembroke Rd.

Cromwell Rd.

Warwick Rd.

Logan Pl.

EARLS COURT

Cromwell Rd.

Queen's Gate

West Cromwell Rd.

Kenway Rd.

GLOUCESTER ROAD

Harrington

Trebovir Rd.

Earls Court Rd.

Barkston Gdns.

Colligham Pl.

Collingham Gdns.

Courtfield Gdns.

Harrington Gardens

Gloucester Rd.

Old Brompton Rd.

Onslow Gardens

Nevern Square

Penywern Rd.

Collingham Gardens

Collingham Road

SOUTH KENSINGTON

Bina Gdns.

Rosary Gdns.

Cranley Gardens

Onslow Gardens

Phillbeach Gdns.

EARLS COURT

Bolton Gdns.

Rd.

Roland Gardens

Gardens

Elm Park

Earls Court Exhibition Building

Eardley Cres.

Kempsford Gdns.

Earls Court Square

Old Brompton

The Little Boltons

The Boltons

Drayton Gardens

Gardens

WEST BROMPTON

Gilston Rd.

Fulham Road

Beaufort St.

Lillie Rd.

Seagrave Rd.

Redcliffe Gardens

Tregunter Rd.

Hollywood Rd.

Park Walk

Sedlescombe Rd.

Ongar Rd.

WEST BROMPTON

Finborough Rd.

Limerston St.

3, 4, 5, 6, 8, 12

1. Albert Memorial
2. Carlyle's House
3. Chiswick House
4. Hampton Court Palace
5. Hogarth's House
6. Kew Gardens
7. Natural History Museum
8. Richmond Park
9. Science Museum
10. Victoria and Albert Museum
11. The Wellington Arch
12. Windsor Castle

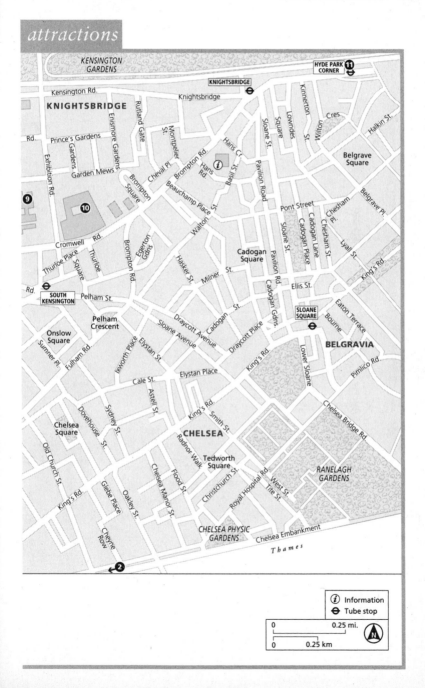

attractions

KENSINGTON GARDENS

HYDE PARK CORNER ⑪

KNIGHTSBRIDGE

Kensington Rd.

Knightsbridge

KNIGHTSBRIDGE

Kinnerton

Lowndes Square

Sloane St.

Wilton

Cres.

Halkin St.

Rd.

Prince's Gardens

Ennismore Gardens

Rutland Gate

Montpelier St.

Cheval Pl.

Brompton Rd.

Hans Cr.

Basil St.

Pavilion Road

Belgrave Square

Exhibition Rd.

Gardens

Garden Mews

Brompton Square

Beauchamp Place

Hans Rd.

ⓘ

Pont Street

Chesham Pl.

Belgrave Pl.

⑨

⑩

Cromwell

Rd.

Brompton Rd.

Egerton Gdns.

Walton

Cadogan Square

Sloane St.

Cadogan Lane

Chesham St.

Lyall St.

King's Rd.

Thurloe Place

Thurloe Square

Thurloe

Hasker St.

Milner St.

Pavilion Rd.

Cadogan Place

Rd.

SOUTH KENSINGTON

Pelham St.

Cadogan St.

Cadogan Gdns.

Ellis St.

Eaton Terrace

Bourne

Onslow Square

Pelham Crescent

Draycott Avenue

Cadogan St.

Draycott Place

SLOANE SQUARE

BELGRAVIA

Summer Pl.

Fulham Rd.

Ixworth Place

Elystan St.

Sloane Avenue

King's Rd.

Lower Sloane

Pimlico Rd.

Cale St.

Astell St.

Elystan Place

Chelsea Square

Dovehouse St.

Sydney St.

King's Rd.

Smith St.

Chelsea Bridge Rd.

Old Church St.

Chelsea Manor St.

Radnor Walk

CHELSEA

Tedworth Square

RANELAGH GARDENS

King's Rd.

Glebe Place

Oakley St.

Flood St.

Christchurch St.

Royal Hospital Rd.

West St.

Tite St.

Cheyne Row

CHELSEA PHYSIC GARDENS

Chelsea Embankment

T h a m e s

② ⟵

ⓘ Information

⊖ Tube stop

0	0.25 mi.
0	0.25 km

Ⓝ

marylebone to notting hill gate

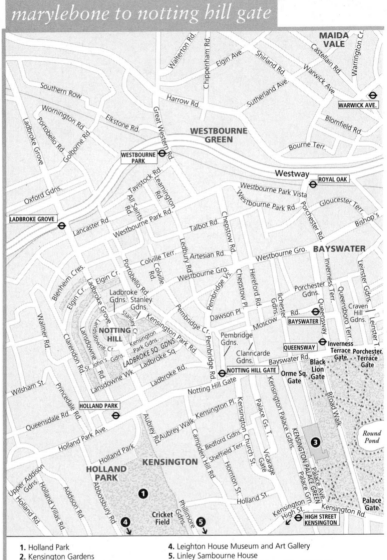

1. Holland Park
2. Kensington Gardens
3. Kensington Palace State Rooms
4. Leighton House Museum and Art Gallery
5. Linley Sambourne House
6. Madame Tussauds Waxworks and the Stardome

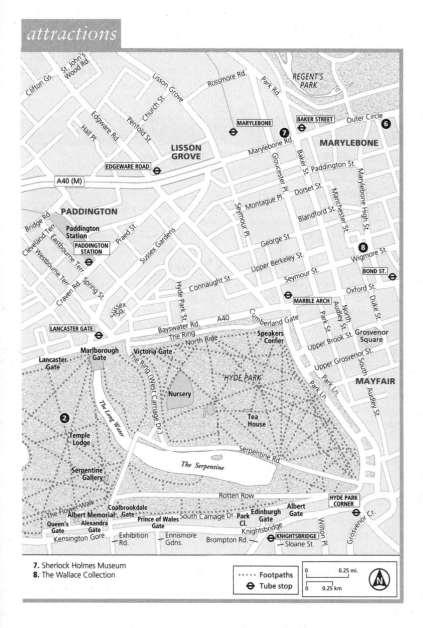

attractions

7. Sherlock Holmes Museum
8. The Wallace Collection

····· Footpaths
Tube stop

0   0.25 mi.
0   0.25 km

MUSEUMS *and* ATTRACTIONS

FOR A LOOK INTO LONDON'S PARKS AND GREEN SPACES, see "Green and Pleasant Lands: Parks of London" on page 250. Also, a profile of Greenwich is at the end of this chapter.

Albert Memorial   ★★

APPEAL BY AGE	PRESCHOOL ★★	GRADE SCHOOL ★★	TEENS ★★
YOUNG ADULTS ★★		OVER 30 ★★	SENIORS ★★

Kensington Gardens, west of Exhibition Road, Kensington, SW7; tube: High Street Kensington

Type of attraction Outdoor memorial to a beloved prince consort. **Admission** Free. **Hours** Daily, dawn–dusk. **When to go** On a sunny day or at night when the floodlights are on. **Special comments** Bring binoculars so you can see the amazing detail of the high parts of the memorial. **Author's rating ★★. How much time to allow** 15 minutes, plus time to hang around on the steps. It's a good people-watching place, right near Kensington Palace.

DESCRIPTION AND COMMENTS This memorial, built by a grieving Queen Victoria after her husband's death from typhoid fever at the age of 42, is as much a monument to the prince as it is to the restoration crews who beavered away under the shroud of canvas for more than a decade while the memorial was returned to its former glory. It had been stripped of its gold in 1915 to confound the zeppelins looking for targets, so we are in the privileged position of being the first generation in almost a century to see it in all its exuberant neo-Gothic gilded glory. Some Londoners find the entire thing hideous and are appalled at the millions of pounds spent on its conservation, but whatever one might think of its artistry, it is a visual knockout. Check it out at night with the floodlights on it to appreciate a view the Victorians were denied.

unofficial **TIP**
Be sure to call the attractions profiled here before you go; opening times can be subject to change without notice.

The memorial can be seen from many angles in Hyde Park and Kensington Gardens, but don't imagine you have experienced its full flavor until you have looked the buffalo square in the eye.

TOURING TIPS Make this part of your Kensington Palace/Gardens and Hyde Park day.

Apsley House (The Wellington Museum)   ★★★

APPEAL BY AGE	PRESCHOOL ★	GRADE SCHOOL ★★	TEENS ★★
YOUNG ADULTS ★★★		OVER 30 ★★★	SENIORS ★★★

149 Piccadilly, W1; ☎ 0207-499-5676; www.english-heritage.org.uk/apsleyhouse; tube: Hyde Park Corner

Type of attraction Former home of the Duke of Wellington. **Admission** £5.30 for adults, £2.70 for children under age 16, £4 for seniors. **Hours**

March–October, Tuesday–Sunday, 10 a.m.–5 p.m.; October–March, closes at 4 p.m.; last entry, half hour before closing. **When to go** Anytime. **Special comments** There is no wheelchair access, and there are multiple steps into the house and between the floors. If you walk along the pedestrian subway below Hyde Park Corner, you can see the story of Apsley House and the Duke of Wellington rendered on the tiles on the wall, a good way to prepare for the visit to the house. **Author's rating ★★★. How much time to allow** 45 minutes to an hour; more if you really love old masters.

DESCRIPTION AND COMMENTS Built between 1771 and 1778 by Robert Adams, this grand house was purchased and upgraded by the Duke of Wellington in 1817 after his military successes in the Napoleonic Wars. An incongruously huge, naked (with fig leaf, of course) statue of the diminutive Napoléon graces a stairwell; an outrageously detailed silver centerpiece runs the length of the very long dining table. While the Hyde Park Corner traffic circle whirls in front of the house, the windows in the back of Apsley House look out onto a serene vista of Hyde Park, the rose gardens, and the occasional horseback riders. Apsley House is of great interest to art lovers, its gallery filled with old masters such as Velázquez, Goya, and Rubens, along with some lesser luminaries. The house is lovingly maintained after having been recently handed over to English Heritage by the Victoria and Albert Museum, and it provides an invaluable education in the decoration of great houses of the day. The basement houses a collection of political cartoons that will teach you about the Duke—one of the towering public figures of his day—and his times.

TOURING TIPS This is a small, in-and-out kind of place, and it fits in well with a walk through Hyde Park and a visit to the Wellington Arch, before you move on through Green and St. James's parks.

Bank of England Museum ★★

APPEAL BY AGE	PRESCHOOL –	GRADE SCHOOL ★★	TEENS ★★
YOUNG ADULTS ★★		OVER 30 ★★	SENIORS ★★

Threadneedle Street, The City, EC2 (museum entrance on Bartholomew Lane); ☎ 0207-601-5545; www.bankofengland.co.uk/museum; tube: Bank

Type of attraction Historical displays tracing the rise of banking and the use of currency. **Admission** Free. **Hours** Monday–Friday, 10 a.m.–5 p.m.; closed weekends and bank holidays. **When to go** Anytime. **Special comments** Disabled-friendly, with portable ramps available on request. **Author's rating ★★. How much time to allow** 1 hour.

DESCRIPTION AND COMMENTS This is the only part of the massive Bank of England—known as the "Old Lady of Threadneedle Street"—that mere mortals can enter. One display shows the evolution of the banknote from 1694—when the bank was formed to lend money to the government to pay for King James II's war against France—to the present; much of the currency used over the centuries can be viewed here. Another display, modeled after the first bank, includes mannequins of wigged clerks and a huge fireplace behind mahogany counters. A video shows real footage from the building of the present bank in the 1930s; interactive computer screens provide a lot of information. Be warned: the displays require quite a bit of reading, as well as a particular interest in money and banking.

Big Ben Clock Tower *(not rated)*

Parliament Square, Westminster, SW1; www.londontouristboard.com; tube: Westminster

Type of attraction Look-only clock tower; enduring symbol of London. **Admission** Visitors can't enter the tower. **Hours** 24 hours a day. **When to go** When you're in the area.

DESCRIPTION AND COMMENTS Big Ben is not an attraction per se, but it is a beautiful piece of architecture that you can set your watch to. It is the most recognizable symbol of the city, and replicas of Big Ben are at the top of most visitors' must-have souvenir lists. The bells play an instantly recognizable tune—known as the Westminster Chimes—on the hour, followed by a wonderful tolling of the time.

In 1834, the old Palace of Westminster burned to the ground, so Parliament decided to build itself a Gothic-style replacement—neo-Gothic was all the rage in those days, as the ugliness of the industrial present cast the past in a nostalgic glow. The clock tower was part of the grand plan, but because of its exacting specifications, construction took some time and was beset by difficulties. "Big Ben" refers in fact to the actual bell that chimes, and it was Big Trouble from the start. The first bell cast cracked almost immediately—probably from the weight of the clapper—and had to be recast to smaller specifications. Likewise, the clock's hands were too heavy to move and also had to be replaced. The bell cracked a second time and remained silent for three years until a solution was found in 1862. Big Ben has been ringing out the famous Westminster Chimes ever since.

kids British Airways London Eye ★★★★★

APPEAL BY AGE	PRESCHOOL ★★★★	GRADE SCHOOL ★★★★★	TEENS ★★★★★
YOUNG ADULTS ★★★★★		OVER 30 ★★★★★	SENIORS ★★★★★

In Jubilee Gardens, next to County Hall by Westminster Bridge, on the south bank of the Thames; ☎ 0870-500-0600; www.londoneye.com; tube: Westminster or Waterloo

Type of attraction The world's highest Ferris wheel. **Admission** £15 for adults, £11 for seniors and the disabled, £7.50 for children ages 5–16, free for kids under age 5; 10% discount for parties of 10 or more or by booking online; £25 for Fast Track. Go to the Web site for other package deals and discounts. **Hours** June–September, daily, 10 a.m.–9 p.m.; October–May, daily, 10 a.m.–8 p.m.; closed for maintenance second week of January. **When to go** Best on a sunny day or clear night; avoid these glassed-in pods on very hot days. In summer, go at 7:30 p.m. The sun sets around 7:45, so you can see what London looks like by day, watch the sun set, and then see London all lit up at night. Also, it's less busy at this time, so you can get onto the Eye virtually straightaway and share the pod with fewer people. **Special comments** Not for those who suffer from vertigo or fear of heights. There is full disabled access to the London Eye and in County Hall, which has wheelchair-accessible toilets. Baby strollers not allowed unless they fold up small; baby carriers available. **Author's rating ★ ★ ★ ★ ★. How much time to allow** If you haven't ordered tickets ahead of time, you may have to wait in line, depending on the season and the weather. If you have reserved tickets (by phone or online), you can pick them up easily, and then you must wait about a half hour for boarding. The rotation takes 30 minutes.

DESCRIPTION AND COMMENTS Definitely London's most successful attraction designed to celebrate the millennium year, the London Eye is a colossal 450 feet high—the largest observation wheel ever built. Conceived as a temporary attraction that would be dismantled after five years, the Eye has become wildly popular, ensuring it a permanent place among the most traditional of London's recreations. Ongoing improvements include a gift shop and a much more efficient system of ticket buying and boarding.

Each of the 32 pods carries about 25 people, with benches for those who wish to sit. The design and the effect are elegant and graceful; the wheel soars above the old buildings of Westminster and the South Bank without striking a discordant note. It revolves slowly and majestically to a zenith of 450 feet, at which point passengers can see a good 25 miles away on a clear day. At the ticket counter, you can purchase a pod-shaped miniguide that identifies all the major landmarks, such as the Houses of Parliament, Windsor Castle, the BT Tower, and St. Paul's.

unofficial **TIP** Most Londoners have taken the arching view of the London Eye to heart and rank it as a graceful addition to the skyline.

TOURING TIPS If you order tickets ahead of time on the Web site or by phone, you can choose the day and the time you wish to "board"; then you show up with your credit card and retrieve the tickets at the County Hall Building, adjacent to the Eye. Combine your visit with a trip to the London Aquarium (especially if you're traveling with children) or Dalí Universe, or lunch at the Marriott Hotel's river-view dining room.

British Library at St. Pancras ★★★★

APPEAL BY AGE	PRESCHOOL –	GRADE SCHOOL ★★	TEENS ★★
YOUNG ADULTS ★★★	OVER 30 ★★★		SENIORS ★★★★

96 Euston Road, North London, NW1; ☎ 0207-412-7332; www.bl.uk; tube: King's Cross

Type of attraction New location of reading rooms (manuscript-archive collections) formerly housed in the British Museum (see profile next page). **Admission**

Free. **Hours** Monday, 9:30 a.m–6 p.m.; Tuesday, 9:30 a.m.–8 p.m.; Wednesday–Friday, 9:30 a.m.–6 p.m.; Saturday, 9:30–5 p.m.; Sunday, 11 a.m.–5 p.m. Special exhibition times vary. **When to go** Anytime. **Special comments** Full wheelchair and disabled access. **Author's rating** ★★★. **How much time to allow** 1–7 hours (it's up to you).

DESCRIPTION AND COMMENTS The embattled (and expensive: £500 million!) project to move the reading rooms from their beautiful longtime niche at the British Museum was one of those necessary concessions to age that no one really wanted to make. However, since the opening, visitors and readers have grudgingly admitted that it is a vast improvement over the cramped old quarters. Even Prince Charles, who scorned the exterior as "a collection of brick sheds groping for significance," was impressed with the interior. The fact is that, however lacking in aesthetics the place may be, it's still a veritable Aladdin's cave of treasures, with more than 13 million books. Manuscripts such as the Lindisfarne Gospels from the tenth century, James Joyce's first draft of *Finnegans Wake,* a copy of the Magna Carta from 1215, the Gutenberg Bible, and a wealth of documents related to the greatest English writer of all, Shakespeare, are only some of the magnificent materials on view here.

The library offers to the public a fine bookstore, a cafe, and special exhibition galleries. The Sir John Ritblat Gallery displays some of the library's most ancient and valuable manuscripts and maps. There's a wondrous room called "Turning the Pages" in which a computer enables you to virtually flip through four gloriously illuminated texts: the Lindisfarne Gospels, the Diamond Sutra, Leonardo da Vinci's notebooks, and the Sforza Hours. You can listen to James Joyce and other authors reading from their work, and to music of all types, too. In the Pearson Gallery of Living Words are educational exhibits, one of which explores the history of writing; another is a reading area, with a good display of children's literature. A few fun interactive offerings include designing a book and checking out the evolution of recorded music.

TOURING TIPS This is not really a tourist attraction—it is for people who love and respect books, so take care whom you take along with you. Sign up for a guided tour to see the parts of the library not open to the public.

 **The British Museum** ★★★★★

APPEAL BY AGE	PRESCHOOL ★★★★	GRADE SCHOOL ★★★★	TEENS ★★★★★
YOUNG ADULTS ★★★★★	OVER 30 ★★★★★		SENIORS ★★★★★

Great Russell Street, Bloomsbury, WC1; ☎ 0207-323-8000/8299; www.thebritishmuseum.ac.uk; tube: Tottenham Court Road

Type of attraction Colossal museum housing treasures of the British Empire. **Admission** Free. **Hours** *Great Court:* Sunday–Wednesday, 9 a.m.–6 p.m., Thursday–Saturday, 9 a.m.–11 p.m. *Galleries:* daily, 10 a.m.–5:30 p.m. (selected galleries are open late Thursdays and Fridays). **When to go** Early mornings. **Special comments**

Get a leaflet from the information desk for details about wheelchair accessibility; wheelchairs are also available to borrow. The Queen Elizabeth II Great Court, opened in December 2000, has improved the museum immensely. **Author's rating ★ ★ ★ ★**. **How much time to allow** 2–4 hours.

DESCRIPTION AND COMMENTS The world's oldest museum houses more than 50,000 items—artifacts of human activities spanning some 2 million years— in 100 galleries. It all began when Sir Hans Sloane bequeathed his remarkable collection of art and artifacts to the state in 1753, and the Earl of Oxford's rare manuscripts were added to the mix. The collection grew rapidly, as it became the scholarly and patriotic thing to do to leave one's finest possessions to the museum, which benefited from England's greatest empire booty-looting years. Even the stolen goods from Napoléon's own empire-building campaigns were placed here after the British defeated the French at Alexandria during the Napoleonic Wars.

At the British Museum, you can travel to the ends of the globe and see just about every little thing that our ancestors thought up along the way: mummies, pottery, clocks, painting, tools of war and peace, sculpture, personal decoration, household goods, treasures of gold and precious stones, and far more. Not only are there artifacts from practically every civilization throughout time, but they are of the greatest historical, cultural, and scientific significance. The Rosetta Stone, the Lindow Man, the Egyptian mummies, and prehistoric pieces are just a few of the finds that have literally changed the world and now reside here.

The building itself contributes to the museum's appeal. Recently remodeled, it features at its center the Queen Elizabeth II Great Court, the largest covered square in Europe, with more than 3,000 panes of glass sheltering an area the size of a soccer field. This courtyard was not always accessible, because it had been gradually filled with the materials of the round domed Reading Room of the British Library. When the library was removed to St. Pancras in 1997 (see preceding profile), the courtyard space was reclaimed.

The museum also offers numerous gift shops, benches and tables on which to rest tired bones, and a restaurant at the top of the courtyard that affords wonderful views of the courtyard and the Reading Room below. Children's activities take place on weekends, and there are occasional workshops for them during the week.

*un*official **TIP**
To make the most of your visit to the British Museum, do study its Web site, which lists the hours of all the shops, cafes, restaurants, exhibitions, and special lectures.

TOURING TIPS The museum is far too big to to cover in one visit, so consult the map and the interests of your group before heading to the galleries, and use the compass multimedia system in the Reading Room to help plan your tour. A good guidebook is sold in the excellent bookstore. And, as with most museums, getting here before the school buses arrive is key. It is hard to gaze with the proper wonder at the Rosetta Stone when you're being jostled by an army of uniformed schoolchildren.

Buckingham Palace   ★★★
(See separate profiles for Queen's Gallery and Royal Mews, both on premises.)

APPEAL BY AGE	PRESCHOOL ★	GRADE SCHOOL ★★	TEENS ★★
YOUNG ADULTS ★★★	OVER 30 ★★★	SENIORS ★★★	

Buckingham Palace Road, Victoria, SW1; ☎ 0207-766-7300; www.royalcollection.org.uk; tube: Green Park

Type of attraction Stately home of the queen. **Admission** £15 for adults, £8.50 for children ages 5–16, free for children under age 5, £13.50 for seniors and students, £38.50 for a family ticket (£1.25 service charge for booking over the phone or Web site). **Hours** July 28–September 28, daily, 9:45 a.m.–6 p.m.; last admission 3:45 p.m. **When to go** If you purchase tickets from the ticket office in Green Park, go at 9 a.m. The queues can be murder. **Special comments** Wheelchair users are required to arrange a visit in advance. We personally wouldn't inflict this tour on a preschooler, although palace reps assure us that the young ones seem to love it. **Author's rating ★★★. How much time to allow** 2–3 hours.

DESCRIPTION AND COMMENTS Buckingham House was purchased by King George III in 1761 from the Duke of Buckingham. Like most real estate, its three most attractive features were location, location, and location. Situated between St. James's and Hyde parks, with a tree-lined avenue affording views of Westminster and even the dome of St. Paul's, it was like a country estate in the city (or near the city, as west of the house was still country). It was a private residence, the official court remaining—as it does to this day, if only in name—that of St. James's, and no doubt one of its attractions was that it was within easy walking distance of St. James's Palace. When George IV ascended the throne, he had his favorite architect, John Nash, remodel it in the lavish style you see today.

There are only two months of the year—August and September (plus a few days at the end of July)—when you can view the state rooms at Buckingham Palace, so make your plans accordingly. In 1996, Queen Elizabeth II decided to open part of the palace to the public to pay for the restoration of Windsor Castle, which was severely damaged by a fire in 1992. By now, they've covered the cost several times over.

It's an amazing spectacle, even more so when you ponder that for all the years of the palace's existence, most loyal subjects of the crown never had a prayer of setting foot in these august precincts, and now they're letting in the likes of you and me to eyeball the queen's goods. And what goods they are: treasures of painting, sculpture, furniture, and decoration beyond description, so we won't even try. (Neither do they. You have to buy the official guidebook to know what you are looking at; there are no signs anywhere.) The views through the numerous French doors are magnificent; you can look out at the back garden, a piece of Ye Olde English Countryside within earshot of the roar of Hyde Park Corner.

TOURING TIPS Don't bring in any bags so you can avoid the security check. Before your tour time, do go buy the official guide from the gift shop, next to the palace at the Queen's Gallery—you'll save yourself a wait on the way into the palace. *We repeat:* it's important to get this book if you want to know what is what, because just as in your own home, there are no labels on the goods. When you book online, you are given a choice among a number of guidebooks that you can order and that will be dispatched to you along with the tickets. The palace employs guides who stand around; they're happy to answer questions and are very knowledgeable. The time designated for your entry will be printed on your ticket, so don't bother lining up until about 15 minutes beforehand. You might wander around St. James's Park in the meantime.

> *unofficial* **TIP**
> *Warning:* Buckingham Palace is not an attraction for everyone, not least because of the lines you have to wait in; even the timed tickets haven't eliminated the queues. It's a lot of money and a lot of effort for what is essentially an inert (though stately) old home.

Burgh House and Hampstead Museum ★★

APPEAL BY AGE	PRESCHOOL ★	GRADE SCHOOL ★	TEENS ★
YOUNG ADULTS ★★		OVER 30 ★★	SENIORS ★★

New End Square, Hampstead, NW3; ☎ 0207-431-0144; www.burghhouse.org.uk; tube: Hampstead

Type of attraction Lovely period home and arts center providing exhibitions, concerts, and lectures. **Admission** Free. **Hours** Wednesday–Sunday, noon–5 p.m.; by appointment on Saturday. **When to go** Anytime. **Author's rating** ★★. **How much time to allow** 1 hour to see Hampstead Museum exhibit; other times depend on lecture or concert lengths.

DESCRIPTION AND COMMENTS The meandering streets of Flask Walk and Well Walk are picturesque reminders of when Hampstead was a thriving spa village. To step out of the sometimes brisk Hampstead breeze, you might stop at this well-maintained Queen Anne home, a modest museum of local history with changing exhibitions. The house is more well known among the locals for its ongoing series of concerts, including opera, chamber music, and jazz (call for a current schedule). Downstairs is a charming tearoom called The Buttery (call ☎ 0207-482-0869 for reservations).

TOURING TIPS See our walking tour of Old Hampstead Village (page 177) for other sights to see in the area.

Carlyle's House ★★★

APPEAL BY AGE	PRESCHOOL ★	GRADE SCHOOL ★★	TEENS ★★
YOUNG ADULTS ★★★		OVER 30 ★★★	SENIORS ★★★

24 Cheyne Row, Chelsea, SW3; ☎ 0207-352-7087; www.nationaltrust.org.uk; tube: Sloane Square

Type of attraction Queen Anne–style home of the Sage of Chelsea. **Admission** £4.50 for adults, £2.30 for children under age 16. **Hours** April–October, Wednesday–Sunday and bank holidays, 11 a.m.–5 p.m.; November–March,

Wednesday–Sunday, 2–5 p.m. **When to go** Any time it's open—call to be sure of hours. **Special comments** It's an old house with steep stairs; no wheelchair access. **Author's rating** ★★★. **How much time to allow** 1 hour.

DESCRIPTION AND COMMENTS It's likely that the name Thomas Carlyle means nothing to most people these days, but he was a great essayist and historian in his own time (1795–1881), known and admired by all the Victorian literati. His house was a salon of luminaries such as Charles Dickens, George Eliot, Alfred Lord Tennyson, and Frédéric Chopin, drawn as much by the Sage of Chelsea's wisdom as by the famous wit of his widely admired wife, Jane. Carlyle's impecunious one-time neighbors, artist James Leigh Hunt and his wife, were in and out of the house constantly, borrowing everything from money to teacups to a fire screen, much to Jane's bemused annoyance. What is marvelous about Carlyle's house, in the absence of any great feeling for its former owners, is that it was made a museum not too long after the scholar's death, and thus contains an abundance of authentic minutiae—a hat hung on a hook, clothing in a drawer—that are lacking in most literary shrines of this sort. A wonderful garden reflects the Victorian reverence for controlled nature. All the furnishings are authentic, and the atmosphere is beyond the wildest dreams of a Victorianaphile.

TOURING TIPS Be sure to look at all the blue plaques around here to see the kinds of neighbors Carlyle enjoyed.

Changing of the Guard ★★

| APPEAL BY AGE | PRESCHOOL ★ | GRADE SCHOOL ★★ | TEENS ★★ |
| YOUNG ADULTS ★★ | | OVER 30 ★★ | SENIORS ★★ |

In the forecourt of Buckingham Palace, at the end of Pall Mall, SW1; www.changing-the-guard.com; tube: Green Park, then walk directly through the park to the palace

Type of attraction A grand old London tradition. **Admission** Free. **Hours** April–July, daily at 11:30 a.m.; August–March, every other day at 11:30 a.m.; check Web site for up-to-the-minute information. **When to go** Arrive by 10:30 a.m. to get a good place by the forecourt railings or at the statue of Queen Victoria, especially in the summer on a nice day. **Special comments** The pageant is canceled in very wet weather. **Author's rating** ★★. **How much time to allow** The actual ceremony lasts 40 minutes, but you should show up an hour earlier for a better view.

DESCRIPTION AND COMMENTS The Queen's Guards, often accompanied by a band, leave Wellington Barracks at 11:27 a.m. and march along Birdcage Walk to the Palace, where they . . . well, change. One shift of guards goes on duty and one goes off, amid all this fanfare. I'm not crazy about this attraction, even though I love horses and history. There's something so annoying about the hordes of people standing around, very few of whom can get a good look at the ceremony, and even the ones pressed against the railings look miserable for all the waiting they've had to do. That said, I can recommend the statue of Queen Victoria for a vantage point that isn't quite as desperate and uncomfortable as the scene around the palace railings. (I'm talking about the summer months, by the way; in the winter, it's not quite so bad.) If it's too crowded for you around the palace, go to the Horse Guards Parade on Horse Guards Parade Road, which is on the far eastern perimeter of St. James's Park (tube: Embankment or Charing Cross). A less elaborate ceremony takes place Monday through Saturday at 11 a.m. and Sunday at 10 a.m. The Queen's Life Guards leave the Hyde Park Barracks Monday through Saturday at 10:30 a.m. and Sunday at 9:30 a.m., and march most impressively through Hyde Park Corner, Constitution Hill, and The Mall.

TOURING TIPS If it's too crowded one day and you can't get a good view, save it for the next. The small Guards Museum, at the Wellington Barracks on Birdcage Walk, is open daily from 10 a.m. to 4 p.m.; entrance fee is £3; ☎ 0207-414-3271; **www.theguardsmuseum.com.** It may be of interest to military enthusiasts and many young boys, and it has a decent gift shop of Guards memorabilia.

Charles Dickens Museum ★

APPEAL BY AGE	PRESCHOOL ★	GRADE SCHOOL ★	TEENS ★
YOUNG ADULTS ★		OVER 30 ★★	SENIORS ★★

48 Doughty Street, Bloomsbury, WC1; ☎ 0207-405-2127; www.dickensmuseum.com; tube: Russell Square

Type of attraction Literary shrine to the great Victorian author. **Admission** £5 for adults, £4 for students and seniors, £3 for children, £14 for families. **Hours** Monday–Saturday, 10 a.m.–5 p.m.; Sunday, 11 a.m.–5 p.m. **When to go** Anytime. **Special comments** The house contains numerous steps and no wheelchair access. **Author's rating ★. How much time to allow** 40 minutes.

DESCRIPTION AND COMMENTS I am a big Dickens fan, and I was hoping for more from this museum; it is sad that London, the city that Dickens made real for so many readers, doesn't have a better temple to honor him. Dickens actually lived in this house for only two years, so his spirit certainly does not walk these floors in the way you sense Carlyle's does in his historic house. There are manuscript pages that are exciting to see, lots of wonderful illustrations from his books, and portraits of the writer, and these make it worth the trip. The gift shop sells some fine old and new editions of Dickens and some of his contemporaries. Watch the video in the basement first; it's very good. Also, check the Web site to see what kind of events and special exhibits are on, which include dramatic readings and displays related to all things Dickens. One of the more inventive recent exhibitions was entitled "Victorian Beards"; make of that what you will.

TOURING TIPS Check the Web site for special events, such as readings and walks.

Chiswick House ★★★

APPEAL BY AGE	PRESCHOOL ★	GRADE SCHOOL ★	TEENS ★
YOUNG ADULTS ★★	OVER 30 ★★		SENIORS ★★

Burlington Lane, West London, W4; ☎ 0208-995-0508; www.chgt.org.uk; tube: Turnham Green; British Rail: Chiswick

Type of attraction Stately home with classic gardens. **Admission** £4 for adults, £2 for children under age 16. **Hours** April–October, Wednesday–Friday and Sunday, 10 a.m.–5 p.m., Saturday until 2 p.m.; November–March, by appointment only. **When to go** In good weather; the garden is splendid. **Special comments** Limited disabled access; call for details. **Author's rating** ★★★. **How much time to allow** 1 hour.

DESCRIPTION AND COMMENTS It's a bit of a hike from either the train station in Chiswick or the tube at Turnham Green, but for anyone interested in Palladian design and 18th-century splendor, this is the place. Built in 1725 by Lord Burlington and William Kent, it has at its heart an octagonal room with a classically symmetrical dome. The house's original purpose was more to show off Burlington's extensive art collection than to live in, but most of those treasures have long since been carted off to museums. However, the decoration, carvings, and statuary that remain are magnificent, and the William Kent ceilings are as sumptuous as those he painted at Kensington Palace. In summer, the gardens are spectacular, filled with wonderful follies—mock ruins that were all the rage in the 18th and 19th centuries—as well as ponds, statues, benches, and formal gardens.

TOURING TIPS Combine with a trip to Hogarth's House (see page 211).

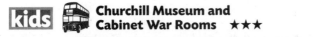

kids Churchill Museum and Cabinet War Rooms ★★★

APPEAL BY AGE	PRESCHOOL ★	GRADE SCHOOL ★★	TEENS ★★★
YOUNG ADULTS ★★★	OVER 30 ★★★★		SENIORS ★★★★

Clive Steps, King Charles Street, Whitehall, SW1; ☎ 0207-930-6961; www.iwm.org.uk (click on "Churchill Museum & Cabinet War Rooms"); tube: Westminster or St. James's Park

Type of attraction World War II shelter for Churchill and his cabinet, with an extensive display of WWII memorabilia and Churchilliana. **Admission** £11 for adults, free for children under age 16, £9 for seniors and students; admission includes audio guide. **Hours** April–September, daily, 9:30 a.m.–6 p.m. **When to go** Anytime. **Special comments** Good disabled access, including wheelchairs on loan and accessible toilets. **Author's rating** ★★★. **How much time to allow** 1–2 hours.

DESCRIPTION AND COMMENTS This is the shelter in which Winston Churchill met with his staff, heads of state, and military personnel during the six years of World War II, when Hitler's bombs fell with grim regularity on London. Churchill's historic radio messages to buck up the public were broadcast from this site, and desperate decisions of uncertain, possibly deadly outcome were strategized in these rooms. From the sandbags that line the front of the shelter to the old telephones and notepaper on Churchill's desk, this is an unusually close encounter with the reality of the war in London. When the war ended, the lights were turned off and the door shut, and the rooms remained exactly as they were left until the 1980s, when they were opened to the public. In 2003, the Churchill suite was opened; this was where the prime minister and his wife, Clementine, slept, dined, and entertained during the long nights of the Blitz. The recent Churchill Project has sunk £13.5 million into upgrading the existing structure and into opening the first museum dedicated exclusively to the indomitable prime minister. Children will enjoy the interactive exhibits. A place for refreshments, the Switchroom cafeteria, is decorated with photographic artifacts. This attraction offers a good audio tour, or you can get a booklet with which to go through the rooms. This is a must for the WWII veteran or buff.

TOURING TIPS Combine with a visit to St. James's Park.

Clink Prison Museum ★

APPEAL BY AGE	PRESCHOOL †	GRADE SCHOOL ★	TEENS ★
YOUNG ADULTS ★	OVER 30	★	SENIORS ★

† Too creepy for preschoolers.

1 Clink Street, South London, SE1; ☎ 0207-403-0900; www.clink.co.uk; tube: London Bridge

Type of attraction Re-creation and exhibition of a medieval prison. **Admission** £5 for adults; £3.50 for seniors, students, and children under 16; £12 for families. **Hours** Monday–Friday, 10 a.m.–6 p.m.; Saturday and Sunday, 10 a.m.–6 p.m. **When to go** Anytime. **Special comments** This attraction is not accessible to wheelchairs or baby strollers, as the entrance to the basement site is down a rather dark flight of stairs, and the exhibit itself includes a number of narrow doorways that must be stepped over. **Author's rating ★. How much time to allow** 30 minutes.

DESCRIPTION AND COMMENTS Be warned: there's much less to this attraction than meets the eye, despite recent efforts to upgrade the entertainment value, and we advise you to give it a pass unless you are deeply interested in the history of everything. The Clink began as a dungeon for disobedient clerics, debtors, and prostitutes. The exhibition presents itself as a re-created medieval dungeon and includes some dismal cell reproductions, diagrams of medieval torture devices, and fact boards on some of the prison's prior inhabitants. Though one might think the ghoulish subject matter would be of high interest to grade-school kids and teens, most of the information must be read from the mounted displays, something most kids grow weary of too quickly.

TOURING TIPS If you do decide to explore this area, include a stop at Southwark Cathedral and Shakespeare's Globe Theatre, both within only a few minutes' walk of the museum.

Dalí Universe   ★★★★

APPEAL BY AGE	PRESCHOOL ★★★	GRADE SCHOOL ★★★	TEENS ★★★★
YOUNG ADULTS ★★★★		OVER 30 ★★★★	SENIORS ★★★★

County Hall Gallery, Riverside Building, South Bank; ☎ 0207-620-2720; www.daliuniverse.com; tube: Westminster or Waterloo

Type of attraction Retrospective of surrealist master, plus related exhibits. **Admission** £12 for adults, £8 for children ages 8–16, £5 for children ages 4–7, free for children under 4, £10 for seniors and students, £30 for families. **Hours** Daily, 10 a.m.–6:30 p.m. **When to go** Anytime. **Special comments** Wheelchair access available at entrance along Queens Walk. **Author's rating ★★★★**. **How much time to allow** 1 hour.

DESCRIPTION AND COMMENTS This fantastic gallery honors surrealist master Salvador Dalí. While certainly not as impressive as the Dalí Museum in Figueres, Spain, it is certainly as comprehensive as the Dalí Museum in Paris. His elephant-on-stilts statue stands outside, soaring gracefully in the air as it looks over the Thames to the Houses of Parliament. Inside are more than 500 of his works, including the famous red sofa in the shape of seductive lips, the witty lobster telephone, and many of his best-known and best-loved canvases. There is also a good exhibition of some personal artifacts, including letters, photos, and scribblings. Dalí Universe contains the largest collection of the artist's sculptures from 1935 to 1984, and the gift shop sells high-quality reproductions of many of them, almost impossible to resist—fans will leave the shop burdened with gifts, postcards, mouse pads, desk toys, T-shirts, and more. (There is something whimsical and ironic about Dalí's art that makes these kinds of knickknacks more fun and appropriate than, say, a Mona Lisa tie, which is just embarrassing.) The gallery is intelligently and creatively curated and designed, making the most of lighting and backgrounds to create a temple of which Dalí would most likely have approved.

TOURING TIPS Combine with visits to any of the South Bank attractions, such as the London Aquarium, the London Eye, and the Saatchi Gallery.

Design Museum   ★★

APPEAL BY AGE	PRESCHOOL ★	GRADE SCHOOL ★	TEENS ★
YOUNG ADULTS ★★		OVER 30 ★★★	SENIORS ★★

28 Shad Thames, Butler's Wharf, SE1; ☎ 0207-378-6055; www.designmuseum.org; tube: Tower Hill or London Bridge

Type of attraction 4 floors featuring the design of everyday items. **Admission** £7 for adults, £4 for students and seniors, free for children under 12. **Hours** Daily, 10 a.m.–5:45 p.m. **When to go** Anytime. **Special comments** Wheelchair accessible. **Author's rating ★★**. **How much time to allow** 1 hour–90 minutes.

DESCRIPTION AND COMMENTS The Design Museum features changing exhibits of design from all possible areas of life, from shoes to shovels, highlighting the work of today's cutting-edge architects, graphic artists, clothing designers, and all manner of innovators in the manufacture of furniture, fabrics, electronics, appliances, jewelry, tableware—you name it.

Created by restaurant and furniture king Terence Conran and situated on the south bank of the Thames by Tower Bridge, the Design Museum is well attended and appreciated by Londoners and tourists, who flock here to look at the mass-produced designs of the 20th century with which we live in close, even intimate, contact, without always noticing what they look like. One need only look at the collection of evolving TV sets to see that our household items have their own histories, which are inextricably linked to our domestic memories. Cars, office furniture, radios, and household utensils are all part of a permanent collection, which is added to regularly. New ideas and design breakthroughs are highlighted here.

The Blueprint Café has splendid views and decent food; in fact, it's a destination restaurant for many. The gift shop is absolutely brilliant—rarely will you find such a variety of designers and their items in one place—and worth a visit, whether you go to the museum or not.

TOURING TIPS Walk around the Thames waterfront; it's an interesting and vibrant part of London.

Dr. Johnson's House ★★

APPEAL BY AGE		PRESCHOOL ½		GRADE SCHOOL ★		TEENS ★
YOUNG ADULTS ★			OVER 30 ★		SENIORS ★	

17 Gough Square, The City, EC4; ☎ 0207-353-3745; www.drjohnsonshouse.org; tube: Blackfriars

Type of attraction Literary attraction in historic house. **Admission** £4.50 for adults, £1.50 for children, £3.50 for seniors and students, £10 for families. **Hours** May–September, Monday–Saturday, 11 a.m.–5:30 p.m.; October–April, Monday–Saturday, 11 a.m.–5 p.m. **When to go** Anytime. **Special comments** No wheelchair access; steep stairs. **Author's rating** ★★. **How much time to allow** 27 minutes for video, 10–15 minutes for the house.

DESCRIPTION AND COMMENTS I like Samuel Johnson more than the average bloke on the block, but even I wasn't overly impressed by this house, the only surviving London domicile of the 17 he lived in. I might have felt differently had the admission been free; however, I do respect and applaud the fact that this house on prime property has managed to avoid the wrecking ball for 250 years. This alone makes it worth the visit and the price. Dr. Johnson spent 11 years in this house working on his famous dictionary, as well as bopping around London with his biographer, Boswell, at his heels, dropping bons mots and shillings in the coffeehouses and taverns of his beloved London. The collection of mezzotints and books on the good doctor is impressive. You must watch the video, very well done and interesting, which does make the remarkable Johnson, as well as Boswell, come to life. Special exhibits (such as "The Hidden Life of Georgian Theatre") and various lectures related to important political and cultural issues of the day can be fascinating.

TOURING TIPS If you're a true Johnson buff, consider taking a train to Lichfield, in Staffordshire, to see the Dr. Johnson museum there—this is the very house in which he was born and his father ran a bookstore (on the ground floor). It has more Johnsonalia on its five floors than the London house, and is located in a town famous for its grand cathedral and village charm. Go to **www.lichfield.gov.uk/sjmuseum** for more information.

Freud Museum ★★

APPEAL BY AGE	PRESCHOOL ★	GRADE SCHOOL ★★	TEENS ★
YOUNG ADULTS ★★		OVER 30 ★★	SENIORS ★★

20 Maresfield Gardens, South Hampstead, NW1; ☎ 0207-435-2002; www.freud.org.uk; tube: Finchley Road

Type of attraction English home of famous psychoanalyst Sigmund Freud. **Admission** £5 for adults, £3 for students, free for children under age 12. **Hours** Wednesday–Sunday, noon–5 p.m. **When to go** Anytime. **Special comments** Limited access for disabled; no lift to upper floor. **Author's rating** ★★. **How much time to allow** 2 hours.

DESCRIPTION AND COMMENTS The house at 20 Maresfield Gardens, Hampstead, was the home of Dr. Sigmund Freud, the father of psychoanalysis, for the last year of his life, after he fled the Nazis in Vienna in 1938. It continued to be home to his daughter, Anna, until her death in 1982, and on her request it now celebrates the life and work of her father. Inside, each room is carefully decorated as it had been in 1938, and the museum contains all the possessions from the home in Vienna in which the psychiatrist had lived for more than 47 years. The exhibition's centerpiece is Freud's library and study, including his famous analytic couch and numerous antiquities. The gift shop sells books and photographs as well as amusing joke items such as Freudian Slippers, which have the doctor's face on them.

TOURING TIPS A wonderfully informative video is available for viewing upstairs. The 45-minute film, partially narrated by Anna Freud, contains silent black-and-white footage of Freud at home in Vienna as well as a description of the family's harrowing escape in 1938.

Guildhall (including Clock Museum, Art Gallery, and Library Bookshop) ★★

APPEAL BY AGE	PRESCHOOL ★	GRADE SCHOOL ★★	TEENS ★★
YOUNG ADULTS ★★		OVER 30 ★★	SENIORS ★★

Gresham Street, The City, EC4; ☎ 0207-332-1456; www.cityoflondon.gov.uk; tube: St. Paul's, Mansion House, or Bank

Type of attraction Corporate headquarters for the City of London; appeals to fans of architecture and London history. **Admission** Free. **Hours** *Guildhall:* Monday–Friday, 10 a.m.–5 p.m. *Clock Museum, Art Gallery, and Library Bookshop:* Monday–Saturday, 10 a.m.–5 p.m.; Sunday, noon–4 p.m.; closed Christmas Day, Boxing Day, and New Year's Day. **When to go** Anytime. **Special comments** Partial access for disabled. **Author's rating** ★★. **How much time to allow** 60–90 minutes.

DESCRIPTION AND COMMENTS The Guildhall has witnessed traitors' trials and heroes' welcomes, freedom ceremonies and glittering state occasions. The seat of London's municipal government for more than 800 years, it is still used for official ceremonies, state banquets, and the annual installation of the lord mayor of London. Although surrounded by 20th-century government offices and largely reconstructed after a World War II bombing, the Great Hall still impresses. Its walls are original and date to the 15th century. An array of monuments lines the hall in honor of national figures from the past three centuries, and banners of the 12 Great Livery Companies hang from above. The complex houses more than 700 examples of timekeeping in its Clock Museum; its Art Gallery displays the Corporation of London's impressive collection of works depicting London life from the 15th century to the present.

TOURING TIPS The 15th-century crypt and 19th-century Old Library are generally off-limits to the public, but it is well worth asking to see them. Guided tours include these spots.

kids HMS *Belfast* ★★

APPEAL BY AGE	PRESCHOOL ★★	GRADE SCHOOL ★★★	TEENS ★★★
YOUNG ADULTS ★★		OVER 30 ★★	SENIORS ★★

Morgans Lane, Tooley Street, South London, SE1; ☎ 0207-940-6328; www.iwm.org.uk; tube: London Bridge

Type of attraction Perfectly preserved Royal Navy battleship from World War II, permanently moored in the Thames. **Admission** £9.95 for adults, £6.15 for seniors and students, free for children under age 16. **Hours** March–October, daily, 10 a.m.–6 p.m.; November–February, daily, 10 a.m.–5 p.m. **When to go** Weekdays; call to see if any class trips are scheduled. **Special comments** Ship is accessible to disabled, but many areas are nonetheless impassable for wheelchairs. **Author's rating** ★★. **How much time to allow** 90 minutes.

DESCRIPTION AND COMMENTS A bit of floating history, the HMS *Belfast* was built in 1938 and pressed into service at the D-day landings. It was decommissioned in the 1960s and is now run by the Imperial War Museum. This huge battleship is a popular tourist attraction, although its appeal is not universal. You can explore all seven levels of the *Belfast* and check out the boiler room, cabins, and gun turrets, as well as exhibitions and videos about life on board in 1943 and the history of the Royal Navy. Children of all ages tend to love this ship, and those interested in World War II will find it an enlightening experience.

TOURING TIPS Dress warmly—the wind can kick up on the Thames.

Hampton Court Palace ★★★★★

APPEAL BY AGE	PRESCHOOL ★★	GRADE SCHOOL ★★★	TEENS ★★★★
YOUNG ADULTS ★★★★★		OVER 30 ★★★★★	SENIORS ★★★★★

East Molesey, Surrey, approximately 12 miles outside of central London; ☎ 0870-751-5175; www.hrp.org.uk/hamptoncourtpalace; tube: Richmond, then R68 bus; British Rail (accessible from Waterloo Station): Hampton Court

Type of attraction London's most impressive royal palace. **Admission** £13 for adults, £10.50 for seniors and students, £6.50 for children ages 5–15, £36 for families; prices include admission to the gardens and maze. **Hours** March 25–October 27, daily, 10 a.m.–6 p.m.; October 28–March 24, the palace closes at 4:30 p.m. **When to go** Anytime. **Special comments** Disabled access, including ramps to the Tudor kitchens, access to some areas of the gardens, elevators to the first floor, and equipped toilets. **Author's rating** ★★★★★. **How much time to allow** Head out early to give yourself the full day to enjoy Hampton Court and time to arrive back in London for dinner.

DESCRIPTION AND COMMENTS One of the nicest things about Hampton Court Palace is its location. If you've been running all over the city, deciphering bus schedules and tube maps, a trip to the outskirts of the metropolis is a relaxing treat.

Cardinal Thomas Wolsey, the powerful and influential Lord Chancellor to Henry VIII, built Hampton Court Palace in 1516 and proceeded to live lavishly there. In 1528, after Henry commented sourly on the extravagance of such a home for a member of the clergy, Wolsey offered it to the king. After the cardinal failed to secure from the Pope Henry's much-desired annulment from Catherine of Aragon in 1529, Henry accepted his offer, no doubt with malicious glee (Wolsey was lucky he kept his head, although he died rather conveniently en route to London to stand trial for treason in 1530). Henry preferred the riverside palace to that of Westminster, and he enlarged the already grandiose home extensively, adding the enormous Tudor kitchens and redesigning the chapel. Alterations were also made in the following century by the great architect Christopher Wren under the direction of William and Mary, who also oversaw the making of the maze, possibly a re-creation of an earlier one planted by the cardinal. A later overhaul, led by William Kent for George II, added yet another distinct stylistic period to the place. In 1838, at the very start of her long reign, Queen Victoria declared the restoration that had commenced in 1796 to be complete, and she opened the palace to the public. The result of these centuries of home improvements is unique, allowing palace visitors to clearly distinguish some of the most important design styles in England's history.

The palace is organized into six walking tours; in addition, there are the gardens and mazes to explore. With all this to see, your best bet is to decide whether you want to start inside or out. After an hour or two inside the vast halls, you may need to get outside for a bit and then return to more fully enjoy the rest of the palace. Costumed guides offer tours of Henry VIII's apartments, the King's Rooms, and, in summer, the Queen's Apartments. Taking one or more of these tours is always a good way to start your visit, as the fascinating story of Hampton Court is vividly brought to life by experienced historians and actors. If you prefer to head out on your own, audio guides of Henry's apartments and the Tudor kitchens are also available at no additional cost.

Of significant interest in Henry's Great Hall are the hammer-beam ceiling and stunning medieval tapestries. The rather plain hallway leading to the king's chapel is the Haunted Gallery, said to be the wandering ground for the restless ghost of Henry's fifth wife, Catherine Howard, who had run down this hall shrieking for her husband to save her from an order of execution by decapitation.

Outside, you have a wide choice of garden styles to match the rooms they surround. The grandest of these is William III's Fountain Garden; on the south side is the Privy Garden. Beyond this are the sunken Pond Gardens and the Tudor-style Knot and Herb Gardens, while on the opposite side of the palace you can venture into the less manicured Wilderness with its evergreens and the ever-popular maze, beloved by children who couldn't care less about the palace. It was originally laid out in 1714.

TOURING TIPS Hampton Court is easily reached by train from Waterloo or Wimbledon Station, but if you have time, a more interesting approach to the palace is by water. Boat tours of the Thames run in the summer from Richmond (for a half-hour ride) or Westminster (for an hour-long excursion). For river-tour schedules and pricing information, call ☎ 0207-930-4721.

Hogarth's House ★★

| APPEAL BY AGE | PRESCHOOL ★ | GRADE SCHOOL ★ | TEENS ★★ |
| YOUNG ADULTS ★★ | | OVER 30 ★★ | SENIORS ★★ |

Hogarth Lane, Great West Road, West London, W4; ☎ 0208-994-6757; www.hiddenlondon.com/hoghouse.htm; tube: Turnham Green; British Rail: Chiswick

Type of attraction The satirist and painter's summer home, filled with memorabilia, fine art, and the artist's engravings. **Admission** Free. **Hours** April–October, Tuesday–Friday, 1–5 p.m.; Saturday and Sunday, 1–6 p.m.; November–March (except January), Tuesday–Friday, 1–4 p.m.; Saturday and Sunday, 1–5 p.m.; closed Mondays and the month of January. **When to go** Anytime, but sunny days are best. **Special comments** Disabled accessible. **Author's rating** ★★. **How much time to allow** 1 hour.

DESCRIPTION AND COMMENTS If you go to Chiswick House in the morning, you might want to visit Hogarth's House in the afternoon. Formerly a quiet country retreat for the brilliant painter and satirist William Hogarth, it is now located on a particularly busy section of the A4 motorway, known as the Hogarth roundabout. More than 200 of Hogarth's most famous prints are here, including *Marriage à la Mode*, *A Rake's Progress*, and *A Harlot's Progress*. It's quite delightful to take your time looking at these witty prints in this setting, which the master called home for 15 years until his death in 1764 (his grave is a short walk away, if you're so inclined). This is a beautiful house with a fine garden, and it boasts the largest collection of Hogarthiana in the world.

TOURING TIPS Make this visit part of your trip to Chiswick House (see page 204).

Houses of Parliament: ★★★
House of Lords and House of Commons

APPEAL BY AGE	PRESCHOOL ★	GRADE SCHOOL ★★	TEENS ★★★
YOUNG ADULTS ★★★	OVER 30 ★★★★		SENIORS ★★★★

Parliament Square, SW1; ☎ 0870-906-3773; www.parliament.uk (click on "Visiting"); tube: Westminster

Type of attraction Britain's working chambers of government; tours in August and September only. **Admission** £12 for adults, £5 for children ages 5–15, £8 for seniors, £30 for families. **Hours** *House of Lords:* the public is admitted to the Strangers' Gallery Monday–Wednesday, beginning at 2:30 p.m.; Thursday, beginning at 3 p.m.; and occasionally on Friday, beginning at 11 a.m. *House of Commons:* Monday–Wednesday, 2:30–10:30 p.m.; Thursday, 11:30 a.m.–7:30 p.m.; Friday, 9:30 a.m.–3 p.m. Check whether the HOC is in session by calling ☎ 0207-219-4272. Question Time (accessible by special prebooked tickets) takes place Monday–Wednesday, 2:30–3:30 p.m., and Thursday, 11:30 a.m.–12:30 p.m. The prime minister answers questions 3–3:30 p.m. *Summer Opening:* This is a new opportunity for overseas visitors to tour during August and September; Monday, Tuesday, Friday, and Saturday, 9:15 a.m–4:40 p.m.; Wednesday and Thursday, 1:15–4:40 p.m.; £7 for adults; £5 for students, seniors, and children under age 16; £22 for families. **When to go** During Summer Opening or whenever else you can get in. **Special comments** Security is tight here; allow at least 30 minutes to clear checkpoints. Do not bring food, drinks, cell phones, or pagers. Cameras are allowed as long as they are stored—absolutely no photography is permitted. **Author's rating ★★★. How much time to allow** 1–2 hours (plus time to clear security), depending on how long you'd like to observe the debates.

DESCRIPTION AND COMMENTS The first Parliament, convened in 1254, consisted of lords, bishops, abbots, knights, and local citizens. Today's Parliament, based closely on its predecessors, includes the sovereign, the House of Lords (which used to consist of hereditary peers but is now made up of members who've been elected or appointed to their positions), and the House of Commons (members elected from their respective English, Welsh, Scottish, and Northern Irish communities). The current buildings in which they meet, built between 1840 and 1860, have become the most recognized trademarks of London. Parliament burned down in the mid-19th century and was rebuilt in its present neo-Gothic splendor by architect Sir Charles Barry and his assistant, Augustus Pugin, who was responsible for much of the intricate decoration. Pugin went mad after years of working on what must have been an exhausting project—just look at all the details of the exterior.

You can see Parliament in session on C-SPAN and certain BBC channels, and it is a most refreshing sight: the prime minister will be questioned, chastised, or challenged directly by the ministers in often rowdy sessions that seem much more of an exercise in democracy than the carefully controlled press conferences of the current American president.

TOURING TIPS Call or use the Web site to plan your visit, because admission policies are currently being updated, and the place may be temporarily closed to visitors. For now, overseas visitors can attend debates and watch judicial hearings and committees throughout the year, but they can tour Parliament only during the Summer Opening (see opposite page for details).

unofficial **TIP**
The July 2005 terrorist attacks have had security officials weighing the dangers of allowing public access to the Houses of Parliament against the long-held democratic belief that government must be transparent. Call or check the Web site for any changes to the visiting schedule.

If you can't get into the Houses of Parliament for any reason, visit **Jewel Tower** (Abingdon Street, by Westminster Abbey; ☎ 0207-222-2219), where you can see, for a small fee, an interactive virtual-reality tour of both Houses. It's open 10 a.m. to 4 p.m. in winter and 10 a.m. to 6 p.m. in summer.

Imperial War Museum ★★

APPEAL BY AGE	PRESCHOOL ★★	GRADE SCHOOL ★★	TEENS ★★½
YOUNG ADULTS ★★½	OVER 30 ★★★	SENIORS ★★★	

Lambeth Road, South London, SE1; ☎ 0207-416-5320; www.iwm.org.uk; tube: Elephant and Castle or Lambeth North

Type of attraction Exhibitions highlighting 20th-century British military actions. **Admission** Free. **Hours** Daily, 10 a.m.–6 p.m. **When to go** Anytime. **Special comments** Limited access for guests with disabilities; to reserve a wheelchair, call ☎ 0207-416-5397. **Author's rating ★★**. **How much time to allow** 1 hour.

DESCRIPTION AND COMMENTS Housed in the infamous former insane asylum known as Bedlam, the Imperial War Museum is an oddly appropriate present tenant, dedicated to the madness that is war. It is a sobering place, especially the section on the liberation of Bergen-Belsen, part of the permanent exhibit on the Holocaust completed in 2000. Overall, it can be hard not to be upset by the displays of such awful hardware of destruction: guns, tanks, zeppelins, V-2 rockets, bombers. You gain insight into the horror of war through the re-creation of the sights and sounds and smells of the Blitz, a clock counting down the numbers of war deaths in this century, and the nightmare of life in a World War I trench, but then it seems you are invited to appreciate the machinery of it.

TOURING TIPS After experiencing war, go bask in the Peace Garden (dedicated by the Dalai Lama in May 1999), which shares the grounds with the Imperial War Museum.

Kensington Palace State Rooms ★★★½

APPEAL BY AGE	PRESCHOOL ★★	GRADE SCHOOL ★★	TEENS ★★★
YOUNG ADULTS ★★★	OVER 30 ★★★½		SENIORS ★★★½

Kensington Gardens, Broad Walk; ☎ 0207-937-9561; www.hrp.org.uk;
tube: High Street Kensington

Type of attraction Stately home in the middle of Kensington Gardens. **Admission**
£12 for adults, £6 for children ages 5–16, free for children under age 5, £10 for
seniors and students, £33 for families. **Hours** April–September, daily, 10 a.m.–
6 p.m.; October–March, daily, 10 a.m.–5 p.m. **When to go** Mornings in summer;
anytime in winter. **Special comments** There are wheelchair-accessible toilets and
a ramp to the Orangery, but many steps inside the palace; upstairs is inaccessible.
Author's rating ★ ★ ★ ½. How much time to allow 1½ hours.

DESCRIPTION AND COMMENTS Kensington Palace is the former home of Diana,
Princess of Wales, and the place where Princess Victoria was told that
she had become queen (check out the size of the bedroom the teenage
princess shared with her mother—you can only imagine how thrilled she
was to move to "Buck House" in 1837). It's not a grandiose palace like
Buckingham, but in many ways that makes it more interesting. It was
built in 1605 and sold to King William and Queen Mary in 1689 as a
country escape from the noxious fumes of Whitehall, which were aggra-
vating the King's asthma. The monarchs immediately hired Christopher
Wren and Nicholas Hawksmoor to improve the house. Queen Anne
later added more improvements, such as the Orangery, which was her
"summer supper house," and acres of flowers and meadows (which are
now the surrounding Kensington Gardens). It was George I who turned
what was essentially a country estate into a palace, and it's fascinating to
note the difference between the homey oak-paneled dining room of
William and Mary and the over-the-top decor of William Kent's innova-
tions. King George II and Queen Caroline made extensive additions to
the gardens that can be enjoyed today, such as Broad Walk, the Round
Pond, and the Serpentine. In 1841, the gardens were opened to the public, when the palace became a source of "grace and favour" apartments
for offshoots of the royal family, such as the late Princess Margaret, the
newly divorced Diana, the Duke and Duchess of Kent, and the very old
Princess Alice, aunt to the Queen, who died in 2004 at the age of 104
and lived through the bombardments of both WWI and WWII.

There are fine examples of furniture and brilliant trompe l'oeil ceiling paintings and murals by William Kent. Two oddities that must be
seen are the wind-dial by which King William III could tell how fast his
ships might be approaching and the massive clock in the Cupola Room
that used to play tunes by Handel, Corelli, and Geminiani—though this
is no longer the case, the clock nonetheless represents a marvelous
marriage of 16th-century technology and art.

TOURING TIPS Make this part of a day in the park. Early birds may find the palace less crowded, but it's also nice to come later in the day and follow up your visit with tea at the Orangery next door. Take advantage of the audio tour, which is very thorough and interesting.

Kenwood House (The Iveagh Bequest) ★★★

APPEAL BY AGE	PRESCHOOL ★	GRADE SCHOOL ★★★	TEENS ★★★
YOUNG ADULTS ★★★	OVER 30 ★★★		SENIORS ★★★

Hampstead Lane, Hampstead Heath, NW3; ☎ 0208-348-1286;
www.english-heritage.org.uk; tube: Archway or Golders Green

Type of attraction World-class art gallery in an elegant old Georgian villa. **Admission** Free. **Hours** April–October, daily, 10 a.m.–5 p.m.; November–March, daily, 11 a.m.–4 p.m. **When to go** Anytime, but preferably on weekdays and in good weather so you can enjoy the heath. **Special comments** Limited wheelchair access for ground floor only. **Author's rating ★★★**. **How much time to allow** 2 hours in the house, plus time for tea or a walk around the grounds and on the heath. It makes for a great day out in good weather, not so much in the rain.

DESCRIPTION AND COMMENTS Kenwood is the most elegant exponent of architect Robert Adams's early-Georgian design. He was commissioned by Lord Mansfield to turn the original 1700 brick house into what you see today, and it took from 1764 until 1779 to get it just right. It is gorgeous, with Adams and Chippendale furniture and decoration, masterpieces on the walls, and exceptional views all year long.

After passing from one Lord Mansfield to the next until the line died out, Kenwood was by 1923 ownerless and being eyed by developers, who would have made a right mess of the wondrous surrounding heath. The house was saved from the depredations of progress by brewery magnate Edward Guinness, Earl of Iveagh, who filled it with his extensive collection of 17th-century Dutch and Flemish and late-18th-century British paintings, including works by Sir Joshua Reynolds, George Romney, J. M. W. Turner, Gainsborough, and Raeburn. His bequest of the house and its contents was a great act of patronage: quite a few unmissable old masterpieces are displayed here, such as Rembrandt's *Self-Portrait* and Vermeer's *The Guitar Player*.

TOURING TIPS Combine this visit with a trip to Hampstead Village and the heath. Bring a blanket and food, or stop in at the excellent cafe, which serves hot and cold food in a charming floral courtyard.

Leighton House Museum and Art Gallery ★★

APPEAL BY AGE	PRESCHOOL ★	GRADE SCHOOL ★	TEENS ★★
YOUNG ADULTS ★★	OVER 30 ★★		SENIORS ★★

12 Holland Park Road, Kensington, W14; ☎ 0207-602-3316;
www.rbkc.gov.uk/leightonhousemuseum;
tube: High Street Kensington, then bus 9, 10, 27, 33, or 49 to
Odeon Cinema; then walk through Holland Park

Type of attraction House of Pre-Raphaelite painter Lord Frederic Leighton. **Admission** £3 for adults; £1 for children, students, and seniors; £6 for families. **Hours** Monday–Saturday, 11 a.m.–5:30 p.m.; closed Tuesday. **When to go** Anytime. **Special comments** No wheelchair access; many steps to top floor. **Author's rating ★★. How much time to allow** 30 minutes.

DESCRIPTION AND COMMENTS If you are a true lover of the Pre-Raphaelites—Frederic Leighton, Edward Burne-Jones, John Millais, and others—this is a must-see. Lord Leighton, whose magnificent painted hallway can be seen in the Victoria and Albert Museum, dedicated his home as "a private palace devoted to art." The main attraction is the Arab Hall, a Victorian fantasy of the Middle East, with Isniuk tiles, elaborately carved and gilded woodwork, and a mosaic frieze; a sunken fountain in the middle of the room furthers the impression of a courtyard straight out of the pages of *The Arabian Nights.* The top floor is Leighton's old studio, and the huge windows, skylights, and dome were clearly the heart's desire of any 19th-century painter. On the lower floor is a good collection of Victorian paintings, including Leighton's *Roman Mother;* upstairs you can see temporary exhibits of a widely varied nature. The house is sadly lacking in furniture and knickknacks, and one wishes for more of the decorative exuberance that must have resided when Leighton lived here.

TOURING TIPS Combine a visit here with a trip to Holland Park and the Linley Sambourne House, profiled next (tickets to the Sambourne House are available only at Leighton House).

Linley Sambourne House   ★★★

APPEAL BY AGE	PRESCHOOL ★	GRADE SCHOOL ★★	TEENS ★★
YOUNG ADULTS ★★★	OVER 30 ★★★		SENIORS ★★★

18 Stafford Terrace, Kensington, W8; ☎ 0207-602-3316; www.rbkc.gov.uk/linleysambournehouse; tube: High Street Kensington

Type of attraction Perfectly preserved home of Victorian *Punch* cartoonist. **Admission** £6 for adults; £4 for students and seniors; £1 for ages 17 and under. **Hours** Wednesday–Monday, 11 a.m.–5:30 p.m.; closed Tuesday. **When to go** Weekends for costumed tours. Weekday bookings can be made by appointment. **Special comments** Lots of stairs and no wheelchair access. **Author's rating ★★★. How much time to allow** 1–2 hours.

DESCRIPTION AND COMMENTS This place is a veritable time machine, plunking one smack down in the middle of the late Victorian–early Edwardian era, with the sumptuous clutter that incited the backlash of modernism. William Morris designs adorn both walls and floors, and there are a few stained-glass windows to admire. (A predominant emotion on seeing the vast collection of clocks, vases, gimcracks, and knickknacks is pity for the poor servant in charge of dusting.) The immense aesthetic weight of all the pretty possessions can be a bit tiring, but it is an amazing piece of preservation, and the tours, conducted by guides in period costume, are fun. On the last Thursday of every month, £20 will buy you tickets to either the 6 p.m. or 8 p.m. "twilight encounter" tour, called "Intrude on

History." More performance than tour, it's based on family diaries that reveal the scandals and secrets of life in the house in 1899.

TOURING TIPS The weekend tours, conducted by actors in costume, are your best bet. Combine with a trip to Holland Park and/or to the Leighton House Museum (see previous profile), which is where you buy tickets for the Sambourne House.

kids London Aquarium   ★★★★

APPEAL BY AGE	PRESCHOOL ★★★★	GRADE SCHOOL ★★★★	TEENS ★★★
YOUNG ADULTS ★★★½		OVER 30 ★★★½	SENIORS ★★★

County Hall, Riverside Building, Westminster Bridge Road, SE1; ☎ 0207-967-8000; www.londonaquarium.co.uk; tube: Westminster or Waterloo

Type of attraction Wonderland of sea life on the south bank of the Thames. **Admission** £13.25 for adults, £11.25 for seniors and students, £9.75 for children ages 3–14, free for children under age 3, £44 for families. Tickets can be purchased online 24 hours in advance, but not on the day you plan to go. Booking online allows you fast-track entry. **Hours** Daily, 10 a.m.–6 p.m. (last entry at 5 p.m.). **When to go** Avoid weekends and school holidays if possible; go early. **Special comments** Fully accessible for disabled persons. To avoid steps, go around building to Belvedere Road to reach entrance. Picnic area available. **Author's rating ★★★★**. **How much time to allow** 2–3 hours.

DESCRIPTION AND COMMENTS On the south bank of the Thames River, in what was once London's County Hall, you will find three dimly lit and atmospheric floors of enormous tanks filled with sea life and freshwater fish of every kind. The Atlantic tank holds 800,000 liters of water and tons of sharks, eels, and stingrays. There's a petting pool for kids to stroke manta rays, who actually seem to invite these caresses. In the Pacific tank reside more sharks, rays, groupers, and smaller fish. The piranha tank is interesting, especially at dinnertime, when you get to see what a real-life feeding frenzy looks like (call ahead to find out feeding times for various fish).

This is not the most amazing aquarium in the world by a long shot, even if its claim that you would have to cover 38,337 miles (how do they arrive at that number?) to see all these fish in their natural habitats is true. If you have access to a good aquarium where you live, you might as well leave this one off your list, but it has been proved to us time and again that when it comes to taming small children, fish take the cake. Plus, the surrounding area is a blast, with the London Eye and all the wonders of the South Bank and the Thames at your disposal. Check the Web site for a variety of special talks, exhibits, and activities.

TOURING TIPS There's a McDonald's next door, with its own entrance to the aquarium. A gift shop has souvenirs for every budget.

London Dungeon   ★★★

APPEAL BY AGE	PRESCHOOL †	GRADE SCHOOL ★★	TEENS ★★★★
YOUNG ADULTS ★★		OVER 30 ★★	SENIORS ★

† Too scary for preschoolers.

28–34 Tooley Street, South Bank, SE1; ☎ 0207-403-7221; www.thedungeons.com; tube: London Bridge

Type of attraction Over-the-top yuckfest with historical pretensions. **Admission** £19.95 for adults, £14.95 for seniors and students, £13.95 for children ages 5–14, free (though not advisable) for kids under 5. **Hours** July–August, daily, 9:30 a.m.–7 p.m.; September–June, daily, 10:30 a.m.–5 p.m. **When to go** Weekdays as soon as it opens, since it gets pretty crowded midday; and weekends are tough, with lines that go around the block. **Special comments** Wheelchair access; don't bring small children; kids under 15 must be accompanied by an adult. **Author's rating ★ ★ ★. How much time to allow** 90 minutes.

DESCRIPTION AND COMMENTS I am the first one to line up for the weird and the horrible, but this place hit me the wrong way. It seems to have more potential than presence, despite the obvious and artful effort they have put forth to make themselves worthy of the long lines waiting to get in. The relentless gore without context was disturbing, and the Jack the Ripper Experience was just plain cheesy. The hordes of French teenage boys who were there during my visit seemed to find it hilarious, cheering wildly when we saw a dummy guillotined—as their ancestors must have done. There are two scary rides—Extremis: Drop Ride to Doom, wherein after being sentenced to hang, you'll suddenly plunge to the ground, and Traitor! Boat Ride to Hell, which is a trip to the unknown in the dark. Be prepared to get wet. The best part was the gift shop, where I picked up a life-size skull candle and some fun Halloween stuff. If you want to get a sense of just what this place is about, call the phone number and listen to the hilariously bad "scary" recorded greeting voice with the warning that London Dungeon is not recommended for those of a nervous disposition.
TOURING TIPS Book online to avoid the murderous queues—you can pay extra for fast-track entry.

kids London Transport Museum   ★★★★

APPEAL BY AGE	PRESCHOOL ★★★★	GRADE SCHOOL ★★★★	TEENS ★★★
YOUNG ADULTS ★★★		OVER 30 ★★★	SENIORS ★★★

39 Wellington Street, off Covent Garden Piazza, WC2; ☎ 0207-565-7299; www.ltmuseum.co.uk; tube: Covent Garden or Leicester Square

Type of attraction Fun, interactive museum of trams, buses, and trains of old and new London. **Admission** £8 for adults, £6.50 for seniors and students, free for accompanied children under age 16. **Hours** Saturday–Thursday, 10 a.m.–6 p.m.; Friday, 11 a.m.–9 p.m. **When to go** Anytime. **Special comments** Wheelchair and stroller access; cafe and gift shop. **Author's rating ★ ★ ★ ★. How much time to allow** 1 hour.

DESCRIPTION AND COMMENTS Recently refurbished with new galleries and interactive exhibits, this is one of the better kid venues in London, and adults love it, too. Although many might yawn at the idea of a museum dedicated to that most prosaic feature of urban life, public transportation, this museum is so cleverly and earnestly organized that it's impossible not to get swept up in the fun of it. From horse-drawn stagecoaches and omnibuses to buses that you can pretend to drive and Underground switches you can pretend to throw, it's like an indoor playground with education slipped in. You're given a ticket to be stamped at each of the numbered sites until you've filled up your card and seen all there is to see. There are videos of old-time trams and buses and a short film on the touching last trip of the last tram in London, with everyone singing "Auld Lang Syne." There's so much for adults to learn here, too, such as why the fares on buses and trains in London have to be so complicated; and that 40,000 people took the first Underground line on its first day in 1863. (Alas, we don't find out why you can wait forever for your bus and then three will come all at once.)

The gift shop has a huge selection of postcards and Underground posters and a wealth of books about London's transport. You can get just about anything with the London Underground map on it, even underpants.

TOURING TIPS Buy the museum guide if you have children under age 12— there's a fun pull-out section with games and educational pursuits in it. Combine this trip with a visit to Covent Garden, also fun for the kids, especially on weekends. Call or visit the Web site to check for lectures, tours, films, and family activities.

kids London Zoo ★★★★

| APPEAL BY AGE | PRESCHOOL ★★★★★ | GRADE SCHOOL ★★★★★ | TEENS ★★★★½ |
| YOUNG ADULTS ★★★★ | | OVER 30 ★★★★ | SENIORS ★★★ |

Regent's Park; ☎ 0207-722-3333; www.londonzoo.co.uk; tube: Camden Town

Type of attraction Modernized old zoo set at the edge of Regent's Park. **Admission** £14.50 for adults, £11 for children ages 3–15, free for age 2 and under, £13 for seniors and students. Children under age 16 must be accompanied by an adult. **Hours** Daily, 10 a.m.–5:30 p.m. in summer; closes at 4 p.m. in winter. **When to go** When it's warm and not raining. **Special comments** Wheelchair access. **Author's rating** ★★★★. **How much time to allow** 2 hours.

DESCRIPTION AND COMMENTS Covering 36 acres, the London Zoo was voted the best attraction in the city by a reader's poll in *Time Out London*. The recently completed Gorilla Kingdom cost more than £5 million, the most money the zoo has spent in more than 40 years. It is home to western lowland gorillas and tree-dwelling monkeys and is situated next to an enclosure of other African primates and a variety of reptiles. The zoo has tried hard to be the best it can be and has created a small but full environment of hooved, winged, and four-legged friends. The argument against the confinement of beasts rages on, but it has been shown that without zoos such as this, even more creatures would be extinct. Certainly many naturalists, conservationists, and environmentalists have been inspired in their choice of career by a childhood visit to a zoo. When people experience the magnificence of these endangered species, they may be moved to do something about the problem, or at least to not participate in the sale or trade of ivory, animal skins, or exotic food. What's more, the zoo has done a lot to make a more natural habitat for its animals, even though English climate bears no relation to the climate of some of these creatures' birthplaces.

Opened in 1828, the London Zoo has clearly evolved from the old animals-in-cages standard. The reptile house—which appeared in the first *Harry Potter* book, when the hero discovered he could speak the language of snakes—is magnificent, with cobras, pythons, and even alligators in nicely designed environments, plus a teaching center with snakeskins and things made from the hides of unfortunate animals. The aquarium is also quite comprehensive and well housed. There are a lot of monkeys as well as a petting zoo for children. The shop is fantastic and will fulfill all your animal-paraphernalia needs, with books, stuffed animals, knickknacks, gimcracks, and gewgaws.

TOURING TIPS Take a taxi from Baker Street or even from your hotel: public transport is insufficient for people who need to be let out in front of the entrance.

Madame Tussauds Waxworks and the Stardome ★★★

APPEAL BY AGE	PRESCHOOL ★★	GRADE SCHOOL ★★★	TEENS ★★★★
YOUNG ADULTS ★★★★		OVER 30 ★★★	SENIORS ★★

Marylebone Road, Marylebone, NW1; ☎ 0870-400-3000 to book tickets in advance; www.madame-tussauds.com; tube: Baker Street

Type of attraction World-famous display of wax figures. **Admission** Ticket prices vary depending on the time of day you visit. Peak times are 9 a.m.–3 p.m. If you book over the phone, ticket prices for peak times are slightly cheaper (£19 for adults and £15 for children ages 5–15) than if you purchase them at the door (£25 for adults and £21 for children). The door prices lower to £21 (adults) and £17 (children) between 3 and 5 p.m., and lower even further to £16 (adults) and £11 (children) between 5 and 5:30 p.m. (Just to make it even more complicated, tickets cost £2 less if you forgo the Chamber Live, the renamed Chamber of Horrors, which now features "live" serial killers.) Children under age 5 get in free. If you're planning on visiting Madame Tussauds and the London Eye, you can save £7 by purchasing a ticket for both attractions for £32.50. A family ticket can be purchased online for £96, which covers 2 adults and 2 children or 1 adult and 3 children. **Hours** Monday–Friday, 9:30 a.m.–5:30 p.m.; 9 a.m.–6 p.m. on weekends, bank holidays, and summer weekdays. Open every day of the year, except Christmas Day. **When to go** Madame Tussauds advises visiting in the afternoon, but there always seems to be a line no matter what the time, even a half hour before it opens. Go a day, before or book over the phone or online to get a timed fast-track ticket. Weekends are unpredictable: sometimes more and sometimes less crowded. **Special comments** Limited wheelchair access; call in advance: ☎ 0870-400-3000. **Author's rating ★★★. How much time to allow** 2 hours.

DESCRIPTION AND COMMENTS Madame Tussauds waxworks were undoubtedly more interesting in the days before film, when one really didn't know what the great personages of the day looked like. However, it is still interesting to see their actual dimensions. You will start out in the Star Studded room, where you can pose for a fashion shoot with Kate Moss or squeeze Brad Pitt's tush. Then you might want to enter the Big Brother Diary room, where you and your companions may be asked to spell out YMCA with your bodies or convince Big Brother that you're martial-arts experts. When you leave the Star Studded room, be prepared to run into some pirates and maybe come nose to nose with Captain Jack Sparrow. There is a fascinating display of how the waxworks are made and how each individual strand of hair is planted in the figures' heads. A new interactive Sports Zone allows you to either take on the penalty challenge and score a goal or practice your putting technique with Tiger Woods. Sadly, the London Planetarium was replaced by the Stardome, which shows *The Wonderful World of Stars,* an animated film about how aliens view celebrities on Earth. Avoid it if you can! When you come out into the gift shop, you can get a wax mold of your hand made.

There is a pretty silly ride in a miniature black taxi that rushes you through the history of London (from Elizabeth I till now), with prerecorded narration in one of five languages. I accidentally pressed the flag of Japan and got the whole tour in Japanese—once you choose the language, you cannot change it. I got to take the ride again, but once is more than enough. The Chamber Live is entered through a gate with the Dante inscription "All Hope Abandon, Ye Who Enter Here!"—a sentiment perhaps more fitting for the end of the queue outside. It is a sobering and disturbing exhibit, which even manages to approximate the smell of unwashed bodies and despair (also reminiscent of the queue outside) in the prison section. They've tried to jazz it up a lot with actors playing serial killers, who jump out at you when you least expect it.

But of all the horrors, murderers, and bloodiness, there is surely nothing more chilling than the display of Madame Tussaud herself, lantern held aloft, searching a mountain of decapitated bodies for the head of her former employer, Marie Antoinette. The young Marie Grosholtz Tussaud started out in the late 1700s assisting a doctor who specialized in making wax anatomy forms. Her talent for portraiture was so extraordinary that she was hired to teach art to the children of the doomed king and queen of France. When the French Revolution came, she was imprisoned (rooming with the future Empress Josephine) and marked for the guillotine. Madame Tussaud was saved by those who wanted her to remain alive long enough to make death masks of the aristocrats, many of whom she had known personally. She spent many a night poking through the bloody corpses for the heads she was commissioned to work on. What a way to make a living.

TOURING TIPS Book a ticket in advance by phone or in person, so that you can avoid the lines or at least minimize waiting time.

kids The Monument ★★★

APPEAL BY AGE	PRESCHOOL	GRADE SCHOOL ★★	TEENS ★★★
YOUNG ADULTS ★★★		OVER 30 ★★★	SENIORS VARIES

Monument Street, The City, EC3; ☎ 0207-626-2717; www.themonument.info; tube: Monument

Type of attraction Tower commemorating the Great Fire of 1666. *Note:* The Monument will be closed for a major overhaul until late 2009. All visitor information will change. Please check the Web site for updates.

DESCRIPTION AND COMMENTS At 202 feet (61 meters) high, The Monument was once as visible as St. Paul's Dome, which was certainly no coincidence, as Christopher Wren designed both (aided, in the case of The Monument, by Dr. Robert Hooke). The Roman Doric column was built in 1677 to commemorate the Great Fire of 1666, which was actually responsible for making Wren one of London's most prolific architects. If laid down on its side, The Monument would reach directly to the spot on Pudding Lane where the fire started (exactly 202 feet, or 61 meters, from the base). It also has a precise linear relationship to St. Paul's, no doubt a touch that Wren relished.

A £4.5 million refurbishment project, to be completed in late 2009, will install new visitor facilities (including a live feed of the views from the top for those who cannot ascend the 311 steps) and include cleaning and repairs on the stonework, plus regilding of The Monument's golden orb. The project has been featured on the BBC Web site, and if the track record of construction and repair work in London is anything to go by, it will probably be viewable well into 2010.

The 311 steps to the top take about five minutes to walk, though it seems much longer. There are three or four window seats on which to take a breather while ascending. The view is quite fine—spectacular, in fact—and this is the best possible place from which to see Tower Bridge, whose managers recently took stewardship of The Monument. Sadly, the views of the Tower of London and the whole of St. Paul's have been severely compromised by newer buildings. In any case, the exertion and the compromised views haven't stopped more than 10,000 people from climbing to the top each year, and once The Monument has reopened, it may attract even more climbers. Look down the stairwell when you get to the top—it's like an M. C. Escher drawing or a scene out of Alfred Hitchcock's *Vertigo*.

TOURING TIPS Bring a camera.

kids Museum of London ★★★★★

APPEAL BY AGE	PRESCHOOL ★★★	GRADE SCHOOL ★★★	TEENS ★★★
YOUNG ADULTS ★★★★★		OVER 30 ★★★★★	SENIORS ★★★★★

London Wall and Aldersgate, The City, EC2; ☎ 0870-444-3851; www.museumoflondon.org.uk; tube: St. Paul's or Barbican

Type of attraction Museum that covers thousands of years of London history. **Admission** Free, although there is a charge for special exhibits. **Hours**

Monday–Saturday, 10 a.m.–5:50 p.m.; Sunday, noon–5:50 p.m. **When to go** Anytime, but you may be navigating around large groups of schoolchildren if you go too early on weekdays while school is in session; after 2:30 p.m., they're gone. **Special comments** Good handicapped accessibility, with a number of ramps and lifts for all floors. Some galleries will remain closed until 2009 for refurbishment. **Author's rating** ★★★★★. **How much time to allow** 2–3 hours.

DESCRIPTION AND COMMENTS The Museum of London tells the story of London from its first settlers back in 4,000 BC to the present, using a variety of eye-catching displays and fascinating reconstructions. The chronologically themed tour route lets each visitor explore more closely the time periods he or she finds most intriguing. This museum is extremely kid-friendly, offering some interactive and tactile displays. A few not-to-be-missed exhibits include a large section of London's fourth-century town wall, located outside but incorporated into the museum's Roman London exhibition through a window overlook; the 1757 gilded Lord Mayor's Coach; and re-created 19th-century street scenes and shops.

A real cell from Newgate Prison is perfectly chilling, and the Victorian shops give one the strangest, most impossible sense of déjà vu. The displays about the years of the Blitz are riveting as well. If you are even slightly interested in London's history, this museum is a must-see; if you're not, you will be after a visit. The gift shop carries a huge assortment of books, including the best collection of historical fiction around as well as nonfiction about London and English history for all ages. There's a good cafe, too.

TOURING TIPS For an introduction to many of the exhibitions and information on current exhibits, check the museum's Web site. Also, call ahead to find out how many schools are booked on the day of your visit—if there are a lot, come after 2:30 p.m.

National Gallery ★★★★★

APPEAL BY AGE	PRESCHOOL ★	GRADE SCHOOL ★★★	TEENS ★★★
YOUNG ADULTS ★★★★★	OVER 30 ★★★★★		SENIORS ★★★★★

Trafalgar Square, West End, WC2; ☎ 0207-747-2885; www.nationalgallery.org.uk; tube: Leicester Square or Charing Cross

Type of attraction Splendid art gallery encompassing 700 years of European painting. **Admission** Free, though there is a charge for special exhibits. **Hours** Daily, 10 a.m.–6 p.m.; late view, Wednesday till 9 p.m. **When to go** The quietest times are weekday mornings and the Wednesday late view. Avoid major exhibits on weekends. **Special comments** Wheelchair accessible. **Author's rating** ★★★★★. **How much time to allow** As much as you can physically handle.

DESCRIPTION AND COMMENTS This is one of those amazing art museums, like the Louvre, in which you get to see the original of some utterly familiar image—Holbein's *The Ambassadors,* Van Gogh's *Sunflowers,* Monet's *Water-Lily Pond*—practically every time you turn around. It holds about 2,300 works from 700 years of European art; you can spend hours gazing at paintings by Titian, Rembrandt, Caravaggio, Vermeer, Velázquez,

Michelangelo, da Vinci, Van Eyck, and other old masters too numerous to mention. As if that weren't enough, the East Wing is filled with Impressionists, featuring some 50 paintings on a sort of permanent loan from the Tate Gallery. You'll see Pissarro, Gauguin, Degas, Seurat, Corot, and others. The collection is laid out methodically, and excellent inscriptions accompany each painting. The special exhibits are always worth the fee, and by all means get yourself a headset to listen to the tour.

The National Gallery was founded in 1824 under King George IV, when the government purchased 38 important paintings—of artists such as Raphael, Van Eyck, and Rembrandt—from the estate of banker John Julius Angerstein. The building was commissioned with a few strange bequest conditions on the architecture, such as the cupola crowning the front portico, initially ridiculed as a mustard pot, with the two bell towers on either side looking like salt-and-pepper shakers. The architect, William Wilkins, was also asked to use a portion of a former royal palace in his design, so the slightly ungainly appearance may owe to these arbitrary requirements.

The modern Sainsbury Wing houses the oldest paintings, dating from 1260 to 1510. (Don't miss Jan Van Eyck's *Arnolfini Portrait,* and look for the artist reflected in the mirror.) The West Wing displays paintings dating from 1510 to 1600, including Tintoretto's *St. George and the Dragon.* The North Wing, which houses paintings from 1600 to 1700, is filled with works by Rembrandt and other 17th-century geniuses whose paintings have an almost supernatural power that no reproduction can capture. The East Wing takes us from 1700 up to 1920, with Canaletto's and Turner's land- and seascapes giving way to the English portraits and social scenes of Gainsborough, Reynolds, and the prodigious Hogarth, whose series *Marriage à la Mode* can be seen here. The Impressionist rooms are always crowded with fans admiring Rousseau's *Surprised!* (aka *Tiger in a Tropical Storm*), Renoir's *Umbrellas,* Van Gogh's *Chair,* and so many more. Picasso is represented in the East Wing as well, though there are no really major works of his here except for *Minotauromachia.*

The self-service Espresso Bar in the basement serves excellent snacks, sandwiches, and salads, and features 14 touch-screen interactive terminals that show and tell you all about the museum's art while you sip your cappuccino. The National Dining Rooms in the Sainsbury Wing on Level One serve a wonderful afternoon tea and are upscale without being intimidating; and the National Café is a brasserie with table service as well as take-out options. The three gift shops are must-visits, filled with the most wonderful collection of books, postcards, and calendars. Try to get your hands on one of the National Gallery's Advent calendars, which conceal masterpieces under each day's tear-off flap. One of the museum's most exciting (and potentially ruinous to the pocketbook) retail endeavors is the Print on Demand service, at the rear of the Sainsbury Wing gift shop. Here you can get high-resolution printouts in any number of sizes, from postcard up to poster, of just about anything from the magnificent collection. Besides the computer database that you can use for searches, there is also a huge volume handy in which you can look up pictures in the old style. It's an exhaustive index that allows you to search for, say, paintings of dogs or seascapes, as well as by artist or period. You'll find plenty of postcards and posters as it is, but if you want a reproduction of a more obscure work, this service is a dream come true.

TOURING TIPS Take advantage of the lectures and recorded tours available here; they are great aids. Remember, when looking at the collection, to keep an eye out for that special piece of art that sings to you, and have it reproduced at the gift shop to bring home with you. It's money well spent.

kids National Maritime Museum and Queen's House ★★★★
(See also profile for Royal Observatory, Greenwich, page 232.)

APPEAL BY AGE	PRESCHOOL ★★★	GRADE SCHOOL ★★★★	TEENS ★★★
YOUNG ADULTS ★★★★		OVER 30 ★★★★	SENIORS ★★★★

Romney Road, Greenwich, SE10; ☎ 0208-858-4422; www.nmm.ac.uk; take Docklands Light Railway: Greenwich

Type of attraction Largest maritime museum in the world. **Admission** Free; fee for special events and exhibits. **Hours** Daily, 10 a.m.–5 p.m.; open until 6 p.m. in summer. **When to go** Anytime on weekdays; early in the day on weekends. **Special comments** It's a steep walk up the hill to the museums, but once you get there it is accessible with elevators for the disabled, touch-talks for the visually impaired, and sign-interpreted talks; call for details. **Author's rating ★★★★**. **How much time to allow** 2–3 hours for the museum and 1–2 hours for Queen's House.

DESCRIPTION AND COMMENTS The National Maritime Museum is part of the larger Maritime Greenwich World Heritage Site, which includes the Queen's House and the Royal Observatory. Its new galleries, courtesy of a £20 million face-lift, include lots of interactive displays exploring the impact of the oceans on our daily lives, as well as our destructive impact on the seas. Exhibitions include the re-creations of steerage and first-class cabins and deck sections from an ocean liner, thousands of ship models, hundreds of navigational instruments, and galleries devoted to the history of British naval conquests and accomplishments. Of particular interest to adults is the elaborate Horatio Nelson exhibition, which pays homage to the famous admiral who defeated Napoléon at the Battle of Trafalgar; the very uniform in which Nelson was killed is one of the most priceless items here. Kids will have to be dragged out of the All-Hands Gallery, a fascinating interactive collection of exhibits, tools, and experiments of nautical principles. The fun includes raising and lowering signal flags, working a crane to load a ship's cargo, and attempting some deep-sea engineering.

The Queen's House, adjacent to the museum, has undergone major refurbishment. The triumph of 17th-century architect Inigo Jones, it is said to be England's first home built in the classical style. Now a venue for the appreciation of maritime-related artwork, it houses regular exhibits including a comprehensive exhibition on Queen Elizabeth I, friend to sailors and pirates alike. The interior of the house has been restored to the days of Charles II, and the Royal Apartments on the upper floor are especially dazzling.

TOURING TIPS The museum offers a wide range of children's educational workshops and activities, many free of charge. For details and a full schedule of planned events, check the excellent Web site.

National Portrait Gallery ★★★★

APPEAL BY AGE	PRESCHOOL ★	GRADE SCHOOL ★★	TEENS ★★★★
YOUNG ADULTS ★★★★		OVER 30 ★★★★	SENIORS ★★★★

2 St. Martin's Place, West End, W2; adjacent to the National Gallery; ☎ 0207-306-0055; www.npg.org.uk; tube: Leicester Square or Charing Cross

Type of attraction Collection of the most famous faces in British history. **Admission** Free; £5 and up for special exhibits. **Hours** Monday–Wednesday and Saturday–Sunday, 10 a.m.–6 p.m.; Thursday and Friday, 10 a.m.–9 p.m. **When to go** Anytime. **Special comments** Very accessible to disabled individuals. **Author's rating ★★★★. How much time to allow** 2–3 hours.

DESCRIPTION AND COMMENTS Of all the museums London has to offer, the National Portrait Gallery holds particular appeal, as it's compact and people-oriented. It's also located in the middle of a very interesting area: across the street from St. Martin-in-the-Fields Church and next to the National Gallery, just off Trafalgar Square. The gallery is quite manageable in a couple of hours, unlike the eight miles of the Victoria and Albert or the endless rooms of the National Gallery. Its size allows for relaxed browsing without the feeling that you must rush or you won't see everything. The NPG gives the casual student of England a direct line to its history through the faces of its most interesting and important people. It's a veritable Who's Who of England that includes the lean faces of the early medieval kings; the Tudors, with Holbein's images of Henry VIII and his many wives; the Stuarts in the 17th century; the 19th-century Victorians; and, finally, portraits and photos of the current royal family. As you take this visual voyage through the ages, notice the changing styles of portraiture and the kinds of people each age deemed worthy of portraiture. You will see people from a variety of disciplines—science, literature, politics, art, and entertainment—whose contributions to English life reached far beyond this small island. With the help of the NPG sound guides, the amount of history you absorb will change the way you perceive London's most famous sights. A good restaurant on the top floor offers glorious views over Trafalgar Square and beyond.

TOURING TIPS In addition to the pricey roof restaurant, there is also the Portrait Café in the basement. Combine your visit with a trip to the

National Gallery next door. Buy posters or have prints made to order of your favorite famous Brits.

kids **Natural History Museum** ★★★

APPEAL BY AGE	PRESCHOOL ★★★	GRADE SCHOOL ★★★★	TEENS ★★★
YOUNG ADULTS ★★★		OVER 30 ★★★	SENIORS ★★★

Cromwell Road, South Kensington, SW7; ☎ 0207-942-5000; www.nhm.ac.uk; tube: South Kensington

Type of attraction Museum with exhibits on the history of the natural world. **Admission** Free. **Hours** Monday–Saturday, 10 a.m.–5:50 p.m.; Sunday, 11 a.m.– 5:50 p.m. **When to go** Weekends can be quite crowded, so go early. **Special comments** Complete disabled access. **Author's rating** ★★★. **How much time to allow** 2 hours or more.

DESCRIPTION AND COMMENTS As part of the South Kensington cultural revolution of the 19th century, the Natural History Museum was formed by the British Library's collections of Sir Hans Sloane, which were divvied up, with the artifacts of the natural world sent to South Ken in the 1860s. It's a grand old institution, housed in a majestic building that in itself makes the visit worthwhile. Notice the animal statues on the outside and the terra-cotta monkeys and other beasts climbing on stone vines in the lobby. It has all the hallmarks of a Gothic cathedral, an impression that architect Alfred Waterhouse intended to inspire the proper reverence for nature. This is a huge place full of many surprises and some really fine examples of educational curation, such as the Green Zone, ecology-focused galleries in which you can walk through a rain forest, and the Darwin Centre, with 22 million specimens of everything from amoebas to monkeys. The museum has plenty of permanent interactive displays and temporary exhibits, some of which have been very good, such as the one on human biology. The geology-focused Red Zone galleries (entrance on Exhibition Road) are entered via a long escalator that goes through a model of the Earth. The see-and-touch educational exhibits in this section include an earthquake simulator housed in a re-created supermarket from Kobe, Japan, the site of a devastating 1995 quake. The older artifacts are more quietly dioramas of exotic animals, including the extinct dodo bird; cabinets full of butterflies; and all the bounty brought back from the far-flung reaches of the British Empire, much of which is utterly irreplaceable and of great scientific importance. The wonderful dinosaur exhibit is impressive, set up so that one follows along paths and climbs up stairs, which keeps kids active and happy while the parents can take the time to read the information posted there. The gift shops carry excellent children's educational toys and books, as well as geological booty.

TOURING TIPS Be sure to look at the entire front of the building on Cromwell Road—in a witty reflection of the statues of artists that adorn the front of the neighboring Victoria and Albert Museum, the Natural History Museum has statues of animals on its facade. If the line at the Cromwell Road entrance is long, enter at the Red Zone on Exhibition Road.

Old Bailey (Central Criminal Courts)   ★★

APPEAL BY AGE	PRESCHOOL †	GRADE SCHOOL †	TEENS ★★
YOUNG ADULTS ★★	OVER 30 ★★★		SENIORS ★★★

† *Not appropriate for children.*

Old Bailey Street, The City, EC4; ☎ 0207-248-6858, ask for List Office; www.old-bailey.com; tube: St. Paul's

Type of attraction London's court of justice. **Admission** Free, although you can book a guide for a fee (call ☎ 0120-651-3919); children under age 14 not admitted. **Hours** Monday–Friday, 10:30 a.m.–4:30 p.m.; closed for lunch 1–2 p.m. **When to go** During the times listed above, but note that the public gallery in each courtroom has a limited number of seats, and bailiffs may not allow access once court is in session. **Special comments** Security searches are routine. Do not bring backpacks, cameras, food, cell phones, or pagers. These items are prohibited, and there is no cloak room for storing them. **Author's rating ★★**. **How much time to allow** As much time as your interest in the proceedings dictates.

DESCRIPTION AND COMMENTS Although most interesting to those with a background in law, the cases held in London's Old Bailey are criminal cases, and just about anyone will find both the content of the cases and the etiquette of the British courtroom intriguing. Bewigged and traditionally robed barristers address each other as "friend" and the judge as "milord," politely asserting their cases while the defendant sits at the rear of the courtroom, visibly separated from the "gentlemen's proceedings" going on in front of him. Be warned: you are not likely to see dramatic outbursts of the *Law and Order* kind.

The Old Bailey was built on the site of Newgate Prison, the noxious and notorious prison that held criminals and public executions from the 12th century until it was destroyed in 1902. This court saw the spectacle of Oscar Wilde's trial–"the butterfly broken on a wheel"–as well as those of the Yorkshire Ripper and American physician–wife killer Hawley Harvey Crippen. Public hangings took place often in the 18th and 19th centuries, with people paying dearly for a "good" view of the proceedings, a lucrative business for people in the neighborhood whose windows looked into the courtyard. In 1787, transportation to Australia became common for felons, reducing the number of hangings. In the mid- to late 20th century, capital punishment in the United Kingdom was eschewed and finally outlawed.

TOURING TIPS The entrance to the public galleries is off Newgate Street and down Old Bailey, past the original court building and its contemporary addition, to Warwick Passage on the left. Call ahead to find out which cases are currently on the docket and at what point in the proceedings they are. Dial the number above and ask for the List Office, or check online at the Web site. For a good background on the history of the Old Bailey, go to **www.oldbaileyonline.org.**

Old Operating Theatre, Museum, and Herb Garret ★★★½

APPEAL BY AGE	PRESCHOOL †	GRADE SCHOOL ★	TEENS ★★
YOUNG ADULTS ★★½		OVER 30 ★★★½	SENIORS ★★★½

† Not appropriate for preschoolers.

9A St. Thomas's Street, South Bank, SE1; ☎ 0207-955-4791; www.thegarret.org.uk; tube: London Bridge

Type of attraction Haunting museum of old medical equipment and an early Victorian operating room. **Admission** £5.25 for adults, £4.25 for seniors and students, £3 for children under age 16, £12.95 for families. **Hours** Daily, 10:30 a.m.– 5 p.m. **When to go** Anytime. **Special comments** The stairs in this old house are very, very steep. There is no wheelchair access. **Author's rating ★★★½. How much time to allow** 1 hour.

DESCRIPTION AND COMMENTS In a tiny old house on a street by London Bridge is one of the most fascinating medical museums in London. You must climb some rather treacherous steps to reach the musty old attic in which you'll find displayed many of the gruesome medical instruments used before the days of anesthesia. Around the room are sheaths of herbs—comfrey for healing bones, pennyroyal for nausea, willow bark from which aspirin was derived, and elderflowers for whatever ails you.

The centerpiece of the museum is the operating theater from the early 19th century, a case study for postoperative infection from the days before Dr. Joseph Lister figured out the germ theory. Under the wooden operating table is a box of sawdust, which the surgeon would kick around the table as he worked to catch the blood; there's also a small washbasin in which hands were washed *after* the operation. The room is ringed by semicircular levels of observation areas into which medical students would be crammed like sardines to stand and watch. The gift shop is packed with interesting books on herbal remedies, as well as some really cool knickknacks, T-shirts, and fun stuff like pens in the shape of syringes.

TOURING TIPS Take your time and read the descriptions—you'll be glad you live in the modern world. Not for the queasy or sensitive.

Queen's Gallery, Buckingham Palace ★★★

APPEAL BY AGE	PRESCHOOL ★	GRADE SCHOOL ★	TEENS ★★★
YOUNG ADULTS ★★★		OVER 30 ★★★	SENIORS ★★★

Buckingham Palace, SW1; ☎ 0207-766-7301; www.royalcollection.org.uk; tube: Victoria, Green Park, or St. James's Park

Type of attraction Rotating exhibition of a fraction of the Queen's treasures. **Admission** £8 for adults, £4 for children ages 5–17, £7 for seniors and students, £20 for families. **Hours** Daily, 10 a.m.–5:30 p.m.; occasionally closed between exhibitions, so call ahead. **When to go** Anytime, but it can be very crowded in summer. **Special comments** Quite a collection of treasures accumulated over the centuries by England's monarchy; a mere fraction of all the booty that fills the many royal residences in Great Britain. One is forced to consider the question of who is the proper owner of all this loot: the nation whose taxes helped acquire the collection or the crowned heads whose net worth is increased by them? **Author's rating ★ ★ ★. How much time to allow** 1 hour.

DESCRIPTION AND COMMENTS The new Queen's Gallery is an impressive piece of renovation and curating. Once a rather down-at-the-heels and uninspired building, it was whipped into shape in 2002. Rooms were built in the grand style of the Buckingham Palace state rooms yet are completely modern and practical, with wheelchair access and well-designed restrooms. The pieces at the gallery are a movable feast and may be moved from one royal storehouse to another without warning, but you can count on seeing sketches by da Vinci and paintings by old masters, extraordinary furniture, gold table services, sculpture, porcelain, and priceless bibelots from every corner of the empire. The bulk of the current exhibits was accumulated under Charles II and mad George III, whom you would think certainly had other things on their minds besides objets d'art and paintings. You will always be impressed by whatever the Queen's Gallery is showing because there is such bounty in her treasure vaults to choose from: 20,000 drawings by old masters, such as Holbein, Canaletto, da Vinci, Michelangelo, Carracci, and more; 10,000 old masters' paintings, including such artists as Rembrandt, Vermeer, Holbein, Brueghel, Van Eyck, and Rubens; royal portraits by Gainsborough, Reynolds, and Wilkie, as well as magnificent equine portraits by George Stubbs; 30,000 English watercolors; a possible half-million prints; and countless sculptures, glass and porcelain works, books, and Fabergé trinkets. An excellent on-site gift shop sells royal memorabilia.

TOURING TIPS Leave your backpacks and pocketbooks at the hotel: a very slow security drill requires having your bags examined and then checked in to the coatroom.

Royal Academy of Arts   ★★★½

APPEAL BY AGE	PRESCHOOL ★	GRADE SCHOOL ★★	TEENS ★★
YOUNG ADULTS ★★★½	OVER 30 ★★★½		SENIORS ★★★½

**Burlington House, Piccadilly, W1; ☎ 0207-300-8000 or
0207-300-5760 for recorded info; www.royalacademy.org.uk;
tube: Piccadilly Circus or Green Park**

Type of attraction Venue for the world-famous Summer Exhibition of contemporary artists, record-breaking exhibitions of major artists and art themes, and a small but fine permanent collection of past academicians. **Admission** Prices vary with each exhibition but run about £8 for adults, £7 for seniors, £6 for students, £3 for children ages 12–18, £2 for children ages 8–11, and free for children age 7 and under. **Hours** Daily, 10 a.m.–6 p.m.; open until 10 p.m. on Friday. **When to go** The largest crowds will appear when there's a very popular exhibition; weekends are normally crowded. Go in the morning if possible. **Special comments** Wheelchair access. **Author's rating ★ ★ ★ ½. How much time to allow** It depends on the exhibit, but 2 hours is a good estimate.

DESCRIPTION AND COMMENTS The academy is housed in the beautiful old Burlington House, on Piccadilly. The courtyard features some exhibit of modern sculptures, usually marvelously at odds with the Palladian grandeur of the surrounding 18th-century-palazzo–style buildings. This was England's first art school, founded by Gainsborough and Reynolds, among others, in 1768. To be counted among the academicians was the highest mark of success. Today, the academy continues its tradition as a venue for new artists by hosting the 200-year-old Summer Exhibition, in which painters and sculptors compete for the honor of displaying their work to an appreciative audience, many of whom come to buy. The summer show is a bit of a hodgepodge that is scorned by many critics and journalists and most of the artists who didn't get in the exhibit. But everyone keeps trying to win a place on the wall.

The exhibits are usually excellent. Some of the temporary shows have been so wildly popular that the academy has had to resort to timed ticket entry; when Monet's work was shown some years back, public demand for tickets was so great that the academy was kept open 24 hours a day. A permanent collection includes work from past academicians, as well as its most significant treasure, Michelangelo's marble frieze *Madonna and Child with the Infant St. John.*

TOURING TIPS For £73 you can become a Friend of the Royal Academy, which allows you use of the very pleasant Friends' Room and free admission for you plus one adult guest and up to four family children. Most importantly, you can jump the queue for the blockbuster exhibitions. You also get to feel quite virtuous as a much-needed patron of the arts. Call the academy ahead of time, or just come to the Friends' Desk and sign up. Of course, this may be a bit more than you would want to commit, given you are on holiday, but this institution does need support.

kids Royal Mews, Buckingham Palace ★★½

APPEAL BY AGE	PRESCHOOL ★★	GRADE SCHOOL ★★★	TEENS ★★
YOUNG ADULTS ★★		OVER 30 ★★	SENIORS ★★

Buckingham Palace Road, SW1; ☎ 0207-766-7302;
www.royalcollection.org.uk; tube: St. James's Park or Victoria

Type of attraction Repository for the royal carriages and the queen's horses. **Admission** £7 for adults, £6 for seniors, £4.50 for children age 17 and under, £18.50 for families. **Hours** March 24–July 27 and September 29–October 28, daily except Friday, 11 a.m.–4 p.m.; July 28–September 28, daily, 10 a.m.–5 p.m. Subject to sudden closures, so be sure to call first. **When to go** See hours above. **Special comments** Good wheelchair access. **Author's rating** ★★½. **How much time to allow** 40 minutes.

DESCRIPTION AND COMMENTS It's a small attraction and of limited appeal to many, but we urge any horse fancier to go take a look, if only to see the cleanest, most elegant stables in the entire world. Designed by John Nash, the mews retain a Georgian perfection, with freshly painted pale-yellow stalls and lots of lovely wrought-iron lamps. The horses are just as magnificent as you would expect: strong, well bred, and glossy. The royal coaches and automobiles are just mind-boggling, especially the gold state coach built for George II in 1761, which is still used ceremonially. Some of the most admirable tack and saddles ever made are also on display, along with sketches and photos of royal public occasions.

TOURING TIPS Try to make this part of your trip to Buckingham Palace and/or the Queen's Gallery—we guarantee that out of the three, this will be the kids' favorite. Combined tickets with the Queen's Gallery will save you 50p off the cost of buying the two separately.

kids Royal Observatory, Greenwich ★★★

APPEAL BY AGE	PRESCHOOL ★	GRADE SCHOOL ★★★	TEENS ★★★
YOUNG ADULTS ★★★		OVER 30 ★★★	SENIORS ★★★

Blackheath Avenue, hilltop of Greenwich Park; ☎ 0208-312-6565; www.nmm.ac.uk (click "What's on" and then "Royal Observatory"); Docklands Light Railway: Greenwich

Type of attraction Location of the world's prime meridian (0 degrees longitude). **Admission** Free; fees for special events, exhibits, and planetarium shows. **Hours** Daily, 10 a.m.–5 p.m. **When to go** Anytime. **Special comments** Not all of the observatory buildings are fully accessible to visitors with disabilities. **Author's rating ★★★**. **How much time to allow** 1–2 hours, or a full day's outing to see the adjacent Queen's House, the National Maritime Museum, and the park.

DESCRIPTION AND COMMENTS In 1675, Charles II appointed John Flamsteed his Astronomer Royal, with the specific mandate to create better navigational maps for the British Empire. Christopher Wren then designed and built an observatory for him on the highest point of the King's royal hunting grounds in Greenwich. Today, this small complex of buildings is a popular museum. You can place yourself in two hemispheres at the same time as you straddle the prime meridian, a favorite photo op for visitors. The museum's oldest part, Flamsteed House, is the restored home of the first Astronomer Royal. Its main galleries chronicle the bizarre methods once used to help ships' captains determine their location at sea and the increasingly important race to discover longitude. The remaining buildings contain a number of astronomical tools and telescopes, including the 28-inch Greenwich refracting telescope, the largest of its kind in the United Kingdom and the seventh largest in the world.

TOURING TIPS Go on a nice day and enjoy walking around Greenwich. Picnic in the surrounding park; and be sure to get a gander at the view of London from the top of the hill.

Saatchi Gallery ★★★

APPEAL BY AGE	PRESCHOOL ★	GRADE SCHOOL ★★	TEENS ★★★★
YOUNG ADULTS ★★★		OVER 30 ★★★	SENIORS ★★★

Type of attraction Contemporary-art space. *Note:* The gallery is moving from its present site to the Duke of York Headquarters in Chelsea and will reopen in mid-2008. Check **www.saatchi-gallery.co.uk** for more information.

DESCRIPTION AND COMMENTS The relocation of the Saatchi Gallery from the old County Hall on the south bank of the Thames to a new 50,000-square-foot space on King's Road in Chelsea will be cause for much joy among West Londoners. No doubt the ribbon-cutting ceremony sometime in 2008 will be a noteworthy media event, star-studded and quirky. The old gallery's 2003 opening celebration featured a performance-art piece in which 200 naked people mingled happily with celebs—it was perhaps the most cheerful display of nudity in history. We can't imagine how they'll top that at the reopening.

The great patron of Young British Artists, Charles Saatchi, has spent most of the past two decades plunking down thousands of pounds for cutting-edge, controversial works such as Damien Hirst's shark in formaldehyde and Tracey Emin's unmade bed (a piece that was famously tidied up by a maintenance man who didn't know that the trash strewn over the bed was part of the installation). No matter where or in what kind of configuration the collection ends up, you must bring a sense of humor and an open mind to the gallery. There is plenty to be amused by in the Saatchi collection, and the cheekiness of the young (or rather, now-aging) British artists known as the Britpack can only be admired. Although Charles Saatchi's holdings are heavy with such contemporary British artists, his intent is to create a center for modern art that may—depending on its exhibitions—rival the Tate Modern.

🚌 St. Paul's Cathedral ★★★

APPEAL BY AGE	PRESCHOOL	★	GRADE SCHOOL	★★	TEENS	★★
YOUNG ADULTS ★★★	OVER	30	★★★	SENIORS	★★★	

Ludgate Hill, The City, EC4; ☎ 0207-236-4128; www.stpauls.co.uk; tube: St. Paul's or Mansion House

Type of attraction London's most prominent cathedral. **Admission** Cathedral, galleries, and crypt entry, £9.50 for adults, £8.50 for seniors and students, £3.50 for children 7–16, free for children under age 7, £22.50 for families. Self-guided tours (with cassette) and guided tours are available for an extra charge. **Hours** Open for sightseeing Monday–Saturday, 8:30 a.m.–4:30 p.m.; galleries open at 9:30 a.m.; choral evensong occurs Monday–Saturday at 7 p.m. and Sunday at 5:15 p.m. Call the cathedral for other service times and for information on closures due to weddings or baptisms. **When to go** Early in the day on weekdays to avoid the crowds and catch the best chances for clear-sky views from the dome. **Special comments** Good disabled access to cathedral's nave and crypt, but there is no elevator access to the galleries. **Author's rating ★★★. How much time to allow** 1–3 hours, depending on whether you plan to climb to the top of the dome and see every nook and cranny.

DESCRIPTION AND COMMENTS A Roman temple to the goddess Diana once stood on the site of the present St. Paul's, but even such ancient sanctity did not put the succeeding buildings out of harm's way: the first church was destroyed by fire around AD 660, and the second was demolished by

Vikings. A huge wooden cross was struck by lightning in 1382, and in 1561 a spire was also toppled by lightning. During Henry VIII's reformation, the church turned into a kind of public marketplace. A bishop described the nave in 1560: "The south side for Popery and Usury; the north for Simony [buying and selling pardons]; and the horse-fair in the middle for all kinds of bargains, meetings, brawlings, murders, conspiracies; and the font for ordinary payments of money." The Great Fire of 1666 destroyed the third incarnation of St. Paul's Cathedral, along with four-fifths of the city. Christopher Wren was drafted to design its replacement, and this became his masterpiece. The cathedral was finished in the course of 35 years, and its stone English-baroque style, despite being dwarfed by the encroachments of skyscrapers, still dominates the neighborhood. At 360 feet, the dome is one of the highest in the world and second in size only to St. Peter's Basilica's in Rome. Its lantern weighs a massive 850 tons.

Inside the cathedral are mosaics and frescoes, *Light of the World* by Holman Hunt, Jean Tijou's grand sanctuary gates, and the intricate choir-stall carvings designed by master woodcraftsman Grinling Gibbons. The crypt is the resting place of, among other notables, Lord Admiral Horatio Nelson, the Duke of Wellington, and Wren himself, whose son composed the Latin inscription on his tomb that translates: "Reader, if you seek his monument, look around."

The 530 steps that take you to the top of St. Paul's are worth the effort, especially if you are lucky enough to visit on a clear, or even sunny, day. It is an easy walk to the Whispering Gallery, on the first of the three levels, where words whispered on one one side of the gallery can be clearly heard on the other. On the second level, the external Stone Gallery provides telescopes and benches, but it is the uppermost Golden Gallery that offers the most spectacular views of London. To see them, however, you must submit to considerably more nerve-racking climbing.

TOURING TIPS If your interest in Christopher Wren is inspired by St. Paul's, other examples of his 17th-century work are in the vicinity. Closest to the cathedral are St. Mary-le-Bow (Cheapside), St. Bride's (Fleet Street), and Christ Church (Newgate Street), which has only its tower remaining (a lovely garden now fills what was once the nave). Also visit St. Bartholomew the Great, on Little Britain Street; it's London's oldest monastic church.

kids Science Museum ★★★★

APPEAL BY AGE	PRESCHOOL ★★★★	GRADE SCHOOL ★★★★	TEENS ★★★★
YOUNG ADULTS ★★★★		OVER 30 ★★★★	SENIORS ★★★★

Exhibition Road, South Kensington, SW7; ☎ 0870-870-4868; www.sciencemuseum.org.uk; tube: South Kensington

Type of attraction Abundant collection of scientific and technological odds and ends that add up to a fascinating experience. **Admission** Free; charge for IMAX and special exhibits. **Hours** Daily, 10 a.m.–6 p.m. **When to go** Avoid school holidays and weekends, unless you arrive right at opening. **Special comments**

Wheelchair access and facilities. **Author's rating ★ ★ ★ ★**. **How much time to allow** As much as you can spare—you could easily spend all day here, there's so much to see. If you're bringing children who want to play in the interactive areas, plan to spend at least 2 hours.

DESCRIPTION AND COMMENTS You don't need any particular interest in things scientific to love this comprehensive collection displaying the progress of technology and science from the dawn of time to today. You can see an early hourglass or the *Apollo 10* Command Module, and everything in between. Exhibits range from something as sweet as a miniature field with tiny moving plows to a stupendously huge mill engine in the middle of the East Hall. You can watch Foucault's pendulum swinging away in the staircase by the East Hall or check out a replica of a turn-of-the-20th-century pharmacy in the area that focuses on the art of medicine.

The basement is designed for young children: there's a hands-on gallery where children between ages 3 and 6 can splash around (hands only) in a long sluice of water, clamber across a bridge, or build things with giant LEGOs, among many other activities. You may never get them out of that play area, which may be why the museum suggests starting at the top and moving downward.

TOURING TIPS If you arrive and find a line, go down the street to the Natural History Museum or cross Exhibition Road to the Victoria and Albert, and come back later in the afternoon.

Shakespeare's Globe Theatre ★★★★

APPEAL BY AGE	PRESCHOOL ★	GRADE SCHOOL ★★	TEENS ★★
YOUNG ADULTS ★★★	OVER 30 ★★★★		SENIORS ★★★★

21 New Globe Walk, Bankside, SE1; ☎ 0207-401-9919; www.shakespeares-globe.org; tube: Mansion House or Blackfriars

Type of attraction Magnificently reconstructed Shakespearean theater. **Admission** The Globe Exhibition and guided tour cost £10 for adults, £8.50 for seniors and students, £6.50 for children ages 6–15, and are free for children age 5 and under. Family tickets cost £28; tours run every half hour. Prices for performances run from £5 (standing room) to £32 (tiered seating). **Hours** Daily, 10 a.m.– 5 p.m.; check with the box office for performance times and dates. **When to go** Anytime. **Special comments** The exhibition is easily accessible for individuals in wheelchairs. **Author's rating ★ ★ ★ ★**. **How much time to allow** 1–2 hours for exhibition and tour.

DESCRIPTION AND COMMENTS Brilliantly reconstructed as an almost exact replica of its former self, the Globe officially opened in 1998 and is a delightful place to learn about the world's greatest playwright, William Shakespeare. In his day, Shakespeare's plays were also performed at the Rose and occasionally at the Swan, but it was at the Globe that Shakespeare made his literary name. The tour of the theater, often led by actors and very well done, provides marvelous details about Elizabethan theater and the notoriously debauched Bankside area. Performances run in the summer months and are held outdoors under natural light, as they used to be. The Globe Exhibition is beneath the theater. As of this writing, the extensive renovation has yet to be unveiled, but the exhibition area will be enlarged and improved, with important additions made to the permanent displays. The exhibits are dedicated to the life and times of the Bard; given that so little is known about Shakespeare's life, his times take center stage. There are impressive reproductions of medieval tools that were actually used in the building of the theater. The complex also contains a cafe, as well as a more upscale restaurant with a view of the river and the city.

TOURING TIPS The box office says that the best seats for performances are not seats at all but the standing area in front of the stage, where the "groundlings" stand; the actors may mingle, and the rain may pour (don't worry; you can buy rain ponchos on-site). Personally, we prefer the seats, which are authentic and not all that comfy, but as a groundling you do get a strong sense of what theatergoing was like in the old days (very convivial and festive).

Sherlock Holmes Museum   ★★★

APPEAL BY AGE	PRESCHOOL ★	GRADE SCHOOL ★	TEENS ★★★
YOUNG ADULTS ★★★	OVER 30 ★★★		SENIORS ★★½

221b Baker Street, Marylebone, NW1; ☎ 0207-935-8866; www.sherlock-holmes.co.uk; tube: Baker Street

Type of attraction Real Victorian home of the fictional detective. **Admission** £6 for adults, free for children age 6 and under. **Hours** Daily, 9:30 a.m.–6 p.m. **When to go** Anytime, especially if you're waiting for Madame Tussauds to open or are on your way to the London Zoo. **Special comments** No wheelchair access; stairs are steep and numerous. **Author's rating** ★★★. **How much time to allow** 30–40 minutes.

DESCRIPTION AND COMMENTS I am a Sherlock Holmes fan, and I am also a sucker for anything from the 19th century. But even if you're neither of the above, I think you'll find this a charming little curiosity. The short self-guided tour through the little house is like stepping back in time: fires are laid in all the rooms, which are bursting with Victorian knickknacks, art, curios, and furniture. It is a funny experience, seeing a fictional place brought to life; by the time you leave, you may think there really was a Sherlock Holmes. The decor is wonderful: there's the violin Holmes played close at hand in the study, leg irons on the bed by a valise half packed, a medical corner for Dr. Watson, a remarkable early typewriter, and a turn-of-the-century telephone. Even the attic is perfect, stuffed with leather goods, hatboxes, and other household items we're all too young to remember. Props from the stories are displayed with appropriate quotes from the books, and there's an extraordinary chess set in gold and silver with characters from the books as the pieces.

TOURING TIPS Read at least one Sherlock Holmes story before visiting; it will add to the flavor and appreciation of the museum.

Sir John Soane's Museum ★★★★

APPEAL BY AGE	PRESCHOOL †	GRADE SCHOOL ★	TEENS ★★★
YOUNG ADULTS ★★★★		OVER 30 ★★★★	SENIORS ★★★½

† Not appropriate for young children.

13 Lincoln's Inn Fields, Holborn, WC2; ☎ 0207-440-4263; www.soane.org; tube: Holborn (Central and Piccadilly lines)

Type of attraction Fascinating and eccentric collection of sculpture, art, and antiquities belonging to the neoclassical architect Sir John Soane. **Admission** Free. **Hours** Tuesday–Saturday, 10 a.m.–5 p.m.; open the first Tuesday of each month 6–9 p.m., with some of the rooms lit by candles. **When to go** Anytime, although an excellent tour of the museum takes place Saturday at 2:30 p.m. (£5, limited to 20 people). **Special comments** The museum is not handicapped accessible, because it was formerly the private home of Sir John Soane and the directions were to leave it the way he'd had it. This attraction is not recommended for very young children with a tendency to touch everything. The number of visitors must be limited, and you may have to queue to take the tour unless you arrive at opening time. **Author's rating ★★★★. How much time to allow** 1½–2½ hours.

DESCRIPTION AND COMMENTS Many Londoners consider this their favorite museum. As small as it is, there are treasures to be found in every conceivable cranny. You can visit this residence over and over and still find new things to admire. Sir John Soane bought and reconstructed the Georgian homes at 12, 13, and 14 Lincoln's Inn Fields, situated just a stone's throw from one of the early Inns of Court, and he began filling them with a rather eccentric collection of art and antiquities. Soane's architectural talent is seen in the unique floor plan of number 13, which includes a glass-domed roof and central atrium that illuminates three floors as well as the dining room and breakfast parlor, both of which incorporate a display of mirrors that reflect light and cleverly create the illusion of spaciousness.

The collection includes William Hogarth's famous series of prints called *A Rake's Progress* and *An Election* in an impressive picture gallery of false walls and hidden doors. A mock medieval monk's parlor contains gloomy casts and gargoyles, and a priceless sarcophagus of Seti I is surrounded by rows of antique statuary. Saturday's hour-long tour takes you through all of this and into number 12 as well, where you can see Soane's enormous research library, complete with his architectural plans for the Bank of England, Whitehall, and parts of the treasury, along with numerous models of Pompeian temples.

TOURING TIPS If you can't manage the Saturday tour, definitely strike up a conversation with one of the museum curators—they're very friendly and love to talk about the plethora of items acquired by Sir John Soane. Call about the candlelit late opening.

Somerset House (including Courtauld Gallery ★★★★
Gilbert Collection, and Hermitage Rooms)

APPEAL BY AGE PRESCHOOL ★★★ GRADE SCHOOL ★★★ TEENS ★★★
YOUNG ADULTS ★★★★ OVER 30 ★★★★ SENIORS ★★★★

Strand, West End, WC2;
Somerset: ☎ 0207-845-4600; www.somersethouse.org.uk;
Courtauld: ☎ 0207-848-2777; www.courtauld.ac.uk;
Gilbert: ☎ 0207-420-9400; www.gilbert-collection.org.uk;
Hermitage: ☎ 0207-845-4600; www.hermitagerooms.com;
tube: Covent Garden, Holborn, or Temple (except Sundays)

Type of attraction Magnificent edifice with river views, a classical courtyard, a river terrace, and 3 separate art galleries. **Admission** Free for Somerset House and grounds. A 3-day pass is a good deal at £12 for adults, £11 for students and seniors, and free for children age 17 and under, and entitles you to 3 consecutive days' entrance to the Courtauld Gallery, the Gilbert Collection, and the Hermitage Rooms, as well as discounts in the 3 gift shops on site, the Admiralty Restaurant, and the Deli. Individual tickets for each of the 3 venues cost £5 for adults, £4 for students and seniors, and free for children age 17 and under. **Hours** Somerset House and all galleries are open daily, 10 a.m.–6 p.m. During the summer, the house itself, the terrace, and the courtyard stay open on Friday till 10 p.m. **When to go** The courtyard and terrace are splendid on a sunny day; inside, the galleries are great anytime, but see special comments about the Hermitage Rooms. **Special comments** The house and the galleries are all wheelchair accessible. Because the Hermitage Rooms are small, the tickets are sold for timed slots, on the hour and on the half hour; about 60 at a time can go in. Also, check the Hermitage Web site to be sure they are not in the middle of staging a new exhibit; the exhibits are shown in 10-month cycles. **Author's rating** ★★★★. **How much time to allow** This depends on whether you go to any or all of the art galleries and on how long you stroll around or linger in the cafes or on the terrace. The 3-day-pass scheme makes complete sense here, as you might suffer from sensory overload if you hit all three collections in one day.

DESCRIPTION AND COMMENTS Somerset House is one of the great jewels in London's architectural and historical crown. It was opened to the public in 2000, after a lengthy and expensive renovation that included adding the Gilbert Collection and the Hermitage Rooms to its long-standing Courtauld Institute of Art. The original Somerset House was an ostentatious monument to ambition built in 1547 by Henry VII's brother-in-law, Edward Seymour, Duke of Somerset and Lord Protector to his nephew, the young and sickly King Edward VI. Somerset was the de facto ruler of England during Edward VI's short reign, and like so many who flew too close to the Tudor flame, he ended up headless on Tower Hill. The mansion then became a property of the crown and was a riverside residence enjoyed by royals from Elizabeth I to the wife of Charles II. After architect Christopher Wren refurbished it in 1685, it entered a long period of decline, which led to its demolition in 1775 to make way for the grand public-works building that housed learned academies and government offices, a preponderance of which were the financial sectors that merged into the Inland Tax Revenue. Although Somerset House took some hits during the Blitz, the multipurpose property you see today is true to its Georgian design. In addition to the galleries, it now houses a fair number of cafes, gift shops, and places to sit and watch the Thames flow by. The on-site Admiralty Restaurant is very upscale and a destination on its own. In winter, the courtyard fountain is converted to a skating rink.

The Courtauld Gallery originated with textile magnate Samuel Courtauld's private collection from the 1930s but has grown considerably since then. It is most famous for its priceless Impressionist works, which include Van Gogh's *Self-Portrait with Bandaged Ear,* Degas's *Two Dancers on a Stage,* Renoir's *La Loge (The Theater Box),* and Manet's *Déjeuner sur l'herbe (Picnic on the Grass).* The medieval and early-Renaissance works in Galleries 1 and 2 are also quite impressive, with paintings by Brueghel, Bellini, and Rubens.

The Gilbert Collection is a museum of decorative arts, housing Sir Arthur Gilbert's mammoth treasure trove of gold, silver, and mosaics. The silver items here rival those in the Victoria and Albert's collection, and there is no other museum with a larger store of "micro-mosaic" tables, artwork, and snuff boxes.

The Hermitage Rooms display selections from the great Hermitage Museum of St. Petersburg, Russia. If you are a museum lover, this is a must-go—it's a long way to St. Petersburg.

TOURING TIPS The Courtauld offers an educational booklet called "Courtauld Gallery Trail," available at the admissions desk, which instructs children (ages 5 to 12) in the study of the gallery's fine-art collection.

Southwark Cathedral ★★½

APPEAL BY AGE	PRESCHOOL ★½	GRADE SCHOOL ★★	TEENS ★★
YOUNG ADULTS ★★½		OVER 30 ★★½	SENIORS ★★½

Montague Close, Southwark, SE1; ☎ 0207-367-6700; www.dswark.org; tube: London Bridge

Type of attraction Small medieval cathedral with famous historical and cultural links. **Admission** Free; suggested minimum donation of £4/person. **Hours** Monday–Friday, 8 a.m.–6 p.m.; Saturday and Sunday, 9 a.m.–6 p.m. **When to go** Anytime. **Special comments** Disabled access; permits must be obtained from welcome desk for photography or videotaping. **Author's rating ★★½. How much time to allow** 1–2 hours.

DESCRIPTION AND COMMENTS Although it has been a cathedral since 1905, parts of this building date back to the 12th century, when it was the Augustinian priory church of St. Mary Overie. In the intervening centuries, the cathedral was frequented by many notables of their day. William Shakespeare attended Mass here regularly, and his brother, Edward, is interred in the choir aisle. A chapel is dedicated to the founder of Harvard University,

John Harvard, who was born in Southwark and baptized in the church in 1607. The cathedral also houses the tomb of poet John Gower, a contemporary of Chaucer, and a memorial to Shakespeare that includes a glorious mid-20th-century stained-glass window depicting almost two dozen of Shakespeare's most famous characters.

TOURING TIPS Southwark Cathedral makes a nice stop if you are wandering around the Southwark area, especially if you've already been to Shakespeare's Globe Theatre. On weekends, a fantastic open-air food market sets up shop under the bridge next to the cathedral.

 **Tate Britain** ★★★★

APPEAL BY AGE	PRESCHOOL ★	GRADE SCHOOL ★★	TEENS ★★★
YOUNG ADULTS ★★★★		OVER 30 ★★★★	SENIORS ★★★★

Millbank, on Thames, SW1; ☎ 0207-887-8888; www.tate.org.uk; tube: Pimlico

Type of attraction Museum of English painters. **Admission** Free, although donations are eagerly accepted; there's a charge for special exhibits. **Hours** Daily, 10 a.m.–5:50 p.m. **When to go** Anytime, but avoid midday if there's a big exhibition. **Special comments** Access-for-disabled leaflet available at information desks. Parking spaces and wheelchairs are available but must be booked ahead. **Author's rating** ★★★★. **How much time to allow** 2 hours or more.

DESCRIPTION AND COMMENTS The old Tate Gallery morphed into the Tate Britain in the spring of 2000, when its collection of international modern art was moved across the river to the new Tate Modern (see separate profile following) at the Bankside Power Station. This left Tate Britain with a significant collection of English painters and sculptors from the 16th to the early 20th centuries. The building itself is quite impressive, one of London's greatest exteriors. Look for Poseidon situated between a lion and a unicorn on the roof, stately columns adorning the entrance, and halls of beautiful marble and design. All the great British artists are here: Hogarth, Stubbs, Reynolds, Blake, Burne-Jones, Constable, and even an honorary Englishman, American expat James Whistler. The pride of the collection is J. M. W. Turner, whose paintings and memorabilia fill the Clore Gallery. The gift shop sells an excellent selection of books, gifts, and postcards, and the cafe and more-formal dining room are top-notch. A ferry service across the street from the museum will take you to the London Eye and then on to the Tate Modern. The pier was designed by the same people who gave us the London Eye, and the boat itself was decorated with the help of artist Damien Hirst.

TOURING TIPS Take the shuttle boat from the pier in front of Tate Britain to get to the London Eye or Tate Modern, or just for the fun of it.

Tate Modern ★★★★★

APPEAL BY AGE	PRESCHOOL ★★★	GRADE SCHOOL ★★★	TEENS ★★★★★
YOUNG ADULTS ★★★★★		OVER 30 ★★★★★	SENIORS ★★★★

25 Sumner Street, Bankside, SE1; ☎ 0207-887-8888; www.tate.org.uk; tube: Southwark or Blackfriars

Type of attraction Museum of international modern art. **Admission** Free, except for special exhibitions, lectures, and films. **Hours** Sunday–Thursday, 10 a.m.–6 p.m.; Friday and Saturday, 10 a.m.–10 p.m. **When to go** Anytime. **Special comments** Individuals with wheelchairs or strollers should use the north entrance from the river walkway or the west entrance on Holland Street. Call to reserve a parking space or wheelchair: ☎ 0207-887-8888. **Author's rating** ★★★★★. **How much time to allow** 2–4 hours.

DESCRIPTION AND COMMENTS Housed in the old Bankside Power Station, the Tate Modern opened to loud acclaim in 2000. This national museum's nucleus was formed from the old Tate Gallery's modern-art collection, from 1900 to the present day. Dalí, Picasso, Matisse, Duchamp, Warhol, and Rothko are all represented here, as are so many other masters of modern art. This former utility megalith has been put to good use, housing enormous art installations and sculptures, and the views across the Thames are wonderful, taking in the Millennium Bridge and St. Paul's. There are good—often great—exhibits here, two cafes and an espresso bar, a large shop by Turbine Hall, and an overall interesting architectural conversion from power station to art gallery. The cavernous Turbine Hall showcases changing art installations on a giant scale. Look for a display of all the items dredged up from the Thames when the building was constructed—a visual history of the discarded and lost. There was a recent funfest installed here comprising five slides that you flew down on mats, giving you the thrill of zooming from the top of the building to the ground floor. Exhibits like this make you really love modern art and adore the whimsy of this very cool museum.

TOURING TIPS Walk across the Millennium Bridge to St. Paul's for a nice contrast between centuries. Or jump on the ferry that goes to the London Eye and the Tate Britain. Be prepared to spend a lot of time hanging out here—the people-watching possibilities are as rich as the art.

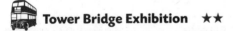 **Tower Bridge Exhibition** ★★

APPEAL BY AGE	PRESCHOOL ★	GRADE SCHOOL ★	TEENS ★
YOUNG ADULTS ★★	OVER 30 ★★		SENIORS ★★

Tower Bridge, Tower Hill (The City), SE1; ☎ 0207-403-3761; www.towerbridge.org.uk; tube: Tower Hill or London Bridge

Type of attraction History of the bridge and a walk across the top of it. **Admission** £5 for adults, £3 for children ages 5–15, £4.50 for seniors and students, £10 to £14 for families. **Hours** April–September, daily, 10 a.m.–6:30 p.m.; October–March, daily, 9:30 a.m.–6 p.m. (last admission is 75 minutes before closing). **When to go** Early morning or around 4 p.m. **Special comments** Disabled access; call for details and to make plans. **Author's rating** ★★. **How much time to allow** 90 minutes.

DESCRIPTION AND COMMENTS This is the bridge that everyone thinks is London Bridge, and allegedly what the American investors thought they were getting when they bought a bridge in the 1970s to put up in the Arizona desert. They must have been quite disappointed to get the real, boring London Bridge (though they hotly deny that they made such a dumb mistake, and you've got to admit that this story has all the earmarks of an urban myth, merrily supporting the stereotype of the rich, clueless Yankee). Built in 1894, Tower Bridge remains a beautiful piece of architecture as well as a marvel of engineering. It is adequately appreciated from the ground, and that may be enough if you encounter an interminable line at the entrance. But if you can get in without waiting for more than half an hour, it's worth a look. The proprietors seem to be straining to provide a tour of some length, with a kind of corny multimedia trip through time to the bridge's inception, but the old films are fun to watch, and the history of how they ended up using this design is interesting. Once you are on the walkway high above the Thames, with views everywhere, you can't help but be glad you visited.

TOURING TIPS If there's a huge line—one that reaches out onto the bridge—go enjoy the south-riverside cafes and stores, or go to the Tower of London and return when the crowds disperse, which, according to the staff, is usually around 4:15 p.m.

kids Tower of London ★★★★★

APPEAL BY AGE PRESCHOOL ★★★★ GRADE SCHOOL ★★★★★ TEENS ★★★★
YOUNG ADULTS ★★★★★ OVER 30 ★★★★★ SENIORS ★★★★★

Tower Hill, The City, EC3; ☎ 0870-756-6060; www.hrp.org.uk;
tube: Tower Hill

Type of attraction Ancient, history-rich fortress on the banks of the Thames. **Admission** £16 for adults, £13 for seniors and students, £9.50 for children ages 5–16, free for children under age 5, £45 for families. Book online to avoid queuing. **Hours** March–October, Monday–Saturday, 9 a.m.–6 p.m.; Sunday, 10 a.m.–6 p.m. (last admission at 5 p.m.); November–February, Sunday and Monday, 10 a.m.–5 p.m.; Tuesday–Saturday, 9 a.m.–5 p.m. (last admission at 4 p.m.). **When to go** The lines get pretty ferocious in the summer; line up early or go later in the day. **Special comments** Lots of difficult stairs and passageways. A limited number of wheelchairs is available; ask at the group-ticket office. **Author's rating** ★★★★★. **How much time to allow** 3 hours or more.

DESCRIPTION AND COMMENTS OK, I admit it: this is in many people's minds one of the biggest tourist traps in London. But methinks they just don't appreciate the genuine historical importance of this place and can't see the castle for the tourists and gift shops. The first time I entered the Tower of London through the Middle Tower, I literally went weak in the knees. For an American with more than a passing interest in English history, a trip to the tower is a transcendent experience. Yes, it is undeniably tourist-ridden, but I have never found that to be a mitigating factor in my awe and appreciation of it. Yes, it is usually packed with howling schoolchildren and grumpy parents; yes, there are gift shops and snack bars all over the place; and yes, some of the attempts at historical verisimilitude are corny. But this is still one of the most important sites in all of England. Numerous guidebooks will tell you that it's hard to feel the essential grimness of the place with all the happy sightseers around, but I say that with a little imagination and focus, you can sense the ghosts that plague this place of imprisonment, torture, and death.

As anyone who has been here at night after closing time can tell you, the place is lousy with ghosts, and not the happy kind. Thomas Macaulay, the 19th-century historian, wrote of the small burial ground by the Chapel of St. Peter Ad Vincula: "In truth, there is no sadder spot on earth as this little cemetery. Death is there associated, not, as in Westminster Abbey and St Paul's, with genius and virtue, but with whatever is darkest in human nature and in human destiny, with the savage triumph of implacable enemies, with the inconstancy, the ingratitude, the cowardice of friends, with all the miseries of fallen greatness and of blighted fame." It does make you shiver when you think of the roll call of the imprisoned and beheaded: Saint Thomas More; Lady Jane Grey and her husband; queen consorts Anne Boleyn and Catherine Howard; and a host of lords and ladies whose only crime was to end up on the wrong side of kings, queens, plotting courtiers, or power-mad churchmen. There were also kings of Scotland and France, William Wallace (alias Braveheart), King Henry VI, the two little princes murdered in their sleep (allegedly by their uncle, Richard III), Sir Walter Raleigh, and countless victims of religious persecutions. It is, for all its present serenity and beauty, a place soaked in centuries of blood and cruelty.

The tower was built as a simple fortification on the Thames in 1066 by William the Conqueror and grew over the years to include 13 different towers and numerous houses, walks, armories, barracks, and greens, all surrounded by a moat. The moat was drained in 1843 due to its mephitic stink and fatal contagions, and green lawns were planted in its place. The Yeoman Warders, also known as Beefeaters, have been guarding the castle—its prisoners and its treasures—since 1485. Thirty-five of them currently live and work at the tower, all retired armed-service officers (the first woman Yeoman Warder was admitted to service in September 2007). There are warder talks and free tours daily; the Lanthorn Tower and the Middle Tower have information boards outlining the day's talks, tours, and events. Actors in period costumes also wander about, striking up conversations in character; children get a huge kick out of this, as they tend to be unembarrassed about chatting up these funny folk. There are currently eight of the famous ravens in residence at the tower, their ancestors having been cared for by Yeoman Warder Raven Masters for more than 600 years; the birds' wings are clipped to prevent their leaving. Legend holds that if the ravens should ever leave, the tower will fall and England with it.

One of the most famous sights at the tower is the Crown Jewels. However, while the crowns and scepters are interesting as historic emblems, they are strangely lifeless. The display isn't nearly as gratifying as reading the scratched graffiti—in English and Latin—of the unfortunate prisoners in Beauchamp Tower, or sitting under a tree in one of the greens absorbing the atmosphere. It's a good place to hang around, so take your time. The audio tours are great and can be done at your own pace, and the guidebook is an excellent investment.

TOURING TIPS A security check slows down the entrance, even if you have prebooked fast-track tickets; if possible, leave your knapsack or bag at home when you visit. Check out the Web site **www.tower-of-london .com** to get a preview of many of the strange tales about the tower, complete with atmospheric music and little-known facts about the traditions of the tower keepers. Also visit **www.toweroflondontour.com** before visiting to whet your appetite and learn a few things.

kids V&A Museum of Childhood ★★★

APPEAL BY AGE	PRESCHOOL ★★★★	GRADE SCHOOL ★★★★	TEENS ★★★
YOUNG ADULTS ★★★		OVER 30 ★★★	SENIORS ★★★

Cambridge Heath Road, East End, E2; ☎ 0208-983-5200; www.vam.ac.uk/moc; tube: Bethnal Green

Type of attraction Largest toy museum in the world. **Admission** Free. **Hours** Daily, 10 a.m.–5:45 p.m. **When to go** Anytime. **Special comments** Check the Web site to find out what activities are on—it makes a big difference to kids' enjoyment of the museum when they have something special to do, such as attending a puppet workshop, making crafts of all kinds, or going on a treasure hunt in the galleries. **Author's rating ★★★. How much time to allow** Depends on which activities your children engage in, but an hour and a half will cover a stroll around the museum.

DESCRIPTION AND COMMENTS Housed in a building directly across the street from the Bethnal Green tube station, the Museum of Childhood is part of the Victoria and Albert Museum, which over the years has contributed thousands of items from its vast stores to expand this museum, which opened in 1872. The building itself is based on the iron framework of a temporary museum created for the Great Exhibition of 1851, which stood on the Victoria and Albert's current site. (The mosaic floor was constructed using the labor of women prisoners from Woking Gaol.) The Museum of Childhood has an unparalleled collection of children's toys and accessories from the 16th century to the present: dollhouses, model trains, hobbyhorses, old mechanical games and toys, dolls of every possible kind, teddy bears, even old-fashioned prams and nursery furniture. Not surprisingly, children seem to prefer pumping the mechanical toys full of coins to admiring the antiques behind glass, which is why the museum has been steadily expanding the fun interactive stuff for kids. A recent refurbishment freshened up the site remarkably, with clever children-centric exhibits and hands-on activities.

TOURING TIPS Pick up some unusual birthday or Christmas presents for kids in the gift shop.

kids 🚌 **Victoria and Albert Museum** ★★★★★

| APPEAL BY AGE | PRESCHOOL ★★ | GRADE SCHOOL ★★★ | TEENS ★★★★ |
| YOUNG ADULTS ★★★★★ | OVER 30 ★★★★★ | SENIORS ★★★★★ |

Cromwell Road (second entrance on Exhibition Road), South Kensington, SW7; ☎ 0207-942-2000; www.vam.ac.uk; tube: South Kensington

Type of attraction Breathtaking collection of decorative arts and design displayed throughout 8 miles of galleries. **Admission** Free; fees for special exhibits. **Hours** Daily, 10 a.m.–5:45 p.m.; on Fridays, selected galleries are open until 10 p.m., with free gallery talks and ticketed lectures (costing £7.50–£18). **When to go** Anytime. **Special comments** Wheelchair access is from the Exhibition Road entrance; there are ramps over most of the many small sets of steps. **Author's rating** ★★★★★. **How much time to allow** As much as possible.

DESCRIPTION AND COMMENTS The museum, in an attempt to shrug off its refined layer of dust, has been playing to the younger generations with stylish, contemporary exhibitions and educational activities. The big exhibits have been sourced from 20th-century trends and schools of design. The major face-lift of the last few years is just now healing, and it has transformed the museum in so many ways that if you haven't been in a few years you'll hardly recognize the old girl.

The Victoria and Albert possesses a vast assortment of treasures connected only by the fluid concept of decorative art: armor, religious artifacts, stained glass, sculptures, wood carvings, jewelry, musical instruments, ironwork, furniture, silver, gold, glasswork, clothing, paintings, photographs—you name it. If it was made by human hands, the V&A has a place for it, whether in permanent displays or in the many special exhibits staged throughout the year.

The original V&A was part of Prince Albert's grand scheme to make South Kensington a center for arts, science, and learning. When it opened in 1852, funded by the Great Exhibition of 1851, Albert envisioned the South Kensington Museum, as it was known then, to be a repository of applied arts—items that happily married beauty to utility or form to function, a school of thought championed by William Morris, who famously declared that he would have nothing in his house that was not useful or that he did not consider beautiful. The founding principle of the museum was impossible to stick to from the start, as treasures began arriving from all over the empire and via thousands of legacies.

By 1899, the old housing for the collection was clearly unfit, and work began on the present building, named by Queen Victoria, who never neglected an opportunity to honor her long-departed husband. She didn't live to see it completed ten years later, but she presides over its Cromwell Road entrance like a secular version of the Virgin Mary, who tops the Brompton Oratory church next door. The building is a real beauty inside and out, and any visit to the museum should always include a few moments to appreciate the edifice's architectural artistry and craftsman-ship. The British Galleries are a must-see, as are Raphael's cartoons, the Dacre Beasts, the dress collection, and the stained glass.

TOURING TIPS Friday nights feature the V&A's Late View, with a limited number of galleries open, a lecture in the beautiful old lecture hall, and a gallery talk. The cafe is open, and there is often live music. On week-ends and school holidays, you and your kids can enjoy such activities as a treasure hunt throughout the museum or making crafts.

The Wallace Collection ★★★

APPEAL BY AGE	PRESCHOOL ★	GRADE SCHOOL ★	TEENS ★★
YOUNG ADULTS ★★★	OVER 30 ★★★		SENIORS ★★★

Hertford House, Manchester Square, Marylebone, W1; ☎ 0207-563-9500; www.wallacecollection.org; tube: Bond Street

Type of attraction Collection of 19th-century Anglo-French art. **Admission** Free. **Hours** Daily, 10 a.m.–5 p.m. **When to go** Anytime. **Special comments** Good disabled access including an outdoor ramp, elevators to the upper floors, and mostly uncluttered rooms in which it is easy to maneuver. **Author's rating** ★★★. **How much time to allow** 1–3 hours.

DESCRIPTION AND COMMENTS The Wallace Collection is tucked away in a lovely Georgian square between Regent's and Hyde parks. The second Marquess of Hertford leased the home, now Hertford House, in 1797, for the excellent duck shooting for which the area was well known. Today, Hertford House holds the combined acquisitions of five generations of Marquesses and Marchionesses of Hertford.

The treasures are displayed throughout this French-style château's two main floors, and some of the objects are especially noteworthy. In various rooms of the house are Louis XIV furniture and art; European Renaissance armor; and some of the finest European paintings to be seen anywhere in the world. In what's known as the Long Picture Gallery hang works by such masters as Titian, Fragonard, Poussin, Rembrandt, Rubens, and Velázquez. Yet even if the house were empty of art, it would still be worth visiting to see the carved mantelpieces and elegant design of this architectural paragon of a bygone era.

Interesting temporary exhibits, educational facilities, and a restau-rant make the Wallace a great small museum.

TOURING TIPS Free public lectures and tours on various aspects of the col-lection are given on weekdays and weekends. Tours usually last about 45 minutes and provide good insight into the styles and history of the artists and their times. If you're on a tight schedule, call for touring times, or just arrive and wander on your own until a tour begins.

The Wellington Arch ★★

APPEAL BY AGE	PRESCHOOL –	GRADE SCHOOL ★	TEENS ★
YOUNG ADULTS ★	OVER 30 ★★		SENIORS ★★

In the middle of Hyde Park Corner roundabout, SW1; ☎ 0207-973-3494;

www.english-heritage.org.uk (search for "Wellington Arch");
tube: Hyde Park Corner

Type of attraction War memorial containing architectural and London-related items. **Admission** £3.20 for adults, £1.60 for children, £2.40 for seniors and students. **Hours** April–October, Wednesday–Sunday, 10 a.m.–5 p.m.; November–March, Wednesday–Sunday, 10 a.m.–4 p.m. **When to go** On a sunny day. **Special comments** The entrance is on the south side inside the arch: a small doorway with no banners or big signs announcing its position. You reach the island either through the subways or at the street crossing in front of the Lanesborough Hotel. **Author's rating** ★★. **How much time to allow** Depending upon your interest, 30 minutes–1 hour.

DESCRIPTION AND COMMENTS This is one of those specialty museums for either architectural historians or London obsessives. It was designed in the 1820s by Decimus Burton to commemorate England's victory over Napoléon, and was originally located at Buckingham Palace. The statue of Wellington that once topped the arch was replaced by the magnificent *Peace Descending on the Quadringa of War*, which gives Hyde Park Corner such a stunning aspect. It's a relatively inexpensive visit, and if you combine it with a jaunt to Apsley House across the way (see page 194), it will leave you feeling as if you know all there is to know about this particular corner of London. A couple of films that run in loops feature shots of Hyde Park Corner from the horse-and-cart era to the present. But the best thing about the arch is the view from the observation platforms. Seeing the tennis courts in the "backyard" of Buckingham Palace was a first for me; the views of the London Eye and Westminster are nice, too.

TOURING TIPS If you walk from Apsley House to the arch via the below-ground path (follow the signs for Green Park), you get the story of the Duke of Wellington recapitulated in tile on the walls, as well as an hour-to-hour description of the battle of Waterloo.

Westminster Abbey ★★★★

APPEAL BY AGE	PRESCHOOL ★	GRADE SCHOOL ★★★	TEENS ★★★★
YOUNG ADULTS ★★★★		OVER 30 ★★★★	SENIORS ★★★★

20 Dean's Yard, just off Parliament Square, Westminster, SW1;
☎ 0207-222-5152; www.westminster-abbey.org;
tube: St. James's Park or Westminster

Type of attraction England's historically most important church. **Admission** Free admission for services or to visit the nave and cloisters; royal chapels and tombs: £10 for adults; £7 for students, seniors, and children ages 11–16; £24 for families. Entry fee includes visit to the Westminster Abbey Museum. **Hours** Royal chapels are open Monday–Friday, 9:30 a.m.–3:45 p.m.; Saturday, 9:30 a.m.–1:45 p.m. (closing times given are for last admission). Museum hours are Monday–Saturday, 10 a.m.–3:30 p.m. The abbey is closed before special services and on Sunday (except for services), December 24–28, Good Friday, and Commonwealth Observance Day.

When to go Early mornings on weekdays, especially during the busy summer months. If you really hate crowds in close spaces, make a quick call to be sure you aren't arriving at the same time as 1 or 2 giant tour groups. **Special comments** Audio guides are available in eight languages for £4, Monday–Friday, 9:30 a.m.–3 p.m., and Saturday, 9:30 a.m.–1 p.m. Guided tours cost £5 plus entry fee. **Author's rating** ★★★★. **How much time to allow** 1½–2 hours for audio guides; 5 p.m. evensong lasts about 45 minutes.

DESCRIPTION AND COMMENTS Because the 900-year-old abbey is one of the most popular tourist sights in London, the key here is to avoid touring when it is mobbed. When you are moving in a sluggish single-file line through the chapels, you lose sight of the beauty of the interiors, the sheer numbers of people buried here (more than 3,000), and the incredible amount of history that this building has seen. Instead, try to start or end your day with a visit.

The main entrance to the abbey is through the North Transept, which gives a rather disjointed image of the abbey on first glance. As soon as you go in, head straight for the West Front door so you can see the abbey as it was meant to be viewed. From this perspective you can appreciate the majesty of the tallest nave in England (at 102 feet). In front of you is the Tomb of the Unknown Soldier, and to your right is a 14th-century portrait of Richard II, the oldest known image of a monarch painted from life. Heading toward the North Transept, also called Statesmen's Aisle, walk along Musician's Aisle until you reach the end, from which you can visit the smaller chapels of Elizabeth I and Innocents Corner. In the Henry VII Chapel you will see a fantastic display of English perpendicular architecture. The elaborately carved choir stalls here are dedicated to the Knights of the Order of the Bath, whose banners and helmets decorate the stalls.

As you head along the south aisle of the Henry VII Chapel, you can see the tombs of Mary, Queen of Scots (reburied in the abbey by her son, James I, and in unfortunate proximity to the tomb of Queen Elizabeth I); William and Mary; Queen Anne; and Charles II. Walking back toward the nave, you pass the Coronation Chair, the oak throne that has been used in nearly every royal coronation since then. Tucked under it for 700 years was the Stone of Scone (or Destiny), a prize stolen from Scotland and triumphantly displayed, but which in 1996 made the historic trip home to Edinburgh Castle. The South Transept of Poet's Corner contains the grave slabs of, among many others, Geoffrey Chaucer; Robert Browning; Alfred, Lord Tennyson; Charles Dickens; Rudyard Kipling; and Thomas Hardy, as well as impressive memorials to William Shakespeare and George Frideric Handel. The last person to have been buried here was Sir Laurence Olivier, who died in 1989.

After exploring the abbey's interior, be sure to find your way out to the cloisters, where the monks worked, studied, and lived. Visiting on a cold day gives you insight into the hearty constitution these early scholars must have had. Today, the cloisters contain a small shop and cafe. English Heritage also runs a small area just off the east cloisters. This includes the Chapter House, which was the original meeting place of the House of Commons until the time of Henry VIII, and the Pyx Chamber, which served as the sacristy and royal treasury of the earliest church (the *pyx* was the wooden box in which coins of the realm were kept).

TOURING TIPS Before you enter Westminster Abbey, take the time to enjoy its lesser-known neighbor. Many people head straight for the entrance and fail to even notice St. Margaret's Church (1523), which shares the churchyard. This tiny church's simple and uncluttered interior contrasts sharply with the abbey's appearance as an overflowing mausoleum.

> *unofficial* **TIP**
> Photography is not permitted in any part of Westminster Abbey at any time. Leave cameras and knapsacks at the hotel; the security checks will slow you down.

Our favorite way to experience Westminster Abbey is to arrive around 3:30 p.m. and then wander the cloisters (especially the lovely Little Cloister) before returning to the nave to wait for the 5 p.m. evensong. It is worth waiting at the head of the line (which starts to form at about 4:15 p.m.) as the first evensong attendees are seated in the stately choir stalls, where the atmosphere and view of the Westminster boys' choir are the best.

Windsor Castle ★★★★

APPEAL BY AGE	PRESCHOOL ★	GRADE SCHOOL ★★	TEENS ★★
YOUNG ADULTS ★★★★	OVER 30 ★★★★		SENIORS ★★★★

Windsor, Hertfordshire, outside London; ☎ 0207-766-7304; www.royal.gov.uk (click "Art & Residences," then "Royal Residences"); British Rail: Waterloo Station to Windsor Riverside

Type of attraction Queen Elizabeth II's country house, a mighty fine old castle. **Admission** £14.20 for adults, £12.70 for seniors and students, £8 for children ages 5–16, free for children under age 5, £36.50 for families (when the State Apartments are closed, admission to the castle is about half the quoted prices). **Hours** March–October, daily, 9:45 a.m.–5:15 p.m., last admission at 4 p.m.; November–February, daily, 9:45 a.m.–4:15 p.m., last admission at 3 p.m.; St. George's Chapel closed Sundays. **When to go** *Always* call first. Windsor Castle is subject to regular, annual, and sudden closures due to various royal ceremonies and events. The month of June is particularly susceptible to this sort of thing. Otherwise, go anytime, but show up early before the tour groups. **Special comments** Limited wheelchair access; lots of walking. **Author's rating** ★★★★. **How much time to allow** Half a day, plus time to wander in the town of Windsor (it can easily be a full day out).

DESCRIPTION AND COMMENTS In November 1992, the world saw news footage of Windsor Castle with smoke and flames pouring out from behind its crenellated keep, foremen running to and fro with priceless paintings and furniture. The fire destroyed more than 100 rooms, and it took five years to repair the terrible damage done to the ancient castle. Even if you don't normally like gaping at castles, you might make an exception of Windsor, for the restoration of the gutted and devastated castle—burned to its medieval stone walls, with roofs collapsed—is a marvel in itself, and the exhibition that describes the process is remarkable.

William the Conqueror, who also built the Tower of London, chose this site in Windsor for a fortress to protect London from western invaders. The castle has been continually inhabited for the past 900 years, and structural additions and deletions—many due to fire—have been made over that time.

It is presently a place of overwhelming splendor and tremendous riches, which might be best summed up by the awesome Queen Mary's Dolls' House. This is big luxury on a small scale: Sir Edward Lutyens designed the multistory dollhouse in the 1920s, and it took three years and 1,000 craftsmen and artists to complete it. It has running water, electric lights, a working elevator, actual miniature books, fine art and furniture, every kind of servant dressed in livery, carpet cleaners, tiny bottles filled with real wine, and even two tiny thrones with crowns on them.

Another attraction at Windsor is St. George's Chapel, started in 1475; it's a stunning example of great medieval architecture, with stained-glass windows of unparalleled beauty. Ten monarchs are buried within its precincts, inside stupendously crafted sarcophagi. The crests and banners of the Knights of the Order of the Garter are all about, and you get a feel for the ritual and pageantry that have propped up the ruling classes of England for centuries.

TOURING TIPS Make time to wander around the pleasant town of Windsor.

GREEN *and* PLEASANT LANDS:
Parks of London

ON WEEKENDS, WHEN THE MUSEUMS and tourist attractions are packed, go to the parks and enjoy the fruits of the British mania for nature, both tame and wild. Part of London's appeal as a city is its careful conservation of greenery—whether in the city's many squares or its enormous parks. For more information, contact the **Royal Parks** agency (☎ 0207-298-2000; **www.royalparks.gov.uk**).

Green Park
Between Piccadilly and Constitution Hill (between Hyde Park and St. James's Park); enter at Hyde Park Corner; tube: Green Park

Type of park Expanse of green lawn and old trees. **Admission** Free. **Hours** Daily, 5 a.m.–midnight. **When to go** Anytime; summer is especially pleasant, with deck chairs for rent and the local workers enjoying lunch in the sun.

DESCRIPTION AND COMMENTS Like St. James's Park, Green Park was reclaimed from the marshy meadows that surrounded the Tyburn River as it made its way south to the Thames. Originally purchased by Henry VIII for enclosed grazing and hunting, the land was made into a formal park in 1667. It became a favorite place for duels, lovers' trysts, military parades, ballooning, and people-watching. Green Park was opened to the public in 1826, and since then people have loved strolling along the east end of the

PARK	DESCRIPTION
Green Park	Between Hyde Park and St. James's Park (Mayfair)
Hampstead Heath	Enormous expanse of country (North London)
Highgate Cemetery	Atmospheric Victorian graveyard (North London)
Holland Park	54-acre landscaped park (West London)
Hyde Park	350-acre people's park (Knightsbridge to Bayswater)
Kensington Gardens	Gardens, walkways, fountains, palace (Kensington to Notting Hill)
Kew Gardens (The Royal Botanic Gardens)	Botanical extravaganza (West London)
Regent's Park	Elegant 490-acre park (North London)
Richmond Park	London's largest park (West London)
St. James's Park	Oldest royal park in London (Whitehall to Victoria)

park, admiring the fine mansions there and ending up at Buckingham Palace and St. James's Park. There are no flower beds here (they were allegedly removed by order of King Charles II's queen, in a jealous fury over some flower-related indiscretion of her philandering husband), but the lawn's crocuses in spring more than make up for that lack, and the 950 magnificent plane, oak, poplar, chestnut, and other varieties of trees are pleasing enough. You may rent chairs in the spring, summer, and fall. Refreshments are sold at the Buckingham Palace end of the park, and toilets can be found by the Green Park tube station.

Hampstead Heath
Hampstead; tube: Highgate, then take the number 210 bus to West Gate

Type of park Enormous expanse of country in Greater London area. **Admission** Free. **Hours** Daily, 8 a.m.–dusk. **When to go** Anytime; and be sure to check out Kenwood House (see page 215).

DESCRIPTION AND COMMENTS   Though Hampstead Heath is not a park per se, it is a most remarkable place nonetheless, covering a staggering 1,600 acres of undeveloped land and offering glorious views over London. There are hills, lakes, wild woods, and landscaped gardens. Hampstead Heath has so much to offer, not the least of which is Kenwood House, a stately home and fine-art museum at the northernmost top of the heath. The Men's and Ladies' Ponds for swimming in the summer are part of a set of lakes along the Highgate border of the heath. There's also a pond for model boats and one for bird-watching. The highest point is Parliament Hill, which is one of the best vantage points from which to watch Guy Fawkes Day fireworks. It's hard to remember you are in a metropolis in some parts of the heath, where mansions on hills look like castles and conspire to make you feel you are in a storybook. You can enjoy a good lunch at the Kenwood House's outdoor cafe in the summer or stay inside the cozy retreat in winter.

Highgate Cemetery

Located on either side of Swains Lane in Highgate, adjacent to Waterlow Park; ☎ 0208-340-1834; www.highgate-cemetery.org; tube: Archway (Northern line)

Type of park Overgrown Victorian graveyard. **Admission** West Cemetery (access is as part of guided tours only), £5; East Cemetery, £2; £1 photo permit (£5 for guided tour on weekends). **Hours** *West Cemetery:* April–September, tours are given Monday–Friday at 2 p.m.; Saturday and Sunday, 11 a.m.–4 p.m. hourly. October–March, tours are given on weekends only, hourly, 11 a.m.–3 p.m. *East Cemetery:* April–September, daily, 10 a.m.–5 p.m.; October–March, daily, 10 a.m.–4 p.m. **When to go** Anytime, although only 20 people are allowed on each weekend hourly tour. Also, the cemetery closes for funerals, so call before you set out.

DESCRIPTION AND COMMENTS Opened in 1839, Highgate Cemetery became *the* place for London's wealthy Victorian families, intellectuals, and artists to be buried. One of seven cemeteries designed and opened during this time of continued population growth, it remains one of the most elaborate and stirring examples of Victorian statuary excess. Overgrown and badly vandalized, the West Cemetery was closed in 1975 and is now diligently cared for by the Friends of Highgate Cemetery. Lush vegetation fills what was once an open, rolling hillside, and volunteers are kept busy clearing overgrown pathways and graves. The extensive foliage creates eerie shadows; these, combined with the cracked and toppled grave markers everywhere, give the cemetery its fabulously Gothic atmosphere, which makes it a favorite subject for black-and-white photographers. Tour guides are well versed on the many famous residents of the cemetery and relate a number of historical anecdotes that explain the elaborate and symbolic Victorian statuary. The cemetery's creepiest section includes the Egyptian Avenue and the Terrace Catacombs. Buried here are Karl Marx, Christina Rossetti, George Eliot, and other greats, all watched over by magnificent angels of stone.

You can wander on your own in the East Cemetery, but it holds a less eerie charm. Tours were offered for the first time in summer 2007, but on a very circumscribed schedule (check the Web site for further developments). The epitaphs in both cemeteries can be funny, sad, fascinating, and memorable. You need to pay a £1 fee to take photos. It's best to go early in the day, preferably on a day with some sun, as the shadowy effects can create artistic photographic images.

kids **Holland Park**

Holland Park, between Kensington and Shepherd's Bush; tube: Holland Park Avenue (then a ten-minute walk to park), or Kensington High Street and take westbound bus 9, 10, 27, 28, 31, or 49

Type of park 54-acre landscaped park with a Japanese garden. **Admission** Free. **Hours** Daily, 7:30 a.m.–dusk. **When to go** Anytime. Camellias, roses, irises, and other flowers blossom in spring; there are dahlias in summer and changing leaves in autumn.

DESCRIPTION AND COMMENTS Holland Park once housed the magnificent Holland House, more castle than mansion, where the literati of the early 19th century flocked to mix with politicians and aristocrats. The house was bombed during World War II, but fascinating monuments to the past remain: the surviving wings of Holland House, one of which houses a youth hostel; the wrought-iron gates that formed the entrance to the estate; the Orangery; the Ice House from the 1770s; the summer ballroom that is now a fancy, overpriced restaurant called The Belvedere; the old stables; and the many walks and enclosures that make up Holland Park.

There is a wonderful variety of flora and fauna here, thanks to Lord Holland—a venerable Victorian gentleman—and his great interest in planting and wildlife. He can be seen in the National Portrait Gallery, as styled by his good friend G. F. Watts. More than 60 wild bird species have been spotted in the park, along with peacocks, who share the Yucca Lawn with numerous rabbits. A serene Japanese garden is a wonderful addition to the park, and the over-the-top adventure playground is a must-stop for families with young children.

kids Hyde Park

Bordered by Park Lane, Knightsbridge, and Bayswater Road; tube: Hyde Park Corner

Type of park 350-acre park with expansive lawns. **Admission** Free. **Hours** Daily, dawn–dusk. **When to go** Anytime; there are roses in summer, crocuses and daffodils in spring, fall foliage in autumn, and atmospheric bare trees in winter.

DESCRIPTION AND COMMENTS During the dissolution of the monasteries in 1536, Henry VIII grabbed a hunk of land from the manor of Hyde and enclosed it for his hunting pleasure. James I opened the park to aristocrats, who took the air daily, a habit that persisted into the early 20th century with Rotten Row—originally *Route du Roi*, or King's Road—resounding with the beating of hooves and the chatter of the idle class. Kensington Gardens was once part of Hyde Park—and it is still separated only by a roadway—but in the mid-1700s, Queen Caroline appropriated 200 acres to make suitable gardens for Kensington Palace.

Hyde Park today is a wonderful escape from the high-decibel traffic noise of its bordering streets, Park Lane, Knightsbridge, and Bayswater. You enter the park from any of those streets, and within minutes of walking toward the Serpentine, the watery heart of the park, a delightful quiet descends. There's so much to do in Hyde Park: Besides the kids' playground that is conveniently located next to an exercise ring for the horses of the Queen's Guards, there are biking and in-line-skating paths through and around the edge of the park; cricket and soccer pitches abound; and for a fee you can use the tennis courts or paddle- and rowboats, or even ride along Rotten Row on horseback. During the warm months, rent a lawn chair for a picnic, or grab a bite to eat at the Lido or the cafeteria at the east end of the Serpentine. The Rose Walk by Hyde Park Corner is magnificent in June, and the Italian Piazza, with fountains and statues, is wonderful at all times. Speaker's Corner, at the northeast end of the park, is hopping on Sunday, often featuring born-again Christians—no longer preaching on soapboxes or overturned buckets—exhorting the heathen to repent. The Queen's Guards rehearse their ceremonies in Hyde Park, on the south by Prince's Gate. It's an astonishing thing to be walking through the park and suddenly be set upon by a regiment of plume-hatted horsemen.

By the Serpentine, you will find the problem-plagued memorial fountain to Diana, Princess of Wales, a round oval in the form of a ditch, filled with running water. Intended to be a place where children could splash and play, the memorial was closed a week after it opened because leaves were clogging it; then kids started slipping on the algae on the bottom, and before you knew it, there was a fence and guards all around trying to prevent lawsuits.

If you want to get from South Kensington to Piccadilly or from Knightsbridge to Marble Arch, do yourself a favor and walk through Hyde Park. Filled with memorials, statues, gardens, and nooks, it's a great place to explore.

kids Kensington Gardens
Kensington Gore; tube: Kensington High Street

Type of park Gardens, walkways, fountains, statues, and a palace. **Admission** Free. **Hours** Daily, dawn–dusk. **When to go** Anytime, especially when Kensington Palace and the Orangery are open. In spring and summer there is the flower walk and in fall, great foliage.

DESCRIPTION AND COMMENTS Kensington Palace will probably be forever associated with the extraordinary event of public mourning for Diana, Princess of Wales, in 1997, when in the days after her death in Paris people arrived and laid flowers in front of the palace that was her home. By week's end there was a sea of blooms and cellophane in front of the gates; the trees nearby were festooned with pictures, poems, and flowers; and candles burned everywhere. In the gardens' northwest corner is a permanent tribute to the "People's Princess": a state-of-the-art playground, always filled to capacity with happy children, with a pirate's ship to climb on. Diana's monument is by the Serpentine in Hyde Park (see previous profile).

By the side of the palace is a lovely sunken garden that can be looked at but not entered. In front of the Orangery, which is a good place for lunch or tea, are topiary trees that recall the Restoration; the Round Pond on which children have sailed toy boats for generations brings *Mary Poppins* vividly to mind. There is also a fanciful statue of Peter Pan; author J. M. Barrie lived right by the park, and the island in the middle of the lake is clearly the model for the Island of the Lost Boys. If you're in the mood for modern art, the Serpentine Gallery has changing exhibits, a bookshop, and a cafe.

Kew Gardens (The Royal Botanic Gardens)
Southwest London on the Thames; tube: Kew Gardens

Type of park Botanical extravaganza with 30,000 species of plants and flowers planted over 300 acres; follies, water features, and conservatories. **Admission** £12.25 for adults, £10.25 for seniors and students, free for children under age 17. **Hours** April–September, daily, 9:30 a.m.–6:30 p.m.; September and October, daily, 9:30 a.m.–5:30 p.m.; November–February, daily, 9:30 a.m.–3:45 p.m. See **www.kew.org** for more information. **When to go** Any time of the year, although summer is the best time to get your money's worth.

DESCRIPTION AND COMMENTS Developed in the 18th century for the pleasure of the monarchy, the Royal Botanic Gardens were perfectly timed to be the greenhouse for botanical specimens brought back by bold explorers such as Captain James Cook, who gave us the once-exotic geranium. Since then the gardens have gone from strength to strength as one of the world's most remarkable and serious centers of botanical research.

The enormous glass Palm House is a treasure trove of exotic tropical plants, with two levels on which to wander through the huge fronds and steamy atmosphere. A tropical aquarium in the basement furthers the impression that you're in a foreign clime. The Waterlily House is a testament to the wide-ranging journeys of the English explorers. The Temperate House is an even more impressive structure than the Palm House, twice as large and containing plants from each and every continent, some of which were planted at Kew in the middle of the 19th century.

Two art galleries, Kew Palace, a Japanese pagoda, and numerous follies and conservatories make the gardens an outing for the whole day.

 **Regent's Park**

At end of Baker Street; for south entrance, take the tube to Regent's Park or Baker Street

Type of park Playground of 490 acres with 6,000 trees. **Admission** Free. **Hours** Daily, 5 a.m.–dusk. **When to go** Anytime; there are flower gardens in spring and in summer, autumn leaves.

DESCRIPTION AND COMMENTS Named for George IV when he was mad King George III's understudy monarch, or acting regent, Regent's Park was designed by John Nash as part of the grand plan for a garden city of terraced mansions with bucolic views. Started in 1811, the scheme ultimately failed, with only a portion of the terrace houses sold (and those were said to be of substandard quality). However, by 1835, the park was flourishing and was opened to the public. Although the neighborhood may not have turned out exactly as Nash planned, it's still beautiful, and few can resist the grace and beauty of the classically inspired white mansions looking out on the magnificent landscape from Cumberland Terrace.

Within the park you will find the home of the U.S. ambassador to Great Britain, donated by heiress Barbara Hutton and suitably fenced and secured; a boating lake with ornamental bridges and an island; a lake by Queen Mary's Gardens, which include a waterfall and an open-air theater; a number of lodges; a mosque; Regent's Canal; and, of course, the London Zoo, which no child can resist. In the summer there are concerts on the Bandstand and plays at the theater, bird-watching walks, puppet shows, open-air festivals, and outdoor refreshments. The Royal Horse Artillery can be seen occasionally on Cumberland Green.

Richmond Park
Southwest London; tube: Richmond Station, then take bus 72, 265, 371, or 415

Type of park London's largest park, with deer and ancient oak trees. **Admission** Free. **Hours** Daily, 7 a.m.–dusk. **When to go** Anytime, though winter is cold.

DESCRIPTION AND COMMENTS Richmond Park is a gargantuan 2,470-acre preserve in which 400 fallow deer and 250 red deer live and graze. It is a piece of rolling countryside where wildlife still roams freely a stone's throw (7 miles from Charing Cross) from the center of a major metropolitan city. Richmond had its first royal connection with King Edward in the 13th century; Henry VII also took refuge there, and during his reign its name was changed from Sheen to Richmond. In 1625, surrounding lands were seized and walled to give King Charles I a country respite from the plague. His wall created much ill will among the neighbors, who had been used to grazing their animals on the land and using the common roads. The king tried to compensate by allowing foot traffic through the park and permitting the local poor to gather deadwood for their hearth fires. After the Civil War in the 1650s, the House of Commons voted to leave the park as undeveloped land, and so it has remained ever since. The royals and the public fought various skirmishes over right of access, disputes that were put to rest on the death of the last royal ranger, Edward VII, in 1910. Today, Richmond Park is a testament to the admirable environmental protectionism of the British and provides for visitors a wonderfully unchanged picture of a medieval hunting ground.

Refreshments are sold at the Pembroke Lodge Cafeteria from April through October, from 10 a.m. to 5:30 p.m. (till 7 p.m. on weekends).

unofficial **TIP**
Be aware that the deer in Richmond Park are not completely harmless and can be aggressive if they are bothered while tending young or during rutting season.

Many seasonal events take place in the park—check a newspaper or *Time Out London* to see when, what, and where. Pembroke Lodge often stages lunchtime concerts. It's a bit of a hike from central London, so you may need to budget a whole day for the outing. It's no fun for unwilling walkers.

 **St. James's Park**

East of Buckingham Palace gates; tube: St. James's Park

Type of park Oldest royal park in London. **Admission** Free. **Hours** Daily, 5 a.m.–midnight. **When to go** Any time is excellent, but summer is the most floral, and there are concerts on the bandstand between May and August.

DESCRIPTION AND COMMENTS St. James's is certainly London's most royal of parks, lying as it does between Buckingham and St. James's palaces. The views from Buckingham Palace and from the bridge in the middle of the lake are just magical—it looks like our fondest fantasy of an enchanted fairy-tale kingdom, with the turrets and steeples of White-hall in the distance. St. James's is the place to see birds; the famous pelicans are here, as well as a huge assortment of other unusual feathered friends, and kids have a great time spotting them. A leper hospital, called St. James's, was erected here in the 1400s. The Tyburn River flowed through this area, so the land was marshy and unsuitable for much more than hunting until King James I drained and planted the area as a pleasure garden, filling it with pelicans and other *rara aves*. He also established an exotic menagerie there, with crocodiles and elephants, for his court's entertainment. When Charles II returned from exile in France, he redesigned the park in a more formal French manner and opened it to the public. It was embraced enthusiastically and began its long life as a favorite spot for Londoners to meet and stroll—although it did have its darker days when muggers prowled the bushes, prostitutes conducted their business, and washerwomen dried their laundry on the shrubbery. Its appeal was upgraded when George IV rebuilt Buckingham House as a royal palace and had John Nash make the park a more natural-looking place.

There is a children's playground at the southwest corner of the park, and at the recently opened refreshment establishment, Inn the Park, you can either sit down for a table-service lunch or save some money and go for the cafeteria option next door (same food, big difference in price). Green-and-white-striped deck chairs can be rented by the hour between April and September.

GREENWICH PARK

IN 1863, AMERICAN AUTHOR NATHANIEL HAWTHORNE described the quiet town of Greenwich as "beautiful,—a spot where the art of man has conspired with Nature." No doubt he was thinking about how the green hills of **Greenwich Park** create an inspiring backdrop for Christopher Wren's splendid **Royal Naval College** and Inigo Jones's equally noble **Queen's House,** while Wren's other Greenwich project, the **Royal Observatory,** is serenely sited on the park's highest hill. Greenwich has undergone a recent renaissance, as rising rents in central London have pushed businesses and homeowners farther afield. Thanks to the Underground's Jubilee Line and Docklands Light Railway, Greenwich is one of the least difficult commutes from the outlying boroughs (you can even get a water taxi!). The streets are atmospheric and fun for strolling; whether you wander down historic **Croom's Hill** or past **St. Alfrege's** near the town center, the area has retained much of its cozy village atmosphere. Weekends bring craft and antiques lovers of all kinds to converge on the busy **Greenwich Market.**

Dating from 1433, Greenwich Park is steeped in royal history, and the Palace of Placentia once graced the riverside where the Royal Naval College now stands. Henry VIII and all three of his children—Mary I, Elizabeth I, and Edward IV—were born here. In 1616, Inigo Jones began building the Queen's House as a Palladian country home at the bottom of the park for Charles II's wife, Henrietta Maria; Christopher Wren followed this project with the hilltop observatory and the Naval College, which elegantly frames the Queen's House today. Walk the Greenwich foot tunnel under the Thames (a five- to ten-minute trek) for a perfect view of Greenwich from the opposite bank of the river. You can catch the Docklands Light Railway (DLR) from the Island Gardens station nearby. Just north of the town center is the colossal **O$_2$ Centre** (formerly the Millennium Dome), which is London's newest megavenue for concerts, games, and conventions. Many of the athletic events of the 2012 Summer Olympics will take place in this area, adding quite a bit of modern significance to this old London village.

GETTING THERE

A FEW MILES DOWNRIVER FROM LONDON, Greenwich makes a delightful day trip. The town center houses a wide variety of shops as well as a diverse selection of restaurants, from Vietnamese to Mexican to English pub food. On weekends, the Greenwich Market offers craft stalls, a flea market, and a secondhand-book market.

To get to Greenwich, catch Docklands Light Railway, a fully automated and electric overland-tram-car type of transport that leaves from Bank Street or Tower Hill. The trip takes about 20 minutes from either station and in the summer includes a recording that guides you through the wharfs and docks of London's East End, leaving you at the Greenwich Pier or the *Cutty Sark.* Alternatively, take the Underground's Jubilee Line to the Cutty Sark station. Another, more leisurely and entertaining travel option is the guided riverboat ride along the Thames, past views of St. Paul's Cathedral, Tower Bridge, and Docklands. Boats leave from Westminster, Charing Cross, and Tower Pier for Greenwich approximately every 45 minutes; the trip takes 40 minutes to an hour, depending on where you embark. For more information, contact **Thames Executive Charters** (☎ 0134-232-2440; **www.tfl.gov.uk** [click on "River" and then "River Timetables"]).

Finally, you can contact the **Greenwich Tourist Information Centre** (☎ 0870-608-2000; **www.greenwich.gov.uk** [click on "Visit Greenwich"]) or stop by in person at 46 Greenwich Church Street, London, SE10, with questions about guided tours in Greenwich, special events, or any additional information you may need.

PART SEVEN

CHILDREN'S LONDON

LONDON *with* KIDS

LONDON IS A FANTASTIC CITY FOR CHILDREN of all ages, with so much to appreciate. And precisely because it has so much to offer, trying to plan your London trip can be a daunting task. It can also be frustrating to find out that your children are tired or simply uninterested in the sights that excite you. Fortunately, there's a great solution: a bus tour, a boat tour, an amphibious tour, or a private tour guide. These four methods of sightseeing provide a convenient overview of London, allowing you to figure out what merits your attention and time.

BUS TOURS Double-decker-bus tickets are good for 24 hours and allow you to hop on and off along a variety of routes. Two tour-bus companies duke it out in the London tourist market: the **Big Bus Company** (☎ 0207-233-9533; **www.bigbus.co.uk**) and the **Original London Sightseeing Tour** (☎ 0208-877-1722; **www.theoriginaltour.com/kids_club**). The latter is the slightly more child-friendly of the two, offering complimentary kids' packs. Both the Big Bus and Original London sell tickets for London attractions, and both offer complimentary river cruises. The biggest drawback to the bus tours is the long queuing at popular stops on weekends or on hot days.

Queues tend not to be a problem, however, on **Transport for London** public buses, which provide another, much more economical option. Check out the **London for Free** Web site (**www.londonforfree .net/bustour/bustour.shtml**) for a suggested route and itinerary. Children age 15 and under ride free, but it can get tricky for teens without identification, so bring copies of their passports. Adults will need to purchase a daily bus pass or an **Oyster card** (see Part Five, Getting Around, for more information).

BOAT CRUISES **City Cruises** (☎ 0207-740-0400; **www.citycruises.com**) offers excursions from 20 minutes to 2½ hours long. They also offer a hop-on, hop-off River Red Rover ticket similar to the tour buses', so you can get on and off at your leisure. Another convenient river cruise is available at the **London Eye** (☎ 0870-500-0600; **www.london eye.com**). The **Tate to Tate** river shuttle (☎ 0207-887-8888; **www .tate.org.uk/tatetotate**) is an economical way to travel the Thames, running daily between the Tate Britain (Millbank) and Tate Modern (Bankside) museums, with a stop at the London Eye (Waterloo) All of these river-cruising options are available year-round, but check schedules as they are revised seasonally.

AMPHIBIOUS TOURS **Duck Tours** (☎ 0207-928-3132; **www.londonduck-tours.co.uk**) have made it across the pond. The converted military vehicles known as duck boats are in fact more indigenous to London than the States, having been used to cross the English Channel in the D-Day landings. Combination boat-bus tours start behind the London Eye for a road trip around the City of Westminster before diving into the Thames and returning to the Eye.

TOUR GUIDES These are the most expensive option but easily the most convenient when you're traveling with kids. A tour guide can usually cater to your itinerary and can buy tickets for you as well; plus, most guides will pick you up from and drop you back off at your hotel. Guide services can also be arranged at the concierge desks of most hotels, so don't forget to check out pricing and packages with your hotel when you make a reservation. To get additional information online, visit **www.londontourguides.com** or **www.blue-badge-guides.com**.

PLANNING *and* TOURING TIPS

THE BRILLIANT "LONDON FOR FAMILIES" brochure from **London Town.com** provides a kid's-eye view of London and its attractions (download at **www.londontown.com/London_for_Families.pdf**), while the Web site **www.whatson4kids.com** is dedicated solely to children's activities in London. Here are a few more tips to bear in mind when planning a vacation with little (and not-so-little) ones:

unofficial **TIP**
If your school-age children can't afford to miss any school, take your vacation as soon as the school year ends in June or before school starts in September.

BEFORE YOUR TRIP
Time of Year to Visit

If there's any way to swing it, avoid the crowded summer months. Try to go between late September and November or between early April and mid-June. If you have children of varying ages and your school-age kids are good students, consider taking the older ones out of school so you can visit during the less expensive, less congested off-season. Arrange special study assignments relating to the many educational aspects of London.

Where to Stay

The best area to stay when you're carting kids around is near a park—**Hyde Park, Holland Park,** and **Kensington Gardens** are good choices. Kids who complain about tired feet and hunger in a museum will perk up amazingly when they see a swing set, have some room to run wild, or can watch horsies ride by. South Kensington works out well because of its proximity to Hyde Park, Kensington Gardens, and the "big three": the Victoria and Albert Museum, Science Museum, and Natural History Museum.

With small children, it's good to plan ahead, but as any parent of under-5s knows, you also need to be extremely flexible. Try to get a hotel within a few minutes' walk to a tube station. Naps and relief from the frenetic pace of touring London are indispensable. Even if you do get some good downtime in a park, there is no true substitute for returning to the familiarity and security of your own hotel. Children too large to sleep in a stroller will relax and revive better if you get them back to their room.

unofficial **TIP**
The health club attached to the Rembrandt Hotel (see page 120) has a perfect pool for children, as well as designated hours for their splash-time amusement. (Ask about times and restrictions on kids in the pool.)

You may want to choose a hotel that has a swimming pool. A lot of visitors to London assume that, like those in so many American destinations, the big London hotels will have pools. Nothing could be further from the truth. A few of the expensive ones do, but more to the point, many hotels can steer you to a public pool or have some arrangement with a health club. Call ahead to find out if there are any age restrictions on swimming. A pool can be a lifesaver for both you and your kids, keeping everyone happily busy and healthily exercising in between the sightseeing.

Setting Limits and Making Plans

The best way to avoid arguments and disappointments is to develop a (flexible) game plan before you go. Establish some general guidelines for each day, and try to get everybody excited about them. Be sure to include the following:

1. Wake-up time and breakfast plans.
2. Departure times for the parts of London you plan to explore.
3. Necessary items to take.
4. A policy for splitting up the group or for staying together.
5. A clearly understood strategy for what to do if the group gets separated or someone becomes lost.
6. Estimates of morning touring time, including fallback plans in case an attraction is too crowded or unexpectedly closed.
7. A policy on what you can afford for snacks, lunch, and refreshments. This is a very important consideration in this very expensive city.
8. A target time for returning to your hotel for a rest.

9. If you rest, a target time for resuming touring and for how late you will stay out.

10. Plans for dinner.

11. A policy for shopping and buying souvenirs. (Be prepared to go over your original budget.)

Recommended Projects

A "LONDON BOOK" A great idea to get the kids paying attention and having fun is to start a "London book" before you even leave. Pick out a blank book big enough to paste lots of things in (but not so huge as to waste pages, as often happens), and write down the itinerary; paste in pictures of planes, get the airline cabin crew to sign it, and so on. Then, everywhere you go, collect stubs and pamphlets, and take plenty of photos. Get film or digital cards developed at any quickie photo lab, and spend the evening helping with the scrapbook. Drawings, poems, thoughts, a leaf from Holland Park, a feather from the Serpentine—all these things can make a beautiful scrapbook that children will always love to look through. Get disposable cameras so your children can take their own photos; you'll be surprised at how much more they'll go in for sightseeing when it has such a personal creative purpose.

LONDON STICKER BOOKS These are considerably easier to find in England (at Waterstone's bookshops and the Natural History Museum gift store) than in the States, but *The Ultimate London Sticker Book* and *The Usborne London Sticker Book* are both available at Amazon.com. Not only are these fun in and of themselves, but your kids can use the stickers to decorate their own scrapbooks or make postcards home more colorful.

Recommended Movies

- **All ages** *101 Dalmatians* (*not* the animated one)
- **Ages 4+** *Mary Poppins, The Little Princess* (the Shirley Temple version)
- **Ages 8+** *The Adventures of Sherlock Holmes*
- **Ages 12+** *Oliver!* (the 1968 musical, *not* the dark Roman Polanski film *Oliver Twist* from 2005), *The Prince and the Pauper, A Christmas Carol* (the Muppets version is less scary than the old one with Alistair Sim), *Princess Caribou*

Recommended Books

- **Ages 0–7** *Katie in London* by James Mayhew, *Madeline in London* by Ludwig Bemelmans, *This Is London* by Miroslav Sasek
- **Ages 5–8** *The Story of London* by Richard Brassey, *The Great Fire of London (How Do We Know About?)* by Deborah Fox
- **Ages 7+** Terry Deary's *Horrible Histories* series (*Cruel Kings and Mean Queens, Loathsome London,* etc.), *The Story of London: From Roman Capital to Capital City* by Jacqui Bailey and Christopher Maynard
- **Ages 9+** *Bloody Tower: The Diary of Tilly Middleton, London 1553–1559* by Valerie Wilding; *London Eye Mystery* by Siobhan Dowd

PACKING

STROLLERS You may be able to check in your stroller at the gate, but don't think you'll see it again immediately upon exiting the plane. Unless you were able to bring your stroller on board, it won't be accessible until baggage claim. So be prepared for toddlers to walk or be carried in your arms, and bring baby carriers on the planes for infants.

unofficial **TIP**
At this time, London airports are still extremely careful with handheld luggage. Give yourself time and leftover pounds to buy formula, milk, or other liquid beverages after you pass security. Also, make sure you can get by with a single carry-on (purses count as one bag) when you leave England. You may have been allowed more than one when you departed for London, but for now you may have to pare down to one on your trip out of the U.K. (rules vary from airline to airline).

WHEELED CARRY-ONS This type of luggage works really well on flat surfaces, not so well on stairs. Many airplanes that arrive in London land on the tarmac and deplane with mobile stairs, and you must ride a bus to the terminal. Take this into consideration when packing your carry-ons.

220-VOLT VS. 110-VOLT Everything from baby monitors to rechargeable batteries for items like Game Boys and iPods can be affected by the difference in voltage. Check your electrical appliances before you arrive, and make sure to bring appropriate adapters or transformers. At most hotels you can borrow these, but it's reassuring to know that you're covered in case you can't. (See Part 2, Planning Your Visit, for more information.)

FORMULA The kind of baby formula available in your country will most likely differ from the kind sold in the United Kingdom. Bring your infant's favorite powdered version to be safe; if that's impractical, buy several varieties after you land, and conduct a "taste test" to figure out which one your baby likes best.

PACIFIERS Bring extras, as you may not find your child's brand of choice once you arrive. Pacifier cords ("binky cords") are also helpful.

DVDS AND DVD PLAYERS These make fantastic traveling companions and can usually be recharged on 110- or 220-volt current (don't forget to bring a plug adapter). Be aware, though, that if you bring your own player or laptop to London and you decide to rent DVDs while you're here, your equipment needs to be multiregion or able to accept Region 2 discs. Likewise, if you bring DVDs from home and pop them in a hotel or rental player, they may not work unless they're Region 2.

unofficial **TIP**
The best advice: if you bring your own DVD player, bring your own DVDs; otherwise, rent or buy secondhand Region 2 discs in London for use in hotel players.

HEALTH AND MEDICAL CARE If you have a child who requires medication, pack plenty of it and bring it on the plane in a carry-on bag. A bottle of liquid Dramamine will come in handy to fight off motion sickness, which can affect kids who are normally fine in a car but may get sick in a plane, train, or boat.

A small first-aid kit, available at most pharmacies, will handle most minor cuts, scrapes, and splinters, and is easy to pack. Grown-up and children's aspirin or Tylenol, a thermometer, arnica cream (for bruises and scrapes), teething gel, cough syrup, baby wipes, a plastic spoon, a battery-powered night-light, and pacifiers will round out a small kit of health-related items for people traveling with children or infants. in England, the most popular paracetamol (acetaminophen, aka Tylenol) elixir for infants is called Calpol or Panadol Junior and is sold everywhere. Bring copies of your children's medical insurance and immunization records when you travel, too.

DOCUMENTS Make copies of your children's passports, and store them in a safe place. Additionally, if your caregiver is traveling solo with your children, you should prepare a notarized letter stating that the caregiver has permission to travel with your children.

DURING YOUR TRIP

RAIN, SUNBURN, AND DEHYDRATION London's weather is changeable. Although it's not often terribly hot, it can get quite warm in the sun, and you can get a beauty of a sunburn. Carry a small bottle of sunscreen, or smear some on before you go out—and don't forget to slather the skin you might be exposing once you shed some of your layers of clothes. Remember to take a bottle of water to rehydrate the happy campers. Rain is the biggest surprise in London; you never know when it's going to come, but chances are it will, if only for a sprinkle. When dressing the kids to go out, layering is advisable.

BLISTERS AND SORE FEET These are common complaints for visitors of all ages, so wear comfortable, well-broken-in shoes. If you or your children are unusually susceptible to blisters, carry some precut moleskin bandages, which offer the best possible protection and won't sweat off. When you feel a hot spot, stop, air out your foot, and place a bandage over the area before a blister forms. **Dr. Scholl's** moleskins are available at many London pharmacies, as are **Compeed Blister Plasters.** The latter are a bit expensive, but they offer great blister protection and speed up healing, too. Sometimes small children won't tell their parents about a developing blister until it's too late, so check out your preschooler's feet a couple of times a day—this penny's worth of prevention will be worth many pounds of cure to you and them.

unofficial **TIP**
The best and lightest rain protection is a plastic poncho; you can carry a few and not have as much weight or bulk as with a couple of umbrellas.

IF YOU BECOME SEPARATED Before venturing out of your hotel room, sit down with your kids and discuss what they should do if they get separated from you while touring a museum or attraction. Tell them to find a uniformed guard and ask for help. Point out that the main entrances of most London attractions have information desks where they should go if they get lost.

Dress smaller kids in distinctive colors so you can find them with a quick scanning. It is also prudent to attach a label to each child's shirt indicating his or her name, your name, and the name of your hotel or the name and address of a local friend in London. A less elegant solution is to write your child's name and other relevant information on a strip of masking tape. Hotel-security professionals suggest printing the info in small letters and affixing the tape to the outside of the child's shirt five inches or so below the armpit.

AGE CONSIDERATIONS Many of London's attractions are clearly geared toward older kids or adults. A parent's challenge while traveling is to make excursions appealing to all the ages in your group. Achieving this goal is pretty easy at a zoo or park playground, but at some of the kiddie-style attractions, you may need to split up and rendezvous later at exhibits that everyone can enjoy. The more-adult-oriented museums may require orchestrating some counting games or "I Spy" for the toddlers.

> *unofficial* **TIP**
> Almost every major museum in London has kids' activity days, especially during the summer.

REST AND RELAXATION Building in rest time is very important to ensure that the remainder of your vacation runs smoothly. It is also important when you consider ticket prices for some of the attractions—nothing is worse than, say, shelling out numerous pounds for a family of four at the London Zoo only to find that the kids can't walk another step, or hiring a babysitter for the evening to catch the West End play you always wanted to see and then falling asleep during the performance. Tour in the early morning, and return to your hotel midday for lunch and possibly a lie-down.

Don't pooh-pooh jet lag: children seem to suffer from it less than the adults, but they can be thrown off-kilter by the time change, the travel, and the foreign surroundings.

Try to get kids adjusted to the time change by exposing them to plenty of sunlight and not letting them nap too long during the day. The best way to quickly acclimate to a new time zone is to wake up at the same time you wake up at home, even though 7:30 a.m. in London may be "really" midnight for your body. Remember—it usually takes one day to recover from each hour of time change.

GETTING AROUND Probably the most fun way to do so is to take a double-decker bus. Sitting on the top deck of a double-decker is a great way to see London, as it affords plenty of sights and stimulation for the kids. The problem with buses used to be is that you might get stuck in traffic. However, since Ken Livingstone became mayor, the dedicated "bus lanes" are ubiquitous, making bus travel a lot quicker.

> *unofficial* **TIP**
> Neglecting to relax and unwind is the surest way to get the whole family in a snit and ruin the day.

The old Routemaster double-deckers have been mostly phased out in favor of modern, wheelchair- and stroller-friendly single-level and double-decker buses. If you feel nostalgic, you can still find Routemaster buses on two specially designed Heritage Routes: **Route 9** (Royal Albert Hall–Hyde Park Corner–Piccadilly Circus–Trafalgar Square–Strand–Aldwych) and **Route 15** (Trafalgar Square–Strand–Aldwych–Fleet Street–Cannon Street–Monument–Tower Hill).

unofficial **TIP**
Buses and tube trains have clearly indicated priority seating for the elderly, the handicapped, or those with small children. So if you have two small kids in tow and no one has offered you a seat, you have every right to ask someone to move.

The quickest way to get around is on the tube. However, the system is neither disabled- nor stroller-friendly. Strollers can be negotiated on the escalators, but there are a lot of stairs to deal with when changing trains. This is fine if there are two or more adults in your group, but if you're alone you could be left struggling to get up and down the stairs. You'd be surprised how many other passengers are quick to scurry by rather than offer a helping hand. And If you're expecting, don't expect people to surrender their seats to you. Consult Transport for London's online **Journey Planner** (**journeyplanner.tfl.gov.uk**) for help in choosing the best route with the fewest possible problems.

unofficial **TIP**
Unfortunately, most bus conductors will not take your word as proof of your teen's age.

Travel is free for children age 5 years and under on all buses, tubes, and local trains. Under-16s ride free on buses and pay children's fares on other forms of transport until 10 p.m., after which time they pay adult fares. Because it can be hard for a bus conductor to gauge how old an adolescent is, 14- and 15-year-olds are required to produce proof of age—a passport or copy of one—or a Child Photocard, which can be obtained from any post office. Bring a passport-sized photo and proof of age, and you'll be good to go.

For short hops with the kids, a black cab might be the best idea (if walking is not an option, of course). Children love the jump seats, and most strollers can fit into these spacious cabs with their passengers undisturbed. Black cabs can even accommodate most tandem strollers (but not the side-by-side models).

unofficial **TIP**
A caveat: during the day, traffic can be bad in the central areas (Oxford Street, Marble Arch, Covent Garden, Piccadilly, Bayswater, Knightsbridge, Chelsea, and Kensington), and taxis are not cheap.

TICKETS One perk of traveling in London with toddlers is that under-3s or under-5s can accompany adults for free at most attractions that charge admission. However, buying tickets for a family quickly adds up, even with toddlers. The cost of some attractions can be alleviated somewhat with the purchase of a family ticket for two adults and two children.

If you know your travel plans will involve many of the charging attractions, consider buying a

London Pass (www.londonpass.com), which gets you free priority entry into 56 such attractions. The pass is available in one-, two-, three-, and six-day adult and child versions; for a few extra pounds, you can buy passes that also include free travel on London public transport.

RECOMMENDED ATTRACTIONS *and* ITINERARIES

THE LISTS BELOW INCLUDE ONLY A LOOSE AGE GUIDE—obviously, some kids will enjoy certain attractions more than others. We've left out some of the activities that one can do in any city, such as visiting arcades and amusement parks.

THE TOP TEN MOST POPULAR SIGHTS FOR CHILDREN

1. **The British Airways London Eye** (all ages; 45-minute "flights")
   Kids' tip: Splurge on the Fast Track tickets if traveling with small children. These tickets enable you to essentially jump the queue, and they include a guidebook in the price (£25, free for kids under age 5). Book Fast Track tickets 14 hours in advance, or call ☎ 0870-800-0500 the day of your visit to check availability.

2. **Science Museum** (all ages) ***Kids' tip:*** Under-5s will enjoy The Garden in the basement. The Pattern Pod is also a fun spot for toddlers through 8-year-olds; it's somewhat hidden, tucked behind the IMAX ticket entrance. Book early for IMAX, especially on rainy days, summer months, and holidays.

3. **London Aquarium** (all ages) ***Kids' tip:*** Toddlers and preschoolers are very entertained here. Older kids might find this aquarium unexceptional but will enjoy the ray-petting tank.

4. **Natural History Museum** (all ages) ***Kids' tip:*** Be prepared to queue for the dinosaur gallery. If there are long lines at the main entrance on Cromwell Road, head around the corner to the side entrance on Exhibition Road.

5. **London Zoo** (all ages) ***Kids' tip:*** Don't miss the newly opened Gorilla Kingdom, a modern zoological enclosure that has brought London's 180-year-old zoo into the 21st century. Buy tickets in advance during the summer and on weekends, when there are almost always queues.

6. **Tower of London** (over-5s) ***Kids' tip:*** The tower's size is daunting, so check out the Historic Royal Palaces Web site (**www.hrp.org.uk/Tower OfLondon/planyourvisit/suggesteditineries.aspx**) to help you choose what you want to see most. Under-5s will usually be entertained by the ravens that hang out near the White Tower.

7. **HMS *Belfast*** (over-5s, although toddlers treat it as an adventure!)
   Kids' tip: The tours can take 1½–2 hours, so plan accordingly.

8. **London Transport Museum** (all ages, even teens)

Kids' tip: This museum was a hit before its refurbishment and has improved considerably since it reopened in late 2007.

9. **Royal Observatory** (over-5s) *Kids' tip:* Smaller children can have a hard time reclining their chairs to truly appreciate the show at the Peter Harrison Planetarium.

10. **V&A Museum of Childhood** (under-10s) *Kids' tip:* Pick up a cutout activity book or old-fashioned scrapbook at the gift shop for playtime fun in the hotel room.

ALSO SEE . . .

1. **Royal Mews** (all ages) *Kids' tip:* You may want to call first (☎ 0207-766-7302) to see if the Cleveland Bays and Windsor Grays will be in the stables during your visit.

2. **British Museum** (over-5s) *Kids' tip:* Check out the children's gift shop for inexpensive treasures to bring home.

3. **Tower Bridge Exhibition** (toddlers to teens) *Kids' tip:* Check out the Tower Bridge Web site (**www.towerbridge.org.uk/TowerBridge/ English/BridgeLifts/schedule.htm**) to see if you can schedule your visit when the bascules are raised or lowered.

4. **London Dungeon** (best for gore-loving adolescents) *Kids' tip:* Children must be more than 1.2 meters (about 4 feet) tall to ride the newly opened Extremis: Drop Ride to Doom.

5. All the military museums for children of that bent: the **Cabinet War Rooms, Imperial War Museum, Guards Museum, National Army Museum,** and the **Royal Air Force Museum** (all ages) *Kids' tip:* These will appeal to mostly over-5s, although the Imperial War Museum allows tiny ones running-around space and buttons to press at random.

6. **South Bank Centre** (all ages) *Kids' tip:* See "Best Day Out for all the Family," next page.

7. **Museum of London** (grade-school age) *Kids' tip:* The "London's Burning" special exhibit (**www.museumoflondon.org.uk/English/Events Exhibitions/Special/LondonsBurning**) explores the most famous disaster in London's history; try to catch it before it departs in 2009.

8. **Shakespeare's Globe Theatre** (ages 8–12) *Kids' tip:* "Childsplay" workshops are held some Saturdays at 1:30 p.m. Call ☎ 0207-401-9919 for bookings, or visit **www.shakespearesglobe.org/calendar ofevents/alleducationevents** for dates.

9. **The Old Operating Theatre, Museum, and Herb Garret** (ages 8–12) *Kids' tip:* Not for the squeamish, and probably not very entertaining for under-5s, but fabulous for those darkling tweenies hungry for information and historical artifacts.

10. **V&A Theatre Collections** (over-5s) *Kids' tip:* This brand-new facility (opened in November 2007) offers hands-on exhibits for kids; call or check the Web site (**www.vam.ac.uk/tco**) for more information.

BEST DAY OUT FOR ALL THE FAMILY
The South Bank

This stretch of the south bank of the River Thames provides something for the whole family: traffic-free outdoor and indoor space for children to run around in; film, theater, and music; an art gallery; street artists; restaurants; a classic view of the river and the architectural visions that line its banks; the **London Eye; Shakespeare's Globe; Tate Modern;** the **Oxo Tower;** and much, much more.

BEFORE YOU LEAVE If you're in London during the summer, phone ahead and plan your visit to coincide with a free outdoor-theater event in the **National Theatre Square** behind the National Theatre building (☎ 0207-452-3400); you can also prebook tickets for the London Eye online (**www.londoneye.com**) or by calling ☎ 0870-500-0600.

GETTING THERE Take the Underground (or overground) train to Waterloo, and follow the exit signs to the South Bank.

CHOOSE TWO OR THREE OF THE FOLLOWING ACTIVITIES:

- Head straight for the **London Eye.** If you've booked a ride on the Eye or the queues don't look too long, this could be a good time to take your unmissable "flight." **The London Aquarium** is to your left if you're facing the river.

- As you head east along the river bank, there are often street artists and stalls lining the **pedestrian river path.** You'll enjoy the riverside views, and it's only a few minutes before you come across the Brutalist 1960s architecture for which the South Bank Centre is infamous. Throughout the year, the **Royal Festival Hall** has free lunchtime foyer music (12:30 p.m. to 2 p.m.), ranging from solo recitals to jazz bands, in a large, open space in which children can move and even run around. This way, adults get to snatch a bit of culture (with a glass of wine or bowl of pasta from the bar or cafe) without making the kids sit still. If you have to leave because of some small rebellion from the little ones, at least you haven't wasted the price of a concert ticket.

- Peruse the **secondhand-book stalls** under the bridge in front of the National Film Theatre. The food in the NFT cafe is reasonable, and with outdoor seating, this can be an ideal place for a snack.

- Next is the National Theatre, and on your right is **National Theatre Square,** where free outdoor performances take place in the summer months. This spot is perfect for families since behind the seating is an installation that looks like a group of rocks, which children love to climb on. However, if you have under-3s with you, it's best to skip this and move on along the river.

- **Gabriel's Wharf** is a row of old buildings that have been turned into an arty enclave. It's a wonderful place for families, because it's a fairly enclosed space and feels very child-friendly; has crafty shops sporting handmade clothes, paintings, and jewelry; and offers a choice of restaurants for lunch. A wood-carving shop called **Noah's Ark** leaves its creations out in the middle of the square, and toddlers love to climb and ride on them, which is allowed. The pizza restaurant has high chairs.

- Next to Gabriel's Wharf is a small grassed area used for the annual **Coin Street Festival,** a culturally themed series of free events taking place throughout the summer, involving music, dance, street theater, fairground rides, and food (☎ 0207-401-2255).

- Then comes the **Oxo Tower:** take the lift to the eighth floor; turn right out of the lift and then right again, passing through the back of the restaurant, and step out onto the observation gallery, which offers breathtaking views of London. Formerly a turn-of-the-century power station, the Oxo Tower now houses art galleries, shops, and retail studio space where the public can watch designers at work.

- Making your way farther east along the South Bank, you'll come across **Shakespeare's Globe Theatre,** which offers tours; the **Tate Modern,** which offers children's activities (and a huge space to run around in); and the **Millennium Footbridge,** which affords wonderful views up and down the river and leads to **St. Paul's Cathedral.** Be warned, however, that by this time small legs will be aching, and there's still the walk back to Waterloo Station, unless you want to continue to London Bridge and hail a taxicab. If it is a Thursday, Friday, or Saturday and you're hungry, stop at London's oldest food market, the **Borough Market,** before you board a cab or the tube.

SERVICES *for* FAMILIES

RENTAL EQUIPMENT AND CHILD CARE

CHELSEA BABY HIRE (☎ 0208-789-9673; **www.chelseababyhire.co.uk**) and **Nappy Express** (☎ 0208-361-4040; **www.nappyexpress.co.uk**) rent cribs, high chairs, and double strollers (or buggies, as they're known here), along with toys, household products, and more.

Most hotels will be able arrange a babysitter to look after the children in your hotel room. You might also try a child-care service, such as **Sitters** (toll free from the United Kingdom, ☎ 0800-389-0038; outside the U.K., ☎ +44-192-347-5539; **www.babysitter.co.uk**). You'll pay a three-month membership fee of £12.75 upon completing your first booking, a booking fee of £4, and an hourly fee that starts at £5.50. (Sitters recently merged with Childminders of London, and now they only offer an evening service.) **Universal Aunts** (☎ 0207-738-8937; **www.universalaunts.co.uk**) can deal with any domestic need or crisis, as a good auntie should, including short-term babysitting. **Hopes and Dreams Montessori Nursery School** (☎ 0207-833-9388; **www.hopesand dreams.co.uk**), a babysitting and nanny agency, also operates a day nursery for kids, complete with organic food and big fun.

PARKS AND PLAYGROUNDS

BATTERSEA PARK (Albert Bridge Road, Battersea, SW11; tube: Sloane Square, then bus 19 or 137) This park has a boating lake, an adventure playground, and a small art gallery, plus a refurbished children's zoo with well-cared-for animals (and some new ones your kids can pet). One of the best ways to tour this 200-acre-plus park is from a recumbent bicycle; rentals are available at **London Recumbents** (Ranger's Yard, Dulwich Park, SE21 7BQ; ☎ 0208-299-6636; **www.londonrecumbents .co.uk**). If you and your family have fun on these cycles, you may want to take them for a spin at **Dulwich Park,** too.

CORAM FIELDS (93 Guildford Street, Bloomsbury, WC1; ☎ 0207-837-6138; tube: Russell Square) This famous playground only allows adults with an accompanying child—and they mean it. Built in 1936 on the site of the old foundling hospital, it's got a wide variety of play equipment to suit all ages. Animals are on view, and it's open 9 a.m. to dusk.

HAMPSTEAD HEATH (Highgate Road, Camden, NW3; ☎ 0207-482-7073; (tube: Hampstead or Highgate) By far the most natural of all the open spaces in London, this park is dotted with woods, meadows, rivers, hills, and more than 30 ponds, 3 of which are used for swimming and some of which even allow fishing. The most popular part of Hampstead Heath is **Parliament Hill,** from which you will see the familiar panoramas of London, from the distant Canary Wharf to the BT Tower, with St. Paul's and skyscrapers from The City in between. The fields on the summit of Parliament Hill also provide one of the best kite-flying spots in London.

HOLLAND PARK (tube: Holland Park) Has peacocks and an impressive multilevel adventure playground with an area for kids under age 8.

HYDE PARK (tube: High Street Kensington) There's a nice playground on the south side of the park near the riding ring, where you may see the Queen's Horse Guards exercising their steeds (not to mention the regular traffic of folks on horseback). The swans and ducks of Hyde Park's famous **Serpentine** happily share the lake with the new **Serpentine Solar Shuttle** as well as rowboats and pedalos (paddle boats)—especially if there are breadcrumbs in it for them. The **Lido** (☎ 0207-706-3422) has a kids' pool in the summer and will be the site of the swimming portion of the 2012 Summer Olympics' triathlon competition. Kids and parents will want to see the **Peter Pan statue** on a path by the water; gazing out at the lake, you can't help but be reminded of the island of the Lost Boys in this beautiful part of the park, where *Peter Pan* creator James Barrie spent many happy days.

KENSINGTON GARDENS (tube: High Street Kensington) The gardens are home to the excellent **Diana, Princess of Wales Memorial Playground** at the north end of Broad Walk; there's a huge (and spectacularly popular) wooden ship for kids to play on. Over by Kensington Palace at the **Round Pond** (as any *Mary Poppins* reader knows), you can follow the voyages of remote-control model boats, usually skippered by very serious grown-ups.

REGENT'S PARK (tube: Regent's Park) Has three playgrounds and two boating lakes, one of which is expressly for children. At the north end of the park is the **London Zoo;** less exotically (and less expensively), there are always lots of birds, squirrels, and dogs (on leashes) to admire in this charming park. Expect to see surprise concerts, ice-cream carts, gazebos, and the odd festival or fair.

RICHMOND PARK (tube: Richmond) London's largest park and Europe's largest walled urban park was the old hunting ground of King Charles I. Today the "Queen's Deer" have free rein of the park along with human visitors. In addition to the typical biking and horseback riding, you can partake in fishing, golf, or power kiting. On certain days, you may be able to catch a rugby or polo match near the **Roehampton Gate.**

ST. JAMES'S PARK (tube: Green Park) Has a smallish playground by **Birdcage Walk** and plenty of pelicans and other birds to watch.

unofficial **TIP**
The 3 p.m. feeding of the pelicans at St. James's Park is very popular.

SYON PARK AND LONDON BUTTERFLY HOUSE (tube: Gunnersbury or Kew Bridge rail, then bus 267 or 237) This estate is open daily, 10 a.m. to 5:30 p.m. Older kids might like the **Butterfly House,** but the younger ones seem to relish the **Aquatic Experience** (☎ 0208-847-4730), which features fish, reptiles, amphibians, and other small animals in their natural habitats. There's also **Snakes and Ladders** (☎ 0208-847-0946), an indoor adventure playground with a new out-door "Assault Course." Check out the miniature steam train in the gardens. Call ☎ 0208-560-0881 for Syon Park information and ☎ 0208-560-0378 for Butterfly House information.

GARDENS

A 300-PLUS-ACRE HAVEN ALONG THE THAMES, the **Royal Botanic Gardens, Kew** (Kew, Richmond, TW9; ☎ 0208-332-5655; **www.kew.org;** (tube or rail: Kew Gardens) has been named a UNESCO World Heritage Site. A ticket on the **Kew Explorer** is a perfect way to see the gardens plus an easy way to get to **Climbers and Creepers,** a splendid indoor–outdoor playground. A recently published guide-book called "Kid's Kew" helps 7-to-11-year-olds get the most out of their visit to the gardens.

ACTIVITIES

BALLET AND OPERA

BOTH ART FORMS CAN BE FOUND at the **Royal Opera House** (Covent Garden, WC2; ☎ 0207-240-1200; tube: Covent Garden). Tickets for many performances are hard to come by and pricing is steep, but you can wait in line outside the Piazza Entrance in Covent Garden for returned tickets on the morning of a show.

BOOKSTORES

CALL THE FOLLOWING TO CHECK ON children's summertime activities and storytelling: **Books Etc.** (Whiteleys Center, Bayswater, W2; ☎ 0207-229-3865; tube: Queensway or Bayswater) and **Children's Book Centre** (237 Kensington High Street, Kensington, W8; ☎ 0207-937-7497; tube: High Street Kensington). Also see **Daisy & Tom** under "Shopping for Children," page 279. They have a huge, wonderful selection of children's books, as well as a puppet show. Borough libraries such as **Kensington Chelsea Libraries** (**www.rbkc.gov.uk/Libraries/childrens library**) offer special activities and readings for a range of ages.

BRASS RUBBINGS

 The **Brass Rubbing Centre** (Trafalgar Square, WC2; ☎ 0207-930-9306; tube: Leicester Square) in the crypt of St. Martin-in-the-Fields offers a wonderful treat for kids age 6 and up. They can make their own souvenirs by rubbing a waxy color stick over paper to reveal the beautiful carved brasses with medieval motifs such as knights, dragons, and crests. **All Hallows by the Tower** (Byward Street, EC3; ☎ 0207-481-2928; **www.allhallowsbythetower.org.uk;** tube: Tower Hill) is another option. Built in AD 675, the church has an interesting history. John Quincy Adams, the sixth president of the United States, was married here, and William Penn, the founder of Pennsylvania, was baptized here. Check out the museum (an audio tour is available); it's good for kids because it covers all sorts of exciting historical events, including the Great Fire of London (1666), complete with sound effects. Brass rubbing is done Monday through Saturday, 2 p.m. to 4 p.m., but call first to be sure the church hasn't been closed for a function.

CINEMA

FLAGSHIP MOVIE PALACES (Leicester Square, WC2; tube: Leicester Square) The three grand cinemas of Leicester Square—the **Empire Leicester Square** (5–6 Leicester Square, WC2H 7NA; ☎ 0871-471-4714; **www.empirecinemas.co.uk**), the **Odeon Leicester Square–Odeon Mezzanine** (24–26 Leicester Square, WC2H 7JY; ☎ 0871-224-4007; **www.odeon.co .uk**), and the **Vue West End** (3 Cranbourn Street, WC2H 7AL; ☎ 0871-224-0240; **www.myvue.com**)—have grand ticket prices to match. However, it's hard not to enjoy the frenzy of fanfare and celebrity spotting at big-time, red-carpet film premieres.

unofficial **TIP**
Don't arrive at the Odeon Leicester Square too late—you will want to catch the pre-movie musical entertainment, played on a Compton organ.

IMAX Cinemas Kids and adults alike love the tall screens, 3-D action, and stomach-dropping cinematography of an IMAX experience. Two screens in London showcase these movies: the **BFI IMAX** Cinema (1 Charlie Chaplin Walk, South Bank, SE1; ☎ 0207-902-1234; **www.bfi.org.uk/imax;** tube: Waterloo) and the **Science Museum IMAX 3D Cinema** (Exhibition Road, South Kensington,

SW7; ☎ 0870-840-4771; **www.sciencemuseum.org.uk/imax;** tube: South Kensington).

KIDS LONDON CINEMA SCREENINGS Several London cinemas offer these special screenings for kids and parents with babies. They're a great marketing tool, especially the "baby screenings," since movie viewing often becomes a dim memory for new parents. For more information, visit **www.viewlondon.co.uk/cinemas/kids-london-cinema-screenings-feature-637.html.**

CYCLING

THE **London Bicycle Tour Company** (1a Gabriels Wharf, 56 Upper Ground, SE1; ☎ 0207-928-6838; tube: Southwark or Blackfriars) conducts daily bicycle tours; you can also opt to rent bikes and come up with your own tour. **Transport for London** publishes free cycling guides that you can pick up at most tube stations. You can also order the guides (in the United Kingdom: ☎ 0207-222-1234; outside the U.K.: ☎ +44-207-222-1234) or plan your own itinerary online (go to **www.tfl.gov.uk/tfl/roadusers/cycling/cycleroutes**).

ICE SKATING

QUEENS ICE RINK AND BOWL (17 Queensway, Bayswater, W2; ☎ 0207-229-0172; tube: Queensway or Bayswater) This big rink is part of a fun complex that also offers bowling. Children should be able to fit into a children's size-6 skate.

IN-LINE SKATING

ORGANIZED SKATES The truly adventurous can tour London during one of several weekly organized skating events. The **Friday Night Skate** (**www.thefns.com**) started the fad with a variety of routes that can follow the Underground or the real estate on a London Monopoly game. Good skaters can get exercise and a unique sightseeing experience. The **Easy Peasy Skate** (**www.easypeasyskate.com**) occurs on Saturdays at Battersea Park, while the Sunday **Rollerstroll** (**www.rollerstroll.com**) usually starts at Hyde Park.

For a full description of sports and exercise venues, see Part Eleven, Exercise and Recreation.

unofficial **TIP**
A number of facilities rent in-line skates, but for convenience try **Slick Willies** (12 Gloucester Road, South Kensington, SW7; ☎ 0207-225-0004; www.slickwillies .co.uk; tube: Gloucester Road). Once you pick up your skates, go to Hyde Park for some practice.

PAINT YOUR OWN POTTERY

ART 4 FUN-COLOUR ME MINE (172 West End Lane, West Hampstead, NW6; ☎ 0207-794-0800; **westhampstead.colourmemine.com;** tube: West Hampstead) This studio offers ceramics, mosaics, glass painting, and bead stringing. Drop in with your kids—even teenagers will be entertained—or bring your baby to get a foot or hand impression done.

POTTERY CAFÉ (735 Fulham Road, Fulham, West London, SW6; ☎ 0207-736-2157; **www.pottery-cafe.com;** tube: Fulham Broadway; bus: #14 toward Fulham) Offers a good selection of ceramic items to paint and fire; you can also decorate drinking glasses or glass vases. Afternoon tea is served in the courtyard. There is another branch in Richmond (322 Richmond Road, TW1 UD2; ☎ 0208-744-3000; bus: #33 or #420).

THEATER

WEST END When it comes to musical theater for families, **The Lion King** rules, but if you want a more-London-themed outing, **Mary Poppins** or the newly staged version of J. R. R. Tolkien's **Lord of the Rings** might be the ticket. Other shows that are popular with children include **Stomp, Wicked,** and **Blue Man Group.** Consult the **Society of London Theatre**'s Web site (**www.officiallondontheatre.co.uk**) or *Time Out London* for performance times.

LITTLE ANGEL THEATRE (14 Dagmar Passage, off Cross Street, Islington, N1; ☎ 0207-226-1787; **www.littleangeltheatre.com;** tube: Angel or Highbury & Islington) The city's only permanent puppet theater, in operation for 40 years, is a delightful venue with a 100-seat auditorium. Weekend shows by the resident or visiting puppet companies are offered, as well as shows during Christmas and half-term holidays.

POLKA THEATRE FOR CHILDREN (240 The Broadway, Wimbledon, SW19; ☎ 0208-543-4888; **www.polkatheatre.com;** tube: Wimbledon; British Rail: South Wimbledon) This venue seats 300 and also has an 80-seat "adventure room" for children under age 5, a small but unusual playground, a cafe, and a gift shop; excellent disability access.

PUPPET THEATRE BARGE (Blomfield Road [opposite no. 35], Maida Vale, W9; ☎ 0207-249-6876; **www.puppetbarge.com;** tube: Warwick Avenue) is a floating puppet show featuring wonderful string marionettes. The barge is moored in Little Venice, Maida Vale, from November to May. Shows run on weekends and during school holidays, beginning at 3 p.m. From July to October, the theater travels on the Thames River, with shows at Henley-on-Thames, Marlow, and Richmond; call or visit the Web site to find out where and when. Advance reservations are recommended.

UNICORN THEATRE (147 Tooley Street, Southwark, SE1; ☎ 0207-645-0560; **www.unicorntheatre.com;** tube: London Bridge) Founded in 1947, the Unicorn has grown into an exciting institution in a well-designed venue with two stages. The writing and production are as good as anything you'll find in the West End, and the plays are geared to intelligent children of all ages. There are also art exhibits of children's work; family days of theater-oriented activities; and a wide variety of educational opportunities for the budding thespian, playwright, or director in your family.

WALKING TOURS

DECLAN MCHUGH'S TOURS McHugh, a professional actor and researcher, provides two distinctly different tours for kids age 12 and over. The more popular one is the horror-filled **Blood and Tears Walk** (**www.shocking london.com**), usually conducted six times a week on Monday, Wednesday, Thursday, and Friday; it starts at the Barbican tube station and ends at the Holburn tube station. McHugh's **Shakespeare City Walk** (**www .shakespeareguide.com**) is usually conducted on Mondays and Fridays, starting and ending at the Blackfriars tube station.

LONDON WALKS (P.O. Box 1708, London, NW6; ☎ 0207-624-3978; **www.walks.com**) This popular walking-tour company offers several itineraries; most, however, are geared towards adults. The **Harry Potter Tours** are the exception, appealing to children and parents alike.

WHERE *to* EAT

KIDS NEED A BIT OF ENTERTAINING to keep them happy in a restaurant, and they generally require something fried and finger-fed. Most youngsters will be happy as clams at the outdoor cafes in the parks, or with a picnic of sandwiches from one of the "sarnie" shops such as **Pret à Manger** (the best-quality take-out sandwiches, with locations all over town). Chains such as **Boots, M&S, Sainsbury's, Starbucks,** and **Waitrose** all sell ready-made sandwiches and drinks—buy a bagful, plus some crisps and drinks, and Bob's your uncle, as they say.

If you require a proper sit-down with table service, here are some kid-friendly places to eat. None are at the top of any serious gourmand's list, but they'll serve your children with a smile.

BIG EASY (332–334 King's Road, Chelsea, SW3; ☎ 0207-352-4071; tube: Sloane Square) Geared to little ones, with a special menu plus crayons to keep those hands busy. Kids' meals start at £5 and include unlimited soft drinks and some chocolate gooey thing.

ED'S EASY DINER (Multiple locations throughout London; **www .edseasydiner.co.uk**). At Ed's children receive their own Junior Bites menu. The newer restaurants have wider aisles that can better accommodate strollers; some even have stroller parking. The food is imitation American diner cuisine (think Johnny Rockets).

GOURMET BURGER KITCHEN (Multiple locations; **www.gbkinfo.com/ GBK_Locations.htm**) Kids' fare is officially limited to the Junior burger and Junior Chicken sandwich, but with at least another 12 beef burgers and 4 chicken sandwiches on the menu, it's hard to go wrong—especially when your meal is washed down with a scrumptious GBK milk shake.

HARD ROCK CAFE (150 Old Park Lane, Mayfair, W1; ☎ 0207-629-0382; **www.hardrock.com;** tube: Green Park or Hyde Park Center) Has lots of loud music and rock memorabilia festooning every available surface. It may not be suitable for very young children—the music rocks hard, as you would imagine. Special kids' menu; crayons provide a distraction.

ITSU (Multiple locations; **www.itsu.co.uk**) Stop here for true fast food: as soon as you sit down, hungry kids can start grabbing sushi off the conveyor belt. *Sushi?* Naysayers may cry "No way!," but we can tell you that this place is big with kids, especially on weekends. The grilled-chicken teriyaki skewers are usually a safe bet for the squeamish. Check out **Yo Sushi!** as well (see facing page).

MAXWELL'S (8–9 James Street, West End, WC2; ☎ 0207-395-5804; tube: Covent Garden) In a great location, near the Covent Garden piazza; offers a special kids' menu, crayons, balloons, and more. During some holidays, they decorate the restaurant and provide seasonally festive menus.

PIZZA EXPRESS (Multiple locations; **www.pizzaexpress.com**) It's hard to beat the Piccolo Menu, offering three kids' courses for £5.25. The *pizzaiolos* in Pizza Express's open kitchens provide plenty of dough-tossing entertainment, too.

RAINFOREST CAFE (20 Shaftesbury Avenue, Soho, WC2; ☎ 0207-434-3111; **www.therainforestcafe.co.uk;** tube: Piccadilly Circus). An American import, this is a great place for little ones, with its kids' menu (burgers, ribs, sandwiches) and special treats for parties (face painting, goodie bags, and more), all in a jungle-esque setting with a rumbling faux volcano that erupts intermittently. (If you're on a budget, try to keep the little ones out of the gift shop.)

STICKY FINGERS (1A Phillimore Gardens, Kensington, W8; ☎ 0207-395-5805; **www.stickyfingers.co.uk;** tube: High Street Kensington) Owned by ex–Rolling Stone Bill Wyman, this eatery offers a children's menu with burgers, ribs, chicken, and more. Sundays are best, with face painting, balloons, and a generally fun atmosphere.

SMOLLENSKY'S (Canary Wharf, Tower Bridge and 105 The Strand, West End, WC2; ☎ 0207-497-2101; **www.smollenskys.com;** tube: Charing Cross) This is the perfect place for kids, especially for Saturday and Sunday lunch. There's a play area, on-site child care for the really young ones, and endless entertainment, including magicians, clowns, face painting, computer games, and more.

T.G.I. FRIDAY'S (6 Bedford Street, West End, WC2; ☎ 0207-379-0585; **www.tgifridays.co.uk;** tube: Covent Garden or Charing Cross) Another family-friendly U.S. import, offering balloons, crayons, children's menus, even free organic baby food. On weekends, there is face painting and a magic show.

TEXAS EMBASSY CANTINA (1 Cockspur Street, West End, SW1; ☎ 0207-925-0077; **www.texasembassy.com;** tube: Charing Cross) Authentic Tex-Mex place near the National Gallery and Trafalgar Square. Children are made to feel very welcome, and the emphasis on cheese and carbs in the cuisine is right up most young people's alley. Desserts are wonderful. The witty Wild West decor makes any meal seem festive.

YO SUSHI! (Multiple locations; **www.yosushi.com**) Like its conveyor-belt-sushi counterpart, Itsu (see left), this restaurant is the ideal place to quickly satiate a hungry family.

SHOPPING *for* CHILDREN

TOYS

CONRAN SHOP (Michelin House, 81 Fulham Road, Chelsea, SW3; ☎ 0207-589-7401; 55 Marylebone High Street, Marylebone, W1U; ☎ 0207-723-2223) Kid shopping is at its best when there are items of interest for adults, too. These modern urban-design stores have unique toy sections. The Chelsea branch is housed in the gorgeous Art Deco Michelin House; the Marylebone branch is in converted stables.

DAISY & TOM (81 King's Road, Chelsea, SW3; ☎ 0207-352-5000; tube: Sloane Square) Big children's store with toys, books, clothes, crafts, nursery furniture, a carousel, and a kids-only hair salon.

DAVENPORT'S MAGIC SHOP (7 Charing Cross Underground Concourse, Strand, WC2; ☎ 0207-836-0408; tube: Charing Cross) Still going strong after 100 years of selling all things magical.

EARLY LEARNING CENTRES (Multiple locations; **www.elc.co.uk**) True to their name, these stores sell beautifully designed developmental and educational toys, such as wooden puzzles and abaci with painted numbers and pictures.

HABITAT (Multiple locations; **www.habitat.co.uk**) This chain of home stores might seem an odd spot to shop for toys, but they do carry unusual kid's items under their own brand name. Check out the wooden double-decker buses and black taxis.

HAMLEYS (188–196 Regent Street, West End, W1; ☎ 0207-734-3161; **www.hamleys.com;** tube: Oxford Street or Piccadilly Circus). With its seven floors, Hamleys is said to be the largest toy store in the world—it is often compared with New York City's FAO Schwarz. Kids will go stark-raving mad with toy lust, which is sure to be fanned by the many demonstrations of fun stuff all over the store.

HARRODS (87–135 Brompton Road, Knightsbridge, SW1; ☎ 0207-730-1234; **www.harrods.com;** tube: Knightsbridge) Carries a remarkable selection of dolls, games, and action toys, but remember that most of this stuff is made in China and can be had for a fraction of what Harrods charges. Your kids will be amazed by the selection of pint-sized automobiles. You'll be amazed that people actually buy them.

unofficial **TIP**
The escalators just inside Harrods's Entrance 10 (off Hans Road) are the most direct route to the toy department on the fourth floor.

SNAPDRAGON (25 Bute Street, South Kensington, SW7; ☎ 0207-584-2330; tube: South Kensington) Sells lots of interesting European toys and small, inexpensive gimcracks.

BOOKS

CHILDREN'S BOOK CENTRE (237 Kensington High Street, Kensington, W8; ☎ 0207-937-7497; **www.childrensbookcentre.co.uk;** tube: High Street Kensington) The name is misleading—in addition to books, you can find computer games, board games, and dress-up attire.

NATURAL HISTORY MUSEUM GIFT STORE (Cromwell Road, South Kensington, SW7; ☎ 0207-942-5000; tube: South Kensington) Informative educational books for young and old can be found in the gift stores throughout the museum, but the shop just to the right of the Cromwell Road entrance has the best selection.

WATERSTONE'S (Multiple locations; **www.waterstones.com**) This bookstore chain has shops especially for kids in a number of larger venues, such as the Science Museum and on the fourth floor of Harrods. All Waterstone's stores have vast children's sections, with some of England's best pop-up, bath-safe, cloth, wooden, and weirdly shaped kids' books—all written in Brit-speak, which is a goof for kids back home.

CLOTHING

KIDSWEAR STORES TEND TO BE LIKE INFANTS and young children themselves—here one minute, gone the next. Most of the shops listed in the first and second editions of this *Unofficial Guide* have gone belly-up, so it's wise to call before you venture to the ones listed here. The following stores are included not so much because they represent good deals—the prices can be as breathtaking as the clothes—but because they have interesting and distinctive European selections from Petit Bateau, Petite Ourse, Laura Ashley, and other British and French designers.

AMAIA (14 Cale Street, Chelsea, SW3; ☎ 0207-590-0999; tube Sloane Square or South Kensington). Designer togs made of gorgeous fabrics that are richly textured with various trimmings, such as buttons, rickrack, and lace. The prices are high, but innovative designs and fine craftsmanship don't come cheap.

BRORA (Multiple locations; **www.brora.co.uk**) Specializes in cashmere and woolen clothes for newborns and young children, along with an established adult line.

CARAMEL (291 Brompton Road, South Kensington, SW3; ☎ 0207-589-7001; tube: South Kensington) Lots of trendy gear for children up to approximately 8 years of age. They have a little sale box that, depending on your luck, can yield a treasure or two.

CLEMENTINE (73 Ledbury Road, Notting] Hill, W11; ☎ 0207-243-6331; tube: Notting Hill Gate or Westbourne Park) Carries French and Italian clothes for children of all ages.

IANA (186 King's Road, Chelsea, SW3; ☎ 0207-352-0060; tube: Sloane Square). This chain of Italian children's stores recently opened its first branch in the United Kingdom.

LILLYWHITES (24–36 Lower Regent Street, Piccadilly, SW1; ☎ 0870-333-9600 tube: Piccadilly Circus) A London store open until 9 p.m.—who'd have thunk it! This fact alone makes Lillywhites worth a visit, especially with its location on Piccadilly Circus. This sporting-goods store is the best place to pick up souvenir kits and get a soccer-team shirt for fans back home.

OILILY (9 Sloane Street, Knightsbridge, SW1; ☎ 0207-823-2505; www.oilily.nl; tube: Knightsbridge) Oilily is a bright and cheerful collection from a popular Dutch design team. It's very 1960s in a pop-art way, featuring beautiful patterns and well-decorated basics. Choose from one-of-a-kind knit sweaters, gorgeous baby blankets, cool shoes, affordable hats, and precious baby bags.

PETIT BATEAU (106–108 King's Road, Chelsea, SW3; ☎ 0207-838-0818; tube: Sloane Square) This venerable French company has been dressing European infants in its luxurious cotton onesies and sweet fashions for years, and now teenagers have rediscovered the label, making PB T-shirts must-haves.

TARTINE ET CHOCOLAT (66 South Molton Street, Mayfair, W1; ☎ 0207-629-7233; tube: Bond Street) This Parisian boutique is the place to go if you're looking for conservative outfits: double-breasted coats, velvet dresses, lots of blues for baby boys, and lots of pinks for baby girls.

SHOES

BUCKLE MY SHOE (Harvey Nichols, Second Floor, 67 Brompton Road, Knightsbridge, SW1; ☎ 0207-235-5000; tube: Knightsbridge) Delights aplenty for tiny feet—funky animal-print slippers, glittery sandals. Not cheap, but so adorable!

INSTEP (Multiple locations; www.instepshoes.co.uk) The shoes here are designed in-house or made in Italy. Choose from gorgeous decorative footwear for babies who have yet to put a foot down, good learning-to-walk shoes, and plenty of styles for older kids.

BABY GOODS

MOTHERCARE (Multiple locations; www.mothercare.com) The West End store (526–528 Oxford Street, W1; ☎ 0845-365-0515) is always heaving with expectant and established parents stocking up on cribs, bedding, strollers, high chairs, bottles, diapers, toys, and more. Particularly handy are the bathroom stalls (big enough to push strollers into), a feeding area with bottle warmers, and a special room for nursing mothers complete with rocking chairs and a water dispenser.

NURSERY WINDOW (83 Walton Street, Chelsea, SW3; ☎ 0207-581-3358; www.nurserywindow.co.uk; tube: South Kensington). Not-too-pricey shop specializing in nursery furnishings: cribs, bedding, curtains, and even wallpaper. All fabrics are designed and printed in the United Kingdom. There's also a mail-order service.

JOHN LEWIS/PETER JONES (Multiple locations; **www.johnlewis.com**) There's a reason you can always find a last-minute nursery-shopping new parent in the infant section: the items here have been carefully selected, so you don't have to spend your time wading through ten different versions of essentially the same thing. The John Lewis clothing line is utilitarian but smart, and different from what you would find in other stores.

ACCESSORIES

ACCESSORIZE (Multiple locations; **www.monsoon.co.uk/icat/acces sorize**) This store can now be found on almost every London high street along with its parent store, Monsoon. It's a spot where young girls are guaranteed to find an excuse to spend their extra cash. Shop here for purses, scarves, hats, jewelry, hair accessories, and more.

DESIGNERS GUILD (267 and 277 King's Road, Chelsea, SW3; ☎ 0207-351-5775; **www.designersguild.com;** tube: Sloane Square) Tricia Guild's flagship store is actually two: a showroom housing fabrics, wallcoverings, and paint collections, and a home store with everything from furniture to jewelry. This is the only place to go in London if you're redecorating a children's room—the Designers Guild Kids and Designers Guild Baby lines of papers, paint, and textiles perfectly showcase Guild's love of color. Bring home some of the Queen's Foot Guards with the "Quick March" collection.

OCTOPUS (28 Carnaby Street, Soho, W1F; ☎ 0207-287-3916; tube: Oxford Street; 130 King's Road, Chelsea, SW3; ☎ 0207-589-1111; tube: Sloane Square) *Quirky* and *fun* best describe the colorful accessories you'll find in an Octopus store. Whether it's funky watches, recycled luggage, or dried-flower-laminated purses, Octopus's eclectic, design-focused merchandise has been sourced from all over the world.

KIDS' LONDON *by the* SEASONS

RAINY-DAY LONDON

IT CAN TAKE WEEKS TO EXPLORE every floor and each exhibit in some of London's museums. You may prefer to go to a play area in a museum and let the kids run wild when the rain keeps you from the parks. For 5-and-unders, try the **Army Museum Kids' Zone** (Royal Hospital Road, Chelsea, SW3; ☎ 0207-730-0717; **www.national-army-museum.ac.uk/kids;** tube: Sloane Square). This playspace is free, but it is small and entries are timed. *Note:* Call before you visit—lots of private parties are held here, and there is only a limited number of tickets per session.

HOT LONDON

AIR-CONDITIONING IS A FOREIGN CONCEPT in this part of the world, so seek some London water features—the **Serpentine Lido** in Hyde Park, for instance, or the **Diana, Princess of Wales Memorial Fountain** abutting it. Younger children are often permitted to venture into the fountain and reflecting pool at the **Victoria and Albert Museum**'s **Madejski Garden.** Adults can dip their feet in as well or opt to spectate from the shade of one of the cafe tables along the perimeter of this picturesque courtyard.

If you want to go for the bigger water, rent a skiff on the Thames in Richmond and experience a London pastime that has been popular for centuries. Contact **Richmond Bridge Boathouses** (1–3 Bridge Boathouses, Richmond, TW9; ☎ 0208-948-8270; **www.richmondbridgeboat houses.com;** tube: Richmond).

For a cool snack, try the gelato at **Oddono's** (14 Bute Street, South Kensington, SW7; ☎ 0207-052-0732; **www.oddonos.com;** tube: South Kensington). This Italian *gelateria* bustles with customers regardless of the temperature. You can also find Oddono's at **Selfridges** department store, but the cold stuff is made fresh daily in the windowed *cucina* at the Bute Street store. If gelato is just a tad too healthy, go for an all-out sugar fix at **Ben's Cookies** (multiple locations; **www.bens cookies.com**). Get one of their cool milk shakes to wash down one or more of their renowned cookies.

COLD, BLUSTERY LONDON

Harrods (87–135 Brompton Road, Knightsbridge, SW1; ☎ 0207-730-1234; **www.harrods.com;** tube: Knightsbridge) is like a London museum: you can spend days here and not see everything (or buy anything—but good luck with that). It is also a haven during cold weather, as Harrods houses 28 places to eat, including 2 of the best places in London for hot chocolate. **Ladurée,** on the ground floor, is a Champs-Elysées import serving rich, thick hot chocolate, plus macaroons in dozens of flavors for accompaniment. On the second floor you'll find the **Harrods Chocolate Bar,** with a special menu of delicacies and vats of churning chocolate to contemplate.

If you've been saddled with miserable weather for most of your London trip and you're desperate for the kids to expend their energy, you need to find the nearest **Gambado** play space (multiple locations; **www.gambado.com**). These supermarket-sized indoor entertainment venues (for children age 11 and under) have trampolines, merry-go-rounds, bumper cars, and other fun stuff.

FRIGID LONDON

IT RARELY DIPS BELOW 32°F HERE, but if it does, bundle up and revel in good ice at one of the seasonal outdoor rinks. Seasonal ice skating used to be confined to **Somerset House** (**www.somersethouse icerink.org.uk**) in the winter, but lately winter outdoor rinks have been cropping up all over London. Two of the more popular ones are

unofficial **TIP**
Ice conditions at skating rinks can be spotty, but if you're having trouble getting an edge, it's most likely due to poorly maintained rental skates. Ask that the blades on your pair be sharpened, or request another pair.

Hampton Court Ice Rink (**www.hamptoncourt icerink.com**) and the rink at the **Natural History Museum** (**www.nhm.ac.uk/visit-us/whats-on/ ice-rink-and-christmas-fair**).

FREE LONDON

ADMISSION TO MAJOR LONDON MUSEUMS is free except for special exhibitions. Bring your own snacks, as most museums have, in addition to their own cafes, "picnic" areas for people who are brown-bagging it. People-watching at **Covent Garden** is free and fun, and fantastic street performers congregate here year-round. The Web site **London for Free** (**www.londonforfree.net**) is dedicated to the pursuit of things to do in London for less than £3.

EXHAUSTED LONDON

IN A WORD, *bus*! You can see the major attractions and not leave your seat except if you elect to change routes.

PART EIGHT

DINING *and* RESTAURANTS

THERE'S AN OLD JOKE about what awaits Europeans in the afterlife: in Heaven, the police are English, the chefs are French, the mechanics are German, the lovers are Italian, and everything is organized by the Swiss. In Hell, however, the police are German, the chefs are British, the mechanics are French, and everything is organized by the Italians. Well, that old saw has become as outdated as lederhosen and berets. There were more than a few tears shed into a soufflé or two in Paris when *Restaurant* magazine named London the new food capital of the world in 2005. Never one to let England get an edge in the ancient rivalry between the two, France reclaimed her crown in 2007 with 12 of the 50 best restaurants in the world.

Contests aside, London is still a serious foodie's paradise—in fact, it just keeps getting tastier (and more expensive, of course) to tuck into a magnificent meal in England's capital—and you don't really have to go Michelin-stargazing to be well fed. The winner of the 2005 *Restaurant* survey was the triple-Michelin-starred **Fat Duck**, an hour outside of London (High Street, Bray, Berkshire; ☎ 0162-858-0333; **www.fatduck .co.uk**), where the chef is celebrated for unusual combinations (snail porridge, anyone?) and his revolutionary "molecular cooking" methods. The Fat Duck waddled down to number two in 2007, but the six other U.K. restaurants that made the list are smack-dab in the center of London: **Nobu, Hakkasan, Restaurant Gordon Ramsay, Le Gavroche, St. John,** and the **River Café. (Maze, Zuma,** and **Sketch** made it to the next 50 of the 100 best restaurants, but who's counting?)

It's a big shift for the Brits, whom the French used to mock as *les rosbifs* for their dreadful propensity toward large sides of overcooked cow. For centuries, food in London, and in all of the United Kingdom, was famous for its brutally unyielding awfulness: great lumps of indifferently prepared beef, vegetables boiled beyond all recognition, potatoes whose only concession to taste was being drowned in butter (or worse, in oily margarine) and salted to within an inch of their lives.

The best that could be said about British cuisine until recently was that it had wonderfully whimsical names: toad-in-the-hole, bubble and squeak, spotted dick, bangers and mash, fruit fool, ploughman's lunch, bacon buttie, and Poor Knights of Windsor—respectively, sausage in a Yorkshire-pudding center with onion gravy; a fried patty of mashed potatoes and Brussels sprouts or cabbage; dessert cake with currants covered in vanilla custard; sausage and mashed potatoes; whipped cream and mashed fruit over crumbled meringue; Cheddar or Stilton cheese, butter, and pickled onion or chutney on thick bread; bacon on a roll; and French toast. To be sure, all of this is good, if artery-clogging, comfort food, but the colorful names can't change the unsophisticated, workmanlike nature of these dishes.

Traditionally, the great restaurants in London earned their stars and rosettes on a Gallic menu, with chefs strictly trained in classical French cooking—the exquisite cuisines from around the old British Empire weren't taken seriously until relatively recently. But now Indian, Chinese, South Asian, Caribbean, and Middle Eastern chefs need no longer struggle with soufflés or roux to be celebrated by the food establishment, and the result has been a new vibrancy upon the traditional linen tablecloths of London. There's a bigger range of global gastronomy than ever before. Continental cuisines—Provençal, Belgian, Eastern European, Scandinavian, Mediterranean—are all represented at one level or another in London, from dodgy tapas bars and pierogi dives to caviar-and-blini cafes and elegant Danish fish eateries.

Nowadays, even old-fashioned British nursery food is taken with the greatest seriousness, again at every price level, with handmade specialty sausages and garlic-potato puree putting a new shine on the old bangers and mash or bubble and squeak. It's all about a relatively recent phenomenon that's called "modern European cooking." Nearly everyone who pays attention to gastronomic trends will use some version of this term. Defining it precisely . . . well, that's another matter. But here's a rough working definition: top-quality ingredients that may—but don't necessarily—come from any corner of the globe and that are imaginatively combined and transformed through classic Continental cooking techniques into well-presented, often whimsical, dishes.

If dining out in London is better than ever, it is also more expensive than ever—for Londoners, for Europeans, and especially for traveling

unofficial **TIP**
Modern European is the most interesting food being cooked in London now, and restaurants of this type figure prominently in these listings.

Americans, with the dollar taking a bruising against the pound sterling. It is nearly impossible to find an outstanding three-course meal with a bottle of wine for less than £35 a head, and even meals at fairly basic restaurants have an annoying tendency to cost twice that amount if you drink anything more interesting than tap water or the house wine. We wish it weren't so, but the high cost of eating in London, combined with dreadful exchange rates, shows no sign of abating.

If you're after a cheap meal in an interesting part of town, look no farther than **Brick Lane** (tube: Aldgate East), a street filled with *balti* (curry) houses, Indian restaurants from every state in India, and very good deals. On weekends you'll be accosted every few steps by some cheerful fellow pressing you to eat at this or that restaurant, offering discounts of anywhere from 10% to 40%. We are skeptical about these deals, but the fact is that you can feed a group of four satisfactorily for under £10 a person. Walk the entire expanse before settling on any one restaurant; the touts are always good for a quick, friendly conversation.

In the meantime, those who seek high quality at moderate prices should pay special attention to the list of gastropubs in the "More Recommendations" section (see page 290). Refurbished in a simple style, these old-fashioned pubs place the greatest emphasis on good food rather than beer and crisps (potato chips). The top gastropubs are

unofficial **TIP**
Gastropubs are some of London's best bets for inexpensive eating in relaxed surroundings.

usually off the beaten track (one reason they can charge lower prices), but you should seek them out if you don't mind a bit of extra traveling. You will also find plenty of small, no-frills cafes where you can get an excellent breakfast, panini, or pizza plus beverage for about £5.

There are other ways to cut costs. Lunch is considerably cheaper than dinner, and many of the upscale establishments offer prix fixe lunch or pre-theater menus with limited choices but much lower prices—it's the only way many of us can afford to try out the famous chefs' restaurants. With drinks making up a large part of many bills, look for house wines, or order by the glass if that's all you want. And don't feel obliged to order a bottle of water (always marked up outrageously) if tap water will please you just as well: London's water is perfectly potable. If you're dining with children at a restaurant without a kids' menu (not at all a standard feature in London bistros), ask if a child-sized portion can be prepared; many restaurants will be happy to oblige.

Aside from the ghastly expense, the other big complaint about eating in London restaurants is the often dicey service, and there's a lot of merit in the complaint. The cafes and restaurants here are flooded with young people from all over the European Union, looking to improve (or learn) the English language, and snap-to-it professionalism is not always part of the package. You may find yourself waiting a long time for your order to be taken, and getting a bill may require an absurd amount of effort. (I have often left a

unofficial **TIP**
Waiters will probably ask "Still or sparkling?" when you order H_2O—just politely specify tap water.

restaurant in annoyance after waiting 15 minutes without even being acknowledged, only to find the same problem at the next place.) And while chefs' cooking skills have certainly improved, the perennial shortage of well-trained, conscientious waiters can ruin even the best-tasting meal. At expensive restaurants this should not (in theory) be an issue at all, but at others—well, you may be lucky and you may not. You certainly should complain about bad service, but don't expect much in the way of compensation or even apology.

Do remember, however, that there are also some cultural differences at work here. For instance, whereas in the States you will be offered the bill when it seems evident that you are finished, the European model is much more relaxed, and it is considered bad manners to bring a check unless it's requested; people like to relax over coffee and an unsolicited bill seems like a summons to move along. Of course, when you've asked for the bill and are forced to cool your heels, one trick is to get up, put your coat on, and start for the door—that tends to get quicker results than flashing the international semaphore for "check, please" ever does.

One final word is in order: there's almost nonstop change in the London restaurant world. Restaurants accept reservations one day and announce their closure the next. Chefs grab their knives and make a run for newer pastures at alarming speed. Menus are overturned and signature dishes erased without warning. New management moves in on well-established operations. The pace of change means that some of the information herein will likely have gone stale by the time you hold this book in your hands. Needless to say, this is out of our control, but we do hope you get a few great meals no matter who's running the kitchen—or even if you have to try the place next door to the defunct eatery or boarded-up bistro that we raved about in these pages.

The RESTAURANTS

RATING OUR FAVORITE LONDON RESTAURANTS

WE HAVE DEVELOPED DETAILED PROFILES for the best and most interesting (in our opinion) restaurants in town. Each profile features an easily scanned heading that allows you, in just a second, to check out the restaurant's name, cuisine, star rating, cost, quality rating, and value rating.

OVERALL RATING This rating encompasses the entire dining experience: the style, service, and ambience in addition to the taste, presentation, and quality of the food. Five stars is the highest rating possible and connotes the best of everything. Four-star restaurants are exceptional, and three-star restaurants are well above average. Two-star restaurants are good. One star is used to indicate an average restaurant that demonstrates an unusual capability in some area of specialization—for example, an otherwise unmemorable place that has great barbecued chicken.

COST Our expense description provides a comparative sense of how much a complete meal will cost. For our purposes, a complete meal consists of an appetizer, entree, and dessert. Drinks and tips are excluded.

Inexpensive	Less than £20 per person
Moderate	£20–£50 per person
Expensive	More than £50 per person

QUALITY Food quality is rated on a scale of one to five stars, five being the best rating attainable. The quality rating is based expressly on the taste, freshness of ingredients, preparation, presentation, and creativity of food served. There is no consideration of price. If you want the best food available and cost is not an issue, you need look no further than the quality ratings.

VALUE RATING If, on the other hand, you are looking for both quality *and* value, then you should check the value rating. The value ratings are defined as follows:

★★★★★	Exceptional value; a real bargain
★★★★	Good value
★★★	Fair value; you get exactly what you pay for
★★	Somewhat overpriced
★	Significantly overpriced

PAYMENT We've listed the type of payment accepted at each restaurant using the following codes: AE equals American Express (Optima), CB equals Carte Blanche, D equals Discover, DC equals Diners Club, JCB equals Japan Credit Bureau, MC equals Master-Card, and V equals VISA.

WHO'S INCLUDED Restaurants in London change owners at an alarming rate. So, for the most part, we've tried to confine our list to establishments with a proven track record over a fairly long period of time. The exceptions here are the newer off-spring of the demigods of the culinary world—these places are destined to last, at least until our next update. Also, the list is highly selective; there are myriad restaurants in this sprawling metropolis. The omission of a particular place does not necessarily indicate that the restaurant is bad, only that either we did not feel it ranked among the best in its genre or we have not visited it

unofficial **TIP**
Despite the increasing globalization of commerce, you should not automatically assume that a given restaurant accepts American Express, Carte Blanche, Diners Club, and/or Japan Credit Bureau. The high fees charged by AE, along with the relative rarity of the other cards, mean that some restaurants may have abandoned one or more of them, so be sure to call for an update.

enough to make a fair assessment. Detailed profiles of individual restaurants follow in alphabetical order at the end of this chapter.

MORE RECOMMENDATIONS

Chinese

- **Fung Shing** (15 Lisle Street, West End, WC2;
  ☎ 0207-437-1539; tube: Piccadilly)
  Capable of producing memorable dishes.
- **Harbour City** (46 Gerrard Street, West End, WC2;
  ☎ 0207-439-7120; tube: Piccadilly)
  Serves superb dim sum and is good in the evenings as well. Very popular with the local Chinese community.
- **Hunan** (51 Pimlico Road, Pimlico, SW1;
  ☎ 0207-730-5712; tube: Sloane Square)
  One of London's few Hunan specialists; essential for devotees of that spicy cuisine.

Fish/Fish and Chips

- **Back to Basics** (21A Foley Street, West End, W1;
  ☎ 0207-436-2181; tube: Goodge Street)
  A small, buzzy place that has been packing in locals for sensationally good, and sometimes very innovative, fish cookery; very reasonable prices, too.
- **Geales** (2 Farmer Street, Notting Hill, W8;
  ☎ 0207-727-7969; tube: Notting Hill)
  Long established and consistently good. This popular spot in fashionable Notting Hill is almost always crowded.
- **Poissonnerie de l'Avenue** (82 Sloane Avenue, South Kensington, SW3;
  ☎ 0207-589-2457; tube: South Kensington)
  A lovely restaurant specializing in fish (there is a fish market next door) done in modern English and French style. Very elegant.

French

- **Mon Plaisir** (21 Monmouth Street, West End, WC2;
  ☎ 0207-836-7243; tube: Covent Garden)
  Ranks among London's longest-established French restaurants. Serves simple bistro fare, centering on steak and *frites* (French fries); decent prices and generally very sound quality.
- **Racine** (239 Brompton Road, South Kensington, SW3;
  ☎ 0207-584-4477; tube: Knightsbridge)
  A lovely place serving bistro food of the highest quality, and at reasonably fair prices. The chef is Henry Harris, who formerly worked at Bibendum (see page 308).
- **1 Lombard Street** (1 Lombard Street, The City, EC3;
  ☎ 0207-929-6611; tube: Bank)
  A big brasserie and a smaller, pricier dining room in a building that

London Restaurants by Cuisine

CUISINE/NAME	OVERALL RATING	COST	QUALITY RATING	VALUE RATING
AMERICAN				
Automat American Brasserie	★★★★	Mod	★★★★½	★★★½
Gourmet Burger Kitchen	★★★	Inexp	★★★★	★★★★
ASIAN				
E&O	★★★½	Mod/Exp	★★★★	★★
Wagamama	★★★	Inexp	★★★★	★★★★
BELGIAN				
Abbaye	★★½	Inexp/Mod	★★½	★★★
Belgo Centraal	★★	Inexp/Mod	★★	★★½
BRITISH				
Richard Corrigan at Lindsay House	★★★★★	Very Exp	★★★★½	★★★½
Fifteen Dining Room and Trattoria	★★★★½	Exp	★★★★★	★★★½
The Wolseley	★★★★	Mod/Exp	★★★★	★★★
Tom's Kitchen	★★★★	Mod	★★★★½	★★★
Rules	★★★	Mod/Exp	★★★	★★★
S&M Cafe	★★★	Inexp	★★½	★★★★
Boisdale of Belgravia	★★½	Mod	★★★	★★½
CARIBBEAN				
Cottons Islington	★★★	Inexp	★★	★★★
CHINESE				
Yauatcha	★★★★½	Exp	★★★★½	★★★
EASTERN EUROPEAN				
Baltic	★★★	Mod	★★★	★★★
Borshtch 'n' Tears	★★★	Mod/Exp	★★★½	★★½
The Tiroler Hut	★★★	Mod	★★★½	★★★
Daquise	★★	Inexp	★★	★★★
FRENCH				
Le Gavroche	★★★★★	Exp	★★★★★	★★★
Sketch	★★★★★	Exp	★★★★★	★★★
Brasserie St. Quentin	★★★½	Mod/Exp	★★★	★★½
Aubaine	★★½	Mod	★★★½	★

London Restaurants by Cuisine (continued)

CUISINE/NAME	OVERALL RATING	COST	QUALITY RATING	VALUE RATING
FRENCH (CONTINUED)				
Café Crêperie	★★	Inexp	★★	★★★
Chez Gérard at the Opera Terrace	★★	Inexp/Mod	★★★	★★★
FUSION				
The Providores and Tapa Room	★★★½	Mod/Exp	★★★★	★★★
INDIAN				
Café Spice Namaste	★★★★	Mod/Exp	★★★★	★★★
La Porte des Indes	★★★½	Exp	★★★★	★★★
Rasa	★★★½	Mod	★★★½	★★★★
Tamarind	★★★½	Mod	★★★½	★★★
Veeraswamy	★★★	Mod	★★★	★★★½
Masala Zone	★★	Inexp/Mod	★★★½	★★★★
GREEK				
Halepi Restaurant and Kebab House	★★★½	Inexp/Mod	★★★★	★★★★
Cafe Corfu	★★★	Mod	★★★½	★★★
ITALIAN				
The River Café	★★★★½	Exp	★★★★	★★
Daphne's	★★★★	Exp	★★★★	★★★★
Toto's	★★★½	Mod/Exp	★★★½	★★★½
Carluccio's Caffè	★★★	Mod	★★★	★★★
Orsini	★★★	Mod	★★★	★★½
Strada	★★★½	Inexp	★★★	★★★
Buona Sera at the Jam	★★½	Mod	★★½	★★★
Cipriani London	★★½	Exp	★★	★★½
JAPANESE				
Nobu	★★★★★	Exp	★★★★★	★★
Matsuri	★★★½	Mod/Exp	★★★½	★★

CUISINE/NAME	OVERALL RATING	COST	QUALITY RATING	VALUE RATING
MODERN EUROPEAN				
Clarke's	★★★★½	Exp	★★★★½	★★★
Michael Moore Restaurant	★★★★½	Exp	★★★★	★★★
Orrery	★★★★	Exp	★★★★	★★★
Bibendum	★★★½	Exp	★★★½	★★
The Ivy	★★★½	Mod	★★★★	★★★½
Blueprint Café	★★★	Mod	★★★½	★★
Le Caprice	★★★	Mod	★★★½	★★★
PIZZA				
Strada	★★★½	Inexp	★★★	★★★
Mulberry Street	★★★	Mod	★★★½	★★★
Pizza Express	★★	Inexp	★★	★★★★½
SANDWICHES				
Pret à Manger	★	Inexp	★★	★★★★
SEAFOOD				
fish!	★★	Inexp/Mod	★★½	★★★½
SPANISH				
Moro	★★★★	Mod	★★★★	★★★★
Cambio de Tercio	★★★	Mod	★★★	★★★
TEX-MEX				
Texas Embassy Cantina	★★½	Mod	★★★	★★★
Navajo Joe's	★★	Mod	★★½	★★★
THAI				
The Thai Restaurant & Bar	★★★	Inexp/Mod	★★★	★★★
VEGETARIAN				
Eat and Two Veg	★★★½	Inexp	★★★★	★★★★
Food for Thought	★★★½	Inexp	★★★½	★★★★

LONDON RESTAURANTS BY NEIGHBORHOOD

THE CITY AND SOUTH THAMES
Baltic
Blueprint Café
Café Spice Namaste
Moro
Pret à Manger

COVENT GARDEN
Navajo Joe
Food for Thought

EAST END
Fifteen Dining Room and Trattoria

HAMMERSMITH/KENSINGTON
River Café

KNIGHTSBRIDGE TO SOUTH KENSINGTON AND CHELSEA
Abbaye
Aubaine
Bibendum
Borshtch 'n' Tears
Brasserie St. Quentin
Buona Sera at the Jam
Café Crêperie
Cambio de Tercio
Daphne's
Daquise
Gourmet Burger Kitchen
Orsini
The Thai Restaurant & Bar
Tom's Kitchen
Toto's

MARYLEBONE TO NOTTING HILL GATE
Carluccio's Caffè
Clarke's
E&O
Eat and Two Veg
Michael Moore Restaurant

Orrery
The Providores and Tapa Room
S&M Cafe

NORTH LONDON
Cafe Corfu
Cottons Islington
Halepi Restaurant and Kebab House
Mulberry Street
Pizza Express
The Tiroler Hut

WEST END
Automat American Brasserie
Belgo Centraal
Chez Gérard at the Opera Terrace
Cipriani London
fish!
The Ivy
La Porte des Indes
Le Caprice
Le Gavroche
Masala Zone
Navajo Joe
Nobu
Rasa
Richard Corrigan at Lindsay House
Rules
Sketch
Strada
Tamarind
Texas Embassy Cantina
Veeraswamy
Wagamama
The Wolseley
Yauatcha

WESTMINSTER AND VICTORIA
Boisdale of Belgravia
Matsuri

began life as a bank; the cooking can be sensational, and the location is good if you're exploring The City (London's financial district).

- **Restaurant Gordon Ramsay** (68–69 Royal Hospital Road, Chelsea, SW3; ☎ 0207-352-4441; tube: Sloane Square)

Boasts three Michelin stars, an extraordinarily talented—and now, thanks to his TV shows in the U.K. and the U.S., very famous—chef, and a small space that means tables are hard to come by (you have to reserve a month in advance). But it's probably the best restaurant in London, so if the dizzying prices (outside the set lunch) don't scare you, it's worth a last-minute call to see if they've had a cancellation.

- **The Square** (6–10 Bruton Street, Mayfair, W1; ☎ 0207-495-7100; tube: Green Park or Bond Street)
Some people consider the modern European cooking here among the best in London. Only the pricey wine list and occasional wobbles of service excluded it from the main entries, but it should be a top choice for a special, expensive meal.

Gastropubs and Wine Bars

- **Cork & Bottle Wine Bar** (44–46 Cranbourn Street, West End, WC2; ☎ 0207-734-7807; tube: Leicester Square)
The food is nothing special, but the wine list is amazing, and the Leicester Square location is as central as you can get. This is why the cramped basement rooms are always packed. Good for a light bite and a drink before or after a movie or play.
- **The Cow** (89 Westbourne Park Road, Notting Hill, W11; ☎ 0207-221-0021; tube: Ladbroke Grove)
Prices are not especially low, but quality is especially high at this popular place near Notting Hill.
- **The Eagle** (159 Farringdon Road, The City, EC1; ☎ 0207-837-1353; tube: Farringdon)
The first of the gastropubs and still one of the best; if you're nearby, pop in for classy Italian-French cooking.
- **The Havelock Tavern** (57 Masbro Road, Shepherd's Bush, W14; ☎ 0207-603-5374; tube: Shepherd's Bush)
A popular local pub in a nice residential area; it has great atmosphere and great food.

Indian

- **Benares** (12 Berkeley Square, Mayfair, W1; ☎ 0207-629-8886; tube: Green Park)
The creation of Atul Kochhar, formerly of Tamarind (see page 343) and universally regarded as one of London's greatest Indian chefs; swanky setting and location that serves staggeringly good food.
- **Shezan** (16–22 Cheval Place, Knightsbridge, SW7; ☎ 0207-584-9316; tube: Knightsbridge)
A bit pricey, but it serves only *halal* (ritually fit) meat and has a traditional menu based on its 40 years in business—none of those newfangled "modern Indian" dishes. Good mulligatawny soup and curries.
- Star of India (154 Old Brompton Road, South Kensington, SW5; ☎ 0207-351-3594; tube: Gloucester Road)

Unpredictable, but when the place is on form, the food is wonderful and the ambience is appealingly shabby-elegant.

Italian and Pizza

- **Condotti** (4 Mill Street, Mayfair, W1; ☎ 0207-499-1308; tube: Green Park)
  In an expensive area, this is a cheap source of good pizza in an attractive space; the proprietor was one of the founders of Pizza Express (see page 335).
- **Locanda Locatelli** (8 Seymour Street, Marylebone, W1; ☎ 0207-935-9088; tube: Marble Arch)
  One of London's very best Italian restaurants. Fairly pricey and incredibly difficult to get into, but it's worth a try if you want spectacular cooking in attractive surroundings.

Japanese

- **Itsu** (103 Wardour Street, Soho, W1; ☎ 0207-479-4790; tube: Piccadilly)
  Kaiten sushi restaurant—dishes are circulated on a conveyor belt and you pick what you want as it goes around. Puts a European spin on its sushi; trendy, attractive, and very popular with local office workers. There's another Itsu in South Kensington at the corner of Draycott and Walton streets (☎ 0207-590-2400).
- **Kulu Kulu** (76 Brewer Street, Soho, W1; ☎ 0207-734-7316; tube: Piccadilly Circus)
  The first of London's *kaiten* sushi places. Some of the best sushi in town, and cheap, too.
- **Misato** (11 Wardour Street, Soho, W1; ☎ 0207-734-0808; tube: Piccadilly)
  A small, simple place in Chinatown for a quick meal; don't expect anything astounding, but quality is good and prices are low.

Middle Eastern and Turkish

- **Al Hamra** (31–33 Shepherd Market, Mayfair, W1; ☎ 0207-493-1954; tube: Green Park)
  Popular with tourists and locals alike. This Middle Eastern restaurant specializes in *meze* (assorted small dishes); sometimes disappoints, but when it's good, it's very good. And the neighborhood is charming.
- **Fakhreddine** (85 Piccadilly, Mayfair, W1; ☎ 0207-493-3424; tube: Green Park)
  Has the great advantage of a beautiful view over Green Park, and a recent renovation gave it a much-needed face-lift. Great *meze* and Sunday brunch.
- **Patogh** (8 Crawford Place, Marylebone, W1; ☎ 0207-262-4015; tube: Marble Arch or Edgware Road)
  Simple in decor but exceptional in cuisine, Patogh is one of the better Middle Eastern restaurants in an area that's crowded with them. No liquor license, but you can bring your own.

- **Ranoush Juice Bar** (43 Edgware Road, Bayswater, W2;
  ☎ 0207-723-5929; tube: Edgware Road)
  This is London's first juice bar and still a source of excellent sandwiches,
  kebabs, and desserts, as well as a lovely range of delicious fruity
  drinks; great budget food.

South Asian

- **Awana Restaurant** (85 Sloane Avenue, South Kensington, SW3;
  ☎ 0207-584-8880; tube: South Kensington)
  Marvelous Malaysian restaurant featuring spicy noodle dishes, curries,
  and excellent appetizers. Elegant decor, good service, and unstartling
  prices make this a good romantic dinner destination as well as a great
  place for a friendly lunch.
- **Nahm** (Halkin Hotel, Halkin Street, Belgravia, SW1;
  ☎ 0207-333-1234; tube: Hyde Park Corner)
  Easily London's best Thai restaurant—and its most expensive by a long
  shot. Lunch is affordable; dinner is only for people who really love
  Thai cooking and are willing to pay around £50 a head before drinks.
- **Patara** (181 Fulham Road, South Kensington, SW3;
  ☎ 0207-351-5692; tube: South Kensington)
  Located on the increasingly swanky stretch of Fulham Road at Sydney
  Street, this Thai restaurant is a solid choice. Good service, fine food,
  and not so hard on the wallet.

RESTAURANT PROFILES

Abbaye ★★½

BELGIAN	INEXPENSIVE/MODERATE	QUALITY ★★½	VALUE ★★★

102 Old Brompton Road, South Kensington, SW7;
☎ 0207-373-2403; tube: Gloucester Road or South Kensington

Customers Locals. **Reservations** Only for large parties. **When to go** Late
breakfast, lunch, or dinner. **Entree range** £8–£18. **Payment** AE, CB, MC, V.
Service rating ★★. **Friendliness rating** ★★★★. **Bar** Standing only. **Wine
selection** OK. **Dress** No dress code. **Disabled access** Yes. **Hours** Daily,
10:30 a.m.–10:30 p.m.

SETTING AND ATMOSPHERE Cozy Old European inn atmosphere, with oak
   tables, wood paneling, and a nice outdoor area .
HOUSE SPECIALTIES Mussels; huge selection of Belgian beer, sausages, fish.
OTHER RECOMMENDATIONS *Gauffre* (Belgian dessert waffles), *bittenballen*
   (meatballs), smoked fish, salads.
SUMMARY AND COMMENTS Many people would tell you that the raison d'être
   of a Belgian restaurant is the beer, and by God, have they ever got
   the beer here: scores of lovely lagers—the Champagnes of *les bières*—
   some of which are served in a wonderful mug called the Pauwel Kwat,
   an elegant curved-waist glass placed in a wooden stand. But beer is just

a beverage to many of us nondevotees, and Abbaye is also a great choice for food: fresh salads that are a cut above the others in the price range, waffles and desserts, schnitzel, and sandwiches. The atmosphere is another recommendation: it's cozy and very European in vibe, and on the rare sunny day, the outside tables evoke a kind of modified beer garden. The service is friendly, and the price is right.

Aubaine ★★½

FRENCH (BISTRO)	MODERATE	QUALITY ★★★½	VALUE ★

260–262 Brompton Road, South Kensington, SW7; ☎ 0207-052-0100; www.aubaine.co.uk; tube: South Kensington

Customers French locals and Francophiles, bread addicts, and ladies who lunch. **Reservations** Recommended, except for breakfast. **When to go** Breakfast, lunch, or dinner. **Entree range** £8–£19.50. **Payment** AE, MC, V. **Service rating** ★★★. **Friendliness rating** ★★. **Bar** No. **Wine selection** Excellent for such a small place. **Dress** Casual. **Disabled access** Yes. **Hours** Monday–Saturday, 8 a.m.–11 p.m.; Sunday, 9 a.m.–10 p.m.

SETTING AND ATMOSPHERE Bright and light country French, fresh flowers on zinc tables, with an on-the-ball staff; very popular at lunch and dinner.

HOUSE SPECIALTIES Exquisite variety of French bread and patisserie; *filet de boeuf tartare.*

OTHER RECOMMENDATIONS Club Aubaine steak tartine.

ENTERTAINMENT AND AMENITIES Sidewalk tables in good weather, take-out bakery, and various condiments for sale.

SUMMARY AND COMMENTS Opened in 2005, Aubaine has been quietly gaining in popularity among the locals who were accustomed to frequenting the nearby Le Brasserie and Patisserie Valerie when they wanted a French bistro meal or croissant. The attraction has a lot to do with the superb bread, the good service, and the decent range of choices from a French country–type menu. Although it is hard to forgive the loss of the marvelous Italian tiled walls of the old restaurant that had been here for so long, the new decor is bright and countrified, redolent of an old-fashioned Provençal restaurant. The menu relies on time-honored French favorites such as coquilles St. Jacques and coq au vin. There is a nice collection of *tartines,* open-faced sandwiches with a variety of toppings, such as smoked salmon with cucumber salad and Brie with walnuts and honey. The breakfasts are excellent: eggs Benedict, granola, omelets, *croque monsieur,* and of course the classic Continental breakfast of breads and jam, croissant, and coffee. The prices reflect the chichi neighborhood, and one may balk at spending £9.75 for a wild-mushroom-and-Gruyère-cheese sandwich, but it appears that a lot of people are willing to spend the extra pence (£16.25 for the *boeuf tartare*) to eat raw steak in mad-cow England.

Automat American Brasserie ★★★★

AMERICAN	MODERATE	QUALITY ★★★★½	VALUE ★★★½

the city dining and nightlife

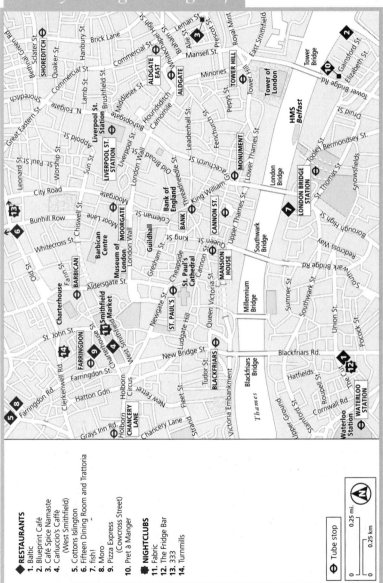

♦ **RESTAURANTS**
1. Baltic
2. Blueprint Café
3. Café Spice Namaste
4. Carluccio's Caffè
   (West Smithfield)
5. Cottons Islington
6. Fifteen Dining Room and Trattoria
7. fish!
8. Moro
9. Pizza Express
   (Cowcross Street)
10. Pret à Manger

■ **NIGHTCLUBS**
11. Fabric
12. The Fridge Bar
13. 333
14. Turnmills

⊖ Tube stop

0   0.25 mi.
0   0.25 km

Ⓐ

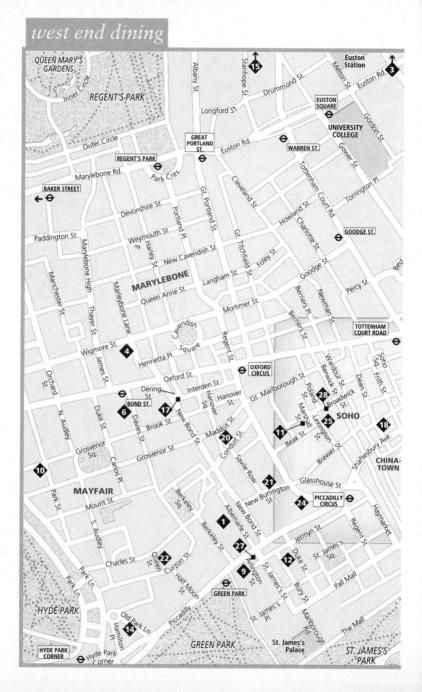

west end dining

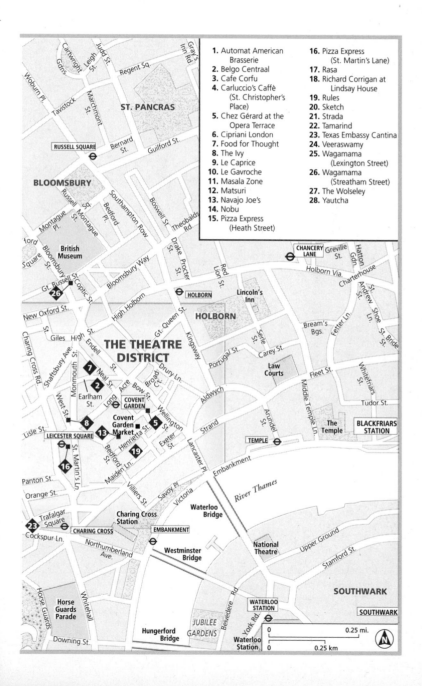

1. Automat American Brasserie
2. Belgo Centraal
3. Cafe Corfu
4. Carluccio's Caffè (St. Christopher's Place)
5. Chez Gérard at the Opera Terrace
6. Cipriani London
7. Food for Thought
8. The Ivy
9. Le Caprice
10. Le Gavroche
11. Masala Zone
12. Matsuri
13. Navajo Joe's
14. Nobu
15. Pizza Express (Heath Street)

16. Pizza Express (St. Martin's Lane)
17. Rasa
18. Richard Corrigan at Lindsay House
19. Rules
20. Sketch
21. Strada
22. Tamarind
23. Texas Embassy Cantina
24. Veeraswamy
25. Wagamama (Lexington Street)
26. Wagamama (Streatham Street)
27. The Wolseley
28. Yautcha

knightsbridge to south kensington

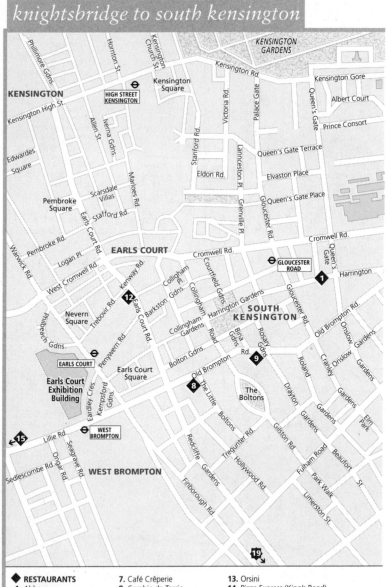

◆ RESTAURANTS
1. Abbaye
2. Aubaine
3. Bibendum
4. Borshtch 'n' Tears
5. Brasserie St. Quentin
6. Buona Sera at the Jam

7. Café Crêperie
8. Cambio de Tercio
9. Carluccio's Caffè
   (Old Brompton Road)
10. Daphne's
11. Daquise
12. Gourmet Burger Kitchen

13. Orsini
14. Pizza Express (King's Road)
15. The River Café
16. The Thai Restaurant & Bar
17. Tom's Kitchen
18. Toto's

dining and nightlife

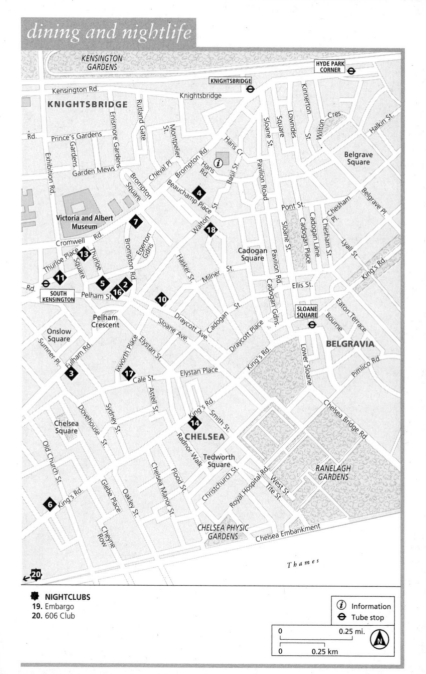

marylebone to notting hill gate

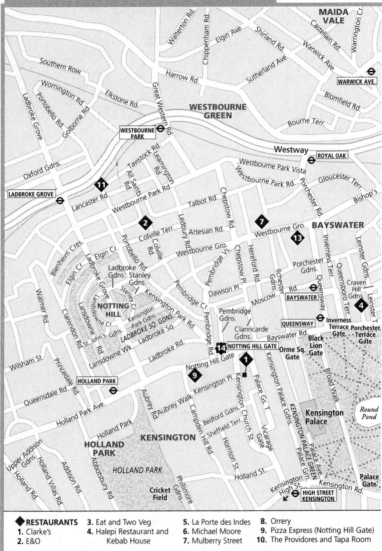

◆ **RESTAURANTS**
1. Clarke's
2. E&O
3. Eat and Two Veg
4. Halepi Restaurant and Kebab House
5. La Porte des Indes
6. Michael Moore
7. Mulberry Street
8. Orrery
9. Pizza Express (Notting Hill Gate)
10. The Providores and Tapa Room

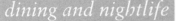

dining and nightlife

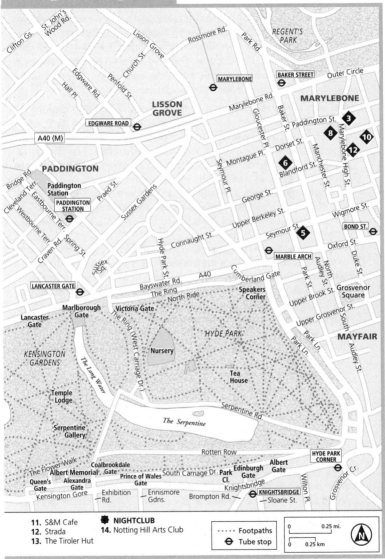

11. S&M Cafe
12. Strada
13. The Tiroler Hut

☘ **NIGHTCLUB**
14. Notting Hill Arts Club

····· Footpaths
⊖ Tube stop

0   0.25 mi.
0   0.25 km

33 Dover Street, Mayfair, W1; ☎ 0207-499-3033;
www.automat-london.com; tube: Green Park

Customers Homesick Americans, visiting celebs, and hearty eaters. **Reservations**
Yes. **When to go** Breakfast or lunch. **Entree range** £7–£28. **Payment** AE, MC, V.
Service rating ★★★★★. **Friendliness rating** ★★★★★. **Bar** Dinner only.
Wine selection Good. **Dress** Casual. **Disabled access** Yes. **Hours** *Breakfast:*
Monday–Friday, 7–11 a.m.; *lunch:* Monday–Friday, noon–3 p.m.; *brunch:* Saturday
and Sunday, 11 a.m.–4 p.m.; *dinner:* Monday–Saturday, 6–11 p.m.

SETTING AND ATMOSPHERE Astonishingly authentic early-20th-century re-
creation and reinterpretation of America's oldest remaining diner, which
is in Ohio (see the movie *Road to Perdition* for views of the original). Oak
panels, black-and-white-tiled floors, and polished steel. Even the letter-
ing on the bathroom doors speaks volumes of verisimilitude. It's an
unmissable piece of architectural authority and whimsy.

HOUSE SPECIALTIES Burgers, mac and cheese (like none you'll ever find outside of Grandma's kitchen, provided she's a great cook), chicken noodle
soup, pancakes, home fries, hash browns, and various cuts of Nebraska
corn-fed beef.

OTHER RECOMMENDATIONS Creamed spinach; milk shakes; clam chowder; all
of the desserts, particularly the Pavlova, cheesecake, and mud pie.

SUMMARY AND COMMENTS While there have been various anemic attempts to
approximate a genuine Yankee diner here, no one in London has yet gotten it quite right—until now. Not that this joint is about imitation (it's in
Mayfair rather than on the side of a country road; need we say more?);
the Automat is a glorious dream-memory of the classic American diner
that has all but disappeared from the United States. It hits some high
notes for the homesick transatlantic in its food, pleasing the aesthetic
souls of U.S. visitors, expats, and cultured internationals at the same time.
The hash browns and home fries are not the greasy spuds that wait in
readiness at the back of a short-order grill, and the macaroni and cheese
features upscale options of bacon bits or spinach, but it's the thought that
counts—and there is a limit to nostalgia when it comes to food.

The restaurant has been lovingly designed, with witty elements of
the classic country roadside diner made elegantly beautiful. Unless you
knew that the owner, architect, and designer is Carlos Almada of New
York's MK Club (among other Manhattan successes), you might be surprised at the beautiful people who eat here: Anna Wintour has been
seen in front of a plate, and Scarlett Johanssen has been observed tuck-
ing into one as well. It is definitely worth a visit for breakfast pancakes
or waffles, or lunch, soup, and sandie. Dinner is geared to carnivores
who miss a taste of heartland beef, but vegetarians may also apply. Stay
tuned for the new club and New York–themed restaurant that Mr.
Almada is creating underneath the Automat, and prepare to be dazzled.

Baltic ★★★

| POLISH | MODERATE | QUALITY ★★★ | VALUE ★★★ |

74 Blackfriars Road, South London, SE1; ☎ 0207-928-1111; www.balticrestaurant.co.uk; tube: Southwark or Waterloo

Customers Diverse, mostly young locals. **Reservations** Recommended. **When to go** Lunch or dinner. **Entree range** £15–£17. **Payment** AE, DC, MC, V. **Service rating** ★★★. **Friendliness rating** ★★★★. **Bar** Yes. **Wine selection** Small but good and very reasonable. **Dress** Casual. **Disabled access** Yes. **Hours** Monday–Friday, 12:30–2:30 p.m. and 7–11:15 p.m.; Saturday and Sunday, 7–11:15 p.m.

SETTING AND ATMOSPHERE Small rooms and plain decor; popular at both lunch and dinner, and very welcoming.

HOUSE SPECIALTIES Traditional Polish dishes such as blinis, dumplings, and herring; extensive vodka list.

OTHER RECOMMENDATIONS Vodka.

ENTERTAINMENT AND AMENITIES Jazz Sunday evenings, 7–11 p.m.

SUMMARY AND COMMENTS London has a long tradition of hosting émigrés from Eastern and Central Europe, who have brought with them the richness of their national cuisines. Baltic is part of that tradition, but it is not a traditional restaurant: the setting is very contemporary and so is the food, despite paying due respect to classic Polish fare. This gives a meal at Baltic a welcome element of surprise, and it also means you can eat more healthily here than at many restaurants serving this type of cuisine, some of which seem to specialize mainly in heavy cooking oil. For many customers, Baltic, like sister restaurants Chez Kristof and Wodka, is preeminently a vodka bar: aficionados can choose from 35 varieties, including vodkas flavored on the premises (such as vanilla or pear). There's a good wine list, and beers as well. For interesting, flexible eating with a different twist, Baltic is a great spot—and justly popular.

kids Belgo Centraal ★★

BELGIAN	INEXPENSIVE/MODERATE	QUALITY ★★	VALUE ★★½

50 Earlham Street, West End, WC2; ☎ 0207-813-2233; www.belgo-restaurants.com; tube: Covent Garden

Customers Locals and tourists. **Reservations** Recommended. **When to go** Lunch or dinner. **Entree range** £8.95–£18. **Payment** AE, CB, D, DC, MC, V. **Service rating** ★★. **Friendliness rating** ★★½. **Bar** No. **Wine selection** Adequate; beers are outstanding. **Dress** Casual. **Disabled access** Yes. **Hours** Monday–Thursday, noon–11:30 p.m.; Friday and Saturday, noon–midnight; Sunday, noon–10:30 p.m.

SETTING AND ATMOSPHERE Big, high-ceilinged subterranean room with a view of the kitchen and a deliberate air of conviviality.

HOUSE SPECIALTIES *Croquettes de fromage, salade liègoise,* Châteaubriand for two, Belgian braised meats, mussels in all guises, crêpes and waffles.

OTHER RECOMMENDATIONS The beer list.

SUMMARY AND COMMENTS Belgo is a success story with a simple formula: sell Belgian food and drink at low prices—with a helpful array of special offers to keep them even lower—and get the waiters to dress in monks' robes. Not everyone's a fan, and the food (especially more-complicated dishes) can be of variable quality, but the simpler mussel dishes are usually just fine. What's more, you can wash them down with a generous array of the great beers of Belgium. Belgo is not the great bargain it once was, and the novelty has long since worn off; moreover, the business has had its ups and downs. But with a lunchtime deal of £5.95, Belgo Centraal (and its other branch, Belgo Noord, 72 Chalk Farm Road, NW1; ☎ 0207-267-0718) continues to offer reasonable food at fairly reasonable prices.

kids Bibendum ★★★½

MODERN EUROPEAN   EXPENSIVE   QUALITY ★★★½   VALUE ★★

Michelin House, 81 Fulham Road, South Kensington, SW3;
☎ 0207-581-5817; www.bibendum.co.uk; tube: South Kensington

Customers Locals, tourists, and people with money to burn. **Reservations** Recommended. **When to go** Lunch for the cheapest option, dinner for that special occasion. **Entree range** £28.50 (plus VAT and beverages, so expect to spend about 25% extra) for 3-course set lunch; main dinner entrees, £16.50–£27.50. **Payment** AE, D, DC, MC, V. **Service rating ★★★★. Friendliness rating ★★★★. Bar** No. **Wine selection** Excellent but expensive. **Dress** Smart casual. **Disabled access** Yes. **Hours** Monday–Friday, noon–2:30 p.m. and 7–11:30 p.m.; Saturday, 12:30–3 p.m. and 7–11:30 p.m.; Sunday, 12:30–3 p.m. and 7–10:30 p.m.

SETTING AND ATMOSPHERE A bright, spotless, high-ceilinged Art Deco room in what was formerly the headquarters of the Michelin Tire Company. The decor is simple and contemporary, with comfortable chairs; two huge stained-glass windows of the Michelin Man make the venue unique. (Check out the painted tiles on the exterior of the building.)

HOUSE SPECIALTIES *Escargots de Bourgogne,* sautéed foie gras with Armagnac jelly, lobster-and-fennel salad, roast quail, grilled calf's liver, *poulet de Bresse à l'estragon.*

OTHER RECOMMENDATIONS Set lunch (£28.50 for three courses), fish and chips.

SUMMARY AND COMMENTS Bibendum was the first restaurant in Sir Terence Conran's empire, and it remains one of the most pleasant dining rooms in London. Like all of Conran's restaurants, the legend outstrips the reality, with the food being less of a transcendent experience than a simply, solidly, satisfying no-brainer. You can come here for lunch or dinner knowing that you'll get adequately prepared food made with the highest-quality ingredients, served with consummate professionalism that still manages to be friendly. The menu is a bit all over the place, with a basic orientation that is French and classic, but Asian influences appear as well, as does solid Britishness (the fish and chips, the least expensive main course, are among the best in London).

The real complaint: cost. Bibendum isn't ripping anyone off with the food prices—attention to detail is expensive, especially when success depends heavily on top-quality ingredients—but wine is marked up without mercy, making an evening meal here a very costly exercise. A recent lunch for two, sans alcohol, sans dessert, and with two courses ordered off the special menu, came to a whopping £70. A less expensive option is the small oyster bar and cafe (both downstairs) where you can eat quickly and lightly without doing violent damage to your budget.

kids Blueprint Café ★★★

MODERN EUROPEAN	MODERATE	QUALITY ★★★½	VALUE ★★

Design Museum, 28 Shad Thames, South London, SE1; ☎ 0207-378-7031; www.blueprintcafe.co.uk; tube: London Bridge or Tower Bridge

Customers Mostly locals. **Reservations** Recommended. **When to go** Lunch or dinner. **Entree range** £12.50–£19.50; set lunch: 2 courses from £15 to £19.50, 3 courses £29.50. **Payment** AE, D, DC, JCB, MC, V. **Service rating** ★★★. **Friendliness rating** ★★★. **Bar** Yes. **Wine selection** Very good. **Dress** Informal. **Disabled access** Yes. **Hours** Monday–Saturday, noon–3 p.m. and 6–11 p.m.; Sunday, noon–3 p.m.

SETTING AND ATMOSPHERE This attractive, modern room with big windows overlooking the Thames hosts a trendy clientele.

HOUSE SPECIALTIES Polenta, grilled bream, razor clams with a parsley crust.

OTHER RECOMMENDATIONS Pork with fennel.

SUMMARY AND COMMENTS The Blueprint is one of many restaurants in the Shad Thames area with a sweeping view of the river, and for this reason alone it's worth a visit. The food is more or less consistently good, year after year: modern in style and with heavy emphasis on the Mediterranean, especially Italy. The seasons and the market are king here, so the menu changes twice daily to reflect what's available. Fish, pasta, and home-curing are strong points. The wine list is not huge but is carefully chosen and easily accommodates diners on a budget. In warm weather, beg for a table on the terrace.

Boisdale of Belgravia ★★½

BRITISH	MODERATE	QUALITY ★★★	VALUE ★★½

15 Eccleston Street, Belgravia, SW1; ☎ 0207-730-6922; www.boisdale.co.uk; tube: Victoria

Customers Tourists, jazz lovers, and affluent locals. **Reservations** Recommended. **When to go** Lunch or dinner. **Entree range** £13.50–£25. **Payment** AE, CB, D, DC, MC, V. **Service rating** ★★★½. **Friendliness rating** ★★★½. **Bar** Yes. **Wine selection** Good. **Dress** Smart casual. **Disabled access** No. **Hours** Monday–Saturday, noon–2:30 p.m. and 7–midnight.

SETTING AND ATMOSPHERE Attractive Regency dining room with dark wood and red paneling, interesting antique prints on the wall, clublike ambience, garden at rear open in warm weather.

HOUSE SPECIALTIES Anything with a Scottish element, such as smoked salmon, smoked grouse, venison, Highland lamb, Aberdeen Angus beef.

OTHER RECOMMENDATIONS Set menus.

ENTERTAINMENT AND AMENITIES Late jazz bar, live music.

SUMMARY AND COMMENTS Boisdale has established itself as London's most serious champion of the food and drink of Scotland. The emphasis is on great ingredients, whether raw or cured, presented to their best advantage. You can go for the simplicity of an Aberdeen Angus steak (from small to gargantuan), grilled and served with béarnaise or Bloody Mary sauce, or you can venture into more-modern territory if you're feeling adventurous. The kitchen does well with both approaches, and the cozy atmosphere makes a warmly attractive setting. If you're game enough to try haggis, one of Scotland's national dishes, this is probably the place to do it. And if you're game for game, there are seasonal specials on all kinds of fish, fowl, and antlered beasts. Whiskey lovers should note that Boisdale's Back Bar, open throughout the day, serves London's largest selection of single-malt scotch.

Borshtch 'n' Tears ★★★

RUSSIAN	MODERATE/EXPENSIVE	QUALITY ★★★½	VALUE ★★½

46 Beauchamp Place, Knightsbridge, SW3; ☎ 0207-584-9911; tube: Knightsbridge

Customers Expatriate Russians, both oligarchs and students; locals; party people. **Reservations** Yes. **When to go** Dinner only, except on weekends. **Entree range** £12–£22 (not counting caviar). **Payment** MC, V. **Service rating** ★★★. **Friendliness rating** ★★★★. **Bar** Yes. **Wine selection** Extensive; try the Georgian wine. **Dress** Casual. **Disabled access** No. **Hours** Monday–Friday, 5:30 p.m.–1:30 a.m.; Saturday and Sunday 1 p.m.–1 a.m.

SETTING AND ATMOSPHERE Reopened in 2007 after a redecoration, B 'n' T has lost none of its old-fashioned style and has added some much-needed comfort and amenities. Plus, the residue from decades of power smoking was removed right after the tobacco ban came into effect.

HOUSE SPECIALTIES Blinis, borscht, pierogis.

OTHER RECOMMENDATIONS Schnitzel, stroganoff.

ENTERTAINMENT AND AMENITIES Live Russian music every night, and the inevitable dancing.

SUMMARY AND COMMENTS Amazingly, this restaurant has been open since 1965, when it was a favorite with the legendary boozers and party animals of the day. Something about the cheerful vulgarity of the place struck—and continues to strike—a robust note of dissonance in this chichi, overposh neighborhood in Knightsbridge. Plus, the Russian music is made to get drunk to, and the heavy Slavic food perfect for absorbing mass quantities of vodka that flow like a natural aquifer here. It's not just a party though; it's also the best restaurant in London for authentic Russian food (pre-Communist) such as pierogis and strong beet soup—the "Borshtch" of the eatery's name. We can only speculate that the "Tears" are the natural by-product of the vodka and Russian music, possibly not accessible to non-Russians.

Brasserie St. Quentin ★★★½

FRENCH	MODERATE/EXPENSIVE	QUALITY ★★★	VALUE ★★½

243 Brompton Road, South Kensington, SW3; ☎ 0207-589-8005;
www.brasseriestquentin.co.uk; tube: South Kensington or Knightsbridge

Customers Locals, businesspeople, gastronomes, old conservatives. **Reservations** Yes for dinner, no for lunch. **When to go** Anytime, but the set lunch is a good deal. **Entree range** £11.50–£20.50. **Payment** AE, MC, V. **Service rating** ★★★★. **Friendliness rating** ★★★★½. **Bar** Yes, but just when waiting for a table. **Wine selection** Excellent. **Dress** Casual. **Disabled access** Yes. **Hours** Daily, noon–2:30 p.m. and 6:30–10 p.m.

SETTING AND ATMOSPHERE A very Parisian interior, with red-leather banquettes and smoked-glass mirrors; it's a quiet sort of place with unpretentious classiness.

HOUSE SPECIALTIES Escalope of Cranborne pork with Parmesan crust and a fried egg; roast Lough Neagh eel with horseradish cream and lamb's lettuce; sautéed scallops with pancetta, green beans, and sesame dressing; Morecambe Bay shrimp; salt-marsh lamb from Holker in Cumbria.

OTHER RECOMMENDATIONS Hot chocolate fondant with burnt-orange ice cream; raspberry brûlée; *mille-feuille* of fruits with citrus *sabayon;* set menus (or *table d'hôte,* as they call it).

ENTERTAINMENT AND AMENITIES Private room downstairs; full range of wines and liqueurs.

SUMMARY AND COMMENTS Brasserie St. Quentin is an old survivor on this strip of the Brompton Road that has been under attack from one particular greedy developer for the past decade. More than 25 years old, it's owned by a consortium of friends and gourmand colleagues. The Marquess of Salisbury is one of the shareholders, and his estates in Dorset supply St. Quentin with traditional-breed pork products, roe deer, and other game. The cooking is of a high caliber, and it always puzzles us why so many people flock to the other French restaurant next door rather than head straight for this, superior in many ways, brasserie. The set lunch menus are a great deal: £17.50 for two courses, £19.50 for three. Our favorite St. Quentin story is that once, when Maggie Thatcher had dinner there a few years back, the other diners rose to their feet in silent homage as she was leaving.

Buona Sera at the Jam ★★½

ITALIAN	MODERATE	QUALITY ★★½	VALUE ★★★

289a King's Road, SW3; ☎ 0207-352-8827; tube: Sloane Square

Customers Families, couples. **Reservations** Yes. **When to go** Any evening. **Entree range** £8–£15. **Payment** MC, V. **Service rating** ★★★★. **Friendliness rating** ★★★½. **Bar** Yes. **Wine selection** Adequate. **Dress** Casual. **Disabled access** No. **Hours** Monday, 6 p.m.–midnight; Tuesday–Friday, noon–3 p.m. and 6 p.m.–midnight; Saturday and Sunday, noon–midnight.

SETTING AND ATMOSPHERE An ideal setting for a romantic dinner for two. Raised wooden cubicles, which you must get to by climbing up a ladder, afford a lot of privacy. The lighting is dim. Side racks are adorned with spices and hanging garlic cloves.

HOUSE SPECIALTIES Steak, spaghetti with seafood.

OTHER RECOMMENDATIONS Lasagna.

SUMMARY AND COMMENTS This is one of our favorite London restaurants, not so much for the food as for the atmosphere. Although the food is solid Italian fare, it is not gourmet cuisine, a fact also reflected in the reasonable prices. If you go, reserve a top booth—sitting on a raised table is a unique experience, and it can feel as goofy as it is romantic, depending on whom you are breaking bread with. (But beware: the steep ladders demand youth or fitness.) Buona Sera is often packed to the rafters, so book in advance. The servers are very friendly and often engage in small talk—a rarity among waitstaff in London—and they make you feel very welcome.

Cafe Corfu ★★★

GREEK	MODERATE	QUALITY ★★★ ½	VALUE ★★★

17 Pratt Street, Camden Town, NW1; ☎ 0207-267-8088; www.cafecorfu.com; tube: Camden Town

Customers Locals, homesick Greek visitors and expats, Grecophiles. **Reservations** Recommended for evening and weekends. **When to go** 8 p.m. dinner, so you can catch the *tsifteteli* belly dancing and musical entertainment. **Entree range** £9–£12. **Payment** MC, V. **Service rating ★★★. Friendliness rating ★★★★. Bar** Yes. **Wine selection** All Greek wine, with lots of retsina and ouzo, plus interesting blended wines. **Dress** Casual. **Disabled access** Yes. **Hours** Tuesday–Friday, noon–10:30 p.m.; Saturday, 5–11:30 p.m.; Sunday, noon–11:30 p.m. (closed Monday except for private parties).

SETTING AND ATMOSPHERE Simple and modern, but who notices? The real decorations are the dancers and beautiful food.

HOUSE SPECIALTIES *Moussaka, spanakopita, tzatziki,* fresh fish, Halloumi cheese, lamb or chicken kebabs—a veritable pantheon of great Greek dishes, updated with flair.

OTHER RECOMMENDATIONS *Baklava,* octopus, fritters.

SUMMARY AND COMMENTS Opened in 1999 by a pair of Greek siblings, this authentic Greek restaurant features regional island cuisine (the grandfather of the proprietors came from Corfu), Greek wines (the nectar of the gods), ambrosial desserts, kickin' coffee, and a marvelous party atmosphere worthy of Zorba's favorite *bouzouki* joint. Two sets of *tsifteteli* (Greek belly dancing) a night make the place a riotous party, and after a few ouzos, patrons are happy to join in. The food is fresh, interesting, and well worth the trip to Camden.

kids Café Crêperie ★★

FRENCH CRÊPERIE	INEXPENSIVE	QUALITY ★★	VALUE ★★★

2 Exhibition Road, South Kensington, SW7; ☎ 0207-589-8947; www.kensingtoncreperie.com; tube: South Kensington

Customers Tourists, French people, locals. **Reservations** No. **When to go** On a sunny day to sit outside, or anytime but lunch. **Entree range** £5–£10. **Payment** AE, MC, V. **Service rating** ★★★. **Friendliness rating** ★★½. **Bar** No. **Wine selection** No. **Dress** Casual. **Disabled access** Yes. **Hours** Daily, 9 a.m.–9 p.m.

SETTING AND ATMOSPHERE No-frills French crêpe joint—small dining room, a few tables outside.

HOUSE SPECIALTIES Galettes with any filling you want; sweet crêpes.

OTHER RECOMMENDATIONS Crêpe with almonds, cream, and real maple syrup. Get one to go if there is no table available.

ENTERTAINMENT AND AMENITIES Watching the chef make the crêpes.

SUMMARY AND COMMENTS From a crêpe cart outside a pub in West Hampstead, the owners of this authentically French *crêperie* took their rollicking success and opened a little shop in South Kensington. If you've ever traveled through France, you will know the genre: a menu of savory galettes, which are made with a darker flour, and sugary-sweet white-flour crêpes. Café Crêperie also serves desserts, salad, and sandwiches, but none are much to write home about.

What you want from this quick-hit place is, say, a ham-and-cheese galette followed by any of the dessert crepes: chocolate with chantilly cream (whipped cream), nuts and honey, syrup and butter, or the simple perfection of a *crêpe sucre,* with fine sugar sprinkled on it. I have seen many young picky eaters transformed into Francophiles at their first taste of one of these sweet crêpes.

Café Spice Namaste   ★★★★

INDIAN	MODERATE/EXPENSIVE	QUALITY ★★★★	VALUE ★★★

16 Prescot Street, The City, E1; ☎ 0207-488-9242; www.cafespice.co.uk; tube: Tower Hill or Tower Gateway

Customers Mostly locals, especially businesspeople and aficionados. **Reservations** Recommended. **When to go** Lunch or dinner. **Entree range** £14–£18. **Payment** AE, CB, D, DC, JCB, MC, V. **Service rating** ★★★★. **Friendliness rating** ★★★★. **Bar** Yes. **Wine selection** Good. **Dress** Casual. **Disabled access** Yes. **Hours** Monday–Friday, noon–3 p.m. and 6:15–10:30 p.m.; Saturday, 6:30–10:30 p.m.; closed Sundays and bank holidays.

SETTING AND ATMOSPHERE A nicely redecorated, high-ceilinged room in a 19th-century building. The Ginger Garden next to the restaurant looks like Goa in the City and features a mosaic tiled bar as well as an outdoor tandoori oven.

HOUSE SPECIALTIES Unusual curries from various Indian regions; tandoori dishes; breads; vegetarian dishes.

OTHER RECOMMENDATIONS Weekly-changing specialty menus.

SUMMARY AND COMMENTS Cyrus Todiwala (known as the "Svengali of Spice") has made Café Spice Namaste one of London's best places to find really serious Indian food. Indeed, he is one of the prime "modernizers" of this favorite British cuisine, raising standards in every aspect over the nondescript curry houses of the bad old days. The dishes on the regular menu cover nearly every area of the Indian subcontinent and are distinguished by their subtle, complex spicing and relative rarity in European recipes. There is also a weekly specialty menu spotlighting a particular region, and the wine list is notable for its serious attention to matching every style of food on the menu.

There is no resting on laurels here—the awards and citations keep pouring in, and Todiwala continues to challenge London's diners to get out of the "curry in a hurry" frame of mind. One cannot help reflecting on the fact that Indians were blending extraordinary spices at the same time that Brits were scratching peat out of a bog. The idea that Indian food is a single cuisine featuring a handful of cardamom and saffron is quickly put to rest here, as exotic tastes from the pan-Asian school of cooking are given a place on the plate.

kids Carluccio's Caffè ★★★

ITALIAN	MODERATE	QUALITY ★★★	VALUE ★★★

St. Christopher's Place, Marylebone, W1; ☎ 0207-935-5927;
tube: Bond Street
12 West Smithfield, EC1;☎ 0207-329-5903; tube: Farringdon
1–7 Old Brompton Road, SW7; ☎ 0207-581-8101; tube: South Kensington;
www.carluccios.com

Customers Locals. **Reservations** Recommended. **When to go** Lunch or dinner. **Entree range** £6–£10.95. **Payment** AE, MC, V. **Service rating** ★★★½. **Friendliness rating** ★★★★. **Bar** No. **Wine selection** Small and inexpensive. **Dress** Casual. **Disabled access** Some locations. **Hours** Monday–Friday, 8 a.m.–11 p.m.; Saturday, 9 a.m.–11 p.m.; Sunday, 10 a.m.–10:30 p.m. (All central London branches adhere approximately to this schedule.)

SETTING AND ATMOSPHERE Simply decorated deli-style rooms, bustling all hours of the day; long shared tables as well as smaller, more private seating; friendly and informal.

HOUSE SPECIALTIES Breads, antipasti, pasta, salads, simple meat and fish dishes.

OTHER RECOMMENDATIONS Lasagna, tiramisù.

SUMMARY AND COMMENTS The 12 branches of this successful chain are nearly always full to bursting. The formula works, and the reason is simple and obvious: this is top-quality, mostly very simple food served in pleasant (if somewhat noisy) surroundings with an absolute minimum of fuss. Cheerful waitstaff may want to place you at one of the long, cafeteria-style tables, and if there's nothing else available, you won't mind a bit. Pasta is a particularly strong point, as you would expect, and you can eat lightly on just an antipasto such as bruschetta served with roasted or grilled vegetables (£3.95). Being open all day is another major attraction, especially because the baked goods and the coffee are of exceptional quality. There

2

is also a deli counter where you can get takeout, as well as baked goods, ground espresso, olive oils, and anything Italian you can think of. If you're eating in, leave some room for one of the delicious desserts.

Cambio de Tercio ★★★

SPANISH MODERATE QUALITY ★★★ VALUE ★★★

163 Old Brompton Road, South Kensington, SW5; ☎ 0207-244-8970; tube: Gloucester Road

Customers Locals. **Reservations** Recommended. **When to go** Lunch or dinner. **Entree range** Lunch £14–£16. **Payment** AE, MC, V. **Service rating** ★★★★. **Friendliness rating** ★★★★. **Bar** No. **Wine selection** Excellent, mostly Spanish. **Dress** Casual. **Disabled access** Restaurant only. **Hours** Monday–Saturday, 12:30–2:30 p.m. and 7–11:30 p.m.; Sunday, 7–11 p.m.

SETTING AND ATMOSPHERE A crowded yet cozy basement room decorated with bullfighting motifs.

HOUSE SPECIALTIES Oxtail, hake, suckling pig, tapas.

OTHER RECOMMENDATIONS Chorizo, soup of the day.

SUMMARY AND COMMENTS Cambio de Tercio is one of London's best Spanish restaurants. The kitchen is equally adept at preparing staple dishes, using the best and most authentic imported ingredients, and at reinterpreting classics with a modern slant. Lovers of tapas, the "little dishes" with which Spanish people love to begin an evening's festivities, should note that the selection and quality here are excellent—and the choice of sherries, the perfect partner for this kind of eating, is similarly broad. The kitchen has undergone a few personnel changes over the years, but standards have remained high. And though there have been loud grumbles about service from some quarters, they are neither numerous nor serious enough to keep Cambio off your list of possibilities. Dessert lovers should note that while Spain does not always excel in that department, Cambio de Tercio almost always does.

kids Chez Gérard at the Opera Terrace ★★

FRENCH (BISTRO) INEXPENSIVE/MODERATE QUALITY ★★★ VALUE ★★★

The Market, The Piazza, West End, WC2; ☎ 0207-379-0666; www.santeonline.co.uk; tube: Covent Garden

Customers Locals and tourists. **Reservations** Recommended. **When to go** Lunch or dinner (restaurant); for an early pre-theater dinner. **Entree range** £12–£22; set menu: £16 for 2 courses, £19 for 3. **Payment** AE, CB, D, DC, MC, V. **Service rating** ★★½. **Friendliness rating** ★★★½. **Bar** Yes. **Wine selection** Good. **Dress** Casual. **Disabled access** No. **Hours** Monday–Saturday, noon–11:30 p.m.; Sunday, noon–10:30 p.m.

SETTING AND ATMOSPHERE Conservatory overlooking Covent Garden market with an open-air terrace in warm weather.

HOUSE SPECIALTIES Steak, especially Châteaubriand and *onglet* (hanger steak), served with *pommes frites*.

OTHER RECOMMENDATIONS Simple bistro-style dishes such as oysters, fish soup, snails, and Bayonne ham with pickles.

SUMMARY AND COMMENTS Chez Gérard has a very simple formula: French-style steak, French-style *pommes frites* (better known as French fries), and French-style service. They usually do it very well, though there are variations from branch to branch, and prices remain low enough to keep most people happy even if they run into occasional problems with cooking or service. Fish eaters will always find at least one dish aimed at them, as will vegetarians, but these are the most variable options in terms of quality, and they are not—let's be frank—what Chez Gérard is about. Don't come here expecting the meal of a lifetime (although the Gatwick and Heathrow branches are your best bet for airport eating); if you're a steak lover, however, this could be your home away from home.

Cipriani London ★★½

ITALIAN	EXPENSIVE	QUALITY ★★	VALUE ★★½

23–25 Davies Street, Mayfair, W1; ☎ 0207-399-0500; www.cipriani.com; tube: Bond Street

Customers Businesspeople, anorexic celebs, ladies who lunch, boulevardiers. **Reservations** Yes. **When to go** Lunch is less expensive. **Entree range** £12–£33. **Payment** AE, DC, MC, V. **Service rating** ★★★. **Friendliness rating** ★★★½. **Bar** Yes. **Wine selection** Good. **Dress** Smart casual. **Disabled access** Yes. **Hours** Daily, noon–3 p.m. and 6 p.m.–midnight.

SETTING AND ATMOSPHERE Elegant but unstuffy, with weird chairs that are too low for the tables. There's a kind of Continental loucheness not found in many similar London restaurants. The hard walls of the room make for terrible acoustics, and a high noise level gives it a buzz it might not otherwise have. Heads swivel like the revolving door itself each time a new arrival is disgorged; the eternal hope of celeb-spotting seems contagious in this restaurant.

HOUSE SPECIALTIES Beef carpaccio, steak tartare, veal Milanese, club sandwich.

OTHER RECOMMENDATIONS Tiramisù, homemade tagliolini, *risotto alla primavera*.

SUMMARY AND COMMENTS We decided to try Cipriani the day after all the former Spice Girls helped celebrate David Beckham's birthday here—not necessarily a great recommendation, as none of those women seem to do much in the way of eating. But it was as good a reason as any. The reputation of Harry's Bar in Venice, granddaddy to all the Harry Cipriani–sponsored sprogs in New York (not to mention the outpost in Hong Kong), gives the London restaurant a not-altogether-justified stamp of approval. It may be very different at dinner, but with lunch specials running from £28 to £35 for a three-course meal, we couldn't make the kind of financial commitment needed for din-din. It was hopping during a Friday lunch, with all tables filled and people three deep at the bar. The service was no more special than the bread, and of the two, the latter came as more of a surprise: boring breadsticks and a kind of English muffin advertised as a brioche. Not promising. The carpaccio was excellent, no doubt about it, and the tiramisù was right on the money, but generally speaking, when you're paying £22 for a hamburger, you expect some magic with your meal. The only sorcery evident at Cipriani was its sleight of hand in making £89 disappear for an essentially dull lunch of pasta and salad for two, with no alcohol and only one dessert. But Cipriani is there to stay, so something must be working. It's a crapshoot . . . do you feel lucky?

Clarke's ★★★½

MODERN EUROPEAN   **EXPENSIVE**   **QUALITY ★★★★**½   **VALUE ★★★**

124 Kensington Church Street, Kensington, W8; ☎ 0207-221-9225; www.sallyclarke.com; tube: Notting Hill Gate

Customers Mostly locals. **Reservations** Essential. **When to go** Lunch or dinner. **Entree range** Lunch from £16; set dinner menu, £49 for 4 courses. **Payment** AE, D, DC, MC, V. **Service rating ★★★★**½. **Friendliness rating ★★★★**. **Bar** No. **Wine selection** Outstanding. **Dress** Casual. **Disabled access** Restaurant, yes; toilets, no. **Hours** Monday, 12:30–2 p.m.; Tuesday–Friday, 12:30–2 p.m. and 7–10 p.m.; Saturday brunch, 11 a.m.–2 p.m.; dinner, 7–10 p.m.; closed Sunday.

SETTING AND ATMOSPHERE Upstairs room is tiny and intimate; downstairs is big and bustling, with a view of the kitchen.

HOUSE SPECIALTIES Dinner menu changes daily, but expect the best of ingredients made in a professional and tantalizing style. Brunch on Saturday is great, and the bread is so good they've opened a bakery and specialty-food shop, Clarke & Clarke's, that sells its wares to the high-end groceries of London, as well as restaurants. Clarke's Breads turns out 2,000 loaves a night.

OTHER RECOMMENDATIONS Lunch features variations on corn-fed chicken, Cornish haddock, grilled veal, roasted lamb, Irish organic salmon, and more. Try the cheesecake.

SUMMARY AND COMMENTS No one in Britain understands California cooking better than Sally Clarke, who worked there years ago (at Chez Panisse and elsewhere) before moving back to London and opening her own place. She bases her cooking on the seasons and on what's available at the market on a given day. Thus, dinner menus change every day (and reservations are only accepted 24 hours in advance, so she knows how much to buy), with a short *carte* at lunchtime and fixed menus (following the example of Chez Panisse) at dinner. For years you ate whatever Sally was serving at dinner—it was called a "no choice four-course dinner menu"—but after more than two decades, she is now offering options. The menu is strong in seasonal and regional foods: buffalo mozzarella is flown in from Naples twice weekly, shellfish comes by train from Scotland, and meat is sourced from some of England's most enlightened and ecological farmers. Because the ingredients are the best that money can buy, the preparation is straightforward—simple but perfectly executed roasting, chargrilling, and baking keep tastes honest and calories low. But before you slip into those tight jeans for dinner, remember that the homemade bread and pastries will blow any diet right out of the water. Phone in advance to find out what's on the menu for dinner; given enough warning, they will happily provide alternatives if you have food issues. The wine list is superb but not especially high priced. Clarke's is not at all cheap, but at its price level it is one of the best restaurants in London.

Cottons Islington ★★★

CARIBBEAN	INEXPENSIVE	QUALITY ★★	VALUE ★★★

70 Exmouth Market (off Rosebery Avenue), Islington-Clerkenwell, EC1; ☎ 0207-833-3332; tube: Angel

Customers Island boys and girls, locals, and rummies. **Reservations** For large parties. **When to go** Lunch or dinner. **Entree range** £7–£14.50 (lunch), £5–£12.95 (evening). **Payment** AE, CB, DC, MC, V. **Service rating** ★★½. **Friendliness rating** ★★★. **Bar** Excellent cocktail bar, the Rum Club, downstairs. **Wine selection** Not as great as the rum selection, but very good. **Dress** Casual to flamboyant. **Disabled access** Limited. **Hours** Monday–Friday, noon–4 p.m. and 5:30–11 p.m.; Saturday, 6–11 p.m.; Sunday, noon–11 p.m.

SETTING AND ATMOSPHERE Three separate bar areas; some open-air seating under heated canopies; comfortable and lively contemporary feel.

HOUSE SPECIALTIES West Indian favorites like jerk chicken, fish fritters, Jamaican patties, goat curry, and plantains are available, but you know you're not in Negril when you check out the panfried vegetables with couscous and a coconut sauce.

OTHER RECOMMENDATIONS Chickpea-and-pumpkin curry with grilled roti, marinated chicken strips, ginger-and-lime crème brûlée. The cocktails—even if you opt out of the rum—are to die for.

SUMMARY AND COMMENTS One of the best Caribbean restaurants in a city long settled by a big West Indian population, Cottons opened just a couple of years ago and has made a splash with the locals and those seeking some reminder of endless sunny days and warm white sands. They serve authentic Caribbean food updated with fresh ingredients and a few modern European twists. High-quality local produce and imported overproof rum give Cottons a huge advantage over most island-beach-resort restaurants, which you might not be able to ascertain—or indeed care much about—after you've chugged a £25 jug of the Reggae Rum Punch.

Daphne's ★★★★

ITALIAN	EXPENSIVE	QUALITY ★★★★	VALUE ★★★★

112 Draycott Avenue, South Kensington, SW3; ☎ 0207-589-4257; www.daphnes-restaurant.co.uk; tube: South Kensington

Customers Locals, businesspeople, men and women of leisure. **Reservations** For dinner. **When to go** Anytime. **Entree range** £10–£25; set lunch menu, £16.75. **Payment** AE, DC, MC, V. **Service rating** ★★★★. **Friendliness rating** ★★★★★. **Bar** For customers waiting on a table. **Wine selection** Excellent; French and Italian. **Dress** No code. **Disabled access** Yes for restaurant, no for bathroom. **Hours** Monday–Friday, noon–3 p.m. and 5:45–11 p.m.; Saturday, noon–3:30 p.m. and 5:30–11:30 p.m.; Sunday, noon–4 p.m. and 5:30–10:30 p.m.

SETTING AND ATMOSPHERE Upscale Tuscan feel; a back room features a small fireplace, and a roof skylight opens on nice days.

HOUSE SPECIALTIES Chargrilled squid with Tuscan sausage, veal tartare, grilled scallops, perfect pasta.

OTHER RECOMMENDATIONS Iced berries covered in hot white-chocolate sauce, *panna cotta*, ravioli, meatballs with potatoes, creamed polenta.

SUMMARY AND COMMENTS Owned by the same group that runs The Ivy, Le Caprice, and a host of other great restaurants in London, Daphne's is a sterling example of democratic friendliness mixed with professional service and perfectly prepared Italian cuisine. Visiting on a rainy day, damply bedraggled and all alone, I was given the most polite and attentive service I have found in London. Most shockingly, as a middle-aged American woman, I was given a choice between a good table and a great table by the window; accordingly, I took the latter. Accustomed to second-class treatment in third-class restaurants when dining alone at peak lunch or dinner times, I was absurdly gratified by the warmth of the reception. (Granted, one should always be assured of good manners when visiting a good restaurant, but sadly, that's just not always the case.) Not only was I treated with the great goodwill that should be a hallmark of all relations in the service industry, but the maître d' was alert enough to bring me, unbidden, the newspaper—a nice touch. Daphne's was once an overly fashionable restaurant, which was off-putting to me. It took me a dozen years of living a three-minute walk away to finally eat there—and I predict this will become a well-trodden path.

The bill does add up when you stray from the well-priced set menu, but it was worth it. Ordering a starter of butternut ravioli with pumpkin seeds and a balsamic reduction proved that they know how to do pasta with flair. For the entree, I ordered meatballs with roasted potatoes in tomato sauce, reasoning that this is one of those dishes that can go horribly wrong in all but the best chefs' hands, and I needed to take the measure of this eatery efficiently. The kitchen picked up the challenge with ease and ran it to the finish line. I will not linger here on the fulsome beauty and divine flavor of the *panna cotta*—another reliable diagnostic of Italian-chef pop quizzes (for French restaurants, crème brûlée and omelets provide a similar kind of DNA evidence)—but I certainly lingered while I ate it. The desserts are all extraordinary, but special mention must go to the iced mixed berries drowned in a warm white-chocolate sauce that winningly teases out flavors you might never have thought possible in a raspberry-blueberry-whatever-berry dessert. I was charmed by the whole experience of Daphne's, and I reckon that if I stick to the set menu at lunch, I just might be able to make it my weekly treat.

Daquise ★★

POLISH	INEXPENSIVE	QUALITY ★★	VALUE ★★★

20 Thurloe Street, South Kensington, SW7; ☎ 0207-589-6117; tube: South Kensington

Customers Homesick Slavs, locals, comfort-food seekers. **Reservations** No. **When to go** Anytime. **Entree range** £6–£12. **Payment** MC, V. **Service rating** ★★★★. **Friendliness rating** ★★★★. **Bar** No. **Wine selection** Adequate. **Dress** Casual. **Disabled access** Yes. **Hours** Daily, 11:30 a.m.–11 p.m.

SETTING AND ATMOSPHERE Small and old-fashioned, with banquettes lining the walls. Woody Allen used the restaurant in a scene from an upcoming film project.

HOUSE SPECIALTIES Potato pancakes, stroganoff, schnitzel, pierogis.

OTHER RECOMMENDATIONS Hungarian goulash in a giant potato pancake.

SUMMARY AND COMMENTS Daquise has been around for a long time, and long may she continue. It's a completely unpretentious restaurant with authentically heavy Polish food, and for once in London, the Polish waitstaff matches the cuisine. Probably not coincidentally, the servers at Daquise seem happier than those at the many non-Slavic restaurants populated by young Polish émigrés. The food is always good and plentiful, which means that weight watchers should watch it. The desserts are unbelievably heavy—strudel loaded with nuts, cheese, and apples; cheesecake with a chocolate-graham-cracker crust and topped with a nut-and-caramel caloric explosion. And when that comes—after, say, a plate of potato pancakes served with sour cream and homemade applesauce, pierogis, and maybe a cream-laden stroganoff—prepare to be wheeled home, fat but happy.

E&O ★★★½

ASIAN FUSION	MODERATE/EXPENSIVE	QUALITY ★★★★	VALUE ★★

14 Blenheim Crescent, Notting Hill, W11; ☎ 0207-229-5454; www.ricker-restaurants.com; tube: Notting Hill or Ladbroke Grove

Customers Elegant Notting Hillbillies. **Reservations** Recommended. **When to go** Dinner, for a look at the beautiful people. **Entree range** £9–£28 (for lobster); dim sum, £3–£8. **Payment** AE, DC, MC, V. **Service rating** ★★★. **Friendliness rating** ★★★. **Bar** Yes. **Wine selection** Good. **Dress** Casual. **Disabled access** Yes. **Hours** Monday–Friday, 12:15–3 p.m. and 6:15–11 p.m.; Saturday, 12:15–4 p.m. and 6:15–11 p.m.; Sunday, 12:30–4 p.m. and 6:15–10:30 p.m.

SETTING AND ATMOSPHERE Zen-like simplicity with linen-tablecloth elegance.

HOUSE SPECIALTIES Roasted black cod with miso, caramelized pork, steamed whole sea bass, pad thai.

OTHER RECOMMENDATIONS Vegetarian dishes, dim sum, desserts.

ENTERTAINMENT AND AMENITIES Watch the beautiful people on diets actually eat the delicious food.

SUMMARY AND COMMENTS This is one of four restaurants dreamed up by Aussie Will Ricker, whose success in London's cutthroat dining scene has been impressive, helped in part by the celebs who put E&O in the news, and in the main by the painstaking presentation of the often carb-free, wheat-free, and dairy-free—but never taste-free—dishes. The pan-Asian menu showcases unusual combinations in dim sum, such as water chestnut–date *gyoza*, as well as the old standbys of bang-bang chicken, satay, and spareribs. Main dishes should be ordered with abandon and shared by the table; the vegetarian fare is particularly good. The desserts are delicious: vanilla-and-lemongrass crème brûlée, seasonal fruit sorbets, and a special chocolate pudding (tell the waiter early on, as it takes 20 minutes to prepare). Curries, sashimi, tempura, and Oriental salads are all artfully placed on the plates and are a real treat for the palate.

The other Ricker restaurants are **Eight over Eight,** with more of a Chinese emphasis (392 King's Road, Chelsea, SW3; ☎ 0207-349-9934); **Great Eastern Dining Room** (54–56 Great Eastern Street, The City, EC2A; ☎ 0207-613-4545); and **Cicada** (132–136 St. John Street, The City, EC1; ☎ 0207-608-1550). Opening in 2008: **Mandalay** (75 Page Street, Westminster, SW1; see Web site on previous page for details and updates).

Eat and Two Veg ★★★½

VEGETARIAN	INEXPENSIVE	QUALITY ★★★★	VALUE ★★★★

50 Marylebone High Street, W1;☎ 0207-258-8595; www.eatandtwoveg.com; tube: Baker Street

Customers Vegans and vegetarians, locals. **Reservations** For large parties, weekends, and dinner. **When to go** Breakfast, lunch, or dinner. **Entree range** £5–£12. **Payment** MC, V. **Service rating** ★★★. **Friendliness rating** ★★★. **Bar** Good cocktails. **Wine selection** Impressive, especially for a seriously vegetarian restaurant. **Dress** No code. **Disabled access** Yes. **Hours** Monday–Saturday, 9 a.m.–11 p.m.; Sunday, 10 a.m.–10 p.m.

SETTING AND ATMOSPHERE Airy, attractive, upscale dinerlike look, with tables as well as booths and an open grill; homey, unfussy atmosphere.

HOUSE SPECIALTIES Classic dishes made with vegetable protein or tofu, such as Lancaster hotpot, schnitzel, veggie burgers; Sunday Nut Roast Special.

OTHER RECOMMENDATIONS Bread-and-butter pudding, Crispy Aromatic Duck (Beijing "duck" made with gluten), full English breakfast with soy bacon or sausages.

SUMMARY AND COMMENTS Vegetarians and vegans in London have been scratching their heads for the past two decades wondering why, in this capital city with probably more herbivores than in, say, San Francisco or Phuket, the best meat-free restaurants on offer here tended to be grad-student type cafeterias where you can forget about wine, style, and comfort. Eat and Two Veg has filled that gap in the market beautifully: it's centrally located in busy Marylebone; it's designed with élan and an eye to efficiency; and it has a huge menu compared with the places that feature the daily legume casserole, the daily stir-fry, and the daily tofu option. Here you can get eggs, veggie burgers, pastas, soups, salads, faux-meat dishes, stews, cottage pies, and luscious desserts all day and night. It's got the kind of urban buzz that city folk go for when dining out, and between the good table service, the sophisticated variety of potables, and the stylish atmosphere, it provides a peaceable kingdom in which lamb and lion, carnivore and vegan, can sit down together to eat in harmony and gustatory goodwill. Your meat-and-potatoes friend won't moan about being deprived of the "main dish," and vegetarian dining companions won't be thinking sadly of butchered innocents being tucked into by tablemates. There's not a mad cow in sight. It's win–win, especially when the bill comes: the prices are very reasonable for this part of town.

Fifteen Dining Room and Trattoria ★★★★½

BRITISH	EXPENSIVE	QUALITY ★★★★★	VALUE ★★★½

13 Westland Place, Hackney, N1; ☎ 0871-330-1515; www.fifteen.net; tube: Old Street (Exit 1)

Customers Everyone and anyone. **Reservations** No reservations for the Trattoria; reserve a week in advance for dinner at the Dining Room. **When to go** Whenever you can. **Entree range** *Trattoria:* lunch or dinner from £15, breakfast, £4–£14; *Dining Room:* lunch, £15–£18; set menu from £23; dinner tasting menu (6 courses), £60. **Payment** AE, MC, V. **Service rating** ★★★★. **Friendliness rating** ★★★★½. **Bar** No. **Wine selection** Excellent wine, some sold by the glass. **Dress** Casual. **Disabled access** Trattoria, yes; downstairs, no. **Hours** *Trattoria:* Monday–Saturday, 7:30–11 a.m., noon–3 p.m., 6–9:30 p.m.; Sunday, noon–3:30 p.m.; *Dining Room:* Daily, noon–3 p.m. and 6:30–9:45 p.m.

SETTING AND ATMOSPHERE New York downtown-funky vibe, with distressed wide-board hardwood floors, simple furniture, faux graffiti on the walls, and a long window on the kitchen, which is the real star here. There are some very groovy booths, too, kind of space-age, which are a destination of choice for Fifteen fans. The ground-floor Trattoria is more buzzy and close-quartered; it's warm and cheerful, and the chefs walk among you more than in the Dining Room.

HOUSE SPECIALTIES The Dining Room changes its à la carte and set lunch menus according to what's available seasonally; dinner is a set menu or tasting menu with Fifteen's signature dishes. Some examples include beef shin and horseradish ravioli, fisherman's stew, leg of lamb cooked for 12 hours, and risotto or pasta dishes.

OTHER RECOMMENDATIONS Any of the desserts, which change with the season, but you can expect the following all year round: tiramisù, apple tart with truffle-honey ice cream, and rice pudding with some wicked extras.

SUMMARY AND COMMENTS Jamie Oliver now has a total of four Fifteen restaurants: in London, Amsterdam, Cornwall, and Melbourne. All are charitable organizations with the goal of giving potentially lost kids the skills to find their place in the world. Oliver's Fifteen Foundation has graduated an army of skilled chefs and staff, many of whom now have their own restaurants or work in some of the world's best kitchens. Jamie's dream—now an ongoing reality—was to take a number of at-risk kids, either homeless or in foster care, and train them to be great chefs. Shrewdly, he did this on TV, which gave the scheme a big boost, both in supporters and applicants. Jamie (all of England is on first-name terms with him) has also shown equally impressive innovation in improving school lunches. His saving-the-world-one-meal-at-a-time philosophy has shown hard, practical results: his work in the cafeterias of state-funded schools proved, in a matter of weeks, that eating fresh and healthy meals on a regular basis can improve a child's attendance, attention, behavior, and grades. Astonishingly, some parents kicked back, with a handful of malcontent—and possibly insane—mothers passing their kids potato chips, greasy French fries, candy, and other assorted crap through the school gates. Ah, England. (See **www.feedmebetter.com** for more information on this program.)

Jamie's activism means that eating at Fifteen is not merely a selfish gastronomic pleasure but a donation toward his admirable projects, with all profits going to the Fifteen Foundation. What's in it for us? Well, the food, obviously. It's fantastic. If you know anything about Jamie Oliver, you know that the market determines the menu, with only the freshest ingredients making it onto his cutting boards. The Trattoria serves breakfast, lunch, and dinner, with à la carte selections that change daily. The more formal Dining Room offers exquisite tasting menus, set lunches, and dinners. The food can best be described as modern British with an Italian prejudice, probably best summed up in the ravioli stuffed with Label Anglais free-range chicken, mascarpone, and roast garlic, or the indescribably fluffy potato gnocchi with Scottish mushrooms. Do make a reservation, and prepare for an admittedly expensive but oh-so-virtuous—and delicious—meal.

kids fish! ★★

FISH AND SHELLFISH   INEXPENSIVE/MODERATE   QUALITY ★★½   VALUE ★★★½

Cathedral Street, London Bridge, SE1; ☎ 0207-407-3803; www.fishdiner.co.uk; tube: London Bridge

Customers Locals and tourists, fish-loving families. **Reservations** Recommended. **When to go** Lunch or dinner. **Entree range** £10.95–£16.95. **Payment** AE, D, DC, JCB, MC, V. **Service rating** ★★★. **Friendliness rating** ★★★½. **Bar** In some branches, but designed for customers waiting on tables. **Wine selection** Small, adequate, inexpensive. **Dress** Casual. **Disabled access** Yes. **Hours** Monday–Thursday, 11:30 a.m.–11 p.m.; Friday–Sunday, noon–11 p.m.

SETTING AND ATMOSPHERE Informal, modern dining rooms with a view of the kitchen.

HOUSE SPECIALTIES Fresh fish and plenty of it, plainly cooked and market-fresh.

ENTERTAINMENT AND AMENITIES Watching the chefs at work.

SUMMARY AND COMMENTS As an island nation, England has always been mad about fish, even if its favorite incarnation, fish and chips, has long been more about grease and carbs than protein. At fish! you are invited to have it your way, and not in the Burger King style. The emphasis is on buying top-quality fish, steaming or grilling it, and allowing customers to choose a side vegetable and a sauce (salsa, hollandaise, herb-and-garlic butter, and so on). Appetizers are along the lines of deviled whitebait, calamari, prawn cocktail, and crab cakes. Though not at all fancy, this is a good, reliable restaurant that won't break the bank.

Food for Thought ★★★½

VEGETARIAN	INEXPENSIVE	QUALITY ★★★½	VALUE ★★★★

**31 Neal Street, Covent Garden, WC2; ☎ 0207-836-0239;
tube: Covent Garden**

Customers Local vegetarians and vegans. **Reservations** Not accepted. **When to go** Arrive at the stroke of noon or after 2 p.m.—the heart of lunch hour gets extremely, uncomfortably crowded, with people waiting on the rickety steps to the basement dining room. **Entree range** £5–£7. **Payment** Cash only. **Service rating** Not applicable (service is cafeteria-style). **Friendliness rating** ★★★. **Bar** No. **Wine selection** BYOB. **Dress** Casual. **Disabled access** No. **Hours** Monday–Saturday, noon–8:30 p.m.; Sunday, noon–5 p.m.

SETTING AND ATMOSPHERE Spartan yet pleasant withal; wooden tables are often shared. A bohemian-hippie-student vibe.

HOUSE SPECIALTIES Stir-fried vegetables with tofu and brown rice, vegan and wheat-free cakes, vegetable stews and casseroles.

OTHER RECOMMENDATIONS Salad with tahini dressing.

SUMMARY AND COMMENTS This is another one of those time capsules that reminds me of some of the great natural-foods restaurants in San Francisco, back when meat-free, wheat-free, or no-dairy diets were considered exotic. The food is served up cafeteria-style; you may have to stand in a queue that can go all the way up the stairs (the dining room is in the basement of an old Georgian building) and out the front door. Indeed, Food for Thought opened in 1974, when Neal Street and the surrounding area were full of head shops and storefront mystics (there's still a crystal shop and an astrology shop there), and it answered the needs of chronically broke students, artists, and rebels with its dirt-cheap, delicious, and filling vegan and vegetarian dishes: stir-fries, brown rice, pasties, and salads, all served in a mellow atmosphere. With vegetarianism having become more mainstream than ever, this restaurant has managed to hold on to its lease in the ever-rising rents of the area around Seven Dials by sticking to its tried-and-true methods: they use good local produce, change the menu each day (except for the brown-rice-and-stir-fried-vegetable option), and give you good value for your money. If I'm having a large dinner party with a few vegans present, I let Food for Thought do the cooking—they always get it right. For a healthy and inexpensive pre-theater meal within easy walking of most of the West End playhouses, this is the place.

Gourmet Burger Kitchen ★★★

AMERICAN	INEXPENSIVE	QUALITY ★★★★	VALUE ★★★★

**163–165 Earls Court Road, Earls Court, SW5; ☎ 0207-373-3184;
www.gbkinfo.com; tube: Earls Court; multiple locations throughout
central London**

Customers Burger lovers, locals, Yankees, office workers doing takeout. **Reservations** No. **When to go** Lunch or dinner. **Entree range** £6–£10. **Payment**

MC, V. **Service rating** ★★. **Friendliness rating** ★★½. **Bar** No. **Wine selection** So-so. **Dress** Casual. **Disabled access** Yes. **Hours** Monday–Friday, noon–11 p.m.; Saturday, 11 a.m.–11 p.m.; Sunday, 11 a.m.–10 p.m.

SETTING AND ATMOSPHERE Totally utilitarian, with plain, clean, solid decor. Atmosphere is cafeteria chic. Well, actually, there's not much atmosphere to speak of, but nothing to complain about either.

HOUSE SPECIALTIES Burgers, burgers, burgers.

OTHER RECOMMENDATIONS Milk shakes, falafel, veggie options, French fries.

SUMMARY AND COMMENTS This chain points to a new trend in eating (we won't say "dining") in London: no table service, everything sold separately (which can add up), and concentration on one central item—in this case, the hamburger. They're not fooling around with that central item either—GBK serves what is arguably the best burger in London: a good-sized but not ridiculously overlarge beef patty, cooked over a flame and served in a delicious sesame-seed-covered bun. Homemade ketchup and a mayonnaise sauce add to the included extras (onions, lettuce, and tomato). The extreme variety of burgers (Thai chicken, Greek lamb, veggie burgers, falafel, mushroom, chorizo) is a bit unnecessary if you're in the market for a good old cheeseburger, but nontraditionalists may appreciate the wild selection of toppings, which include such surprises as kiwi, pineapple, blue cheese, and pesto sauce, as well as the more-pedestrian avocado, bacon, and chili.

Halepi Restaurant and Kebab House   ★★★½

GREEK	INEXPENSIVE/MODERATE	QUALITY ★★★★	VALUE ★★★★

18 Leinster Terrace, Bayswater, W2; ☎ 0207-262-1070; www.halepi.co.uk; tube: Bayswater

Customers Locals, regulars, Greek expats, and visitors. **Reservations** Weekends or for large parties. **When to go** Anytime. **Entree range** £10–£20. **Payment** MC, V. **Service rating** ★★★★. **Friendliness rating** ★★★★. **Bar** No. **Wine selection** Greek, Portuguese, and French. **Dress** Casual. **Disabled access** None for bathroom. **Hours** Daily, noon–midnight.

SETTING AND ATMOSPHERE Reassuringly unmodernized, Halepi is intimate and homey, with wood paneling and red banquettes; you'll feel as if you are in an old Greek *bouzoukia.*

HOUSE SPECIALTIES *Kleftikon* (baked lamb *à la grecque*), grilled prawns, kebabs; hard-to-find Greek sausages; unbelievably good *baklava.*

OTHER RECOMMENDATIONS Fish *meze,* beef *stifado,* anything from the grill.

SUMMARY AND COMMENTS Owned by the Kazolides family, Halepi has been serving London since 1966; the wife of the original owner still makes the transcendentally delicious baklava and runs the kitchen. The good old Greek favorites are featured—*spanakopita, moussaka, dolmades,* and *taramasalata*—but mainly it's the ingredients that are the stars here. The food is fresh and perfectly seasoned, and it hits the highest standards of any global cuisine as far as taste goes. The grilled prawns are always perfect, and the Halloumi cheese is also grilled in such a way that its simple flavor doesn't require any sauces or condiments to make it shine—but do dip it into the mixed *meze* of hummus, taramasalata, and *tzatziki:* all are homemade and a meal in themselves. It's a no-fuss, no-pretense kind of a place. Regulars who've been coming here for most of their lives will no doubt insist on being wheeled in on a walker or in a wheelchair in their extreme old age, for one last honey-dripping baklava. Friendly, professional service, reasonable prices, and the sense that Mama—or, in this case, Yaya ("Grandma" in Greek)—is in the kitchen and cooking for her family make Halepi one of the nicest, most reliable restaurants in London.

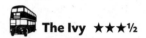 **The Ivy** ★★★½

| MODERN EUROPEAN | MODERATE | QUALITY ★★★★ | VALUE ★★★½ |

1–5 West Street, West End, WC2; ☎ 0207-836-4751; www.the-ivy.co.uk; tube: Leicester Square

Customers Mostly locals, which include the theater folk after 10 p.m. **Reservations** Essential. **When to go** Lunch or dinner. **Entree range** £10–£40. Set lunch Saturday and Sunday, £27 for 3 courses. **Payment** AE, D, DC, JCB, MC, V. **Service rating** ★★★★. **Friendliness rating** ★★★. **Bar** For diners only. **Wine selection** Very good. **Dress** No dress code. **Disabled access** Restaurant only. **Hours** Monday–Saturday, noon–3 p.m. and 5:30 p.m.–midnight; Sunday, noon–3:30 p.m. and 5:30 p.m.–midnight.

SETTING AND ATMOSPHERE Exceptionally comfortable wood-paneled room with stained-glass windows; discreet and refined, but not stuffy.

HOUSE SPECIALTIES Steak tartare, calf's liver, smoked salmon with scrambled eggs, shepherd's pie, eggs Benedict, grilled or fried fish.

OTHER RECOMMENDATIONS Burgers; sautéed foie gras with caramelized apples and a raisin jus; vegetarian and vegan options; raspberry Pavlova and baked Alaska; set lunch.

SUMMARY AND COMMENTS Getting a table at The Ivy is famously difficult, as it's one of London's favorite restaurants and rich hunting grounds for the paparazzi. If you're planning a trip and are dying to eat here, it's advisable to reserve in advance. The popularity of The Ivy is based not on herd instincts among the hungry rich and famous—there are plenty of mediocre restaurants whose point is for people to see and be seen—but on this uncomplicated fact: it's a supremely wonderful place. The food is mostly simple but always executed with great skill, and the prices are not astronomical (which works for the underpaid theater crews who pop in after performances). Service is professional and efficient, occasionally even friendly. The room is comfortable, the menu is extensive, and, yes, you might just see a face or two from *Hello!* magazine or the cover of your *Playbill* while enjoying your eggs Benedict or fish and chips. But don't stare, please. That wouldn't be in keeping with Ivy etiquette.

La Porte des Indes ★★★½

| INDIAN | EXPENSIVE | QUALITY ★★★★ | VALUE ★★★ |

32 Bryanston Street, Marylebone, W1; ☎ 0207-224-0055;
www.laportedesindes.com; tube: Marble Arch

Customers Celebrants, romantic couples, tourists. **Reservations** Recommended
but not essential. **When to go** Anytime. **Entree range** £15–£30; set menu from
£34–£38; vegetarian menu, £32–£36. **Payment** AE, DC, MC, V. **Service rating**
★★★★. **Friendliness rating** ★★★½. **Bar** Jungle Bar, inspired by Singapore's
Raffles Hotel. Throw your peanut shells on the floor. **Wine selection** Good. **Dress**
Casual. **Disabled access** Limited. **Hours** Monday–Friday, noon–2:30 p.m. and
7–11:30 p.m.; Saturday, 7–11:30 p.m.; Sunday, noon–3:30 p.m. and 6–10:30 p.m.

SETTING AND ATMOSPHERE Decadent Raj splendor, with a waterfall, many different dining rooms (all beautifully appointed), and skylights.

HOUSE SPECIALTIES Shrimp, mangoes, green chiles, ginger, and poppy seeds in
coconut curry; grilled lamb chops marinated in "aphrodisiac" spices; crab
Malabar; *makal palak pakora* (fritters of chickpea flour, spinach, and corn).

OTHER RECOMMENDATIONS Grilled lobster *anarkali; gulab jamun* (deep-fried
milk-curd nuggets in cinnamon and rose syrup).

ENTERTAINMENT AND AMENITIES Private rooms; a variety of beautiful vistas
within the main dining rooms; Sunday jazz brunch.

SUMMARY AND COMMENTS Let it be said straightaway that one comes first for
the decor and comes back for the food. The waterfall, the Jungle Bar,
and the fabled exuberance of the decor make you feel as if you're on
the set of a Bollywood extravaganza. It's a bit expensive, but it's worth the
cost—the food is as gorgeous as the decor. As the name implies, La Porte
des Indes is French-influenced, with food that focuses on the former
French colonies of India. Eight specialist chefs make sure that each of
the regional cuisines rings true. They are very accommodating about the
degree of spiciness in the dishes, but Western palates should take care with
the vindaloos and other hot dishes. The service is good and the wine
respectable, and the set menus are a good way to try everything, although
it's probably less expensive to share a few à la carte dishes.

La Porte is owned by Blue Elephant International, which seems to have
perfect pitch when it comes to interpreting Eastern food for Western gastronomes, and whoever does the decorating here should win an award.

Le Caprice   ★★★

| MODERN EUROPEAN | MODERATE | QUALITY ★★★½ | VALUE ★★★ |

Arlington House, Arlington Street, Mayfair, SW1; ☎ 0207-629-2239;
www.caprice-holdings.co.uk; tube: Green Park

Customers Celebrities, affluent locals. **Reservations** Recommended. **When to
go** Dinner or Sunday brunch. **Entree range** £15–£25. **Payment** AE, D, DC, MC, V.
Service rating ★★★. **Friendliness rating** ★★★. **Bar** Yes. **Wine selection**
Short but good. **Dress** No dress code. **Disabled access** Yes, but not to toilets.
Hours Monday–Saturday, noon–3 p.m. and 5:30 p.m.–midnight; Sunday, noon–
3:15 p.m. and 6 p.m.–midnight.

SETTING AND ATMOSPHERE Lively yet low-key, modern room that is pleasant
but of no great distinction.

HOUSE SPECIALTIES Nearly everything on the menu, especially the fish and chips, salmon cakes, gnocchi pomodoro, and eggs Benedict.

OTHER RECOMMENDATIONS Chargrilled squid.

SUMMARY AND COMMENTS Le Caprice has a well-deserved reputation for serving food that reaches a high standard pretty consistently. But that is not the main reason Londoners come here, even if it helps. Le Caprice is supremely fashionable in a low-key kind of way. It's a place where no one raises an eyebrow if the next table is occupied by a princess, two movie stars, and a Nobel Prize–winning novelist—well, at least not in a way you would notice. This is surely one of the reasons why the rich, fashionable, and celebrated love the place so much, just as they love its sister restaurant, The Ivy (see page 326). For us mortals, the possibility of stargazing might be a bonus. But we've paid three visits with nary a star in sight and have loved the place anyway. It is comfortable and well run, and the food is mostly outstanding. And when it isn't outstanding, it's still very good. Dinners are buzzy, while Sunday brunch is more laid-back.

🚌 Le Gavroche ★★★★★

FRENCH (HAUTE CUISINE)   EXPENSIVE   QUALITY ★★★★★   VALUE ★★★

43 Upper Brook Street, Mayfair, W1; ☎ 0207-408-0881; www.le-gavroche.co.uk; tube: Marble Arch

Customers Wealthy locals, serious gourmets, and tourists. **Reservations** Essential. **When to go** Lunch or dinner. **Entree range** £28–£40. **Payment** AE, CB, DC, MC, V. **Service rating** ★★★★★. **Friendliness rating** ★★★★. **Bar** Yes, for diners only. **Wine selection** Excellent. **Dress** Smart casual; jackets for men. **Disabled access** No. **Hours** Monday–Friday, noon–2 p.m. and 6:30–11 p.m.; Saturday, 6:30–11 p.m.

SETTING AND ATMOSPHERE This downstairs room offers intimate comfort at both lunch and dinner; it's indisputably grand, and you will unconsciously sit up straighter as you are eased smoothly into your seat. It's got that gracious old-world elegance that tells you straight off you are in for an extraordinary dining experience.

HOUSE SPECIALTIES *Soufflé suissesse* (Gruyère-cheese soufflé); *agneau de lait rôti* (roast lamb); *coquilles St. Jacques grillée*; artichoke filled with foie gras; hot foie gras and crispy pancake of duck flavored with cinnamon; steamed lobster with pasta; perfect crème brûlée.

OTHER RECOMMENDATIONS Set lunch.

SUMMARY AND COMMENTS Le Gavroche is one of London's most famous and most expensive restaurants. It is classic in every sense, even though the menu has been "modernized" in recent years. The service is among the best in London, priding itself on knowing what customers want before they themselves know they want it, and the care taken with every detail is gratifying. Menus without prices are given to those who are obviously guests of someone; plates of tiny but elaborate *amuses-bouches* (hors d'oeuvres) are laid at your table; a palate-clearing sorbet is often served between courses; and the painstaking desserts alone would justify a visit.

All this comes at a truly frightening price outside the set lunch, which at £46 per person includes three courses, half a bottle of wine, water and coffee, and service. Sure, that's pretty expensive, too, but with main courses alone costing £30 on average, lunch is the only way most people can afford Le Gavroche. It's worth that one splash-out, because this is a great restaurant of the old-fashioned, perfectionist kind. Bread, ice creams and sorbets, premeal tidbits—they're all outstanding. And the all-French cheese board is probably the best in London. Come here if you want to treat yourself. And if you're feeling particularly flush (and very hungry), there is a heavenly tasting menu for £90.

Masala Zone ★★

| INDIAN | INEXPENSIVE/MODERATE | QUALITY ★★★½ | VALUE ★★★★ |

9 Marshall Street, Soho, W1; ☎ 0207-287-9966; tube: Oxford Circus
47 Earls Court Road, Kensington, SW5; ☎ 0207-373-0220;
tube: Earls Court
80 Upper Street, Islington, N1; ☎ 0207-359-3399; tube: Angel;
www.masalazone.com

Customers Locals, mostly office workers at lunch. **Reservations** Not accepted. **When to go** Anytime. **Entree range** £5–£9.50, *thalis*, £8–£12. **Payment** MC, V. **Service rating** ★★★. **Friendliness rating** ★★★★. **Bar** No. **Wine selection** Cheap and good. **Dress** Casual. **Disabled access** Yes. **Hours** Monday–Friday, noon–2:45 p.m. and 5:30–11 p.m.; Saturday, 12:30–11 p.m.; Sunday, 6–10:30 p.m.

SETTING AND ATMOSPHERE Open-plan cafeteria-style; light, modern decor.

HOUSE SPECIALTIES *Thalis* (complete meals comprising samplings of numerous dishes), snacks, mango *lassi* (a traditional Indian dairy beverage) and Indian lemonade.

OTHER RECOMMENDATIONS *Paratha* and *naan* (flatbreads), vegetarian *thali*.

SUMMARY AND COMMENTS Part of the restaurant group that owns Veeraswamy (see page 347), Chutney Mary's, and Amaya, Masala Zone opened in 2001 with a novel approach: high-quality, adventurous, and sometimes unorthodox Indian-style food at very low prices—the cuisine is advertised as "earthy street food." It has gone from strength to strength, never wavering in its commitment to quality, freshness, and precise, friendly service. One of the best things about Masala Zone is the flexibility of the food: you can have a full meal or a "light bite" if your appetite is small. There's a grilled club sandwich—chicken, bacon, egg, cheese, and mayo—if that's all you want, and satisfying bowls of noodles for a heartier meal. Because of the no-reservations policy, you may have trouble getting a table at peak lunch and dinner times. If you love high-quality Indian food and don't want to spend a fortune for it, Masala Zone is a worthy choice. And the Soho branch's central location, close to Theatreland, makes it all the more attractive.

Matsuri   ★★★½

JAPANESE	MODERATE/EXPENSIVE	QUALITY ★★★½	VALUE ★★

15 Bury Street, St. James, SW1; ☎ 0207-839-1101;
www.matsuri-restaurant.com; tube: Green Park

Customers Locals and tourists. **Reservations** Recommended. **When to go** Lunch or dinner. **Entree range** £16–£50. **Payment** AE, CB, DC, MC, V. **Service rating** ★★★½. **Friendliness rating** ★★★½. **Bar** Yes. **Wine selection** Adequate; beer and sake are better. **Dress** Casual. **Disabled access** Yes, for diners only. **Hours** Daily, noon–2:30 p.m. and 6–10:30 p.m.

SETTING AND ATMOSPHERE   Big, spacious main dining room and smaller sushi bar; elegant but relaxed.

HOUSE SPECIALTIES   Sushi and teppanyaki.

SUMMARY AND COMMENTS   London has its full share of big Japanese restaurants catering to businesspeople with expense accounts as big as the Grand Canyon. Matsuri also attracts a business crowd given its location in the heart of St. James, a stone's throw from the Ritz, but the prices are relatively reasonable (£14 to £21 for a daily special set lunch) and the quality is high. Sushi and sashimi, expertly prepared, can be ordered either à la carte at the bar or in various permutations of a set meal. Most of the space is given over to teppanyaki tables, where your choice of fish, meat, and vegetables is prepared and cooked for you on a sizzling hot table—very theatrical, and also very good. There's even a nod toward fusion cooking in the form of tuna tartare, foie gras "Japanese," and little dishes such as deep-fried chicken. The list of specialty-brand sakes is intriguing, if high-priced. But, then, top-quality Japanese never comes cheap—and given the raw-fish emphasis, nor should it.

Michael Moore Restaurant   ★★★★½

MODERN EUROPEAN	EXPENSIVE	QUALITY ★★★★	VALUE ★★★

19 Blandford Street, Marylebone, W1; ☎ 0207-592-1222;
www.michaelmoorerestaurant.com; tube: Baker Street

Customers Locals and gastronomes. **Reservations** Yes. **When to go** Anytime. **Entree range** £14–£30, set lunch menu, £16–£19. **Payment** AE, MC, V. **Service rating** ★★★★. **Friendliness rating** ★★★★★. **Bar** Yes. **Wine selection** Excellent. **Dress** Casual. **Disabled access** Yes. **Hours** Monday–Friday, noon–3 p.m. and 6:30–11 p.m.; Saturday, 6:30–11:30 p.m.

SETTING AND ATMOSPHERE   This small room has the vibe of an intimate French bistro but is not overly close. The owners are looking for a larger venue, and wherever the restaurant ends up, it will no doubt be equally elegant and unfussily comfortable.

HOUSE SPECIALTIES   Pork belly and lobster, seared scallops, vegetarian selections.

OTHER RECOMMENDATIONS   All the desserts, especially the strawberry soup with floating island.

SUMMARY AND COMMENTS Michael Moore is a culinary veteran, having worked in many of the great kitchens of London, New York, and Toronto, and a nicer guy couldn't have put together a greater restaurant. It's small and intimate, and new digs are being researched as we speak, so check on the address when you make a reservation. The food is painstakingly prepared and exquisitely presented, and the desserts are worth the price of admission. Unlike many other chef-centric restaurants, this one graciously gives a nod to vegetarians, with a ragoût of potatoes, white beans, and asparagus flavored with lemongrass, as well as a good risotto. You may just get a visit from the chef himself, a real Londoner with no airs and a "souf of da rivah" sense of humor. The French maître d' is extremely gracious and warm and full of helpful suggestions. The tasting menu is a wonderful treat, though perhaps a bit expensive; at lunchtime you can get a crack at some truly innovative modern-European dishes for a fraction of the dinner cost. The menu changes all the time, but trust us: whatever is being served up is sure to please.

Moro ★★★★

SPANISH/MIDDLE EASTERN   MODERATE   QUALITY ★★★★   VALUE ★★★★

34–36 Exmouth Market, The City, EC1; ☎ 0207-833-8336; www.moro.co.uk; tube: Farringdon or Angel

Customers Locals, both young and old. **Reservations** Recommended. **When to go** Anytime. **Entree range** £16.50–£18. **Payment** AE, D, MC, V. **Service rating** ★★★. **Friendliness rating** ★★★½. **Bar** Yes, with tapas menu. **Wine selection** Very good. **Dress** Casual. **Disabled access** Yes. **Hours** Monday–Saturday, 12:30–2:30 p.m. and 7–10:30 p.m.; tapas served all day.

SETTING AND ATMOSPHERE Casual and lively; high-ceilinged room with simple decor.

HOUSE SPECIALTIES Everything cooked in the wood-fired oven, such as cod with saffron rice, caramelized onions, and tahini; charcoal-grilled dishes like lamb kebab with egg-and-mint salad and bulgur; homemade breads and yogurt; tarts and other desserts.

OTHER RECOMMENDATIONS Vegetarian dishes, well-chosen Spanish cheeses, braised dishes.

SUMMARY AND COMMENTS Since opening in 1997, Moro has become one of the most popular restaurants in London. Located on the pedestrianized street of Exmouth Market, it's a bit off the beaten track as far as sightseeing is concerned, but the area continues to grow more and more trendy. Moro has played no small part in this. It is a destination restaurant because the food is outstanding, and the prices are very reasonable for cooking of this quality. Based on the cuisine and culture of Moorish Spain, when the country was under Islamic rule, the food has big, bold flavors and generous spicing. You can never tell what you'll find at Moro, because the menu changes weekly. Everything's delicious. This is not a place for a quiet evening, but definitely a place for a memorable meal.

Mulberry Street ★★★

| PIZZA | MODERATE | QUALITY ★★★½ | VALUE ★★★ |

84 Westbourne Grove, Notting Hill, W2; ☎ 0207-313-6789;
www.mulberrystreet.co.uk; tube: Bayswater

Customers Pizza lovers. **Reservations** Yes. **When to go** Anytime. **Entree range**
£6.50–£17. **Payment** AE, MC, V. **Service rating** ★★★★. **Friendliness rating**
★★★½. **Bar** Yes. **Wine selection** Adequate. **Dress** Casual. **Disabled access** No.
Hours Daily, noon–midnight.

SETTING AND ATMOSPHERE Colorful wall mural of New York designed by
Victoria Dawe; more than 100 seats on two floors, with comfortable
purple-leather booths that can seat up to 16, perfect for a family; open
gallery kitchen. You can sit at the bar, have a slice of pizza and a genuine
American root beer or cream soda, and read the paper or watch sports
on the flat-screen TV. Staff is very friendly.

HOUSE SPECIALTIES Authentic New York pizza, full New York breakfast, Mom's
homemade cupcakes.

OTHER RECOMMENDATIONS Spaghetti with meatballs.

SUMMARY AND COMMENTS This is a great restaurant, one that bills itself as
London's only authentic New York pizzeria. You can buy either pizza
by the slice for £3.50 or a massive 20-incher for around £17. The New
York Hot Pizza—pepperoni with green and jalapeño peppers—is highly
recommended. The attention to detail is interesting: the water used in
the pizza dough is filtered and tested to conform to New York City
water standards—and as everyone knows, the main ingredient of the
Big Apple's inimitable bagels and pizza crust is the city's excellent water.
If you want to be totally un–New York about it, go for the Beluga King
Pizza, covered in chopped egg, onion, and Beluga caviar—there's no
price for this on the menu, and of course, if you have to ask how much
it costs, you can't afford it. Closer to the traditions of the actual Mulberry Street in New York's Little Italy are the chicken and eggplant
Parmesan pizzas. Ray's Famous it ain't, but it's more authentic than any
pizzeria outside the Tri-Borough area.

kids Navajo Joe's ★★

| UPSCALE TEX-MEX | MODERATE | QUALITY ★★ | VALUE ★★★ |

34 King Street, West End, WC2; ☎ 0207-240-4008;
www.navajojoe.co.uk; tube: Covent Garden

Customers Locals, business lunchers, after-work partiers, tourists. **Reservations**
Not necessary. **When to go** Anytime. **Entree range** £10–£17. **Payment** AE, DC,
MC, V. **Service rating** ★★★. **Friendliness rating** ★★★★. **Bar** Fabulously well
stocked, with good munchies available. **Wine selection** Decent. **Dress** Casual.
Disabled access Yes. **Hours** Daily, noon–midnight.

SETTING AND ATMOSPHERE Western-accented, with wooden tables and a
warm glow, helped along by the enormous candle "sculptures" on the

bar, made by the dripping wax of hundreds of burning candles over the years.

HOUSE SPECIALTIES Lobster-and-mango nachos, barbecue glazed ribs, spicy chicken wings, asparagus-and-mushroom enchiladas, fajitas for two.

OTHER RECOMMENDATIONS Rib-eye steak with béarnaise sauce, baked vanilla-bean cheesecake.

ENTERTAINMENT AND AMENITIES Lots of camaraderie in the early evening as workers from Covent Garden pile up at the bar. Music a little American-centric, circa 1960s and '70s; DJ on weekend nights.

SUMMARY AND COMMENTS There are so many restaurants to choose from in the Covent Garden area, sometimes you just have to give up and go for an American meal. And Navajo Joe does it pretty well, better than its sister restaurant Cactus Blue in Chelsea, in my opinion, although the menus are very similar. The restaurant occupies a big, high-ceilinged storefront off Covent Garden, with a loft upstairs, a big bar in the front, and tables sprinkled around in such a way as to give a sense of intimacy. The food is a strange combination of old Tex-Mex standbys with new twists (pulled-duck nachos with plum salsa, tequila-and-lime chicken chimichangas) and a kind of no-man's-land cuisine (mushroom-and-mascarpone ravioli, sea bass served on a banana leaf with green curry and rice). The vanilla-bean cheesecake is probably the best I've had in London, resembling the Junior's cheesecakes in Brooklyn that always set the standard for me. You can also have what they call "Amusements" anytime, or small noshes such as steak teriyaki, spring rolls, spicy meatballs, and so on, for £10 for a selection of three, or two for £7.

Nobu ★★★★★

"NEW-STYLE" JAPANESE   EXPENSIVE   QUALITY ★★★★★   VALUE ★★

The Metropolitan Hotel, 19 Old Park Lane, Mayfair, W1;
☎ **0207-447-4747; www.noburestaurants.com; tube: Hyde Park Corner**

Customers Businesspeople, tourists, the occasional celebrity. **Reservations** Essential. **When to go** Lunch or dinner. **Entree range** £10–£30. **Payment** AE, CB, DC, MC, V. **Service rating** ★★★★. **Friendliness rating** ★★★. **Bar** Yes. **Wine selection** Very good. **Dress** Fashionable. **Disabled access** Yes. **Hours** Monday–Friday, noon–2:15 p.m. and 6–10:15 p.m.; Saturday, 6–11:15 p.m.; Sunday, 6–9:45 p.m.

SETTING AND ATMOSPHERE Ultraminimalist decor for an ultrachic clientele.

HOUSE SPECIALTIES Special appetizers such as yellowtail sashimi with jalapeño-and-tomato rock-shrimp seviche; traditional sushi and sashimi.

OTHER RECOMMENDATIONS Tempura; special dishes such as *wagyu* and foie gras *gyoza;* Inaniwa pasta salad with lobster.

SUMMARY AND COMMENTS Nobu is a one-of-a-kind restaurant, with 15 locations worldwide. If you have ever been to a Nobu in Tokyo, Hong Kong, Melbourne, Mykonos, Milan, the Bahamas, New York City, Los Angeles, Miami, Dallas, Honolulu, or Las Vegas, you are well aware of Matsuhisu Nobuyuki's extraordinary reworking of Japanese cuisine (and the extraordinary prices as well). Three things come to mind, the most important of which is the startling innovation that almost invariably sends diners into raptures. This is like no other Japanese food, taking in influences from every corner of the globe, especially South America. But it is innovation that works, which is what counts. The second thing is chic: Nobu attracts entertainment people, and you may get to see one or two when you eat here. The third thing is the daunting expense. If you order a full meal, it's hard to come away without spending £60 or more on food alone, and it won't even fill you up. Consequently, Nobu doesn't rate well for value. In fact, in a newspaper's celebrity questionnaire called "My London," Nobu is invariably the response to "What was your most expensive meal in London?" But it is a special place, and everyone should visit once. Consider going for a sushi lunch, which shouldn't set you back more than £25 a head as long as you avoid alcohol.

Orrery ★★★★

MODERN EUROPEAN   EXPENSIVE   QUALITY ★★★★   VALUE ★★★

55 Marylebone High Street, Marylebone, W1; ☎ 0207-616-8000; www.orreryrestaurant.co.uk; tube: Baker Street

Customers Affluent locals from all over London. **When to go** Lunch or dinner. **Entree range** £19–£29, tasting menu, £59. **Payment** AE, D, DC, JCB, MC, V. **Service rating** ★★★★★. **Friendliness rating** ★★★★★. **Bar** Yes. **Wine selection** Outstanding but expensive. **Dress** Smart. **Disabled access** Yes. **Hours** Monday–Saturday, noon–3 p.m. and 7–11 p.m.; Sunday, 7–10:30 p.m.

SETTING AND ATMOSPHERE Long, narrow second-floor room with skylight; small adjacent bar; open-air terrace (in good weather) with nice view of the churchyard opposite.

HOUSE SPECIALTIES Somerset lamb with aubergine puree; wild Cornish sea bass with twice-cooked Belgian endive; filet of beef with oxtail pastille; roast squab with poached blackberries.

OTHER RECOMMENDATIONS Light dinner menu on the terrace, weather permitting (summer months only); set lunch and Sunday set dinner menus (£25–£80); *menu gourmand* (£59). Desserts are amazing; try the raspberry soufflé.

SUMMARY AND COMMENTS Orrery is part of the large Conran group and is universally regarded as the best of its restaurants for those seeking high-quality cooking in intimate surroundings. The restaurant is small by Conran standards; the emphasis here is on the food rather than the buzz. And the kitchen consistently meets the high standards it sets for itself: the cooking often reaches dazzling heights in inventiveness, seasoning, and presentation. On the other hand, the prices are as dazzling as the food. It is alarmingly easy to spend £75 a head for a full meal with wine, and if you take on the five-star reaches of the fine but costly wine list, you can go a lot higher than that. But they also have many wines by the glass, and the set lunch is a bargain by anyone's standards. With service that combines military precision with a genuinely warm welcome, Orrery is one of London's top stars.

A small *épicerie* (grocer) downstairs serves cafe food, breakfast, and meals at a long communal table. They also sell deli-type prepared food, which you can buy for a dinner party (and claim credit for), as well as spices, wine, and pantry items.

kids Orsini ★★★

ITALIAN CAFE	MODERATE	QUALITY ★★★	VALUE ★★½

8a Thurloe Place, South Kensington, SW7; ☎ 0207-581-5553; tube: South Kensington

Customers Locals and museumgoers. **Reservations** Not accepted. **When to go** Breakfast, lunch, or afternoon coffee. **Entree range** Lunch £5–£10. **Payment** MC, V. **Service rating** ★★. **Friendliness rating** ★★★. **Bar** Basic mixed drinks, Italian liquors, beer, and wine. **Wine selection** Italian table red or white; specials weekly. **Dress** No dress code. **Disabled access** For downstairs and outdoor tables only. **Hours** Daily, 8 a.m.–10 p.m.

SETTING AND ATMOSPHERE Temporary art exhibits decorate the walls; wooden tables and chairs on two floors. Casual, very Italian.

HOUSE SPECIALTIES Daily pasta and meat specials using fresh products, such as mozzarella and aubergine fettuccine; homemade soups; panini; breaded (or grilled) chicken cutlets with salad; great cappuccino, fresh-squeezed orange juice.

OTHER RECOMMENDATIONS Homemade desserts.

SUMMARY AND COMMENTS Located across the street from the Victoria and Albert Museum on a leafy stretch of road, Orsini is a family-run eatery that provides good homemade food and the authenticity of a cafe in Naples. Even in the face of astronomical rent and service hikes throughout the neighborhood, it has managed to hang in there. It's a favorite with locals, museumgoers, and visitors staying at the nearby Rembrandt Hotel. Daily specials are always a treat: porcini mushrooms, clams, and artichokes make sporadic appearances in unique dishes. The friendly service, provided by good-looking young Europeans, can be a bit unpredictable, but the sense of Mediterranean relaxation is part of the charm. In the best tradition of Italy, children are more than welcome, strollers and all. The prices reflect the high rents of the area, but it's still a good value, and no one raises an eyebrow if you linger over an espresso for hours.

kids Pizza Express ★★

PIZZA	INEXPENSIVE	QUALITY ★★	VALUE ★★★★½

80–81 St. Martin's Lane, West End, WC2; ☎ 0207-836-8001; tube: Charing Cross
26 Cowcross Street, West End, EC1; ☎ 0207-490-8025; tube: Farringdon
25 Millbank, Pimlico, SW1; ☎ 0207-976-6214; tube: Millbank
The Pheasantry, 152 King's Road, Chelsea, SW3; ☎ 0207-351-5031; tube: Sloane Square
137 Notting Hill Gate, Notting Hill, W11; ☎ 0207-229-6000; tube: Notting Hill Gate

70 Heath Street, North London, NW3; ☎ 0207-433-1600; tube: Hampstead; www.pizzaexpress.co.uk

Customers Locals and tourists. **Reservations** Not necessary. **When to go** Anytime. **Entree range** £5.95–£11. **Payment** AE, DC, MC, V. **Service rating** ★★★. **Friendliness rating** ★★★½. **Bar** In some locations, not in others. **Wine selection** Minimal. **Dress** Casual. **Disabled access** Yes. **Hours** Daily, 11 a.m.–midnight.

SETTING AND ATMOSPHERE Relaxed, unpretentious, and very child-friendly.

HOUSE SPECIALTIES All the salads are excellent, the *salade niçoise* in particular.

OTHER RECOMMENDATIONS The garlic-bread balls are very good, if filling.

SUMMARY AND COMMENTS We've provided specific information for branches in several neighborhoods, but trust us when we say that no matter where you are, there is likely a Pizza Express nearby—these pizzerias are almost as ubiquitous in London as Starbucks is in the States, and they offer the same kind of predictable, quality-controlled fare. The formula is very simple: 16 types of pizza, a couple of baked pasta dishes and salads, and a few side dishes. The thin-crust pizzas are smallish by American standards but reliably good; the pasta dishes are acceptable but not really what you should come here for; the salads are not at all bad, if a little skimpy, and come with pizza-dough balls. In short, this is not a place to visit for a special meal but, rather, when you want something cheap and fast. Pizza Express is especially good for children, who are always made welcome.

kids Pret à Manger ★

SANDWICHES, ETC.	INEXPENSIVE	QUALITY ★★	VALUE ★★★★

1 Great Tower Street, The City, EC3; ☎ 0207-932-5265; www.pret.com; tube: Tower Hill or Monument; many other London locations

Customers Locals and tourists. **Reservations** Not necessary. **When to go** Breakfast, lunch, or snack. **Entree range** £3.50–£6. **Payment** AE, CB, D, MC, V. **Service rating** ★★★. **Friendliness rating** ★★★½. **Bar** No. **Wine selection** No. **Dress** Casual. **Disabled access** Yes. **Hours** Daily, 8:30 a.m.–6 p.m.

SETTING AND ATMOSPHERE Sandwich shop.

HOUSE SPECIALTIES Daily specials are good; old favorites include the avocado and pine-nut wraps.

HOUSE SPECIALTIES Vegetarian sushi selections.

SUMMARY AND COMMENTS Pret à Manger isn't a restaurant but an outlet for fast food, mostly sandwiches, and part of a chain of more than 150 in the capital (and many more outside London and overseas). Sandwiches range from ultrasimple egg salad (called "egg mayonnaise" in Britain) to wraps filled with hummus and red-pepper salad or avocado and pine nuts; there's also a great vegetarian sushi and deluxe sushi. In an attempt to stay up to the minute with current diet fads, the menu now offers such noshes as no-bread mozzarella and no-bread poached salmon and egg (which may not help calorie counters: there's not much in the way of lo-cal sandwiches). The salads, while small by Yankee standards, are varied and yummy, and you can put your own dressing on most of them. Cakes and desserts are decent; coffee is of high quality. Pret is good, it's cheap, it's quick, and it's everywhere. If you just want a quick, light refueling, this is one place to get it. Plus, they give whatever food is left at the end of the day to shelters and soup kitchens—a gesture far too rare in today's food-wasting culture.

The Providores and Tapa Room ★★★½

FUSION   MODERATE/EXPENSIVE   QUALITY ★★★★   VALUE ★★★

109 Marylebone High Street, Marylebone, W1; ☎ 0207-935-6175; www.theprovidores.co.uk; tube: Bond Street

Customers Mostly locals. **Reservations** Essential. **When to go** Lunch or dinner. **Entree range** Tapa Room, £4–£12; The Providores, £10–£24. **Payment** AE, MC, V. **Service rating** ★★★★½. **Friendliness rating** ★★★. **Bar** No. **Wine selection** Excellent. **Dress** Casual. **Disabled access** Yes. **Hours** *Tapa Room:* Monday–Friday, 9 a.m.–11:30 p.m.; Saturday, 10 a.m.–10:30 p.m.; Sunday, 10 a.m.–10 p.m. *The Providores:* Monday–Friday, noon–3 p.m. and 6–10:30 p.m.; Saturday and Sunday, noon–3 p.m. and 6–10 p.m.

SETTING AND ATMOSPHERE Modern decor—warm minimalism with a New Zealand theme.

HOUSE SPECIALTIES Varying menu might offer sweet potato, feta, and caramelized-red-onion tortilla with smoked tomato–vanilla relish; baked goat-milk ricotta with grilled asparagus; five-spiced roast Barbary duck breast; berbere-spiced kangaroo fillet on a shiitake, basil, and Halloumi fritter with tahini and yogurt; roast monkfish on chorizo mash with artichoke and bean salsa.

SUMMARY AND COMMENTS Just looking at the list of specialties may tell you you're on unfamiliar territory. But while the dishes may sound strange, the genius of the chefs ensures that even the oddest-sounding combinations work beautifully on the plate. Asian influences are effortlessly and expertly absorbed into The Providores's highly individualist cooking. You can go in for breakfast, brunch, or a light snack in the Tapa Room, or a full meal in the main restaurant. Prices are not ultralow, even in the Tapa Room, a mellow eatery with a great breakfast menu (including the delicious sweet-brown-rice-and-apple porridge) and all-day tapas such as shiitake-and-Halloumi fritters with pomegranate-cumin yogurt. The higher prices upstairs are not out of line for restaurants of this quality. If you have a sense of culinary adventure, head straight for The Providores.

Rasa ★★★½

INDIAN/VEGETARIAN   MODERATE   QUALITY ★★★½   VALUE ★★★★

6 Dering Street, West End, W1; ☎ 0207-629-1346; www.rasarestaurants.com; tube: Oxford Circus

Customers Locals and aficionados. **Reservations** Recommended. **When to go** Lunch or dinner. **Entree range** £6.25–£12.95. "Feasts" menus from £20 per person. **Payment** AE, CB, D, MC, V. **Service rating** ★★★½. **Friendliness rating** ★★★. **Bar** Yes. **Wine selection** Small but good. **Dress** Casual. **Disabled access** Restaurant only. **Hours** Monday–Saturday, noon–3 p.m. and 6–11 p.m.

SETTING AND ATMOSPHERE Pleasant modern interior, simply decorated, friendly and informal.

HOUSE SPECIALTIES Southern Indian vegetarian dishes.

OTHER RECOMMENDATIONS Breads, pickles, and chutneys.

SUMMARY AND COMMENTS One of six Rasa restaurants in London, the West End outpost is one of the more upscale venues in which to enjoy the beauties of Keralan (southern Indian) cuisine. This was once a strictly vegetarian restaurant, but Rasa's success has persuaded them to add northern Keralan meat and seafood dishes to the menu. You can ask them to put together a Kerala feast, which will provide a good balance and range of dishes featuring different flavors and textures. Or choose for yourself among the *dosas* (filled pancakes), curries, and side dishes of rice, vegetables, and exquisite bread. The food is filling but not stodgy, and no one who eats it comes away unimpressed.

Richard Corrigan at Lindsay House   ★★★★★

BRITISH	VERY EXPENSIVE	QUALITY ★★★★½	VALUE ★★★½

21 Romilly Street, Soho, W1; ☎ 0207-439-0450;
www.lindsayhouse.co.uk; tube: Leicester Square or Piccadilly Circus

Customers Mostly locals. **Reservations** Recommended. **When to go** Lunch or dinner. **Entree range** Lunch £12–£20; dinner offers set menu from £27 for pre-theater to £68 for tasting menu. **Payment** AE, CB, D, MC, V. **Service rating** ★★★★. **Friendliness rating** ★★★★. **Bar** No. **Wine selection** Excellent but expensive. **Dress** Smart casual. **Disabled access** No. **Hours** Monday–Friday, noon–2:30 p.m. and 6–11 p.m.; Saturday, 6–11 p.m.

SETTING AND ATMOSPHERE Two stories of a 1740s town house are decorated with quiet, unstuffy elegance, like a beautiful home or members' club.

HOUSE SPECIALTIES An ever-changing menu offers such dishes as monkfish *en croûte* with béarnaise sauce; caramelized veal sweetbreads; braised pig's cheek with pork belly and pineapple; gnocchi with fontina and wild mushrooms; steamed fillets of sole with *beurre fondue,* salsify, and brown shrimp; and roasted scallops with spiced chicken and pea shoots. Desserts may include peanut parfait with roast banana and caramel ice crème, rice pudding with pears poached in lavender, or a lime soufflé.

SUMMARY AND COMMENTS Richard Corrigan, the chef at Lindsay House, has long had devoted followers for his robust, sophisticated approach to modern cooking. Corrigan is Irish, and his native tradition shows in a love of pork, offal, and Irish ingredients such as black pudding. But his cooking is also based in French classicism, and it is both refined and adventurous, with unusual combinations of foods and tastes adding up to a sublime experience. Desserts are a strong point. Prices are predictably high, but hardly extortionate for what you get; the pre-theater set menu at £27 is, in fact, a bargain. If you like hearty cooking raised to the level of culinary art, chances are you'll love the Lindsay House. They'll cook especially for vegetarians if asked.

 **The River Café** ★★★★½

TUSCAN ITALIAN   **EXPENSIVE**   **QUALITY** ★★★★   **VALUE** ★★

Thames Wharf, Rainville Road, Hammersmith, W6; ☎ 0207-386-4200; www.rivercafe.co.uk; tube: Hammersmith

Customers People with very deep pockets or on expense accounts, celebs, local worthies, foodies. **Reservations** Essential. **When to go** Anytime; try for a table outside. **Entree range** £27–£31. **Payment** AE, DC, MC, V. **Service rating** ★★★★. **Friendliness rating** ★★★★. **Bar** For waiting diners. **Wine selection** Good but, like everything, expensive. **Dress** Smart casual. **Disabled access** Yes. **Hours** Daily, 12:30–3:30 p.m. and 7–11 p.m. (last booking at 9 p.m.).

SETTING AND ATMOSPHERE   A wall of floor-to-ceiling glass doors and windows lines one side of the long, narrow dining room, and on the other side is the busy kitchen, a kind of short-order-diner affair. The tone is unpretentious and functional. Seats in the garden are coveted on warm days.

HOUSE SPECIALTIES   Changing menu reflects seasonal freshness of produce.

OTHER RECOMMENDATIONS   Risotto, pasta of the day, any of the fish (John Dory fillet wood-roasted with olives, or chargrilled Scottish salmon with artichoke *fritti*), desserts.

ENTERTAINMENT AND AMENITIES   Outside, there's the Thames (less exciting than you'd hope); inside there's the cooking going on behind the counter. They sell olive oil and cookbooks. Valet parking service.

SUMMARY AND COMMENTS   Having heard so much about the River Café for so long, I finally got a chance to try it at the urging of an out-of-town friend who footed the bill (thank goodness). It's hard to get reservations, but if you book enough in advance it's possible (just don't try changing it—we were unable to change the booking from two people to three, even a week ahead). The cafe has been owned and run by Rose Gray and Ruth Rogers for the past two decades; their simple menu of Tuscan dishes, prepared with perfectly fresh seasonal produce, led to extraordinary, unflagging success and thousands of imitators: the River Café cookbooks are the bible of many a foodie, and the influence of this restaurant on London dining has been profound. The recipes are sensationally excellent, though not grand or showy. The specials of the day are always good: I shared an appetizer of grilled scallop with anchovies and lentils that, despite my general avoidance of anchovies, was superb, awakening taste buds I didn't know I had. However, the prices are frankly astronomical for what is essentially an upgrade of typical Tuscan peasant fare. A three-course meal with dessert (and without wine) can easily cost £70 before the 12.5% service charge is added. It's safe to say that the bill can kill the overall pleasure of the meal, as one reflects on the small portions and the general workaday ambience. However, for true seekers of good cooking, or for anyone whose rich uncle wants to buy him or her a meal, the River Café is a must-try: since it opened in 1987, its simple, healthy philosophy has exerted a huge influence on modern British eating habits.

 ## Rules ★★★

BRITISH	MODERATE/EXPENSIVE	QUALITY ★★★	VALUE ★★★

35 Maiden Lane, West End, WC2; ☎ 0207-836-5314; www.rules.co.uk; tube: Covent Garden or Charing Cross

Customers More tourists than locals. **Reservations** Recommended. **When to go** Dinner is best. **Entree range** £17–£28. **Payment** AE, DC, JCB, MC, V. **Service rating** ★★★. **Friendliness rating** ★★★. **Bar** No. **Wine selection** Small but good. **Dress** Casual. **Disabled access** Yes. **Hours** Monday–Saturday, noon–11:30 p.m.; Sunday, noon–10:30 p.m.

SETTING AND ATMOSPHERE   Ornate old-fashioned decor with Victorian prints and statues. It's rather wonderful.

HOUSE SPECIALTIES   Game dishes, Aberdeen Angus beef.

OTHER RECOMMENDATIONS   Châteaubriand, béarnaise sauce, and asparagus; Scottish salmon with cauliflower, pea shoots, and shallot puree; grilled calf's liver; steak, kidney, and oyster pudding; rib of beef; Yorkshire pudding; warm chocolate pudding with rose petal and pistachio ice-cream cornet; sticky date and toffee pudding.

SUMMARY AND COMMENTS   Rules has been serving food from this location since 1798. That by itself is not a reason to recommend it, and for years the restaurant served indifferently cooked game and beef to tourists seeking a taste of tradition. But for some years now it has been run very well by John Mayhew, who brought in great chefs and smart customers and has turned the historic eatery into something special, with a menu that combines classic game and meat cookery with up-to-the-minute modern touches. The menu changes regularly, which is a good sign, and fish lovers will find more choice than ever. The selection of "feathered and furred game" (some from the owner's Lartington Estate in the High Pennines, which also occasionally supplies beef and pork) is as good as you'll find anywhere in London. Vegetarians should probably go elsewhere. If you want to try a classic rib of beef or steak-and-kidney pie (with or without oysters), Rules is one of your best bets.

S&M Cafe ★★★

BRITISH	INEXPENSIVE	QUALITY ★★½	VALUE ★★★★

268 Portobello Road, Notting Hill, W1; ☎ 0208-968-8898; www.sandmcafe.co.uk; tube: Ladbroke Grove

Customers Artsy Notting Hill types. **Reservations** Not accepted. **When to go** Lunchtime. **Entree range** £6.25–£8.95. **Payment** MC, V. **Service rating** ★★★. **Friendliness rating** ★★½. **Bar** Yes. **Wine selection** Adequate. **Dress** Casual. **Disabled access** No. **Hours** Monday–Thursday, 9 a.m.–11 p.m.; Friday and Saturday, 9 a.m.–11:30 p.m.; Sunday, 9 a.m.–10:30 p.m.

SETTING AND ATMOSPHERE Much like that of a diner or cafe, the setting is very simple: black painted floor with red checkers, red benches, wooden chairs, blue painted tabletop with Heinz ketchup and HP sauce set in the center.

HOUSE SPECIALTIES Selection of bangers and mash, botanically brewed soft drinks such as ginger beer, Victorian lemonade.

OTHER RECOMMENDATIONS Shepherd's pie, haddock fish cakes.

SUMMARY AND COMMENTS S&M is short for "sausage and mash," and they do indeed make the best sausages and mash in town. You can choose from pork, leek-and-chile, lamb-and-mint, or honey-mustard sausages; vegetarians can opt between spinach and Cheddar or mushroom and tarragon. Who needs five stars when you can have S&M at affordable prices?

Sketch: Gallery & Glade; Lecture Room & Library; Parlour ★★★★★

FRENCH	EXPENSIVE	QUALITY ★★★★★	VALUE ★★★

9 Conduit Street, Soho, W1; ☎ 0870-777-4488; www.sketch.uk.com; tube: Oxford Circus or Bond Street

Customers Gourmands, businesspeople, celebs, deep-pocketed locals. **Reservations** Yes. **When to go** Anytime; tea is excellent. **Entree range** Depends on the venue; from £9 lunch in the Parlour to £125 in Library for dinner tasting menu. **Payment** AE, MC, V. **Service rating** ★★★★. **Friendliness rating** ★★★★. **Bar** Yes. **Wine selection** Upmarket, extensive. **Dress** Smart casual. **Disabled access** Yes. **Hours** Check Web site or call; hours vary according to venue.

SETTING AND ATMOSPHERE *Wow.* From the witty sculpture on the doorstep commemorating July 1, 2007, the first day of the London smoking ban, with ashtrays mounted on a bicycle wheel, to the egg pods of the Gallery bathrooms, this is a seriously funny old place. In the foyer, a bench and a chair emerge from (or melt into) a block of plaster; in the Glade, a series of round mirrors mounted near the ceiling revolve slowly, picking up the glint of jewels on the wall; a chandelier of branches reaches like a mad-hatter Philip Treacy confection across the skylight; and artfully composed lakes of paint run winningly down the stairs to the upstairs restaurant, which is yet another glorious combination of art and architecture. Still with us?

HOUSE SPECIALTIES Whatever Michelin-star-winning chef Pierre Gagnaire has taken in his *toque blanche* to create. More earthbound are the re-creations of classics such as the gnocchi with tomato-and-strawberry marmalade and gorgonzola, the vegetarian *croque monsieur* on black bread, the steak tartare with potato fondant, and the roast duck with spiced-prune-and-blackcurrant coulis.

OTHER RECOMMENDATIONS Anything here is sure to be delicious, but special mention must be given to any and all of the pastries, scones, and finger sandwiches (on minibaguettes made on the premises) of the fabulous Afternoon Tea.

SUMMARY AND COMMENTS Sketch has in its short life become something of a must-see in London. Whether it's for tea or lunch or a crushingly expensive tasting-menu dinner, Sketch has something for every serious diner, as well as something to tickle the funny bone of art connoisseurs. The 18th-century town house between Regent and New Bond streets was purchased by the successful owner of Momo's, who brought in a team of cutting-edge artists and architects to go wild on this beautiful building. They left the elegant bone structure and period details and added decoration that is whimsical, beautiful, and appealing. This exuberance is perfectly appropriate to the time period of the original building, when Georgians tended toward an anything-goes self-expression.

But enough about the setting—it's the food that keeps people coming back. Sketch is among *Restaurant* magazine's top 50 restaurants in the world for 2007, thanks to the partnership of Mourad Mazouz and Pierre Gagnaire, who is considered one of the top chefs on the planet. The dining rooms feature a number of themes: the Glade serves lunch (entrees from £10; the typical bill ends up around £30-plus per person); the Gallery next to it features art exhibitions in the day and becomes a club with DJ at night; the Parlour is for light lunch and heavy afternoon tea (£30 per person), with a head-spinning selection of teas and pastries, and it becomes a bar at cocktail hour and in the evening; the Lecture Room and Library upstairs is home to the Gourmet Rapide Lunch (two courses for £30, three courses for £35), and in the evening this is where you'll enjoy the fine-dining experience of dinner, in which a tasting menu may be considered well worth the £100-plus per head. Whether you are an epicurean in search of a mind-blowing meal, or a schlub who wants to see it all, you will be happy you checked out Sketch.

kids Strada ★★★½

ITALIAN/PIZZA	INEXPENSIVE	QUALITY ★★★	VALUE ★★★

31 Marylebone High Street, Marylebone Village, W1; ☎ 0207-935-1004; www.strada.co.uk

Customers Local office workers, families, tourists. **When to go** Lunch or dinner. **Entree range** £6.50–£14.50. **Payment** MC, V. **Service rating** ★★★. **Friendliness rating** ★★★. **Bar** No. **Wine selection** Adequate. **Dress** Casual. **Disabled access** Yes. **Hours** Monday–Friday, noon–2:30 p.m. and 6:30–10:45 p.m.; Saturday, 6:30–10:45 p.m.; Sunday, noon–2:45 p.m.

SETTING AND ATMOSPHERE Informal Italian.

HOUSE SPECIALTIES Pasta and pizza.

OTHER RECOMMENDATIONS Salads, soups, simple appetizers, risotto.

SUMMARY AND COMMENTS Pizza Express (see page 335) may have more branches and a higher public profile, but when it comes to pizza, everyone in the know will assure you that Strada is the better bet. But it's not just the wood-oven-baked thin-crust pizza that attracts a local customer base: the menu features a range of dishes, with good choice at every course. The level of cooking is generally very sound, with good meals served in friendly, lively surroundings by a young (usually) Italian wait-staff. Prices are low by London standards, and the ingredients really taste of Italy. Moreover, Strada positively adores children in true Italian fashion. Don't expect fireworks, but do expect to be well fed and well looked after.

Tamarind ★★★½

INDIAN	MODERATE	QUALITY ★★★½	VALUE ★★★

20 Queen Street, Mayfair, W1; ☎ 0207-629-3561; www.tamarindrestaurant.com; tube: Green Park

Customers Locals and tourists. **Reservations** Recommended. **When to go** Lunch or dinner. **Entree range** £12.95–£24. **Payment** AE, CB, D, DC, MC, V. **Service rating** ★★★. **Friendliness rating** ★★★. **Bar** Yes. **Wine selection** Very good. **Dress** Smart. **Disabled access** No. **Hours** Lunch Sunday–Friday, noon–2:45 p.m.; Dinner Monday–Saturday, 6–11:30 p.m.; Sunday, 6:30–10:30 p.m.

SETTING AND ATMOSPHERE Chic, stylish decor sets the tone.

HOUSE SPECIALTIES Venison with turnips; roast duck breast; salad of tandoori chicken and grilled *paneer* in a honey-lemon marinade with chiles and avocado; carrot fudge with melon seeds and raisins served with vanilla ice cream.

OTHER RECOMMENDATIONS Pre-theater set menu from 6 to 7 p.m., £24; set lunch (based on seasonal produce), £16.95 for two courses, £18.95 for three, and £24 for a multicourse tasting menu.

SUMMARY AND COMMENTS Tamarind has always produced excellence in every department, from chutneys and pickles (available for sale) to breads and rice, and on to the meat, fish, and vegetable dishes that make this one of the best Indian eateries in London. (Vegetarians could do very well just ordering rice, bread, and a selection of side dishes.) It's not inexpensive—aside from the set menu, a three-course meal with all the right sides can easily cost £45 before drinks. Part of the expense is paying for the setting, for a large and polished team of waiters, and for rent in one of London's most exclusive areas. But it's also paying for the best ingredients, cooked with exceptional skill and attention. And we defy you to find a better set-lunch deal at any of the other fancy one-Michelin-starred restaurants in town (that's right, Tamarind has a Michelin star!). If you want to find out how good Indian restaurant cooking can be and you don't mind paying "European" prices for the pleasure, this is one of the three or four best places to do it.

kids Texas Embassy Cantina ★★½

TEX-MEX	MODERATE	QUALITY ★★★	VALUE ★★★

2 Cockspur Lane, West End, SW1; ☎ 0207-925-0077; www.texasembassy.com; tube: Charing Cross

Customers Tourists, teenage Londoners, expat Americans. **Reservations** For large parties. **When to go** Anytime. **Entree range** £7–£13, set menu £20 per

person. **Payment** AE, DC, MC, V. **Service rating** ★★★. **Friendliness rating** ★★.
Bar Yes. **Wine selection** Bottlings from California and parts of Latin America.
Dress Casual. **Disabled access** Yes. **Hours** Daily, noon–midnight.

SETTING AND ATMOSPHERE Faux Wild West, with weird stuff on the walls and
floors; old American license plates, painted footsteps that you follow to
the bathroom, lights strung gaily all over, and Western music blaring.

HOUSE SPECIALTIES Fajitas, nachos, chimichangas, burritos, and so on, in
Texas-sized portions. Ribs, steaks, and chicken, cooked in Tex-Mex style.

OTHER RECOMMENDATIONS José Cuervo, frozen margaritas, and other crazy
tequila-based cocktails.

ENTERTAINMENT AND AMENITIES Gift shop selling items that you don't need.

SUMMARY AND COMMENTS OK, so it's not *entirely* believable Tex-Mex food,
but Texas Embassy does give it their best shot, and does it better than
most similar establishments in London. And the drinks are pretty great,
as are the nachos. With the walls covered in oddities and mad decorations, coming in here lifts your mood a bit, and it's a big hit with children.
There's a kids' menu, which, considering the size of the regular portions,
is a dang good idea. The building once housed the White Star Shipping
Line (the company that launched the *Titanic*) and is not the actual site
of the real Texas Embassy, which was in nearby St. James. Another draw
is that this eatery is near Trafalgar Square and convenient to everything.
In the summer they put lots of tables out, and the liquor and laughs
flow freely.

The Thai Restaurant & Bar ★★★

THAI	INEXPENSIVE/MODERATE	QUALITY ★★★	VALUE ★★★

93 Pelham Street, South Kensington, SW7;
☎ **0207-584-4788; tube: South Kensington**

Customers Locals and museumgoers. **Reservations** Only for large parties.
When to go Lunch or dinner. **Entree range** £8–£15. **Payment** CB, MC, V. **Service
rating** ★★. **Friendliness rating** ★★★. **Bar** Yes. **Wine selection** OK. **Dress** No
dress code. **Disabled access** Restaurant only, not restrooms. **Hours** Monday–
Sunday, 11:30 a.m.–11:30 p.m.

SETTING AND ATMOSPHERE Small, attractive room with beautiful Thai carvings
and orchids on the tables.

HOUSE SPECIALTIES Very good *pad thai.*

OTHER RECOMMENDATIONS Vegetable spring rolls; banana or apple fritters.

SUMMARY AND COMMENTS This small Thai restaurant does an excellent pad
thai that is a weekly special in my house. The waitstaff are unfailingly
polite, and the set menus for lunch are extremely well priced for the
area as well as for the quantity and quality of the food. The appetizers
are always good, and if the spring rolls are sometimes a bit too greasy,
well, they're authentic in any case. The Thai won't send you into parox-
ysms of delight, but it is a respectable and reliably good restaurant
featuring my favorite Thai dishes, plus some unusual desserts for which
you should be sure to save room.

The Tiroler Hut   ★★★

AUSTRIAN	MODERATE	QUALITY ★★★½	VALUE ★★★

27 Westbourne Grove, Notting Hill, W2; ☎ 0207-727 3981; www.tirolerhut.co.uk; tube: Bayswater

Customers International crowd. **Reservations** A must! **When to go** Friday or Saturday night. **Entree range** £10–£16.50. **Payment** MC, V. **Service rating** ★★★. **Friendliness rating** ★★★★★. **Bar** Yes. **Wine selection** Austrian, French, Hungarian. **Dress** Casual. **Disabled access** No. **Hours** Tuesday–Saturday, 6:30 p.m.–1 a.m.; Sunday, 6:30–11 p.m; closed Monday.

SETTING AND ATMOSPHERE Family-run basement restaurant; staff are all clad in lederhosen and other traditional Austrian dress. Joseph, your host, is sure to give you a lively evening with his accordion (Wednesday through Sunday), a highly original cowbell show (9 p.m.), and, if you're lucky, some yodeling. The walls of the restaurant are packed with Austrian paraphernalia. The tablecloths are checkered red and white, with candles lit in wine bottles. *Very* kitschy.

HOUSE SPECIALTIES Bratwurst, sauerkraut, roast pork, dumplings.

OTHER RECOMMENDATIONS Hungarian goulash with spaetzle, cakes, and strudel.

SUMMARY AND COMMENTS The Tiroler Hut is more than a restaurant; it's also a place to be entertained by lively, boisterous ringmaster–maître d' Joseph Friedmann (who can even play "The Entertainer" on his accordion). If you love goulash, this is one of the few places you can get it in London, and everything else on the menu is equally fantastic—there's even plenty for vegetarians to choose from. Beer comes in huge steins. The atmosphere is unique in that most diners are smiling, laughing, and encouraged to talk to each other. The last time I went there, a bride-to-be was having her bachelorette night, and Joseph asked each of the single men in the restaurant to go up and kiss her on the cheek.

Tom's Kitchen   ★★★★

BRITISH	MODERATE	QUALITY ★★★★½	VALUE ★★★

27 Cale Street, Chelsea, SW3; ☎ 0207-349-0202; www.tomskitchen.co.uk; tube: Sloane Square

Customers Locals, businesspeople. **Reservations** For lunch and dinner. **When to go** Anytime; breakfast is good. **Entree range** £5–£16. **Payment** AE, MC, V. **Service rating** ★★★★. **Friendliness rating** ★★½. **Bar** Cocktails at dinner. **Wine selection** Excellent. **Dress** Casual. **Disabled access** Yes. **Hours** Monday–Friday, breakfast 7–10 a.m.; Saturday and Sunday, brunch 10 a.m.–3 p.m.; Monday–Friday, lunch noon–3 p.m.; dinner from 6 p.m.

SETTING AND ATMOSPHERE Very charming room covered in gleaming white-porcelain tiles, with wood and marble accents and oak tables; provincial French yet with a distinctly posh vibe. Huge Cartier-Bresson–style black-and-white photos adorn the walls and depict the suppliers of the fresh produce at work: these witty portraits include the owner of the Dayleford Organic Farm perching on a tree bough with a herd of beef at his feet; Richard Vine, the appropriately named greenhouse supplier, shown with his head popping up out of a sea of salad leaves, a magnifying glass enlarging his eye; and an atmospherically brooding portrait of a man and his chickens.

HOUSE SPECIALTIES Hamburgers, sausage and mash, salads.

OTHER RECOMMENDATIONS Try any of the desserts—the thyme-and-lemongrass *panna cotta* sounds crazy but is complexly perfect.

SUMMARY AND COMMENTS Tom Aikens, owner of the eponymous gastro-cathedral down the street off Chelsea Green, has opened a less intimidating eatery that serves a smokin' breakfast as well as a great lunch and dinner at a fraction of the cost of his fancy restaurant. It's a very relaxing place, lively and always busy, and the food is made with only the finest products England has to offer. No fireworks in the kitchen, no pretension or over-the-top presentation—just reliably fresh, excellently prepared dishes that are the crème-de-la-comfort-food and then some.

Toto's ★★★½

ITALIAN	MODERATE/EXPENSIVE	QUALITY ★★★½	VALUE ★★★½

Lennox Gardens Mews (off Walton Street), Knightsbridge, SW1; ☎ 0207-589-0075; tube: Knightsbridge or South Kensington

Customers Local celebs and poshies, businesspeople, ladies who lunch. **Reservations** Yes. **When to go** Anytime. **Entree range** £14–£23. **Payment** AE, DC, MC, V. **Service rating** ★★★★. **Friendliness rating** ★★★★. **Bar** Yes. **Wine selection** Excellent. **Dress** Casual. **Disabled access** No. **Hours** Daily, 12:30–3 p.m. and 7–11 p.m.

SETTING AND ATMOSPHERE Lush and elegant, this ancient building has been restored just enough and no more. Decor is beautifully subtle, with black-and-white photos of various scenes from recent eras. The mantelpiece is antique, original, and exquisite. Huge windows and a soaring ceiling make this one of the nicest rooms in London, and the outdoor garden is like something out of Fellini's *Amarcord*. The owner and service staff are all delightful and professional—no snooty vibe here at all.

HOUSE SPECIALTIES Filet steak with foie gras, homemade pasta, amazing bread basket, tiramisù.

OTHER RECOMMENDATIONS Any of the specials.

SUMMARY AND COMMENTS Knightsbridge residents can hardly swing a cat without hitting one or two fancy Italian restaurants, but those in the know skip the San Lorenzo crowd and abjure the nearby Scalini to relax in the reliably warm and welcoming atmosphere of Toto's, knowing that fine dining is another given here. Service is impeccable without being overbearing, and the food is high-end Italian at its best. A rotating special menu assures a new taste treat every day, and touches such as the complimentary glass of sparkling wine, the generous basket of assorted breads, and numerous fresh side orders are not to be taken for granted in London's upmarket restaurants. Best of all is the gorgeous dining room—the foyer has an old tree right in the center, and the main dining room is bright and airy while maintaining a genuine medieval feeling—museums would fight over the original carved fireplace. The lunch menu offers two courses for £21 and three courses for £23. Go for the extra course so you can try the dessert.

Veeraswamy ★★★

INDIAN	MODERATE	QUALITY ★★★	VALUE ★★★½

Mezzanine Floor, Victory House, 99 Regent Street, Piccadilly, W1;
☎ **0207-734-1401; www.veeraswamy.com; tube: Piccadilly Circus**

Customers Mostly locals. **Reservations** Recommended. **When to go** Lunch or dinner. **Entree range** £10–£15; set menus £16.50 and up. **Payment** AE, CB, DC, MC, V. **Service rating** ★★★★. **Friendliness rating** ★★★★. **Bar** No. **Wine selection** Very good. **Dress** No dress code. **Disabled access** Yes; street entrance added in 2007. **Hours** Monday–Friday, noon–2:30 p.m. and 5:30–11:30 p.m.; Saturday, 12:30–3 p.m. and 5:30–11:30 p.m.; Sunday, 12:30–3 p.m. and 5:30–10:30 p.m.

SETTING AND ATMOSPHERE Stylish, colorful room overlooking Regent Street; mostly young, fashionable crowd.

HOUSE SPECIALTIES Mussels in coconut-and-ginger sauce; supreme of chicken with sesame; Malabar lobster curry with fresh turmeric and raw mango; chicken curry with saffron and Himalayan screw pine essence; tandoori chicken *tikka* sautéed in a sauce of tomato and onion; green-chile-and-cheese *naan*.

OTHER RECOMMENDATIONS Breads; condiments; set lunch (in addition to à la carte menu), Monday through Saturday, £16.50 and up; Sunday lunch of Indian favorites, £20 for three courses. There are also pre- and post-theater menus, £16.50 for three courses.

SUMMARY AND COMMENTS Veeraswamy, Britain's first Indian restaurant, has been on this site since the 1920s. It was taken over and revamped by the quality-conscious Masala Zone people who also own Chutney Mary and Amaya. They modernized everything from decor (re-renovated in 2007) to menu to wine list, and the result is one of London's better Indian restaurants. (And for those of you who are interested in tradition, there are fascinating sepia photos on the wall of how it used to be.) The attractively modern room, its pale wood contrasting with deep, well-chosen color, is a far cry from the decor of most Indian restaurants in London.

Service is provided a young, multiethnic crew, and the kitchen specialists prepare dishes of their own region. This means that each dish is likely authentic, whatever part of India it represents. Vegetable and fish/meat/chicken dishes are given equal prominence and cooked with equal care, making Veeraswamy a particularly good place to come with a mixed group of vegetarians and meat eaters. Prices are fair, compared with those of other Indian restaurants at this level, and set-price offerings make them even better. If your time is limited and you can eat at only one Indian place, you can't go wrong here.

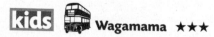

kids Wagamama ★★★

| ASIAN | INEXPENSIVE | QUALITY ★★★★ | VALUE ★★★★ |

4A Streatham Street, Bloomsbury, WC1; ☎ **0207-323-9223;**
tube: Tottenham Court Road
10A Lexington Street, West End, W1; ☎ **0207-292-0990;**
tube: Oxford Circus or Piccadilly Circus; www.wagamama.com

Customers Mostly locals. **Reservations** Not accepted. **When to go** Anytime.
Entree range £6.50–£9.50. **Payment** AE, D, JCB, MC, V. **Service rating** ★.
Friendliness rating ★★. **Bar** No. **Wine selection** Minimal. **Dress** Casual.
Disabled access Not at the locations above, but see profile. **Hours** Monday–
Saturday, noon–11 p.m.; Sunday, 12:30–10:30 p.m.

SETTING AND ATMOSPHERE Spartan room with communal seating at long tables.
HOUSE SPECIALTIES Soup noodles, fried noodles, dumplings.
OTHER RECOMMENDATIONS Desserts are surprising; try the ice-cream *gyoza*.
SUMMARY AND COMMENTS Wagamama has spoken to the zeitgeist of London,
growing from the original restaurant on Streatham Street to close to a
hundred worldwide. The expansion tells the story of a phenomenal success based on a simple idea: produce a menu that focuses on just a few
things, make them consistently well, and cut out the frills so you can sell
them cheap. The focus is on noodles, mostly Japanese varieties such as
ramen and udon, although each year the menu grows longer, with deep-
fried *katsu* of all kinds, salads, curry, fried rice, raw salad, *gyoza*—all sorts
of solid pan-Asian dishes, and lots of fruit-and-vegetable-juice combos.
The frills that disappear are personal space (you sit at long tables with
other diners) and flexibility. You're in a machine at Wagamama, and it's
no place to dawdle. But the meals are cheap, well made, and filling, and
you can be in and out very quickly when you're on the go. Complaints
almost always deal with service, which has little to do with personalized
attention and much more with keeping the machine working smoothly.
Kids like the informality of the place, and, recognizing this, the restaurant now offers a kids' menu with nonyucky food they might like (such
as breaded chicken and noodles) at prices you'll definitely like (around
£5). *Note:* Some other locations have disabled access.

The Wolseley ★★★★

| MODERN BRITISH | MODERATE/EXPENSIVE | QUALITY ★★★★ | VALUE ★★★ |

160 Piccadilly, West End, W1; ☎ **0207-499-6996; www.thewolseley.com;**
tube: Green Park

Customers Celebs, ladies who lunch, local businesspeople. **Reservations** Essential.
When to go Morning, noon, or night, though morning is the least expensive time.
Entree range £6.75–£29.50. **Payment** AE, DC, MC, V. **Service rating** ★★★★.
Friendliness rating ★★★½. **Bar** Yes, and very attractive it is. **Wine selection**

Excellent. **Dress** Smart casual. **Disabled access** Yes. **Hours** Monday–Friday, 7 a.m.–midnight; Saturday, 9 a.m.–midnight; Sunday, 9 a.m.–11 p.m.

SETTING AND ATMOSPHERE Gorgeous, if a bit cavernous, sharing a lovely stretch of Piccadilly with The Ritz.

HOUSE SPECIALTIES Oysters, crab hash with lemon aioli; steak *frites*.

OTHER RECOMMENDATIONS Any of the *plats du jour;* wiener schnitzel; panfried gnocchi; desserts.

SUMMARY AND COMMENTS This grand cafe on Piccadilly opened in 2003 and hasn't had a slow day since. The owners named this eatery after the company that commissioned the 1921 building as a car showroom before it became a Barclay's Bank. It's filled with A-, B-, and C-list celebrities, some of whom rate the small dining room up the staircase at the back. It's distinguished without being intimidating, and the prices of the well-prepared dishes are not ridiculously out of this world—you can order a hamburger for £9.75 without inviting a sneer from the waiter. The panfried gnocchi with pesto and spring vegetables is so delicious I tried to make it myself, but there is no way that a home-cooked job would measure up.

The efficient service and attention of the waiters, coupled with the buzzy energy in the dining room, definitely add to the enjoyment of The Wolseley's reliably great food. You'll need to reserve a table well in advance of your visit, so make the call—they don't take e-mail reservations. If you can't get in for lunch or dinner, I urge you to check out the fine breakfast, served from 7 a.m. (9 a.m. on weekends); the postlunch all-day menu; or a late-afternoon tea that costs about 10 quid less than the same thing at the many fancy hotels in the area.

Yauatcha ★★★★½

CHINESE AND DIM SUM   EXPENSIVE   QUALITY ★★★★½   VALUE ★★★

15–17 Broadwick Street, Soho, W1; ☎ 0207-494-8888; tube: Oxford Circus

Customers Expense accounters, Soho businesspeople, trendies. **Reservations** Yes. **When to go** Anytime. **Entree range** Dim sum dishes, £4–£22. **Payment** AE, DC, MC, V. **Service rating** ★★★★. **Friendliness rating** ★★. **Bar** Tearoom for customers waiting on a table. **Wine selection** Excellent. **Dress** Casual. **Disabled access** No. **Hours** *Tearoom:* Monday–Saturday, 10 a.m.–11 p.m.; *dining room:* Monday–Saturday, 11 a.m.–11 p.m.; Sunday, 11 a.m.–10 p.m.

SETTING AND ATMOSPHERE Extraordinary modern, almost sci-fi decor, with enormous fish tanks and moody lighting.

HOUSE SPECIALTIES Dim sum and plenty of it; mango spring rolls; chicken feet in chile–black bean sauce; crispy duck roll; crystal buns; *shumai.*

OTHER RECOMMENDATIONS Desserts.

ENTERTAINMENT AND AMENITIES People-watching, fish-tank-gazing, and visiting the unusual restrooms.

SUMMARY AND COMMENTS Yauatcha is an achingly hip spot that cost £4.5 million to decorate (you may find yourself wondering where the money went—except for the fish tanks, it's very minimalist). It certainly is dramatic and interesting and edgy, but the real star here is the dim sum, translated from owner Alan Yau's native Hong Kong into a vernacular that is authentic yet au courant. The dishes themselves are not expensive, but watch what you order, as the bill can climb very steeply, very easily.

The dim sum is served not on the traditional trolley but on bamboo trays by waitstaff whose uniforms were created by the costume designer for the film *Crouching Tiger, Hidden Dragon*. You'd be forgiven for thinking the waiters, regardless of their clothes, could be a bit friendlier and less abrupt, but if you've ever eaten in Hong Kong, you'd know the norm there is get 'em in, feed 'em up, get 'em out. There was originally a 90-minute maximum for eating, and you'd be refused dessert if your time was up. But thanks to the patronage of the Beautiful People, that rule's less rigid these days; the idea of some crouching-tiger waiter telling the dragonlike Naomi Campbell to vacate her table *now* is hilariously unlikely.

PART NINE

ENTERTAINMENT *and* NIGHTLIFE

The LONDON SCENE

FEW WORLD CITIES CAN RIVAL LONDON for the overall quality and quantity of its theaters, opera, ballet, concert halls, jazz venues, cinemas, cabarets, casinos, comedy clubs, television, nightclubs, pubs, restaurants, and street entertainment. England has a bit of a schizophrenic culture, one in which BBC adaptations of literary masterpieces share the airwaves with people eating spiders on *I'm a Celebrity, Get Me Out of Here!* The art scene, too, ranges from the sublime to the ridiculous: Tracy Emin's unmade bed commands higher prices than a David Hockney or Lucian Freud portrait, and a leather purse filled with concrete by an artist who calls himself Bob and Roberta Smith is flogged for £50. This all-encompassing embrace of cutting-edge and kooky as well as traditional and classic is what makes London's entertainment culture so marvelously mad.

This enthusiasm for wildly divergent entertainment may stem from the diversity of London's population. Although the city at its heart remains English in character, it has, since World War II, become a microcosm of the defunct British Empire, with one person in five now hailing from an ethnic minority. It is precisely these various Middle Eastern, Indian, Asian, and Afro-Caribbean influences that have made London at least as vibrantly international as New York.

Soho, an old district of said West End, has long been the epicenter of London's nightlife, with its preponderance of famous theaters, cinemas, pubs, clubs, and restaurants. But London's culture and night fun are by no means limited to this neighborhood. Pick up copies of *Time Out London, What's On,* or *Metro Life,* the Thursday supplement of the *Evening Standard,* to see what's going on where and when.

unofficial **TIP**
Forward-thinking types can check out **www.timeout.com/london** or **www.londontown.com** in the weeks before they visit to hone their lists of things to do in London.

THEATER

LONDON THEATER FALLS INTO THREE CATEGORIES: the **West End,** London's equivalent to New York City's Broadway; **off–West End** (ditto); and **fringe,** which is roughly similar to New York's off-Broadway.

THE WEST END

ALTHOUGH "WEST END" REFERS TO AN AREA of central London, it also indicates cultural status, encompassing the **National Theatre,** which is south of the Thames, and the **Old Vic,** which is also outside of shouting distance of Piccadilly Circus. West End theaters, with their massive overheads, tend to bet on the safe side with proven, popular musicals and mainstream productions, but plenty of other London venues are willing to take creative risks, with dramas ranging from the sublime to the puzzling, including the odd star vehicle (for example, Daniel Radcliffe, star of the *Harry Potter* movies, took his clothes off in a production of *Equus* in 2007). The West End actually sells almost three times as many tickets a year as all the Greater London League football teams combined—which is saying a lot, as the English are bonkers over their football.

Try **www.officiallondontheatre.co.uk** for a listing of current plays, plus reviews, phone numbers, and tips. Choose the production venue, then click on a seating plan of the theater, which is very useful when ordering tickets. The *stalls* are the seats on the same level as the stage; *dress circle* is the first balcony; and *upper circle* is the second balcony, known as the nosebleed seats in bigger theaters, although in the smaller venues a front-row upper-circle ticket is always better than a rear-row stalls seat.

 Don't even think of buying a ticket from a tout (essentially a scalper), because you'll be charged an unfair price compared with the legitimate discount tickets sold at the **tkts** booth, operated by the Society of London Theatre. Half-price and well-discounted tickets are available for more than 30 performances daily. To see details of what's on each day, visit **www.tkts.co.uk.**

In the middle of Leicester Square in the Clock Tower building, tkts is the only official ticket-discount booth in London, guaranteeing real bargains for a range of theatrical performances on the day of the show. (No, you cannot get these tickets in advance.)

You will be charged a a service fee of £2.50 per ticket; payment is by cash or credit card (MasterCard, VISA, Switch/Maestro, or Solo; traveler's checks are not accepted). Please note that tkts may impose a limit of four tickets per customer depending on the show. The booth is open Monday through Saturday from 10 a.m. until 7 p.m. and on Sunday between noon and 5 p.m.

Tickets for the big West End shows can be relatively expensive, ranging from £19 to £60 (and beyond). If it's a hot new production you want to see (usually a musical like *Mary Poppins* or *The Sound of Music*), you aren't likely to find half-price tickets available, so you will need to book through **Ticketmaster** (☎ 0207-344-4444; **www.ticketmaster .co.uk**) or **Keith Prowse Ticketing** (☎ 0870-840-1111; **www.keithprowse.com**), or call the theater box office directly. However, booking fees add around 10%—or up to a punishing 20% in some cases—to the price of a ticket, and many theaters charge a telephone-booking fee. The least expensive way to acquire a ticket is to turn up at the box office in person about an hour before curtain time, hoping for a ticket return.

unofficial **TIP**
When seeking out discount theater tickets, go only to the tkts booth—*not* one of the many shopfronts around Leicester Square that call themselves "discount" or "half price" but actually offer no deals at all.

Many theaters offer half-price tickets on Mondays and for dress rehearsals; some also grant concessions (discounts) to students and seniors. Queuing for return or standby tickets before a performance can sometimes yield discounts as well. **LastMinute.com** (**www.last minute.com/site/entertainment/theatre**) is another good resource for finding half-price tickets to some of the top shows of the season. Certain dates and restrictions apply.

The **London Symphony Orchestra** has also reduced its prices and has introduced a £5 concert ticket. West End–Broadway impresario Cameron Mackintosh has even cut some ticket prices for the massive musicals he produces (although you will still get skinned for a good seat on a Saturday night).

The **National Theatre** (South Bank, SE1; box office, ☎ 0207-452-3000; information, ☎ 0207-452-3400; **www.nationaltheatre .org.uk;** tube: Waterloo) operates three theaters—the **Cottesloe, Lyttelton,** and **Olivier**—that present plays in repertory as well as special events with live music or dance DJs. In 2003, Trevor Nunn yielded his position as director to Nicholas Hytner, whose first change was to drop the politically loaded "Royal" from the theater's title. The presentations encompass not only classical but new and neglected plays from the whole of world drama. On the lighter side, the National also offers musicals and even the occasional production for children, six days a week throughout the year. The box office is open Monday through Saturday, 10 a.m. to 8 p.m.; ticket prices range from £10 to £40.

unofficial **TIP**
Try to get standby tickets a half hour before the performance you want to see.

The **Royal Court Theatre** (Sloane Square, SW1; ☎ 0207-565-5000; **www.royalcourttheatre.com;** tube: Sloane Square) has long been the most important venue for new writers of every nationality; the *New York Times* has called it "the most important theatre in Europe." The Royal Court Young Writers Programme participates in exchange residencies with other countries and stages new productions in many cities around the world. The theater opened in 1956 with John Osborne's *Look Back in Anger,* considered ground zero of the "Angry Young Men" generation of playwrights, novelists, and filmmakers.

The Royal Court has also staged plays by such international authors as Bertolt Brecht, Eugene Ionesco, Samuel Beckett, and Jean-Paul Sartre. You could even witness the debut of a new production by Václav Havel, Caryl Churchill, or David Hare here. There are two performance spaces: the Downstairs main theater and the Upstairs studio. Performances are held Monday through Saturday at 7:30 p.m.; Saturday matinees are held at 3:30 p.m. Tickets cost £9 to £27.50 Tuesday through Saturday, £9 to £15 on Friday and for previews and matinees, and £7.50 on Monday (£9 if you book in advance). A limited number of £5 tickets are available to guests age 25 and younger.

The authentic re-creation of **Shakespeare's Globe Theatre** (New Globe Walk, SE1; ☎ 0207-401-9919; **www.shakespeares globe.org;** tube: Blackfriars), close to its original site, is the achievement of American expat actor Sam Wanamaker, who, sadly, died shortly before the restoration was completed. It is an extraordinary accomplishment, and as fascinating to students of historical architecture as it is to Bard buffs. The theater was re-created using only the tools available to the original builders: imagine dovetailing joints without electricity! Although the basement museum, home of the world's largest exhibition devoted to Shakespeare and the theater of his time, remains open year-round (except for December 24 and 25), the roofless Globe's theatrical season is limited to April through October. The box office is open Tuesday through Saturday, 10 a.m. to 6 p.m. Matinees are Saturday at 2 p.m. and Sunday at 1 p.m. or 6:30 p.m. (times alternate weekly). Tickets are £5 to £32. The cheap tickets are for standing in the yard in front of the stage—not a viable option for many people, but a lot of fun for those with stamina (and a rain poncho). Check out the Globe exhibition (October 10 through April 17, 10 a.m. to 5 p.m.; April 18 to October 9, 9 a.m. to 12:30 p.m. and 1 p.m. to 5 p.m.; noon to 5 p.m. Sunday), to get a complete picture of what London life was like in the 1500s. A guided tour is included in your visit, available every half hour from 9 a.m. to 12:30 p.m. daily (the last tour on Sunday is at 11:30 a.m.). Entrance for adults is £9; seniors and students, £7.50; and children, £6.50. Or you can get a family ticket for £20.

OFF–WEST END

OFF–WEST END THEATERS OFTEN PROVIDE the most outstanding productions in terms of creativity because they afford writers, directors, and actors an artistic freedom that may be lacking in some of the more commercially motivated organizations. With emphasis firmly on the modern and avant-garde, the **Almeida** (Almeida Street, N1; ☎ 0207-359-4404; **www.almeida.co.uk;** tube: Angel) features cerebral drama from top writers and actors. It came under the direction of former Royal Shakespeare Company head Michael Attenborough when it reopened in spring 2003. Tickets are £6 to £30. The intimate 105-seat **Bush Theatre** (Shepherd's Bush Green, W12; ☎ 0207-610-4224; **www.bushtheatre.co.uk;** tube: Shepherd's Bush or Goldhawk Road) is considered the next most important spot (after the Royal Court) for productions by new writers, many of whom have gone on to greater successes. Tickets are £6 to £14. The **Donmar Warehouse** (41 Earlham Street, WC2; ☎ 0207-369-1732; **www.donmarware house.com;** tube: Covent Garden) became an exciting venue in the late 1990s under the artistic direction of Sam Mendes; taking over from him in early 2003 was Michael Grandage, who continues to stage provocative drama. Tickets are £12 to £29. Home to gay-and-lesbian-themed productions, the **Drill Hall** (16 Chenies Street, WC1; ☎ 0207-307-5060; **www.drillhall.co.uk**; tube: Goodge Street) welcomes everyone. The atmosphere of this intimate theater is brilliant. Monday evenings are for women only. Tickets are £10 to £16. A small theater located above a pub, the **Gate** (The Prince Albert, 11 Pembridge Road, W11; ☎ 0207-229-0706; **www.gatetheatre.co.uk;** tube: Notting Hill Gate) has a fine reputation for its low-budget yet high-quality dramas from all over the world. Budding actors and directors relish the opportunity to work here and will happily do so for free, so great are the kudos. Performances run Monday through Saturday; tickets are £10 to £20. The **King's Head** (115 Upper Street, N1; ☎ 0207-226-1916; tube: Angel), London's most venerable pub theater, frequently puts on top-quality, small-scale plays, revues, and musicals. It's a fine pub as well. Its founder and guiding spirit, Dan Crawford, died in 2005, but the shows will undoubtedly go on. Tickets are £10.50 to £22.50. **Regent's Park Open Air Theatre** (Regent's Park, NW1; ☎ 0207-486-2431; **www.open airtheatre.org.uk;** tube: Baker Street) caters to those who like their theater alfresco. Set in the middle of the eponymous park and furnished with a bar and snacking facilities, this charming summer theater is an ideal venue in which to see the company's vastly entertaining version of *A Midsummer Night's Dream*. The season kicks off the first week of June, and tickets are £12 to £40.

    Riverside Studios (Crisp Road, W6; ☎ 0208-237-1111; **www.riversidestudios.co.uk;** tube: Hammersmith) overlooks the River Thames near Hammersmith Bridge. There are three studio spaces: one seats 400, another seats 150, and the third is in permanent use for a TV show. In addition to the theatrical and dance productions, there is a repertory cinema, a gallery, and a cafe overlooking the river. The **Soho Theatre** (21 Dean

unofficial **TIP**
Always prepare for the vagaries of British weather. Outdoor performances will be canceled in torrential rain but will soldier on in the usual drizzle, so bring a rain poncho.

Street, Soho, W1; ☎ 0207-478-0100; **www.sohotheatre.com;** tube: Tottenham Court Road) has been happily at home in a modern and well-appointed space for the last few years, producing topical new plays as well as occasional stand-up comedy and readings by authors. Standing in the shadows of the Old Vic theater, **Young Vic** (66 The Cut, SE1; ☎ 0207-928-6363; **www.youngvic.org;** tube: Southwark) attracts big-name actors and touring companies such as the Royal Shakespeare Company. Shows run Monday through Saturday; tickets are £15 to £40.

FRINGE

FRINGE THEATER CAN BE FOUND THROUGHOUT London but, like British weather, is variable and generally patchy in quality. Still, the following theaters do provide the occasional ray of dramatic sunshine:

The small **Chelsea Theatre** (King's Road, SW10; ☎ 0207-352-1967; **www.chelseatheatre.co.uk;** tube: Sloane Square, then bus 19, 22, 211, or 319; or South Kensington, then bus 45 or 49) focuses on exciting new plays that run seven to eight weeks at a time. Performances are held Monday through Saturday at 8 p.m. Tickets are £8 to £12. The **Finborough** (Finborough Arms, Finborough Road, SW10; ☎ 0207-373-3842; **www.finboroughtheatre.itgo .com;** tube: Earls Court), a small pub venue, hosts new writers, some of whom have ended up in the West End or on Broadway. Performances are Tuesday through Saturday at 7:30 p.m.; Sunday matinees occur at 3:30 p.m. Tickets are £12. For previews and Tuesday performances, all seats are £8. Credit cards are *not* accepted. Being so close to Piccadilly, **Jermyn Street Theatre** (16b Jermyn Street, SW1; ☎ 0207-287-2875; **www.jermyn streettheatre.co.uk;** tube: Piccadilly Circus) is a great alternative to a big West End production. This intimate 70-seat venue hosts a mixture of shows, but musicals are the main feature. Performances are daily at 7:30 p.m.; Sunday matinees are at 3 p.m. Tickets are £12 to £18. The **New End Theatre** (27 New End, NW3; ☎ 0207-794-0022; **www.newendtheatre.co.uk;** tube: Hampstead), in lovely Hampstead, offers reliably interesting productions. Tickets range from £15 to £18. New writing and a thriving bar can be found in at the legendary **Old Red Lion** (416 St. John Street, EC1; ☎ 0207-837-7816; **www.oldredliontheatre.co.uk;** tube: Angel). Tickets are around £10.

unofficial **TIP**
Although dinner jackets and tiaras are no longer standard attire when attending the theater, the British middle class still appears to dress with care for certain events, and black tie remains mandatory for any gala charity night at which royals may be present. Certainly, suits and smart dresses are often seen in West End and off–West End theaters, but you will not feel out of place in the egalitarian uniform of sneakers (called "trainers" here), baseball cap, and jeans.

LAUGHS *in* LONDON

THE BRITISH FREQUENTLY CONGRATULATE themselves on their well-developed, often idiosyncratic sense of humor, and justly so;

surely no other country has produced so many generations of comic novelists of the caliber of Lawrence Sterne, Henry Fielding, Charles Dickens, Jane Austen, Evelyn Waugh, Nancy Mitford, and, of course, the divine P. G. Wodehouse, to name only a few.

Although British sitcoms are currently in the doldrums, the BBC has an unrivaled roster of past triumphs. If you're staying in one evening, try renting videos of *Black Adder, Jeeves and Wooster, Drop the Dead Donkey, I'm Alan Partridge, French and Saunders, The Comic Strip, The Fast Show, Slap the Pony, Absolutely Fabulous, Stella Street, Little Britain, The Office,* or Ricky Gervais's *Office* follow-up, *Extras,* a comedy that trains a jaundiced eye on the low end of the film business, with wickedly funny, self-mocking cameos by big-name actors. Although most native Brits and expats find most of the above seriously funny, it's hard to gauge how well they travel— some foreigners are mystified by them, as comedy tends to be culture specific; Americans have been known to flinch from the boarding-school-bully brutality of British humor.

London has more comedy outlets than most cosmopolitan cities. The humor on display varies in quality, including traditional impro-visation as well as physical, surreal, and observational comedy. Most venues provide food and drink—both of which help if the acts are dreadful. Tee-hee aficionados will appreciate the **London Comedy Festival** in May (☎ 0870-011-9611; **www.londoncomedyfestival.com**).

Amused Moose Soho (Moonlighting Nightclub, 17 Greek Street, Soho, London W1; ☎ 020 7287 3727; **www.amusedmoose.com;** tube: Piccadilly Circus or Tottenham Court Road) has shows at 8:30 p.m. on Monday, Wednesday, and Thursday and 8 p.m. on Saturday and Sunday. Tickets are reasonably priced, from £5 to £10.

Comedy Café (66 Rivington Street, EC2; ☎ 0207-739-5706; **www.comedycafe.co.uk;** tube: Old Street), one of the handful of clubs in London devoted entirely to comedy, takes the generous precaution of granting free admission on Wednesday, when new acts make their debuts. The club is open Wednesday through Saturday; tickets are £8 on Thursday, £5 on Friday, and £15 on Saturday. Comedy Café offers a

> *unofficial* **TIP**
> London comedy clubs boast that their acts are "first-date friendly," which presumably means you won't be hounded or heckled as part of the act.

"party package" that rather endearingly includes party hats as well as admission, a three-course dinner, and entrance to the weekend disco; packages cost £14.50 on Wednesday, £22.50 on Thursday, £19.50 on Friday, and £29.50 on Saturday. The **Comedy Store** at Haymarket House (1A Oxendon Street, SW1; ☎ 0207-344-0234; **www.thecomedystore.co.uk;** tube: Piccadilly Circus) is the venue from which alternative comedy exploded onto British television screens. Such stars as Jennifer Saunders (of *French and Saunders* and *Absolutely Fabulous* fame), Ben Elton, and Rik Mayall began their careers here. It's still the best club on the circuit. Open Tuesday through Sunday; tickets range from £15 to £18, and on the last Monday of the month, the cost is only £5 for the King Gong amateur night show. **Jongleurs** (The Cornet, 49 Lavender Gardens, SW11; ☎ 0207-564-2500; **www.jongleurs.com;** tube: Clapham Junction) is as popular as the Comedy Store, with an impressive lineup of performances that aren't all stand-up. Friday shows start at 8:45 p.m., followed by a disco and late bar until 1 a.m.; Saturday performances begin at 7:15 p.m., with a late show at 11:15 p.m. Another branch in North London, **Jongleurs Camden Lock** (Dingwalls, Middle Yard, Camden Lock, Camden High Street, NW1; ☎ 0207-564-2500; tube: Camden Town or Chalk Farm), is comfortable and busy, so book in advance. Shows on Friday start at 8:45 p.m., followed by a disco; on Saturday, performances start at 7:15 p.m. and 11:15 p.m. Tickets are £12 to £15 on Friday and £15 to £20 on Saturday.

◼| CLASSICAL MUSIC

ARGUABLY THE MUSIC CAPITAL OF THE WORLD, London is endowed with four highly regarded orchestras, two internationally renowned arts establishments, numerous ensembles, and a correspondingly wide range of concerts.

Although the Barbican's **London Symphony Orchestra** remains the capital's leading ensemble, the South Bank Centre's **London Philharmonic Orchestra** has been gaining in strength. Then, too, the **Royal Philharmonic Orchestra** enjoys a distinguished history despite having to get by without public funding.

Many of the world's leading musicians flock to London stages, often for the city's frequent music festivals, especially the **Henry Wood Promenade Concerts** (affectionately known as "the Proms"), held annually from July to September at the **Royal Albert Hall** (Kensington Gore, SW7; ☎ 0207-589-3203 or 589-8212; **www.royalalberthall.com;** tube: Gloucester Road or South Kensington). The Albert is a prodigious Victorian building that hosts pop gigs, opera, ballet, Cirque du Soleil, and even pro-wrestling bouts. Tickets range from £6 to £80. An impressive exterior restoration opened up the original entrance on the opposite side of Kensington Gore; the sweeping steps afford a view of the friezes and other details that define Victorian grandeur.

The refurbished **Royal Opera House** (Covent Garden, WC2; recorded information; ☎ 0207-304-4000; box office, ☎ 0207-240-1200; **www.royalopera.org;** tube: Covent Garden) is worth a visit just to see the beautiful building (tours available). The presentations include classical productions of operas and ballets, and the price of the tickets is wonderfully varied: from £4 to £180.

Wigmore Hall (36 Wigmore Street, W1; ☎ 0207-935-2141; **www.wigmore-hall.org.uk;** tube: Bond Street) is the best place in town to hear piano recitals and chamber groups. Although the hall was modernized not long ago, Wigmore continues to serve up largely traditional fare. Tickets are £5 to £40.

You might enjoy the lunchtime concert held every second Thursday at the converted church of **St. John's Smith Square** (Smith Square, SW1; ☎ 0207-222-1061; **www.sjss.org.uk;** tube: Westminster). St. John's, near the Houses of Parliament, is nestled in an area of antique civility and possessed of a magical ambience. Tickets are £10 to £15, £5 for students.

It is easy to lose one's way down the labyrinthine corridors of that monster of modernism the **Barbican Centre** (Silk Street; ☎ 0207-638-8891 or 0207-638-4141; **www.barbican.org.uk;** tube: Barbican). Still, it has superb acoustics, is home to the London Symphony Orchestra, and hosts the "Great Orchestras of the World," making it worth a music lover's effort. Other great orchestras that perform a wide range of classical music at the Barbican include the BBC Symphony Orchestra, the City of London Sinfonia, and the English Chamber Orchestra. Tickets start at £6.50.

Perched just above the Thames, next to Waterloo Bridge, is the **South Bank Centre** (Belvedere Road, South Bank, SE1; box office, ☎ 0207-960-4242; recorded information, ☎ 0207-633-0932; **www.sbc.org.uk;** tube: Waterloo). Its Royal Festival Hall (RFH1) is the main auditorium for symphony concerts; the smaller Queen Elizabeth Hall (RFH2) hosts stripped-down opera and chamber-music productions; recitals as well as ensemble performances take place in the intimate setting of the adjacent Purcell Room (RFH3). The South Bank Centre comes complete with restaurants, cafes, bars, and book and record shops. Ticket prices vary from £6 to £80.

Weather permitting, there is nothing more English than listening to classical music outdoors in the summer air, beside a great castle or on the grounds of a fragrant park. The **Hampton Court Palace Festival** takes place in June (Hampton Court, East Molesey, Surrey; ☎ 0207-344-4444; **www.hamptoncourtfestival.com;** British Rail: London Waterloo to Hampton Court Station; Hampton Court riverboat: Westminster or Richmond to Hampton Court Pier). Tickets are £15 to £85.

unofficial **TIP**
The lawns of historic Hampton Court Palace along the Thames make a perfect picnic ground.

The **Holland Park Theatre** (Holland Park, Kensington High Street, W8; box office, ☎ 0207-602-7856; information, ☎ 0207-603-1123; **www.operahollandpark.com;** tube: High Street Kensington or Holland Park) stages an array of music, theater, and dance performances in one of London's loveliest parks. Guests are sheltered from the harmful effects of storm and sun by an enveloping canopy. Open June through August; tickets are £21, £38, and £43.

Kenwood Lakeside Concerts (Kenwood House, Hampstead Lane, NW3; ☎ 0208-233-7435; **www.picnicconcerts.com;** tube: Golders

Green or East Finchley to courtesy bus on concert nights) are best enjoyed on the nights when they punctuate the shows with fireworks. Held during July and August on the grounds of Kenwood House in Hampstead Heath, these concerts are among London's most delightful events. Tickets vary from £17 to £26, and seating is either in deck chairs or on the grass (bring a blanket and a picnic).

DANCE *and* BALLET

WHEN ONE THINKS OF DANCE IN LONDON, a flood of terpsichorean images comes pirouetting to mind: *The Red Shoes*, Fonteyn and Nureyev, Fred and Adele Astaire, Sadler's Wells, the Royal Ballet, and Covent Garden. The wonderful movie *Billy Elliot* was reinvented for the stage in 2005, becoming the biggest smash hit of that year in the West End.

Dance grew steadily in popularity throughout the 1990s, abetted by several festivals. **Dance Umbrella** (☎ 0208-741-5881; **www.dance umbrella.co.uk**), featuring contemporary dance from all over the world, normally runs during September and October for six weeks. The events are hosted at various locations across London; ticket prices vary according to the venue.

Two of the largest and most active dance venues are the **Barbican Centre** and the **South Bank Centre** (see "Classical Music," page 358, for contact information).

The **Royal Ballet** hosts productions in the main theater of the Royal Opera House (see entries for this venue in the "Classical Music" and "Opera" sections). Expect to see performances of such classics as *Don Quixote, The Nutcracker, La Bayadère, Giselle,* and *Romeo and Juliet*. Tickets are £5 to £180.

The refurbishment of **Sadler's Wells** (Rosebury Avenue, EC1; ☎ 0207-863-8000; **www.sadlerswells.com;** tube: Chancery Lane) has been completed at last, and the more intimate and central **Peacock Theatre** (Portugal Street, off Kingsway, WC2; ☎ 0207-314-8800; tube: Holborn), which served as the interim house during the refurbishment, is now a permanent branch of the main theater. Sadler's Wells has extensive concession areas, state-of-the-art flying and lighting equipment, an ultraflexible stage and an 80-seat orchestra pit. Tickets are £10 to £45.

Vast in scale yet graceful in outline, the **London Coliseum** (St. Martin's Lane, WC2; ☎ 0207-632-8300; **www.eno.org;** tube: Charing Cross) is the home of the English National Opera for most of the year and also presents such leading dance companies as the English National Ballet and the Royal Ballet during their Christmas and summer seasons. Alongside the Coliseum's more modern and challenging productions, you can always be certain of a Christmastime presentation of *The Nutcracker*. (See separate listing in "Opera," page 361.)

unofficial **TIP**
The Peacock Theatre and Sadler's Wells tend to feature more-contemporary ballet performances.

OPERA

THE MAIN THEATER OF THE **Royal Opera House** (see "Classical Music," page 358, for contact information) is home to the Royal Ballet, but within the complex are two more-intimate venues for opera and dance: the **Linbury Studio Theater,** with 420 seats, and the **Clore Studios,** a 200-seat space that is ideal for workshops and performances. At these smaller theaters, one can see opera stripped to its essentials and for a more affordable price than the great productions in the main theater. Disability access has also improved. There is also the enticing Amphitheatre Bar and Restaurant, whose terrace overlooks Covent Garden. Ticket prices range from £5 for lunchtime performances and some severely restricted views of evening performances to £180 for the best seats. Go to **www.royalopera.org** for the latest information.

Home to the English National Opera, the **London Coliseum** (St. Martin's Lane, WC2; ☎ 0207-632-8300, **www.eno.org;** tube: Charing Cross) is a grand venue that tries to promote a populist image with affordable ticket prices. Please note that the English National Ballet takes over the Coliseum from mid-December through mid-January. Tickets run from £10 to £74.

LIVE JAZZ, POP, *and* ROCK

LONDON IS A MATRIX OF PERFORMING TALENT, and on any given Saturday night there will be well over 100 gigs being played throughout the city. Tickets vary in price from a fiver or less for small gigs to more than £100 for a top pop attraction. (In 2007, Barbra Streisand caused palpitations and shock-horror with tickets that ranged from £150 to more than a grand for her U.K. farewell concerts—bye-bye indeed.)

The thriving London jazz scene has, over the years, given the world such international luminaries as John McLaughlin, George Shearing, and Dave Holland, a fact that is indicative of the talent found here. Numerous restaurants, bars, pubs, and cafes continue to pleasantly enhance their atmospheres with live jazz music; see *Time Out London* and the *Evening Standard*'s *Metro Life* magazine for details. Among the leading jazz venues for largely local talent (all of which are profiled in the following club section) are **Ronnie Scott's,** the **606 Club, Jazz Café,** and **Pizza Express.**

The **Barbican** and **South Bank Centre** often present top international stars, and two big jazz festivals are held in the autumn: the **Soho Jazz Festival** and the **Oris London Jazz Festival.**

The **Notting Hill Carnival,** held in late August, is Europe's largest street festival, its huge sound systems pumping out reggae,

unofficial **TIP**
As with the theater, you should never buy concert tickets from scalpers—the practice is illegal, and the merchandise is probably forged. It is always best to purchase tickets from the concert venue itself. You will usually not be charged a booking fee if you pay with cash.

rap, and drum bass. Be warned, though: this event is not for the agora-phobic or timid—there are entirely too many muggers, pickpockets, and deranged people pumped full of alcohol for it to suit every sensibility, and the neighborhood streets have become so overwhelmed that the mayor might just get his wish to move the carnival to Hyde Park.

Gargantuan rock stages include the spectacularly renovated 11,000-seat **Wembley Arena** (Empire Way, Wembley, Middlesex; ☎ 0208-902-8833 or 0870-739-0739; **www.wembley.co.uk** or **www.whatsonwembley.com;** tube: Wembley Park);

unofficial **TIP**
Smaller-scale concert venues are preferable in every way.

the 20,000-seat **Earls Court Exhibition Centre** (Warwick Road, SW5; ☎ 0207-385-1200; **www.eco.co.uk;** tube: Earls Court); and London's latest megavenue, the 20,000-capacity **02 Arena** (The 02, Peninsula Square, London SE10; ☎ 0871-984-0002; outside the U.K., 00-44-(0)-161-385-3211; **www.the02.co.uk;** tube: Jubilee Line to North Greenwich for the 02). Of course, the sheer vastness of these coliseums tends to undermine the sonic and visual aspects of performance, and the refreshments are overpriced. Still, if you want to catch the monsters of rock and pop, these are the monster venues you'll have to hit.

Now part of the Carling Group, an entertainment conglomerate, **Brixton Academy** (211 Stockwell Road; London SW9; ☎ 0207-771-3000 or 0870-771-2000; **www.brixton-academy.co.uk;** tube: Brixton) has a 4,300-person capacity, with a seated balcony and standing room at ground level. Many popular bands perform here, and the place has a good atmosphere. Tickets vary from £10 to £26.

The midsized **Shepherd's Bush Empire** (Shepherd's Bush Green; W12; ☎ 0207-771-2000; **www.shepherds-bush-empire.co.uk;** tube: Shepherd's Bush) was the BBC Television Theatre before developing into a top popular music spot with an excellent sound system; it too is now part of the Carling Group. The Empire has a three-tiered seating arrangement, and the first balcony has better views than the ground floor. Expect to pay about £10 to £30 for tickets.

unofficial **TIP**
Warning: The Brixton Academy lies within one of London's dodgier areas, so use common sense and don't go wandering around after the gig.

◼ DANCE CLUBS

LONDON HAS A REPUTATION AS THE DANCE-CLUB capital of Europe, and with good reason. Whatever kind of night you are looking for, you'll no doubt find it—and more—in London. In fact, when going out in London, you should expect the unexpected. The city's nightclubs offer everything from the beatnik beat of cool jazz at **Pizza Express** and Ronnie Scott's to house, electro, and trance madness at **Turnmills, Fabric,** and **Pacha,** not to mention the plenitude of nomadic

underground rave sites. You'll also find everything in between: from pop and rock at **SEone**
and **On-Anon** to scene-making at the wickedly
expensive 24, Paper, and **Koko.** And don't neglect
the parties after the parties at places like the **Egg.**

The covers that most clubs charge can be shockingly expensive
when added to the cost of drinks, so take a deep breath and even
deeper pockets when you go out. You can expect to pay a cover of
between £5 and £10 at clubs that close at 3 a.m. and between £12 and
£20 at clubs that carry on until 6 a.m. The busiest period for most
clubs is between 11:30 p.m. and 2 a.m., so if you arrive early and the
club is completely empty, don't panic—grab a table or spot at the bar
and wait: a club that is quiet at 11 p.m. will be packed to the rafters
by midnight. If you intend to dine at the club, we recommend booking a table for 10 p.m., after which time you will be permitted to stay
on for the dancing. Not all clubs serve dinner; call for information.

The following clubs (profiled in the next section) are known as the
more reliable top venues in London: **Café de Paris, Fabric, Ministry of
Sound,** and **Turnmills.** Of course, nightlife being as fickle and fashionable as it is, even these stalwarts can be here-today-gone-tomorrow
without warning, so do check up-to-date listings
such as those at **www.timeout.com/london.**

Many nightspots try to filter out the riffraff
by styling themselves as "members" clubs. One-off
admissions depend on the club's popularity, clientele, and exclusivity. Clubs like **Chinawhite,** a longtime celebrity haunt, enforce strict members-only
policies on some nights but will let you in on other
nights if you are smartly dressed and look desirable.

Some clubs, even if they are members-only, will
let you in if you get on the guest list in advance; other advantages
include reduced admission and skipping the queue. To get on a guest
list, try calling or e-mailing the club directly. **Kensington Roof Gardens**
(☎ 0207-368-3999; **www.roofgardens.com;** tube: High Street Kensington), for example, allows one-off admission if you contact them in
advance. You can also visit **www.londonclubsguestlist.com, www.allin
london.co.uk/guestlists, www.viewlondon.co.uk, www.hrmguestlists.com,**
or **www.exclusivelondon.co.uk** to get on other clubs' guest lists.

🚌 BARS *and* PUBS

THE BRITISH ARE, GENERALLY SPEAKING, formidable drinkers—they
consume more alcohol than any of their Western European neighbors—
and the pub has stood since time immemorial as an institution that is
integral to the British experience. Since World War I, Britain has had
strict alcohol-licensing laws, initially put in place to ensure that laborers

would not turn up to work late or hung over. On November 24, 2005, new legislation was passed allowing pubs and bars to apply to local authorities for late licenses, allowing them to operate during the hours of their choice, up to and including 24 hours. The change was introduced partly in a bid to put an end to the binge-drinking culture, which is a pretty peculiar way of trying to control the uncontrollable. (And no, it hasn't worked—if anything, public drunkenness has devolved; just look around the West End at the end of a night.)

Most pubs serve a variety of beer, including lager (light Continental beer), bitter (an appropriately named Anglo-Saxon ale), mild (concocted with chocolate malt), cider (fermented apple juice), and shandy (half lager, half lemonade). Best of all are real ales, the boozy equivalent of organic whole-meal bread.

Pub food can also be surprisingly good, depending on the overall quality of the pub itself. Most pubs are strongly historical in ambience, festooned with attractive 18th- and 19th-century bric-a-brac, etched-glass privacy screens, flagstone floors, and deliriously over-carved mahogany or oak bars. In winter, many pubs have a roaring fire and, in summer, a beer garden.

LONDON BAR AND PUB PROFILES
Alphabet Bar

61–63 Beak Street, W1F; ☎ 0871-075-1606; www.alphabetbar.com; tube: Piccadilly Circus

---

Cover charge None. **Dress** Trendy. **Food available** Yes. **Hours** Monday–Friday, noon–11 p.m.; Saturday, 4 p.m.–11 p.m.

DESCRIPTION Artworks drape the walls upstairs; downstairs, comfy leather seats are home to media-industry regulars.

Charles Dickens Inn

St. Katherine's Dock, Wapping, E1; ☎ 0871-332-4923; tube: Tower Hill

---

Cover charge None. **Dress** Casual. **Food available** Upstairs in the pizzeria. **Hours** Monday–Saturday, 11 a.m.–11 p.m.; Sunday, noon–11 p.m.

DESCRIPTION An alternate and enjoyable way to get to this pub is to take a riverboat cruise (£6) from Embankment to St. Katherine's Dock. Originally a brewery, the Charles Dickens Inn is housed in the ground floor of a three-story timber building built in 1793, overlooking a dock of luxury yachts. Comfy leather sofas, friendly staff. The pub's namesake was never actually a patron (that honor goes to The Eagle, profiled on the next page); nevertheless, this bar is well worth a visit, especially on a nice summer's day. Plays anything from 1980s music to house depending on what day you go; reasonably priced.

Cittie of Yorke Tavern

22 High Holborn, WC1V; ☎ 0207-242-7670; tube: Chancery Lane

London Bars and Pubs at a Glance

NAME	ADDRESS
Alphabet Bar	Beak Street, W1
Charles Dickens Inn	St. Katherine's Dock, Wapping, E1
Cittie of York Tavern	High Holborn, WC1
Coach & Horses	Greek Street, W1V
The Eagle	Shepherdess Walk, Hoxton, N1
Elbow Room Pool Lounge and Bar	Westbourne Grove, W2
Fifty Five Bar and Lounge	Jamestown Road, Camden Town, NW1
Hilton Hotel (Trader Vic's, Windows, and Zeta Bar)	Park Lane, W1
Mandarin Bar	Mandarin Oriental Hotel, Knightsbridge, SW1
Old Bank of England	Fleet Street, EC4
Prospect of Whitby	Wapping Wall, E1
Ye Old Cheshire Cheese	Fleet Street, EC4
Ye Olde Mitre Tavern	Ely Court, EC1

Cover charge None. **Dress** Casual. **Food available** Until 9 p.m. **Hours** Monday–Saturday, 11 a.m.–11 p.m.; closed Sundays.

DESCRIPTION This tavern operates in a building dating from 1430, when it was part of a monastery. It's unimpressive on entry, but take a walk to the back, where a vaulted ceiling covers intimate wooden booths and suspended wine barrels.

Coach & Horses
29 Greek Street, W1V; ☎ 0207-437-5920; tube: Leicester Square or Piccadilly Circus

Cover charge None. **Dress** Casual. **Food available** Typical pub grub such as fish and chips, pork or chicken pie, and great sandwiches. **Hours** Monday–Thursday, 11 a.m.–11:30 p.m.; Friday and Saturday, noon–10:30 p.m.

DESCRIPTION This is the pub that inspired Keith Waterhouse's play *Jeffrey Bernard Is Unwell*. Bernard, a real-life newspaper journalist, was a regular—to excess—at the Coach & Horses; the play's title refers to the message that would run in place of his *Spectator* column whenever he got too soused to write it. Not glamorous by any means, but for a taste of a traditional old English pub, it's definitely worth a visit.

The Eagle
2 Shepherdess Walk, City Road, Hoxton, N1; ☎ 0871-332-5131; tube: Old Street

Cover charge None. **Dress** However you want. **Food available** Noon–10 p.m.
Hours Sunday–Thursday, noon–midnight; Friday and Saturday, noon–1 a.m.

DESCRIPTION Though you'd never know it from the name, Charles Dickens
was a regular here. Traditional atmosphere (wooden bar, grand pillars)
and good food. From June to September, a barbecue and DJ draw the
local crowd into the beer garden. If you have dull friends, you can take
advantage of the board games, including Operation!

Elbow Room Pool Lounge and Bar

**103 Westbourne Grove, W2, and other locations; ☎ 0207-221-5211;
www.elbow-room.co.uk; tube: Bayswater**

Cover charge None. **Dress** Casual. **Food available** Until 10 p.m. **Hours** Monday–
Saturday, noon–11 p.m.; Sunday, noon–10:30 p.m.; 2-for-1 cocktails weekdays,
bottles and wine, 5–8 p.m.

DESCRIPTION Elbow Room is a bar, nightclub, and pool hall with the slogan
"the rebirth of pool." The color scheme gives it a relaxed feel, with
calm-enhancing half-peachy, half-green walls; purple-felt American-
style pool tables; and red-velvet curtains. American-style snacks such as
burgers and nachos are available. There's often a long wait for the pool
table, and you're limited to an hour's play, but during the wait you can
sit in the private booths with plasma TVs.

Fifty Five Bar and Lounge

**31 Jamestown Road, Camden Town, NW1; ☎ 0207-424-9054;
www.fiftyfivebar.co.uk; tube: Camden Town**

Cover charge None. **Dress** Trendy. **Food available** Only snacks (nuts and crisps).
Hours Monday–Friday, 5 p.m.–12:30 a.m.; Saturday and Sunday, 1 p.m.–12:30 a.m.
2-for-1 happy hour 6–8 p.m., with 160 cocktails to choose from.

DESCRIPTION You can not only enjoy drinking the cocktails, but you'll also
get a kick out of watching them being made, as here the bartenders
specialize in juggling bottles. (The bartenders themselves aren't hard to
look at either.) Leading bands play live blues five nights a week.

Hilton Hotel

**Park Lane, W1; ☎ 0207-493-8000; www.hilton.com;
tube: Hyde Park Corner or Green Park**

Cover charge *Trader Vic's, Windows Bar and Restaurant:* None. *Zeta Bar:* £10 after 10
p.m. Thursday–Saturday; none Sunday–Wednesday. **Dress** Smart casual–upscale.
Food available Yes; reservations required at Windows. **Hours** *Trader Vic's:* Monday–
Saturday, 5 p.m.–12:45 a.m.; Sunday, 5–10:30 p.m. *Windows Bar and Restaurant:*
Monday–Friday, 12:30–2:30 p.m. and 5:30 p.m.–2 a.m.; Saturday, 5:30 p.m.–
3 a.m. *Zeta Bar:* Monday–Tuesday, noon–1 a.m.; Wednesday–Friday, noon–3 a.m.;
Saturday, 5 p.m.–3 a.m.; Sunday, 5–10:30 p.m.

DESCRIPTION One venue, three great individual bars. If Britain's inclement
weather causes you to yearn for sunnier climes, you might enjoy **Trader**

Vic's (☎ 0207-208-4113) for an ersatz night on a South Pacific island. Home of the mai tai cocktail and delicious food, Vic's is something of a mood lagoon. Alternately, you could venture up to the Hilton's 28th floor to the chichi and romantic **Windows Bar and Restaurant** (☎ 0207-208-4021), which offers a great view of London. Please note the dress code (no jeans or sneakers), and you will need to make reservations if you wish to eat. Finally, the latest addition to the Hilton bar scene is the Zen-trendy **Zeta Bar** (it has a separate entrance on Hertford Street; ☎ 0207-208-4067). Cocktails are the specialty here—either nonalcoholic, delicious, health-inducing "liquid lunches" or the more lethal alcoholic variety. Good bar food is also available. As the night wears on, the door code gets stricter—but as long as you look affluent or trendy, you should have no problem getting in.

Mandarin Bar
Mandarin Oriental Hotel, 66 Knightsbridge, SW1; ☎ 0207-235-2000; tube: Knightsbridge

Cover charge £5 for non-hotel guests after 10:30 p.m. **Dress** Smart casual. **Food available** Canapés only. **Hours** Monday–Saturday, 11 a.m.–2 a.m.; Sunday, 11:30 a.m.–midnight.

DESCRIPTION   Think classy. Think elegant. Located in the aesthetically impressive Mandarin Oriental, Mandarin Bar was rated London's number-one hotel bar in *Time Out London* magazine. Leather armchairs and walls lined with beige silk define the decor; bottles are showcased behind frosted glass. Attracts a very hip crowd. Regular live jazz.

Old Bank of England
194 Fleet Street, EC4; ☎ 0207-430-2255; tube: Temple

Cover charge None. **Dress** Casual. **Food available** Noon–9 p.m. **Hours** Monday–Friday, 11 a.m.–11 p.m.; closed weekends.

DESCRIPTION   A majestic Italianate temple to Mammon, built as a branch of the Bank of England in 1888. Marble, soaring ceilings, and huge chandeliers make this a pub of a very different color.

Prospect of Whitby
57 Wapping Wall, E1; ☎ 0207-481-1095; tube: Wapping

Cover charge None. **Dress** Whatever. **Food available** Noon–9:30 p.m. daily; dishes include soups, savory pies, sausage and mash, and chicken *tikka*. **Hours** Monday–Saturday, noon–11 p.m.; Sunday, noon–10:30 p.m.

DESCRIPTION   If you want to include a visit to an archetypal old-world inn on your agenda, you couldn't do better than this pub, which dates back to 1520 and is mentioned in Samuel Pepys's diary. Prospect of Whitby is renowned for its Elizabethan pewter bar, flagstone floors, cast-iron hearths, and small, round windows.

Ye Old Cheshire Cheese
145 Fleet Street, EC4; ☎ 0207-353-6170; tube: Blackfriars

Cover charge None. **Dress** Casual. **Food available** Steak-and-kidney pie and other pub fare. **Hours** Daily, noon–11 p.m.

DESCRIPTION A haven for journalists and scribblers of all types since before 1666, when it was singed by the Great Fire, Ye Old Cheshire Cheese is a storybook tavern replete with blazing fires, nooks and crannies, wooden floors, sundry bars, and dining sections often populated by tour-bus habitués. And well they might have a visit: it is a must-see even for teetotalers; mind your head as you walk beneath the low ceilings of the little warrens.

Ye Olde Mitre Tavern
**Ely Court, Hatton Garden, EC1; ☎ 0207-405-4751;
tube: Chancery Lane/Farringdon**

Cover charge None. **Dress** Casual. **Food available** Renowned for its toasted sandwiches. **Hours** Monday–Friday, 11 a.m.–11 p.m.; closed weekends.

DESCRIPTION Open since 1547, this hard-to-find tavern is an atmospheric little hideaway with a pervasive sense of Elizabethan England.

SEX *in the* CITY

SOHO IS THE SEX CENTER OF LONDON, and the area around Old Compton Street hosts quite a few sex shops and strip clubs. Beware of unlicensed venues, though, for they are quite literally tourist traps. A common practice of these establishments is to plant a sirenlike hostess at the door; after she lures her victim inside for a drink and a show, the hapless fellow subsequently discovers that the bill for her orange juice and his beer comes to some astronomically unreasonable figure—and there are always belligerent security staff on hand to ensure that customers pay up.

If you don't fancy the Soho scene, which is frankly still a bit sleazy despite local cleanup campaigns, the next safest bet would be the erotic shows held at the following venues. These are mainly "saucy" cabaret shows and lap-dance clubs.

FOR YOUR EYES ONLY (11 White Horse Street, W1; ☎ 0808-100-8899; www.fyeo.co.uk; tube: Green Park; 28 Abbey Road, Park Royal, NW10; ☎ 0208-965-7699; tube: Park Royal) This is the place to go if you want your dancers to go the "full monty." It's open Monday through Wednesday, 7:30 p.m. to 2:30 a.m.; Thursday through Saturday, 7:30 p.m. to 3 a.m.

STRINGFELLOW'S (16 Upper St. Martin's Lane, Covent Garden, WC2; ☎ 0207-240-5534; www.stringfellows.com; tube: Leicester Square) Peter Stringfellow's club plays host to the mass-market sort of celebrity: soap stars, footballers, and AMWs (actresses-models-whatevers). The place is rife with 1980s glamour and pleasant enough in its way, particularly since Stringfellow's came into possession of a table-dancing license. It's open Monday through Saturday, 7:30 p.m. to 3 a.m.

SOPHISTICATS AT VOLTANE (1 Marylebone Lane, W1; ☎ 0208-201-8804 or 201-8968; tube: Bond Street) This gentlemen's club has a distinctly Parisian decadence about it. In addition to the twice-nightly Catgirl cabaret, the club also provides table dancing, caviar girls, and cocktail waitresses. Because this is a private club, it's recommended that you call first to see if you can get a reservation. It's open Monday through Friday, 8:30 p.m. to 3 a.m.

GAMING *in the* UNITED KINGDOM

THE GAMING INDUSTRY IN GREAT BRITAIN is one of the most carefully regulated in the world. All casinos across England, Scotland, and Wales are licensed under the Gaming Act of 1968, which stipulates that unless a player is already a member or the guest of a member, he or she must register at the casino a full day before entering to play. The Gaming Act is designed to protect the public purse from the perils of compulsive gambling. Or, in the strictest legalese: it is a legal requirement that the membership application form is signed on the premises of the casino. Players must present a passport, driver's license, or other suitable identification; authorization of all new memberships takes 24 hours.

The casinos of **London Clubs International** begin with the magnificent **50 St. James** (50 St. James Street, SW1; ☎ 0207-491-4678; tube: Piccadilly), which opened in 1828 as London's first gaming club and is, along with the legendary **Les Ambassadeurs Club** (5 Hamilton Place, W1; ☎ 0207-495-5555; www.clublci.com; tube: Hyde Park), at the top end of the market. These exclusive and lavishly appointed clubs are frequented by royalty, the aristocracy, and celebrated figures from the world of entertainment. Both clubs are open daily, 2 p.m. to 4 a.m. The dress code prohibits jeans, and men are expected to wear coats and ties in the evenings.

Midmarket venues include the **Rendezvous Casino** (14 Old Park Lane, W1; ☎ 0207-491-8586; www.clublci.com; tube: Hyde Park), with its spacious gaming floor, French-influenced bistro, and relaxed sports bar; and the **Sportsman Casino** (40 Bryanston Street, W1; ☎ 0207-414-0061; www.clublci.com; tube: Hyde Park), designed in the style of a Mississippi riverboat. Both clubs are open from about noon until 6 a.m.; gaming begins at 2 p.m. The dress code is smart casual; no jeans are allowed. Coats and ties are required for men in the evening.

The mass-market **Golden Nugget Casino** (22 Shaftesbury Avenue, W1; ☎ 0207-439-0099; **www.clublci.com;** tube: Piccadilly) is the largest and busiest casino in the London Clubs group. It offers a fast-moving environment and fast food to go with it. The atmosphere of this casino is both friendly and informal. Games include roulette, baccarat, blackjack, and stud poker; open daily, 2 p.m. to 6 a.m.

FREELOADER'S FORUM

VISITORS TO LONDON RAPIDLY DISCOVER the disparity in prices between goods and services purchased in England and pretty much anywhere else in the world, a fact that makes the bonanza of free activities taking place throughout London just that much more of a welcome surprise.

FREE MUSIC

MANY CHURCHES IN CENTRAL LONDON, such as **St. John's** (Waterloo Road; tube: Waterloo), **St. Martin-in-the-Fields** (St. Martin's Place; tube: Leicester Square or Charing Cross), and **St. Pancras Church** (Euston Road; tube: Euston) offer free lunchtime classical concerts and recitals, as do music schools such as the **Royal College of Music** (Prince Consort Road, SW7; ☎ 0207-591-4314; **www.rcm.ac.uk;** tube: Gloucester Road or High Street Kensington) and the **Royal Academy of Music** (Marylebone Road; ☎ 0207-873-7300; **www.ram.ac.uk;** tube: Marylebone or Baker Street). Performances at the Royal College of Music are held Monday through Thursday at 1:05 p.m., and during the school year they are held evenings at 7 p.m. Performances at the Royal Academy of Music are held daily at 1:05 and 5:05 p.m.

You can also hear a mixture of musical delights at the aptly named **Freestage at the Barbican** (Silk Street, EC2; ☎ 0207-638-8891; **www .barbican.org.uk;** tube: Barbican) and at the South Bank Centre's **National Theatre** (South Bank, SE1; ☎ 0207-452-3000; **www.national theatre.org.uk;** tube: Waterloo or Westminster) and **Royal Festival Hall** (South Bank, SE1; ☎ 0207-960-4242; **www.sbc.org.uk;** tube; Westminster or Waterloo). Performances at the Barbican take place daily at 1 p.m.; the National Theatre features music in the foyer area Monday through Friday at 6 p.m., and on Saturday at 1 p.m. and 6 p.m. Performances in the foyer of the Royal Festival Hall run daily from 12:30 to 2:30 p.m.; they also feature jazz on Friday evenings at 7 p.m.

The **100 Club** (100 Oxford Street, W1; ☎ 0207-636-0933; tube: Oxford Street) presents a well-liked series of swing and traditional gigs during Friday lunchtimes. Some bookshops also present free music. *Time Out London* always carries an abundance of listings for free gigs all around the city at its Web site (**www.timeout.com/ london**) and in the weekly magazine (on sale at reputable newsagents every Wednesday).

FREE COMEDY

BECAUSE THE PRACTICE OF ADDING CANNED laughter to television soundtracks has been universally condemned, the BBC now requires a constant supply of jolly spectators willing to be audience members for its comedy productions. For free tickets, contact the **BBC Ticket Unit** at Room 30, Design Building, BBC TV Centre, Wood Lane, W12 7RJ; ☎ 0208-576-1227; **www.bbc.co.uk/whatson/tickets.**

▌ NIGHTCLUB PROFILES

Bar Rumba

SWEATY SOHO DANCETERIA

36 Shaftesbury Avenue, Soho, W1; ☎ 0207-287-6933; www.barrumba.co.uk; tube: Piccadilly Circus

Cover £3–£12; free before 10 p.m. on most nights. **Prices** Fair to middling. **Dress** Smart casual (no jeans or sneakers). **Food available** Nibbles and snacks. **Hours** Monday–Friday, 5 p.m.–3.30 a.m.; Saturday, 7 p.m.–6 a.m.; Sunday, 8 p.m.–1 a.m.

WHO GOES THERE A lot of different types—the club holds a maximum of 455 people—but mainly hip-hop and R&B lovers.

WHAT GOES ON Opened in 1993, Bar Rumba is still going strong. It has a bleeding-edge sound system and hosts London's premier drum-and-bass night every Thursday. Check the Web site to see what's going on. There are salsa lessons on Tuesday night, followed by the best salsa and merengue in town; £2 Cuba Libre cocktails all night long; an eclectic mix of hip-hop and R&B on four turntables on Fridays; and a bit of everything on Saturdays, including funk, soul, house, and R&B. Early-evening promotions include live bands and comedy nights.

SETTING AND ATMOSPHERE Recently refurbished; updated touches include mood lighting and comfy leather couches.

IF YOU GO Get on the guest list by e-mailing **della@thebreakfastgroup.co.uk.**

Café de Paris

LONDON'S MOST RENOWNED CLUB

3–4 Coventry Street, Soho, W1; ☎ 0207-734-7700; www.cafedeparis.com; tube: Piccadilly Circus

Cover £15 before 11 p.m., £20 after. **Prices** Expensive but worth it. **Dress** Elegant. **Food available** The restaurant is open on Saturday nights. You can book a table between 6 p.m and 8 p.m. (call ☎ 0207-395-5806 to make reservations). French cuisine, of course. **Hours** Friday and Saturday, 10 p.m.–3 a.m.

WHO GOES THERE Everyone who's anyone in London.

WHAT GOES ON What *doesn't* go on? It's got cabaret, theme nights, and Champagne-sipped-from-golden-slippers-type decadence and splendor. Live jazz music accompanies dinner, after which a DJ spins records

London Nightclubs

NAME	DESCRIPTION	NEIGHBORHOOD
Bar Rumba	International tunes and salsa	Soho
Café de Paris	London's most renowned club	Soho
Chinawhite	Celeb haunt	Soho
Dover Street Restaurant and Bar	Large jazz restaurant and bar	Mayfair
Embargo	Chelsea dance club	Chelsea
The End	Dance to the world's best underground	Holborn
Fabric	"Bodysonic" dance floor (vibrates beneath your feet)	Farringdon
The Fridge Bar	Brixton's most celebrated disco	Brixton Hill
Grill Room at Café Royal	Dress-up nights and cocktails	Piccadilly
Guanabara	Gateway to Brazil	Holborn
Hanover Grand	Popular discotheque	Mayfair
Heaven	Gayish dance club	Charing Cross
Jazz Café	Modern jazz club	Camden Town
Kabarets Prophecy	Award-winning Soho celeb spot	Soho
Metro Night Club	Venerable live-rock dive	Marylebone
Ministry of Sound	The U.K.'s most famous disco	Elephant and Castle
Notting Hill Arts Club	Arty and intimate clubhouse	Notting Hill
Pacha	World's most famous club brand	Victoria
Pizza Express Live	Intimate jazz club and restaurant	Soho
Ronnie Scott's	London's premier jazz club	Soho
606 Club	Jazz club and restaurant	Chelsea
333	Three floors of fun in trendy Hoxton	Shoreditch
Turnmills	The disco where all nightclubbers end up	Clerkenwell
24 London	State-of-the-art techno-bar	Oxford Circus
Zoo Bar	Bar and dance club	Leicester Square

for the more athletically inclined. The cafe is furnished with numerous bars, all terribly chic and deliciously sexy. Friday is funky house night.

SETTING AND ATMOSPHERE Since its launch in the 1920s, Café de Paris has been synonymous with high society—even the queen has given a party there. The luminous performers have included Marlene Dietrich, Maurice Chevalier, Fred Astaire, Noël Coward, Frank Sinatra, and the divine ecdysiast Dita von Teese. Plush, opulent, and elegant, the cafe's Art Deco design, including luxurious red sofas, was influenced by the operas *Don Giovanni* and *La Bohème*. A 50-foot bar encompasses the oval ballroom, and the restaurant is highly regarded.

IF YOU GO Dress to the nines: you will be dining, drinking, and dancing in style. You may, however, need to know the right people to get in. Therefore, we suggest that you circumvent all the nonsense at the door by booking a table for dinner. Please do not turn up in your baseball cap and sneakers.

Chinawhite

CELEBRITY GROUND ZERO

6 Air Street, W1B; ☎ 0207-343-0040; www.chinawhite.com; tube: Piccadilly Circus

Cover £20. **Prices** Expensive. **Dress** Smart—no sneakers or jeans. **Food available** Asian specialties. **Hours** Monday–Saturday, 9 p.m.–3 a.m.

WHO GOES THERE Glitzy A-listers.

WHAT GOES ON Superficial chat about who is good looking and rich enough to be there. Great place to go if you want to flaunt your new Gucci bag and pretend to be shallow for the evening.

SETTING AND ATMOSPHERE Highly artistic and colorful. Oriental styles and Chinese daybeds mixed with theatrical flair; unique lighting and cushions everywhere.

IF YOU GO Browse through a few tabloids beforehand so you'll be able to recognize the subjects of the latest scandals. Chinawhite is members-only; to get on the Thursday- or Friday-night guest list, e-mail **guest lists@vickib.co.uk.**

Dover Street Restaurant and Bar

LARGE AND JUSTLY POPULAR JAZZ RESTAURANT AND BAR

8–10 Dover Street, Mayfair, W1; ☎ 0207-491-7509; www.doverst.co.uk; tube: Green Park

Cover £10–£20. **Prices** Reasonable. **Dress** Smart casual; jeans and sneakers are not permitted. **Food available** Lunch menu offers a good deal; French and Mediterranean cuisine served until 2 a.m. **Hours** Monday–Thursday, 6 p.m.– 3 a.m.; Friday and Saturday, 7 p.m.–3 a.m.

WHO GOES THERE Personalities from the worlds of stage, film, television, and sport mingle with white-collar workers.

WHAT GOES ON Fine dining, live music, dancing, and DJ-ing.

SETTING AND ATMOSPHERE One of London's most atmospheric restaurants and jazz, blues, and R&B venues for more than 25 years, Dover Street has recently been refurbished to become the largest club of its kind in the capital. This place swings.

IF YOU GO Stick to the dress code.

Embargo

CHELSEA'S ALWAYS-IN-VOGUE DESIGNER DANCE CLUB

533B King's Road, Chelsea, SW10; ☎ 0207-351-5038; www.barclub.com/embargo; tube: Sloane Square

west end nightlife

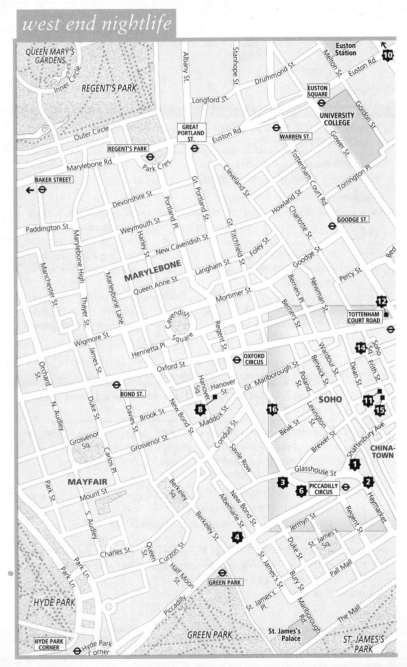

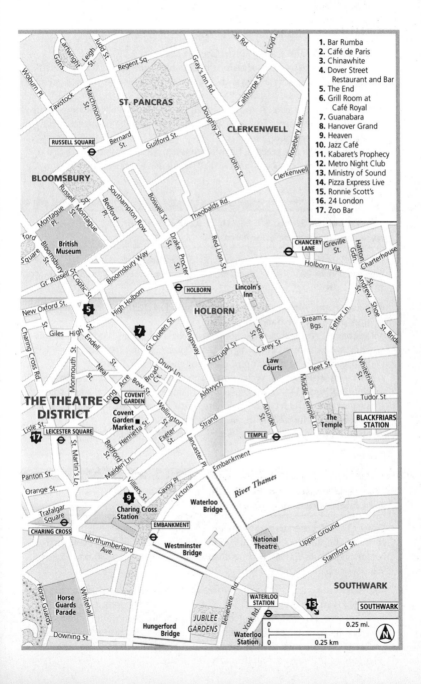

1. Bar Rumba
2. Café de Paris
3. Chinawhite
4. Dover Street Restaurant and Bar
5. The End
6. Grill Room at Café Royal
7. Guanabara
8. Hanover Grand
9. Heaven
10. Jazz Café
11. Kabaret's Prophecy
12. Metro Night Club
13. Ministry of Sound
14. Pizza Express Live
15. Ronnie Scott's
16. 24 London
17. Zoo Bar

Cover £10 on weekends. **Prices** reasonable. **Dress** Stylish, smart casual. **Food available** No. **Hours** Tuesday–Thursday, 10 p.m–2 a.m.; Friday and Saturday, 10 p.m.–3 a.m.; closed Sunday and Monday.

WHO GOES THERE The young, single Chelsea set.

WHAT GOES ON Despite the occasionally difficult doorkeepers, Embargo still draws a very young and trendy crowd that dances the night away to thunderous house DJs.

SETTING AND ATMOSPHERE A modern designer club with high ceilings, iron posts, and mirrors, Embargo is often attended by beautiful young women of posh pedigree.

IF YOU GO Get on the guest list; Embargo is a private members' club (go to the Web site and click on "Guestlist" to fill out a request form).

The End

UNDERGROUND-DANCE HAUNT

18 West Central Street, WC1A 1JJ, ☎ 0207-419-9199; www.endclub.com; tube: Holborn

Cover £12–£16 depending on the night; £15 advance tickets available at the Web site. **Prices** Reasonable. **Dress** No code. **Food available** No. **Hours** Nightly, 10 p.m.–7a.m.

WHO GOES THERE A friendly international crowd of clubbers who know their music and love to dance till dawn.

WHAT GOES ON You can hear some of the world's best underground at this club, which is open every night. DJs play everything from cutting-edge house, electro, and techno to dark, rolling drum-and-bass.

SETTING AND ATMOSPHERE Walk down the iconic stairs, and you enter a different world—the wickedly dark main room boasts a killer sound system and an electric atmosphere, with the infamous blue DJ booth slap-bang in the middle of the dance floor.

IF YOU GO You can also nip upstairs to the End's sister bar, AKA, for a cocktail.

Fabric

"BODYSONIC" DANCE CLUB

77a Charterhouse Street, EC1M 3HN, ☎ 0207-336-8898; www.fabriclondon.com; tube: Farringdon

Cover £12–£16 depending on the night. The Fabricfirst program offers discounts on admission and lets you jump the queue; see Web site for details. **Prices** Reasonable. **Dress** Casual. **Food available** No. **Hours** Friday, 9:30 p.m.–5 a.m.; Saturday, 10 p.m.–7 a.m.

WHO GOES THERE London's committed partygoers and hot-off-the-press-vinyl lovers.

WHAT GOES ON DJ worship—dance till 5 a.m. in a huge warehouselike space.

SETTING AND ATMOSPHERE Three separate rooms feature different DJs. The "bodysonic" dance floor in Room One allows you to feel the bass frequencies of the music all through your body.

IF YOU GO   Enter a trance with the easygoing in-crowd.

The Fridge Bar

BRIXTON'S MOST CELEBRATED DISCO

Town Hall Parade, Brixton Hill, SW2; ☎ 0207-326-5100; www.fridge.co.uk; tube: Brixton

Cover £5–£16 depending on the night; see Web site for details. **Prices** Average. **Dress** Casual. **Food available** Fast. **Hours** Daily, 10 p.m.–6 a.m.

WHO GOES THERE   The clientele varies according to what's on during any given night, but the Fridge has been playing host to the gay-and-lesbian market for some time now.

WHAT GOES ON   Dancing and trancing out to techno, drag nights, disco, you name it.

SETTING AND ATMOSPHERE   With a vast dance floor, a huge bar, capacious balconies, and plenty of variety in the theme nights, the Fridge is a place to really let it all hang out. Highly recommended for the open-minded. Renowned DJs spinning every night. Call for special-event information. On some nights, only those over age 22 or 23 are admitted.

IF YOU GO   Call a respectable minicab company to get home (see Part Five Getting Around, for our recommendations).

Grill Room at Café Royal

DRESS-UP THEME NIGHTS IN ELEGANT SURROUNDINGS

68 Regent Street, Piccadilly, W1; ☎ 0207-439-1865; www.grill-room.com; tube: Piccadilly or Oxford Circus

Cover Varies depending on the night. **Prices** Expensive. **Dress** Smart casual or appropriate to the theme of the night. **Food available** Pricey menu. **Hours** Tuesday–Saturday, 10 p.m.–3 a.m.

WHO GOES THERE   The young, well-heeled set out for a party.

WHAT GOES ON   Built in 1865, this grand establishment plays host to an array of exciting events, depending on your choice of music, such as the very popular Modern Times, a 1920s night (dress like guys or dolls and you'll be sure to get in), and rock-and-roll night (again, dressing the part, that is, rockabilly-style, increases your chances of entry). Friday and Saturday mix up a dance-worthy musical cocktail of hip-hop and R&B.

SETTING AND ATMOSPHERE   Exquisitely restored Belle Époque splendor.

IF YOU GO   Get on a guest list or book a table for dinner; call the number above or e-mail **info@grill-room.com** for more information.

Guanabara

GATEWAY TO BRAZIL

Parker Street, corner of Drury Lane, WC2B; ☎ 0207-242-8600; www.guanabara.co.uk, tube: Holborn

Cover £5. **Prices** Reasonable. **Dress** Sexy. **Food available** South American. **Hours** Monday–Saturday, 5 p.m.–2:30 a.m.; Sunday, 5 p.m.–midnight. Happy hour with half price on selected drinks, Monday–Thursday, 5–7:30 p.m.; Friday and Saturday, 5–7 p.m.

WHO GOES THERE Beautiful people who can really move.

WHAT GOES ON Sparkly professional dancers groove to a mix of live *baile* funk, samba, and homegrown jazz played by Brazilian musicians.

SETTING AND ATMOSPHERE Spacious, modern interior with roomy dance floor; relaxed, happy vibe.

IF YOU GO It's a seriously fun night out. Guanabara sources the exotic fruits for its delicious cocktails from eco-farms in the Amazon. Don't leave without trying one of their famous *caipirinhas,* made with sugar, lime, and *cachaça,* a Brazilian rum made from sugar cane.

Hanover Grand

POPULAR DISCOTHEQUE

6 Hanover Street, Mayfair, W1; ☎ 0207-499-7977; www.hanovergrand.com; tube: Oxford Circus

Cover £8–£20. **Prices** Uppish. **Dress** Smart casual. **Food available** No. **Hours** Daily, 10:30 p.m.–5 a.m.

WHO GOES THERE Fashionistas during the week, while the house set attends on Friday and Saturday.

WHAT GOES ON Different evenings include Fresh 'n' Funky on Wednesday, SchoolDisco.com on Friday, Carwash on Saturday, and dancing aplenty any day of the week.

SETTING AND ATMOSPHERE The club holds 800 people, with two dance floors and five bars on three levels.

IF YOU GO Don't dress down on weeknights.

 ## Heaven

GAY PARADISE THAT STRAIGHTS LINE UP FOR

The Arches, Villiers Street, Charing Cross, WC2; ☎ 0207-930-2020; www.heaven-london.com; tube: Embankment or Charing Cross

Cover £6–£15. **Prices** Average. **Dress** Flamboyant. **Food available** Coffee-bar-type sandwiches and munchies. **Hours** Daily, 10:30 p.m.–3 a.m.; Friday and Saturday, 10 p.m.–6 a.m.

WHO GOES THERE Party animals of all sexual persuasions.

WHAT GOES ON This was originally a gay club, but London quickly twigged that the fun quotient was sky-high here, and now everyone is dying to get into Heaven. Check the Web site for special nights.

SETTING AND ATMOSPHERE The crowded rooms pulsate to techno music.

IF YOU GO Arrive before 10:30 p.m.—Heaven is notorious for the length of its queues.

Jazz Café

MODERN CLUB GEARED TOWARD RAP, SOUL, FUNK, AND JAZZ

5 Parkway, Camden Town, N1; ☎ 0207-916-6060; www.jazzcafe.co.uk; tube: Camden Town

Cover £8–£27.50 according to the popularity of the act. **Prices** Average. **Dress** Anything goes. **Food available** Modern European dinner menu. **Hours** Nightly, 7 p.m.–2 a.m.

WHO GOES THERE Crowd ranges from ages 20 to 55, depending on whether jazz or rap is featured.

WHAT GOES ON This club's name is something of a misnomer, as is the radio station Jazz FM's—both entities attempt to confer the superior artistic status of jazz on lesser forms of music. Thus, on any given night the Jazz Café may have rap, soul, or funk bands performing rather than jazz groups. We therefore suggest consulting the listings in *Time Out London* or *Metro Life* magazine before you go, or you may end up with Vonda Shepard or Blackalicious when you were up for a Michael Brecker–type evening.

SETTING AND ATMOSPHERE The bar leads onto the dance floor, near which a few seats are available. The restaurant is situated on the balcony overlooking the stage; projectors transmit arty neon images onto the awnings.

IF YOU GO Tell the soul band that's performing that you thought you were coming to a jazz club and then ask them to attempt a rendition of John Coltrane's "Giant Steps."

Kabarets Prophecy

AWARD-WINNING MEMBERS-ONLY NIGHTSPOT

16–18 Beak Street, Soho, W1; ☎ 0207-439-2229; www.kabaretsprophecy.com; tube: Piccadilly

Cover £10 before midnight, £20 after, but you *must* be on the guest list to gain entry—at the Web site, click on "Calendar," then click on the night when you want to visit, or e-mail **thegaffer@kabaretsprophecy.com. Prices** High; the minimum bill for a table is £500! **Dress** This year's designer duds or vintage. **Food available** Dinner and late-night snacks. **Hours** Monday, Wednesday–Saturday, 11 p.m.–3 a.m.

WHO GOES THERE A slightly older, very fashionable mix of society and celebs on the weekends. Monday at Kabaret is Paris Hilton's fave night out in London—consider yourself warned.

WHAT GOES ON This member's club with a reasonable attitude toward non-members was named World's Best Nightclub by *Wallpaper** magazine and Best Cocktail Bar in the United Kingdom by the *Independent* newspaper. Kabarets Prophecy is the ultimate deluxe playpen in the heart of Soho. Its technology is awe-inspiring, with sounds and lights that are almost space-age in their cutting edge. It's got a maximum capacity of 200, which makes it both intimate and exclusive, so don't take it personally if you can't get on the guest list on a weekend night. An eclectic mix of people and great music create perfect synergy.

SETTING AND ATMOSPHERE The interior boasts a striking LED backdrop and a bar motif studded with Swarovski crystals.

IF YOU GO No ogling the celebs, and definitely no cell phone–camera clicking (except perhaps in the case of Miss Hilton).

Metro Night Club

AUTHENTIC HEADBANGER DIVE WITH IMPRESSIVE ROCK-AND-ROLL HISTORY

19 Oxford Street, Marylebone, W1; ☎ 0207-437-0964; tube: Oxford Circus

Cover Depends on who's playing. **Prices** Cheap. **Dress** Very casual. **Food available** None. **Hours** Again, depends on who's playing; closes at 4 a.m.

WHO GOES THERE Live-music lovers who aren't particular about fashion or decor.

WHAT GOES ON This is a good old Soho rock-and-roller where Queen and Black Sabbath played in the early days and where you just might catch the next big act. A DJ spins punk, metal, and rock from 11 p.m. till the wee hours.

SETTING AND ATMOSPHERE Metro is small, and it's not going to win any design awards, which is part of its old-fashioned, down-and-dirty funky-bar charm. No one's out to impress here except the performers.

IF YOU GO Make sure you're up for whatever live act is playing.

 **Ministry of Sound**

THE UNITED KINGDOM'S MOST FAMOUS DISCO

103 Gaunt Street, Elephant and Castle, SE1; ☎ 0207-378-6562; www.ministryofsound.com; tube: Elephant and Castle

Cover £15–£20 Friday and Saturday, depending on the gig; e-mail **mhunter@ ministryofsound.com** for info and guest-list requests. **Prices** Expensive. **Dress** Chic and stylish; no hoods, caps, athletic shoes, or sportswear. **Food available** No. **Hours** Friday, 10:30 p.m.–6 a.m.; Saturday, midnight–8 a.m.

WHO GOES THERE Young-to-youngish clubbers, cool and funky types ready to worship the high-quality DJs.

WHAT GOES ON The sweaty rooms are filled with a youngish crowd bopping to techno, hip-hop, funky house, and garage. Check the Web site or the listings pages of local publications to see what's on.

SETTING AND ATMOSPHERE Ministry of Sound is housed in a converted warehouse in the Elephant and Castle district. The bigger dance room, called "the box," is painted black from floor to ceiling, with flat-screen TVs and a hefty sound system.

IF YOU GO Get on the guest list to shorten your waiting time, or arrive before 11 p.m., when the queue gets out of control.

Notting Hill Arts Club

MUSIC AND ART IN INTIMATE BASEMENT

21 Notting Hill Gate, Notting Hill, W11; ☎ 0207-460-4459;
www.nottinghillartsclub.com; tube: Notting Hill Gate

Cover Free before 8 p.m., £5–£8 thereafter. **Prices** Cheap. **Dress** Casual to paint-spattered. **Food available** Bar snacks and toasted sandwiches. **Hours** Monday–Wednesday, 6 p.m.–1 a.m.; Thursday and Friday, 6 p.m.–2 a.m.; Saturday, 4 p.m.–2 a.m.; Sunday, 4 p.m.–1 a.m.

WHO GOES THERE Alternative types, artists, musicians, and the slightly odd.

WHAT GOES ON This small basement club is in the heart of West London's Notting Hill. In our opinion, there are far better clubs where you can choose to spend the evening. The basement is dingy and dark, the crowd a bit too alternative for our tastes, the door staff less than inviting.

SETTING AND ATMOSPHERE If you like cramped, dark, very loud spaces, then you'll love this place. If not, head to Pacha or Fabric.

IF YOU GO Dress down!

Pacha

WORLD'S MOST FAMOUS CLUB BRAND

Terminus Place, Victoria, SW1, ☎ 0207-833-3139;
www.pachalondon.com; tube: Victoria

Cover Varies. **Prices** Expensive. **Dress** No official code, but guests are advised to dress smartly or trendily. **Food available** No. **Hours** Friday and Saturday, 10 p.m.–6 a.m.

WHO GOES THERE The chic, the glamorous, the gorgeous.

WHAT GOES ON Clubbing with style to house music. Scantily clad dancers gyrate on a podium.

SETTING AND ATMOSPHERE Pacha's authentic 1920s decor makes it much more elegant than warehouse-type clubs like Fabric. From the balcony that surrounds the one main dance floor, you can either look up and admire the impressive stained-glass ceiling or look down and admire the good-looking crowd on the dance floor.

IF YOU GO It'll put a smile on your face.

Pizza Express Live

INTIMATE JAZZ CLUB AND RESTAURANT

10 Dean Street, Soho, W1; ☎ 0207-439-8722;
www.pizzaexpresslive.co.uk; tube: Tottenham Court Road

Cover £15–£27, depending on the band. **Prices** Average. **Dress** Casual. **Food available** Pizza, pasta, lasagna, salade niçoise, and the like. **Hours** Nightly, 7:45 p.m–midnight; shows begin at 9 p.m.

WHO GOES THERE Pizza and jazz lovers of both the tourist and local variety.

WHAT GOES ON Eighty percent of the bands booked are Americans of the status of Tal Farlow, Art Farmer, Kenny Garrett, and Roy Haynes. The club also books top British talent such as Martin Taylor and Guy Barker.

SETTING AND ATMOSPHERE Pizza Express Live is an intimate basement venue equipped with modern stage lighting and sound. The environment is friendly, sophisticated, and relaxed.

IF YOU GO Order pizza—it's what they do best.

Ronnie Scott's

LONDON'S PREMIER JAZZ CLUB

47 Frith Street, Soho, W1; ☎ 0207-643-4525; www.ronniescotts.co.uk; tube: Tottenham Court Road

Cover Varies; £20–£25 is normal for a Saturday; £10 for students. **Prices** A little lower than average. **Dress** Smart. **Food available** Full menu of modern European cuisine and à la carte as well. **Hours** Nightly, 8 p.m.–3 a.m.

WHO GOES THERE Yuppies, buppies, musicians, jazz junkies, arty types.

WHAT GOES ON Affluent diners and drinkers come to hear the world's best jazz musicians in the downstairs club, while the younger set tends to congregate on and around the upstairs dance floor. Doors open at 8 p.m., and the live shows start at 9:30 p.m. Cover price usually includes both sets.

SETTING AND ATMOSPHERE Since it opened in 1959, Ronnie's has been the top jazz club in the United Kingdom, inspired in atmosphere and setting by the old jazz dives of Greenwich Village in its beatnik heyday, where Ronnie Scott performed in the 1950s. It's as close as London will ever get to the classic sort of jazz club you've seen in films (minus the smoke).

IF YOU GO Prepare for an enjoyable evening.

606 Club

HIGHLY REGARDED JAZZ CLUB AND RESTAURANT OPEN FOR MORE THAN 25 YEARS

90 Lots Road, Chelsea, SW10; ☎ 0207-352-5953; www.606club.co.uk; tube: Sloane Square

Cover No cover per se, but a music charge (£7 per person Monday–Thursday, £9 Friday and Saturday, and £8 Sunday) is added to your bill at the end of the night. **Prices** Modest to reasonable. **Dress** Casual. **Food available** An extensive European-based menu featuring a wide selection of meat, fresh fish, and vegetarian meals. The cuisine at the 606 has been praised by the *Sunday Times* and TV's *Restaurant Show,* among others. **Hours** Monday–Wednesday, 7:30 p.m.–midnight; Thursday, 8 p.m.–1:30 a.m.; Friday and Saturday, 8 p.m.–2 a.m.; Sunday, 8 p.m.–midnight.

WHO GOES THERE Beboppers and bohemians, young and old.

WHAT GOES ON Two jazz groups play each night from Monday through Wednesday, 7:30 p.m. until midnight. The headliner band plays from around 8 p.m. until 11 p.m. The entertainers are selected from a variety of up-and-coming players and more-established musicians. Music ranges from traditional to contemporary, with an emphasis on the modern.

SETTING AND ATMOSPHERE A basement club with a relaxed atmosphere, the 606 is a great place to take a date for a late supper and a bottle of wine.

ᴵꟳ ʸᴼᵁ ᴳᴼ Don't ask any of the bands to play "Tie a Yellow Ribbon."

333

THREE FLOORS OF FUN IN HIP, HAPPENING HOXTON

333 Old Street, Hoxton, EC1; ☎ 0207-739-5949; www.333mother.com; tube: Old Street

Cover £5–£10. **Prices** Middling. **Dress** Something cool, in every sense of the word. **Food available** Snacks. **Hours** *Bar:* Monday–Friday, 8 p.m.–3 a.m.; *club and bar:* Friday and Saturday, 10 p.m.–5 a.m.

ᵂᴴᴼ ᴳᴼᴱˢ ᵀᴴᴱᴿᴱ Upmarket socialites, artsy folk, students, and music maniacs.

ᵂᴴᴬᵀ ᴳᴼᴱˢ ᴼᴺ This old building in trendy Hoxton houses a no-frills, three-story musicfest—something different every night. Expect queues. The basement usually plays techno and drum-and-bass, while the main room bounces from house to electro to reggae. Upstairs is Mother Bar, offering a plusher, more chilled environment—a great place to hang out.

ˢᴱᵀᵀᴵᴺᴳ ᴬᴺᴰ ᴬᵀᴹᴼˢᴾᴴᴱᴿᴱ Charming yet weirdly retro club with a great dance floor and a sense of humor. Go to the Web site to get a sense of the kind of joint this is.

ᴵꟳ ʸᴼᵁ ᴳᴼ Like Goldilocks, try out all the rooms to see which one fits best.

Turnmills

THE DISCO WHERE ALL NIGHTCLUBBERS END UP

63B Clerkenwell Road, Clerkenwell, EC1M 5NP; ☎ 0207-250-3409; www.turnmills.co.uk; tube: Farringdon

Cover £5–£15, depending on the night. **Prices** Lowish. **Dress** Casual. **Food available** Bar grub. **Hours** Friday, 10:30 p.m.–7:30 a.m.; Saturday, 10 p.m.–5 a.m.

ᵂᴴᴼ ᴳᴼᴱˢ ᵀᴴᴱᴿᴱ Disco freaks, acid-house lovers, trance-heads. Turnmills also hosts Trade, Britain's top gay night.

ᵂᴴᴬᵀ ᴳᴼᴱˢ ᴼᴺ Friday-night institution Saturday nights flip between Together's festival-esque madness and the straight-up house beats of resident Bob Sinclair.

ˢᴱᵀᵀᴵᴺᴳ ᴬᴺᴰ ᴬᵀᴹᴼˢᴾᴴᴱᴿᴱ Turnmills is built above the old River Fleet, which smugglers used to use. The club itself features low ceilings, brickwork, and state-of-the-art sound and lighting.

ᴵꟳ ʸᴼᵁ ᴳᴼ There's every chance that you won't stop dancing till the sun comes up the next morning.

24 London

STATE-OF-THE-ART TECHNO-BAR

24 Kingly Street, Oxford Circus, W1B; ☎ 0207-494-9835; www.24london.eu;tube: Oxford Circus

Cover £20. **Prices** Expensive. **Dress** Fashionable. **Hours** Thursday–Saturday, 10 p.m.–3 a.m.

ᵂᴴᴼ ᴳᴼᴱˢ ᵀᴴᴱᴿᴱ Trendy, good-looking crowd.

WHAT GOES ON 24 is a new club concept and the most high-tech venue in London. Wall projections transform the venue into oceans, canyons, or even the fiery pits of hell. If you touch the bar, a light will shoot across to you alerting the bartender that you are there.

SETTING AND ATMOSPHERE Breathtaking, unique, and impressive.

IF YOU GO E-mail **guestlist@24london.eu** to get on the guest list.

Zoo Bar

BAR AND DANCE CLUB

13–17 Bear Street, Leicester Square, WC2; ☎ 0207-839-4188; www.zoobar.co.uk; tube: Leicester Square

Cover £3 Monday–Wednesday after 9 p.m.; £4 Thursday; £5 Friday and Saturday after 9 p.m., £8 after 11 p.m. If you're on the guest list, entry is free before 10 p.m. and half price after. **Prices** Average; about £4 a drink, less at happy hour. **Dress** Trendy but flexible (jeans and trainers allowed). **Food available** Snacks. **Hours** Monday–Thursday, 4 p.m.–3 a.m.; Friday, 4 p.m.–3:30 a.m.; Saturday, noon–3:30 a.m.; Sunday, 3 p.m.–2 a.m.

WHO GOES THERE Eclectic range of regulars, from laborers to lawyers; plenty of young tourists. Guests age 18 and up welcome; proof of ID required.

WHAT GOES ON A mixed bag; very laid-back. Everyone is out to have a great time. There are happy hours every night, along with good dance music. Zoo Bar recently finished a much-needed face-lift and has added air-conditioning, which can come in handy on the dance floor even in the middle of winter.

SETTING AND ATMOSPHERE Two floors of fun. The first floor has a bar area in which to mingle and meet friends; the basement floor has a huge dance floor surrounded by a few smaller bars to ease traffic flow.

IF YOU GO Beware the throngs of Leicester Square on weekends—it really is a zoo, so hold on to your valuables. E-mail **info@zoobar.co.uk** to get on the guest list.

PART TEN

SHOPPING

AT A TIME WHEN POUNDS are worth twice as much as dollars, it may seem like madness to spend money on anything in London but lodging, food, theater tickets, and museum fees. Currency-exchange rates and the high cost of British goods are something we can't control, any more than we can control the weather, but in the same way that we know how to make the best of a rainy day with umbrellas or raincoats, we can learn to spend our money wisely in the shops of London.

unofficial **TIP**
At this writing, one British pound sterling equals $2.02 U.S.

The high prices in London have to do with the fact that England is an island without much manufacturing, meaning that goods must be delivered. There is also a shocking tradition of noncompetitive price-fixing among big retailers, but that is being challenged by some newcomers. Add to that the 17.5% value-added tax (VAT) and the astronomical rents that shops in central London pay, and you have a seriously false economy of inflated prices and deadly costs of living—and visiting.

unofficial **TIP**
If you come to London during the big sales months of January and August, you just might be able to pay fair-to-good prices for stuff you can't get at home. These sales are a retail tradition to make way for the next season of goods, but you can also expect some closing-down sales, minor spur-of-the-moment sales, or just plain desperate-to-sell sales during any given month.

So as not to completely dash your shopping dreams, let us hasten to emphasize that London has a vibrant shopping scene, with stores, stalls, and shops as far as the eye can see and plenty of goods that you may not find elsewhere, such as Liberty scarves, bespoke shirts from Harvie & Hudson, books published only in England, and various European products, are catnip to the worldly shopper.

Many Londoners are addicted to buying things secondhand. London is fairly bursting with charity shops, vintage-clothing venues, and designer-resale emporiums that embrace the principles of recycling, anticonsumerism, and good old-fashioned thrift while still offering chic and trendy clothing, objets d'art, books, accessories, and jewels. While it would be madness for any but the richest or bravest to venture onto Bond Street in search of designer duds or jewelry, we can all have the thrill of the hunt and the triumph of bagging bargains without breaking the bank.

But if breaking the bank *is* on your itinerary, we've listed plenty of world-class shops particular to London—homegrown designers, boutique perfumeries, antiques purveyors, stationers, and jewelers— for which a credit card with a sky-high spending limit is a must.

WISE BUYS *in* LONDON

THE FOLLOWING ITEMS are worth buying in London because of their high quality or unavailability elsewhere. See our "Where to Find . . ." section later in this chapter for information on shops that sell these items.

Antiques

If you can handle waking before dawn to get to the early-morning **Bermondsey Market** or check out the **Camden Passage** on Wednesdays, you'll find a lot of English and European antiques at relatively decent prices. There are also antiques centers, wonderful warrens of individual stalls selling everything from military artifacts to vintage charms for bracelets.

Bath Products and Perfumes

Bath oils, salts, soaps, and scents abound in London, made by **Culpeper, Neal's Yard Remedies, Molton Brown, Floris, Jo Malone, Lush,** and **Penhaligon,** among others, and there are always lesser-known products making a name for themselves that you can find at stores such as **Space.NK** and **Harvey Nichols.** There are also many new and creative perfumers in business who will whip up a unique fragrance just for you or who sell interesting concoctions of their own. Not cheap, but you won't find them anywhere outside of Paris or Grasse.

Bone China

Look in the stalls on **Portobello Road** in Notting Hill on Saturday market day for patterns you can't find at home. Even **Harrods** has deals at sale times, and its stock is enormous. (We know that you can find Spode china at T.J. Maxx for about $10 a plate, but you won't find the old stuff in discontinued patterns there, or any of the beautiful Staffordshire china you can pick up in antiques stalls.)

Books

London is a city of readers, with thousands of bookstores catering to all possible interests. You can get books here that are only published in England, antiquarian volumes in gorgeous sets, and crates full of secondhand books. The *Harry Potter* and *Lord of the Rings* books published here are more attractive to the serious fan because of their un-Americanized spelling, punctuation, vocabulary, and idioms.

unofficial TIP
Around the British Museum are specialty bookshops that have managed to keep in business despite the steady encroachment of big chain booksellers like Waterstone's and WHSmith.

Children's Clothing

kids Some kids' clothing may be, if not cheaper, of better quality and value than in the States. English smock dresses and French baby clothes are beautiful, and you don't have to pay VAT on children's wear. Many big-name designers (**Dior, Jigsaw,** and **Paul Smith,** to name a few) are now making children's clothing, a trend to which well-heeled Londoners have taken enthusiastically. **Lillywhites,** the sporting-goods store in Piccadilly Circus, sells the soccer shirts of British teams and will personalize them with your kid's name (sporty children will love this, but make sure you know which team they're into).

Designer Clothing

Secondhand, that is. Resale shops offer "preowned" Chanel, Prada, Dolce & Gabbana, Gucci, Vivienne Westwood, Giorgio Armani, Voyage, and more for a fraction of the original price. A lot of ladies seem to have worn these clothes twice and moved on to the next big thing, and it's a happy day indeed when someone of your size and taste drops off bags of discarded clothes or shoes. The hunt is part of the fun.

Fabrics

England has long been known for its gorgeous fabrics: Tudor crewel work is often reproduced, as are the exquisite Arts and Crafts designs of William Morris & Co. **Sanderson, Liberty, Anna French, Designers Guild, Osborne & Little,** and **Colefax & Fowler** are all world-renowned names in the fabric business. You can also find antique fabrics, ribbons, and trimming at specialty shops or at auction.

Souvenirs of London

Yes, they're cheaper here than anywhere, naturally. The best buys are on the street in stalls: **Oxford Street, Leicester Square, Soho** (Tottenham Court Road), and **Piccadilly Circus** are the places to look. For quirkier or more-upscale finds, hit the gift shops of **Westminster Abbey,** the **British Museum,** the **Queen's Gallery, Hampton Court Palace,** the **Victoria and Albert Museum,** or the **Tower of London.**

TIME *to* SHOP

STORES IN CENTRAL LONDON open late and close early. The usual times are 10 a.m. to 6 p.m., with a few opening at 9 a.m. (but closing at 5 p.m.), and a very few, like Waterstone's bookstores, staying open until 9:30 p.m. (the Piccadilly branch stays open until 11:30 p.m.). Some places, such as those in Covent Garden and some fashionable stores, don't open until 10:30 or 11 a.m.

There is a "late" night for shopping in London. Stores stay open until 7 or 8 p.m. on Thursdays or Wednesday on Oxford Street, Regent Street, Knightsbridge, and Chelsea's King's Road. Sunday has finally joined the rest of the week as a shopping day, with most stores (except for some big department stores and small businesses) opening for at least a half day, from noon to 5 or 6 p.m. Street markets follow their own muse as far as opening hours and days go; most markets are open on weekends only (Portobello Market takes place on Saturday).

PAYING UP

MOST SHOPS TAKE ALL THE MAJOR CREDIT CARDS. Some stores will take traveler's checks in British sterling, but they don't even want to hear about U.S.-dollar checks. Even if the staff are kind enough to cash them, chances are they will do so at a rate unfavorable to you (two notable exceptions are **Harrods** and **Marks and Spencer,** which have good exchanges rates).

The credit card is a mixed blessing. On the plus side, you'll have a record of your purchases, and the exchange rate will be that of the day your purchase clears your credit-card company or bank, not the day when you bought something (go to **www.xe.com** to find out the daily exchange rate). Be careful about which card you use: many credit cards now hit you with a foreign-currency exchange charge of 1% to 2.5% on each purchase made outside your home country. This is a total rip-off that can run into a huge amount of money between hotel costs, restaurants, and shopping trips. The best solution to such highway robbery is to use your bank card to get cash to pay for the bulk of your purchases. Paying in cash at some small shops, antiques stalls, and the occasional hotel could even net you a bit of a discount— so by all means give it a try.

unofficial **TIP**
Bring your passport to cash traveler's checks at an American Express office.

AS FOR VAT . . .

VALUE-ADDED TAX IS THE MIND-BOGGLING 17.5% charge the British government adds to the cost of all goods and services except for books, food, and children's clothing. Most goods will have the VAT already figured into the price on the tags, but other items, especially those sold at fancy knickknack or antiques shops, try to skirt the sticker shock by placing a discreet "+VAT" after all those zeros. If you have your goods shipped directly from the store, the VAT will be deducted from the price, but you'd have to be paying a lot of money to balance the costs of shipping. There's also the added cost of duty on expensive imported goods when you arrive in the United States. You are allowed to bring in $400 per person of goods duty free, and families may combine this allowance, so that a family of five is allowed $2,000 worth of goods. The next $1,000 worth of goods gets charged a flat 10%—after that it will vary according to what type of import you're bringing.

Yes, you may be able to recoup some of the VAT you've paid, but it requires a bit of footwork. Let's sketch it out briefly for you, and you'll get more detail below: First, be sure that the shop where you make your purchase participates in the refund scheme—it's a completely voluntary retail service. Then the shop must fill out the official form or its own version of the VAT 407 form or a VAT Retail Export Scheme sales receipt (a regular sales receipt is not accepted). You have to show the goods to customs at the airport, so don't pack them in your check-in luggage (unless, of course, they're too big for a carry-on) or wrap them too well—customs will have to examine your purchases to make sure the documents match the goods before they'll certify the forms. Once armed with the stamped forms, you take them to a VAT Refund counter at the airport, where you'll get the refund, minus some handling fees. For more details, we'll let Her Majesty's Revenue and Customs Department explain it all.

VAT Refunds: The Official Story

Here are the highlights from a pamphlet titled "Notice 704/1, Tax-free Shopping: VAT Refunds for Travellers Departing from the European Community (EC) September 2004," produced by Her Majesty's Revenue and Customs Department and reproduced here with her kind permission.

1. What is the VAT Retail Export Scheme?

When you visit the United Kingdom (UK) you will pay Value Added Tax (VAT) on most things that you buy. The VAT Retail Export Scheme allows you to claim a VAT refund on most goods that you buy and export from the European Community (EC). The shopkeeper may deduct an administration fee before making any refund.

2. Do I qualify to use the Scheme?

Yes if you are an overseas visitor:
  (a) an overseas visitor is a traveller who is not established in the European Community (EC).
  (b) Non-EC residents studying or working in the UK or EC residents may also qualify to use the scheme if they intend to permanently leave the EC for a minimum period of 12 months.

3. What goods can I buy under the Scheme?

You can buy any goods under the Scheme on which you pay VAT except:
• new or used motor vehicles;
• a boat that you intend to sail to a destination outside the EC;
• goods over £600 in value exported for business purposes (a form C88 must be used for these);

- goods that will be exported as freight;
- goods requiring an export licence (except antiques);
- unmounted gemstones;
- bullion (over 125 grams);
- mail-order goods including Internet sales.

In addition you cannot obtain a refund of tax on goods which are consumed, or partly consumed, in the EC such as perfume; or service charges such as hotel expenses.

4. Where can I buy tax-free goods?

From any shop operating the VAT Retail Export Scheme.

5. What do I do when I buy tax-free goods?

At the time you buy the goods the retailer will ask you to provide proof that you are eligible to use the Scheme. For example, the retailer will ask to see your passport. You will then be asked to complete and sign some simple details on a refund form.

You must have one of these forms; till receipts alone are not acceptable. The form should be completed at the time you buy the goods in the presence of the retailer. You cannot ask another person to complete and sign these details on your behalf. You should also agree with the shop how your refund will be repaid to you.

6. When must I export the goods?

You must export the goods from the EC by the last day of the third month following that in which the goods were purchased.

7. What must I do when I leave the UK?

(a) *Leaving for an immediate destination outside the EC:*

If you are not travelling to any other country within the EC, you must present your goods and the refund form to UK Customs at your port or airport of departure. Items that will be checked in as hold baggage must be produced to Customs before you check in your baggage.

During busy periods, queues are likely and you should allow yourself plenty of time in which to produce the goods and refund form prior to departure. This is particularly important if you are exporting goods in your hold baggage as any extra time allowed should be in addition to your advised check in time.

When Customs are satisfied that all the conditions of the Scheme have been met, they will certify and return your refund form to you.

8. What should I do if there is no Customs presence?

In most cases you will be able to locate a Customs Officer to certify your form. However, some of the smaller UK ports and airports do not have a 24-hour Customs presence. At such places there will be either a telephone to ring the officer or a clearly marked Customs post box to deposit your form. Customs will collect the form and if they are satisfied that all the conditions have been met, they will certify it and return it to the retailer to arrange your refund.

There is no facility to have your form certified in your country of destination.

10. How do I obtain my refund?

After your VAT refund form has been certified by Customs you can either:

- post the form back to the retailer to arrange payment of your refund;
- post the form back to a commercial refund company to arrange payment of your refund;
- hand your form to a refund booth to arrange immediate payment.

Whichever method is used should have been agreed between yourself and the retailer when you bought the goods.

Your refund may be reduced by an administration charge. This charge should be clearly shown on your refund form.

If you do not receive your refund within a reasonable time you should write to the retailer—not to Customs and Excise.

unofficial **TIP**
Important: You will not receive a refund of VAT if the refund document is not fully completed. You must produce the goods and the refund document to Customs when you leave the European Union. *No goods = no refund.*

SALESPEOPLE'S ATTITUDES *and* BEHAVIOR

RETAIL WORKERS IN LONDON ARE (although one hates to generalize about such things) among the most laid-back in the world. It's not that they don't want to make a sale; it's just that they don't want to be perceived as pushing anyone to buy something. Except at a few upscale stores, where the staff are rigorously trained to look like they give a damn, salespeople in London will surprise and perhaps bewilder you with their laissez-faire attitudes. There's nothing malicious or lackadaisical about them; this simply isn't a culture in which overeager selling is admired. Even the famously funny Cockney sales patter you might still hear in some East End markets or from street vendors is more a tradition of being quick and clever than it is of making a sale. The correct response is to be equally laid-back rather than demanding and rude—London salespeople are masters of the cold dismissal, and you *won't* win.

The CHAIN REACTION

NOWADAYS, JUST ABOUT EVERY SHOPPING STREET in every post code seems to be dominated by chain stores: Tesco's or Sainsbury's grocery outlets; Starbucks or Costa Coffee; McDonald's or Burger King; Pizza Express; Car Phone Warehouse; Pret à Manger; Boots the Chemist; Accessorize; Marks and Spencer; Waterstone's bookstores; and Ryman's stationery shops. The statistics are chilling to small-business retailers: economists estimate that by 2050 the mom-and-pop shop is likely to be as obsolete as the chimney sweep.

But there's a slowly growing backlash: many of the proud independents have reopened in less expensive areas of London, such as the East End, Hoxton, Camden, Clerkenwell, Brick Lane (Cheshire Street), and Greenwich, or they've set themselves up in a stall at a covered market, which functions as an eccentric shopping mall. There are still plenty of the kind of Old Curiosity Shops that Dickens wrote about—they just may be a bit more off the beaten track than they used to be.

The following shopping areas are mostly in and around central London. Please note that all these areas may have a wide range of possibilities; you may find an on-sale bargain on the very chic Bond Street or run into nothing but rip-offs in the market stalls. We can't predict these things. But even if you're just window-shopping, we think you'll like the vibe and the energy of this briskly commercial city. London started out as a trading post and has kept the tradition of wheeling and dealing alive ever since. Whether you're into Jimmy Choo or Birkenstock, Paul Smith or Primark, London's got you covered.

The BIG SHOPPING NEIGHBORHOODS

COVENT GARDEN
(tube: Covent Garden or Leicester Square)

COVENT GARDEN IS ONE OF THE MORE FUN PLACES to wander around. There's usually a remarkable busker somewhere around the piazza, entertaining with music, sidewalk art, or daredevilry. You'll find plenty of places to sit with a cuppa and take in the urban energy around the elegant arcade, the very site where Henry Higgins met his Cockney flower girl, Eliza Doolittle.

Neal Street and **Neal's Yard** comprise a fun shopping area as well, with plenty of hip little shops, such as the cosmetics and makeup store **Pout,** an amusement park for young beauties; the **Natural Shoe Store,** a purveyor of foot-friendly shoes; and some good cafes. Get your horoscope chart cast at the **Astrology Shop,** or fulfill all your crystal and New Age needs at **Mysteries** on Monmouth Street (cool retro clothes stores on that street, too). There are also plenty of clothing and shoe stores for the urban cool cat and teenager, along with **Filofax** for the busy professional.

WESTBOURNE GROVE, NOTTING HILL, KENSINGTON, KENSINGTON CHURCH STREET
(tube: High Street Kensington)

KENSINGTON CHURCH IS THE STREET OF ANTIQUES, with shops stretching from **Kensington High Street** all the way to **Notting Hill Gate.** It's a great place to window-shop and cruise in and out of stores whose displays that your fancy. As with all antiques stores, the inventory is always changing, but a few places specialize in certain periods and styles. There are also wonderful mirror stores and a fab crystal-chandelier place. The prices can be quite high on this street, as the rents have gone through the roof, but it's fun to look, and you never know when you'll find something you really love. A couple of the charity shops here are definitely worth a look in, given that they're in such an upscale neighborhood.

KENSINGTON HIGH STREET (tube: High Street Kensington)

YOUNG FASHIONISTAS LOVE "Ken" High Street for picking up the latest fashions at **Topshop, Miss Sixty, Diesel, American Apparel, H&M,** and **Urban Outfitters.**

PORTOBELLO ROAD (tube: Notting Hill Gate)

THIS AREA IS HOME TO THE WORLD-FAMOUS antiques and what-not market on Saturday, but every day of the week there are antiques shops, clothing and shoe shops, and the fabulous vintage-clothing shop **One of a Kind Too.**

WESTBOURNE GROVE (tube: Notting Hill Gate and Queensway)

HEADING EAST FROM PORTOBELLO is a retail and residential area that's experienced a real renaissance in the past few years. While it used to be known chiefly for the well-stocked health-food store **Planet Organic,** it's now got chic and wonderful shops all up and down it, including a good restaurant called **202** that doubles as a clothing-and-design shop for **Nicole Farhi.** The **Notting Hill Charity Shop** on this street also has rich pickings, and there's a bounteous flower stall located by a grade-listed (historically significant) public loo. Chic boutiques abound, the biggest one with the most cutting-edge designers being the three-story boutique called **Question Air.**

If you head up Ledbury Road to **Artesian Road,** make a right on Needham Road and drop in at the new perfumery **Miller Harris,** where you can have a scent mixed just for you. Down the street is **Alice & Astrid** for wild retro lingerie. Bakeries, antiques shops, and specialty food stores round out this vibrant area.

KNIGHTSBRIDGE (tube: Knightsbridge)

YOU CAN PRETTY MUCH FORGET ABOUT SHOPPING here if you want to get a deal, unless you go to the little neighborhood north of Brompton Road, which boasts three designer-consignment shops. The best, or at least the biggest and most likely to have sales, is **Pandora,** and up the street are **Salou** and **The Dress Box.** Off the north side of Brompton Road is **Beauchamp Place** (pronounced "Beecham"), a swiftly changing street these days due to punishingly high rents and an ever-changing economy.

Walton Street has jewelers, a slew of interior decorators' shops full of wonderful curiosities, and a couple of decent restaurants. Try

Patrizia Wigan Designs for *Alice in Wonderland*–esque smocked dresses and other classic children's clothing. **Stephanie Hoppen** features old portraits whose faces have been erased and replaced with dog faces—very strange, and very popular with Americans, apparently. **Chelsea Textiles Ltd.** carries fiercely expensive and awesomely beautiful hand-embroidered reproductions of 17th- and 18th-century linens. Everyone on the street is happy to ship their products all around the world, so if you want to buy new or antique children's furniture at **Dragons of Walton Street,** you can get the VAT refund and have something sent home.

Sloane Street connects Knightsbridge with Sloane Square in Chelsea (on Sloane Square and Sloane Street is a new **Tiffany's,** which looks over at the department store **Peter Jones**). The Knightsbridge end of the street is teeming with every hot designer you can think of. Like a mini–Bond Street, it's home to **Chanel, Dior, Dolce & Gabbana, Valentino, Prada, Christian Lacroix, Max Mara, Gianfranco Ferré, Giorgio Armani, Alberta Ferretti, Hermès, Gucci,** and more. If you're looking for more-obscure designers, there's always **Harvey Nichols** on the east corner of Sloane Street or **Harrods** just a few blocks west on the Brompton Road. Sloane Street just smells of money, which is sweetened by the perfumes of **Jo Malone**'s fabulous flagship shop.

OXFORD AND REGENT STREETS, MARYLEBONE VILLAGE (tube: Oxford Circus and Marble Arch)

THOUGH THE AREA IS DOMINATED BY CHAIN STORES, you won't want to miss **Selfridges,** which is fantastic, inside and out, and getting better all the time—you can even get a tattoo there these days. **John Lewis, Marks and Spencer, Debenhams, Gap, Virgin Megastores**—all have their flagship stores on Oxford Street. A little past Oxford Circus is the multifloored, always busy **Topshop,** with fab clothes for young fashionables, but others will prefer to head down **Regent Street** and stop in at **Liberty,** the Tudor-style department store with fascinating architecture and some interesting goods. Stop by **Hamleys** for toys and children's books available only in England. Legendary **Carnaby Street** (off Regent Street) is worth exploring as well, but the old days of groovy independent designers and head shops are long gone—now it's got **Puma, O'Neill, Diesel, Soccer Scene, Rugby Scene,** and young street-wear labels such as **High Jinks** and **Mambo.** Take your teens and have a coffee at a sidewalk cafe while they do their thing.

Off Oxford Street is **St. Christopher's Place,** a charming pedestrian alley that leads to **Marylebone Village,** which has been given the old gentrification slap of paint and retail upgrades over the past few years. It's now got the ubiquitous chain stores, but it has also won a nod from *Time Out London* as one of its Best Shopping Streets. **Daunt Books** is an old independent bookshop with an eclectic and interesting collection of titles, and **Aveda** offers natural beauty and bath products, as well as a health-food cafe whose dishes are divine. **Rococo** has expanded from its King's Road chocolate shop to open a branch here, and it's an excellent place to buy nicely presented gifts or to feed your cocoa addiction. At the northernmost end of the street is **calmia** (yes, it's a small *c*), where rich spiritual seekers go to drop a few hundred quid on yoga props and clothing or schedule soothing body treatments.

CHELSEA: KING'S ROAD (tube: Sloane Square)

THIS WAS THE PLACE TO BE IN THE 1960S AND '70S, when Mary Quant set up shop to sell her revolutionary miniskirts and Vivienne Westwood kept changing the name of her and Malcolm MacLaren's punk boutique. Having settled on the eponymous **Vivienne Westwood,** the shop still has the fast-moving backward clock outside, and the floor inside still slants dangerously.

King's Road is long and full of quickly changing boutiques and trendy stores, but some places will, one can only hope, always be there. Starting at the Vivienne Westwood end (the western part near **World's End**) and heading toward Sloane Square, you'll find charity shops; **Oxfam, Trinity Hospice,** and **Imperial Cancer Fund** offer the occasional great buy. Some fabric stores along the way include **Anna French, Thomas Dare, Osborne & Little,** and **Designers Guild. Wilde Ones** is a fun shop to browse in, very peaceful and full of crystals, incense, and New Age books. **Lello Bracio, Johnny Moke,** and the **Natural Shoe Store** offer the latest in shoes, both comfortable and stylish. **Old Church Galleries** has wonderful old and rare prints, and there are some good antiques and reproduction places along the way, including **Antiquarius,** a market housing many stalls with lots of goods.

Duke of York Square opened in 2003 and continues to fill its mall space with upscale stores. At the moment, the **London Furniture Store** is the largest emporium on the complex, with reasonably priced and interesting home decor. There's also a **Patisserie Valerie** for cappuccino, **Yves Delorme** for luscious sheets and towels, and a large **Joseph** boutique.

At the end of King's Road, at **Sloane Square,** is **Peter Jones,** the stolid department store, brother to Oxford Street's **John Lewis.** To the south of King's Road is **Chelsea Green,** a very smart area with shops including **Jane Asher Party Cakes,** for all your baking needs; **Cath Kidson,** purveyor of clothing, wallets, duvets, and pillows dressed in her trademark cheerful prints; and the very hot designer **Colette Dinnegan,** whose prices will leave you gasping for air.

Down **Elystan Street** are two brilliant designer-resale shops, **La Scala** and **Sign of the Times,** where you might just find an old Voyage dress for 45 quid, plus scads of expensive shoes at a fraction of their original price.

NEW AND OLD BOND STREETS (tube: Bond Street)

WOW, WHAT A STRETCH OF RETAIL REAL ESTATE these streets are! Starting from Oxford Street, **New Bond Street** begins with a battery of designer shops and clothing boutiques, designer-shoe stores, fine art, jewelry (**Asprey, Tiffany,** and **Cartier,** natch), and so on. **Smythson**

of Bond Street is a stationery store that begs your jaw to drop with its £45 pigskin mini–note holder. **Old Bond** is more of the same: exactly the same, in fact, in the cases of **Donna Karan, Chanel, Joseph, Ralph Lauren, Giorgio Armani, Versace,** and others. Old Bond is also home to **Prada, Dolce & Gabbana, Gucci** and the chauffeured Rolls-Royces of such world-class shoppers as the Beckhams and Elton John. Recently opened shops in this area, also known as the "Golden T," include **Stella McCartney, Gibo,** and **Alexander McQueen.** At the end of the street is the historic and charming **Burlington Arcade,** whose tenants wax and wane as regularly as the credit rating of a shopping addict.

SOUTH KENSINGTON: BROMPTON CROSS
(tube: South Kensington)

THE AREA IS MARKED BY THE OLD **Michelin House,** home to the **Conran Shop** (housewares, toiletries, fabrics, furniture, stationery, children's stuff, and books) and the restaurants **Bibendum** and its sister, the **Oyster Bar.** At Brompton Cross you'll also find **Chanel, Jimmy Choo, Jean Paul Gaultier, Joseph, Ralph Lauren,** and other, smaller boutiques: **Whistles, Paul & Joe, Tokio, Jigsaw,** and **Space.NK Apothecary** (actually a cosmetics shop).

From Brompton Cross to Edith Grove, **Fulham Road** is lined with shops selling fashion, antiques, and housewares. Moving west on Fulham, you pass **Agnès B., Jigsaw,** and **Jigsaw Junior** for women's and children's fashions. **Butler & Wilson** is a fun place to browse and shop, and many of its prices are not over the moon. The jeweler **Theo Fennell** and the **Wedding Shop,** with its worn-once secondhand dresses, precede the block devoted to expensive antiques. The **Pan Bookshop,** an independent bookstore past the cinema, carries an impressive assortment of signed editions.

In addition to the aforementioned neighborhoods, London has many other smaller and perfectly fascinating areas for shopping; you're bound to come across your own personal preferences as you wander around. Don't neglect the more far-flung neighborhoods, such as the **East End, Greenwich, Hampstead, Ealing, Hackney,** and **Putney Green**—there are plenty of places all over the city where you can do some serious damage to your credit card.

MARKETS

THESE COVER A GOOD BIT OF GROUND, so rather than addresses, we've given tube stops, from which signs direct you most efficiently.

APPLE MARKET (tube: Covent Garden) Open daily from 9 a.m. to 5 p.m., this is a permanent market on the south side of the piazza. Set up in stalls, it includes everything from crafts to woolens, with a juice bar and other food stands thrown in. The brick structure that once housed the fruit, vegetable, and flower sellers is now given over to clothing, silverware, old photos and prints, handcrafts, jewelry, and whatever else the wind blows in that day. At the **Jubilee Market,** at the west end of the main arcade of Covent Garden, you'll find a medium-sized antiques market, with bric-a-brac, jewelry, antique prints, and curios on Mondays only, from 7 a.m. to 5 p.m.

BERMONDSEY MARKET (Bermondsey Square; tube: London Bridge and Borough) goes back to 1855 and originally operated in Islington. Open Fridays only from 4 a.m. to 2 p.m., Bermondsey (also known as the New Caledonian Market) gives preference to the early bird, which means arriving in pitch darkness to vie with dealers buying antiques of every description and value, including clothing and jewelry. Bring plenty of cash—no credit cards are taken here. And you should take a taxi before sunrise as the tube doesn't start running until around 5:30 a.m., not to mention the fact that a taxi is the safest option. Ask to be let off at the corner of Bermondsey Street and Long Lane. If you do go later by tube, take the Northern Line to London Bridge, exiting on Tooley Street and walking past the London Dungeon until you get to Bermondsey Street, where you will make a right and walk down it for about ten minutes till you see the market. Many stalls are closed by 9 a.m., but some remain open till 2 p.m. Lots of antiques shops on nearby **Tower Bridge Road** have regular business hours.

BRICK LANE MARKET (Brick Lane; tube: Aldgate East, Shoreditch, or Liverpool Street) This East End market is open only on Sundays from 8 a.m. to 1 p.m. It is still kind of basic, without much of the sexy stuff like antiques and curios, but it does have its fans. As the East End grows more fashionable, the market shares in the gentrification, with hip, young designer gear vying with chipped crockery for your attention. For lunch, walk down Brick Lane and prepare to be accosted by Pakistanis and Indians touting their restaurants with offers of discounts—there are scores of curry joints and restaurants here.

CAMDEN MARKET (Camden Town; tube: Camden Town) This has become one of London's biggest tourist attractions, which means big crowds on weekdays and weekends. An absolute must for teens and 20-somethings, this market sells cheap and trendy clothing, jewelry, and records. Camden is sort of a latter-day Haight-Ashbury, complete with head shops, local crafts, incense, Indian fabrics, and lots of curious-looking young people. There are plenty of food stalls and cafes in the area, and lots of outdoor seating in warm weather. Open daily, the **Victorian Market Hall** has three floors of shops and stalls of everything from London souvenirs to antiques to books—something for everyone in a charming and festive atmosphere. The street part of Camden Market is open Thursday and Friday from 9 a.m. to 5 p.m. and weekends from 10 a.m. to 6 p.m.

CAMDEN PASSAGE MARKET (Camden Passage, off Upper Street; tube: Angel) Not to be confused with the previous market, Camden Passage offers an interesting array of antiques and collectibles in outdoor stalls. It's open Wednesday from 10 a.m. to 2 p.m. and Saturday from 10 a.m. to 5 p.m., but the Passage itself has permanent antiques stores open all week (visit **www.antiquescamdenpassage.co.uk** for more information).

GREENWICH MARKETS (There are three easy ways to get to Greenwich from central London: by ferry [from the Westminster Pier], Docklands Light Railway [DLR], and the Jubilee Line on the Underground. Follow signs to the market, which is a short walk from the Greenwich stop for each method of transport.) There's no better way to pass a Sunday than by taking a boat up the Thames from Westminster to Greenwich. A few well-priced markets in Greenwich are open on Saturday and Sunday from 9 a.m. to 6 p.m. You should have no trouble finding them, because the town is small and you just can't miss them. There's the crafts market in the center of town; the **Bosun's Yard** market, which also sells crafts and such; the **Canopy Antiques Market,** which is really a flea market with plenty of interesting junk; and the **Greenwich Antiques Market,** with many stalls of vintage clothes as well as a variety of collectibles and antiques.

PETTICOAT LANE MARKET (Middlesex Street and environs; tube: Liverpool Street) Open only on Sunday from 9 a.m. to 2 p.m., Petticoat Lane Market used to be located on a street of that name until Victorian sensibilities became too delicate to handle the reference to ladies' unmentionables. Today there are tons of stalls lining a number of streets in the area, selling clothing, shoes, household goods, crafts, and what have you.

PORTOBELLO MARKET (tube: Notting Hill Gate) Located on Portobello Road, from the Notting Hill end to the Ladbroke Grove end, this is really several markets in one. The **antiques market** is held on Saturday from 7 a.m. to 6 p.m.; the **general market** is open Monday through Wednesday from 9 a.m. to 5 p.m.; and **clothing and knickknacks** are for sale on Friday from 7 a.m. to 4 p.m., Saturday from 8 a.m. to 5 p.m., and Sunday from 9 a.m. to 4 p.m. On Saturday, at the Notting Hill end, in addition to the antiques stalls galore, the stores that are often closed on weekdays are open for business. It's a major scene, so come early.

ST. MARTIN-IN-THE-FIELDS MARKET (St. Martin's Lane; tube: Charing Cross) Have a look around when you're in the Trafalgar Square area, as this market is in the same area. It's mostly clothing and teen stuff, although one might find some nice and inexpensive secondhand velvet jackets from the 1970s. Lots of neo-hippie gear.

SPITALFIELDS MARKET (Commercial Street between Lam and Brushfield; tube: Liverpool Street) The old Sunday Market, alas, has been disbanded in favor of more-regular shops and permanent stalls. There are interesting shops, to be sure, but the good old days of fried-food stalls and the occasional dog show on Sundays are gone. Still, you may want to take a look around if you're going to the Petticoat Lane and/or Brick Lane markets.

WALTHAMSTOW (Walthamstow High Street; tube: Walthamstow Central) Open Monday through Saturday from 8 a.m. to 6 p.m., Walthamstow is billed as Europe's **longest daily street market,** with 450 stalls and 300 shops. It's mostly ordinary consumer goods for bargain prices—food, clothes, electrical equipment, and the like—but it is fun to see. It also offers lots of stalls serving delicious food and, in the summer, live entertainment. It's far off the beaten track, but if you combine it with a visit to the **William Morris House** or **Hatfield House,** it could be a good day out.

DEPARTMENT STORES

THESE ARE MOST LIKE THE AMERICAN STORES we know so well, although they're more expensive.

DEBENHAMS (334–338 Oxford Street, West End, W1; ☎ 0207-580-3000; **www.debenhams.com;** tube: Bond Street) It has the usual fashion, cosmetics, and a few designers. The store has numerous locations in London, the United Kingdom, and around the world in addition to the Oxford Street flagship.

FORTNUM & MASON (181 Piccadilly, Mayfair, W1; ☎ 0207-734-8040; **www.fortnumandmason.co.uk;** tube: Green Park) You might not think of this as anything other than a food emporium, but in fact F&M has floors that carry clothing, clocks, and gifts above its ground floor stocked with jellies and jams. The interior is beautiful, and the cream tea is classic. Make sure you cross the street a few minutes before the hour to see the enchanting movement of the mechanical clock on the building, with its velvet-coated Georgian-era mannequin popping out for a look at the pullulating traffic on Piccadilly.

HARRODS (87 Brompton Road, Knightsbridge, SW1; ☎ 0207-730-1234; **www.harrods.com;** tube: Knightsbridge) Harrods made its reputation in the mid–19th century as a retailer unparalleled in the empire, capable of satisfying every possible whim: it once famously delivered a camel to a customer. Kids go mad for the overwhelming World of Toys, with its miniature automobiles and all the toys demonstrated by staff. The food halls, which stay open till 11 p.m., are filled with produce and prepared food from all over the world.

HARVEY NICHOLS (109–125 Knightsbridge, SW1; ☎ 0207-235-5000; **www.harveynichols.com;** tube: Knightsbridge) "Harvey Nicks" offers floors of designer clothes, plus a good restaurant on the fifth-floor food hall. The out-of-this-world window displays change regularly.

JOHN LEWIS/PETER JONES (*John Lewis:* 278–306 Oxford Street, West End, W1; ☎ 0207-629-7711; tube: Oxford Circus; *Peter Jones:* Sloane Square, SW1; ☎ 0207-730-3434; tube: Sloane Square; **www.johnlewis .co.uk**) There's nothing fancy or trendy here, but both stores (same company, different branding) carry a bit of everything at good prices, from picture hooks to computers.

 LIBERTY (210–220 Regent Street, West End, W1; ☎ 0207-734-1234; **www.libertyoflondon.co.uk;** tube: Oxford Circus) A wonderful store in the Tudor style that perks up the Georgian cool of Regent Street, Liberty is full of interesting items and home to a famous line of fabrics.

MARKS AND SPENCER (main branch, 458 Oxford Street, Marble Arch, W1; ☎ 0207-935-7954; **www.marksandspencer.com;** tube: Bond Street) M&S, or "Marks and Sparks," carries a lot of good stuff. Under its own St. Michel name brand, it provides food and fashion. Solid, if unimaginative, clothing is offered in every possible size, and the underwear, while not cheap, is plentiful and well loved (rumor has it that 70% of all Londoners get their dainties here). Branches are everywhere.

 SELFRIDGES (400 Oxford Street, Marble Arch, W1; ☎ 0870-837-7377; **www.selfridges.co.uk;** tube: Marble Arch) This department store thoroughly lives up to the grand promise of its extravagant Art Deco facade and arty window dressing. Designer wear, silver, beauty products, and furniture, along with a glorious food hall, make this a fun and satisfying shopping experience. Selfridges gives new meaning to "cutting edge" with its very own tattoo-and-body-piercing parlor.

WHERE *to* FIND . . .

ANTIQUES

FROM WHITECHAPEL TO HAMMERSMITH, London boasts a multitude of wonderful antiques stores, so many, in fact, that entire books are devoted to listing them. What we'll point you toward in this book are the antiques arcades that are so plentiful in London, letting you browse the myriad treasures to be found—jewelry, books, clothing, furniture, clocks, silver, decorative arts, knickknacks, and more. See pages 396–399 for information about the larger markets that sell antiques—**Bermondsey, Camden Passage,** and **Portobello.** For even more markets, read on.

Alfie's Antique Market (13–5 Church Street, Marylebone, NW8; ☎ 0207-723-6066; **www.alfiesantiques.com;** tube: Edgware Road) is open Tuesday–Saturday, 10 a.m.–6 p.m.

Antiquarius (131–141 King's Road, Chelsea, SW3; ☎ 0207-351-5353; **www.antiquarius.co.uk;** tube: Sloane Square) is open Monday–Saturday, 10 a.m.–6 p.m.

Bourbon-Hanby Antiques Centre (151 Sydney Street, Chelsea, SW3, on the corner of King's Road; ☎ 0207-352-2106; **www.antiques.co.uk/ bourbon-hanby;** tube: Sloane Square) is open Monday–Saturday, 10 a.m.–6 p.m. and Sunday, 11 a.m.–5 p.m.

Gray's Antiques Market and **Gray's Mews Market** (off Oxford Street at 58 Davies Street, Mayfair, W1; ☎ 0207-629-7034; **www.graysan-tiques.com;** tube: Bond Street) is open Monday–Friday, 10 a.m.–6 p.m.

London hosts numerous antiques fairs over the course of the year. Check the following Web sites for more information:

www.antiques-london.com   www.antiquesnews.co.uk

www.antiquesweb.co.uk   www.portobelloroad.co.uk

www.lapada.co.uk   www.bada.org

AUCTION HOUSES

THESE CAN BE A LOT OF FUN, and you can also find some amazing items, as the treasures of the empire continue to pass through acquisitive hands. Bargains aren't terribly common because the auction houses know what they're doing and how to do it, but you can give it a go. Call to find out what's being sold and when, and peruse the catalogs to familiarize yourself with the prices.

The giants of the auction business in London (and in the world) include the following:

Bonhams has two London auction houses: the one in Knightsbridge (Montpelier Street, SW7; ☎ 0207-629-1602, **www.bonhams.com;** tube: Knightsbridge) and the head office in Mayfair (101 New Bond Street, W1; ☎ 0207-629-6602; tube: Bond Street); **Christie's** (85 Old Brompton Road, SW7; ☎ 0207-581-7611; **www.christies.com;** tube: South Kensington); and **Sotheby's** (34–35 New Bond Street, W1; ☎ 0207-293-5000; **www.sothebys.com;** tube: Bond Street; and Sotheby's Olympia, (Hammersmith Road, W14; ☎ 0207-293-5555; tube: Olympia Kensington).

Less expensive but just as much fun is **Lots Road,** off New King's Road, the westernmost end of King's Road in Chelsea (71–73 Lots Road, SW10; ☎ 0207-376-6800; **www.lotsroad.com;** tube: Sloane Square, then bus 11; or Fulham Broadway and walk 10 or 15 minutes; a cab is probably best, though). There are two sales on Sundays: one of modern furniture and the other of antique furniture or household items. Viewing starts on Thursday morning until the auction starts at 2 p.m. Sunday. You won't find museum-quality goods here, but neither will you be bankrupted.

The Bidding Game

For each of the hundreds of auctions these houses hold, there is an exhibition of the goods to be sold. Open to one and all at no charge, these exhibitions are worth attending even if you aren't in the market for treasure. Catalogs of the pieces up for auction are available in print at the auction houses for a small to middling cost, or online for free (though sometimes without illustrations). This is where you can get a handle on provenance, price, and possibility of purchase. You can buy without attending an auction through an absentee bidding service or by telephone.

Going in person to the auction is the most fun, however, whether you buy or not. When you arrive, you must register and receive your numbered bidding paddle. Lots are brought out in numerical order; the auctioneer will describe the item and start the bidding at about

unofficial **TIP**
Be sure to discuss delivery terms with the auction house when you pay for your purchase—some houses have the nerve to start charging you for storage after a couple of days.

two-thirds of the estimated price in the catalog. Raise your paddle to bid; the auctioneer will acknowledge it and then continue asking for higher bids. Bids increase in increments of about 10%. When no more bids are accepted, the hammer comes down and the auctioneer pronounces the item "sold" before calling out the number of the winning paddle. If you've won, go to the cashier and pay for your new trinket with credit card, cash, bank transfer, or an approved personal check. The total cost is your bid plus tax and a buyers' premium (a percentage of the cost paid to the auction house). The auction house will deliver your prize for a fee, but it may be a few days before you can pick it up.

BEAUTY AND BATH STORES

CULPEPER (8 The Market, Covent Garden Piazza, WC2; ☎ 0207-379-6698—hang on, it switches from fax to telephone; **www.culpeper.co.uk;** tube: Covent Garden) sells bath salts, oils, teas, spices, essential oils—they've got it all here. There's also a branch at 21 Bruton Street (Mayfair, W1; ☎ 0207-629-4559), plus other locations around London. **Shu Uemura** (55 Neal Street, West End, WC2, ☎ 0207-240-7635; **www.shu uemura.com;** tube: Covent Garden) is held in high esteem by many professional makeup artists; this shop has everything for the international beauty, from cosmetics to massages. Go to **Pout** for a makeover as well as the latest in makeup (34 Shelton Street, WC2, 0207-379-0379; **www .pout.co.uk;** tube: Covent Garden). Lush (11 The Market, Covent Garden Piazza, WC2; ☎ 0207-240-4570; **www.lush.co.uk;** tube: Covent Garden) is a wonderful place for chocolate massage bars, soaps by the hunk, fizzy bath "bombs," and homemade oatmeal masks. Like many other shops listed here, Lush has multiple locations all over the city.

Neal's Yard Remedies (15 Neal's Yard, West End, WC2; ☎ 0207-379-7222; **www.nealsyardremedies.com;** tube: Covent Garden) is a great place for homeopathic remedies, fresh herbs, essential oils, soaps, and hair-care products, all in beautiful blue-glass bottles. The other branches are too numerous to mention, so call or visit the Web site for information. **Space.NK Apothecary** (37 Earlham Street, West End, WC2; ☎ 0207-379-7030; **www.spacenk.co.uk;** tube: Covent Garden) is a body and beauty-products boutique. The apothecary also has many branches, so call or go online for additional locations.

For **Dr. Hauschka** products, stop into a health-food store in Chelsea Market called **Here** (125 Sydney Street, SW3, ☎ 0207-351-4321; tube: Sloane Square or South Kensington), which also carries other holistic-type products.

For men's gifts or men's pampering treatments, don't miss the genteel, traditional Mayfair establishment **Geo. F. Trumper** (9 Curzon Street, Mayfair, W1; ☎ 0207-499-1850; **www.trumpers.com;** tube: Green Park). It's like stepping into a time capsule, with gleaming dark oak and glass cases displaying the highest quality shaving and personal-care accessories in the world. Trumper's deluxe straight-razor shave is light-years away from the typical daily lather and scrape.

BOOKSTORES

Chains

London has many chain booksellers with a multitude of branches. Call to find the one nearest you: **Books Etc.** (☎ 0207-404-0261; **www.booksetc.co.uk**); **Borders Books & Music** (☎ 0207-379-6838; **www.borders.com**); **WHSmith** (☎ 0207-261-1708; **www.whsmith .co.uk**); and **Waterstone's** (☎ 0207-434-4291; **www.waterstones.com**), which is the best of the lot.

Independents

The **Pan Bookshop** (158 Fulham Road, Chelsea, SW10; ☎ 0207-373-4997; **www.thepanbookshop.co.uk;** tube: South Kensington, then bus 14 toward Fulham) carries lots of signed editions of recently published books. **Daunt Books** (83 Marylebone High Street, Marylebone, W1, and three other locations; ☎ 0207-224-2295; **www.dauntbooks.co.uk;** tube: Baker Street) is a beautiful store to browse in, offering recently published titles and good travel books. No trip to London would be complete without a stop at London's oldest bookstore, **Hatchards** (187 Piccadilly, Mayfair, W1; ☎ 0207-439-9921; **www.hatchards.co.uk;** tube: Piccadilly Circus). Established in 1797 and housed in a beautiful four-story building, Hatchards has an endearingly serious atmosphere and stocks some very weighty tomes. Fans of the madcap Mitford sisters must make a beeline to **Heywood Hill** (10 Curzon Street, Mayfair, W1; ☎ 0207-629-0647; **www.heywoodhill.com;** tube: Green Park), where shopgirl Nancy Mitford held court during the Blitz. And we can't forget the famous **Foyles** (113–119 Charing Cross, Soho, WC2; ☎ 0207-437-5660; **www.foyles.co.uk;** tube: Tottenham Court). Formerly a mad teetering pile of all kinds of books, old and new, it has been updated to four floors (with a lift, no less) of soberly organized books on every subject under the sun.

Then there are the more unusual specialty bookstores. **Atlantis Bookshop** (49A Museum Street, Bloomsbury, WC1; ☎ 0207-405-2120; **www.theatlantisbookshop.com;** tube: Tottenham Court Road) caters to a clientele interested in psychic research, witchcraft, and supernatural phenomena. **Book Thrift** (22 Thurloe Street, South Kensington, SW7; ☎ 0207-589-2916; tube: South Kensington) specializes in fine-arts books at a fraction of their original cost. The **European Bookshop** (5 Warwick Street, Soho, W1; ☎ 0207-734-5259; **www.esb.co.uk;** tube: Piccadilly Circus) sells books and mags in most European languages. **Grant & Cutler** (55–57 Great Marlborough Street, Marylebone, W1; ☎ 0207-734-2012; **www.grantandcutler.com;** tube: Oxford Street) carries books, videos, cassettes, and more. About 200 languages are represented, so you're certain to find something you can understand.

One of the oldest rare-book dealers is located in a grand, spooky old town house in Berkeley Square. **Maggs Bros.** (50 Berkeley Square, Mayfair, W1; ☎ 0207-493-7160; **www.maggs.com;** tube: Green Park), in business since 1853, has a staff of 20 specialists in seven departments and carries first editions of old, important books. The prices on some of their precious stock can hit six figures.

Billed as "The Science Fiction Entertainment Store," **Forbidden Planet** (179 Shaftesbury Avenue, West End, WC2; ☎ 0207-420-3666; **www.forbiddenplanet.com;** tube: Tottenham Court Road) has it all, from toys to videos to every kind of printed matter you can imagine. **French's Theatre Bookshop** (52 Fitzroy Street, West End, W1; ☎ 0207-387-9373; **www.samuelfrench-london.co.uk;** tube: Warren Street) is a must for the drama student or aficionado.

Librairie La Page French Bookshop has everything for the French student, young and old (7 Harrington Road, South Kensington, SW7; ☎ 0207-589-5991; **www.librairielapage.com;** tube: South Kensington). **Politico's Bookshop** (8 Artillery Row, Mayfair, SW1; ☎ 0207-828-0010; **www.politicos.co.uk;** tube: St. James's Park) stocks political paraphernalia, plus a fine selection of biographies, reference works, and history texts. **Stanfords** (12–14 Long Acre, West End, WC2; ☎ 0207-836-1321; **www.stanfords.co.uk;** tube: Leicester Square) has the biggest collection of maps, globes, and travel books you're likely to ever see. The **Talking Book Shop** (11 Wigmore Street, Marylebone, W1; ☎ 0207-491-4117; **www.talkingbooks.co.uk;** tube: Bond Street) is one of our favorites, with hours and hours of unabridged great fiction and nonfiction, from cassette taped classics to this year's best-sellers as well as books on CD. They may not be cheaper than other shops, but they offer more unabridged books than you'll see outside of a library. The **Dover Bookshop** (18 Earlham Street, West End, WC2; ☎ 0207-836-2111; **www.doverbooks.co.uk;** tube: Covent Garden) is a fabulous resource for arcane books of old as well as interesting copyright-free illustrations, many of them on CD.

Secondhand-book Shops

It would behoove anyone interested in idly browsing out-of-print books to take a stroll down **Charing Cross Road** or around **Soho** to look into the many used-book shops spilling over with the titles of yesteryear. The prices are reasonable; sometimes you'll find a bargain bin selling six books for a fiver or some such deal. On the **South Bank** by the National Theatre, you'll find great deals on secondhand books at stalls that remain open till around sundown.

For anything from old paperbacks to antique first editions, try **Any Amount of Books** (62 Charing Cross Road, West End, WC2; ☎ 0207-240-8140; **www.anyamountofbooks.com;** tube: Leicester Square); **Gloucester Road Bookshop** (123 Gloucester Road, South Kensington, SW7; ☎ 0207-370-3503; tube: Gloucester Road); **Skoob Books** (15 Sicilian Avenue, Holborn, WC1; ☎ 0207-404-3063; **www.skoob.com;** tube: Holborn); and **Unsworths Antiquarian Booksellers** (15 Bloomsbury Street, Bloomsbury, WC1; ☎ 0207-436-9836; **www.unsworths.com;** tube: Tottenham Court Road).

HOME DECOR AND ACCESSORIES

SUMMERHILL AND BISHOP (100 Portland Road, Kensington, W11; ☎ 0207-221-4566; tube: Holland Park) carries kitchen goods from France and unusual gifts such as candles spelling *amour* and *ange,* and glasses etched with *amitie.* A fun place to browse.

The **Conran Shop** (Michelin House, 81 Fulham Road, South Kensington, SW3; ☎ 0207-589-7401; **www.conran.com;** tube: South Kensington) deals in furniture, household goods, fabric, and all manner of modern bric-a-brac for bed, bath, kitchen, and nursery. The **London Silver Vaults** (53–64 Chancery Lane, The City, WC2; ☎ 0207-242-3844; tube: Chancery Lane) is actually 40 shops selling silver, old and new, for every budget.

If you're into modern design, the **Design Museum Shop** (Design Museum, Shad Thames, SE1; ☎ 0207-940-8753; **www.designmuseum.org;** tube: Tower Hill) is a repository of elegantly space-age (and museum-worthy) household goods designed by big names such as Stefan Lindfors and Aldo Rossi. Or you could step back in time at **Thomas Goode** (19 South Audley Street, Mayfair, W1; ☎ 0207-499-2823; **www.thomasgoode.co.uk;** tube: Green Park), where you're guaranteed an authentic upper-crust English shopping experience, with exquisite china, silver, and crystal as well as knickknacks. Have a spot of tea there, too.

DESIGNER CLOTHES

FOLLOWING IS A LIST OF SOME OF LONDON'S BEST-KNOWN designers, not all of whom sell their clothes in other countries. Some have their own boutiques, but unless you just want to see what they have to offer, you're better off buying at the department stores and boutiques that carry their clothes. If it's an internationally known designer, you're better off buying in the United States, if possible.

Antoni & Alison, Blaak, Boudicca, Hussein Chalayan, Caroline Charles, Jasper Conran, Emma Cook, English Eccentrics, John Galliano, Ghost, Joseph, Katharine Hamnett, Justin Oh, Nicole Farhi, Bella Freud,

Betty Jackson, Sophia Kokosalaki, Markus Lupfer, Stella McCartney, Julien MacDonald, Alexander McQueen, Hamish Morrow, Bruce Oldfield, Red or Dead, Pearce Fionda, Lainey Keogh, Zandra Rhodes, Paul Smith, Tomasz Starzewski, Phillip Treacy (hats only), **Catherine Walker, Amanda Wakeley, Vivienne Westwood,** and **Matthew Williamson** all have stores in London or can be found at **Selfridges, Harvey Nichols, Harrods,** and smaller boutiques (see below). Check the phone book or the Web for locations and numbers.

DESIGNER BOUTIQUES

BROWNS (23–27 South Molton Street, Mayfair, W1; ☎ 0207-491-7833; **www.brownsfashions.com;** tube: Bond Street) stocks up-to-the-minute creations from all the big-name designers. Other boutiques of note include **À La Mode** (10 Symons Street, Chelsea, SW3; ☎ 0207-730-7180; tube: Sloane Square), **Feathers** (176 Westbourne Grove, Notting Hill, W11; ☎ 0207-243-8800; tube: Notting Hill Gate), and **Question Air** (38 Floral Street, West End, WC2; ☎ 0207-836-8220; **www.question-air .com;** tube: Covent Garden; five other branches).

FABRICS

ANNA FRENCH (343 King's Road, Chelsea, SW3; ☎ 0207-351-1126; **www.annafrench.co.uk;** tube: Sloane Square, then bus 11 or 22) sells fabrics for children's rooms, as well as sheer, lacy, and flowery textiles. **Beaumont & Fletcher** (261 Fulham Road, Chelsea, SW3; ☎ 0207-352-5594; **www.beaumontandfletcher.com;** tube: South Kensington, then bus 14) stocks mind-blowing, museum-quality antique fabric (18th- and 19th-century) and sells reproduction fabrics of perfect verisimilitude. **Colefax & Fowler** (110 Fulham Road, Chelsea, SW3; ☎ 0207-244-7427; **www.colefax.com;** tube: South Kensington, then bus 14) is one of the giants in traditional English decoration, with elegant fabrics for upholstering furniture, covering walls, or making curtains. **Osborne & Little** (304–308 King's Road, Chelsea, SW3; ☎ 0207-352-1456; **www.osborneandlittle.com;** tube: Sloane Square) sells traditional and modern designs, all of high quality. **Barnett Lawson** (16–17 Little Portland Street, Soho, W1; ☎ 0207-636-8591; **www.bltrimmings.com;** tube: Oxford Circus) carries an incomparable stock of exotic ribbons, trimmings, and braids to use in upholstery, tying back curtains, or jazzing up a boring piece of clothing. Prices are unbelievably low, and stock is huge.

If you want to make a quilt from Liberty prints, have a look at **Shaukat & Company** (170–172 Old Brompton Road, South Kensington, SW5; ☎ 0207-373-6927; **www.shaukat.co.uk;** tube: Gloucester Road), which stocks stacks and stacks of Liberty squares, most at about a pound per piece, plus a fabulous selection of Indian fabrics and shawls in pretty colors. Another fabric shop with good prices and selection is **Joel & Son Fabrics,** off Edgware Road (73–85 Church Street Market, Marylebone, NW8; ☎ 0207-724-6895; **www.joelandsonfabrics.co.uk**).

LINENS

THE LINEN MERCHANT (11 Montpelier Street, Knightsbridge, SW7; ☎ 0207-584-3654; tube: Knightsbridge) has a range of beautiful bathrobes and bed linens. At the **Monogrammed Linen Shop** (168 Walton Street, Chelsea, SW3; ☎ 0207-589-4033; tube: South Kensington), you can order a personal monogram on expensive, high-quality linen. **The White Company** (8 Symons Street, Chelsea, SW3; ☎ 0207-823-5322; www.thewhitecompany.com; tube: Sloane Square) sells lovely bedclothes, table linens, and some clothing. Ditto the French sheet designer **Yves Delorme** (54 Duke of York Square, King's Road, Chelsea, SW3; ☎ 0207-730-3435; www.yvesdelorme.com; tube: Sloane Square), where elegant patterns are combined with rich, practically edible cotton.

MUSEUM SHOPS

THE SHOPS AT THE **British Museum** carry excellent facsimiles of its treasures, such as the Lewis chess pieces and Roman coins and jewelry. **Hampton Court Palace**'s shop has the best all-around selection of housewares, books, food, and decorative arts. The **Museum of London**'s shop has the best books on London, plus tube maps printed on boxer shorts or T-shirts. The **National Gallery** and **National Portrait Gallery** shops feature reproductions of their art on clothing, mugs, notebooks, stationery, calendars, and fridge magnets, not to mention postcards and posters. Look for the lusciously printed catalogs from temporary exhibits past. The **Natural History Museum** shop is a kids' paradise, featuring tons of plastic and stuffed animals. The **Queen's Gallery** and **Buckingham Palace** shops (open only July 28 to September 28) stock the best royal-related items and a good range of tin plates printed with antique china designs, perfect for alfresco dining. If you can't find a fun, educational gift for an inquisitive child at the **Science Museum** for reasonable prices, then you don't know kids. The shops at both **Tate Museums** sell art books and postcards. Have a look at the **Victoria and Albert Museum** for reproduction jewelry, decorative arts, and books on design and interior decoration, all of which reflect the glory of the collections; they also have lots of little trinkets for Christmas stocking stuffing. The **Tower of London** has a number of gift shops featuring everything from kid's medieval costumes to reproductions of the royal jewels. And **Westminster Abbey** has a quirky shop full of cheap tourist stuff as well as a few genuinely interesting souvenirs.

unofficial **TIP**
All the museum gift shops in London sell excellent chocolate in whimsical packaging.

PERFUMERIES

ONE OF THE GREAT THINGS ABOUT LONDON is its proximity to France, home of a thousand scents. The interest in aromas has wafted across the English Channel, and you can find some of the best perfumes in the world at the following stores. **L'Artisan Parfumeur** (17 Cale Street, Chelsea, SW3; ☎ 0207-352-4196; **www.artisanparfumeur.com;** tube: South Kensington) makes scents for men, women, and children, plus candles. **Jo Malone** (150 Sloane Street, Chelsea, SW1; ☎ 0207-730-2100; **www.jomalone.co.uk;** tube: Sloane Square) is a wildly popular store with remarkable, imaginative scents and creams. **Les Senteurs** (71 Elizabeth Street, Victoria, SW1; ☎ 0207-730-2322; **www.lessenteurs.com;** tube: Victoria or Sloane Square) retails unusual fragrances, straight from France, as well as fine skin-care products. If you're an individualist with strong feelings about what you like in a fragrance, you can get your very own signature scent whipped up at **Miller Harris** in Notting Hill (14 Needham Road, Notting Hill, W11; ☎ 0207-221-1545; **www .millerharris.com;** tube: Notting Hill Gate). **Parfums de Nicolaï** (101a Fulham Road, South Kensington, SW3; ☎ 0207-581-0922; **www.pnicolai .com;** tube: South Kensington), started by a granddaughter of the famous French perfume family Guerlain, sells both men's and women's products as well as candles.

SHOES

BIRKENSTOCK (37 Neal Street, West End, W2; ☎ 0207-240-2783; **www.birkenstock.co.uk;** tube: Covent Garden), the hippie shoe from the 1960s, has never been so popular or mainstream, and the styles have never been better. **Emma Hope** (53 Sloane Square, Chelsea, SW1; ☎ 0207-259-9566; **www.emmahope.co.uk;** tube: Sloane Square) makes elegant, up-to-date footwear. **Jimmy Choo** (169 Draycott Avenue, South Kensington, SW3; ☎ 0207-584-6111; **www.jimmychoo.com**; tube: South Kensington) has become the designer of choice for wealthy, fashionable young women; his shoes have probably trod more red carpets than pavement. Similarly, the red-soled pumps of **Christian Louboutin** (23 Motcomb Street, Belgravia, SW1; ☎ 0207-823-2234; tube: Knightsbridge) are must-haves among the deep-pocketed-diva set. And while we're at it, how about **Manolo Blahnik** (49–51 Old Church Street, Chelsea, SW3; ☎ 0207-352-3863; tube: Sloane Square), whose shoes have been described by a devotee as "better than sex"? Apparently, he's one cobbler who can combine glamour with comfort, which helps explain the eye-popping prices. The newest shoe master on the block is **Georgina Goodman** (12–14 Shepherd Street, Mayfair, W1; ☎ 0207-499-8599; **www.georginagoodman.com;** tube: Green Park), whose Mayfair shop is a splendid space in which to admire the artful, individual handmade shoes in quirky designs (admittedly, not for everyone). **John Lobb Ltd.** (9 St. James Street, Mayfair, SW1; ☎ 0207-930-3664; **www.john lobbltd.co.uk;** tube: Green Park) is the oldest, grandest, and most expensive of the bespoke shoemakers; a pair of Lobb's classic English leather shoes will set you back about £1,500, and it will take months to get them, but we hear they're worth every penny. The **Natural Shoe Store** (325 King's Road, Chelsea, SW3; ☎ 0207-351-3721; **www.nature sko.com;** tube: Sloane Square) stocks the best in comfort brands: Ecco,

Birkenstock, Arche, Krone clogs, and American brands such as Bass, Dexter, and Rockport. (Don't even think of getting the American stuff, but check the prices on the Europeans.)

VINTAGE-CLOTHING AND DESIGNER-RESALE SHOPS

SUCH A GOOD IDEA, THESE SHOPS. They're hit or miss, but you can ease into some world-class designer threads and shoes for a fraction of what they'd cost new. Unfortunately, there tend to be more size 4s than 14s, but shoes and purses will work for anyone. Some good places to try include **Catwalk** (52 Blandford Street, Marylebone, W1; ☎ 0207-935-1052; tube: Baker Street); **The Dresser** (10 Porchester Place, Bayswater, W2; ☎ 0207-724-7212; tube: Marble Arch); **The Loft** (35 Monmouth Street, West End, WC2; ☎ 0207-240-3807; **www.the-loft.co.uk;** tube: Covent Garden); and **Sign of the Times** (17 Elystan Street, Chelsea, SW3; ☎ 0207-589-4774; tube: Sloane Square). When visiting **Pandora** (16–22 Cheval Place, Knightsbridge, SW7; ☎ 0207-589-5289; tube: Knightsbridge), also drop in at, along this same street, **The Dress Box** (8 Cheval Place, Knightsbridge, SW3; ☎ 0207-589-2240) and **Salou** (6 Cheval Place, Knightsbridge, SW3; ☎ 0207-581-2380).

At the corner of Notting Hill Gate and Pembridge Road, right outside the north exit of the Notting Hill Gate tube station, is a row of secondhand shops that all go by the name **Retro Clothing.** There are two women's, two men's, and a home-decorating Retro. The selection is unpredictable, although the prevailing philosophy supports hip, quirky duds and low prices. (From 16 to 34 Pembridge Road and 56 Notting Hill Gate, Notting Hill, W11; ☎ 0207-792-1715 and ☎ 0207-221-1123; tube: Notting Hill Gate). Try either branch of **Bang Bang** (21 Goodge Street, West End, W1; ☎ 0207-631-4191, tube: Tottenham Court Road; 9 Berwick Street, Soho, W1; ☎ 0207-494-2042, tube: Oxford Circus) for some great bargains. Vintage and retro fans know all about **Kingly Court** (49 Carnaby Street, W1; tube: Oxford Circus), which has secondhand, retro, and vintage shops on all three floors. Three of our favorites: **Twinkled** (first floor; ☎ 0207-334-1978; **www .twinkled.net**), **Love Vintage** (top floor; ☎ 0203-214-0044; **www.love vintage.net**), and **Marshmallow Mountain** (ground floor; ☎ 0207-434-9498; **www.marshmallowmountain.com**).

The **Antique Clothing Shop** (282 Portobello Road, Notting Hill, W10; ☎ 0208-964-4830; tube: Ladbroke Grove) has a wonderful range of vintage clothing, spanning the Victorian era through the 1970s. Costumers for films come here to dress their actors, and designers here come for inspiration. Another ultravintage shop is the visually gorgeous **Virginia** (98 Portland Road, Kensington, W11; ☎ 0207-727-9908; tube: Holland Park), specializing in aristocratic fashions and accessories from the late-Victorian period—unless you've got a corset and a very deep pocket, you'll just want to look. For one-stop retro-clothing shopping, go to **Alfie's Antique Market** (13–25 Church Street,

Marylebone, NW8; ☎ 0207-724-7366; **www.alfiesantiques.com;** tube: Edgware Road), where you'll find stalls specializing in various eras (the 1940s and '50s are particularly well represented). Plenty of accessories, too.

Small but crammed with breathtakingly beautiful vintage women's wear, **Cloud Cuckoo Land** (6 Charlton Place, Camden Passage, Camden, N1; ☎ 0207-354-3141) is well worth the trip to Camden, if only to see the owner, Dawn, who gets herself all dolled up in full regalia: the last time we were there, she was dressed as a 1920s flapper, right down to her toenails.

The East End is filled with these shops—too many of them to list. Wander around **Brick Lane** and **Commercial Street,** and you won't believe your eyes.

WOOL AND CASHMERE

WOOLENS FROM SCOTLAND AND IRELAND are more expensive and of better quality than the ubiquitous Chinese material. The best time to buy is during sales. **Liberty, Harrods, Marks and Spencer, Debenhams,** and other big stores carry good selections (see "Department Stores," page 399).

Shi Cashmere (30 Lowndes Street, Knightsbridge, SW1; ☎ 0207-235-3829; **www.shicashmere.com;** tube: Knightsbridge) carries an elegant array of cashmeres, wools, and silks. If you don't see it, you can order it from the Scottish factory.

PART ELEVEN

EXERCISE *and* RECREATION

SPECTATOR SPORTS

THE NATIONAL JUBILATION AND PLANNED CELEBRATIONS surrounding London's selection to host the 2012 Summer Olympics were abruptly and horribly deflated by the July 7, 2005, terrorist attacks on the city, which came the day the good news was announced. In fact, this being London, complaints about the inconvenience of the games have replaced any initial optimism quashed by the attacks—a deep cynicism here recognizes that the only beneficiaries will be property developers and PR firms. Oh, and maybe the gold medalists. Even the Queen, somewhat impolitically, was said to believe that Paris would be the perfect place for it. Expect widely reported disgruntlement and gaffes for the next few years—the new £400,000 logo launched in 2007 met with widespread disapproval.

Never mind: there's more to sport in London than a few overhyped future games, and the dedicated fans among you may enjoy checking out the *real* sports of England: soccer, rugby, and cricket.

SOCCER

SOCCER, OR FOOTBALL ("footie"), as the English call it, is more than a national obsession—it is a religion with serious and often deranged devotees. The days when rival fans would do bloody battle in the streets are mostly gone due to closed-circuit TV, bans on the most violent fans, tight security at games, and reconstruction of the arenas. However, the fever burns as strong as ever. Game tickets for the top teams of the **Premier League** are expensive (£25 to £90), whereas tickets for the teams farther down the league ladder are cheaper (£10 to £18).

unofficial **TIP**
Though pricey, Premier League games are worth the expense—the class of players these days is phenomenal. The spectators themselves are also worthy of close attention: listen to their songs and chants, filled with venomous derision of the visiting team.

The soccer season runs from August to May. Games are 90 minutes long, plus injury time and extra time if it is important that there be a winner (as in, for a cup final). Most clubs take credit-card bookings over the phone, which is crucial for Premier League games. Matches take place on Saturday afternoons and weekday evenings. Wrap up warmly, and bring a rain poncho.

London Premier League teams include the following:

ARSENAL AT THE EMIRATES STADIUM (Avenall Road, N5; ☎ 0207-704-4000; **www.arsenal.co.uk;** tube: Piccadilly Line to Arsenal) Tickets are £32 to £94.

CHELSEA AT STAMFORD BRIDGE (Fulham Road, SW6; ☎ 0207-386-7799; **www.chelseafc.co.uk;** tube: Fulham Broadway) Tickets are £20 to £65 for adults and from £15 for children.

TOTTENHAM HOTSPUR AT WHITE HART LANE (High Road, N17; ☎ 0870-420-5000; **www.tottenhamhotspur.com;** British Rail: White Hart Lane) Tickets are £27 to £71 for adults.

WEST HAM UNITED AT BOLEYN GROUND (Green Street, Upton Park, E13; ☎ 0870-112-2700; **www.whufc.com;** tube: Upton Park). Adult tickets are £34 to £61.

CRICKET

THOUGH IT IS NOW AN INTERNATIONAL SPORT, there is something quintessentially English about the game of cricket. It is sedate, difficult to understand, and full of quaint language. For example, a "maiden over" is a series of six balls, bowled in a swinging over-arm motion, during which no runs are scored. The games sometimes last for days, interrupted frequently by rain and tea. It is considered vulgar to thrash one's opponent by too many runs; when it is clear that the losing team cannot win, the winning side "declares" and gives the other team a chance to recover some of their dignity. You can see this game played by men in white clothing on many a village green during the season, which runs from mid-April to early September, but there are two main cricket venues in London:

unofficial **TIP**
Tickets for international cricket games need to be booked well in advance, but league games, played between local counties, are much easier to get tickets for and are sometimes free.

LORDS CRICKET GROUND (St. John's Wood, NW8; ☎ 0207-432-1000; **www.lords.org;** tube: St. John's Wood) This is the home of the Marylebone Cricket Club (MCC) and is often considered the home of cricket. Tickets range from £5 upward.

BRIT OVAL (Surrey County Cricket Club, Kennington, SE11; ☎ 0871-246-1100 [calls cost 10p per minute]; **www.surreycricket.com;** tube: Northern Line to Oval) International cricket is often played here, and demand is high. Also played here are county matches, which are less expensive than international ones. Tickets start at £12 for adults and £6 for guests under age 16.

RUGBY

THIS IS A BRUTAL AND VIOLENT GAME similar to American football but without the padding. As an old saying goes, "Football is a gentlemen's game played by hooligans, and rugby [union] is a hooligan's game played by gentlemen." Again, the rules are characteristically English: The ball, shaped like an American football, is passed backward or sideways, never forward. The ball is thrown into a mass of huddle players, from which it is booted out. Whoever catches it then dashes along the field to score a "try" (touchdown), which is then converted by kicking it over the goalposts for extra points. The season runs from September to May, and the game is enjoying something of a resurgence in popularity because of the amount of money it now brings in.

Rugby league is the professional form of the sport. (The term is both generic and a proper name: that is, rugby-league football is governed by the Rugby League.) This type of rugby is a fast-moving collision game with lots of open running, big hits, and tackles—basically, the closest thing to American football.

Rugby union is traditionally the amateur form of the game (governed by the Rugby Football Union), with the characteristic scrums, timeouts, and touchdowns, and 15 players per team. However, it now boasts a professional status with the **Guinness Premiership,** a competition among the top rugby-union clubs that draws major crowds. The season runs from August to May. Watch out for the **London Wasps,** the **Saracens,** and the **Sale Sharks.** Wrap up warmly if you go.

The primary rugby venues are as follows:

ATHLETIC GROUND (Kew Foot Road, Richmond, Surrey, TW9; ☎ 0208-940-0397; **www.the-raa.co.uk;** tube: Richmond) These amateur games are free.

ROSSLYN PARK (Upper Richmond Road, Priory Lane, Roehampton, SW15; ☎ 0208-876-6044; **www.rosslynpark.co.uk;** British Rail: Barnes) Tickets are approximately £10 for adults, £5 for seniors, and £3 for children.

TWICKENHAM RUGBY HOUSE (21 Rugby Road, Twickenham, Middlesex, TW1; ☎ 0870-405-2000; **www.rfu.com;** tube: Twickenham) Tickets vary in price depending on the game. Tickets for the Six Nations series held here are very difficult to get and are distributed to the faithful via the various clubs. You can see cup finals for the leagues here, too, for which tickets range between £15 and £35.

BOXING

BIG FIGHTS TAKE PLACE IN BIG VENUES, such as the newly renovated and reopened **Wembley Arena, Royal Albert Hall, London Arena,** and **Earls Court.** Publicity is large scale, and tickets are always expensive. Smaller venues host amateur or semiprofessional fights, which are advertised in local papers, *Time Out London,* or on posters. You can catch a good pro or amateur fight at **York Hall** (Old Ford Road, E2; ☎ 0208-980-4171; tube: Bethnal Green). This place has a serious East End vibe and has hosted amateur matches since 1929. Tickets start at £10. Tickets for pro fights are priced by the promoters. Call **Boxing News** at ☎ 0207-882-1040, or go to **www.sporting-life.com/boxing** for details on what's on, where, and when.

unofficial **TIP**
For all but the most high-profile matches, you can usually get in at Wimbledon by showing up on the day of the event and waiting to buy tickets for the outer courts; you can also buy returned tickets for the next day at good prices.

TENNIS

THE LAST WEEK IN JUNE marks the start of the **Wimbledon** fortnight, and demand for tickets exceeds supply. Tickets must be secured well in advance and are awarded by ballot. To get tickets for Centre Court or Number One Court, you have to write for an application form between September 1 and December 31 to the All England Lawn Tennis Club, P.O. Box 98, Church Road, London, SW19 (☎ 0208-946-2244; **www.wimbledon.com;** tube: District Line to Wimbledon). Tickets range from £36 to £87 for Centre Court and £24 to £65 for Number One Court. All tickets for the last four days are presold; on all other days, a total of 500 tickets are held back for sale at the turnstile on the day of the event, cash only. Bring a hat or umbrella and plenty of sunblock. June is a fickle month for weather.

HORSE RACING

YOU CAN SEE RACING ALMOST EVERY DAY on television, and every high street has at least one betting shop, or "turf accountant," as the Brits like to call them. Gambling is legal here, and bookies offer odds on almost anything, from the gender of the next royal birth to whether it will snow on Christmas Day. A day at the races is as popular with the upper classes (members of which own the horses and can be seen at Royal Ascot wearing hilarious hats that are never worn anywhere else) as it is with the hoi polloi. The flat season runs from April to September, and the jumps, or steeplechase runs, from October to April.

All the tracks are just outside London and are well serviced by rail. Take a coat and umbrella just in case. Most tracks have bars and restaurants, which serve notoriously bad food, so be warned. A day at the races is exactly that; be prepared for a longish haul. Racing venues include those listed below:

ASCOT RACECOURSE (High Street, Ascot, Berks; ☎ 0134-462-2211; **www.ascot.co.uk;** British Rail: Ascot) Admission is £7 to £52, depending on whether you sit in the grandstand or the silver ring. (The royal enclosure, not surprisingly, is closed to commoners.) Good competitive racing can always be seen here. One of the highlights of the year is the week-long **Royal Meeting** (aka **Royal Ascot**). A 2006 revamp gave Ascot Racecourse a new realigned track and grandstand, as well as the honor of being named Large Visitor Attraction of the Year at the 2006 Tourism South East Tourism ExSEllence Awards.

EPSOM (Epsom Downs, Epsom, Surrey; ☎ 0137-247-0047; **www.epsomderby.co.uk;** British Rail: Epsom Downs) Admission is £6 to £23. This is where the **Oaks** and the **Derby** (pronounced "Darby") races are held in June; other races take place throughout the summer. Derby Day is a big betting day in England. Some races feature live music, making them a nice way to spend a summer evening even if you know nothing about horses. Tickets in the Queen's Stand and for Derby Day cost up to £100.

KEMPTON PARK (Staines Road East, Kempton Park; ☎ 0137-247-0047; **www.kempton.co.uk;** British Rail: Sunbury-on-Thames or Kempton Park) Admission is £15 to £21. This course hosts the King George VI Stakes on Boxing Day (December 26) and additional events year-round. Summer evenings are particularly fun, with themes such as Irish music and fireworks. You can bet on and watch the races from the restaurant in the sleek exhibition hall.

WINDSOR MAIDENHEAD ROAD (Windsor, Berks; ☎ 0175-349-8400; **www.windsor-racecourse.co.uk;** British Rail: Windsor or Eton Riverside) Admission is £6 to £25. This is a pretty part of England that's worth visiting in its own right. Windsor Castle (very much in use by Her Majesty) looms beautifully over the course and can be toured as part of your day out.

RECREATIONAL SPORTS

GYMS AND LEISURE CENTERS

THE GYM CULTURE OF WORKING OUT and staying in shape has grown proportionally as the Britons make their way up the scale of overweight nations. London is full of exercise options, some of them quite entertaining, such as evening in-line-skating events, organized sunrise runs in **Hyde Park,** and the popular **London Marathon.**

London visitors needing to pump up their endorphins or maintain a training program will have no problem finding parks for running or sophisticated gyms that charge £20 to £50 for a visitor's day pass. We have room to list only a few facilities here, so look in the Yellow Pages under "Leisure Centres" to find the one nearest you, or speak to your concierge.

unofficial **TIP**
Many hotels, even the budget ones, have access to a gym or sports center or provide their own exercise rooms, which will vary in quality.

Here's a sampling of sports and leisure centers in central London. Please note that most of the leisure centers will expect you to pay a small "induction" fee, and that some of the busier centers have had to limit their gym facilities to members only (call for details).

CHELSEA SPORTS CENTRE (Chelsea Manor Street, Chelsea, SW3, ☎ 0207-352-6985; **www.rbkc.gov.uk/sport;** tube: Sloane Square) Offers a 25-meter pool and aerobics classes. Fees: £3.20 to swim, £4.50 to £5.50 for studio classes, £5.65 for use of the gym, and £6.60 per hour on the badminton court.

THE GYM COVENT GARDEN (30 The Piazza, Covent Garden, WC2; ☎ 0207-836-4835; **www.jubileehallclubs.co.uk;** tube: Covent Garden) This fully equipped gym has been refurbished with a new cardio theater, free weights, and resistance machines, and is in an excellent location. There are also yoga, Pilates, and various exercise classes at reasonable prices. The cost is £10 for a day visit.

LONDON CENTRAL YMCA (112 Great Russell Street, Bloomsbury, WC1; ☎ 0207-343-1700; **www.ymcaclub.co.uk;** tube: Tottenham Court Road). Also very centrally located, and totally comprehensive, with lots of classes. The cost is £15 for a "taster" day visit.

QUEEN MOTHER SPORTS CENTRE (223 Vauxhall Bridge Road, Victoria, SW1; ☎ 0207-630-5522; **www.westminster.gov.uk/leisureandculture;** tube: Victoria) Very central as well, this center has been modernized to the tune of more than £1 million and offers a complete range of facilities, equipment, and classes. Fees: £10 for gym, £5 for fitness classes, and £3 for pool.

PORCHESTER CENTRE (Queensway, Bayswater, W2; ☎ 0207-792-2919; **www.westminster.gov.uk/leisureandculture;** tube: Queensway or Bayswater) Facilities include a 30-meter pool, gym, classes, and a wonderful health spa (Russian steam room, Turkish hot room, sauna, Jacuzzi, and plunge pool). The gym, pool, and spa are open daily; fees: £8 for gym, £5.50 for fitness classes, and £4 for pool.

SEYMOUR LEISURE CENTRE (Seymour Place, Marylebone, W1; ☎ 0207-723-8019; **www.westminster.gov.uk/leisureandculture;** tube: Marble Arch) This center has an Olympic-sized pool, steam rooms, cardio-vascular machines, and exercise classes. Fees: £8 for gym, £9.10 for sauna and steam rooms, £5.15 for fitness classes, and £4.25 for pool.

BICYCLING

YOU TAKE YOUR LIFE INTO YOUR HANDS cycling around the streets of London, even with the marked bicycle lanes, but there are plenty of parks to bike in that are wonderfully stress free and interest rich. The **London Bicycle Tour Company** is the best outfitter of its kind, with a huge inventory of bikes for rent as well as fun guided tours. They are open from 10 a.m. to 6 p.m. and are located on the Thames at

1a Gabriels Wharf, 56 Upper Ground, SE1 (☎ 0207-928-6838; **www .londonbicycle.com**; tube: Blackfriars or Waterloo).

IN-LINE SKATING

ROLLERBLADES ARE POPULAR IN LONDON, with plenty of good paths throughout **Hyde and Battersea parks.** There are hotdoggers with ramps and cones, as well as serious hockey players, alongside the Albert Memorial and on the north side of the Serpentine in Hyde Park, which makes for good spectator sports. On Wednesday and Friday nights in the warmer months, hundreds of skaters start at Hyde Park Corner and glide down London streets in a pack, pumped up by music and whistles. Check **www.thefns.com** for meeting times and locations (for intermediate and above skaters only—they move fast). You can rent roller skates or in-line skates at a number of sports stores; **www.easy peasyskate.co.uk** has links to shops around London. **London Skate Centre** (21 Leinster Terrace, W2; ☎ 0207-7706-8769; **www.lonskate.com;** tube: Queensway or Bayswater) and Slick Willies (12 Gloucester Road, South Kensington, SW7; ☎ 0207-225-0004; **www.slickwillies.co.uk;** tube: Gloucester Road) stock the latest models. Both stores are conveniently located near Hyde Park; prices run around £10 per day or £15 overnight, with a credit-card deposit of £100.

HORSEBACK RIDING

THOUGH THIS ISN'T EXACTLY THE SPORT OF CHOICE for the masses, London has some beautiful places for riding. **Hyde Park** is an old favorite, with well-trodden riding paths like Rotten Row. Check the **British Horse Society** Web site (**www.bhs.org.uk**) for a comprehensive list of stables around London.

The most central stables are the first two following, which share the same mews location:

ROSS NYE STABLES (8 Bathurst Mews, Bayswater, W2; ☎ 0207-262-3791; tube: Lancaster Gate or Paddington) The price is £45 per hour for a ride around Hyde Park (closed Monday) and £55 for individual lessons (Tuesday through Friday only). They won't take anyone younger than age 6 or anyone who weighs more than 200 pounds. The stables are closed for a couple of months in the

unofficial **TIP**
Do not assume that riding in Hyde Park is without danger. You have to traverse a few streets and cross a busy main road to get into the park.

summer. Beginners and experienced riders are allowed, and children are encouraged. The horses here are gorgeous and well cared for, and there are plenty of ponies.

HYDE PARK STABLES (63 Bathurst Mews, Bayswater, W2; ☎ 0207-723-2813; **www.hydeparkstables.com;** tube: Lancaster Gate or Paddington) The cost is £49 for groups and £59 for a solo hour. The staff are very careful, and you may have to prove your abilities before being let off a lead.

WIMBLEDON VILLAGE STABLES (24 High Street, Wimbledon, SW19, ☎ 0208-946-8579; **www.wvstables.com;** tube: Wimbledon) They charge from £45 to £80, depending on the day and how much time and/or instruction you want. The stables are outside central London but worth the trip if you want to avoid riding in automobile traffic. Small classes are offered for beginners, and you will be taken on a rugged ride through Wimbledon Common, Putney Heath, and Richmond Park, all of which are semiwild expanses (look out for deer). This is a much more beautiful experience than Hyde Park, if less convenient.

ICE SKATING

ALTHOUGH IT'S NEVER COLD ENOUGH IN LONDON for any natural bodies of water to ice over, the city looks after its budding Olympians with a fair number of year-round and winter-only rinks. Admission and skate rental are cheap, and skating can be a fun night out. During December and January, a wonderful skating venue is open in the courtyard of the grand old **Somerset House** on the Strand (☎ 0207-845-4600; **www.somerset-house.org.uk;** tube: Temple), with other, less grand outdoor rinks rigged up in a variety of likely places.

BROADGATE ICE RINK (Broadgate Circus, Eldon Street, EC2; ☎ 0207-505-4068; **www.broadgateice.co.uk;** tube: Liverpool Street) Admission plus skate rental is £8 adults, £5 children. This tiny outdoor rink in the middle of London, among the glass castles of the financial district, is open late October through April. There's plenty of room to watch if you don't skate.

QUEENS ICE RINK AND BOWL (17 Queensway, W2; ☎ 0207-229-0172; **www.queensiceandbowl.co.uk;** tube: Bayswater or Queensway) Admission is £9 plus £1 for skate rental. Friday and Saturday nights are disco nights. Good Middle Eastern, Chinese, and Indian restaurants are in the immediate neighborhood for après-skate. For those who aren't so keen on skating, there are bowling lanes, refreshment venues, and arcade games all under the same roof.

SWIMMING

MOST OF THE LEISURE CENTERS listed earlier have swimming pools, but it is worth noting that almost every borough of London has at least one municipally run pool, some of which are more salubrious than others. To find your nearest municipal pool, outdoor pool, or lido, have a look at the interesting Web sites **www.lidos.org.uk** and **www.londonpoolscampaign.com,** both of which will give you an idea of how passionately some Londoners feel about swimming and their glorious history of public pools.

Bearing in mind that no one comes to London for the great swimming, here's a list of some of the better dipping holes, which are worth checking out when it's hot, although they can get crowded:

HAMPSTEAD MIXED PONDS and **THE HIGHGATE MEN'S AND LADIES' PONDS** (Millfield Lane, NW3; ☎ 0207-485-3873; tube: Hampstead or Hampstead Heath; British Rail: Gospel Oak) Admission is free to these ponds, which have been in use for 100 years, though by the time you read this there may be a small fee. (In fact, by the time you read this, the

ponds may be closed to swimmers, but we expect a huge popular resistance.) The facility comprises three ponds in picturesque surroundings: one for men, one for women, and one for both. The segregated ponds are open all year. (Try not to look shocked by the skinny-dipping, which is not compulsory.) The mixed pond is open April through September only.

OASIS SPORTS CENTRE (32 Endell Street, West End, WC2; ☎ 0207-831-1804; **www.gll.org;** tube: Covent Garden or Holborn) Opened originally in 1852 as the Bloomsbury Baths and Washhouses, Oasis became the first all-weather swimming complex in the country with the completion of the indoor facility in 1960. Open Monday through Friday, 6:30 a.m. to 10 p.m.; Saturday and Sunday, 9:30 a.m. to 6 p.m.; admission is £2.90 for adults, £1.10 for children over age 5, and free for children under age 5. There is an indoor pool, an outdoor pool, and a bathing deck for basking on those rare sunny days.

PARLIAMENT HILL LIDO Gordon House Road, NW3; ☎ 0207-485-3873; British Rail: Gospel Oak) This 200-by-90-foot pool on the edge of Hampstead Heath was first opened to the public in 1938 and was upgraded in 2005 and 2006. Admission is £3.50, £1.50 for concessions. This is London's biggest outdoor pool and is recommended for hot days (it's unheated). Open daily, April through September.

SERPENTINE LIDO (Hyde Park; ☎ 0207-706-3422; **www.serpentinelido .com;** tube: Hyde Park Corner, Lancaster Gate, or Marble Arch) The lido is open July through September only, from 10 a.m. to 6 p.m. daily. Near the Diana, Princess of Wales Memorial, this is the most centrally located lido, with fun for the kids in the form of a playground, occasional entertainment, and people-watching possibilities aplenty. Admission is £3.50 for adults and £1 for children.

WATER SPORTS

FOR THOSE WHO ENJOY messing around on the water, there is plenty to do on the Thames and in the surrounding reservoirs and docklands. Thanks to insurance problems, many of the old water-sports clubs no longer offer drop-in fun. But there is still one place that is full-service:

DOCKLANDS SAILING AND WATERSPORTS CENTRE (235a Westferry Road, E14; ☎ 0207-537-2626; **www.dswc.org;** Docklands Light Railway to Crossharbour–London Arena) Offers sailing, dragon-boat racing, power boating, rowing, canoeing, and more. Day passes cost £25. Open daily, 9 a.m. to 9 p.m.

GOLF

THE ENGLISH GOLF UNION (☎ 0152-635-4500; **www.englishgolf union.org**) is an excellent resource for London golf information. Courses outside the city include the following:

RICHMOND PARK PUBLIC GOLF CLUB (Roehampton Gate, Richmond Park, SW15; ☎ 0208-876-3205; **www.richmondparkgolf.co.uk;** British Rail: Barnes) Open weekdays, 7 a.m. to dusk in summer (open 6 a.m. weekends and bank holidays), 7:30 a.m. to dusk in winter; closed Christmas Day. Two 18-hole courses; £18 on weekdays and £25 on weekends. The price drops for games played late in the day.

ROYAL MID-SURREY GOLF CLUB (Old Deer Park, Twickenham Road, Richmond, Surrey; ☎ 0208-940-1894; **www.rmsgc.co.uk;** tube or British Rail: Richmond) This private club with two 18-hole courses welcomes visitors. Admission runs from £30 to £80. Nonmembers can visit from Monday to Friday, 8 a.m. to dusk. The club requires that you be an experienced golfer with a club handicap—no beginners at any time, and no visitors on weekends. Call the Pro Shop at ☎ 0208-939-0148 for tee times.

DUKES MEADOWS GOLF CLUB and **CHISWICK BRIDGE GOLF RANGE** (Dukes Meadows, Dan Mason Drive [formerly Great Chartsey Road], Chiswick, W4; ☎ 0208-994-3314; **www.golflessons.co.uk;** tube: Hammersmith, then bus 190 to Hartington Road) Open daily, 9 a.m. to 10 p.m. There's something for everyone here: a nine-hole course, a 50-bay driving range, a six-hole academy course (child-friendly), and a full teaching center. You can rent golf clubs here, too. The cost to play the nine-hole course is £12 on weekdays, £15 on weekends. On the driving range, you'll pay £5 for a bucket of balls.

TENNIS

ALMOST ALL LONDON PARKS have tennis courts, which cost very little to play on, but you must bring your own racket and balls. There is usually a grass court or two and a few asphalt ones. It's very informal: just turn up on any weekday, and you will almost certainly be able to play. The serious player should look into the **Queen's Club** (Palliser Road, West Kensington, W14; ☎ 0207-385-3421; **www.queensclub .co.uk;** tube: Barons Court or West Kensington) or contact the **Lawn Tennis Association** at ☎ 0207-381-7000 or **www.lta.org.uk** for a listing of all London venues.

ACCOMMODATIONS INDEX

RESTAURANT INDEX

SUBJECT INDEX

Unofficial Guide Reader Survey

If you would like to express your opinion in writing about London or this guidebook, complete the following survey and mail it to:

> *Unofficial Guide* Reader Survey
> P.O. Box 43673
> Birmingham, AL 35243

Inclusive dates of your visit: _____

Members of
your party: Person 1   Person 2   Person 3   Person 4   Person 5
Gender: M F   M F   M F   M F   M F
Age: _____

How many times have you been to London? _____
On your most recent trip, where did you stay? _____

Concerning your accommodations, on a scale of 100 as best and 0 as worst, how would you rate:

The quality of your room?	The value of your room?
The quietness of your room?	Check-in/check-out efficiency?
Shuttle service to the airport?	Swimming pool facilities?

Did you rent a car?   From whom?

Concerning your rental car, on a scale of 100 as best and 0 as worst, how would you rate:

Pick-up processing efficiency?	Return processing efficiency?
Condition of the car?	Cleanliness of the car?
Airport shuttle efficiency?	

Concerning your dining experiences:

Estimate your meals in restaurants per day? _____
Approximately how much did your party spend on meals per day? ____
_____

Favorite restaurants in London: _____
_____

Did you buy this guide before leaving?   while on your trip?

How did you hear about this guide? (check all that apply)

Loaned or recommended by a friend ☐ Radio or TV ☐
Newspaper or magazine ☐   Bookstore salesperson ☐
Just picked it out on my own ☐   Library ☐
Internet ☐

What other guidebooks did you use on this trip?_____
_____
_____
_____

On a scale of 100 as best and 0 as worst, how would you rate them?
_____
_____
_____

Using the same scale, how would you rate the *Unofficial Guide*(s)?

_____

Are Unofficial Guides readily available at bookstores in your area?_____

Have you used other *Unofficial Guides*? _____

Which one(s)? _____
_____
_____

Comments about your London trip or the *Unofficial Guide*(s):
_____
_____
_____
_____
_____
_____
_____
_____
_____
_____
_____
_____
_____
_____
_____
_____
_____
_____
_____